Life Themes
Major Conflicts in Drama

Robert Barton
Annie McGregor

THOMSON

Australia · Canada · Mexico · Singapore · Spain · United Kingdom · United States

Custom Editor:
John Horvath

Project Development Editor:
Lisa Sizemore

Marketing Coordinators:
Lindsay Annett and Sara Mercurio

Production/Manufacturing Supervisor:
Donna M. Brown

Senior Project Coordinator:
Melanie Evans

Pre-Media Services Supervisor:
Dan Plofchan

Rights and Permissions Specialist:
Kalina Hintz

Senior Prepress Specialist:
Deanna Dixon

Cover Design:
Deanna Dixon

Cover Image:
Getty Images

CREDITS

CONTENTS

Life Themes

Love War Generations

Rebellion Dreams Values

Life Theme 1:

Love

Life Theme 1: Love

The old cliché says "love makes the world go 'round," But it's also true that "love stinks" at times.

Love is a kind of warfare.

—Ars Amatoria, Ovid

Featured plays:

Much Ado About Nothing
  by William Shakespeare
M. Butterfly
  by David Henry Hwang

We seem destined to struggle with love within our families, our friends, our community, and even ourselves. But nothing confuses and delights us more than "romantic love." We are obsessed with it. Our passion for passion is universal. Two plays, one by the most famous English playwright and the other by a contemporary Asian American playwright, explore the joys and agonies, the risks and rewards of falling in love.

Much Ado About Nothing

Year: 1598
Genre: Elizabethan Comedy, predominantly prose
Structure: English neo-classicism
Setting: Messina, a seaport town in Sicily

Context:

Queen Elizabeth I (1533-1603). The era of Shakespeare's highest artistic productivity was dominated by Elizabeth Tudor, Queen of England from 1558 until her death in 1603. Only 25 years old when she ascended the throne, Elizabeth was surrounded and pressured by powerful lords to marry and produce an heir. But marriage meant abdicating her power to a husband chosen by others for political reasons. Elizabeth never did this, remaining unmarried until her death at age 70. To keep advisors and enemies quiet, she "entertained" marriage proposals from most of the royal families of Europe. With each suitor, she used all her considerable wit to postpone the actual engagement until he either got tired of waiting for her or showed himself to be unacceptable in some way. Elizabeth was famous for her acerbic wit and would unmercifully tease her would-be husbands in front of the whole court. By 1598, when Shakespeare wrote *Much Ado*, Elizabeth was in her sixties and was clearly not going to be producing any heirs, but she appeared to be much taken by the young courtier the Earl of Essex, a very attractive man several decades her junior. For years, Elizabeth exchanged verbal witticisms with Essex, much like Beatrice and Benedick in the play. Their public exchanges of wit and sarcasm may have influenced the writing of this play, but no playwright, especially one as savvy as Shakespeare, was going to risk mocking the Queen, and so the intelligence and strength of Beatrice and Benedick are emphasized, while rumor, petty bickering, and jealousy (things Elizabeth knew all too well) are shown to be dangerous games to play in the Claudio/Hero subplot.

This play is the first of three romantic comedies (the others are *As You Like It* and *Twelfth Night*) written back-to-back revealing Shakespeare's comic genius at the height of its power. In each, true love finds a way to overcome all obstacles "and they all lived happily ever after", the classic romantic resolution.

As to Shakespeare's own love life, few figures in history have inspired so much research and revealed so little actual information. After hundreds of years of minute, exhaustive study, the actual facts about William Shakespeare's life fill less than one typed page. Although it is dangerous to assume life history from an artist's work, and usually inaccurate, scholars and theatre artists have generally agreed that during this period of the young man's life, he must have been feeling pretty good about his love life.

At the age of 19, young Shakespeare married a 26 year old spinster named Anne Hathaway in the small market town of Stratford-upon-Avon. She was pregnant at the time and fatherhood followed quickly on the heels of husband-hood. By the time he was 21 years old, Shakespeare had three children and a wife nearing thirty. History loses track of him for the next seven years until he is suddenly a well known actor and playwright in London. Exactly what happened during those seven years of silence may never be known, but clearly he somehow made his way to London, got hired into a theatrical company and wrote some successful plays. (By most accounts, he was a serviceable actor, but no "star.") He stayed in London, achieving a reasonable level of wealth and respectability (for a theatre person), and returned to Stratford for his last years, dying before his wife and leaving her only the "second best bed" in his will.

With so little known of the man, it is tempting to use the plays as testaments to his life. Certainly a young man, full of himself, making a name for himself as the hot new playwright in London, wife and children left behind in the sticks, could perhaps find himself entangled in new loves. If the three happy plays of his early years, including this play *Much Ado About Nothing*, are any indication, this young man still believed that love conquered all and that happy endings were possible in the world. If you wish to guess the mood of Shakespeare through his later works, look at *King Lear* and its cynicism about romance and erotic love later in this anthology.

The Playwright:

William Shakespeare was born in 1564, the son of John Shakespeare and Mary Arden. His father was a prosperous merchant who eventually was made an alderman of the market town of Stratford-upon-Avon, where William was born. He probably attended the Stratford grammar school, but did not go on to Oxford or Cambridge Universities. He married Anne Hathaway in 1562 who gave birth to their first child Susannah shortly thereafter. Two years later, Anne gave birth to twins Judith and Hamnet. After a prolific and financially successful career in the theatre, writing some of the greatest drama of the English language, he retired to the town of his birth where he had purchased a large home and several land holdings. He died at the age of 52.

M. Butterfly

> *Year: 1988*
> *Genre: Postmodern Expressionism*
> *Structure: Episodic*
> *Setting: A Paris prison in the present and, in flashbacks, the decade 1960-70 in Beijing and 1966 to the present in Paris.*

Context:

China and the Cultural Revolution. After World War II, China experienced a series of political upheavals which form the background for David Henry Hwang's play *M. Butterfly*. While this play is influenced by more than 3000 years of intricate Chinese history, we will focus on the last 50 years, the period during which the play takes place.

After the Second World War and a long, desperate period of Japanese occupation, two groups struggled for ascendancy in China. By 1949 Mao Tse Tung's Communist forces had won, and the People's Republic of China was born. Long needed agrarian and social reforms were instituted. For the average Chinese citizen, Mao's regime was a marked improvement over anything they had known before under emperors, warlords, and foreign occupiers. Sadly, this changed in the 1960's when he and his wife, Madame Mao, began slowly bleeding the country dry in a movement known as the Great Proletariat Cultural Revolution.

By the mid-1960s, Mao's absolute authority began to erode. In response, he and his allies launched the Cultural Revolution, an attempt to purge any remnant of foreign influence from Chinese culture. In 1966, groups of young people formed Red Guard units and took to the streets in wild and often violent pro-Maoist demonstrations. Before long, the Red Guards were controlling the country, "informing" against anyone who disagreed with them. In exchange for special rations and privileges granted to Red Guard members, children as young as six denounced their own parents, siblings, and neighbors. The centuries-long tradition of honoring one's elders collapsed and

China entered a long, sad decade of internal crisis as Red Guards sought out and destroyed the best and brightest of the Chinese people. Anyone could be targeted but most vulnerable were those who had traveled in the West, had contact with foreigners, spoke a western language, or practiced an art form or business labeled "intellectual" or "elitist."

The methods of the Cultural Revolution are referred to in *M. Butterfly*. Citizens targeted by the Red Guards were forced into "re-education" camps to learn "peasant wisdom." Doctors, scientists, engineers, artists, business people, and teachers were marked as "bourgeois elements" and sent to the camps to do hard labor in the fields. Their families were also tormented, denied housing, food rations, and employment. By the time the Revolution started winding down, China was bereft of the talented and educated people needed to rebuild its social fabric and economy. All too often, the targets were the very revolutionaries who had devoted their lives to Mao and the Communist Revolution. Frenzy grew without restraint until, as Hwang writes, "...*children ruled the Middle Kingdom with complete caprice.*"

During the same period, political and military upheaval in Southeast Asia was drawing the United States into its futile and protracted war against Communist forces in Vietnam. This too is part of the background for the play. Hwang explores how racism and imperialism led to erroneous assumptions on the part of Western diplomats and politicians.

Yet even given the rich political/social setting of the play, it is ultimately about love. Much darker than Shakespeare's vision of romantic love in *Much Ado About Nothing*, Hwang's play explores the ways in which we fall in love with our own fantasies rather than a human being. He also asks us to consider exactly what we would do for love. When Gallimard, the protagonist, meets Song he is immediately smitten with her. We see that Song is deliberately courting him under orders from the government, but Gallimard can only see his most romantic, passionate fantasies coming true through his affair with Song.

Hwang explores the shadow side of love, asking us to think about our own ability to love a fantasy figure more than a real person. He calls his play a "deconstruction" of the opera *Madame Butterfly* and says he was inspired by the following newspaper brief:

> *A former French diplomat and a Chinese opera singer have been sentenced to six years in jail for spying for China after a two-day trial that traced the story of clandestine love and mistaken sexual identity...Mr. Bouriscot was accused of passing information to China after he fell in love with Mr. Shi, whom he believed for twenty years to be a woman. New York Times, May 11, 1986.*

Hwang says he intentionally did no research on this specific case because he was more interested in how it *could* happen than in what actually *did* happen. The play begins in present day Paris with Gallimard in his prison cell, reliving once again the 20 years of happiness he experienced with Song, a performer in the Beijing Opera. Through a series of flashbacks filtered through Gallimard's memories, we go back to China during the 1960s and follow his intensifying romance with Song. Although David H. Hwang's play invites us to think about racism, colonialism, and imperialism, it is at heart a love story, about a love that goes terribly awry because it is based on illusions and fantasies. Yet Gallimard tells us that we are the fools. He has committed treason and is sitting in prison, the laughing stock of the world, as the play begins. But he says he would do it all again because he has "loved and been loved by the perfect woman."

The Playwright.

David Henry Hwang was born in 1957, the son of Chinese immigrants. His father worked as a banker and his mother was a professor of piano. A self-described "valley boy," he grew up in southern California and attended Stanford University. During his senior year at Stanford, he wrote and produced his first play *FOB* (which is short for "fresh off the boat," a disparaging slang used by 2nd and 3rd generation Asian Americans for newly arrived immigrants). He attended Yale School of Drama for two years before moving to New York without completing his degree. He achieved critical acclaim with uncommon speed, until he achieved both critical and commercial success in 1988 with *M. Butterfly.* For *M. Butterfly* Hwang won the Outer Critics Circle Award, the Drama Desk award, and the Tony award for Best Play of 1988. Hwang's plays explore many themes, including love, politics, and generational conflicts. Underlying these themes is an ongoing exploration of the American immigrant experience in plays such as *Dance and the Railroad, Family Devotions,* and *Sound and Beauty.* He has also been a founding member of a West Coast rock band and has written for film and television, including the screenplay for *Seven Years in Tibet*, starring Brad Pitt.

Much Ado About Nothing

by William Shakespeare
Adapted by Robert Barton

Characters

Don Pedro: Prince of Aragon
Don John: his bastard brother
Claudio: a young lord of Florence
Benedick: a young lord of Padua
Leonato: Govenor of Messina
Antonio: his brother
Balthasar: a singer, attendant on Don Pedro
Conrade and **Borachio:** followers of Don John
Friar Francis
Dogberry: master constable
Verges: a constable
Watchmen: servants, attendants, etc.
Hero: daughter of Leonato
Beatrice: niece of Leonato
Margaret and **Ursula:** gentlewomen attendant upon Hero

ACT 1, SCENE 1

[Messina. Before Leonato's house. Enter **LEONATO, HERO,** and **BEATRICE,** with a **MESSENGER.**]

LEONATO: I learn in this letter that Don[1] Pedro of Aragon comes this night to Messina.

MESSENGER: He is very near by. He was not three leagues off when I left him.

LEONATO: How many gentlemen have you lost in this action?

MESSENGER: But few of any sort.

LEONATO: A victory is twice as sweet when the achiever brings home full numbers. I find here that Don Pedro hath bestow'd much honour on a young Florentine called Claudio.

MESSENGER: Much deserved on his part. He hath borne himself beyond the promise of his age, doing in the figure of a lamb, the feats of a lion.

BEATRICE: I pray you, is Signior Benedick return'd from the wars or no?

MESSENGER: O, he's return'd; and as pleasant as ever he was.

BEATRICE: I pray you, how many hath he kill'd and eaten in these wars? Or how many hath he kill'd? For, indeed, I promised to eat all of his killing.

MESSENGER: He hath done good service, lady, in these wars. He is a good soldier.

BEATRICE: Ah, a good soldier to a lady- but what is he to a lord?

MESSENGER: A lord to a lord, a man to a man; stuff'd with all honourable virtues.

BEATRICE: He is indeed a stuff'd man: but for the stuffing[2]—well, we are all mortal.

LEONATO: You must not, sir, mistake my niece. There is a kind of merry war betwixt Signior Benedick and her: they never meet but there's a skirmish of wit between them.

BEATRICE: Alas, in our last conflict four of his five wits went halting off, and now is the whole man govern'd with one, so that if he have wit enough to keep himself warm, for that would be the sole difference between himself and his horse. Who is his companion now? He hath every month a new sworn brother.

MESSENGER: He is most in the company of the right noble Claudio.

BEATRICE: O Lord, he will hang upon him like a disease. God help the noble Claudio! If he have caught the Benedick, it will cost him a thousand pound ere a' be cured.

MESSENGER: Don Pedro is approach'd.

[*Enter* **DON PEDRO, DON JOHN, CLAUDIO, BENEDICK,** and **BALTHAZAR.**]

DON PEDRO: Good Signior Leonato, you are come to meet your trouble[3]? The fashion of the world is to avoid cost and you encounter it.

LEONATO: Never came trouble to my house in the likeness of your grace. You are most welcome.

DON PEDRO: I think this is your daughter.

LEONATO: Her mother hath many times told me so.

BENEDICK: Were you in doubt, sir, that you ask'd, her?

LEONATO: Signior Benedick, no; for then were you a child.

DON PEDRO: Truly, the lady fathers herself. Be happy, lady; for you are like your honourable father.

BENEDICK: If Signior Leonato be her father, she would not have his head[4] on her shoulders for all Messina, as like him as she is.

BEATRICE: I wonder that you will still be talking, Signior Benedick: nobody marks[5] you.

BENEDICK: What, my dear Lady Disdain! Are you yet living?

BEATRICE: Is it possible disdain should die while she hath such food to feed it as Signior Benedick? Courtesy itself must convert to disdain, if you come in her presence.

BENEDICK: Then is courtesy a traitor. But it is certain I am loved of all ladies, only you excepted: and I would that I had not a hard heart; for, truly, I love none.

BEATRICE: A dear happiness to women: they would else have been troubled with a pernicious suitor. I thank God I am of your humour for that: I had rather hear my dog bark at a crow than a man swear he loves me.

BENEDICK: God keep your ladyship still in that mind! So some gentleman or other shall scape a scratch'd face.

BEATRICE: Scratching could not make it worse, and 'twere such a face as yours.

BENEDICK: Well, you are a rare parrot-teacher.[6]

BEATRICE: A bird of my tongue is better than a beast of yours.

BENEDICK: I would my horse had the speed of your tongue. But keep your way, i' God's name; I have done.

BEATRICE: You always end with a jade's trick[7]: I know you of old.

DON PEDRO: This is the sum of all, Leonato. Signior Claudio and Signior Benedick, my dear friend Leonato hath invited you all. I tell him we shall stay here at the least a month; and he heartily prays some occasion may detain us longer!

LEONATO: [*to* **DON JOHN**] Let me bid you welcome, my lord: being reconciled to the Prince your brother, I owe you all duty.

DON JOHN: I thank you: I am not of many words, but I thank you.

LEONATO: Please it your Grace lead on?

DON PEDRO: We will go together.

[*Exeunt all except* **BENEDICK** *and* **CLAUDIO.**]

CLAUDIO: Benedick, didst thou note the daughter of Signior Leonato?

BENEDICK: I noted her not; but I look'd on her.

CLAUDIO: Is she not a modest young lady?

BENEDICK: Do you question me, as an honest man, for my simple true judgment, or would you have me speak after my custom, as being a profess'd tyrant to their sex?

CLAUDIO: No; I pray thee speak in sober judgment.

BENEDICK: Why, i' faith, methinks she's too low for a high praise, too dark for a fair praise, and too little for a great praise.

CLAUDIO: Thou think'st I am in sport: I pray thee tell me truly how thou likest her.

BENEDICK: Would you buy her, that you inquire after her?

CLAUDIO: Can the world buy such a jewel?

BENEDICK: Yea, and a case to put it into.

CLAUDIO: In mine eye she is the sweetest lady that ever I look'd on.

BENEDICK: I can see yet without spectacles, and I see no such matter: now there's her cousin, if she were not possess'd with a fury, exceeds her as much in beauty as the first of May doth the last of December. But I hope you have no intent to turn husband, have you?

CLAUDIO: I would scarce trust myself, though I had sworn the contrary, if Hero would be my wife.

BENEDICK: Is't come to this? In faith, hath not the world one man who will remain firm? Shall I never see a bachelor of threescore again? Look; Don Pedro is return'd to seek you.

[*Enter* DON PEDRO.]

DON PEDRO: What secret hath held you here, that you follow'd not to Leonato's?

BENEDICK: He is in love. With who? Mark how short his answer is—With Hero, Leonato's short daughter.

CLAUDIO: This is so. What say you?

DON PEDRO: Amen, if you love her; for the lady is very well worthy.

CLAUDIO: That I love her, I feel.

DON PEDRO: That she is worthy, I know.

BENEDICK: That I neither feel how she should be loved, nor know how she should be worthy, is the opinion that fire cannot melt out of me: I will die in it at the stake.

DON PEDRO: Thou wast ever an obstinate heretic in scorning beauty.

CLAUDIO: And never could maintain his part, but by the force of his will.

BENEDICK: That a woman conceived me, I thank her; that she brought me up, I likewise give her most humble thanks: but all women shall pardon me. Because I will not do them the wrong to mistrust any, I will do myself the right to trust none. I will live forever a bachelor.

DON PEDRO: I shall see thee yet look pale with love.

BENEDICK: With anger, with sickness, or with hunger, my lord; not ever, ever with love!

DON PEDRO: Well, as time shall try: "In time the savage bull doth bear the yoke."

BENEDICK: The savage bull may; but if ever the sensible Benedick bear it, pluck off the bull's horns[8], and set them in my forehead; and let me be vilely painted; and in great letters with my sign saying, "Here you may see Benedick the married man."

DON PEDRO: Nay, if Cupid have not spent all his quiver in Venice, thou wilt quake for this shortly.

BENEDICK: I look for an earthquake too, then.

DON PEDRO: In the meantime, good Signior Benedick, repair to Leonato's: commend me to him, and tell him I will not fail him at supper; for indeed he bath made great preparation.

BENEDICK: I have almost matter enough in me for such an embassage[9] and so I leave you. [*Exit.*]

CLAUDIO: My liege, your highness now may do me good.

DON PEDRO: My love is thine to teach: teach it but how and thou shalt see how apt it is to learn.

CLAUDIO: Hath Leonato any son, my lord?

DON PEDRO: No child but Hero; she's his only heir. Dost thou affect[10] her, Claudio?

CLAUDIO: 0, my lord,
Before we went unto this recent battle,
I look'd upon her with a soldier's eye,
That liked, but had a rougher task in hand
Than to drive liking to the name of love:
But now I am return'd, and that war-thoughts
Have left their places vacant, in their rooms
Come thronging soft and delicate desires,
All prompting me how fair young Hero is.

DON PEDRO: If thou dost love fair Hero, cherish it;
And I will speak with her and with her father,
And thou shalt have her. There's reveling tonight:
I will assume thy part in some disguise,
And tell fair Hero I am Claudio;
And in her bosom I'll unclasp my heart.
Then after to her father will I speak;
And the conclusion is, she shall be thine.
In practice let us put it presently. [*Exeunt.*]

SCENE 2 (I.II)

[*A room in Leonato's house. Enter, severally,* LEONATO *and* ANTONIO.]

ANTONIO: How now, brother! I can tell you strange news, that you yet dreamt not of.

LEONATO: Are they good?[11]

ANTONIO: They show well outwardly. Walking in my orchard, I overheard the Prince who admitted to Count Claudio that he loved my niece your daughter, and hoped to acknowledge it this night in a dance.

LEONATO: I will acquaint my daughter withal, that she may be the better prepared for an answer, if peradventure[12] this be true. Go you and tell her of it. [*Exeunt.*]

SCENE 3 (I.III)

[*Another room in Leonato's house. Enter* DON JOHN *and* CONRADE.]

CONRADE: My lord! Why are you thus out of measure sad?

DON JOHN: There is no measure to my sadness, therefore it is without limit.

CONRADE: Yet conceal it, my lord.

DON JOHN: I cannot hide what I am: I must be sad when I have cause, and smile at no man's jests; eat when I have stomach, and wait for no man's leisure; sleep when I am drowsy, and tend on no man's business; laugh when I am merry, and cater to no man's humour.

CONRADE: Yea, but you must not make the full show of this. You have of late stood out against your brother, and he hath ta'en you newly into his grace; where it is impossible you should take true root but by the fair weather that you make yourself.

DON JOHN: I had rather be a canker in a hedge than a rose in his grace; and it better fits my blood to be disdain'd than to pretend to love. In this, though I cannot be said to be a flattering honest man, it must not be denied but I am a plain-dealing villain. I am fitted with a muzzle, and enfranchised with a clog[13]; therefore I have decreed not to sing in my cage. If I had my mouth, I would bite; if I had my liberty, I would do my liking: in the meantime let me be that I am, and seek not to alter me.

CONRADE: Can you make no use of your discontent?

DON JOHN: I make all use of it, for I use it only. Who comes here? [*Enter* BORACHIO.]
What news, Borachio?

BORACHIO: I came yonder from the great supper. The Prince your brother is royally entertained by Leonato, and I can give you intelligence of an intended marriage.

DON JOHN: Will it serve for any model to build mischief on? What is he for a fool[14] that betroths himself?

BORACHIO: Marry, it is your brother's right hand man.

DON JOHN: Who, the most exquisite Claudio?

BORACHIO: Even he.

DON JOHN: A proper squire! And who, and who? Which way looks he?

BORACHIO: Marry, on Hero, the daughter and heir of Leonato.

DON JOHN: A very forward little fledgling-chick[15]! How came you to this?

BORACHIO: I overheard heard it agreed upon, that the Prince should woo Hero for himself, and having obtain'd her, give her to Count Claudio.

DON JOHN: Come, come, let us thither: this may prove food to my displeasure. That young upstart hath all the glory of my overthrow: if I can cross him in any way, I bless myself in every way. You are both sure, and will assist me?

CONRADE: To the death, my lord.

DON JOHN: Let us to the great supper: their cheer is the greater that I am subdued. Would the cook were of my mind! Shall we go see what's to be done?

BORACHIO: We'll wait upon your lordship. *[Exeunt.]*

ACT 2, SCENE 1 (II₁)

[A hall in Leonato's house. Enter **LEONATO**, **ANTONIO**, **HERO**, **BEATRICE***]*

LEONATO: Was not Count John here at supper?

ANTONIO: I saw him not.

BEATRICE: How tartly that gentleman looks! I never can see him but I am heart-burn'd an hour after.

HERO: He is of a very melancholy disposition.

BEATRICE: He were an excellent man that were made just in the midway between him and Benedick: the one is too like a painting, and says nothing; and the other too like a spoiled eldest son, evermore tattling.

LEONATO: By my troth, niece, thou wilt never get thee a husband, if thou be so shrewd of thy tongue.

ANTONIO: In faith, she's too curst. God will send you no husband.

BEATRICE: For the which blessing I thank him upon my knees every morning and evening. Lord, I could not endure a husband with a beard on his face: I had rather lie in the woolen.

LEONATO: You may light on a husband that hath no beard.

BEATRICE: What should I do with him? Dress him in my apparel, and make him my waiting-gentlewoman? He that hath a beard is more than a youth; and he that hath no beard is less than a man: and he that is more than a youth is not for me; and he that is less than a man, I am not for him. Therefore, I will instead lead all the apes into hell.[16]

LEONATO: Well, then, go you into hell?

BEATRICE: No; but to the gate; and there will the devil meet me, like an old cuckold, with horns on his head, and say, "Get you to heaven, Beatrice, get you to heaven; here's no place for you maids." So deliver I up my apes, and away to Saint Peter for the

heavens; he shows me where the bachelors sit, and there live we as merry as the day is long.

ANTONIO: *[to* **HERO***]* Now niece, I trust you will be ruled by your father.

BEATRICE: Yes, it is my cousin's duty to make curtsy, and say, "Father, as it please you:"- but yet for all that, cousin, let him be a handsome fellow, or else make another curtsy, and say, "Father, as it please me."

LEONATO: Well, niece, I hope to see you one day fitted with a husband.

BEATRICE: Not till God make men of some other metal than earth. No, uncle, I'll none: Adam's sons are my brethren; and, truly, I hold it a sin to match in my kindred.

LEONATO: Daughter, remember what I told you: if you are solicited in that kind, you know your answer.

BEATRICE: Hear me, Hero: Marriage has three phases: first it is wooing, then wedding, and finally repenting.

LEONATO: Cousin, you apprehend passing shrewdly.[17]

BEATRICE: I have a good eye, uncle; I can see a church by daylight.

LEONATO: The revelers are ent'ring, brother: make good room.

[Enter **DON PEDRO**, **CLAUDIO**, **BENEDICK**, **BALTHAZAR**, **DON JOHN**, **BORACHIO**, **MARGARET**, **URSULA**, *and others, masked; with music.]*

DON PEDRO: *[to* **HERO***]* Lady, will you walk about with your friend?

HERO: So you walk softly, and look sweetly, and say nothing, I am yours for the walk; and especially when I walk away.

DON PEDRO: Speak low, if you speak love. *[Takes her aside.]*

BALTHAZAR: Well, I would you did like me.

MARGARET: So would not I, for your own sake; for I have many ill qualities.

BALTHAZAR: Which is one?

MARGARET: I say my prayers aloud.

BALTHAZAR: I love you the better: the hearers may cry, Amen.

MARGARET: God match me with a good dancer!

BALTHAZAR: Amen.

MARGARET: And God keep him out of my sight when the dance is done! Answer, clerk!

BALTHAZAR: No more words. The clerk is answered. *[They step aside]*

URSULA: I know you well enough; you are Signior Antonio.

ANTONIO: At a word, I am not.

URSULA: I know you by the waggling of your head.

ANTONIO: To tell you true, I counterfeit him.

URSULA: You could never do him so well, unless you were the very man. Here's his hand up and down: you are he, you are he.

ANTONIO: At a word, I am not.

URSULA: Come, come, do you think I do not know you by your excellent wit? Can virtue hide itself? Go to! You are he: graces will appear, and there's an end. *[They step aside]*

BEATRICE: Will you not tell me who told you so?

BENEDICK: No, you shall pardon me.

BEATRICE: Nor will you not tell me who you are?

BENEDICK: Not now.

BEATRICE: That I was disdainful, and that I had my good wit out of the "Hundred Merry Tales"?[18] Well, this was Signior Benedick that said so.

BENEDICK: What's he?

BEATRICE: I am sure you know him well enough.

BENEDICK: Not I, believe me.

BEATRICE: Did he never make you laugh?

BENEDICK: I pray you, what is he?

BEATRICE: Why, he is the Prince's jester: a very dull fool; his only gift is in devising impossible slanders: he both amuses men and angers them, and then *they* laugh at him and beat him.

BENEDICK: When I know the gentleman, I'll tell him what you say.

BEATRICE: Do, do. *[Music within.]* We must follow the leaders.

BENEDICK: In every good thing.

BEATRICE: Nay, if they lead to any ill, I will leave them at the next turning.

[Music. Dance. Exeunt all except **DON JOHN**, **BORACHIO**, *and* **CLAUDIO** *standing alone to one side.]*

DON JOHN: Sure my brother is amorous on Hero, and hath withdrawn her father to speak with him about it. Only one remains.

BORACHIO: And that is Claudio, I know him by his bearing.

DON JOHN: Are not you Signior Benedick?

CLAUDIO: You know me well; I am he.

DON JOHN: Signior, you are very near my brother in his love: he is enamour'd on Hero; I pray you, dissuade him from her, she is no equal for his birth: you may do the part of an honest man in it.

CLAUDIO: How know you he loves Hero?

DON JOHN: I heard him swear his affection.

BORACHIO: So did I too; and he swore he would marry her tonight.

DON JOHN: Come, let us to the banquet. *[Exeunt* **DON JOHN** *and* **BORACHIO**.*]*

CLAUDIO: Thus answer I in name of Benedick, but hear these ill news with the ears of Claudio. 'Tis certain so; the Prince woos for himself. Friendship is constant in all other things but in the office and affairs of love: Therefore all hearts in love speak for themselves. Beauty is a witch! Alas, farewell, Hero!

[Enter **BENEDICK**.*]*

BENEDICK: Count Claudio, come, will you go with me?

CLAUDIO: Whither?

BENEDICK: The Prince hath got your Hero.

CLAUDIO: I wish him joy of her. I pray you leave me.

BENEDICK: How now?

CLAUDIO: Then I'll leave you. *[Exit.]*

BENEDICK: Alas, poor hurt fowl! But, that my Lady Beatrice should know me, and not know me! The Prince's fool! Ha! It may be I go under that title because I am merry. Yea, but surely I am not so reputed. It is the base, bitter disposition of Beatrice that gives false report. Well, I'll be revenged as I may.

[Enter **DON PEDRO**.*]*

DON PEDRO: Now, Signior, where's the count? Did you see him?

BENEDICK: I found him here all melancholy. I told him that your grace had got the good will of this young lady; and I offer'd him my company but he departed.

DON PEDRO: The Lady Beatrice hath a quarrel to you: the gentleman that danced with her told her she is much wrong'd by you.

BENEDICK: O, she misused me past the endurance of a block! An oak but with one green leaf on it would have answer'd her; my very visor[19] began to assume life and scold with her. She told me—not thinking I had been myself—that I was the Prince's jester, and that I was duller than a great thaw; huddling jest upon jest with such impossible conveyance[20] upon me that I stood like a target, with a whole army shooting at me. Every word she speaks stabs: if her breath were as terrible as her terminations, there were no living near her; she would infect to the North Star. I would not marry her for any reward. Come, talk not of her: while she is here, a man may live as quiet in hell as in a sanctuary; and I would sin upon purpose, because I would rather go to hell than endure her! All disquiet, horror, and perturbation follow her!

DON PEDRO: Look, here she comes.

[Enter **CLAUDIO**, **BEATRICE**, **HERO**, *and* **LEONATO**.*]*

BENEDICK: Will your grace command me any service to the world's end? I will go on the slightest errand now to the remote Antipodes that you can devise to send me on; I will fetch you a toothpick now from the furthest inch of Asia; fetch you a hair off the great Khan's beard; do you any impossible embassage to the Pygmies; rather than hold three words' conference with this harpy. You have no employment for me?

DON PEDRO: None, but to desire your good company.

BENEDICK: O God, sir, here's a dish I love not: I cannot endure my Lady Tongue. *[Exit]*

DON PEDRO: Come, lady, come; you have lost the heart of Signior Benedick. You have put him down, lady, you have put him down.

BEATRICE: I would not let him put me down, my lord, lest I should prove the mother of fools. I have brought Count Claudio, whom you sent me to seek.

DON PEDRO: Why, how now, Count! Wherefore are you sad?

CLAUDIO: Not sad, my lord.

DON PEDRO: How then? sick?

CLAUDIO: Neither, my lord.

BEATRICE: The count is neither sad, nor sick, nor merry, nor well; but civil, Count, civil as an orange, and something of that jealous complexion.

DON PEDRO: Here, Claudio, I have woo'd in thy name, and fair Hero is won: I have spoken with her father, and, his good-will obtain'd, name the day of marriage, and God give thee joy!

LEONATO: Count, take of me my daughter and with her my fortunes: his Grace hath made the match, and all grace say Amen to it!

BEATRICE: Speak, Count, 'tis your cue.

CLAUDIO: Silence is the perfectest herald of joy. I were but little happy, if I could say how much. Lady, as you are mine, I am yours.

BEATRICE: Speak, cousin; or, if you cannot, stop his mouth with a kiss, and let not him speak neither. [**CLAUDIO** *and* **HERO** *kiss.]*

DON PEDRO: In faith, lady, you have a merry heart.

BEATRICE: Yea, my lord; I thank it, poor fool, it keeps on the windy side of care. My cousin tells him in his ear that he is in her heart.

CLAUDIO: And so she doth, cousin.

BEATRICE: Ah marriage!—Thus goes every one to the world but I, who may sit in a corner, and cry heigh-ho for a husband!

DON PEDRO: Lady Beatrice, I will get you one.

BEATRICE: I would rather have one of your father's getting. Hath your Grace ne'er a brother like you? Your father begot excellent husbands, if a maid could come by them.

DON PEDRO: Will you have me, lady?

BEATRICE: No, my lord, unless I might have another for working-days: your grace is too costly to wear every day. But, I beseech your Grace, pardon me: I was born to speak all mirth and no matter.

DON PEDRO: To be merry best becomes you; for, out of question, you were born in a merry hour.

BEATRICE: No, sure, my lord, my mother cried; but then there was a star danced, and under that was I born. Cousins, God give you joy!

LEONATO: Niece, will you look to those things I told you of?

BEATRICE: I cry you mercy, uncle. By your Grace's pardon. *[Exit.]*

DON PEDRO: By my troth, a pleasant-spirited lady. Yet she cannot endure to hear tell of a husband.

LEONATO: O, by no means: she mocks all her wooers out of suit.

DON PEDRO: She were an excellent wife for Benedick.

LEONATO: O Lord, my lord, if they were but a week married, they would talk themselves mad!

DON PEDRO: Count Claudio, when mean you to go to church?

CLAUDIO: Tomorrow, my lord: time goes on crutches till love have all his rites.

LEONATO: Not till Monday, my dear son, which is hence just a few days; and a time too brief, too, to prepare.

DON PEDRO: Come, I warrant thee, Claudio, the time shall not go dully by us. I will, in the interim, undertake one of Hercules' labours; which is, to bring Signior Benedick and the Lady Beatrice into a mountain of affection the one with the other. I would fain have it a match. If you three will but minister such assistance as I shall give you direction, we shall fashion it.

LEONATO: My lord, I am for you.

CLAUDIO: And I, my lord.

DON PEDRO: And you too, gentle Hero?

HERO: I will do any modest office, my lord, to help my cousin to a good husband.

DON PEDRO: And Benedick is not the unhopefullest husband that I know. He's noble, valiant, and honest. I will teach you how to humour your cousin, that she shall fall in love with Benedick. And I, with your two helps, will so practice on Benedick, that, in despite of his quick wit and his queasy stomach, he shall fall in love with Beatrice. If we can do this, Cupid is no longer chief archer: his glory shall be ours, for we are the only love-gods. Go in with me, and I will tell you my drift. *[Exeunt.]*

SCENE 2 (II II)

*[Another room in Leonato's house. Enter **DON JOHN** and **BORACHIO**.]*

DON JOHN: It is so; the Count Claudio shall marry the daughter of Leonato.

BORACHIO: Yea, my lord; but I can cross it.

DON JOHN: Any bar, any cross, any impediment will be medicine to me: I am sick in displeasure to him; and whatsoever comes athwart his affection ranges evenly with mine. How canst thou cross this marriage?

BORACHIO: Not honestly, my lord; but so covertly that no dishonesty shall appear in me.

DON JOHN: Show me briefly how.

BORACHIO: I think I told your lordship how much I am in the favor of Margaret, the waiting-gentlewoman to Hero.

DON JOHN: I remember.

BORACHIO: I can, at any unseasonable instant of the night, appoint her to look out at her lady's chamber-window.

DON JOHN: What life is in that, to be the death of this marriage?

BORACHIO: The poison of that lies in you to temper. Go you to the Prince your brother; spare not to tell him that he hath wrong'd his honor in marrying the renown'd Claudio to a contaminated stale, such a one as Hero.

DON JOHN: What proof shall I make of that?

BORACHIO: Proof enough to misuse the Prince, to vex Claudio, to undo Hero, and kill Leonato. Go, then; draw Don Pedro and Claudio alone: tell them that you know that Hero loves me and that you have discover'd thus. They will scarcely believe this without trial: offer them the chance to see me at her chamber-window; hear me call Margaret, Hero, and bring them to see this the very night before the intended wedding, for in the meantime I will so fashion the matter that Hero shall be absent, and there shall appear such seeming truth of Hero's disloyalty, that jealousy shall be call'd assurance, and all the preparation overthrown.

DON JOHN: Be cunning in the working this, and thy fee is a thousand ducats.

BORACHIO: Be you constant in the accusation, and my cunning shall not shame me.

[Exeunt.]

SCENE 3 (II III)

*[Leonato's orchard. Enter **BENEDICK** alone.]*

BENEDICK: I do much wonder that one man, seeing how much another man is a fool when he dedicates his behaviours to love, will, after he hath laugh'd at such shallow follies in others, become the source of his own scorn by falling in love: and such a man is Claudio. I have known when there was no music with him but the drum and the fife; and now had he rather hear the lute and the pipe. I have known when he would have walk'd ten miles to see a good armour; and now will he lie ten nights awake, carving the fashion of a new doublet. He was wont to speak plain and to the purpose, like an honest man and a soldier; and now is he turn'd orthography; his words are a very fantastical banquet, just so many strange dishes. May I be so converted? I think not. Love shall never make me such a fool. One woman is fair, yet I am well; another is wise, yet I am well; another virtuous, yet I am well: but till all graces be in one woman, one woman shall not come in my grace. Rich she shall be, that's certain; wise, or I'll none; virtuous, or I'll never cheapen her; fair, or I'll never look on her; mild or come not near me; noble, of good discourse, an excellent musician, and her hair shall be of what colour it please God! Ha, the Prince and Monsieur Love! I will hide me in the arbour. *[Withdraws]*

[Enter DON PEDRO, CLAUDIO, LEONATO, BALTHAZAR*]*

DON PEDRO: Come, shall we hear this music?

CLAUDIO: Yea, my good lord. How still the evening is.

DON PEDRO: See you where Benedick hath hid himself? Come, Balthazar, we'll hear that song again.

BALTHAZAR: *[sings]*

> Sigh no more, ladies, sigh no more,
> Men were deceivers ever;
>   One foot in sea, and one on shore;
>   To one thing constant never:
>   Then sigh not so,
>   But let them go,
>   And be you blithe and bonny;
>   Converting all your sounds of woe
>   Into Hey nonny, nonny.
>   Sing no more ditties, sing no more,
>   Of dumps so dull and heavy;
>   The fraud of men was ever so,
>   Since summer first was leavy.
>   Then sigh not so, etc.

DON PEDRO: By my troth, a good song.

BALTHAZAR: And an ill singer, my lord.

DON PEDRO: Ha, no, no, faith; thou sing'st well enough.

BENEDICK: *[aside]* If he had been a dog that should have howl'd thus, they would have hang'd him.

DON PEDRO: Balthazar, I pray thee, get us some excellent music for tomorrow night we would have it at the Lady Hero's chamber-window.

BALTHAZAR: The best I can, my lord.

DON PEDRO: Do so: farewell. *[Exeunt* BALTHAZAR*]* Come thither, Leonato. What was it you told me of today—that your niece Beatrice was in love with Signior Benedick?

CLAUDIO: O, aye! *[aside to* PEDRO*]* stalk on, stalk on; the fowl sits. *[aloud]* I did never think that lady would have loved any man.

LEONATO: No, nor I neither; but most wonderful that she should so dote on Signior Benedick, whom she hath in all outward behaviours seem'd ever to abhor.

BENEDICK: *[aside]* Is't possible? Sits the wind in that corner?

LEONATO: By my troth, my lord, I cannot tell what to think of it: but that she loves him with an enraged affection, it is past the infinity of thought.

DON PEDRO: Maybe she doth but counterfeit.

CLAUDIO: Faith, like enough.

LEONATO: O God, counterfeit! There was never counterfeit of passion came so near the life of passion that she displays.

CLAUDIO: *[aside]* Bait the hook well; this fish will bite.

DON PEDRO: You amaze me: I would have thought her spirit had been invincible against all assaults of affection.

LEONATO: I would have sworn it had, my lord; especially against Benedick.

BENEDICK: *[aside]* I should think this a gull[21], but that the gray-bearded fellow speaks it.

DON PEDRO: Hath she made her affection known to Benedick?

LEONATO: No; and swears she never will: that's her torment.

CLAUDIO: Your daughter tells me that she says "How can I that have so oft scorned him, write to him that I love him?"

LEONATO: She'll be up twenty times a night; and there will she sit in her smock till she have writ a full sheet of paper: my daughter tells us all. Then she tore the letter into a thousand halfpence[22]; rail'd at herself, that she should be so immodest to write to one that she knew would reject her.

CLAUDIO: Then down upon her knees she falls, weeps, sobs, beats her heart, tears her hair, prays, curses: "O sweet Benedick! God give me patience!"

LEONATO: She doth indeed; my daughter says so: and the ecstasy hath so much overborne her, that my daughter is afeard she will do a desperate outrage to herself: it is very true.

DON PEDRO: It were good that Benedick knew of it by some other, if she will not discover it.

CLAUDIO: To what end? He would but make a sport of it, and torment the poor lady worse.

DON PEDRO: Shame on him. She's an excellent-sweet lady; and, out of all suspicion, she is virtuous.

CLAUDIO: And she is exceeding wise.

DON PEDRO: In everything but in loving Benedick.

LEONATO: Aye. I am sorry for her, as I have just cause, being her uncle and her guardian.

CLAUDIO: Hero thinks surely she will die; for she says she will die, if he loves her not; and she will die, ere she make her love known.

DON PEDRO: If she should make tender[23] of her love, 'tis very possible he'll scorn it; for the man, as you know all, hath a contemptible spirit. I am sorry for your niece. Shall we go seek Benedick, and tell him of her love?

CLAUDIO: Never tell him, my lord: he will but mock her. Let her wear it out[24] with good counsel.

DON PEDRO: I love Benedick well; and I could wish he would modestly examine himself, to see how much he is unworthy so good a lady.

LEONATO: My lord, will you walk? Dinner is ready.

CLAUDIO: If he do not dote on her upon this, I will never trust my expectation.

DON PEDRO: Let there be the same net spread for her: and that must your daughter and her gentlewomen carry. The sport will be, when they each hold an opinion of the other's dotage, and no such matter: that's the scene that I would see. Let us send her to call him in to dinner.

[Exeunt DON PEDRO, CLAUDIO, *and* LEONATO.*]*

BENEDICK: *[coming forward]* This can be no trick: the conference was sadly borne. They have the truth of this from Hero. They seem to pity the lady: it seems her affections have their full bent. Love me! Why, it must be requited! I hear how I am censured: they say I will bear myself proudly, if I perceive the love come from her; they say too that she will rather die than give any sign of affection. I did never think to marry—I must not seem proud—happy are they that hear their detractions, and can put them to mending. They say the lady is fair, 'tis a truth, and virtuous, 'tis so, and wise—but for loving me—by my troth, it is no addition to her wit, nor to her folly, for I will be horribly in love with her! I may chance have some odd quirks and remnants of wit broken on me, because I have rail'd so long against marriage: but doth not the appetite alter? A man loves the meat in his youth that he cannot endure in his age. The world must be peopled! When I said I would die a bachelor, I did not think I should live till I were married. Here comes Beatrice. By this day, she's a fair lady: I do spy some marks of love in her. *[Enter* BEATRICE.*]*

BEATRICE: Against my will I am sent to bid you come in to dinner.

BENEDICK: Fair Beatrice, I thank you for your pains.

BEATRICE: I took no more pains for those thanks than you take pains to thank me: if it had been painful, I would not have come. You have no stomach²⁵, signior: fare you well. *[Exit.]*

BENEDICK: Ha! "Against my will I am sent to bid you come in to dinner,"—there's a double meaning in that. "I took no more pains for those thanks than you took pains to thank me,"—that's as much as to say, "Any pains that I take for you is as easy as thanks." If I do not take pity of her, I am a villain; if I do not love her, I am a fool. I will go get her picture. *[Exit.]*

ACT 3
ACT 3, SCENE 1 (III i)

*[*LEONATO's *orchard. Enter* HERO, MARGARET *and* URSULA.*]*

HERO: Good Margaret, run thee to the parlour;
There shalt thou find my cousin Beatrice,
Whisper her ear, and tell her, I and Ursula
Walk in the orchard, and our whole discourse
Is all of her; say that thou overheard'st us;
And bid her hide her²⁶ to listen to our purpose.

MARGARET: I'll make her come, I warrant you, presently. *[Exit.]*

HERO: Now, Ursula, when Beatrice doth come,
As we do trace this walkway up and down,
Our talk must only be of Benedick.
When I do name him, let it be thy part
To praise him more than ever man did merit:
My talk to thee must be how Benedick
Is sick in love with Beatrice. *[Enter* BEATRICE, *behind.]* Now begin.

URSULA: This fish shall greedily devour our bait.

HERO: Then go we near her, that her ear lose nothing *[They advance to the bower.]* No, truly, Ursula, she's too disdainful;
Her spirits too coy and wild.

URSULA: But are you sure
That Benedick loves Beatrice so entirely?

HERO: So says the Prince and my betrothed lord.

URSULA: And did they bid you tell her of it, madam?

HERO: They did entreat me to acquaint her of it;
But I persuaded them, if they loved Benedick,
To wish him wrestle with affection,
And never to let Beatrice know of it.

URSULA: Why did you so? Doth he not deserve...

HERO: O god of love! I know he doth deserve
As much as may be yielded to a man:
But Nature never framed a woman's heart
Of prouder stuff than that of Beatrice;
Disdain and scorn ride sparkling in her eyes,
Misprizing²⁷ what they look on; and her wit
Values itself so highly, she cannot love.

URSULA: If she knew his love, she'd make sport at it.

HERO: Why, you speak truth. I never yet saw man,
How wise, how noble, young, how rarely-featured,
But she would turn the man the wrong side out.

URSULA: Sure, sure, such carping is not commendable.

HERO: But who dare tell her so? If I should speak,
She'd mock me into air, kill me with wit!
Therefore let Benedick consume away in sighs,
waste inwardly until he dies.

URSULA: Yet tell her of it: hear what she will say.

HERO: No; rather I will go to Benedick,
And counsel him to fight against his passion.

URSULA: I pray you, be not angry with me, madam, speaking my fancy: Signior Benedick, for shape, for bearing, argument, and valour, goes foremost in report through Italy. Are you married tomorrow, madam then?

HERO: Aye, tomorrow. Come, go in: I'll show thee some attires; and ask thee which is best to furnish me.

URSULA: She's limed²⁸; we have caught her, madam.

HERO: [aside] If it prove so, then loving goes by haps²⁹:
Some Cupid kills with arrows, some with traps.

[Exeunt HERO *and* URSULA.*]*

BEATRICE: *[coming forward]*
What fire is in mine ears? Can this be true?³⁰
Stand I condemn'd for pride and scorn so much?
Contempt, farewell! and maiden pride, adieu!
No glory lives behind the back of such.
And, Benedick, love on; I will requite thee,
Taming my wild heart to thy loving hand:
If thou dost love, my kindness shall incite thee
To bind our loves up in a holy band!

SCENE 2 (III ii)

*[Room—*LEONATO's *house. Enter* DON PEDRO, CLAUDIO, BENEDICK, LEONATO.*]*

DON PEDRO: I do but stay till your marriage and then go I toward Aragon.

CLAUDIO: I'll bring you thither, my lord, if you'll vouchsafe³¹ me.

DON PEDRO: Nay, that would be as great a soil in the new gloss of your marriage, as to show a child his new coat, and forbid him to wear it. I will only be bold with Benedick for his company; for he is all mirth: his heart is so inviolate that Cupid's bow-dare not shoot his arrows at him.

BENEDICK: Gallants, I am not as I have been.

LEONATO: So say I: methinks you are sadder.

CLAUDIO: Could he be in love?

Don Pedro: Impossible! He cannot be in love: if he be sad, he wants money.

Benedick: I have a toothache.

Claudio: Yet say I he is in love.

Don Pedro: There is no appearance of fancy in him. Hath any man seen him at the barber's?

Claudio: No, but the barber's man hath been seen with him.

Leonato: Indeed, he looks younger than he did, by the loss of a beard.

Don Pedro: Nay; he rubs himself with civet[32]: can you smell him out by that?

Claudio: That's as much as to say, the sweet youth's in love.

Don Pedro: The greatest note of it is his melancholy.

Claudio: Nay, but I know who loves him.

Benedick: Yet is this no charm for the toothache. Old signior, walk aside with me: I have studied eight or nine wise words to speak to you, which these hobby-horses must not hear.

[Exeunt **Benedick** *and* **Leonato.***]*

Don Pedro: Hero and Margaret have by this play'd their parts with Beatrice

Claudio: And the two bears will not again bite one another when they meet.

[Enter **Don John.***]*

Don John: My lord and brother, God save you!

Don Pedro: Good evening, brother.

Don John: If your leisure served, I would speak with you.

Don Pedro: In private?

Don John: If it please you: yet Count Claudio may hear: for what I would speak of concerns him.

Don Pedro: What's the matter?

Don John: *[to* **Claudio***]* Means your lordship to be married tomorrow?

Don Pedro: You know he does.

Don John: I know not that, when he knows what I know.

Claudio: If there by *any* impediment, I pray you discover it.

Don John: My brother, I think, holds you well; and in dearness of heart hath helped to effect your ensuing marriage - surely suit ill-spent and labour ill-bestow'd.

Don Pedro: Why, what's the matter?

Don John: I came hither to tell you the lady is disloyal.

Claudio: Who, Hero?

Don John: Even she; Leonato's Hero, your Hero, every man's Hero.

Claudio: Disloyal!

Don John: The word is too good to paint out her wickedness. Wonder not till further proof. Go but with me tonight, you shall see her chamber-window enter'd, even the night before her wedding-day: if you love her then, tomorrow wed her; but it would better fit your honour to change your mind.

Claudio: May this be so?

Don John: If you will follow me, I will show you enough.

Claudio: If I see anything tonight why I should not marry her tomorrow, in the congregation, where I should wed her, there will I shame her.

Don John: I will disparage her no further till you are my witnesses: bear it coldly but till midnight, and let the issue show itself. *[Exeunt.]*

SCENE 3 (III.iii)

[A street. Enter **Dogberry**, *master constable and* **Verges**, *a constable, with the* **Watch**[33].*]*

Dogberry: Are you good men and true?

Verges: Yea, body and soul. Give them their charge, neighbour Dogberry.

Dogberry: First, who think you the most desartless[34] man to be constable?

First watchman: (**Hugh Oatcake**) George Seacoal for he can write and read.

Dogberry: Come hither, neighbour Seacoal. God hath bless'd you with a good name; to be a well-favour'd man is the gift of fortune; but to write and read comes by nature.

Second watchman: (**George Seacoal**) Both which, master constable...

Dogberry: You have: I knew it would be your answer. You are thought here to be the most senseless and fit man for the constable of the watch; therefore bear you the lantern. This is your charge:- you shall comprehend all vagrom men; you are to bid any man stand, in the Prince's name.

Second watchman: How if he will not stand?

Dogberry: Why, then, take no note of him, but let him go; and presently call the rest of the watch together, and thank God you are rid of a knave.

Verges: If he will not stand when he is bidden, he is none of the Prince's subjects.

Dogberry: True, and they are to meddle with none but the Prince's subjects. You shall also make no noise in the streets; for, for the watch to babble and talk is most tolerable and not to be endured.

Second watchman: We will rather sleep than talk: we know what belongs to a watch.

Dogberry: Why, you speak wise, for I cannot see how sleeping should offend. Well, you are to call at all the alehouses, and bid those that are drunk get them to bed.

Second Watchman: How if they will not?

Dogberry: Why, then, let them alone till they are sober: if they make you not then the better answer, you may say they are not the men you took them for.

Second watchman: Well, sir.

Dogberry: If you meet a thief, you may suspect him, by virtue of your office.

Second watchman: If we know him to be a thief, shall we not lay hands on him?

Dogberry: I think the most peaceable way for you, if you do take a thief, is to let him show himself what he is, and steal out of your company.

Verges: If you hear a child cry in the night, you must call to the nurse and bid her still it.

Second watchman: How if the nurse be asleep and will not hear us?

Dogberry: Why, then, depart in peace, and let the child wake her with crying.

Verges: 'Tis very true.

Dogberry: This is the end of the charge. Well, masters, good night.

FIRST WATCHMAN: Well, masters, we hear our charge: let us go sit here upon the church-bench till two, and then all to bed.

DOGBERRY: One word more, honest neighbours. I pray you, watch about Signior Leonato's door; for the wedding being there tomorrow, there is a great coil[35] tonight. Adieu: be vigitant, I beseech you.

[Exeunt DOGBERRY. *Enter* BORACHIO *and* CONRADE.]

BORACHIO: What, Conrade!

FIRST WATCHMAN: *[aside]* Peace! stir not.

BORACHIO: Conrade, I say!

CONRADE: Here, man; I am at thy elbow.

FIRST WATCHMAN: *[aside]* Some treason, masters: yet stand close.

BORACHIO: Therefore know I have earn'd of Don John a thousand ducats. And know that I have tonight woo'd Margaret, the Lady Hero's gentlewoman, by the name of Hero: she leans out at her mistress' chamber-window, bids me a thousand times good night. I should first tell thee how the Prince, Claudio, and my master, planted and placed and possess'd by my master Don John, saw afar off in the orchard this amiable encounter.

CONRADE: And thought *they* Margaret was Hero?

BORACHIO: Yea, and away went Claudio enraged; swore he would meet her, as he was appointed, next morning in church, and there, before the whole congregation, shame her with what he saw o'ernight, and send her home again without a husband.

FIRST WATCHMAN: We charge you, in the Prince's name, stand!

SECOND WATCHMAN: Call up the right master constable. We have here recover'd the most dangerous piece of lechery that ever was known in the commonwealth.

CONRADE: Master, masters —

FIRST WATCHMAN: Never speak: we charge you let us obey you to go with us.

CONRADE: Come, we'll obey you. *[Exeunt.]*

SCENE 4 (IIIiv)

[Room in Leonato's house. Enter HERO, MARGARET, *and* URSULA.]

HERO: Good Ursula, wake my cousin Beatrice, and desire her to rise.

URSULA: I will, lady.

HERO: And bid her come hither.

URSULA: Well. *[Exit.]*

MARGARET: Oh madam, your gown's a most rare fashion, i' faith. I saw the Duchess of Milan's gown that they praise so.

HERO: O, that exceeds, they say.

MARGARET: By my troth, it's but a night-gown in respect of yours. For a fine, quaint, graceful, and excellent fashion, yours is worth ten of hers.

HERO: God give me joy to wear it! For my heart is exceeding heavy.

MARGARET: 'Twill be heavier soon by the weight of a man.

HERO: Fie upon thee! Art not ashamed?

MARGARET: Of what, lady? Is there any harm in "the heavier for a husband"? None, I think, an[36] it be the right husband and the right wife; otherwise 'tis light, and not heavy: ask my Lady Beatrice else; here she comes.

[Enter BEATRICE.]

HERO: Good morrow, coz.

BEATRICE: Good morrow, sweet Hero.

HERO: Why, how now! Do you speak in the sick tune?

BEATRICE: I am all out of tune, methinks. 'Tis almost five o'clock, cousin; 'tis time you were ready. By my troth, I have a cold.

HERO: These gloves the Count sent me; they are an excellent perfume.

BEATRICE: I am stuff'd, cousin; I cannot smell.

MARGARET: A maid, and stuff'd! There's goodly catching of cold.

BEATRICE: O, God help me! God help me! How long have you profess'd apprehension[37]?

MARGARET: Ever since you left it. Doth not my wit become me rarely?

BEATRICE: It is not seen enough. By my troth, I am sick.

MARGARET: Get you some of this distill'd *carduus benedictus*[38], and lay it to your heart: it is the only thing for a cold.

BEATRICE: Benedictus! Why Benedictus? You have some moral in this Benedictus?

MARGARET: Moral! No, by my troth, I have no moral. You may think perchance that I think you are in love: nay, by'r lady, I am not such a fool to think that, but methinks you look with your eyes as other women do.

[Enter URSULA.]

URSULA: Madam, withdraw: the Prince, the Count, Signior Benedick, Don John, and all the gallants of the town, are come to fetch you to church.

HERO: Help to dress me, good coz, good Meg, good Ursula. *[Exeunt.]*

SCENE 5 (IIIv)

[Another room—Leonato's house. Enter LEONATO, DOGBERRY *and* VERGES.]

LEONATO: What would you with me, honest neighbour?

DOGBERRY: Marry, sir, I would have some confidence with you that discerns you nearly.

LEONATO: Brief, I pray you; for you see it is a busy time with me.

DOGBERRY: Marry, this it is, sir—

VERGES: Yes, in truth it is, sir.

LEONATO: What is it, my good friends?

DOGBERRY: Goodman Verges, sir, speaks a little off the matter: an old man, sir, and his wits are not so blunt as, God help, I would desire they were; but, in faith, honest as the skin between his brows.

VERGES: Yes, I thank God I am as honest as any man living that is an old man and no honester than I.

DOGBERRY: Comparisons are odorous, neighbour Verges.

LEONATO: Neighbours, you are tedious.

DOGBERRY: It pleases your worship to say so, but we are the poor Duke's officers; but truly, for mine own part, if I were as tedious as a king, I could find in my heart to bestow it all of your worship.

LEONATO: I would fain know what you have to say.

VERGES: Marry, sir, our watch tonight ha' ta'en a couple of as arrant knaves as any in Messina.

DOGBERRY: A good old man, sir; he will be talking, as they say. When the age is in, the wit is out: God help us! Well said, i' faith, neighbour Verges. Well, God's a good man; an two men ride of a horse, one must ride behind.

LEONATO: I must leave you.

DOGBERRY: One word, sir: our watch, sir, have indeed comprehended two aspicious persons, and we would have them this morning examined before your worship.

LEONATO: Take their examination yourself, and bring it me: I am now in great haste, as it may appear unto you.

DOGBERRY: It shall be suffigance.

LEONATO: Drink some wine ere you go: fare you well. [Enter URSULA.]

URSULA: My lord, they stay for you to give your daughter to her husband.

LEONATO: I'll wait upon them: I am ready.

[Exeunt LEONATO and URSULA.]

DOGBERRY: Go, good partner, go, get you thy pen and inkhorn. We are now to examination these men.

VERGES: And we must do it wisely.

DOGBERRY: We will spare for no wit, only get writing implements to set down our excommunication, and meet me at the jail. [Exeunt.]

ACT 4
ACT 4, SCENE 1 (IVi)

[A church. Enter DON PEDRO, DON JOHN, LEONATO, FRIAR FRANCIS, CLAUDIO, BENEDICK, HERO, BEATRICE, ATTENDANTS.]

FRIAR FRANCIS: You come hither, my lord, to marry this lady?

CLAUDIO: No.

LEONATO: To be married to her, friar. You come to marry her.

FRIAR FRANCIS: Lady, you come hither to be married to this count?

HERO: I do.

FRIAR FRANCIS: If either of you know any inward impediment why you should not be conjoin'd, I charge you, on your souls, to utter it.

CLAUDIO: Know you any, Hero?

HERO: None, my lord.

FRIAR FRANCIS: Know you any, Count?

LEONATO: I dare make his answer,—none.

CLAUDIO: O, what men dare do! what men may do! what men daily do, not knowing what they do! Stand thee by, friar. Father, by your leave: Will you with free and unconstrained soul give me this maid, your daughter?

LEONATO: As freely, son, as God did give her me.

CLAUDIO: And what have I to give you back, whose worth may counterpoise this rich and precious gift?

DON PEDRO: Nothing, unless you render her again.

CLAUDIO: Sweet Prince, you learn[39] me noble thankfulness. There, Leonato, take her back again: Give not this rotten orange to your friend; She's but the sign and semblance of her honour.

Behold how like a maid she blushes here! Would all you who see her not swear that she Were a maid by these exterior shows? She is none: She knows the heat of a lascivious bed; Her blush is guiltiness, not modesty.

LEONATO: What do you mean, my lord?

CLAUDIO: Not to be married, not to knit my soul to an approved wanton.

LEONATO: Dear my lord, if you, in your own proof, have vanquish'd the resistance of her youth, and made defeat of her virginity—

CLAUDIO: I know what you would say: if I have known her, You will say she did embrace me as a husband, To excuse the 'forehand sin. No, Leonato, I never tempted her with word too large; But, as a brother to his sister, show'd Bashful sincerity and comely love.

HERO: And seem'd I ever otherwise to you?

CLAUDIO: Out on thee, seeming! You do seem as chaste As is the purest bud ere it be blown; But you do rage in savage sensuality.

HERO: Is my lord well, that he doth speak so wide?

CLAUDIO: Sweet Prince, why speak not you?

DON PEDRO: What should I speak? I stand dishonour'd, that have gone about To link my dear friend to a common stale.

LEONATO: Are these things spoken? Or do I but dream?

DON JOHN: Sir, they are spoken, and these things are true.

BENEDICK: This looks not like a nuptial.

HERO: True! O God!

CLAUDIO: Let me but move one question to your daughter; And as her father, bid her answer truly.

LEONATO: I charge thee do so, as thou art my child.

CLAUDIO: What man was he talk'd with you yesternight Out at your window betwixt twelve and one? Now, if you are a maid, answer to this.

HERO: I talk'd with no man at that hour, my lord.

DON PEDRO: Why, then are you no maiden. Leonato, I am sorry you must hear: upon mine honour, Myself, my brother, and this grieved count Did see her, hear her, at that hour last night Talk with a ruffian at her chamber-window; Who hath indeed, most like a liberal villain, Confess'd the vile encounters they have had A thousand times in secret.

DON JOHN: Fie, fie! they are not to be named, my lord, Not to be spoke of; thus, pretty lady, I am sorry for thy much misgovernment.

CLAUDIO: O Hero, what a Hero hadst thou been, If half thy outward graces had been placed About the thoughts and counsels of thy heart! But fare thee well, most foul, most fair! Farewell, Thou pure impiety and impious purity! For thee I'll lock up all the gates of love.

LEONATO: Hath no man's dagger here a point for me? [Hero swoons.]

BEATRICE: Why, how now, cousin!

DON JOHN: Come, let us go. These things, come thus to light.

[*Exeunt* **DON PEDRO, DON JOHN, CLAUDIO,**
ATTENDANTS.]

BENEDICK: How doth the lady?
BEATRICE: Dead, I think: help, uncle
Hero! why, Hero!—uncle!—Signior Benedick!—Friar!
LEONATO: Death is the fairest cover for her shame That may be
wish'd for.
BEATRICE: How now, cousin Hero!
FRIAR FRANCIS: Have comfort, lady.
LEONATO: Dost thou look up?
FRIAR FRANCIS: Yea, wherefore should she not?
LEONATO: Wherefore! Why, doth not every earthly thing
Cry shame upon her? Could she here deny
The story that is printed in her blood?
Do not live, Hero; do not ope thine eyes:
Why ever wast thou lovely in my eyes?
This shame derives itself from unknown loins!
O, she is fall'n into a pit of ink,
The wide sea hath not drops to wash her clean!
BENEDICK: Sir, sir, be patient. For my part, I am
So full of wonder, I know not what to say.
BEATRICE: O, on my soul, my cousin is belied[40]!
BENEDICK: Lady, were you her bedfellow last night?
BEATRICE: No, truly, not; although, until last night,
I have this twelvemonth been her bedfellow[41].
LEONATO: Confirm'd, confirm'd! O, torture me no more.
Would the two princes lie? and Claudio lie,
Who loved her so, that, speaking of her foulness,
Wash'd it with tears? Hence from here! Let her die.
FRIAR FRANCIS: Hear me a little, having been too silent.
Call me a fool; trust not my judgment nor
My observations, trust not my age,
My reverence, calling, nor divinity,
If this sweet lady be not guiltless here.
Lady, what man is he you are accused of?
HERO: They know that do accuse me; I know none:
If I know more of any man alive
Than that which maiden modesty doth warrant,
Let all my sins lack mercy! 0 my father,
Prove you that any man with me conversed
At hours unmeet, or that I yesternight
Maintain'd the change of words with any creature,
Refuse me, hate me, torture me to death!
FRIAR FRANCIS: There is some strange misprision in the princes.
BENEDICK: Two of them have the very bent of honour;
And if their wisdoms be misled in this,
The practice of it lives in John the bastard,
Whose spirits toil in frame of villainies.
FRIAR FRANCIS: Now let my counsel sway you in this case.
Your daughter here the princes left for dead,
Let her awhile be secretly kept in,
And publish it that she is dead indeed;
Maintain a mourning ostentation,
And on your family's old monument
Hang mournful epitaphs, and do all rites

That appertain unto a burial.
LEONATO: What shall become of this? What will this do?
FRIAR FRANCIS: She dying, as it must be so maintain'd,
Upon the instant that she was accused,
Shall be lamented, pitied, and excused
Of every hearer: So 'twill fare with Claudio.
The supposition of the lady's death
Will quench the wonder of her infamy:
And if it sort not well, you may conceal her
(As best befits her wounded reputation)
In some reclusive and religious life,
Out of all eyes, tongues, minds, and injuries.
BENEDICK: Signior Leonato, let the Friar advise you.
LEONATO: I'll let thy wisdom lead me in my grief.
FRIAR FRANCIS: 'Tis well consented: presently away;
For to strange sores strangely they strain the cure.
Come, lady, die to live: this wedding-day
Perhaps is but prolong'd: have patience and endure.

[*Exeunt* **FRIAR, HERO, LEONATO, ATTENDANTS**]

BENEDICK: Lady Beatrice, have you wept all this while?
BEATRICE: Yea, and I will weep a while longer.
BENEDICK: I will not desire that.
BEATRICE: You have no reason; I do it freely.
BENEDICK: Surely I do believe your fair cousin is wrong'd.
BEATRICE: Ah, how much might the man deserve of me that
would right her!
BENEDICK: Is there any way to show such friendship?
BEATRICE: A very even way, but no such friend.
BENEDICK: May a man do it?
BEATRICE: It is a man's office, but not yours.
BENEDICK: I do love nothing in the world so well as you: is not
that strange?
BEATRICE: As strange as the thing I know not. It were as possible
for me to say I loved nothing so well as you: but believe me
not; and yet I lie not; I confess nothing, nor I deny nothing. I
am sorry for my cousin.
BENEDICK: I protest I love thee.
BEATRICE: Why, then, God forgive me!
BENEDICK: What offense, sweet Beatrice?
BEATRICE: You have stay'd me in a happy hour: I was about to
protest I loved you.
BENEDICK: And do it with all thy heart.
BEATRICE: I love you with so much of my heart, that none is left
to protest.
BENEDICK: Come, bid me do any thing for thee.
BEATRICE: Kill Claudio.
BENEDICK: Not for the wide world.
BEATRICE: You kill me to deny it. Farewell.
BENEDICK: Tarry, sweet Beatrice.
BEATRICE: I am gone, though I am here—there is no love in
you—nay, I pray you, let me go.
BENEDICK: Beatrice
BEATRICE: In faith, I will go.
BENEDICK: We'll be friends first.
BEATRICE: You dare easier be friends with me than fight with mine
enemy.
BENEDICK: Is Claudio thine enemy?

BEATRICE: Is he not approved in the height a villain, that hath slander'd, scorn'd, dishonour'd my kinswoman? O that I were a man! What, bear her in hand until they come to take hands; and then, with public accusation, uncover'd slander, unmitigated rancour—O God, that I were a man! I would eat his heart in the market-place.

BENEDICK: Hear me, Beatrice—

BEATRICE: Talk with a man out at a window!- A proper saying!

BENEDICK: Nay, but, Beatrice,—

BEATRICE: Sweet Hero!—she is wrong'd, she is slander'd, she is undone.

BENEDICK: Beat-

BEATRICE: Princes and counties! 0 that I were a man for his sake! or that I had any friend would be a man for my sake! But manhood is melted into curtsies, valour into compliment, and men are only turn'd into tongues. I cannot be a man with wishing, therefore I will die a woman with grieving.

BENEDICK: Tarry, good Beatrice. By this hand, I love thee.

BEATRICE: Use it for my love some other way than swearing by it.

BENEDICK: Think you in your soul the Count Claudio hath wrong'd Hero?

BEATRICE: Yea, as sure as I have a thought or a soul.

BENEDICK: Enough, I am engaged; I will challenge him. I will kiss your hand, and so I leave you. By this hand, Claudio shall render me a dear account. As you hear of me, so think of me. Go, comfort your cousin: I must say she is dead: and so, farewell. [*Exeunt.*]

SCENE 2 (IV ɪɪ)

[*A prison. Enter* **DOGBERRY, VERGES,** *the* **WATCH, CONRADE** *and* **BORACHIO.**]

DOGBERRY: Is our whole dissembly appear'd?

VERGES: Nay, that's certain; we have the exhibition to examine. Let the offenders come before master constable.

DOGBERRY: Yea, marry, let them come before me. What is your name, friend?

BORACHIO: Borachio.

DOGBERRY: Pray, write down—Borachio. Yours, sirrah?

CONRADE: I am a gentleman, sir, and my name is Conrade.

DOGBERRY: Write down—master gentleman Conrade.- Masters, do you serve God?

CONRADE: Yea, sir

BORACHIO: We hope.

DOGBERRY: Write down—that they hope they serve God. Let the watch come forth. Masters, I charge you, in the Prince's name, accuse these men.

FIRST WATCHMAN: This man said, sir, that Don John, the Prince's brother, was a villain.

DOGBERRY: What heard you him say else?

SECOND WATCHMAN: Marry that he had received a thousand ducats of Don John for accusing the Lady Hero wrongfully and that Count Claudio did mean, upon his words, to disgrace Hero before the whole assembly, and not marry her.

DOGBERRY: O villain! thou wilt be condemn'd into everlasting redemption for this. What else?

SECOND WATCHMAN: This is all.

VERGES: And this is more, masters, than you can deny. Prince John is this morning secretly stolen away; Hero was in this manner accused, in this very manner refused, and upon the grief of this suddenly died. Master constable, let these men be bound, and brought to Leonato's: I will go before and show him their examination. [*Exit.*]

DOGBERRY: Come, let them be opinion'd.

FIRST WATCHMAN: Let them be in the hands—

CONRADE: Off, coxcomb!

DOGBERRY: God's my life, where's the sexton? let him write down—the Prince's officer, coxcomb.—Come, bind them.— Thou naughty varlet!

CONRADE: Away! you are an ass, you are an ass.

DOGBERRY: Dost thou not suspect my place? dost thou not suspect my years? O that he were here to write me down an ass! but, masters, remember that I am an ass; though it be not written down, yet forget not that I am an ass. No, thou villain, thou art full of piety, as shall be proved upon thee by good witness. I am a wise fellow; and, which is more, an officer; and, which is more, a householder; and, which is more, as pretty a piece of flesh as any in Messina; and one that knows the law, go to; and a rich fellow enough, go to; and a fellow that hath had losses; and one that hath two gowns, and every thing handsome about him.—Bring him away.—O that I had been writ down an ass! [*Exeunt.*]

ACT 5
ACT 5, SCENE 1 (V ɪ)

[*Before Leonato's house. Enter* **LEONATO** *and* **ANTONIO.**]

ANTONIO: If you go on thus, you will kill yourself.

LEONATO: I pray thee, cease thy counsel, advise me not.
Bring me a father that so loved his child,
Whose joy of her is overwhelm'd like mine,
And then you bid him speak of patience.
But there is no such man: for, brother, men
Can counsel and speak comfort to that grief
Which they themselves not feel; but, tasting it,
Their counsel turns to naught. Give me no counsel:
My griefs cry louder than advertisement.

ANTONIO: Yet bend not all the harm upon yourself; Make those that do offend you suffer too.

LEONATO: There thou speak'st reason: nay, I will do so.
My soul doth tell me Hero is belied;
And that shall Claudio know; so shall the Prince,
And all of them that thus dishonour her.

ANTONIO: Here comes the Prince and Claudio hastily.

[*Enter* **DON PEDRO** *and* **CLAUDIO.**]

DON PEDRO: Good day, good day.

CLAUDIO: Good day to both of you.

LEONATO: Hear you, my lords-

DON PEDRO: We have some haste, Leonato.

LEONATO: Some haste, my lord! Well, fare you well, my lord: Are you so hasty now? Well, all is one.

CLAUDIO: Who wrongs him?

LEONATO: Marry, thou dost wrong me; thou dissembler.
Thou hast so wrong'd mine innocent child and me,
That I am forced to lay my reverence by,
And, with grey hairs and bruise of many days,
Do challenge thee to trial of a man.
I say thou hast belied mine innocent child;
Thy slander hath gone deep and through her heart,
And she lies buried with her ancestors,
O, in a tomb where never scandal slept,
Save this of hers, framed by thy villainy!

CLAUDIO: My villainy!

LEONATO: Thine, Claudio; thine, I say.

DON PEDRO: You say not right.

CLAUDIO: I will not have to do with you.

LEONATO: Canst thou so daff[42] me? Thou hast kill'd my child:
If thou kill'st me, boy, thou shalt kill a man.

DON PEDRO: My heart is sorry for your daughter's death:
But, on my honour, she was charged with nothing
But what was true, and very full of proof.

LEONATO: My lord, my lord,—

DON PEDRO: I will not hear you.

LEONATO: No? Come, brother, away. I will be heard.

[Exeunt LEONATO and ANTONIO.]

DON PEDRO: See, see; here comes the man we went to seek. *[Enter Benedick.]*
Welcome, signior: you are almost come to part almost a fray.

CLAUDIO: We had like to have had our two noses snapp'd off by two old men.

DON PEDRO: Leonato and his brother. What think'st thou?

BENEDICK: I came to seek you both.

CLAUDIO: We have been up and down to seek thee; for we are high-proof melancholy, and would fain have it beaten away. Wilt thou use thy wit?

BENEDICK: It is in my scabbard: shall I draw it?

DON PEDRO: As I am an honest man, he looks pale. Art thou sick, or angry? I think he be angry indeed.

BENEDICK: Sir, you are a villain; I jest not: I will make it good how you dare, with what you dare, and when you dare. Do me right, or I will protest your cowardice. You have kill'd a sweet lady, and her death shall fall heavy on you. Let me hear from you.

CLAUDIO: Well, I will meet you, so I may have good cheer.

DON PEDRO: But when shall we set the savage bull's horns on the sensible Benedick's head?

CLAUDIO: Yea, and text underneath, "Here dwells Benedick, the married man"?

BENEDICK: Fare you well, boy: you know my mind. I will leave you now to your feeble wit. My lord, for your many courtesies I thank you: I must discontinue your company: your brother the bastard is fled from Messina. You have among you kill'd a sweet and innocent lady. For my Lord Lackbeard there, he and I shall meet: and till then peace be with him. *[Exit.]*

DON PEDRO: He is in earnest.

CLAUDIO: In most profound earnest; and, I'll warrant you, for the love of Beatrice.

DON PEDRO: And hath challenged thee.

CLAUDIO: Most sincerely.

DON PEDRO: But, soft you, did he not say, my brother was fled?
How now! Two of my brother's men bound! Borachio one!

[Enter DOGBERRY, VERGES, the WATCH, CONRADE and BORACHIO.]

Officers, what offense have these men done?

DOGBERRY: Marry, sir, they have committed false report; moreover, they have spoken untruths; secondarily, they are slanders; sixth and lastly, they have belied a lady; thirdly, they have verified unjust things; and, to conclude, they are lying knaves.

DON PEDRO: First, I ask thee what they have done; thirdly, I ask thee what's their offense; sixth and lastly, why they are committed: and, to conclude, what you lay to their charge.

BORACHIO: Sweet Prince, do you hear me, and let this count kill me. I have deceived even your very eyes: what your wisdoms could not discover, these shallow fools have brought to light; who, in the night, overheard me confessing to this man, how Don John your brother incensed me to slander the Lady Hero; how you were brought into the orchard, and saw me court Margaret in Hero's garments; how you disgraced her, when you should marry her. My villainy they have upon record; which I had rather seal with my death than repeat over to my shame. The lady is dead upon mine and my master's false accusations. I desire nothing but the reward of a villain.

DON PEDRO: Runs not this speech like iron through your blood?

CLAUDIO: I have drunk poison whiles he utter'd it.

DON PEDRO: But did my brother set thee on to this?

BORACHIO: Yea, and paid me richly for the practice of it.

CLAUDIO: Sweet Hero! Oh dear God! How have I wronged thee!

DOGBERRY: Come, bring away the plaintiffs: by this time our Master Verges hath reform'd Signior Leonato of the matter: and, masters, do not forget to specify, when time and place shall serve, that I am an ass. Here, here comes master Signior Leonato.

[Enter LEONATO, ANTONIO, VERGES]

LEONATO: Which is the villain? Let me see his eyes.,

BORACHIO: If you would know your wronger, look on me.

LEONATO: No, not so, villain; thou beliest thyself:
Here stand a pair of honourable men,
A third is fled, that had a hand in it.
I thank you, Princes, for my daughter's death.

CLAUDIO: I know not how to pray your patience;
Yet I must speak. Choose your revenge yourself;
Impose me to what penance your invention
Can lay upon my sin: yet sinn'd I not
But in mistaking.

DON PEDRO: By my soul, nor I:
And yet, to satisfy this good old man,
I would bend under any heavy weight
That he'll enjoin me to.

LEONATO: I cannot bid you bid my daughter live,
That were impossible: but, I pray you both,
Tell all the people in Messina here
How innocent she died; and if your love
Can labour aught in sad invention,

Hang her an epitaph upon her tomb,
And sing it to her bones—sing it tonight
Tomorrow morning come you to my house;
And since you could not be my son-in-law,
Be yet my nephew: my brother hath a daughter,
Almost the copy of my child that's dead,
And she alone is heir to both of us:
Give her the right you should have given her cousin,
And so dies my revenge.

CLAUDIO: O noble sir,
Your over-kindness doth wring tears from me!
I do embrace your offer.

LEONATO: Tomorrow, then, I will expect your coming;

DOGBERRY: Moreover, sir, this plaintiff here, the offender, did call me ass: I beseech you, let it be remember'd in his punishment.

LEONATO: I thank thee for thy care and honest pains.

DOGBERRY: Your worship speaks like a most thankful and reverend youth; and I praise God for you.

LEONATO: There's for thy pains.

DOGBERRY: God save the foundation!

LEONATO: Go, I discharge thee of thy prisoner, and I thank thee.

DOGBERRY: God keep your worship! I wish your worship well; God restore you to health! I humbly give you leave to depart; and if a merry meeting may be wish'd, God prohibit it! Come, neighbour.

[Exeunt DOGBERRY *and* VERGES.*]*

LEONATO: Until tomorrow morning, lords, farewell.

[Exeunt WATCH, BORACHIO, CONTRADE, LEONATO, ANTONIO)*

DON PEDRO: We will not fail.

CLAUDIO: Tonight I'll mourn with Hero.

[Exeunt DON PEDRO *and* CLAUDIO.*]*

SCENE 2 (VII)

[Leonato's garden. Enter BENEDICK *and* MARGARET.*]*

BENEDICK: Pray thee, sweet mistress Margaret, deserve well at my hands by helping me to the speech of Beatrice.

MARGARET: Will you, then, write me a sonnet in praise of my beauty?

BENEDICK: In so high a style, Margaret, that no man living shall come over it; for, in most comely truth, thou deservest it.

MARGARET: To have no man come over me! why, shall I always keep below stairs?

BENEDICK: Thy wit is as quick as the greyhound's mouth—it catches.

MARGARET: And yours as blunt as the fencer's foils, which hit, but hurt not.

BENEDICK: A most manly wit, Margaret; it will not hurt a woman: and so, I pray thee, call Beatrice: I give thee the bucklers.[43]

MARGARET: Give us the swords; we have bucklers of our own. Well, I will call Beatrice to you, who I think hath legs.

BENEDICK: And therefore will come. *[Exit* MARGARET.*]* How pitiful I compose—My poor self in love cannot woo in verse! Marry, I cannot show it in rhyme. I have tried: I can find out no rhyme to "lady" but "baby," an innocent rhyme; for "scorn," "horn,"— a hard rhyme; for "school," "fool,"—a babbling rhyme; very ominous endings: no, I was not born under a rhyming planet! *[Enter* BEATRICE.*]* Sweet Beatrice, wouldst thou come when I call'd thee?

BEATRICE: Yea, signior, and depart when you bid me.

BENEDICK: O, stay but till then!

BEATRICE: "Then" is spoken; fare you well now: and yet, ere I go, let me go with that I came[44]; which is, with knowing what hath pass'd between you and Claudio.

BENEDICK: Only foul words; and thereupon I will kiss thee.

BEATRICE: Foul words is but foul wind and foul wind is but foul breath. I will depart unkiss'd.

BENEDICK: I tell thee plainly, Claudio undergoes my challenge; and either I must shortly hear from him, or I will subscribe him a coward. And, I pray thee now, tell me for which of my bad parts didst thou first fall in love with me?

BEATRICE: For them all together; which maintain'd such a state of evil, that they will not admit any good part to intermingle with them. But for which of my good parts did you first suffer love for me?

BENEDICK: Suffer love—a good epithet! I do suffer love indeed, for I love thee against my will.

BEATRICE: In spite of your heart, I think; alas, poor heart! If you spite it for my sake, I will spite it for yours; for I will never love that which my friend hates.

BENEDICK: Thou and I are too wise to woo peaceably. Now tell me, how doth your cousin?

BEATRICE: Very ill.

BENEDICK: And how do you?

BEATRICE: Very ill too.

BENEDICK: Serve God, love me, and mend. There will I leave you too, for here comes one in haste. *[Enter* URSULA.*]*

URSULA: Madam, you must come to your uncle. Yonder's old coil at home: it is proved my Lady Hero hath been falsely accused, the Prince and Claudio mightily abused; and Don John is the author of all, who is fled and gone. Will you come presently?

BEATRICE: Will you go hear this news, signior?

BENEDICK: I will live in thy heart, die in thy lap, and be buried in thy eyes. And moreover I will go with thee to thy uncle's. *[Exeunt.]*

SCENE 3 (VIII)

[A church. Enter DON PEDRO, CLAUDIO, BALTHASAR, ATTENDANTS.*]*

CLAUDIO: Is this the monument of Leonato?

BALTHASAR: It is, my lord.

CLAUDIO: *[reads from a scroll]*
"Done to death by slanderous tongues
    Was the Hero that here lies;
    Death, in recompense of her wrongs,

Gives her fame which never dies.
So the life that died with shame
Lives in death with glorious fame."
Hang thou there upon the tomb,
Praising her when I am dumb.
Now, music, sound, and sing your solemn hymn.

BALTHASAR: *[Song.]* Pardon, goddess of the night
Those that slew thy virgin knight;
For the which, with songs of woe,
Round about her tomb they go.
Midnight, assist our moan;
Help us to sigh and groan,
Heavily, heavily;
Graves, yawn, and yield your dead,
Till death be uttered,
Heavily, heavily.

CLAUDIO: Now, unto thy bones good night!
Yearly will I do this rite.

DON PEDRO: Good morrow, masters; put your torches out: The
wolves have prey'd; and look, the gentle day,
Before the wheels of Phoebus, round about
Dapples the drowsy east with spots of grey.
Thanks to you all, and leave us: fare you well.

CLAUDIO: Good morrow, masters: each his several way.

DON PEDRO: Come, let us hence, and put on other weeds; And
then to Leonato's we will go.

CLAUDIO: And Hymen now with luckier issue speed's than this for
whom we render'd up this woe! *[Exeunt.]*

SCENE 4 (VIII)

[A room in Leonato's house or the church. Enter LEONATO,
ANTONIO, BENEDICK, FRIAR FRANCIS*]*

FRIAR FRANCIS: Did I not tell you she was innocent?

LEONATO: So are the Prince and Claudio, who accused her.

BENEDICK: Friar, I must entreat your pains, I think.

FRIAR FRANCIS: To do what, signior?

BENEDICK: To bind me, or undo me; one of them. Signior
Leonato, truth it is, good Signior,
Your niece regards me with an eye of favour.
And I do with an eye of love requite her.

LEONATO: The sight whereof I think you had from me,
From Claudio, and the Prince: but what's your will?

BENEDICK: But, your good-will this day to be conjoin'd
In the state of honourable marriage.
In which, good friar, I shall desire your help.

LEONATO: My heart is with your liking.

FRIAR FRANCIS: And my help.
Here comes the Prince and Claudio.

[Enter DON PEDRO *and* CLAUDIO, *with* ATTENDANTS.]*

DON PEDRO: Good morrow to this fair assembly.

LEONATO: Good morrow, Prince; good morrow, Claudio:
We here attend you. Are you yet determined

Today to marry with my brother's daughter?
Call her forth, brother; here's the Friar ready.

[Exit ANTONIO.]*

CLAUDIO: All this I owe you sir and far, far more.

[Enter ANTONIO, *with* BEATRICE, MARGARET, URSULA,
and HERO *masked.]*

Which is the lady I must seize upon?

ANTONIO: This same is she, and I do give you her.

CLAUDIO: Why, then she's mine. Sweet, let me see your face.

LEONATO: No, that you shall not, till you take her hand before this
Friar, and swear to marry her.

CLAUDIO: Give me your hand before this holy Friar: I am your
husband, if you like of me.

HERO: And when I lived, I was your other wife: *[Unmasking.]* And
when you loved, you were my other husband.

CLAUDIO: Another Hero!

HERO: Nothing certainer:
One Hero died defiled; but I do live,
And surely as I live, I am a maid.

DON PEDRO: The former Hero! Hero that is dead!

LEONATO: She died, my lord, but whiles her slander lived.

FRIAR FRANCIS: All this amazement can I qualify;
When after all the holy rites are ended.

BENEDICK: Soft and fair, Friar. Which is Beatrice?

BEATRICE: *[unmasking]* I answer to that name. What is your will?

BENEDICK: Do not you love me?

BEATRICE: Why, no; no more than reason.

BENEDICK: Why, then your uncle, and the Prince, and Claudio
Have been deceived; for they swore you did.

BEATRICE: Do not you love me?

BENEDICK: Troth, no; no more than reason.

BEATRICE: Why, then my cousin, Margaret, and Ursula
Are much deceived; for they did swear you did.

BENEDICK: They swore that you were almost sick for me.

BEATRICE: They swore that you were well-nigh dead for me.

BENEDICK: 'Tis no such matter. Then you do not love me?

BEATRICE: No, truly, but in friendly recompense.

LEONATO: Come, cousin, I am sure you love the gentleman.

CLAUDIO: And I'll be sworn upon't that he loves her; For here's a
paper, written in his hand,
A halting sonnet of his own pure brain,
Fashion'd to Beatrice.

HERO: And here's another,
Writ in my cousin's hand, stol'n from her pocket,
Containing her affection unto Benedick.

BENEDICK: A miracle! here's our own hands against our hearts.
Come, I will have thee; but, by this light, I take thee for pity.

BEATRICE: I would not deny you; but, by this good day, I yield
upon great persuasion; and partly to save your life, for I was
told you were in a consumption.

BENEDICK: Peace! I will stop your mouth. *[Kissing her.]*

DON PEDRO: How dost thou, Benedick, the married man?

BENEDICK: I'll tell thee what, Prince; the world cannot flout at
me for what I have said against marriage; for man is a giddy
thing, and this is my conclusion. For thy part, Claudio, I did
think to have beaten thee; but in that thou art like to be my

kinsman, live unbruised, and love my cousin. Come, come, we are friends. Let's have a dance ere we are married, that we may lighten our own hearts and our wives' heels.

LEONATO: We'll have dancing afterward.

BENEDICK: First, of my word; therefore play, music!-
Prince, thou art sad; get thee a wife, get thee a wife.

[Enter BALTHASAR.]

BALTHASAR: My lord, your brother John is ta'en in flight,
And brought with armed men back to Messina.

BENEDICK: Think not on him till tomorrow: I'll devise thee brave punishments for him. Strike up, pipers!

[Dance. Exeunt.]

NOTES:

[1] Don: a title of respect. In this play, princes, counts, and minor lords may all be called Don.

[2] He is indeed...the stuffing: He is indeed a figure stuffed to resemble a man, but what he's truly made of...

[3] trouble: the expense of entertaining a prince and his followers could, and sometimes did, bankrupt a family. However, the honor and potential future profit attained by such a visit was also considerable.

[4] his head: meaning his grey hair and aged face

[5] Marks: notices

[6] Rare: excellent. parrot teacher: one who repeats the same word/phrase over and over again.

[7] jade's trick: a jade is a bad tempered horse, whose trick is to slip free of the bridle or rope.

[8] bull's horns: traditional sign of a man with an unfaithful wife.

[9] embassage: mission

[10] affect: love

[11] Are they good?: "news" was often plural in Elizabethan usage.

[12] peradventure: by chance

[13] enfranchised with a clog: granted certain freedoms (enfranchised), but with a wooden block on a short leash to restrain him.

[14] What is he for a fool: what kind of fool is he

[15] A very forward little fledgling-chick: probably referring to Claudio as a presumptuous brat.

[16] I will instead...apes into hell.: an Elizabethan proverb: "Old maids lead apes in hell."

[17] Apprehend passing shrewdly: understand unusually clearly.

[18] Hundred Merry Tales: a collection of crudely comic stories popular in Elizabethan London, but a definite insult to Beatrice's wit.

[19] visor: mask

[20] conveyance: quickness

[21] gull: trick

[22] halfpence: a small coin, therefore "tiny pieces"

[23] tender: make an offer

[24] wear it out: get over it

[25] stomach: appetite

[26] her: herself

[27] Misprizing: undervaluing. what: that which

[28] limed: trapped. Liming was the practice of spreading a sticky sub-stance on tree branches in order to catch birds that landed on the branch.

[29] goes by haps: progresses (or not) by chance.

[30] This is the first time Beatrice breaks into poetry, signaling her charming sense of romance, hidden until now.

[31] vouchsafe: allow

[32] civet: perfume derived from the civet cat.

[33] The Watch: several men whose jobs are to walk and watch the streets at night.

[34] The first of Dogberry's many malapropisms, he means "deserving"

[35] coil: a boisterous gathering

[36] an: if

[37] professed apprehension: claimed to be witty

[38] carduus benedictus: the blessed thistle, known as an herbal medicine

[39] learn: teach

[40] belied: sworn against dishonestly

[41] Where Hero and Beatrice spent the night, since not in their usual room, is a plot point Shakespeare ignored.

[42] daft put aside

[43] I give...bucklers: a buckler is a shield with a spike in the center. I means "I admit you've beaten me."

[44] with that I came: what I came for

M Butterfly

by David Henry Hwang

Characters

Rene Gallimard: a French diplomat in China
Song Liling: a performer in the Beijing Opera and Gallimard's lover
Marc: friend of Gallimard
Man #2: friend of Gallimard
Consul Sharpless: friend of Gallimard
Renee: woman Gallimard meets or imagines
Woman at Party: woman Gallimard meets or imagines
Girl in Magazine: woman Gallimard meets or imagines
Comrade Chin: Chinese contact of Song
Suzuki: Chinese contact of Song
Shu Fang: Chinese contact of Song
Helga: Gallimard's wife
M. Toulon: man of authority to Gallimard
Man #1: man of authority to Gallimard
Judge: man of authority to Gallimard

Setting

The action of the play takes place in a Paris prison in the present, and in recall, during the decade 1960 to 1970 in Beijing, and from 1966 to the present in Paris.

ACT 1, SCENE 1

M. GALLIMARD's prison cell. Paris. Present.

Lights fade up to reveal RENE GALLIMARD, 65, in a prison cell. He wears a comfortable bathrobe, and looks old and tired. The sparsely furnished cell contains a wooden crate upon which sits a hot plate with a kettle, and a portable tape recorder. GALLIMARD sits on the crate staring at the recorder, a sad smile on' his face.

Upstage SONG, who appears as a beautiful woman in traditional Chinese garb, dances a traditional piece from the Peking Opera, surrounded by the percussive clatter of Chinese music.

Then, slowly, lights and sound cross fade; the Chinese opera music dissolves into a Western opera, the "Love Duet" from Puccini's Madame Butterfly. *SONG continues dancing, now to the Western accompaniment. Though her movements are the same, the difference in music now gives them a balletic quality.*

GALLIMARD rises, and turns upstage towards the figure of SONG, who dances without acknowledging him.

GALLIMARD: Butterfly, Butterfly...

> *[He forces himself to turn away, as the image of SONG fades out, and talks to us.]*

GALLIMARD: The limits of my cell are as such: four-and-a-half meters by five. There's one window against the far wall; a door, very strong, to protect me from autograph hounds. I'm responsible for the tape recorder, the hot plate, and this charming coffee table.

When I want to eat, I'm marched off to the dining room—hot, steaming slop appears on my plate. When I want to sleep, the light bulb turns itself off—the work of fairies. It's an enchanted space I occupy. The French—we know how to run a prison.

But, to be honest, I'm not treated like an ordinary prisoner. Why? Because I'm a celebrity. You see, I make people laugh.

I never dreamed this day would arrive. I've never been considered witty or clever. In fact, as a young boy, in an informal poll among my grammar school classmates, I was voted "least likely to be invited to a party." It's a title I managed to hold onto for many years. Despite some stiff competition.

But now, how the tables turn! Look at me: the life of every social function in Paris. Paris? Why be modest? My fame has spread to Amsterdam, London, New York. Listen to them! In the world's smartest parlors. I'm the one who lifts their spirits!

> *[With a flourish, GALLIMARD directs our attention to another part of the stage.]*

SCENE 2

A party. Present.

Lights go up on a chic-looking parlor, where a well-dressed trio, two men and one woman, make conversation. GALLIMARD also remains lit; he observes them from his cell.

WOMAN: And what of Gallimard?

MAN 1: Gallimard?

MAN 2: Gallimard!

GALLIMARD: *[To us]* You see? They're all determined to say my name, as if it were some new dance.

WOMAN: He still claims not to believe the truth.

MAN 1: What? Still? Even since the trial?

WOMAN: Yes. Isn't it mad?

MAN 2: *[Laughing]* He says...it was dark...and she was very modest! *[The trio break into laughter.]*

MAN 1: So—what? He never touched her with his hands?

MAN 2: Perhaps he did, and simply misidentified the equipment. A compelling case for sex education in the schools.

WOMAN: To protect the National Security—the Church can't argue with that.

MAN 1: That's impossible! How could he not know?

MAN 2: Simple ignorance.

MAN 1: For twenty years?

MAN 2: Time flies when you're being stupid.

WOMAN: Well, I thought the French were ladies' men.

MAN 2: It seems Monsieur Gallimard was overly anxious to live up to his national reputation.

WOMAN: Well, he's not very good-looking.

MAN 1: No, he's not.

MAN 2: Certainly not.

WOMAN: Actually, I feel sorry for him.

MAN 2: A toast! To Monsieur Gallimard!

WOMAN: Yes! To Gallimard!

MAN 1: To Gallimard!

MAN 2: Vive la différence!

> *[They toast, laughing. Lights down on them.]*

SCENE 3

M. GALLIMARD's cell.

GALLIMARD *[smiling]:* You see? They toast me. I've become patron saint of the socially inept. Can they really be so foolish? Men like that they should be scratching at my door, begging to learn my secrets! For I, Rene Gallimard, you see, I have known, and been loved by...the Perfect Woman.

Alone in this cell, I sit night after night, watching our story play through my head, always searching for a new ending, one which redeems my honor, where she returns at last to my arms. And I imagine you—my ideal audience—who come to understand and even, perhaps just a little, to envy me.

> *[He turns on his tape recorder. Over the house speakers, we hear the opening phrases of* Madame Butterfly.*]*

GALLIMARD: In order for you to understand what I did and why, I must introduce you to my favorite opera: *Madame Butterfly.* By Giacomo Puccini. First produced at La Scala, Milan, in 1904, it is now beloved throughout the Western world.

> *[As GALLIMARD describes the opera, the tape segues in and out to sections he may be describing.]*

GALLIMARD: And why not? Its heroine, Cio-Cio-San, also known as Butterfly, is a feminine ideal, beautiful and brave. And its hero, the man for whom she gives up every-thing, is—*[He pulls out a naval officer's cap from under his crate, pops it on his head, and struts about]*—not very good-looking, not too bright, and pretty much a wimp: Benjamin Franklin Pinkerton of the U.S. Navy. As the curtain rises, he's just closed on two great bargains: one on a house, the other on a woman—call it a package deal.

Pinkerton purchased the rights to Butterfly for one hundred yen—in modern currency, equivalent to about... sixty-six cents. So, he's feeling pretty pleased with himself as Sharpless, the American consul, arrives to witness the marriage.

[MARC, wearing an official cap to designate SHARPLESS, enters and plays the character.]

SHARPLESS/MARC: Pinkerton!

PINKERTON/GALLIMARD: Sharpless! How's it hangin'? It's a great day, just great. Between my house, my wife, and the rickshaw ride in from town, I've saved nineteen cents just this morning.

SHARPLESS: Wonderful. I can see the inscription on your tombstone already: "I saved a dollar, here I lie." *[He looks around]* Nice house.

PINKERTON: It's artistic. Artistic, don't you think? Like the way the shoji screens slide open to reveal the wet bar and disco mirror ball? Classy, huh? Great for impressing the chicks.

SHARPLESS: "Chicks"? Pinkerton, you're going to be a married man!

PINKERTON: Well, sort of.

SHARPLESS: What do you mean?

PINKERTON: This country—Sharpless, it is okay. You got all these geisha girls running around—

SHARPLESS: I know! I live here!

PINKERTON: Then, you know the marriage laws, right? I split for one month, it's annulled!

SHARPLESS: Leave it to you to read the fine print. Who's the lucky girl?

PINKERTON: Cio-Cio-San. Her friends call her Butterfly. Sharpless, she eats out of my hand!

SHARPLESS: She's probably very hungry.

PINKERTON: Not like American girls. It's true what they say about Oriental girls. They want to be treated bad!

SHARPLESS: Oh, please!

PINKERTON: It's true!

SHARPLESS: Are you serious about this girl?

PINKERTON: I'm marrying her, aren't I?

SHARPLESS: Yes—with generous trade-in terms.

PINKERTON: When I leave, she'll know what it's like to have loved a real man. And I'll even buy her a few nylons.

SHARPLESS: You aren't planning to take her with you?

PINKERTON: Huh? Where?

SHARPLESS: Home!

PINKERTON: You mean, America? Are you crazy? Can you see her trying to buy rice in St. Louis?

SHARPLESS: So, you're not serious.

[Pause.]

PINKERTON/GALLIMARD *[As PINKERTON]*: Consul, I am a sailor in port. *[As GALLIMARD]* They then proceed to sing the famous duet, "The Whole World Over."

[The duet plays on the speakers. GALLIMARD, as PINKERTON, lipsyncs his lines from the opera.]

GALLIMARD: To give a rough translation: "The whole world over, the Yankee travels, casting his anchor wherever he wants. Life's not worth living unless he can win the hearts of the fairest maidens, then hotfoot it off the premises ASAP." *[He turns towards MARC]* In the preceding scene, I played Pinkerton, the womanizing cad, and my friend Marc from school...[MARC *bows grandly for our benefit]* played Sharpless, the sensitive soul of reason. In life, however, our positions were usually—no, always—reversed.

SCENE 4
ECOLE NATIONALE. AIX-EN-PROVENCE, 1947.

GALLIMARD: No, Marc, I think I'd rather stay home.

MARC: Are you crazy?! We are going to Dad's condo in Marseille! You know what happened last time?

GALLIMARD: Of course I do.

MARC: Of course you don't! You never know....They stripped, Rene!

GALLIMARD: Who stripped?

MARC: The girls!

GALLIMARD: Girls? Who said anything about girls?

MARC: Rene, we're a buncha university guys goin' up to the woods. What are we gonna do—talk philosophy?

GALLIMARD: What girls? Where do you get them?

MARC: Who cares? The point is, they come. On trucks. Packed in like sardines. The back flips open, babes hop out, we're ready to roll.

GALLIMARD: You mean, they just—?

MARC: Before you know it, every last one of them—they're stripped and splashing around my pool. There's no moon out, they can't see what's going on, their boobs are flapping, right? You close your eyes, reach out it's grab bag, get it? Doesn't matter whose ass is between whose legs, whose teeth are sinking into who. You're just in there, going at it, eyes closed, on and on for as long as you can stand. *[Pause]* Some fun, huh?

GALLIMARD: What happens in the morning?

MARC: In the morning, you're ready to talk some philosophy. *[Beat]* So how 'bout it?

GALLIMARD: Marc, I can't...I'm afraid they'll say no—the girls. So I never ask.

MARC: You don't have to ask! That's the beauty—don't you see? They don't have to say yes. It's perfect for a guy like you, really.

GALLIMARD: You go ahead...I may come later.

MARC: Hey, Rene—it doesn't matter that you're clumsy and got zits—they're not looking!

GALLIMARD: Thank you very much.

MARC: Wimp.

[MARC walks over to the other side of the stage, and starts waving. and smiling at women in the audience.]

GALLIMARD *[To us]*: We now return to my version of *Madame Butterfly* and the events leading to my recent conviction for treason.

[GALLIMARD notices MARC making lewd gestures.]

GALLIMARD: Marc, what are you doing?

MARC: Huh? *[Sotto voce]* Rene, there're a lotta great babes out there. They're probably lookin' at me and thinking, "What a dangerous guy."

GALLIMARD: Yes—how could they help but be impressed by your cool sophistication?

[GALLIMARD pops the SHARPLESS cap on MARC's head, and points him offstage. MARC exits, leering.]

SCENE 5
M. GALLIMARD'S CELL.

GALLIMARD: Next, Butterfly makes her entrance. We learn her age—fifteen...but very mature for her years.

[Lights come up on the area where we saw SONG dancing at the top of the play. She appears there again, now dressed as Madame Butterfly, moving to the "Love Duet." GALLIMARD turns upstage slightly to watch, transfixed.]

GALLIMARD: But as she glides past him, beautiful, laughing softly behind her fan, don't we who are men sigh with hope? We, who are not handsome, nor brave, nor powerful, yet somehow believe, like Pinkerton, that we deserve a Butterfly. She arrives with all her possessions in the folds of her sleeves, lays them all out, for her man to do with as he pleases: Even her life itself— she bows her head as she whispers that she's not even worth the hundred yen he paid for her. He's already given too much, when we know he's really had to give nothing, at all.

[Music and lights on SONG out. GALLIMARD sits at his crate.]

GALLIMARD: In real life, women who put their total worth at less than sixty-six cents are quite hard to find. The closest we come is in the pages of these magazines. *[He reaches into his crate, pulls out a stack of girlie magazines, and begins flipping through them]* Quite a necessity in prison. For three or four dollars, you get seven or eight women. I first discovered these magazines at my uncle's house. One day, as a boy of twelve. The first time I saw them in his closet...all lined up—my body shook. Not with lust no, with power. Here were women—a bashful who would do exactly as I wanted.

[The "Love Duet" creeps in over the speakers. Special comes up, revealing, not SONG this time, but a pinup girl in a sexy negligee, her back to us. GALLIMARD turns upstage and looks at her.]

GIRL: I know you're watching me.

GALLIMARD: My throat...it's dry.

GIRL: I leave my blinds open every night before I go to bed.

GALLIMARD: I can't move.

GIRL: I leave my blinds open and the lights on.

GALLIMARD: I'm shaking. My skin is hot, but my penis is soft. Why?

GIRL: I stand in front of the window.

GALLIMARD: What is she going to do?

GIRL: I toss my hair, and I let my lips part...barely.

GALLIMARD: I shouldn't be seeing this. It's so dirty: I'm so bad.

GIRL: Then, slowly, I lift off my nightdress.

GALLIMARD: Oh, god...I can't believe it. I can't—

GIRL: I toss it to the ground.

GALLIMARD: Now, she's going to walk away. She's going to—

GIRL: I stand there, in the light, displaying myself.

GALLIMARD: No. She's—why is she naked?

GIRL: To you.

GALLIMARD: In front of a window? This is wrong. No—

GIRL: Without shame.

GALLIMARD: No, she must...like it.

GIRL: I like it. .

GALLIMARD: She...she wants me to see.

GIRL: I want you to see.

GALLIMARD: I can't believe it! She's getting excited!

GIRL: I can't see you. You can do whatever you want.

GALLIMARD: I can't do a thing. Why?

GIRL: What would you like me to do...next?

[Lights go down on her. Music of Silence, as GALLIMARD puts away his magazines. Then he resumes talking to us.]

GALLIMARD: Act Two begins with Butterfly staring at the ocean. Pinkerton's been called back to the U. S., and he's given his wife a detailed schedule of his plans. In the column marked "return date," he's written "when the robins nest." This failed to ignite her suspicions. Now, three years have passed without a peep from him. Which brings a response from her faithful servant, Suzuki.

[Comrade CHIN enters, playing SUZUKI.]

SUZUKI: Girl, he's a loser. What'd he ever give you? Nineteen cents and those ugly Day-Glo stockings? Look, it's finished! Kaput! Done! And you should be glad! I mean, the guy was a woofer! He tried before, you know—before he met you, he went down to geisha central and plunked down his spare change in front of the usual candidates—everyone else gagged! These are hungry prostitutes, and they were not interested, get the picture? Now, stop slathering when an American ship sails in, and let's make some bucks—I mean, yen! We are broke!

Now, what about Yamadori? Hey, hey—don't look away—the man is a prince—figuratively, and, what's even better, literally. He's rich, he's handsome, he says he'll die if you don't marry him—and he's even willing to overlook the little fact that you've been deflowered all over the place by a foreign devil. What do you mean, "But he's Japanese?" You're Japanese! You think you've been touched by the whitey god? He was a sailor with dirty hands!

[SUZUKI stalks offstage.]

GALLIMARD: She's also visited by Consul Sharpless, sent by Pinkerton on a minor errand.

[MARC enters, as SHARPLESS.]

SHARPLESS: I hate this job.

GALLIMARD: This Pinkerton—he doesn't show up personally to tell his wife he's abandoning her. No, he sends a government diplomat...at taxpayer's expense.

SHARPLESS: Butterfly? Butterfly? I have some bad—I'm going to be ill. Butterfly, I came to tell you

GALLIMARD: Butterfly says she knows he'll return and if he doesn't she'll kill herself rather than go back to her own people. *[Beat]* This causes a lull in the conversation.

SHARPLESS: Let's put it this way...

GALLIMARD: Butterfly runs into the next room, and returns holding

> *[Sound cue: a baby crying. SHARPLESS, "seeing" this, backs away.]*

SHARPLESS: Well, good. Happy to see things going so well. I suppose I'll be going now. Ta ta. Ciao. *[He turns away. Sound cue out]* I hate this job. *[He exits]*

GALLIMARD: At that moment, Butterfly spots in the harbor an American ship—the Abramo Lincoln!

> *[Music cue: "The Flower Duet." SONG still dressed as BUTTERFLY, changes into a wedding kimono, moving to the music.]*

GALLIMARD: This is the moment that redeems her years of waiting. With Suzuki's help, they cover the room with flowers

> *[CHIN, as SUZUKI, trudges onstage and drops a lone flower without much enthusiasm.]*

GALLIMARD: —and she changes into her wedding dress to prepare for Pinkerton's arrival.

> *[SUZUKI helps BUTTERFLY change. HELGA enters, and helps GALLIMARD change into a tuxedo.]*

GALLIMARD: I married a woman older than myself—Helga.

HELGA: My father was ambassador to Australia. I grew up among criminals and kangaroos.

GALLIMARD: Hearing that brought me to the altar—

> *[HELGA exits.]*

GALLIMARD: —where I took a vow renouncing love. No fantasy woman would ever want me, so, yes, I would settle for a quick leap up the career ladder. Passion, I banish, and in its place—practicality!

But my vows had long since lost their charm by the time we arrived in China. The sad truth is that all men want a beautiful woman, and the uglier the man, the greater the want.

> *[SUZUKI makes final adjustments of BUTTERFLY'S costume, as does GALLIMARD of his tuxedo.]*

GALLIMARD: I married late, at age thirty-one. I was faithful to my marriage for eight years. Until the day when, as a junior-level diplomat in puritanical Peking, in a parlor at the German ambassador's house, during the "Reign of a Hundred Flowers," I first saw her...singing the death scene from *Madame Butterfly.*

> *[SUZUKI runs offstage.]*

SCENE 6

German ambassador's house. Beijing. 1960.

* *The upstage special area now becomes a stage. Several chairs face upstage, representing seating for some twenty guests in*

the parlor. A few "diplomats"—RENEE, MARC, TOULON—in formal dress enter and take seats.

> GALLIMARD *also sits down, but turns towards us and continues to talk. Orchestral accompaniment on the tape is now replaced by a simple piano. SONG picks up the death scene from the point where BUTTERFLY uncovers the harakiri knife.*

GALLIMARD: The ending is pitiful. Pinkerton, in an act of great courage, stays home and sends his American wife to pick up Butterfly's child. The truth, long deferred, has come up to her door.

> *[SONG, playing BUTTERFLY sings the lines from the opera in her own voice—which, though not classical, should be decent.]*

SONG: "Con onor muore/ chi non puo serbar/ vita con onore."

GALLIMARD *[Simultaneously]:* "Death with honor/ Is better than life/ Life with dishonor."

> *[The stage is illuminated; we are now completely within an elegant diplomat's residence. SONG proceeds to play out an abbreviated death scene. Everyone in the room applauds. SONG, shyly takes her bows. Others in the room rush to congratulate her. GALLIMARD remains with us.]*

GALLIMARD: They say in opera the voice is everything. That's probably why I'd never before enjoyed opera. Here...here was a Butterfly with little or no voice—but she had the grace, the delicacy...I believed this girl. I believed her suffering. I wanted to take her in my arms—so delicate, even I could protect her, take her home, pamper her until she smiled. *[Over the course of the preceeding speech, SONG has broken from the upstage crowd and moved directly upstage of GALLIMARD.]*

SONG: Excuse me. Monsieur...? *[GALLIMARD turns upstage, shocked.]*

GALLIMARD: Oh! Gallimard. Mademoiselle...? A beautiful...

SONG: Song Liling.

GALLIMARD: A beautiful performance.

SONG: Oh, please.

GALLIMARD: I usually

SONG: You make me blush. I'm no opera singer at all.

GALLIMARD: I usually don't like Butterfly.

SONG: I can't blame you in the least.

GALLIMARD: I mean, the story.

SONG: Ridiculous.

GALLIMARD: I like the story, but...what?

SONG: Oh, you like it?

GALLIMARD: I...what I mean is, I've always seen it played by huge women in so much bad makeup.

SONG: Bad makeup is not unique to the West.

GALLIMARD: But, who can believe them?

SONG: And you believe me?

GALLIMARD: Absolutely. You were utterly convincing. It's the first time—

SONG: Convincing? As a Japanese woman? The Japanese used hundreds of our people for medical experiments during the war, you know. But I gather such an irony is lost on you.

GALLIMARD: No! I was about to say, it's the first time I've seen the beauty of the story.

SONG: Really?

GALLIMARD: Of her death. It's a...a pure sacrifice. He's unworthy, but what can she do? She loves him...so much. It's a very beautiful story.

SONG: Well, yes, to a Westerner.

GALLIMARD: Excuse me?

SONG: It's one of your favorite fantasies, isn't it? The submissive Oriental woman and the cruel white man.

GALLIMARD: Well, I didn't quite mean...

SONG: Consider it this way: what would you say if a blonde homecoming queen fell in love with a short Japanese businessman? He treats her cruelly, then goes home for three years, during which time she prays to his picture and turns down marriage from a young Kennedy. Then, when she learns he has remarried, she kills herself. Now, I believe you would consider this girl to be a deranged idiot, correct? But because it's an Oriental who kills herself for a Westerner—ah!—you find it beautiful.

[Silence.]

GALLIMARD: Yes...well...I see your point...

SONG: I will never do Butterfly again, Monsieur Gallimard. If you wish to see some real theatre, come to the Peking Opera sometime. Expand your mind.

[SONG walks offstage.]

GALLIMARD *[To us]*: So much for protecting her in my big Western arms.

SCENE 7

M. GALLIMARD'S *apartment. Beijing. 1960.*

Galiimard changes from his tux into a casual suit. **HELGA** *enters.*

GALLIMARD: The Chinese are an incredibly arrogant people.

HELGA: They warned us about that in Paris, remember?

GALLIMARD: Even Parisians consider them arrogant. That's a switch.

HELGA: What is it that Madame Su says? "We are a very old civilization." I never know if she's talking about her country or herself.

GALLIMARD: I walk around here, all I hear every day, everywhere is how old this culture is. The fact that "old" may be synonymous with "senile" doesn't occur to them.

HELGA: You're not going to change them. "East is east, west is west, and..." whatever that guy said.

GALLIMARD: It's just that—silly. I met...at Ambassador Koening's tonight you should've been there.

HELGA: Koening? Oh god, no. Did he enchant you all again with the history of Bavaria?

GALLIMARD: No. I met, I suppose, the Chinese equivalent of a diva. She's a singer in the Chinese opera.

HELGA: They have an opera, too? Do they sing in Chinese? Or maybe in Italian?

GALLIMARD: Tonight, she did sing in Italian.

HELGA: How'd she manage that?

GALLIMARD: She must've been educated in the West before the Revolution. Her French is very good also. Anyway, she sang the death scene from *Madame Butterfly.*

HELGA: *Madame Butterfly!* Then I should have come. *[She begins humming; floating around the room as if dragging long kimono sleeves]* Did she have a nice costume? I think it's a classic piece of music.

GALLIMARD: That's what 1 thought, too. Don't let her hear you say that.

HELGA: What's wrong?

GALLIMARD: Evidently the Chinese hate it.

HELGA: She hated it, but she performed it anyway? Is she perverse?

GALLIMARD: They hate it because the white man gets the girl. Sour grapes if you ask me.

HELGA: Politics again? Why can't they just hear it as a piece of beautiful music? So, what's in their opera?

GALLIMARD: I don't know. But, whatever it is, I'm sure it must be old.

[HELGA exits.]

SCENE 8

Chinese opera house and the streets of Beijing. 1960. The sound of gongs clanging fills the stage.

GALLIMARD: My wife's innocent question kept ringing in my ears. I asked around, but no one knew anything about the Chinese opera. It took four weeks, but my curiosity overcame my cowardice. This Chinese diva—this unwilling Butterfly—what did she do to make her so proud?

The room was hot, and full of smoke. Wrinkled faces, old women, teeth missing—a man with a growth on his neck, like a human toad. All smiling, pipes falling from their mouths, cracking nuts between their teeth, a live chicken pecking at my foot—all looking, screaming, gawking...at her.

[The upstage area is suddenly hit with a harsh white light. It has become the stage for the Chinese opera performance. Two dancers enter, along with **SONG.** **GALLIMARD** *stands apart, watching.* **SONG** *glides gracefully amidst the two dancers. Drums suddenly slam to a halt.* **SONG** *strikes a pose, looking straight at* **GALLIMARD.** *Dancers exit. Light change. Pause, then* **SONG** *walks right of the stage and straight up to* **GALLIMARD.***]*

SONG: Yes. You. White man. I'm looking straight at you.

GALLIMARD: Me?

SONG: You see any other white men? It was too easy to spot you. How often does a man in my audience come in a tie? *[SONG starts to remove her costume. Underneath, she wears simple baggy clothes. They are now backstage. The show is over.]*

SONG: So, you are an adventurous imperialist?

GALLIMARD: I...thought it would further my education.

SONG: It took you four weeks. Why?

GALLIMARD: I've been busy.

SONG: Well, education has always been undervalued in the West, hasn't it?

GALLIMARD: *[Laughing]* I don't think it's true.

SONG: No, you wouldn't. You're a Westerner. How can you objectively judge your own values?

GALLIMARD: I think it's possible to achieve some distance.

SONG: Do you? *[Pause]* It stinks in here. Let's go.

GALLIMARD: These are the smells of your loyal fans.

SONG: I love them for being my fans. I hate the smell they leave behind. I too can distance myself from my people. *[She looks around, then whispers in his ear]* "Art for the masses" is a shitty excuse to keep artists poor. *[She pops a cigarette in her mouth]* Be a gentleman, will you? And light my cigarette.

*[*GALLIMARD *fumbles for a match.]*

GALLIMARD: I don't...smoke.

SONG: *[Lighting her own]* Your loss. Had you lit my cigarette, I might have blown a puff of smoke right between your eyes. Come.

[They start to walk about the stage. It is a summer night on the Beijing streets. Sounds of the city play on the house speakers.]

SONG: How I wish there were even a tiny cafe to sit in. With cappuccinos, and men in tuxedos and bad expatriate jazz

GALLIMARD: If my history serves me correctly, you weren't even allowed into the clubs in Shanghai before the Revolution.

SONG: Your history serves you poorly, Monsieur Gallimard. True, there were signs reading "No dogs and Chinamen." But a woman, especially a delicate Oriental woman—we always go where we please. Could you imagine it otherwise? Clubs in China filled with pasty, big-thighed white women, while thousands of slender lotus blossoms wait just outside the door? Never. The clubs would be empty. *[Beat]* We have always held a certain fascination for you Caucasian men, have we not?

GALLIMARD: But...that fascination is imperialist, or so you tell me.

SONG: Do you believe everything I tell you? Yes. It is always imperialist. But sometimes...sometimes, it is also mutual. Oh—this is my flat.

GALLIMARD: I didn't even—

SONG: Thank you. Come another time and we will further expand your mind.

*[*SONG *exits.* GALLIMARD *continues roaming the streets as he speaks to us.]*

GALLIMARD: What was that? What did she mean, "Sometimes... it is mutual?" Women do not flirt with me. And I normally can't talk to them. But tonight, I held up my end of the conversation.

SCENE 9

GALLIMARD'S *bedroom. Beijing. 1960.* HELGA *enters.*

HELGA: You didn't tell me you'd be home late.

GALLIMARD: I didn't intend to. Something came up.

HELGA: Oh? Like what?

GALLIMARD: I went to the...to the Dutch ambassador's home.

HELGA: Again?

GALLIMARD: There was a reception for a visiting scholar. He's writing a six-volume treatise on the Chinese revolution. We all gathered that meant he'd have to live here long enough to actually write six volumes, and we all expressed our deepest sympathies.

HELGA: Well, I had a good night too. I went with the ladies to a martial arts demonstration. Some of those men when they break those thick boards—[She *mimes fanning herself* whoo-whoo!

*[*HELGA *exits. Lights dim.]*

GALLIMARD: I lied to my wife. Why? I've never had any reason to lie before. But what reason did I have tonight? I didn't do anything wrong. That night, I had a dream. Other people, I've been told, have dreams where angels appear. Or dragons, or Sophia Loren in a towel. In my dream, Marc from school appeared.

*[*MARC *enters, in a nightshirt and cap.]*

MARC: Rene! You met a girl!

*[*GALLIMARD *and* MARC *stumble down the Beijing streets. Night sounds over the speakers.]*

GALLIMARD: It's not that amazing, thank you.

MARC: No! It's so monumental, I heard about it halfway around the world in my sleep!

GALLIMARD: I've met girls before, you know.

MARC: Name one. I've come across time and space to congratulate you. *[He hands* GALLIMARD *a bottle of wine]*

GALLIMARD: Marc, this is expensive.

MARC: On those rare occasions when you become a formless spirit, why not steal the best?

*[*MARC *pops open the bottle, begins to share it with* GALLIMARD.*]*

GALLIMARD: You embarrass me. She...there's no reason to think she likes me.

MARC: "Sometimes, it is mutual"?

GALLIMARD: Oh.

MARC: "Mutual"? "Mutual"? What does that mean?

GALLIMARD: You heard!

MARC: It means the money is in the bank, you only have to write the check!

GALLIMARD: I am—a married man!

MARC: And an excellent one too. I cheated after...six months. Then again and, again, until now—three hundred girls in twelve years.

GALLIMARD: I don't think we should hold that up as a model.

MARC: Of course not! My life—it is disgusting! Phooey! Phooey! But, you—you are the model husband.

GALLIMARD: Anyway, it's impossible. I'm a foreigner.

MARC: Ah, yes. She cannot love you, it is taboo, but something deep inside her heart...she cannot help herself...she must surrender to you. It is her destiny.

GALLIMARD: How do you imagine all this?

MARC: The same way you do. It's an old story. It's in our blood. They fear us, Rene. Their women fear us. And their men—their men hate us. And, you know something? They are all correct.

[They spot a light in a window.]

MARC: There! There, Rene!

GALLIMARD: It's her window.

MARC: Late at night—it burns. The light it burns for you.

GALLIMARD: I won't look. It's not respectful.

MARC: We don't have to be respectful. We're foreign devils.

[Enter SONG, in a sheer robe. The "One Fine Day" aria creeps in over the speakers. With her back to us, SONG mimes attending to her toilette. Her robe comes loose, revealing her white shoulders.]

MARC: All your life you've waited for a beautiful girl who would lay down for you. All your life you've smiled like a saint when it's happened to every other man you know. And you see them in magazines and you see them in movies. And you wonder, what's wrong with me? Will anyone beautiful ever want me? As the years pass, your hair thins and you struggle to hold onto even your hopes. Stop struggling, Rene. The wait is over. [He exits]

GALLIMARD: Marc? Marc?

[At that moment, SONG, her back still towards us, drops her robe. A second of her naked back, then a sound cue: a phone ringing, very loud. Blackout, followed in the next beat by a special up on the bedroom area, where a phone now sits. GALLIMARD stumbles across the stage and picks up the phone. Sound cue out. Over the course of his conversation, area lights fill in the vicinity of his bed. It is the following morning.]

GALLIMARD: Yes? Hello?

SONG [offstage]: Is it very early?

GALLIMARD: Why, yes.

SONG [OFFSTAGE]: How early?

GALLIMARD: It's...it's 5:30. Why are you—?

SONG [offstage]: But it's light outside. Already.

GALLIMARD: It is. The sun must be in confusion today.

[Over the course of SONG's next speech, her upstage special comes up again. She sits in a chair, legs crossed, in a robe, telephone to her ear.]

SONG: I waited until I saw the sun. That was as much discipline as I could manage for one night. Do you forgive me?

GALLIMARD: Of course... for what?

SONG: Then I'll ask you quickly. Are you really interested in the opera?

GALLIMARD: Why, yes. Yes I am.

SONG: Then come again next Thursday. I am playing The Drunken Beauty. May I count on you?

GALLIMARD: Yes. You may.

SONG: Perfect. Well, I must be getting to bed. I'm exhausted. It's been a very long night for me.

[SONG hangs up; special on her goes off GALLIMARD begins to dress for work.]

SCENE 10

SONG LILING'S apartment. Beijing. 1960.

GALLIMARD: I returned to the opera that next week, and the week after that...she keeps our meetings so short—perhaps fifteen, twenty minutes at most. So I am left each week with a thirst which is intensified. In this way, fifteen weeks have gone by. I am starting to doubt the words of my friend Marc. But no, not really. In my heart, I know she has...an interest in me. I suspect this is her way. She is outwardly bold and outspoken, yet her heart is shy and afraid. It is the Oriental in her at war with her Western education.

SONG [offstage]: I will be out in an instant. Ask the servant for anything you want.

GALLIMARD: Tonight, I have finally been invited to enter her apartment. Though the idea is almost beyond belief, I believe she is afraid of me.

[GALLIMARD looks around the room. He picks up a picture in a frame, studies it. Without his noticing, SONG enters, dressed elegantly in a black gown from the twenties. She stands in the doorway looking like Anna May Wong.]

SONG: That is my father.

GALLIMARD [Surprised]: Mademoiselle Song...[She glides up to him, snatches away the picture.]

SONG: It is very good that he did not live to see the Revolution. They would, no doubt, have made him kneel on broken glass. Not that he didn't deserve such a punishment. But he is my father. I would've hated to see it happen.

GALLIMARD: I'm very honored that you've allowed me to visit your home. [SONG curtsys.]

SONG: Thank you. Oh! Haven't you been poured any tea?

GALLIMARD: I'm really not—

SONG [To her offstage servant]: Shu-Fang! Cha! Kwai-lah! [To GALLIMARD] I'm sorry. You want everything to be perfect—

GALLIMARD: Please.

SONG: —and before the evening even begins

GALLIMARD: I'm really not thirsty.

SONG: —it's ruined.

GALLIMARD: [Sharply] Mademoiselle Song!

[SONG sits down.]

SONG: I'm sorry.

GALLIMARD: What are you apologizing for now? [Pause; SONG starts to giggle.]

SONG: I don't know!

[GALLIMARD laughs.]

GALLIMARD: Exactly my point.

SONG: Oh, I am silly. Lightheaded. I promise not to apologize for anything else tonight, do you hear me?

GALLIMARD: That's a good girl. [Shu-Fang, a servant girl, comes out with a tea tray and starts to pour.]

SONG: [To Shu-Fang] No! I'll pour myself for the gentleman! [SHU-FANG, staring at GALLIMARD, exits.]

SONG: No, I...I don't even know why I invited you up.

GALLIMARD: Well, I'm glad you did. [Song looks around the room.]

SONG: There is an element of danger to your presence.

GALLIMARD: Oh?

SONG: You must know.

GALLIMARD: It doesn't concern me. We both know why I'm here.

SONG: It doesn't concern me either. No...well perhaps

GALLIMARD: What?

SONG: Perhaps I am slightly afraid of scandal.

GALLIMARD: What are we doing?

SONG: I'm entertaining you. In my parlor.

GALLIMARD: In France, that would hardly—

SONG: France. France is a country living in the modern era. Perhaps even ahead of it. China is a nation whose soul is firmly rooted two thousand years in the past. What I do, even pouring the tea for you now...it has...implications.

The walls and windows say so. Even my own heart, strapped inside this Western dress...even it says things—things I don't care to hear.

[SONG *hands* GALLIMARD *a cup of tea.* GALLIMARD *puts his hand over both the teacup and* SONG's *hand.*]

GALLIMARD: This is a beautiful dress.

SONG: Don't.

GALLIMARD: What?

SONG: I don't even know if it looks right on me.

GALLIMARD: Believe me

SONG: You are from France. You see so many beautiful women.

GALLIMARD: France? Since when are the European women—?

SONG: Oh! What am I trying to do, anyway?!

[SONG *runs to the door, composes herself, then turns towards* GALLIMARD.]

SONG: Monsieur Gallimard, perhaps you should go.

GALLIMARD: But...why?

SONG: There's something wrong about this.

GALLIMARD: I don't see what.

SONG: I feel...I am not myself.

GALLIMARD: No. You're nervous.

SONG: Please. Hard as I try to be modern, to speak like a man, to hold a Western woman's strong face up to my own...in the end, I fail. A small, frightened heart beats too quickly and gives me away. Monsieur Gallimard, I'm a Chinese girl. I've never...never invited a man up to my flat before. The forwardness of my actions makes my skin burn.

GALLIMARD: What are you afraid of? Certainly not me, I hope.

SONG: I'm a modest girl.

GALLIMARD: I know. And very beautiful. [*He touches her hair*]

SONG: Please—go now. The next time you see me, I shall again be myself.

GALLIMARD: I like you the way you are right now.

SONG: You are a cad.

GALLIMARD: What do you expect? I'm a foreign devil. [GALLIMARD *walks downstage.* SONG *exits.*]

GALLIMARD [*To us*]: Did you hear the way she talked about Western women? Much differently than the first night. She does—she feels inferior to them—and to me.

SCENE 11

The French embassy. Beijing. 1960. GALLIMARD *moves towards a desk.*

GALLIMARD: I determined to try an experiment. In *Madame Butterfly*, Cio-Cio-San fears that the Western man who catches a butterfly will pierce its heart with a needle, then leave it to perish. I began to wonder: had I, too, caught a butterfly who would writhe on a needle?

[MARC *enters; dressed as a bureaucrat, holding a stack of papers. As* GALLIMARD *speaks,* MARC *hands papers to him. He peruses, then signs, stamps or rejects them.*]

GALLIMARD: Over the next five weeks, I worked like a dynamo...I stopped going to the opera, I didn't phone or write her. I knew this little flower was waiting for me to call, and, as I wickedly refused to do so, I felt for the first time that rush of power—the absolute power of a man.

[MARC *continues acting as the bureaucrat, but he now speaks as himself*]

MARC: Rene! It's me!

GALLIMARD: Marc—I hear your voice everywhere now. Even in the midst of work.

MARC: That's because I'm watching you—all the time.

GALLIMARD: You were always the most popular guy in school.

MARC: Well, there's no guarantee of failure in life like happiness in high school. Somehow I knew I'd end up in the suburbs working for Renault and you'd be in the Orient picking exotic women off the trees. And they say there's no justice.

GALLIMARD: That's why you were my friend?

MARC: I gave you a little of my life, so that now you can give me some of yours [*Pause*] Remember Isabelle?

GALLIMARD: Of course I remember! She was my first experience.

MARC: We all wanted to ball her. But she only wanted me.

GALLIMARD: I had her.

MARC: Right. You balled her.

GALLIMARD: You were the only one who ever believed me.

MARC: Well, there's a good reason for that. [*Beat*] C'mon. You must've guessed.

GALLIMARD: You told me to wait in the bushes by the cafeteria that night. The next thing I knew, she was on me. Dress up in the air.

MARC: She never wore underwear.

GALLIMARD: My arms were pinned to the dirt.

MARC: She loved the superior position. A girl ahead of her time.

GALLIMARD: I looked up, and there was this woman...bouncing up and down on my loins.

MARC: Screaming, right?

GALLIMARD: Screaming, and breaking off the branches all around me, and pounding my butt up and down into the dirt.

MARC: Huffing and puffing like a locomotive.

GALLIMARD: And in the middle of all this, the leaves were getting into my mouth, my legs were losing circulation, I thought, "God. So this is it?"

MARC: You thought that?

GALLIMARD: Well, I was worried about my legs falling off.

MARC: You didn't have a good time?

GALLIMARD: No, that's not what I—I had a great time!

MARC: You're sure?

GALLIMARD: Yeah. Really.

MARC: 'Cuz I wanted you to have a good time.

GALLIMARD: I did. *[Pause.]*

MARC: Shit. *[Pause]* When all is said and done, she was kind of a lousy lay, wasn't she? I mean, there was a lot of energy there, but you never knew what she was doing with it. Like when she yelled "I'm coming!" hell, it was so loud, you wanted to go "Look, it's not that big a deal."

GALLIMARD: I got scared. I thought she meant someone was actually coming. *[Pause]* But, Marc?

MARC: What?

GALLIMARD: Thanks.

MARC: Oh, don't mention it.

GALLIMARD: It was my first experience.

MARC: Yeah. You got her.

GALLIMARD: I got her.

MARC: Wait! Look at that letter again!

[GALLIMARD picks up one of the papers he's been stamping, and rereads it.]

GALLIMARD: *[To us]* After six weeks, they began to arrive. The letters.

[Upstage special on SONG, as MADAME BUTTERFLY. The scene is underscored by the "Love Duet."]

SONG: Did we fight? I do not know. Is the opera no longer of interest to you? Please come—my audiences miss the white devil in their midst.

[GALLIMARD looks up from the letter, towards us.]

GALLIMARD: *[To us]* A concession, but much too dignified. *[Beat; he discards the letter]* I skipped the opera again that week to complete a position paper on trade.

[The bureaucrat hands him another letter.]

SONG: Six weeks have passed since last we met. Is this your practice—to leave friends in the lurch? Sometimes I hate you, sometimes I hate myself, but always I miss you.

GALLIMARD: *[To us]* Better, but I don't like the way she calls me "friend." When a woman calls a man her "friend," she's calling him a eunuch or a homosexual. *[Beat; he discards the letter]* I was absent from the opera for the seventh week, feeling a sudden urge to clean out my files.

[Bureaucrat hands him another letter.]

SONG: Your rudeness is beyond belief I don't deserve this cruelty. Don't bother to call. I'll have you turned away at the door.

GALLIMARD: *[To us]* I didn't. *[He discards the letter; bureaucrat hands him another]* And then finally, the letter that concluded my experiment.

SONG: I am out of words. I can hide behind dignity no longer. What do you want? I have already given you my shame.

[GALLIMARD gives the letter back to MARC, slowly. Special on SONG fades out.]

GALLIMARD: *[To us]*: Reading it, I became suddenly ashamed. Yes, my experiment had been a success: She was turning on my needle. But the victory seemed hollow.

MARC: Hollow?! Are you crazy?

GALLIMARD: Nothing, Marc. Please go away.

MARC *[Exiting, with papers]*: Haven't I taught you anything?

GALLIMARD: "I have already given you my shame." I had to attend a reception that evening. On the way, I felt sick. If there is a God, surely he would punish me now. I had finally gained power over a beautiful woman, only to abuse it cruelly. There must be justice in the world. I had the strange feeling that the ax would fall this very evening.

SCENE 12

AMBASSADOR TOULON'S residence. Beijing. 1960. Sound cue: party noises. Light change. We are now in a spacious residence. TOULON, the French ambassador, enters and taps GALLIMARD on the shoulder.

TOULON: Gallimard? Can I have a word? Over here.

GALLIMARD: *[To us]* Manuel Toulon. French ambassador to China. He likes to think of us all as his children. Rather like God.

TOULON: Look, Gallimard, there's not much to say. I've liked you. From the day you walked in. You were no leader, but you were tidy and efficient.

GALLIMARD: Thank you, sir.

TOULON: Don't jump the gun. Okay, our needs in China are changing. It's embarrassing that we lost Indochina. Someone just wasn't on the ball there. I don't mean you personally, of course.

GALLIMARD: Thank you, sir.

TOULON: We're going to be doing a lot more information-gathering in the future. The nature of our work here is changing. Some people are just going to have to go. It's nothing personal.

GALLIMARD: Oh.

TOULON: Want to know a secret? Vice-Consul LeBon is being transferred.

GALLIMARD: *[To us]* My immediate superior!

TOULON: And most of his department.

GALLIMARD: *[To us]* Just as I feared! God has seen my evil heart

TOULON: But not you.

GALLIMARD: *[To us]* —and he's taking her away just as... *[To TOULON]* Excuse me, sir?

TOULON: Scare you? I think I did. Cheer up, Gallimard. I want you to replace LeBon as vice-consul.

GALLIMARD: You—? Yes, well, thank you, sir.

TOULON: Anytime.

GALLIMARD: I...accept with great humility.

TOULON: Humility won't be part of the job. You're going to coordinate the revamped intelligence division. Want to know a secret? A year ago, you would've been out. But the past few months, I don't know how it happened, you've become this new aggressive confident...thing. And they also tell me you get along with the Chinese. So I think you're a lucky man, Gallimard. Congratulations.

[They shake hands. TOULON exits. Party noises out. GALLIMARD stumbles across a darkened stage.]

GALLIMARD: Vice-consul? Impossible! As I stumbled out of the party, I saw it written across the sky: There is no God. Or, no—say that there is a God. But that God...understands. Of course! God who creates Eve to serve Adam, who blesses Solomon with his harem but ties Jezebel to a burning bed—that God is a man.

And he understands! At age thirty-nine, I was suddenly initiated into the way of the world.

SCENE 13

Song Liling's *apartment. Beijing. 1960.* Song *enters, in a sheer dressing gown.*

SONG: Are you crazy?

GALLIMARD: Mademoiselle Song

SONG: To come here—at this hour? After...after eight weeks?

GALLIMARD: It's the most amazing—

SONG: You bang on my door? Scare my servants, scandalize the neighbors?

GALLIMARD: I've been promoted. To vice-consul. *[Pause.]*

SONG: And what is that supposed to mean to me?

GALLIMARD: Are you my Butterfly?

SONG: What are you saying?

GALLIMARD: I've come tonight for an answer: are you my Butterfly?

SONG: Don't you know already?

GALLIMARD: I want you to say it.

SONG: I don't want to say it.

GALLIMARD: So, that is your answer?

SONG: You know how I feel about

GALLIMARD: I do remember one thing.

SONG: What?

GALLIMARD: In the letter I received today.

SONG: Don't.

GALLIMARD: "I have already given you my shame."

SONG: It's enough that I even wrote it.

GALLIMARD: Well, then

SONG: I shouldn't have it splashed across my face.

GALLIMARD: —if that's all true

SONG: Stop!

GALLIMARD: Then what is one more short answer?

SONG: I don't want to!

GALLIMARD: Are you my Butterfly? *[Silence; he crosses the room and begins to touch her hair]* I want from you honesty. There should be nothing false between us. No false pride. *[Pause.]*

SONG: Yes, I am. I am your Butterfly.

GALLIMARD: Then let me be honest with you. It is because of you that I was promoted tonight. You have changed my life forever. My little Butterfly, there should be no more secrets: I love you. *[He starts to kiss her roughly. She resists slightly.]*

SONG: No...no...gently...please, I've never...

GALLIMARD: No?

SONG: I've tried to appear experienced, but...the truth is... no.

GALLIMARD: Are you cold?

SONG: Yes. Cold.

GALLIMARD: Then we will go very, very slowly. *[He starts to caress her; her gown begins to open.]*

SONG: No...let me...keep my clothes...

GALLIMARD: But...

SONG: Please...it all frightens me. I'm a modest Chinese girl.

GALLIMARD: My poor little treasure.

SONG: I am your treasure. Though inexperienced, I am not...

ignorant. They teach us things, our mothers, about pleasing a man.

GALLIMARD: Yes?

SONG: I'll do my best to make you happy. Turn off the lights.

*[*GALLIMARD *gets up and heads for a lamp.* SONG *propped up on one elbow, tosses her hair back and smiles.]*

SONG: Monsieur Gallimard?

GALLIMARD: Yes, Butterfly?

SONG: "Vieni, vieni!"

GALLIMARD: "Come, darling."

SONG: "Ah! Dolce notte!"

GALLIMARD: "Beautiful night."

SONG: "Tutto estatico d'amor ride il ciel!"

GALLIMARD: "All ecstatic with love, the heavens are filled with laughter."

[He turns off the lamp. Blackout.]

ACT 2, SCENE 1

M. Gallimard's *cell. Paris. Present.*

Lights up on Gallimard. *He sits in his cell, reading from a leaflet.*

GALLIMARD: This, from a contemporary critic's commentary on *Madame Butterfly:* "Pinkerton suffers from...being an obnoxious bounder whom every man in the audience itches to kick." Bully for us men in the audience! Then, in the same note: "Butterfly is the most irresistibly appealing of Puccini's 'Little Women.' Watching the succession of her humiliations is like watching a child under torture." *[He tosses the pamphlet over his shoulder]* I suggest that, while we men may all want to kick Pinkerton, very few of us would pass up the opportunity to be Pinkerton.

*[*GALLIMARD *moves out of his cell]*

SCENE 2

GALLIMARD *and* BUTTERFLY's *flat. Beijing. 1960.*

We are in a simple but well-decorated parlor. GALLIMARD *moves to sit on a sofa, while* SONG, *dressed in a chong sam, enters and curls up at his feet.*

GALLIMARD: *[To us]* We secured a flat on the outskirts of Peking. Butterfly, as I was calling her now, decorated our "home" with Western furniture and Chinese antiques. And there, on a few stolen afternoons or evenings each week, Butterfly commenced her education.

SONG: The Chinese men—they keep us down.

GALLIMARD: Even in the "New Society"?

SONG: In the "New Society," we are all kept ignorant equally. That's one of the exciting things about loving a Western man. I know you are not threatened by a woman's education.

GALLIMARD: I'm no saint, Butterfly.

SONG: But you come from a progressive society.

GALLIMARD: We're not always reminding each other how "old" we are, if that's what you mean.

SONG: Exactly. We Chinese—once, I suppose, it is true, we ruled the world. But so what? How much more exciting to be part of the society ruling the world today. Tell me—what's happening in Vietnam?

GALLIMARD: Oh, Butterfly—you want me to bring my work home?

SONG: I want to know what you know. To be impressed by my man. It's not the particulars so much as the fact that you're making decisions which change the shape of the world.

GALLIMARD: Not the world. At best, a small corner.

[TOULON enters, and sits at a desk upstage.]

SCENE 3

French embassy. Beijing. 1961.

GALLIMARD *moves downstage, to* **TOULON's** *desk.* **SONG** *remains upstage, watching.*

TOULON: And a more troublesome corner is hard to imagine.

GALLIMARD: So, the Americans plan to begin bombing?

TOULON: This is very secret, Gallimard: yes. The Americans don't have an embassy here. They're asking us to be their eyes and ears. Say Jack Kennedy signed an order to bomb North Vietnam, Laos. How would the Chinese react?

GALLIMARD: I think the Chinese will squawk

TOULON: Uh-huh.

GALLIMARD: —but, in their hearts, they don't even like Ho Chi Minh.

[*Pause.*]

TOULON: What a bunch of jerks. Vietnam was our colony. Not only didn't the Americans help us fight to keep them, but now, seven years later, they've come back to grab the territory for themselves. It's very irritating.

GALLIMARD: With all due respect, sir, why should the Americans have won our war for us back in '54 if we didn't have the will to win it ourselves?

TOULON: You're kidding, aren't you? [*Pause.*]

GALLIMARD: The Orientals simply want to be associated with whoever shows the most strength and power. You live with the Chinese, sir. Do you think they like Communism?

TOULON: I live in China. Not with the Chinese.

GALLIMARD: Well, I—

TOULON: You live with the Chinese.

GALLIMARD: Excuse me?

TOULON: I can't keep a secret.

GALLIMARD: What are you saying?

TOULON: Only that I'm not immune to gossip. So, you're keeping a native mistress. Don't answer. It's none of my business. [*Pause*] I'm sure she must be gorgeous.

GALLIMARD: Well...

TOULON: I'm impressed. You have the stamina to go out, into the streets and hunt one down. Some of us have to be content with the wives of the expatriate community.

GALLIMARD: I do feel... fortunate.

TOULON: So, Gallimard, you've got the inside knowledge—what do the Chinese think?

GALLIMARD: Deep down, they miss the old days. You know, cappuccinos, men in tuxedos

TOULON: So what do we tell the Americans about Vietnam?

GALLIMARD: Tell them there's a natural affinity between the West and the Orient.

TOULON: And that you speak from experience?

GALLIMARD: The Orientals are people too. They want the good things we can give them. If the Americans demonstrate the will to win, the Vietnamese will welcome them into a mutually beneficial union.

TOULON: I don't see how the Vietnamese can stand up to American firepower.

GALLIMARD: Orientals will always submit to a greater force.

TOULON: I'll note your opinions in my report. The Americans always love to hear how "welcome" they'll be. [*He starts to exit*]

GALLIMARD: Sir?'

TOULON: Mmmm?

GALLIMARD: This...rumor you've heard.

TOULON: Uh-huh?

GALLIMARD: How...widespread do you think it is?

TOULON: It's only widespread within this embassy. Where nobody talks because everybody is guilty. We were worried about you, Gallimard. We thought you were the only one here without a secret. Now you go and find a lotus blossom...and top us all. [*He exits*]

GALLIMARD: [*To us*] Toulon knows! And he approves! I was learning the benefits of being a man. We form our own clubs, sit behind thick doors, smoke—and celebrate the fact that we're still boys. [*He starts to move downstage, to-wards* SONG] So, over the—

[*Suddenly Comrade* CHIN *enters.* GALLIMARD *backs away*].

GALLIMARD: [*To* SONG] No! Why does she have to come in?

SONG: Rene, be sensible. How can they understand the story without her? Now, don't embarrass yourself.

[GALLIMARD *moves down center.*]

GALLIMARD [*To us*]: Now, you will see why my story is so amusing to so many people. Why they snicker at parties in disbelief. Please—try to understand it from my point of view. We are all prisoners of our time and place. [*He exits*]

SCENE 4

GALLIMARD *and* **BUTTERFLY's** *flat. Beijing. 1961.*

SONG [*To us*]: 1961. The flat Monsieur Gallimard rented for us. An evening after he has gone.

CHIN: Okay, see if you can find out when the Americans plan to start bombing Vietnam. If you can find out what cities, even better.

SONG: I'll do my best, but I don't want to arouse his suspicions.

CHIN: Yeah, sure, of course. So, what else?

SONG: The Americans will increase troops in Vietnam to 170,000 soldiers with 120,000 militia and 11,000 American advisors.

CHIN [*Writing*]: Wait, wait. 120,000 militia and—

SONG: —11,000 American

CHIN: —American advisors. [*Beat*] How do you remember so much?

SONG: I'm an actor.

CHIN: Yeah. [*Beat*] Is that how come you dress like that?

SONG: Like what, Miss Chin?

CHIN: Like that dress! You're wearing a dress. And every time I come here, you're wearing a dress. Is that because you're an actor? Or what?

SONG: It's a...disguise, Miss Chin.

CHIN: Actors, I think they're all weirdos. My mother tells me actors are like gamblers or prostitutes or—

SONG: It helps me in my assignment.

[*Pause.*]

CHIN: You're not gathering information in anyway that violates Communist Party principles, are you?

SONG: Why would I do that?

CHIN: Just checking. Remember: when working for the Great Proletarian State, you represent our Chairman Mao in every position you take.

SONG: I'll try to imagine the Chairman taking my positions.

CHIN: We all think of him this way. Good-bye, comrade. [*She starts to exit*] Comrade?

SONG: Yes?

CHIN: Don't forget: there is no homosexuality in China!

SONG: Yes, I've heard.

CHIN: Just checking. [*She exits*]

SONG [*To us*]: What passes for a woman in modern China.

[GALLIMARD *sticks his head out from the wings.*]

GALLIMARD: Is she gone?

SONG: Yes, Rene. Please continue in your own fashion.

SCENE 5

Beijing. 1961-63.

GALLIMARD *moves to the couch where* SONG *still sits. He lies down in her lap, and she strokes his forehead.*

GALLIMARD [To us]: And so, over the years 1961, '62, '63, we settled into our routine, Butterfly and I. She would always have prepared a light snack and then, ever so delicately, and only if I agreed, she would start to pleasure me. With her hands, her mouth...too many ways to explain, and too sad, given my present situation. But mostly we would talk. About my life. Perhaps there is nothing more rare than to find a woman who passionately listens.

[SONG *remains upstage, listening, as* HELGA *enters and plays a scene downstage with* GALLIMARD.]

HELGA: Rene, I visited Dr. Bolleart this morning.

GALLIMARD: Why? Are you ill?

HELGA: No, no. You see, I wanted to ask him...that question we've been discussing.

GALLIMARD: And I told you, it's only a matter of time. Why did you bring a doctor into this? We just have to keep trying—like a crapshoot, actually.

HELGA: I went, I'm sorry. But listen: he says there's nothing wrong with me.

GALLIMARD: You see? Now, will you stop—?

HELGA: Rene, he says he'd like you to go in and take some tests.

GALLIMARD: Why? So he can find there's nothing wrong with both of us?

HELGA: Rene, I don't ask for much. One trip! One visit! And then, whatever you want to do about it you decide.

GALLIMARD: You're assuming he'll find something defective!

HELGA: No! Of course not! Whatever he finds—if he finds nothing, we decide what to do about nothing! But go!

GALLIMARD: If he finds nothing, we keep trying. Just like we do now.

HELGA: But at least we'll know! [*Pause*] I'm sorry. [*She starts to exit*]

GALLIMARD: Do you really want me to see Dr. Bolleart?

HELGA: Only if you want a child, Rene. We have to face the fact that time is running out. Only if you want a child.

[*She exits*]

GALLIMARD [*To* SONG]: I'm a modern man, Butterfly. And yet, I don't want to go. It's the same old voodoo. I feel like God himself is laughing at me if I can't produce a child.

SONG: You men of the West—you're obsessed by your odd desire for equality. Your wife can't give you a child, and you're going to the doctor?

GALLIMARD: Well, you see, she's already gone.

SONG: And because this incompetent can't find the defect, you now have to subject yourself to him? It's unnatural.

GALLIMARD: Well, what is the "natural" solution?

SONG: In Imperial China, when a man found that one wife was inadequate, he turned to another—to give him his son.

GALLIMARD: What do you—? I can't...marry you, yet.

SONG: Please. I'm not asking you to be my husband. But I am already your wife.

GALLIMARD: Do you want to...have my child?

SONG: I thought you'd never ask.

GALLIMARD: But, your career...your

SONG: Phooey on my career! That's your Western mind, twisting itself into strange shapes again. Of course I love my career. But what would I love most of all? To feel something inside me— day and night—something I know is yours. [*Pause*] Promise me...you won't go to this doctor. Who is this Western quack to set himself as judge over the man I love? I know who is a man, and who is not. [*She exits*]

GALLIMARD [*To us*]: Dr. Bolleart? Of course I didn't go. What man would?

SCENE 6

Beijing. 1963.

Party noises over the house speakers. RENEE *enters, wearing a revealing gown.*

GALLIMARD: 1963. A party at the Austrian embassy. None of us could remember the Austrian ambassador's name, which seemed somehow appropriate. *[To* **RENEE***]* So, I tell the Americans, Diem must go. The U.S. wants to be respected by the Vietnamese, and yet they're propping up this nobody seminarian as her president. A man whose claim to fame is his sister-in-law imposing fanatic "moral order" campaigns? Oriental women—when they're good, they're very good, but when they're bad, they're Christians.

RENEE: Yeah.

GALLIMARD: And what do you do?

RENEE: I'm a student. My father exports a lot of useless stuff to the Third World.

GALLIMARD: How useless?

RENEE: You know. Squirt guns, confectioner's sugar, hula hoops...

GALLIMARD: I'm sure they appreciate the sugar.

RENEE: I'm here for two years to study Chinese.

GALLIMARD: Two years?

RENEE: That's what everybody says.

GALLIMARD: When did you arrive?

RENEE: Three weeks ago.

GALLIMARD: And?

RENEE: I like it. It's primitive; but...well, this is the place to learn Chinese, so here I am.

GALLIMARD: Why Chinese?

RENEE: I think it'll be important someday.

GALLIMARD: You do?

RENEE: Don't ask me when, but...that's what I think.

GALLIMARD: Well, I agree with you. One hundred percent. That's very farsighted.

RENEE: Yeah. Well of course, my father thinks I'm a complete weirdo.

GALLIMARD: He'll thank you someday:

RENEE: Like when the Chinese start buying hula hoops?

GALLIMARD: There're a billion bellies out there.

RENEE: And if they end up taking over the world—well, then I'll be lucky to know Chinese too, right? *[Pause.]*

GALLIMARD: At this point, I don't see how the Chinese can possibly take—

RENEE: You know what I don't like about China?

GALLIMARD: Excuse me? No—what?

RENEE: Nothing to do at night.

GALLIMARD: You come to parties at embassies like everyone else.

RENEE: Yeah, but they get out at ten. And then what?

GALLIMARD: I'm afraid the Chinese idea of a dance hall is a dirt floor and a man with a flute.

RENEE: Are you married?

GALLIMARD: Yes.. Why?

RENEE: You wanna...fool around? *[Pause.]*

GALLIMARD: Sure.

RENEE: I'll wait for you outside. What's your name?

GALLIMARD: Gallimard. Rene.

RENEE: Weird. I'm Renee too. *[She exits]*

GALLIMARD *[To us]:* And so, I embarked on my first extra-extramarital affair. Renee was picture perfect. With a body like those girls in the magazines. If I put a tissue paper over my eyes, I wouldn't have been able to tell the difference. And it was exciting to be with someone who wasn't afraid to be seen completely naked. But is it possible for a woman to be too

uninhibited, too willing, so as to seem almost too... masculine?

[Chuck Berry blares from the house speakers, then comes down in volume as **RENEE** *enters, toweling her hair.]*

RENEE: You have a nice weenie.

GALLIMARD: What?

RENEE: Penis. You have a nice penis.

GALLIMARD: Oh. Well, thank you. That's very...

RENEE: What can't take a compliment?

GALLIMARD: No, it's very...reassuring.

RENEE: But most girls don't come out and say it, huh?

GALLIMARD: And also...what did you call it?

RENEE: Oh. Most girls don't call it a "weenie," huh?

GALLIMARD: It sounds very—

RENEE: Small, I know.

GALLIMARD: I was going to say, "young."

RENEE: Yeah. Young, small, same thing. Most guys are pretty, uh, sensitive about that. Like, you know, I had a boyfriend back home in Denmark. I got mad at him once and called him a little weeniehead. He got so mad! He said at least I should call him a great big weeniehead.

GALLIMARD: I suppose I just say "penis."

RENEE: Yeah. That's pretty clinical. There's "cock," but that sounds like a chicken. And "prick" is painful, and "dick" is like you're talking about someone who's not in the room.

GALLIMARD: Yes. It's a...bigger problem than I imagined.

RENEE: I—I think maybe it's because I really don't know what to do with them—that's why I call them "weenies."

GALLIMARD: Well, you did quite well with...mine.

RENEE: Thanks, but I mean, really do with them. Like, okay, have you ever looked at one? I mean, really?

GALLIMARD: No, I suppose when it's part of you, you sort of take it for granted.

RENEE: I guess. But, like, it just hangs there. This little...flap of flesh. And there's so much fuss that we make about it. Like, I think the reason we fight wars is because we wear clothes. Because no one knows—between the men, I mean—who has the bigger...weenie. So, if I'm a guy with a small one, I'm going to build a really big building or take over a really big piece of land or write a really long book so the other men don't know, right? But, see, it never really works, that's the problem. I mean, you conquer the country, or whatever, but you're still wearing clothes, so there's no way to prove absolutely whose is bigger or smaller. And that's what we call a civilized society. The whole world run by a bunch of men with pricks the size of pins. *[She exits]*

GALLIMARD *[To us]:* This was simply not acceptable.

[A high-pitched chime rings through the air. **SONG,** *dressed as Butterfly, appears in the upstage special. She is obviously distressed. Her body swoons as she attempts to clip the stems of flowers she's arranging in a vase.]*

GALLIMARD: But I kept up our affair, wildly, for several months. Why? I believe because of Butterfly. She knew the secret I was trying to hide. But, unlike a Western woman, she didn't confront me, threaten, even pout. I remembered the words of Puccini's Butterfly:

SONG: "Noi siamo gente avvezza/ alle piccole core/ umili e silenziose."

GALLIMARD: "I come from a people/ Who are accustomed to little/ Humble and silent." I saw Pinkerton and Butterfly, and what she would say if he were unfaithful... nothing. She would cry, alone, into those wildly soft sleeves, once full of possessions, now empty to collect her tears. It was her tears and her silence that excited me, every time I visited Renee.

TOULON [*offstage*]: Gallimard!

[TOULON *enters.* GALLIMARD *turns towards him. During the next section,* SONG, *up center, begins to dance with the flowers. It is a drunken dance, where she breaks small pieces of the stems.*]

TOULON: They're killing him.

GALLIMARD: Who? I'm sorry? What?

TOULON: Bother you to come over at this late hour?

GALLIMARD: No...of course not.

TOULON: Not after you hear my secret. Champagne?

GALLIMARD: Um...thank you.

TOULON: You're surprised. There's something that you've wanted, Gallimard. No, not a promotion. Next time. Something in the world. You're not aware of this, but there's an informal gossip circle among intelligence agents. And some of ours heard from some of the Americans

GALLIMARD: Yes?

TOULON: That the U.S. will allow the Vietnamese generals to stage a coup...and assassinate President Diem.

[*The chime rings again.* TOULON *freezes.* GALLIMARD *turns upstage and looks at* BUTTERFLY, *who slowly and deliberately clips a flower off its stem.* GALLIMARD *turns back towards* TOULON.]

GALLIMARD: I think...that's a very wise move! [TOULON *unfreezes.*]

TOULON: It's what you've been advocating. A toast?

GALLIMARD: Sure. I consider this a vindication.

TOULON: Not exactly. "To the test. Let's hope you pass."

[*They drink. The chime rings again.* TOULON *freezes.* GALLIMARD *turns upstage, and* SONG *clips another flower.*]

GALLIMARD [*To* TOULON]: The test?

TOULON [*Unfreezing*]: It's a test of everything you've been saying. I personally think the generals probably will stop the Communists. And you'll be a hero. But if anything goes wrong, then your opinions won't be worth a pig's ear. I'm sure that won't happen. But sometimes it's easier when they don't listen to you.

GALLIMARD: They're your opinions too, aren't they?

TOULON: Personally, yes.

GALLIMARD: So we agree.

TOULON: But my opinions aren't on that report. Yours are. Cheers.

[TOULON *turns away from* GALLIMARD *and raises his glass. At that instant* SONG *picks up the vase and hurls it to the ground. It shatters.* SONG *sinks down amidst the shards of the vase, in a calm, childlike trance. She sings softly, as if reciting a child's nursery rhyme.*]

SONG [*Repeat as necessary*]: "The whole world over, the white man travels, setting anchor, wherever he likes. Life's not worth living,

unless he finds, the finest maidens, of every land..."

[GALLIMARD *turns downstage towards us.* SONG *continues singing.*]

GALLIMARD: I shook as I left his house. That coward! That worm! To put the burden for his decisions on my shoulders!

I started for Renee's. But no, that was all I needed. A schoolgirl who would question the role of the penis in modern society. What I wanted was revenge. A vessel to contain my humiliation. Though I hadn't seen her in several weeks, I headed for Butterfly's.

[GALLIMARD *enters* SONG'S *apartment.*]

SONG: Oh! Rene...I was dreaming!

GALLIMARD: You've been drinking?

SONG: If I can't sleep, then yes, I drink. But then, it gives me these dreams which—Rene, it's been almost three weeks since you visited me last.

GALLIMARD: I know. There's been a lot going on in the world.

SONG: Fortunately I am drunk. So I can speak freely. It's not the world, it's you and me. And an old problem. Even the softest skin becomes like leather to a man who's touched it too often. I confess I don't know how to stop it. I don't know how to become another woman.

GALLIMARD: I have a request.

SONG: Is this a solution? Or are you ready to give up the flat?

GALLIMARD: It may be a solution. But I'm sure you won't like it.

SONG: Oh well, that's very important. "Like it?" Do you think I "like" lying here alone, waiting, always waiting for your return? Please—don't worry about what I may not "like."

GALLIMARD: I want to see you...naked.

[*Silence.*]

SONG: I thought you understood my modesty. So you want me to—what—strip? Like a big cowboy girl? Shiny pasties on my breasts? Shall I fling my kimono over my head and yell "ya-hoo" in the process? I thought you respected my shame!

GALLIMARD: I believe you gave me your shame many years ago.

SONG: Yes—and it is just like a white devil to use it against me. I can't believe it. I thought myself so repulsed by the passive Oriental and the cruel white man. Now I see—we are always most revolted by the things hidden within us.

GALLIMARD: I just mean

SONG: Yes?

GALLIMARD: —that it will remove the only barrier left between us.

SONG: No, Rene. Don't couch your request in sweet words. Be yourself—a cad—and know that my love is enough, that I submit—submit to the worst you can give me. [*Pause*] Well, come. Strip me. Whatever happens, know that you have willed it. Our love, in your hands. I'm helpless before my man.

[GALLIMARD *starts to cross the room.*]

GALLIMARD: Did I not undress her because I knew, somewhere deep down, what I would find? Perhaps. Happiness is so rare that our mind can turn somersaults to protect it. At the time, I only knew that I was seeing Pinkerton stalking towards his Butterfly, ready to reward her love with his lecherous hands. The image sickened me, pulled me to my knees, so I was crawling towards her like a worm. By the time I reached her, Pinkerton... had vanished from my heart. To be replaced by something new, something unnatural, that flew in the face of all I'd learned in the world—something very close to love.

[He grabs her around the waist; she strokes his hair.]

GALLIMARD: Butterfly; forgive me.
SONG: Rene...
GALLIMARD: For everything. From the start.
SONG: I'm...
GALLIMARD: I want to—
SONG: I'm pregnant. *[Beat]* I'm pregnant. *[Beat]* I'm pregnant.

[Beat.]

GALLIMARD: I want to marry you!

SCENE 7

GALLIMARD *and* BUTTERFLY's *flat. Beijing: 1963. Downstage,* SONG *paces as* COMRADE CHIN *reads from her notepad. Upstage,* GALLIMARD *is still kneeling. He remains on his knees throughout the scene, watching it.*

SONG: I need a baby.
CHIN *[From pad]:* He's been spotted going to a dorm.
SONG: I need a baby.
CHIN: At the Foreign Language Institute.
SONG: I need a baby.
CHIN: The room of a Danish girl...What do you mean, you need a baby?!
SONG: Tell Comrade Kang—last night, the entire mission, it could've ended.
CHIN: What do you mean?
SONG: Tell Kang—he told me to strip.
CHIN: Strip?!
SONG: Write!
CHIN: I tell you, I don't understand nothing about this case anymore. Nothing.
SONG: He told me to strip, and I took a chance. Oh, we Chinese, we know how to gamble.
CHIN *[writing]:* "...told him to strip."
SONG: My palms were wet, I had to make a split-second decision.
CHIN: Hey! Can you slow down?! *[Pause.]*
SONG: You write faster, I'm the artist here. Suddenly, it hit me—All he wants is for her to submit. Once a woman submits, a man is always ready to become 'generous.'"
CHIN: You're just gonna end up with rough notes.
SONG: And it worked! He gave in! Now, if I can just present him with a baby. A Chinese baby with blond hair—he'll be mine for life!
CHIN: Kang will never agree! The trading of babies has to be a counterrevolutionary act!
SONG: Sometimes, a counterrevolutionary act is necessary to counter a counterrevolutionary act.

[Pause.]

CHIN: Wait.
SONG: I need one...in seven months. Make sure it's a boy.

CHIN: This doesn't sound like something the Chairman would do. Maybe you'd better talk to Comrade Kang yourself.
SONG: Good. I will. *[*CHIN *gets up to leave.]*
SONG: Miss Chin? Why, in the Peking Opera, are women's roles played by men?
CHIN: I don't know. Maybe, a reactionary remnant of male—
SONG: No. *[Beat]* Because only a man knows how a woman is supposed to act.

*[*CHIN *exits.* SONG *turns upstage, towards* GALLIMARD.*]*

GALLIMARD: *[Calling after* CHIN]: Good riddance! *[To* SONG] I could forget all that betrayal in an instant, you know. If you'd just come back and become Butterfly again.
SONG: Fat chance. You're here in prison, rotting in a cell. And I'm on a plane, winging my way back to China. Your President pardoned me of our treason, you know.
GALLIMARD: Yes, I read about that.
SONG: Must make you feel...lower than shit.
GALLIMARD: But don't you, even a little bit, wish you were here with me?
SONG: I'm an artist, Rene. You were my greatest...acting challenge. *[She laughs]* It doesn't matter how rotten I answer, does it? You still adore me. That's why I love you, Rene. *[She points to us]* So—you were telling your audience about the night I announced I was pregnant.

*[*GALLIMARD *puts his arms around* SONG's *waist. He and* SONG *are in the positions they were in at the end of Scene 6]*

SCENE 8

Same.

GALLIMARD: I'll divorce my wife. We'll live together here, and then later in France.
SONG: I feel so... ashamed.
GALLIMARD: Why?
SONG: I had begun to lose faith. And now, you shame me with your generosity.
GALLIMARD: Generosity? No, I'm proposing for very selfish reasons.
SONG: Your apologies only make me feel more ashamed. My outburst a moment ago!
GALLIMARD: Your outburst? What about my request?!
SONG: You've been very patient dealing with my...eccentricities. A Western man, used to women freer with their bodies
GALLIMARD: It was sick! Don't make excuses for me.
SONG: I have to. You don't seem willing to make them for yourself. *[Pause.]*
GALLIMARD: You're crazy.
SONG: I'm happy. Which often looks like crazy.
GALLIMARD: Then make me crazy. Marry me. *[Pause.]*
SONG: No.
GALLIMARD: What?
SONG: Do I sound silly, a slave, if I say I'm not worthy?
GALLIMARD: Yes. In fact you do. No one has loved me like you.
SONG: Thank you. And no one ever will. I'll see to that.

GALLIMARD: So what is the problem?

SONG: Rene, we Chinese are realists. We understand rice, gold, and guns. You are a diplomat. Your career is skyrocketing. Now, what would happen if you divorced your wife to marry a Communist Chinese actress?

GALLIMARD: That's not being realistic. That's defeating yourself before you begin.

SONG: We must conserve our strength for the battles we can win.

GALLIMARD: That sounds like a fortune cookie!

SONG: Where do you think fortune cookies come from?

GALLIMARD: I don't care.

SONG: You do. So do I. And we should. That is why I say I'm not worthy. I'm worthy to love and even to be loved by you. But I am not worthy to end the career of one of the West's most promising diplomats.

GALLIMARD:, It's not that great a career! I made it sound like more than it is!

SONG: Modesty will get you nowhere. Flatter yourself, and you flatter me. I'm flattered to decline your offer. [She exits]

GALLIMARD [To us]: Butterfly and I argued all night. And, in the end, I left, knowing I would never be her husband. She went away for several months—to the countryside, like a small animal. Until the night I received her call.

[A baby's cry from offstage. SONG enters, carrying a child.]

SONG: He looks like you.

GALLIMARD: Oh! [Beat; he approaches the baby] Well, babies are never very attractive at birth.

SONG: Stop!

GALLIMARD: I'm sure he'll grow more beautiful with age. More like his mother.

SONG: "Chi vide mail a bimbo del Giappon..."

GALLIMARD: "What baby, I wonder, was ever born in Japan"—or China, for that matter

SONG: "...occhi azzurrim?"

GALLIMARD: "With azure eyes"—they're actually sort of brown, wouldn't you say?

SONG: "E il labbro."

GALLIMARD: "And such lips!" [He kisses SONG] And such lips.

SONG: "E i ricciolini d'oro schietto?"

GALLIMARD: "And such a head of golden"—if slightly patchy—"curls?"

SONG: I'm going to call him "Peepee."

GALLIMARD: Darling, could you repeat that because I'm sure a rickshaw just flew by overhead.

SONG: You heard me.

GALLIMARD: "Song Peepee"? May I suggest Michael, or Stephan, or Adolph?

SONG: You may, but I won't listen.

GALLIMARD: You can't be serious. Can you imagine the time this child will have in school?

SONG: In the West, yes.

GALLIMARD: It's worse than naming him Ping Pong or Long Dong or—

SONG: But he's never going to live in the West, is he?

[Pause.]

GALLIMARD: That wasn't my choice.

SONG: It is mine. And this is my promise to you: I will raise him, he will be our child, but he will never burden you outside of China.

GALLIMARD: Why do you make these promises? I want to be burdened! I want a scandal to cover the papers!

SONG [To us]: Prophetic.

GALLIMARD: I'm serious.

SONG: So am I. His name is as I registered it. And he will never live in the West.

[SONG exits with the child.]

GALLIMARD [To us]: It is possible that her stubbornness only made me want her more. That drawing back at the moment of my capitulation was the most brilliant strategy she could have chosen. It is possible. But it is also possible that by this point she could have said, could have done...anything, and I would have adored her still.

SCENE 9

Beijing. 1966

A driving rhythm of Chinese percussion fills the stage.

GALLIMARD: And then, China began to change. Mao became very old, and his cult became very strong. And, like many old men, he entered his second childhood. So he handed over the reins of state to those with minds like his own. And children ruled the Middle Kingdom with complete caprice. The doctrine of the Cultural Revolution implied continuous anarchy. Contact between Chinese and foreigners became impossible. Our flat was confiscated. Her fame and my money now counted against us.

[Two dancers in Mao suits and red-starred caps enter, and begin crudely mimicking revolutionary violence, in an agit-prop fashion.]

GALLIMARD: And somehow the American war went wrong too. Four hundred thousand dollars were being spent for every Viet Cong killed; so General Westmoreland's remark that the Oriental does not value life the way Americans do was oddly accurate. Why weren't the Vietnamese people giving in? Why were they content instead to die and die and die again?

[TOULON enters.]

TOULON: Congratulations, Gallimard.

GALLIMARD: Excuse me, sir?

TOULON: Not a promotion. That was last time. You're going home.

GALLIMARD: What?

TOULON: Don't say I didn't warn you.

GALLIMARD: I'm being transferred...because I was wrong about the American war?

TOULON: Of course not. We don't care about the Americans. We care about your mind. The quality of your analysis. In general, everything you've predicted here in the Orient...just hasn't happened.

GALLIMARD: I think that's premature.

TOULON: Don't force me to be blunt. Okay, you said China was ready to open to Western trade. The only thing they're trading out there are Western heads. And, yes, you said the Americans would succeed in Indochina. You were kidding, right?

GALLIMARD: I think the end is in sight.

TOULON: Don't be pathetic. And don't take this personally. You were wrong. It's not your fault.

GALLIMARD: But I'm going home.

TOULON: Right. Could I have the number of your mistress? [Beat] Joke! Joke! Eat a croissant for me.

[TOULON exits. SONG, wearing a Mao suit, is dragged in from the wings as part of the upstage dance. They "beat" her, then lampoon the acrobatics of the Chinese opera, as she is made to kneel onstage.]

GALLIMARD [Simultaneously]: I don't care to recall how Butterfly and I said our hurried farewell. Perhaps it was better to end our affair before it killed her.

[GALLIMARD exits. COMRADE CHIN walks across the stage with a banner reading: "The Actor Renounces His Decadent Profession!" She reaches the kneeling SONG. Percussion stops with a thud. Dancers strike poses.]

CHIN: Actor-oppressor, for years you have lived above the common people and looked down on their labor. While the farmer ate millet

SONG: I ate pastries from France and sweetmeats from silver trays.

CHIN: And how did you come to live in such an exalted position?

SONG: I was a plaything for the imperialists!

CHIN: What did you do?

SONG: I shamed China by allowing myself to be corrupted by a foreigner...

CHIN: What does this mean? The People demand a full confession!

SONG: I engaged in the lowest perversions with China's enemies!

CHIN: What perversions? be more clear!

SONG: I let him put it up my ass! [Dancers look over, disgusted.]

CHIN: Aaaa-ya! How can you use such sickening language?!

SONG: My language... is only as foul as the crimes I committed...

CHIN: Yeah. That's better. So—what do you want to do now?

SONG: I want to serve the people. [Percussion starts up, with Chinese strings.]

CHIN: What?

SONG: I want to serve the people! [Dancers regain their revolutionary smiles, and begin a dance of victory.]

CHIN: What?!

SONG: I want to serve the people!!

[Dancers unveil a banner: "The Actor Is Rehabilitated!" SONG remains kneeling before CHIN, as the dancers bounce around them, then exit. Music out.]

SCENE 10

A commune. Hunan Province. 1970.

CHIN: How you planning to do that?

SONG: I've already worked four years in the fields of Hunan, Comrade Chin.

CHIN: So? Farmers work all their lives. Let me see your hands.

[SONG holds them out for her inspection.]

CHIN: Goddamn! Still so smooth! How long does it take to turn you actors into good anythings? Hunh. You've just spent too many years in luxury to be any good to the Revolution.

SONG: I served the Revolution.

CHIN: Serve the Revolution? Bullshit! You wore dresses! Don't tell me—I was there. I saw you! You and your white vice-consul! Stuck up there in your flat, living off the People's Treasury! Yeah, I knew what was going on! You two...homos! Homos! Homos! [Pause; she composes herself] Ah! Well...you will serve the people, all right. But not with the Revolution's money. This time, you use your own money.

SONG: I have no money.

CHIN: Shut up! And you won't stink up China anymore with your pervert stuff. You'll pollute the place where pollution begins—the West.

SONG: What do you mean?

CHIN: Shut up! You're going to France. Without a cent in your pocket. You find your consul's house, you make him pay your expenses

SONG: No.

CHIN: And you give us weekly reports! Useful information!

SONG: That's crazy. It's been four years.

CHIN: Either that, or back to rehabilitation center!

SONG: Comrade Chin, he's not going to support me! Not in France! He's a white man! I was just his plaything

CHIN: Oh yuck! Again with the sickening language? Where's my stick?

SONG: You don't understand the mind of a man.

[Pause.]

CHIN: Oh no? No I don't? Then how come I'm married, huh? How come I got a man? Five, six years ago, you always tell me those kind of things, I felt very bad. But not now! Because what does the Chairman say? He tells us I'm now the smart one; you're now the nincompoop! You're the blackhead, the harebrain, the nitwit! You think you're so smart? You understand "The Mind of a Man"? Good! Then you go to France and be a pervert for Chairman Mao!

[CHIN and SONG exit in opposite directions.]

SCENE 11

Paris. 1968-70. GALLIMARD enters.

GALLIMARD: And what was waiting for me back in Paris? Well, better Chinese food than I'd eaten in China. Friends and relatives. A little accounting, regular schedule, keeping track of traffic violations in the suburbs....And the indignity of students shouting the slogans of Chairman Mao at me—in French.

HELGA: Rene? Rene? [She enters, soaking wet] I've had a...a problem. [She sneezes]

GALLIMARD: You're wet.

HELGA: Yes, I...coming back from the grocer's. A group of students, waving red flags, they

[GALLIMARD fetches a towel.]

HELGA:—they ran by, I was caught up along with them. Before I knew what was happening

[GALLIMARD *gives her the towel.*]

HELGA: Thank you. The police started firing water cannons at us. I tried to shout, to tell them I was the wife of a diplomat, but—you know how it is... [*Pause*] Needless to say, I lost the groceries. Rene, what's happening to France?

GALLIMARD: What's—? Well, nothing, really.

HELGA: Nothing?! The storefronts are in flames, there's glass in the streets, buildings are toppling—and I'm wet!

GALLIMARD: Nothing!... that I care to think about.

HELGA: And is that why you stay in this room?

GALLIMARD: Yes, in fact.

HELGA: With the incense burning? You know something? I hate incense. It smells so sickly sweet.

GALLIMARD: Well, I hate the French. Who just smell—period!

HELGA: And the Chinese were better?

GALLIMARD: Please—don't start.

HELGA: When we left, this exact same thing, the riots—

GALLIMARD: No, no...

HELGA: Students screaming slogans, smashing down doors

GALLIMARD: Helga

HELGA: It was all going on in China, too. Don't you remember?!

GALLIMARD: Helga! Please! [*Pause*] You have never understood China, have you? You walk in here with these ridiculous ideas, that the West is falling apart, that China was spitting in our faces. You come in, dripping of the streets, and you leave water all over my floor. [*He grabs* HELGA'S *towel, begins mopping up the floor*]

HELGA: But it's the truth!

GALLIMARD: Helga, I want a divorce.

[*Pause;* GALLIMARD *continues, mopping the foor.*]

HELGA: I take it back. China is...beautiful. Incense, I like incense.

GALLIMARD: I've had a mistress.

HELGA: So?

GALLIMARD: For eight years.

HELGA: I knew you would. I knew you would the day I married you. And now what? You want to marry her?

GALLIMARD: I can't. She's in China.

HELGA: I see. You want to leave. For someone who's not here, is that right?

GALLIMARD: That's right.

HELGA: You can't live with her, but still you don't want to live with me.

GALLIMARD: That's right. [*Pause.*]

HELGA: Shit. How terrible that I can figure that out. [*Pause*] I never thought I'd say it. But, in China, I was happy. I knew, in my own way, I knew that you were not everything you pretended to be. But the pretense—going on your arm to the embassy ball, visiting your office and the guards saying, "Good morning, good morning, Madame Gallimard"—the pretense... was very good indeed. [*Pause*] I hope everyone is mean to you for the rest of your life. [*She exits*]

GALLIMARD [*To us*]: Prophetic.

[MARC *enters with two drinks.*]

GALLIMARD [*to* MARC]: In China, I was different from all other men.

MARC: Sure. You were white. Here's your drink.

GALLIMARD: I felt... touched.

MARC: In the head? Rene, I don't want to hear about the Oriental love goddess. Okay? One night—can we just drink and throw up without a lot of conversation?

GALLIMARD: You still don't believe me, do you?

MARC: Sure I do. She was the most beautiful, et cetera, et cetera, blase blase.

[*Pause.*]

GALLIMARD: My life in the West has been such a disappointment.

MARC: Life in the West is like that. You'll get used to it. Look, you're driving me away. I'm leaving. Happy, now? [*He exits, then returns*] Look, I have a date tomorrow night. You wanna come? I can fix you up with—

GALLIMARD: Of course. I would love to come. [*Pause.*]

MARC: Uh—on second thought, no. You'd better get ahold of yourself first.

[*He exits;* GALLIMARD *nurses his drink.*]

GALLIMARD [*To us*]: This is the ultimate cruelty, isn't it? That I can talk and talk and to anyone listening, it's only air—too rich a diet to be swallowed by a mundane world. Why can't anyone understand? That in China, I once loved, and was loved by, very simply, the Perfect Woman. [SONG *enters, dressed as* BUTTERFLY *in wedding dress.*]

GALLIMARD [*to* SONG]: Not again. My imagination is hell. Am I asleep this time? Or did I drink too much?

SONG: Rene?

GALLIMARD: God, it's too painful! That you speak?

SONG: What are you talking about? Rene—touch me.

GALLIMARD: Why?

SONG: I'm real. Take my hand.

GALLIMARD: Why? So you can disappear again and leave me clutching at the air? For the entertainment of my neighbors who—? [SONG *touches* GALLIMARD.]

SONG: Rene? [GALLIMARD *takes* SONG'S *hand. Silence.*]

GALLIMARD: Butterfly? I never doubted you'd return.

SONG: You hadn't... forgotten—?

GALLIMARD: Yes, actually, I've forgotten everything. My mind, you see—there wasn't enough room in this hard head—not for the world and for you. No, there was only room for one. [*Beat*] Come, look. See? Your bed has been waiting, with the Klimt poster you like, and—see? The xiang lu [*incense burner*] you gave me?

SONG: I...I don't know what to say.

GALLIMARD: There's nothing to say. Not at the end of a long trip. Can I make you some tea?

SONG: But where's your wife?

GALLIMARD: She's by my side. She's by my side at last.

[GALLIMARD *reaches to embrace* SONG. SONG *sidesteps, dodging him.*]

GALLIMARD: Why?!

SONG [*To us*]: So I did return to Rene in Paris. Where I found—

GALLIMARD: Why do you run away? Can't we show them how we embraced that evening?

SONG: Please. I'm talking.

GALLIMARD: You have to do what I say! I'm conjuring you up in my mind!

SONG: Rene, I've never done what you've said. Why should it be any different in your mind? Now split—the story moves on, and I must change.

GALLIMARD: I welcomed you into my home! I didn't have to, you know! I could've left you penniless on the streets of Paris! But I took you in!

SONG: Thank you.

GALLIMARD: So...please...don't change.

SONG: You know I have to. You know I will. And anyway, what difference does it make? No matter what your eyes tell you, you can't ignore the truth. You already know too much.

[GALLIMARD *exits.* SONG *turns to us.*]

SONG: The change I'm going to make requires about five minutes. So I thought you might want to take this opportunity to stretch your legs, enjoy a drink, or listen to the musicians. I'll be here, when you return, right where you left me.

[SONG *goes to a mirror in front of which is a wash basin of water. She starts to remove her makeup as stagelights go to half and houselights come up.*]

ACT 3, SCENE 1

A courthouse in Paris. 1986

As he promised, SONG *has completed the bulk of his transformation, onstage by the time the houselights go down and the stagelights come up full. He removes his wig and kimono, leaving them on the floor. Underneath, he wears a well-cut suit.*

SONG: So I'd done my job better than I had a right to expect. Well, give him some credit, too. He's right—I was in a fix when I arrived in Paris. I walked from the airport into town, then I located, by blind groping, the Chinatown district. Let me make one thing clear: whatever else may be said about the Chinese, they are stingy! I slept in doorways three days until I could find a tailor who would make me this kimono on credit. As it turns out, maybe I didn't even need it. Maybe he would've been happy to see me in a simple shift and mascara. But...better safe than sorry.

That was 1970, when I arrived in Paris. For the next fifteen years, yes, I lived a very comfy life. Some relief, believe me, after four years on a fucking commune in Nowheresville, China. Rene supported the boy and me, and I did some demonstrations around the country as part of my "cultural exchange" cover. And then there was the spying.

[SONG *moves upstage, to a chair.* TOULON *enters as a judge, wearing the appropriate wig and robes. He sits near* SONG. *It's 1986, and* SONG *is testifying in a courtroom.*]

SONG: Not much at first. Rene had lost all his high-level contacts. Comrade Chin wasn't very interested in parking-ticket statistics.

But finally, at my urging, Rene got a job as a courier, handling sensitive documents. He'd photograph them for me, and I'd pass them on to the Chinese embassy.

JUDGE: Did he understand the extent of his activity?

SONG: He didn't ask. He knew that I needed those documents, and that was enough.

JUDGE: But he must've known he was passing classified information.

SONG: I can't say.

JUDGE: He never asked what you were going to do with them?

SONG: Nope. [*Pause.*]

JUDGE: There is one thing that the court—indeed, that all of France—would like to know.

SONG: Fire away.

JUDGE: Did Monsieur Gallimard know you were a man?

SONG: Well, he never saw me completely naked. Ever.

JUDGE: But surely, he must've...how can I put this?

SONG: Put it however you like. I'm not shy. He must've felt around?

JUDGE: Mmmmm.

SONG: Not really. I did all the work. He just laid back. Of course we did enjoy more...complete union, and I suppose he might have wondered why I was always on my stomach, but....But what you're thinking is. "Of course a wrist must've brushed... a hand hit...over twenty years!" Yeah. Well, Your Honor, it was my job to make him think I was a woman. And chew on this: it wasn't all that hard. See, my mother was a prostitute along the Bundt before the Revolution. And, uh, I think it's fair to say she learned a few things about Western men. So I borrowed her knowledge. In service to my country.

JUDGE: Would you care to enlighten the court with this secret knowledge? I'm sure we're all very curious.

SONG: I'm sure you are. [*Pause*] Okay, Rule One is: Men always believe what they want to hear. So a girl can tell the most obnoxious lies and the guys will believe them every time— "This is my first time"—"That's the biggest I've ever seen"— or—both, which, if you really think about it, is not possible in a single lifetime. You've maybe heard those phrases a few times in your own life, yes, Your Honor?

JUDGE: It's not my life, Monsieur Song, which is on trial today.

SONG: Okay, okay, just trying to lighten up the proceedings. Tough room.

JUDGE: Go on.

SONG: Rule Two: As soon as a Western man comes into contact with the East—he's already confused. The West has sort of an international rape mentality towards the East. Do you know rape mentality?

JUDGE: Give us your definition, please.

SONG: Basically, "Her mouth says no, but her eyes say yes." The West thinks of itself as masculine—big guns, big industry, big money—so the East is feminine—weak, delicate, poor... but good at art, and full of inscrutable wisdom—the feminine mystique.

Her mouth says no, but her eyes say yes. The West believes the East, deep down, wants to be dominated because a woman can't think for herself.

JUDGE: What does this have to do with my question?

SONG: You expect Oriental countries to submit to your guns, and you expect Oriental women to be submissive to your men. That's why you say they make the best wives.

JUDGE: But why would that make it possible for you to fool Monsieur Gallimard? Please—get to the point.

SONG: One, because when he finally met his fantasy woman, he wanted more than anything to believe that she was, in fact, a woman. And second, I am an Oriental. And being an Oriental, I could never be completely a man.

[*Pause.*]

JUDGE: Your armchair political theory is tenuous, Monsieur Song.

SONG: You think so? That's why you'll lose in all your dealings with the East.

JUDGE: Just answer my question: did he know you were a man?

[*Pause.*]

SONG: You know, Your Honor, I never asked.

SCENE 2

Same.

Music from the "Death Scene" from Butterfly blares over the house speakers. It is the loudest thing we've heard in this play.

Gallimard enters, crawling towards SONG'S *wig and kimono.*

GALLIMARD: Butterfly? Butterfly?

[SONG *remains a man, in the witness box, delivering a testimony we do not hear.*]

GALLIMARD [*To us*]: In my moment of greatest shame, here, in this courtroom—with that...person up there, telling the world.... What strikes me especially is how shallow he is, how glib and obsequious...completely... without substance! The type that prowls around discos with a gold medallion stinking of garlic. So little like my Butterfly.

Yet even in this moment my mind remains agile, flip-flopping like a man on a trampoline. Even now, my picture dissolves, and I see that...witness...talking to me. [SONG *suddenly stands straight up in his witness box, and looks at* GALLIMARD.]

SONG: Yes. You. White man.

[SONG *steps out of the witness box, and moves downstage towards* GALLIMARD. *Light change.*]

GALLIMARD [*to* SONG]: Who? Me?

SONG: Do you see any other white men?

GALLIMARD: Yes. There're white men all around. This is a French courtroom.

SONG: So you are an adventurous imperialist. Tell me, why did it take you so long? To come back to this place?

GALLIMARD: What place?

SONG: This theatre in China. Where we met many years ago.

GALLIMARD: [*To us*] And once again, against my will, I am transported.

[*Chinese opera music comes up on the speakers.* SONG *begins to do opera moves, as he did the night they met.*]

SONG: Do you remember? The night you gave your heart?

GALLIMARD: It was a long time ago.

SONG: Not long enough. A night that turned your world upside down.

GALLIMARD: Perhaps.

SONG: Oh, be honest with me. What's another bit of flattery when you've already given me twenty years' worth? It's a wonder my head hasn't swollen to the size of China.

GALLIMARD: Who's to say it hasn't?

SONG: Who's to say? And what's the shame? In pride? You think I could've pulled this off if I wasn't already full of pride when we met? No, not just pride. Arrogance. It takes arrogance, really—to believe you can will, with your eyes and your lips, the destiny of another. [*He dances*] C'mon. Admit it. You still want me. Even in slacks and a button-down collar.

GALLIMARD: I don't see what the point of

SONG: You don't? Well maybe, Rene, just maybe—I want you.

GALLIMARD: You do?

SONG: Then again, maybe I'm just playing with you. How can you tell? [*Reprising his feminine character, he sidles up to* GALLIMARD] "How I wish there were even a small cafe to sit in. With men in tuxedos, and cappuccinos, and bad expatriate jazz." Now you want to kiss me, don't you?

GALLIMARD [*Pulling away*]: What makes you—?

SONG: —so sure? See? I take the words from your mouth. Then I wait for you to come and retrieve them. [*He reclines on the floor*]

GALLIMARD: Why?! Why do you treat me so cruelly?

SONG: Perhaps I was treating you cruelly. But now—I'm being nice. Come here, my little one.

GALLIMARD: I'm not your little one!

SONG: My mistake. It's I who am *your* little one, right?

GALLIMARD: Yes, I—

SONG: So come get your little one. If you like. I may even let you strip me.

GALLIMARD: I mean, you were! Before...but not like this!

SONG: I was? Then perhaps I still am. If you look hard enough. [*He starts to remove his clothes*]

GALLIMARD: What—what are you doing?

SONG: Helping you to see through my act.

GALLIMARD: Stop that! I don't want to! I don't

SONG: Oh, but you asked me to strip, remember?

GALLIMARD: What? That was years ago! And I took it back!

SONG: No. You postponed it. Postponed the inevitable. Today, the inevitable has come calling. [*From the speakers, Cacophony: Butterfly mixed in with Chinese gongs.*]

GALLIMARD: No! Stop! I don't want to see!

SONG: Then look away.

GALLIMARD: You're only in my mind! All this is in my mind! I order you! To stop!

SONG: To what? To strip? That's just what I'm

GALLIMARD: No! Stop! I want you—!

SONG: You want me?

GALLIMARD: To stop!

SONG: You know something, Rene? Your mouth says no, but your eyes say yes. Turn them away. I dare you.

GALLIMARD: I don't have to! Every night, you say you're going to strip, but then I beg you and you stop!

SONG: I guess tonight is different.

GALLIMARD: Why? Why should that be?

SONG: Maybe I've become frustrated. Maybe I'm saying "Look at me, you fool!" Or maybe I'm just feeling...sexy. *[He is down to his briefs]*

GALLIMARD: Please. This is unnecessary. I know what you are.

SONG: Do you? What am I?

GALLIMARD: A—a man.

SONG: You don't really believe that.

GALLIMARD: Yes I do! I knew all the time somewhere that my happiness was temporary, my love a deception. But my mind kept the knowledge at bay. To make the wait bearable.

SONG: Monsieur Gallimard—the wait is over.

[SONG drops his briefs. He is naked. Sound cue out. Slowly, we and SONG come to the realization that what we had thought to be GALLIMARD's sobbing is actually his laughter.]

GALLIMARD: Oh god! What an idiot! Of course!

SONG: Rene—what?

GALLIMARD: Look at you! You're a man! *[He bursts into laughter again]*

SONG: I fail to see what's funny!

GALLIMARD: "You fail to see—!" I mean, you never did have much of a sense of humor, did you? I just think it's ridiculously funny that I've wasted so much time on just a man!

SONG: Wait. I'm not "just a man."

GALLIMARD: No? Isn't that what you've been trying to convince me of?

SONG: Yes, but what I mean

GALLIMARD: And now, I finally believe you, and you tell me it's not true? I think you must have some kind of identity problem.

SONG: Will you listen to me?

GALLIMARD: Why?! I've been listening to you for twenty years. Don't I deserve a vacation?

SONG: I'm not just any man!

GALLIMARD: Then, what exactly are you?

SONG: Rene, how can you ask—? Okay, what about this? *[He picks up BUTTERFLY's robes, starts to dance around. No music.]*

GALLIMARD: Yes, that's very nice. I have to admit.

[SONG holds out his arm to GALLIMARD.]

SONG: It's the same skin you've worshiped for years. Touch it.

GALLIMARD: Yes, it does feel the same.

SONG: Now—close your eyes.

[SONG covers GALLIMARD's eyes with one hand. With the other, SONG draws GALLIMARD's hand up to his face. GALLIMARD, like a blind man, lets his hands run over SONG's face.]

GALLIMARD: This skin, I remember. The curve of her face, the softness of her cheek, her hair against the back of my hand...

SONG: I'm your Butterfly. Under the robes, beneath everything, it was always me. Now, open your eyes and admit it—you adore me. *[He removes his hand from GALLIMARD's eyes]*

GALLIMARD: You, who knew every inch of my desires—how could you, of all people, have made such a mistake?

SONG: What?

GALLIMARD: You showed me your true self. When all I loved was the lie. A perfect lie, which you let fall to the ground—and now, it's old and soiled.

SONG: So—you never really loved me? Only when I was playing a part?

GALLIMARD: I'm a man who loved a woman created by a man. Everything else—simply falls short.

[Pause.]

SONG: What am I supposed to do now?

GALLIMARD: You were a fine spy, Monsieur Song, with an even finer accomplice. But now I believe you should go. Get out of my life!

SONG: Go where? Rene, you can't live without me. Not after twenty years.

GALLIMARD: I certainly can't live with you—not after twenty years of betrayal.

SONG: Don't be so stubborn! Where will you go?

GALLIMARD: I have a date...with my Butterfly.

SONG: So, throw away your pride. And come...

GALLIMARD: Get away from me! Tonight, I've finally learned to tell fantasy from reality. And, knowing the difference, I choose fantasy.

SONG: I'm your fantasy!

GALLIMARD: You? You're as real as hamburger. Now get out! I have a date with my Butterfly and I don't want your body polluting the room! *[He tosses SONG's suit at him]* Look at these—you dress like a pimp.

SONG: Hey! These are Armani slacks and—! *[He puts on his briefs and slacks]* Let's just say...I'm disappointed in you, Rene. In the crush of your adoration, I thought you'd become something more. More like...a woman.

But no. Men. You're like the rest of them. It's all in the way we dress, and make up our faces, and bat our eyelashes. You really have so little imagination!

GALLIMARD: You, Monsieur Song? Accuse me of too little imagination? You, if anyone, should know—I am pure imagination. And in imagination I will remain. Now get out!

[GALLIMARD bodily removes SONG from the stage, taking his kimono.]

SONG: Rene! I'll never put on those robes again! You'll be sorry!

GALLIMARD: *[To SONG]*: I'm already sorry! *[Looking at the kimono in his hands]* Exactly as sorry...as a Butterfly.

SCENE 3

M. GALLIMARD's *prison cell. Paris. Present.*

GALLIMARD: I've played out the events of my life night after night, always searching for a new ending to my story, one where I leave this cell and return forever to my Butterfly's arms.

Tonight I realize my search is over. That I've looked all along in the wrong place. And now, to you, I will prove that my love was not in vain—by returning to the world of fantasy where I first met her.

[He picks up the kimono; dancers enter.]

GALLIMARD: There is a vision of the Orient that I have. Of slender women in chong sams and kimonos who die for the love of unworthy foreign devils. Who are born and raised to be the perfect women. Who take whatever punishment we give them, and bounce back, strengthened by love, unconditionally. It is a vision that has become my life.

[Dancers bring the wash basin to him and help him make up his face.]

GALLIMARD: In public, I have continued to deny that Song Liling is a man. This brings me headlines, and is a source of great embarrassment to my French colleagues, who can now be sent into a coughing fit by the mere mention of Chinese food. But alone, in my cell, I have long since faced the truth.

And the truth demands a sacrifice. For mistakes made over the course of a lifetime. My mistakes were simple and absolute— the man I loved was a cad, a bounder. He deserved nothing but a kick in the behind, and instead I gave him...all my love.

Yes—love. Why not admit it all? That was my undoing, wasn't it? Love warped my judgment; blinded my eyes, re-arranged the very lines on my face...until I could look in the mirror and see nothing but...a woman.

[Dancers help him put on the Butterfly wig.]

GALLIMARD: I have a vision. Of the Orient. That, deep within its almond eyes, there are still women. Women willing to sacrifice themselves for the love of a man. Even a man whose love is completely without worth.

[Dancers assist GALLIMARD in donning the kimono. They hand him a knife.]

GALLIMARD: Death with honor is better than life...life with dishonor. *[He sets himself center stage, in a seppuku position]* The love of a Butterfly can withstand many things—unfaithfulness, loss, even abandonment. But how can it face the one sin that implies all others? The devastating knowledge that, underneath it all, the object of her love was nothing more, nothing less than...a man. *[He sets the tip of the knife against his body]* It is 19__. And I have found her at last. In a prison on the outskirts of Paris. My name is Rene Gallimard—also known as *Madame Butterfly*.

[GALLIMARD turns upstage and plunges the knife into his body, as music from the "Love Duet" blares over the speakers. He collapses into the arms of the dancers, who lay him reverently on the floor. The image holds for several beats. Then a tight special up on SONG, who stands as a man, staring at the dead GALLIMARD. He smokes a cigarette; the smoke filters up through the lights. Two words leave his lips.]

SONG: Butterfly? Butterfly?

[Smoke rises as lights fade slowly to black.]

END OF PLAY

Life Theme 2:

War

Life Theme 2: War

It invigorates hope as all who fight believe their cause to be just. It destroys life as no one fights a war except at a terrible cost.

Older men declare war. But it is youth that must fight and die. And it is youth who must inherit the tribulation, the sorrow, and the triumphs that are the aftermath of war.
—Speech at Republican National Convention
Herbert Hoover, 1944.

Featured plays:

Arms and the Man
  by George Bernard Shaw
Necessary Targets
  by Eve Ensler

The very nature of drama is conflict. When that conflict escalates to the point where entire nations and vast armies are involved, electrifying drama can happen. In our time, film has largely taken over war as plot line since the camera has the potential to capture the full sweep of battle while the theatre must always contain it. However, some of the greatest plays deal with war at the very intimate level of the individual caught in this sad, seemingly unavoidable phenomenon where a cause is considered reason enough to sacrifice countless lives. G. B. Shaw, one of the most honored English playwrights of the late nineteenth and much of the twentieth century (he lived to be nearly 100 years old) has provided us a greatly ironic comic perspective on war. Eve Ensler, one of America's leading contemporary playwrights, looks at a more recent international conflict to explore the devastation that is always war's aftermath. Perhaps coincidentally, but perhaps because of the long, bitter history of conflict in the region, both plays are set in Eastern Europe in the area referred to today as the Balkans.

Arms and the Man

Year: 1894
Genre: Edwardian prose comedy of manners
Structure: Well made in three acts
Setting: The home of the Petkoffs, "the richest and best known family in Bulgaria," in a small town near the Dragonman Pass

Context:

Along with Anton Chekhov and Henrik Ibsen, Shaw is considered one of the fathers of modern realism. He is however, the least likely of the three to employ flat, ordinary dialogue. While his plays are always about something serious, they are also full of sprightly wit, satire and high spirits. Shaw was himself was a Socialist and an active member of the Fabian Society. This organization, founded in 1884, was named for a famous Roman general (Quintus Fabius Maximus) who avoided defeat against Hannibal by simply refusing to fight any decisive battles against him. The Society's current (as of 2004) Web page contains the following mission statement:

> The Fabian Society is the UK's only membership based left of centre think tank. Providing an arena for open-minded debate, the Society's program aims to explore the political ideas and the policy reforms which will define progressive politics in the future. (http://www.fabian-society.org.uk/int.asp)

The idea that one can use one's wits to outsmart opponents and avoid the carnage of battle permeates the Fabian agenda and *Arms and the Man*. The Fabians differ sharply from Communists whose core belief is that violent revolution is the only way for the people to gain power. Fabians believe instead that a series of reforms can accomplish the same thing more effectively. The core concepts of the Society became the philosophical basis of the British Labor party, whose prime minister at the time of this writing, Tony Blair, received severe criticism from within his own Party when he supported American war efforts in Iraq and sent British soldiers into harm's way. For contemporary British society, the Fabian and Labor stance against war had for decades been nearly synonymous. Today, the relationship is clouded. The play *Arms and the Man* is Shaw's witty, acerbic, but ultimately gentle anti-war play with an uncompromising Fabian point of view. No great call for men to come to their senses, no call for humanity to unite in eternal friendship, this play simply points out the terrible waste of it all and the simple fatigue of those sent to fight it.

While the play received a chilly reception when it first opened in London, it has subsequently become one of Shaw's most popular works. This is probably because it was somewhat ahead of its time and initial critics and audiences were not quite ready. Shaw was often ahead of the curve in perspective and in the causes he championed. He received the Nobel prize for literature in 1925. Critic Max Beerbom wrote of *Arms and the Man*:

> What at first struck me as flippancy and fantasy, I now see as a mere striving after sober reality and that the reason why it appeared fantastic was that it did not conform with certain conventions the theatre then took as a necessary part of truth in life. While abreast of his time in form, Shaw was far ahead of his time in matter.

The play has a strikingly contemporary attitude towards war and militarism, refusing to grant a simple response to either. While most anti-war plays present it as unbearably brutal, Shaw chooses to show war as boring, humdrum and unworthy of romantic allure. For example, Shaw gives us the character of Bluntschli, a Swiss mercenary without patriotic ties to either army. Bluntschli cheerfully explains to Raina that everyone knows that the most important man in the army is not the general, but the supply man.

While ostensibly set in Bulgaria, the play is resolutely English in feeling and tone. Shaw avoids patriotic objections from audience members whose memories are enmeshed with fervor over English wars, by setting the play at some distance from their lives. Yet, the behavior of all is undeniably British. There was even a common belief at the time that the two central figures were modeled on actual Englishmen, the war weary Bluntschli on the economist Sidney Webb and the war happy Saranoff on the wealthy world traveler, R. B. Cunninghame Graham.

The play's title is a play on arms (weapons) used in war. It mocks the first lines of Virgil's *Aeneid*: "Arms and the man I sing." In the course of the play, the arms of a woman are substituted for military arms. The switch is considered by all to be most satisfactory.

The Playwright:

Born in 1856 in Dublin, Shaw was the son of a civil servant and a homemaker. Avoiding school because of an inherent distaste for organized training, he made his way to London at the age of 20 and quickly established himself as a writer, critic, and political activist. His early plays include *Mrs. Warren's Profession* and *Widower's House,* both scathing indictments of social hypocrisy, and Arms and the Man, a gentler satire on the lunacy of war. His later works sometimes wavered on the line between discourse and drama, but his masterpieces include *Pygmalion,* which became the musical *My Fair Lady* by Lerner and Loewe, and *Saint Joan,* a revisiting of the famous story of a medieval peasant girl sent by God to save France which Shaw extended into modern times. He won the Nobel Prize for Literature in 1925 and between 1930 and 1950 published his complete works in 36 volumes. He died in 1950 at the age of 94, still writing, working, and goading society to better itself.

Necessary Targets

Year: 2002
Genre: Realism
Structure: Episodic
Setting: A Bosnian refugee camp, 1995

Context:

With *Necessary Targets,* Eve Ensler joins the international arena in the struggle for women's rights. Her most popular work to date, *The Vagina Monologues,* includes as one of its episodes a monologue by a young Bosnian girl trapped in a refugee camp in the aftermath of that recent particularly bloody civil war. Ensler visited the camp in 1995 and recorded her conversations with many of the women there. Their voices and the playwright's experience of their suffering receive full treatment in her work, *Necessary Targets.*

Focusing on the suffering of the innocent, this play features a sophisticated American psychiatrist and a young American trauma counselor who arrive at an East European refugee camp intending to ease the suffering of the women and children interred there. Instead they both discover their own biases and assumptions and learn the meaning of true generosity from the Bosnian women.

Reporting on the Balkan war in 1992, Peter Anderson of the Green Left Weekly said in 1992:

> The war in the former Yugoslavia has taken a tragic toll and nowhere more than in Bosnia-Herzegovina where it is estimated 100,000 Muslims have lost their lives as a result of Serbian aggression. Taken together, the Muslim dead and wounded add up to half a million and one million are refugees or displaced.

The "nation" involved in this conflict, the Kingdom of Serbs, Croats, and Slovenes (renamed Yugoslavia in 1929) was created out of a mish-mash of nations, tribes, and allegiances in the chaotic aftermath of the First World War. Though linked by geographic proximity, a shared history of conquest and oppression by larger, stronger neighbors, and sometimes by political necessity ("the enemy of my enemy is my friend"), the various Balkan factions have never been unified as one people. To attempt here a history of the Balkans is beyond the scope of this introduction. Suffice it to say that as a crossroad between Europe, the Near East and the Russian steppes, this area in Central Europe has known few decades of freedom and peace in its history.

Conquered by the Ottoman Turkish Empire in the 14th century, the area was under Islamic domination along with much of the Mediterranean, North Africa, Greece and Italy and the Middle East. The people of the Balkan area who converted to Islam might have been from any of the various ethnic groups in the region, but in the 20th century conflicts, the Bosnian Muslims were particularly targeted as violent Serb and Croat nationalism grew and the Christian Austro-Hungarian Empire defeated and displaced the Ottoman Turks in 1923

During the Second World War, some nationalistic Serbs, Croats, Bosnians, and Montenegrans (some of the ethnic groups artificially bound together by conquering empires) joined forces with the Nazis to attempt the extermination of Muslims, Jews, gypsies, and other marginalized groups. Others, including Balkan Communists, fought against Germany during the war and received rewards of power and territory from Allies at the end of the war. By 1945, Socialist Yugoslavia was formed under the charismatic leadership of Marshall Tito, who managed to contain the ethnic and religious violence in the region by establishing six theoretically equal "republics": Croatia, Montenegro, Serbia, Slovenia, Bosnia-Herzegovena, and Macedonia. This shaky and tempestuous alliance, supported by the Soviet Union, continued until Tito's death in 1980. Many observers believed his death would lead to immediate disintegration and ethnic fighting, but Yugoslavia continued to survive as a political entity for another decade, perhaps under pressure from the Soviets.

By 1992, however, Yugoslavia was falling apart as predicted. Following the earlier withdrawals of Slovenia and Croatia from the Federation, Bosnia declared its independence which triggered conflict with Serbian nationalists who lived in the region and who were determined to remain within the Yugoslav sphere of influence. Civil war between Bosnian factions and Serbian nationalists broke out and the world first heard the phrase "ethnic cleansing" used to describe the attempted genocide of all Bosnian Muslims, including non-combatants. Fifty years after the Nazis, new concentration camps were built designed to contain and exterminate any who opposed Serbian nationalism.

In 1995, a treaty known as the Dayton Peace Accord created two ethnic homelands within Bosnia: the Bosnian Serb Republic and the Muslim-Croat Federation. Although the agreement was criticized for not specifically addressing the effect of ethnic cleansing on the Muslim population, a NATO peace-keeping force put an end to the overt violence of war and continues its mission to the time of this writing. Though outbreaks of violence occur with mind-numbing regularity (1999, 2000, 2001, 2003, etc) the fate of millions of non-combatants has nominally improved with many being allowed to return to their homes or to build new homes in a welcoming area. But the fate of many Muslim refugees was simple removal from a concentration camp to a refugee camp. As of February 2004, over 750,000 Bosnian refugees were still unable to return to their homes and about half of these (mostly women, children and the elderly) were still in refugee camps. (The other half, over 350,000, are either living in exile or living with relatives within the disputed areas.)

With *Necessary Targets*, Ensler takes us into a little known world and reveals not only the continued suffering of these women and children, but also their enormous strength, dignity, and desire for self-definition. So far in her career as a playwright, Eve Ensler has focused her work on violence against women. Her play *The Vagina Monogues* initiated and inspired the organization of "V-Day", a global movement to stop violence against women. With *Necessary Targets,* she expands that work into the international community, exposing both the specific effects of the Bosnian civil war and the universal suffering of women in war zones.

Meryl Streep, who starred in the New York production of the play, wrote about *Necessary Targets:*

> . . .*Necessary Targets* lets us peer beneath the head scarves of women whom we recognize as our friends, sisters, and daughters. A brave, powerful, and crucial testimony against violence aimed at women as an act of war.

The Playwright.

Eve Ensler is a woman on a crusade. That crusade is to combat violence against women and girls. She speaks passionately of her vision: a world where women and girls can not only survive but thrive. Her first international exposure came with her Obie-award winning play *The Vagina Monogues* which has been translated into over 35 languages and led to the creation of global V-Day. To date volunteer organizations around the world have donated over 25 million dollars to the fight for women's safety and Ensler's work continues as playwright, screenwriter, teacher, spokeswoman, and community activist. She was the executive producer of "What I want my words to do to you," a documentary film about the writing group she began in a women's prison in 1998. The film was accepted into the prestigious Sundance Film Festival in 2003 at which it received the highly respected "Freedom of Expression" award. Her 2005 play *The Good Body* explores the universal efforts of women to alter the shape, size or appearance of their bodies in order to fit in, to be considered attractive. She currently lives in New York City and continues with unflagging energy her campaign to free women and girls from violence, oppression and exploitation around the world.

Arms and the Man

====

by George Bernard Shaw
Edited and Adapted by Robert Barton

Characters

====

Raina Petkoff
Catherine Petkoff
Captain Bluntschli Louka
Nicola
Major Paul Petkoff
Major Sergius Sranoff
Russian Officer

Setting

The home of the Petkoffs, "the richest and best known family in Bulgaria," in a small town near the Dragonman Pass

Act 1: Late November 1885 Raina Petkoff's bedchamber

Act 2: March 6, 1886 Petkoff family garden

Act 3: Same day as Act 2, after lunch The household library

ACT I

Night. A lady's bedchamber in Bulgaria, in a small town near the Dragonman Pass, late in November in the year 1885. Through an open window with a little balcony, a peak of the Balkans, wonderfully white and beautiful in the starlit snow, seems quite close at hand, though it is really miles away. The interior of the room half Bulgarian, half Viennese. Above the head of the bed is a painted wooden shrine with an ivory image of Christ, and a light hanging before it. The principal seat, placed towards the other side of the room and opposite window, is a Turkish ottoman. The counterpane and hangings of the bed, the window curtains, the little carpet, and all the ornamental textile fabrics in the room are oriental and gorgeous. A washstand, with enameled basin and pail and a single towel on the rail at the side, stands against the wall on the side nearest the ottoman and window. The dressing table, between bed and window is covered with a cloth of many colors, with an expensive toilet mirror on it. The door is on the side nearest the bed with a chest of drawers between. This chest of drawers is also covered by a variegated native cloth; and on it there is a pile of novels, a box of chocolate creams, and a miniature easel with a large photograph of an extremely handsome officer, whose lofty bearing and magnetic glance can be felt even from the portrait. The room is lighted by a candle on the chest of drawers, and another on the dressing table with a box of matches beside it.

The double floor length window is hinged doorwise and stands wide open. On the balcony a young lady, intensely conscious of the romantic beauty of the night, and of the fact that her own youth and beauty are part of it, is gazing at the snowy Balkans. She is in her nightgown, well covered by a long mantle of furs, worth, on a moderate estimate, about three times the furniture of her room.

Her reverie is interrupted by her mother, CATHERINE PETKOFF a woman over forty, imperiously energetic, with magnificent hair and eyes, who might be a very splendid specimen of the wife of a mountain farmer, but is determined to be a Viennese lady, and to that end wears a fashionable tea gown on all occasions.

CATHERINE: *[entering hastily; full of good news]* RAINA! *[She pronounces it Rah-eena, with the stress on the ee]*. RAINA! *[She goes to the bed, expecting to find RAINA there]*. Why, where? *[RAINA looks into the room]* Heavens, child! Are you out in the night air instead of in your bed? You'll catch your death. Louka told me you were asleep.

RAINA: *[dreamily]* I sent her away. I wanted to be alone. The stars are so beautiful! What is the matter?

CATHERINE: Such news! There has been a battle.

RAINA: *[her eyes dilating]* Ah! *[She comes eagerly to CATHERINE]*

CATHERINE: A great battle at Slivnitza! A victory! And it was won by Sergius.

RAINA: *[with a cry of delight]* Ah! *[They embrace rapturously]* Oh, mother! *[Then, with sudden anxiety]* Is father safe?

CATHERINE: Of course: he sends me the news. Sergius is the hero of the hour, the idol of the regiment.

RAINA: Tell me, tell me. How was it? *[Ecstatically]* Oh, mother! Mother! Mother! *[She pulls her mother down on the ottoman; and they kiss one another frantically]*

CATHERINE: *[with surging enthusiasm]* You can't guess how splendid it is. A cavalry charge! Think of that! He defied our Russian commanders—acted without orders—led a charge on his own responsibility—headed it himself—was the first man to sweep through their guns. Can't you see it, Raina, our gallant splendid Bulgarians with their swords and eyes flashing, thundering down like an avalanche and scattering the wretched Serbs and their dandified Austrian officers like chaff. And you! You kept Sergius waiting a year before you would be betrothed to him. Oh, if you have a drop of Bulgarian blood in your veins, you will worship him when he comes back.

RAINA: What will he care for my poor little worship after the acclamations of a whole army of heroes? But no matter; I am so happy! So proud! *[She rises and walks about excitedly]* It proves that all our ideas were real after all.

CATHERINE: *[indignantly]* Our ideas real! What do you mean?

RAINA: Our ideas of what Sergius would do. Our patriotism. Our heroic ideals. I sometimes used to doubt whether they were anything but dreams. Oh, what faithless little creatures girls are! When I buckled on Sergius' sword he looked so noble: it was treason to think of disillusion or humiliation or failure. And yet—and yet—*[She sits down again suddenly]* Promise me you'll never tell him.

CATHERINE: Don't ask me for promises until I know what I'm promising.

RAINA: Well, it came into my head just as he was holding me in his arms and looking into my eyes, that perhaps we only had our heroic ideas because we are so fond of reading Byron and Pushkin, and because we were so delighted with the opera that season at Bucharest. Real life is so seldom like that! Indeed never, as far as I knew it then. *[Remorsefully]* Only think, mother, I doubted him. I had an uneasy fear that he might cut a poor figure there beside all those clever officers from the Tsar's court. I was only a prosaic little coward. Oh, to think that it was all true! That Sergius is just as splendid and noble as he looks! That the world is really a glorious world for women who can see its glory and men who can act its romance! What happiness! What unspeakable fulfillment!

[They are interrupted by the entry of LOUKA, a handsome proud girl in a pretty Bulgarian peasant's dress with double apron, so defiant that her servility to RAINA is almost insolent. She is afraid of CATHERINE, but even with her goes as far as she dares.]

LOUKA: If you please, madam, all the windows are to be closed and the shutters made fast. They say there may be shooting in the streets. *[RAINA and CATHERINE rise together, alarmed]* The Serbs are being chased right back through the pass; and they say they may run into town. Our cavalry will be after them, and our people will be ready for them, you may be sure, now they're running away. *[She goes out on the balcony, and pulls the outside shutters too; then steps back into the room.]*

CATHERINE: [businesslike, her housekeeping instincts aroused] I must see that everything is made safe downstairs.

RAINA: I wish our people were not so cruel. What glory is there in killing wretched fugitives?

CATHERINE: Cruel! Do you suppose they would hesitate to kill you—or worse?

RAINA: [to LOUKA] Leave the shutters so that I can just close them if I hear any noise.

CATHERINE: [authoritatively, turning on her way to the door] Oh no, dear; you must keep them fastened. You would be sure to drop off to sleep and leave them open. Make them fast, Louka.

LOUKA: Yes, madam. [She fastens them]

RAINA: Don't be anxious about me. The moment I hear a shot, I shall blow out the candles and roll myself up in bed with my ears well covered.

CATHERINE: Quite the wisest thing you can do, my love. Goodnight.

RAINA: Goodnight. [Her emotion comes back for a moment] Wish me joy. [They kiss] This is the happiest night of my life—if only there are no fugitives.

CATHERINE: Go to bed, dear; and don't think of them. [She goes out]

LOUKA: [secretly; to RAINA] If you would like the shutters open, just give them a push like this [she pushes them: they open: she pulls them to again]. One of them ought to be bolted at the bottom; but the bolt's gone.

RAINA: [with dignity, reproving her] Thanks, Louka; but we must do what we are told. [LOUKA makes a grimace] Goodnight.

LOUKA: [carelessly] Goodnight. [She goes out, swaggering]

[RAINA, left alone, takes off her fur cloak and throws it on the ottoman. Then she goes to the chest of drawers, and adores the portrait there with feelings that are beyond all expression.]

RAINA: [looking up at the picture] Oh, I shall never be unworthy of you any more; my soul's hero; never, never, never. [She replaces it reverently. Then she selects a novel from the little pile of books. She turns over the leaves dreamily; finds her page; turns the book inside out at it; and, with a happy sigh, gets into bed and prepares to read herself to sleep. But before abandoning herself to fiction, she raises her eyes once more, thinking of the blessed reality, and murmurs] My hero! My hero!

[A distant shot breaks the quiet of the night. She starts, listening; and two more shots, much nearer, follow, startling her so that she scrambles out of bed, and hastily blows out the candle on the chest of drawers. Then, putting her fingers in her ears, she runs to the dressing table, blows out the light there, and hurries back to bed in the dark, nothing being visible but the glimmer of the light in the pierced ball before the image, and the starlight seen through the slits at the top of the shutters. The firing breaks out again; there is a startling fusillade quite close at hand. Whilst it is still echoing, the shutters disappear, pulled open from without; and for an instant the rectangle of snowy starlight flashes out with the figure of a man silhouetted in black upon it. The shutters close immediately; and the room is dark again. But the silence is now broken by the sound of panting. Then

there is a scratch; and the flame of a match is seen in the middle of the room.

RAINA: [crouching on the bed] Who's there? [The match is out instantly] Who's there? Who is that?

A MAN'S VOICE: [In the darkness, subduedly, but threateningly] Sh—sh! Don't call out; or you'll be shot. Be good; and no harm will happen to you. [She is heard leaving her bed, and making for the door] Take care: it's no use trying to run away.

RAINA: But who

THE VOICE: [warning] Remember; if you raise your voice my revolver will go off. [commandingly] Strike a light and let me see you. Do you hear? [another moment of silence and darkness as she retreats to the chest of drawers. Then she lights a candle; and the mystery is at an end. He is in a deplorable plight, bespattered with mud and blood and snow, his belt and the strap of his revolver-case keeping together the torn ruins of the blue tunic of a Serbian artillery officer. All that the candlelight and his unwashed unkempt condition make it possible to discern is that he has a strong neck and shoulders and clear quick eyes, trim soldierlike carriage and energetic manner, and with all his wits about him in spite of his desperate predicament; even with a sense of the humor of it, without, however, the least intention of trifling with it or throwing away a chance. Reckoning up what he can guess about RAINA: her age, her social position, her character, and the extent to which she is frightened, he continues more politely but still most determinedly] Excuse my disturbing you; but you recognize my uniform? Serb! If I'm caught I shall be killed. [Menacingly] Do you understand that?

RAINA: Yes.

THE MAN: Well, I don't intend to get killed if I can help it. [Still more formidably] Do you understand that? [He locks the door quickly **but** quietly]

RAINA: [disdainfully] I suppose not. [She draws herself up superbly, and looks him straight in the face, adding, with cutting emphasis] Some soldiers, I know, are afraid to die.

THE MAN: [with grim humor] All of them, dear lady, all of them, believe me. It is our duty to live as long as we can. Now, if you raise an alarm

RAINA: [cutting him short] You will shoot me. How do you know that I am afraid to die?

THE MAN: [cunningly] Ah; but suppose I don't shoot you, what will happen then? A lot of your cavalry will burst into this pretty room of yours and slaughter me here like a pig; for I'll fight like a demon: they shan't get me into the street to amuse themselves with; I know what they are. Are you prepared to receive that sort of company in your present undress? [RAINA, suddenly conscious of her nightgown, instinctively shrinks, and gathers it more closely about her neck. He watches her, and adds, pitilessly] Hardly presentable, eh? [She turns to the ottoman. He raises his pistol instantly, and cries] Stop! [she stops] Where are you going?

RAINA: [with dignified patience] Only to get my cloak.

THE MAN: [passing swiftly to the ottoman and snatching the cloak] A good idea! I'll keep the cloak; and you'll take care that nobody comes in and sees you without it. This is a better weapon than the revolver, eh? [He throws the pistol down on the ottoman]

RAINA: [revolted] It is not the weapon of a gentleman!

THE MAN: It's good enough for a man with only you to stand between him and death. [As they look at one another for a moment, RAINA *hardly able to believe that even a Serbian officer can be so cynically and selfishly unchivalrous, they are startled by a sharp fusillade in the street. The chill of imminent death hushes the man's voice as he adds]* Do you hear? If you are going to bring those blackguards in on me you shall receive them as you are.

> *[Clamor and disturbance. The pursuers in the street batter at the house door, shouting,* Open the door! Open the door! Wake up, you will! *A man servant's voice calls to them angrily from within,* This is MAJOR PETKOFF's house: you can't come in here; *but a renewal of the clamor, and a torrent of blows to the door, end with his letting a chain down with a clank, followed by a rush of heavy footsteps and a din of triumphant yells, dominated at last by the voice of* CATHERINE, *indignantly addressing an officer with,* What does this mean, sir? Do you know where you are? *The noise subsides suddenly.]*

LOUKA: *[outside, knocking at the bedroom door]* My lady! My lady! Get up quickly and open the door. If you don't they will break it down.

> *[The fugitive throws up his head with a gesture of a man who sees that it is all over with him, and drops the manner he has been assuming to intimidate* RAINA.]

THE MAN: *[sincerely and kindly]* No use, dear: I'm done for. *[Flinging the cloak to her]* Quick! Wrap yourself up. They're coming.

RAINA: Oh, thank *you*. *[She wraps herself up with intense relief]*

THE MAN: *[between his teeth]* Don't mention it.

RAINA: *[anxiously]* What will you do?

THE MAN: *[grimly]* The first man in will find out. Keep out of the way; and don't look. It won't last long; but it will not be nice. *[He draws his sabre and faces the door, waiting]*

RAINA: *[impulsively]* I'll help you. I'll save you.

THE MAN: You can't.

RAINA: I can. I'll hide you. *[She drags him towards the window.]* Here, behind the curtains.

THE MAN: *[yielding to her]* There's just half a chance if you keep your head.

RAINA: *[drawing the curtain before him]* S-sh! *[She makes for the ottoman]*

THE MAN: *[putting out his head]* Remember

RAINA: *[running back to him]* Yes?

THE MAN: —nine soldiers out of ten are born fools.

RAINA: Oh! *[She draws the curtain angrily before him]*

THE MAN: *[looking out at the other side]* If they find me, I promise you a fight: a devil of a fight.

> *[She stamps at him. He disappears hastily. She takes off her cloak, and throws it across the foot of the bed. Then, with a sleepy, disturbed air, she opens the door.* LOUKA *enters excitedly.]*

LOUKA: One of those beasts of Serbs has been seen climbing up the waterpipe of your balcony. Our men want to search for him; and they are so wild and drunk and furious. *[She makes for the other side of the room to get as far from the door as possible]* My lady says you are to dress at once, and to—*[She sees the revolver lying on the ottoman, and stops, petrified]*

RAINA: *[as if annoyed at being disturbed]* They shall not search here. Why have they been let in?

CATHERINE: *[coming in hastily]* Raina, darling; are you safe? Have you seen anyone or heard anything?

RAINA: I heard the shooting. Surely the soldiers will not dare come in here?

CATHERINE: I have found a Russian officer, thank Heavens; he knows Sergius. *[speaking through the door to someone outside]* Sir, will you come in now. My daughter will receive you.

> *[A young Russian officer, in Bulgarian uniform, enters, sword in hand.]*

OFFICER: *[with soft, feline politeness and stiff military carriage]* Good evening, gracious lady. I am sorry to intrude, but there is a Serb hiding on the balcony. Will you and the gracious lady your mother please to withdraw whilst we search?

RAINA: *[petulantly]* Nonsense, sir. You can see that there is no one on the balcony. *[She throws the shutters wide open and stands with her back to the curtain where the man is hidden, pointing to the moonlit balcony. A couple of shots are fired right under the window and a bullet shatters the glass opposite* RAINA, *who winks and gasps, but stands her ground; whilst* CATHERINE *screams, and the officer, with a cry of]* Take care! *[rushes to the balcony]*

THE OFFICER: *[on the balcony, shouting savagely down to the street]* Cease firing there, you fools, do you hear? Cease firing, damn you! *[He glares down for a moment, then turns to* RAINA, *trying to resume his polite manner]* Could anyone have got in without your knowledge? Were you asleep?

RAINA: No. I have not been to bed.

THE OFFICER: *[impatiently, coming back into the room]* Your neighbors have their heads so full of runaway Serbs that they see them everywhere. *[Politely]* Gracious lady: a thousand pardons. Goodnight. *[Military bow, which* RAINA *returns coldly. Another to* CATHERINE, *who follows him out.* RAINA *closes the shutters. She turns and sees* LOUKA, *who has been watching the scene curiously.]*

RAINA: Don't leave my mother, Louka, until the soldiers go away.

> *[LOUKA *glances at* RAINA, *at the ottoman, at the curtain; then purses her lips secretively, laughs insolently, and goes out.* RAINA, *highly offended by this demonstration, follows her to the door, and shuts it behind her with a slam, locking it violently. The man immediately steps out from behind the curtain, sheathing his sabre, and closes the shutters. Then, dismissing the danger from his mind in a business like way, he comes affably to* RAINA.]

THE MAN: A narrow shave; but a miss is as good as a mile. Dear young lady: your servant to the death. I wish for your sake I had joined the Bulgarian army instead of the other one. I am not a native Serb.

RAINA: *[haughtily]* No, you are one of the Austrians who set the Serbs on to rob us of our national liberty, and who officer their army for them. We hate them!

THE MAN: Austrian! Not I. Don't hate me, dear young lady. I am a Swiss, fighting merely as a professional soldier. I joined the Serbs because they came first on the road from Switzerland. Be generous; you've beaten us hollow.

RAINA: Have I not been generous?

THE MAN: Noble! Heroic! But I'm not saved yet. This particular rush will soon pass through, but the pursuit will go on all night by fits and starts. I must take my chance to get off in a quiet interval. *[Pleasantly]* You don't mind my waiting just a minute or two, do you?

RAINA: *[putting on her most genteel society manner]* Oh, not at all. Won't you sit down?

THE MAN: Thanks. *[He sits on the foot of the bed]*

> *[RAINA walks with studied elegance to the ottoman and sits down. Unfortunately she sits on the pistol, and jumps up with a shriek. The man, all nerves, shies like a frightened horse to the other side of the room.]*

THE MAN: *[irritably]* Don't frighten me like that. What is it?

RAINA: Your revolver! It was staring that officer in the face all the time. What an escape!

THE MAN: *[vexed at being unnecessarily terrified]* Oh, is that all?

RAINA: *[staring at him rather superciliously as she conceives a poorer and poorer opinion of him, and feels proportionately more and more at her ease]* I am sorry I frightened you. *[She takes up the pistol and hands it to him]* Pray take it to protect yourself against me.

THE MAN: *[grinning wearily at the sarcasm as he takes the pistol]* No use, dear young lady, there's nothing in it. It's not loaded. *[He makes a grimace at it, and drops it disparagingly into his revolver case]*

RAINA: Load it by all means.

THE MAN: I've no ammunition. What use are cartridges in battle? I always carry chocolate instead; and I finished the last cake of that hours ago.

RAINA: *[outraged in her most cherished ideals of manhood]* Chocolate! Do you stuff your pockets with sweets—like a school boy—even in the field?

THE MAN: *[grinning]* Yes. Isn't it contemptible? *[Hungrily]* I wish I had some now.

RAINA: Allow me. *[She sails away scornfully to the chest of drawers, and returns with the box of confectionery in her hand]* I am sorry I have eaten them all except these. *[She offers him the box]*

THE MAN: *[ravenously]* You're an angel! *[he gobbles the contents]* Creams! Delicious! *[He looks anxiously to see whether there are any more. There are none. He can only scrape the box with his fingers and suck them. When that nourishment is exhausted he accepts the inevitable with pathetic good humor, and says with grateful emotion]* Bless you, dear lady! You can always tell an old soldier by the inside of his holsters and cartridge boxes. The young ones carry pistols and cartridges; the old ones, grub. Thank you. *[He hands back the box. She snatches it contemptuously from him and throws it away. He shies again, as if she had meant to strike him]* Ugh! Don't do things so suddenly, gracious lady. It's mean to revenge yourself because I frightened you just now.

RAINA: *[loftily]* Frighten me! Do you know, sir, that though I am only a woman, I think I am at heart as brave as you.

THE MAN: I should think so. You haven't been under fire for three days as I have. I can stand two days without showing it much; but no man can stand three days. I'm as nervous as a mouse. *[He sits down on the ottoman, and takes his head in his hands]* Would you like to see me cry?

RAINA: *[alarmed]* No.

THE MAN: If you would, all you have to do is to scold me just as if I were a little boy and you my nurse. If I were in camp now, they'd play all sorts of tricks on me.

RAINA: *[a little moved]* I'm sorry. I won't scold you. *[Touched by the sympathy in her tone, he raises his head and looks gratefully at her]*

RAINA: *[eagerly turning to him, as all her enthusiasm and her dreams of glory rush back on her]* Did you see the great cavalry charge? Oh, tell me about it. Describe it to me.

THE MAN: You never saw a cavalry charge, did you?

RAINA: How could I?

THE MAN: Ah, perhaps not. No. Of course not! Well, it's a funny sight. First one comes, then two or three close behind him, and then all the rest in a lump.

RAINA: *[her eyes dilating as she raises her clasped hands ecstatically]* Yes, first One! The bravest of the brave!

THE MAN: *[prosaically]* Hm! You should see the poor devil pulling at his horse.

RAINA: Why should he pull at his horse?

THE MAN: *[impatient at so stupid a question]* It's running away with him, of course. Do you suppose the fellow wants to get there before the others and be killed?

RAINA: Ugh! But I don't believe the first man is a coward. I know he is a hero!

THE MAN: *[good humoredly]* That's what you'd have said if you'd seen the first man in charge today.

RAINA: *[breathless, forgiving him everything]* Ah, I knew it! Tell me about him.

THE MAN: He did it like an operatic tenor. A regular handsome fellow, with flashing eyes and lovely moustache, shouting his war-cry and charging like Don Quixote at the windmills. We did laugh.

RAINA: You dared to laugh!

THE MAN: Yes, but when the sergeant ran up as white as a sheet, and told us they'd sent us the wrong ammunition, and that we couldn't fire a round for the next ten minutes, we laughed out of the other side of our mouths. I never felt so sick in my life, though I've been in one or two very tight places. And I hadn't even a revolver cartridge, only chocolate. We'd no bayonets, nothing. Of course, they just cut us to bits. And there was Don Quixote flourishing like a drum major, thinking he's the cleverest thing ever known, whereas he ought to be court martialed for it. Of all the fools ever let loose on a field of battle, that man must be the very maddest. He and his regiment simply committed suicide; only the pistol missed fire; that's all.

RAINA: *[deeply wounded, but steadfastly loyal to her ideals]* Indeed! Would you know him again if you saw him?

THE MAN: Shall I ever forget him!

> *[She again goes to the chest of drawers. He watches her with a vague hope that she may have something more for him to eat. She takes the portrait from its stand and brings it to him.]*

RAINA: That is a photograph of the gentleman—the patriot and hero—to whom I am betrothed.

THE MAN: *[recognizing it with shock]* I'm really very sorry. *[Looking at her]* Was it fair to lead me on? *[He looks at the portrait again]* Yes, that's Don Quixote. Not a doubt of it. *[He stifles a laugh]*

RAINA: [quickly] Why do you laugh?

THE MAN: [apologetic, but still greatly tickled] I didn't laugh, I assure you. At least I didn't mean to. But when I think of him charging the windmills and imagining he was doing the finest thing—[he chokes with suppressed laughter]

RAINA: [sternly] Give me back the portrait, sir.

THE MAN: [with sincere remorse] Of course. Certainly. I'm really very sorry. [He hands her the picture. She deliberately kisses it and looks him straight in the face before returning to the chest of drawers to replace it. He follows her, apologizing.] Perhaps I'm quite wrong, you know, no doubt I am. Most likely he had got wind of the cartridge business somehow, and knew it was a safe job.

RAINA: That is to say, he was a pretender and a coward! You did not dare say that before.

THE MAN: [with a comic gesture of despair] It's no use, dear lady. I can't make you see it from the professional point of view. [As he turns away to get back to the ottoman, a couple of distant shots threaten renewed trouble]

RAINA: [sternly, as she sees him listening to the shots] So much the better for you!

THE MAN: [turning] How?

RAINA: You are my enemy; and you are at my mercy. What would I do if I were a professional soldier?

THE MAN: Ah, true, dear young lady: you're always right. I know how good you've been to me. To my last hour I shall remember those three chocolate creams. It was unsoldierly, but it was angelic.

RAINA: [coldly] Thank you. And now I will do a soldierly thing. You cannot stay here after what you have just said about my future husband; but I will go out on the balcony and see whether it is safe for you to climb down into the street. [She turns to the window]

THE MAN: [changing countenance] Down that waterpipe! Stop! Wait! I can't! I daren't! The very thought of it makes me giddy. I came up it fast enough with death behind me. But to face it now in cold blood—! [He drops his head in his hands in the deepest dejection]

RAINA: [disarmed by pity] Come, don't be disheartened. [She stoops over him almost maternally; he shakes his head] Oh, you are a very poor soldier. A chocolate cream soldier! Come, cheer up! It takes less courage to climb down than to face capture. Remember that.

THE MAN: [dreamily, lulled by her voice] No. Capture only means death, and death is sleep. Oh, sleep, sleep, undisturbed sleep! Climbing down the pipe means doing something—exerting myself—thinking! Death ten times over first.

RAINA: [softly and wonderingly, catching the rhythm of his weariness] Are you as sleepy as that?

THE MAN: I've not had two hours undisturbed sleep since I joined. I haven't closed my eyes for forty-eight hours.

RAINA: [at her wit's end] But what am I to do with you?

THE MAN: [staggering up, roused by her desperation] Of course. I must do something. [He shakes himself pulls himself together, and speaks with rallied vigor and courage.] You see, sleep or no sleep, hunger or no hunger, tired or not tired, you can always do a thing when you know it must be done. Well, that pipe must be got down. [He hits himself on the chest] Do you hear that, you chocolate cream soldier? [He turns to the window]

RAINA: [anxiously] But if you fall?

THE MAN: I shall sleep as if the stones were a feather bed. Goodbye. [He makes boldly for the window; and his hand is on the shutter when there is a terrible burst of firing in the street beneath]

RAINA: [rushing to him] Stop! [She seizes him recklessly, and pulls him quite around.] They'll kill you.

THE MAN: [cooly, but attentively] Never mind. This sort of thing is all in my day's work. I'm bound to take my chance. [Decisively] Now do what I tell you. Put out the candles, so they shan't see the light when I open the shutters. And keep away from the window, whatever you do. If they see me they're sure to have a shot at me.

RAINA: [clinging to him] They're sure to see you. It's bright moonlight. I'll save you. Oh, how can you be so indifferent! You want me to save you, don't you?

THE MAN: I really don't want to be troublesome. [She shakes him in her impatience] I am not indifferent, dear young lady, I assure you. But how is it to be done?

RAINA: Come away from the window. [She takes him firmly back to the middle of the room.] Now listen. You must trust to our hospitality. You do not yet know in whose house you are. I am a Petkoff.

THE MAN: A pet what?

RAINA: [rather indignantly] I mean that I belong to the family of the Petkoffs, the richest and best known in our country.

THE MAN: Oh yes, of course. I beg your pardon. The Petkoffs, to be sure. How stupid of me!

RAINA: You know you never heard of them until this moment. How can you stoop to pretend!

THE MAN: Forgive me. I'm too tired to think, and the change of subject was too much for me. Don't scold me.

RAINA: I forgot. It might make you cry. [He nods, quite seriously. She pouts and then resumes her patronizing tone.] I must tell you that my father holds the highest command of any Bulgarian in our army. He is [proudly] a Major.

THE MAN: [pretending to be deeply impressed] A Major! Bless me! Think of that!

RAINA: Have you ever seen the opera of Ernani?

THE MAN: Is that the one with the devil in it in red velvet, and a soldier's chorus?

RAINA: [contemptuously] No!

THE MAN: [stifling a heavy sigh of weariness] Then I don't know it.

RAINA: I thought you might have remembered the great scene where Ernani, flying from his foes just as you are tonight, takes refuge in the castle of his bitterest enemy, an old Castilian noble. The noble refuses to give him up. His quest is sacred to him.

THE MAN: [quickly, waking up a little] Have your people got that notion?

RAINA: [with dignity] My mother and I can understand that notion, as you call it. And if instead of threatening me with your pistol as you did you had simply thrown yourself as a fugitive on our hospitality, you would have been as safe as in your father's house.

THE MAN: What about your father?

RAINA: He is away at Slivnitza fighting for his country. I answer for your safety. There is my hand in pledge of it. Will that reassure you? [*She offers him her hand*]

THE MAN: [*looking dubiously at his own hand*] Better not touch my hand, dear young lady. I must have a wash first.

RAINA: [*touched*] That is very nice of you. I see that you are a gentleman. You may take my hand. [*She offers it again*]

THE MAN: [*kissing it with his hands behind his back*] Thanks, gracious young lady. I feel safe at last. And now would you mind breaking the news to your mother? I had better not stay here secretly longer than is necessary.

RAINA: If you will be so good as to keep perfectly still whilst I am away.

THE MAN: Certainly. [*He sits down on the ottoman*]

[*RAINA goes to the bed and wraps herself in the fur cloak. His eyes close. She goes to the door. Turning for a last look at him, she sees that he is dropping off to sleep.*]

RAINA: [*at the door*] You are not going asleep, are you? [*He murmurs inarticulately; she runs to him and shakes him*] Do you hear? Wake up. You are falling asleep.

THE MAN: Eh? Falling aslee—? Oh, no, not the least in the world. I was only thinking. It's all right. I'm wide awake.

RAINA: [*severely*] Will you please stand up while I am away? [*He rises reluctantly*] All the time, mind.

THE MAN: [*standing unsteadily*] Certainly. Certainly. You may depend on me.

[*RAINA looks doubtfully at him. He smiles weakly. She goes reluctantly, turning again at the door, and almost catching him in the act of yawning. She goes out.*]

THE MAN: [*drowsily*] Sleep, sleep, sleep, sleep, slee—[*The words trail off into a murmur.*] He wakes again with a shock on the point of falling! Where am I? That's what I want to know. Where am I? Must keep awake. Nothing keeps me awake except danger. Remember that. Danger, danger, danger, dan—[*trailing off again: another shock*] I'm to go to bed, but not to sleep. Not to lie down either, only sit down. [*He sits on the bed. A blissful expression comes into his face*] Ah! [*With a happy sigh he sinks back at full length; lifts his boots into the bed with a final effort and falls fast asleep insantly*]

[*CATHERINE comes in, followed by RAINA.*]

RAINA: [*looking at the ottoman*] He's gone! I left him here.

CATHERINE: Here! Then he just have climbed down from the—

RAINA: [*seeing him*] Oh! [*She points*]

CATHERINE: [*scandalized*] Well! [*She strides to the bed, RAINA following until she is opposite her on the other side.*] He's fast asleep. The brute!

RAINA: [*anxiously*] Sh!

CATHERINE: [*shaking him*] Sir! [*Shaking him again, harder*] Sir!! [*Vehemently, shaking very hard*] Sir!!!

RAINA: [*catching her arm*] Don't mamma. The poor darling is worn out. Let him sleep.

CATHERINE: [*letting go and turning amazed at RAINA*] The poor darling! Raina!!! [*She looks sternly at her daughter.*] [*the man sleeps profoundly*]

ACT 2

The sixth of March, 1886 In the garden of MAJOR PETKOFF'*s house. It is a fine spring morning. The garden looks fresh and pretty. Beyond the paling the tops of a couple of minarets can be seen, showing that there is a valley there, with the little town in it. A few miles further the Balkan mountains rise and shut in the landscape. Looking toward them from within the garden, the side of the house is seen on the left with a garden door reached by a little flight of steps. On the right the stable yard, with its gateway, encroaches on the garden. There are fruit bushes along the paling and house, covered with washing spread out to dry. A path runs by the house, and rises by two steps at the corner, where it turns out of sight. In the middle, a small table, with two bentwood chairs at it, is laid for breakfast with Turkish coffee pot, cups, rolls, etc.; but the cups have been used and the bread is broken. There is a wooden garden seat against the wall on the right.*

[LOUKA, *smoking a cigarette, is standing between the table and the house, turning her back with angry disdain on a man servant who is lecturing her. He is a middle-aged man of cool temperament and low but clear and keen intelligence, with the complacency of the servant who values himself on his rank in servitude, and the imperturtability of the accurate calculator who has no illusions. He wears a white Bulgarian costume; jacket with embroidered border, sash, wide knickerbockers, and decorated gaiters. His name is* NICOLA.]

NICOLA: Be warned in time, Louka: mend your manners. I know the mistress. She is so grand that she never dreams that any servant could dare be disrespectful to her; but if she once suspects that you are defying her, out you go.

LOUKA: I do defy her. I will defy her. What do I care for her?

NICOLA: If you quarrel with the family, I never can marry you. It's the same as if you quarrelled with me!

LOUKA: You take her part against me, do you?

NICOLA: [*sedately*] I shall always be dependent on the good will of the family. When I leave their service and start a shop in Sofia, their custom will be half my capital; their bad word would ruin me.

LOUKA: You have no spirit. I should like to catch them saying a word against me!

NICOLA: [*pityingly*] I should have expected more sense from you, Louka. But you're young. You're young!

LOUKA: Yes, and you like me the better for it, don't you? But I know some family secrets they wouldn't care to have told, young as I am. Let them quarrel with me if they dare!

NICOLA: [*with compassionate superiority*] Do you know what they would do if they heard you talk like that?

LOUKA: What could they do?

NICOLA: Discharge you for untruthfulness. Who would believe any stories you told after that? Who would give you another situation? Who in this house would dare be seen speaking to you ever again? How long would your father be left on his little farm? *[She impatiently throws away the end of her cigarette and stamps on it]* Child, you don't know the power such high people have over the like of you and me when we try to rise out of our poverty against them. *[He goes close to her and lowers his voice]* Look at me, ten years in their service. Do you think I know no secrets? I know things about the mistress that she wouldn't have the master know for a thousand levas. I know things about him that she wouldn't let him hear the last of for six months if I blabbed them to her. I know things about Raina that would break off her match with Sergius if—

LOUKA: *[turning on him quickly]* How do you know? I never told you!

NICOLA: *[opening his eyes cunningly]* So that's your little secret, is it? I though it might be something like that. Well, you take my advice and be respectful, and make the mistress feel that no matter what you know or don't know, she can depend on you to hold your tongue and serve the family faithfully. That's what they like, and that's how you'll make most out of them.

LOUKA: *[with searching scorn]* You have the soul of a servant, Nicola.

NICOLA: *[complacently]* Yes. That's the secret of success in service.

[A loud knocking with a whip handle on a wooden door is heard from the stable yard.]

MALE VOICE OUTSIDE: Hollo! Hollo there! Nicola!

LOUKA: Master! Back from the war!

NICOLA: *[quickly]* My word for it, Louka, the war's over. Off with you and get some fresh coffee. *[He runs out into the stable yard]*

LOUKA: *[as she collects the coffee pot and cups on the tray, and carries it into the house]* You'll never put the soul of a servant into me.

[MAJOR PETKOFF comes from the stable yard, followed by NICOLA. He is a cheerful, excitable, insignificant, unpolished man of about 50, naturally unambitious except to his income and his importance in local society, but just now greatly pleased with the military rank which the war has thrust on him as a man of consequence in his town. The fever of plucky patriotism which the Serbian attack roused in all the Bulgarians has pulled him through the war; but he is obviously glad to be home again.]

PETKOFF: *[pointing to the table with his whip]* Breakfast out here, eh?

NICOLA: Yes, sir. The mistress and Miss Raina have just gone in.

PETKOFF: *[sitting down and taking a roll]* Go in and say I've come; and get me some fresh coffee.

NICOLA: It's coming, sir. *[He goes to the house door. LOUKA, with fresh coffee, a clean cup, and a brandy bottle on her tray, meets him]* Have you told the mistress?

LOUKA: Yes, she's corning.

[NICOLA goes into the house. LOUKA brings the coffee to the table.]

PETKOFF: Well, the Serbs haven't run away with you, have they?

LOUKA: No, sir.

PETKOFF: That's right. Have you brought me some cognac?

LOUKA: *[putting the bottle on the table]* Here, sir.

PETKOFF: That's right. *[He pours some into his coffee.]*

[CATHERINE, who, having at this early hour made only a very perfunctory toilet, wears a Bulgarian apron over a once brilliant but now half worn-out dressing gown, and a colored handkerchief tied over her thick black hair, comes from the house with Turkish slippers on her bare feet, looking astonishingly handsome and stately under all the circumstances. LOUKA goes into the house.]

CATHERINE: My dear. Paul. What a surprise for us! *[She stoops over the back of his chair to kiss him.]* Have they brought you fresh coffee?

PETKOFF: Yes. Louka's been looking after me. The war's over. The treaty was signed three days ago at Bucharest; and the decree for our army to demobilize was issued yesterday.

CATHERINE: *[springing erect, with flashing eyes]* Paul, have you let the Austrians force you to make peace?

PETKOFF: *[submissively]* My dear, they didn't consult me. What could I do? *[She sits down and turns away from him]* but of course we saw to it that the treaty was an honorable one. It declares peace....

CATHERINE: *[outraged]* Peace!

PETKOFF: *[appeasing her]* But not friendly relations, remember that. They wanted to put that in, but I insisted on its being struck out. What more could I do?

CATHERINE: You could have annexed Serbia and made Prince Alexander Emperor of the Balkans. That's what I would have done.

PETKOFF: I don't doubt it in the least, my dear. But I should have had to subdue the whole Austrian Empire first; and that would have kept me too long away from you. I missed you greatly.

CATHERINE: *[relenting]* Ah! *[She stretches her hand affectionately across the table to squeeze his]*

SERGIUS: *[knocking at the stable gates]* Gate, Nicola!

CATHERINE: Oh, don't shout, Paul. It really isn't nice.

PETKOFF: Bosh! *[He shouts louder than before]* Nicola!

NICOLA: *[appearing at the house door]* Yes, sir.

PETKOFF: Are you deaf? Don't you hear Major Saranoff knocking? Bring him round this way. *[He pronounces the name with the stress on the second syllable: SARAHNOFF]*

NICOLA: Yes, Major. *[He goes into the stable yard]*

PETKOFF: You must talk to him, my dear, until Raina takes him off our hands. He bores my life out about our not promoting him. And it's no use. He hasn't the slightest chance of promotion until we're quite sure that the peace will be a lasting one.

NICOLA: *[at the gate, announcing]* Major Sergius Saranoff! *[He goes into the house and returns presently with a third chair, which he places at the table. He then withdraws]*

[MAJOR SERGIUS SARAHNOFF, the original of the portrait in RAINA's room, is a tall romantically handsome man, with the physical hardihood, the high spirit, and the susceptible imagination of an untamed mountaineer chieftain. But his remarkable personal distinctions of a characteristically civilized type would not be out of place in a Parisian salon. The result is Byronism. By his brooding on the perpetual failure, not only of others, but of himself, to live up to his ideals; by his consequent cynical scorn for humanity; by his credulity as to the absolute validity

of his concepts and the unworthiness of the world in disregarding them, he has acquired the half tragic, half ironic air, the mysterious moodiness, the the suggestion of a strange and terrible history that has left nothing but undying remorse. It is clear that here or nowhere is RAINA's *ideal hero.* CATHERINE *is hardly less enthusiastic about him than her daughter, and much less reserved in showing her enthusiasm. As he enters from the stable gate, she rises effusively to greet him.* PETKOFF *is distinctly less disposed to make a fuss about him.]*

PETKOFF: Here already, Sergius! Glad to see you.

CATHERINE: My dear Sergius! *[She holds out both her hands]*

SERGIUS: *[kissing them with scrupulous gallantry]* My dear mother, if I may call you so.

PETKOFF: *[dryly]* Mother-in-law, Sergius; mother-in-law! Sit down and have some coffee.

SERGIUS: Thank you. None for me. *[He gets away from the table with a certain distaste for* PETKOFF's *enjoyment of it, and posts himself with conscious dignity against the rail of the steps leading to the house]*

CATHERINE: You look superb. The campaign has improved you, Sergius. Everybody here is mad about you. We were all wild with enthusiasm about that magnificent cavalry charge.

SERGIUS: *[with grave irony]* Madam, it was the cradle and the grave of my military reputation.

CATHERINE: How so?

SERGIUS: I won the battle the wrong way when our worthy Russian generals were losing it the right way. In short, I upset their plans, and wounded their self-esteem. Two Cossack colonels had their regiments routed on the most correct principles of scientific warfare. Two major-generals got killed strictly according to military etiquette. The two colonels are now major-generals, and I still a simple major.

CATHERINE: You shall not remain so, Sergius. The women are on your side, and they will see that justice is done you.

SERGIUS: It is too late. I have only waited for the peace to send in my resignation.

PETKOFF: *[dropping his cup in his amazement]* Your resignation!

CATHERINE: Oh, you must withdraw it!

SERGIUS: *[with resolute measured emphasis, folding his arms]* I never withdraw.

PETKOFF: *[vexed]* Now who could have supposed you were going to do such a thing?

SERGIUS: *[with fire]* Everyone that knew me. But enough of myself and my affairs. How is Raina? And where is Raina?

RAINA: *[suddenly coming round the corner of the house and standing at the top of the steps in the path]* Raina is here. *[She makes a charming picture as they turn to look at her. She wears an underdress of pale silk, draped with an overdress of thin ecru canvas embroidered with gold. She is crowned with a dainty eastern cap.* SERGIUS *goes impulsively to meet her. Posing regally, she presents her hand. He drops chivalrously on one knee and kisses it.]*

PETKOFF: *[aside to* CATHERINE, *beaming with parental pride]* Pretty, isn't it? She always appears at the right moment.

CATHERINE: *[impatiently]* Yes. She listens for it. It is an abominable habit.

*[*SERGIUS *leads* RAINA *forward with splendid gallantry. When they arrive at the table, she turns to him with a bend of the head; he bows; and thus they separate, he coming to his place, and she going behind her father's chair.]*

RAINA: *[stooping and kissing her father]* Dear father! Welcome home!

PETKOFF: *[patting her cheek]* My little pet girl. *[He kisses her. She goes to the chair left by* NICOLA *for* SERGIUS, *and sits down.]*

CATHERINE: And so you're no longer a soldier, Sergius.

SERGIUS: I am no longer a soldier. Soldiering, my dear madam, is the coward's art of attacking mercilessly when you are strong, and keeping out of harm's way when you are weak.

PETKOFF: I suppose soldiering has to be a trade like any other trade.

SERGIUS: Precisely. But I have no ambition to shine as a tradesman; so I have taken the advice of that captain that settled the exchange of prisoners with us and given it up.

PETKOFF: What! That Swiss fellow? He over-reached us about those horses.

SERGIUS: Of course he over-reached us. His father was a hotel and livery stable keeper; and certainly knew horse-dealing. *[With mock enthusiasm]* Ah, he was a soldier; every inch a soldier! If only I had bought the horses for my regiment instead of foolishly leading it into danger, I should have been a field-marshal now!

CATHERINE: A Swiss? What was he doing in the Serbian army?

PETKOFF: A volunteer, of course. Keen on picking up his profession. *[Chuckling]*

RAINA: Are there many Swiss officers in the Serbian army?

PETKOFF: No, all Austrians, just as our officers were all Russians. This was the only Swiss I came across. I'll never trust a Swiss again. He humbugged us into giving him fifty ablebodied men for two hundred worn out chargers. They weren't even eatable!

SERGIUS: We were two children in the hands of that consummate soldier, Major. Simply two innocent little children.

RAINA: What was he like?

CATHERINE: Oh, Raina, what a silly question!

SERGIUS: He was like a commercial traveller in uniform. Bourgeois to his boots!

PETKOFF: *[grinning]* Sergius; tell Catherine that queer story his friend told us about how he escaped after Slivnitza. You remember. About his being hid by two women.

SERGIUS: *[with bitter irony]* Oh yes. Quite a romance! He was serving in the very battery I so unprofessionally charged. Being a thorough soldier, he ran away like the rest of them, with our cavalry at his heels. To escape their sabres he climbed a waterpipe and made his way into the bedroom of a young Bulgarian lady. The young lady was enchanted. She very modestly entertained him for an hour or so, and then called in her mother lest her conduct should appear unmaidenly. The old lady was equally fascinated, and the fugitive was sent on his way in the morning, disguised in an old coat belonging to the master of the house, who was away at the war.

RAINA: *[rising with marked stateliness]* Your life in the camp has made you coarse, Sergius. I did not think you would have repeated such a story before me. *[She turns away coldly]*

CATHERINE: [also rising] She is right, Sergius. If such women exist, we should be spared the knowledge of them.

PETKOFF: Pooh! Nonsense! What does it matter?

SERGIUS: [ashamed] No, Petkoff: I was wrong. [to RAINA, with earnest humility] I beg your pardon. I have behaved abominbly. Forgive me, Raina. [She bows reservedly] And you too, madam. [CATHERINE bows graciously and sits down. He proceeds solemnly, again addressing RAINA] The glimpses I have had of the seamy side of life during the last few months have made me cynical; but I should not have brought my cynicism here, least of all into your presence, Raina. I—[Here, turning to the others, he is evidently going to begin a long speech when the MAJOR interrupts him]

PETKOFF: Stuff and nonsense. Sergius! A soldier's daughter should be able to stand up without flinching to a little strong conversation. [he rises] Come. It's time for us to get to business. We have to make up our minds how those three regiments are to get back to Philippopolis; there's no forage for them on the Sofia route. [He goes towards the house] Come along. [SERGIUS is about to follow him when CATHERINE rises and intervenes]

CATHERINE: [stopping him playfully] You stay here, my dear Sergius; there's no hurry. I have a word or two to say to Paul. [SERGIUS instantly bows and steps back] Now, dear [taking PETKOFF's arm] come and see the electric bell.

PETKOFF: Oh, very well, very well.

[They go into the house together affectionately. SERGIUS, left alone with RAINA, looks anxiously at her, fearing that she is still offended. She smiles, and stretches out her arms to him.

SERGIUS: [hastening to her] Am I forgiven?

RAINA: [placing her hands on his shoulders as she looks up at him with admiration and worship] My hero! My king!

SERGIUS: My queen! [He kisses her on the forehead]

RAINA: How I have envied you, Sergius! You have been out in the world, on the field of battle, able to prove yourself there worthy of any woman in the world; whilst I have had to sit at home inactive—dreaming—useless—doing nothing that could give me the right to call myself worthy of any man.

SERGIUS: Dearest. All my deeds have been yours. You inspired me. I have gone through the war like a knight in a tournament with his lady looking down at him!

RAINA: And you have never been absent from my thoughts for a moment. [very solemnly] Sergius, I think we two have found the higher love. When I think of you, I feel that I could never do a base deed or think an ignoble thought.

SERGIUS: My lady and my saint! [He clasps her reverently]

RAINA: I trust you. I love you. You will never disappoint me, Sergius. [LOUKA is heard singing within the house. LOUKA comes from the house with her tray. She goes to the table, and begins to clear it, with her back turned to them.] I will get my hat; and then we can go out until lunch time. Wouldn't you like that?

SERGIUS: Be quick. If you are away five minutes, it will seem five hours. [RAINA runs to the top of the steps, and turns there to exchange looks with him and wave him a kiss with both hands. He looks after her with emotion for a moment; then turns slowly away, his face radiant with the loftiest exaltation. The movement shifts his field of vision, into the corner of which there now comes the tail of

LOUKA's double apron. His attention is arrested at once. He takes a stealthy look at her, with his left hand akimbo on his hip. Finally, striking the ground with his heels in something of a cavalry swagger, he strolls over to the other side of the table, opposite her, and says] Louka, do you know what the higher love is?

LOUKA: [astonished] No, sir.

SERGIUS: Very fatiguing thing to keep up for any length of time, Louka. One feels the need of some relief after it.

LOUKA: [innocently] Perhaps you would like some coffee, sir? [She stretches her hand across the table for the coffee pot]

SERGIUS: [taking her hand] Thank you, Louka.

LOUKA: [pretending to pull] Oh, sir, you know I didn't mean that. I'm surprised at you!

SERGIUS: [coming close to the table and drawing her with him] I am surprised at myself, Louka. What would Sergius, the hero of Silvnitza, say if he saw me now? What would Sergius, the apostle of the higher love, say if he saw me now? What would the half dozen Sergiuses who keep popping in and out of me? [Letting go her hand and slipping his arm dexterously round her waist] Do you consider my figure handsome, Louka?

LOUKA: Let me go, sir. I shall be disgraced. [She struggles; he holds her inexorably] Oh, will you let go?

SERGIUS: [looking straight into her eyes] No.

LOUKA: Then stand back where we can't be seen. Have you no common sense?

SERGIUS: Ah! That's reasonable. [He takes her into the stableyard gateway, where they are hidden from the house]

LOUKA: [plaintively] I may have been seen from the windows. Miss Raina is sure to be spying about after you.

SERGIUS: [stung; letting her go] Take care, Louka. I may be worthless enough to betray the higher love; but do not you insult it.

LOUKA: [demurely] Not for the world, sir, I'm sure. May I go on with my work, please, now?

SERGIUS: [again putting his arm around her] You are a provoking little witch, Louka. If you were in love with me, would you spy out of windows on me?

LOUKA: Well, you see, sir, since you say you are half a dozen different gentlemen all at once, I should have a great deal to look after.

SERGIUS: [charmed] Witty as well as pretty. [He tries to kiss her]

LOUKA: [avoiding him] No! I don't want your kisses. Gentlefolk are all alike. You making love to me behind Miss Raina's back, and she doing the same behind yours.

SERGIUS: [recoiling a step] Louka!

LOUKA: It shows how little you really care.

SERGIUS: [dropping his familiarity, and speaking with freezing politeness] If our conversation is to continue, Louka, you will please remember that a gentleman does not discuss the conduct of the lady he is engaged to with her maid.

LOUKA: It's so hard to know what a gentleman considers right. I thought from your trying to kiss me that you had given up being so particular. Ha! Ha! I expect one of the six of you is very like me, sir; though I am only Miss Raina's maid. [she goes back to her work at the table, taking no further notice of him]

SERGIUS: [speaking to himself] Which of the six is the real man? That's the question that torments me. One of them is a hero, another a buffoon, another a humbug, another perhaps a bit of a blackguard. [He pauses, and looks furtively at LOUKA, as he adds, *with deep bitterness]* And one, at least, is a coward; jealous, like all cowards. *[He goes to the table]* Louka.

LOUKA: Yes?

SERGIUS: Who is my rival?

LOUKA: You shall never get that out of me, for love or money.

SERGIUS: Why?

LOUKA: Never mind why. Besides, you would tell that I told you; and I should lose my place.

SERGIUS: *[holding out his right hand in affirmation]* No! On the honor of a—*[he checks himself; and his hand drops, nerveless, as he concludes sardonically]* of a man capable of behaving as I have been behaving for the last five minutes. Who is he?

LOUKA: I don't know. I never saw him. I only heard his voice through the door of her room.

SERGIUS: Damnation! How dare you?

LOUKA: And I tell you that if that gentleman ever comes here again, Miss Raina will marry him, whether he likes it or not. I know the difference between the sort of manner you and she put on before one another and the real manner.

[SERGIUS shivers as if she had stabbed him. Then, setting his face like iron, he strides grimly to her, and grips her above the elbows with both hands.]

SERGIUS: Now listen you to me.

LOUKA: *[wincing]* Not so tight. You're hurting me.

SERGIUS: That doesn't matter. You have stained my honor by making me a party to your eavesdropping. And you have betrayed your mistress.

LOUKA: *[writhing]* Please—

SERGIUS: That shows that you are an abominable little clod of common clay, and with soul of a servant. *[He lets her go as if she were an unclean thing, and turns away, dusting his hands of her, to the bench by the wall, where he sits down with averted head, meditating gloomily]*

LOUKA: *[whimpering angrily with her hands up her sleeves, feeling her bruised arms]* You know how to hurt with your tongue as well as your hands. But I don't care, now I've found out that whatever clay I'm made of, you're made of the same. As for her, she's a liar; and her fine airs are a cheat, and I'm worth six of her. *[She shakes the pain off hardily; tosses her head; and sets to work to put the things on the tray]*

[He looks doubtfully at her. She finishes packing the tray, and laps the cloth over the edges, so as to carry all out together. As she stoops to lift it, he rises.]

SERGIUS: Louka! *[She stops and looks defiantly at him]* A gentleman has no right to hurt a woman under any circumstances. *[With profound humility, uncovering his head]* I beg your pardon.

LOUKA: That sort of apology may satisfy a lady. Of what use is it to a servant?

SERGIUS: *[rudely crossed in his chivalry, throws it off with a bitter laugh, and says slightingly]* Oh! You wish to be paid for the hurt? *[He puts on his shako, and takes some money from his pocket]*

LOUKA: *[her eyes filling with tears in spite of herself]* No! I want my hurt made well.

[With unaffected dignity, she takes her tray, and is approaching the house when RAINA returns, wearing a hat and jacket in the height of the Vienna fashion of the

previous year, 1885. LOUKA *makes way proudly for her, and then goes into the house.]*

RAINA: I'm ready. What's the matter? *[gaily]* Have you been flirting with LOUKA?

SERGIUS: *[hastily]* No, no! How can you think such a thing?

RAINA: *[ashamed of herself]* Forgive me, dear. It was only a jest. I am so happy today. *[He goes quickly to her, and kisses her hand remorsefully.* CATHERINE *comes out and calls to them from the top of the steps.]*

CATHERINE: *[coming down to them]* I am sorry to disturb you, children, but Paul is distracted over those three regiments. He doesn't know how to send them to Philippopolis; and he objects to every suggestion of mine. You must go and help him, Sergius. He is in the library.

RAINA: *[disappointed]* But we are just going out for a walk.

SERGIUS: I shall not be long. Wait for me just five minutes. *[He runs up the steps to the door]*

RAINA: *[following him to the foot of the steps and looking up at him with timid coquetry]* I shall go round and wait in full view of the library windows. Be sure you draw father's attention to me. If you are a moment longer than five minutes, I shall go in and fetch you, regiments or no regiments.

SERGIUS: *[laughing]* Very well. *[He goes in]*

[RAINA watches him until he is out of her sight. Then, with a perceptible relaxation of manner, she begins to pace up and down the garden in a brown study.]

CATHERINE: Imagine their meeting that Swiss and hearing the whole story! The very first thing your father asked for was the old coat we sent him off in. A nice mess you have got us into!

RAINA: *[gazing thoughtfully at the gravel as she walks]* The little beast!

CATHERINE: Little beast! What little beast?

RAINA: To go and tell! Oh, if I had him here, I'd cram him with chocolate creams til he couldn't ever speak again!

CATHERINE: Don't talk such stuff. If Sergius finds out, it will be all over between you.

RAINA: *[with cool impertinence]* Oh, I know Sergius is your pet. I sometimes wish you could marry him instead of me. You would just suit him. You would pet him, and spoil him, and mother him to perfection.

CATHERINE: *[opening her eyes very widely indeed]* Well, upon my word!

RAINA: *[capriciously; half to herself]* I always feel a longing to do or say something dreadful to him—to shock his propriety—to scandalize the five senses out of him. *[To* CATHERINE, *perversely]* I don't care whether he finds out about the chocolate cream soldier or not. I have hope he may. *[She again turns and strolls flippantly away up the path to the corner of the house.]*

[LOUKA comes from the house with a salver, which she carries hanging down by her side.]

CATHERINE: Well?

LOUKA: There's a gentleman just called, Madam. A Serbian officer.

CATHERINE: *[flaming]* A Serb! And how dare he—*[checking herself bitterly]* Oh, I forgot. We are at peace now. Well, if he is an officer why don't you tell your master? He is in the library with Major Saranoff. Why do you come to me?

LOUKA: But he asks for you, madam. And I don't think he knows who you are. He said the lady of the house. He gave me this little ticket for you. *[She takes a card out of her bosom; puts it on the salver; and offers it to* CATHERINE*]*

CATHERINE: *[reading]* Captain Bluntschli? That's a German name.

LOUKA: Swiss, madam, I think.

CATHERINE: *[with a bound that makes* LOUKA *jump back]* Swiss! What is he like?

LOUKA: *[Timidly]* He has a big carpet bag, madam.

CATHERINE: Oh Heavens! He's come to return the coat. Send him away. Say we're not at home. Ask him to leave his address and I'll write to him. Oh, stop. That will never do. Wait! *[She throws herself into a chair to think it out.* LOUKA *waits.]* The master and Major Saranoff are busy in the library, aren't they?

LOUKA: Yes, madam.

CATHERINE: *[decisively]* Bring the gentleman out here at once. *[Peremptorily]* And be very polite to him. Don't delay. Here *[impatiently snatching the salver from her]* Leave that here, and go straight back to him.

LOUKA: Yes, madam. *[going]*

CATHERINE: Louka!

LOUKA: *[stopping]* Yes, madam.

CATHERINE: Is the library door shut?

LOUKA: I think so, madam.

CATHERINE: If not, shut it as you pass through.

LOUKA: Yes, madam *[going]*

CATHERINE: Stop! *[*LOUKA *stops]* He will have to go that way *[indicating the gate of the stableyard]* Tell Nicola to bring his bag here after him. Don't forget.

LOUKA: *[surprised]* His bag?

CATHERINE: Yes, here. As soon as possible. *[Vehemently]* Be quick! *[*LOUKA *runs into the house.* CATHERINE *snatches her apron **off** and throws it behind a bush. She then takes up the salver and uses it as a mirror, with the result that the handkerchief tied round her head follows the apron. A touch to her hair and a shake to her dressing gown make her presentable.]* Oh, how? How? How can a man be such a fool! Such a moment to select! *[*LOUKA *appears at the door of the house, announcing* CAPTAIN BLUNTSCHLI. *She stands aside at the top of the steps to let him pass before she goes in again. He is the man of the midnight adventure in* RAINA's *room, clean, well brushed, smartly uniformed, and out of trouble, but still unmistakably the same man. The moment* LOUKA's *back is turned,* CATHERINE *swoops on him with impetuous, urgent, coaxing appeal]* Captain Bluntschli! I am very glad to see you. But you must leave this house at once. *[He raises his eyebrows]* My husband has just returned with my future son-in-law and they know nothing. If my husband discovers our secret, he will never forgive me and my daughter's life will hardly be safe. Will you, like the chivalrous gentleman and soldier you are, leave at once before he finds you here?

BLUNTSCHLI: *[disappointed, but philosophical]* At once, gracious lady. I only came to thank you and return the coat you lent me. If you will allow me to take it out of my bag and leave it with your servant as I pass out, I need detain you no further. *[He turns to go into the house]*

CATHERINE: *[catching him by the sleeve]* Oh, you must not think of going back that way. *[Coaxing him across the stable gates]* This

is the shortest way out! Many thanks. So glad to have been of service to you. Good-bye.

BLUNTSCHLI: But my bag?

CATHERINE: It shall be sent on. You will leave me your address.

BLUNTSCHLI: True. Allow me. *[He takes out his card-case, and stops to write his address, keeping* CATHERINE *in an agony of impatience. As he hands her the card,* PETKOFF, *hatless, rushes from the house in a fluster of hospitality, followed by* SERGIUS*]*

PETKOFF: *[As he hurries down the steps]* My dear Captain Bluntschli

CATHERINE: Oh Heavens! *[She sinks on the seat against the wall]*

PETKOFF: *[too preoccupied to notice her as he shakes Bluntschli's hand heartily]* Those stupid people of mine thought I was out here, instead of in the—haw! Library *[he cannot mention the library without betraying how proud he is of it]* I saw you through the window. I was wondering why you didn't come in. Saranoff is with me; you remember him, don't you?

SERGIUS: *[saluting humorously, and then offering his hand with great charm of manner]* Welcome, our friend the enemy!

PETKOFF: No longer the enemy, happily. *[Rather anxiously]* I hope you've called as a friend, and not about horses or prisoners.

CATHERINE: Oh, quite as a friend, Paul. I was just asking Captain Bluntschli to stay for lunch, but he declares he must go at once.

SERGIUS: *[sardonically]* Impossible, Bluntschli. We want you here badly. We have to send on three cavalry regiments to Philippopolis, and we don't in the least know how to do it.

BLUNTSCHLI: *[suddenly attentive and business like]* Philippopolis? The forage is the trouble, I suppose.

PETKOFF: *[eagerly]* Yes, that's it. *[To* SERGIUS*]* He sees the whole thing at once.

BLUNTSCHLI: I think I can show you how to manage that.

SERGIUS: Invaluable man! Come along! *[He puts his hand on his shoulder and takes him to the steps,* PETKOFF *following]*

*[*RAINA *comes from the house as* BLUNTSCHLI *puts his foot on the first step.]*

RAINA: Oh! The chocolate cream soldier!

*[*BLUNTSCHLI *stands rigid.* SERGIUS, *amazed, looks at* RAINA, *then at* PETKOFF, *who looks back at him and then at his wife.]*

CATHERINE: *[with commanding presence of mind]* My dear Raina, don't you see that we have a guest here? Captain Bluntschli, one of our new Serbian friends.

*[*RAINA *bows.* BLUNTSCHLI *bows]*

RAINA: How silly of me! *[She comes down the center of the group, between* BLUNTSCHLI *and* PETKOFF*]* I made a beautiful chocolate ornament this morning for the ice pudding, and that stupid Nicola has just put down a pile of plates on it and spoilt it. *[To* BLUNTSCHLI, *winningly]* I hope you didn't think that you were the chocolate cream soldier, Captain Bluntschli.

PETKOFF: *[testily]* Has Nicola taken to drinking? He used to be careful enough. First he shows Captain Bluntschli out here when he knew quite well I was in the library, and then he goes downstairs and breaks RAINA's chocolate soldier. He must— *[*NICOLA *appears at the top of the steps with the bag. He descends,* places it respectfully before BLUNTSCHLI; *and waits for further orders. General amazement.* NICOLA, *unconscious of the effect he is producing, looks perfectly satisfied with himself. When* PETKOFF *recovers his power of speech, he breaks out at him with]* Are you mad, Nicola?

NICOLA: *[taken aback]* Sir?

PETKOFF: What have you brought that for?

NICOLA: My lady's orders, Major. Louka told me that—

CATHERINE: *[interrupting him]* My orders! Why should I order you to bring Captain Bluntschli's luggage out here? What are you thinking of, Nicola?

NICOLA: *[after a moment's bewilderment, picking up the bag as he addresses* BLUNTSCHLI *with the very perfection of servile discretion]* I beg your pardon, Captain, I am sure. *[To* CATHERINE*]* My fault, madam; I hope you'll overlook it. *[He bows, and is going to the steps with the bag, when* PETKOFF *addresses him angrily]*

PETKOFF: You'd better go and slam that bag, too, down on Miss Raina's ice pudding! *[This is too much for* NICOLA. *The bag drops from his hand almost on his master's toes, eliciting an order of]* Begone, you butter-fingered donkey.

NICOLA: *[snatching up the bag, and escaping into the house]* Yes, Major.

CATHERINE: Oh, never mind, Paul. Don't be angry.

PETKOFF: *[blustering]* Scoundrel! He's got out of hand while I was away. I'll teach him. Infernal blackguard! The sack next Saturday! I'll clear out the whole establishment. *[He is stifled by the caresses of his wife and daughter, who hang around his neck, petting him.]*

CATHERINE/RAINA: *[together]* Now, now, now, it mustn't be Wow, wow, wow; not on your Angry. He meant no harm. Be good to First day at home. I'll make another ice Please me dear. Sh-sh-sh-sh! Pudding. Tch-ch-ch!

PETKOFF: *[yielding]* Oh well, never mind. Come, Bluntschli; let's have no more nonsense about going away. You know very well you're not going back to Switzerland yet. Until you do go back you'll stay with us.

RAINA: Oh, do, Captain Bluntschli.

CATHERINE: Of course! I shall be only too delighted if *[appealingly]* Captain Bluntschli really wishes to stay. He knows my wishes.

BLUNTSCHLI: *[in his driest military manner]* I am at madam's orders.

SERGIUS: *[cordially]* That settles it!

PETKOFF: *[heartily]* Of course!

RAINA: You see you must stay.

BLUNTSCHLI: *[smiling]* Well, if I must, I must.

[Gesture of despair from CATHERINE*]*

ACT 3

[In the library after lunch. It is not much of a library. But it is a most comfortable sitting room. A row of three large windows shows a mountain panorama, just now seen in one of its friendliest aspects in the mellowing afternoon light. In the corner next the right hand window a square earthenware stove, a perfect tower of glistening pottery,
rises nearly to the ceiling and guarantees plenty of warmth. The ottoman is like that in RAINA's room, and similarly placed; and the window seats are luxurious with decorated cushions. There is a small writing table with an old canister full of pens and an eggcup filled with ink.

[At the side of this table, which stands to the left of anyone facing the window, BLUNTSCHLI *is hard at work with a couple of maps before him, writing orders. At the head of it sits* SERGIUS, *who is supposed to be also at work, but is actually gnawing the feather of a pen, and contemplating* BLUNTSCHLI's *quick, sure, businesslike progress with a mixture of envious irritation at his own incapacity and awestruck wonder at an ability which seems to him almost miraculous, though its prosaic character forbids him to esteem it. The* MAJOR *is comfortably established on the ottoman, with a newspaper in his hand and the tube of his hookah within easy reach.* CATHERINE *sits at the stove, with her back to them, embroidering.* RAINA, *reclining on the divan, is gazing in a daydream out at the Balkan landscape, with a neglected novel in her lap.*

[The door is on the same side as the stove, farther from the window. The button of the electric bell is at the opposite side, behind BLUNTSCHLI*]*

PETKOFF: *[looking up from his paper to watch how they are getting on at the table]* Are you sure I can't help you in any way, Bluntschli?

BLUNTSCHLI: *[without interrupting his writing or looking up]* Quite sure, thank you. Saranoff and I will manage it.

SERGIUS: *[grimly]* Yes, we'll manage it. He finds out what to do; draws up the orders; and I sign 'em. Division of labor! *[*BLUNTSCHLI *passes him a paper]* Another one? Thank you. *[He plants the paper squarely before him; sets his chair carefully parallel to it; and signs with his cheek on his elbow and his protruded tongue following the movements of his pen]* This hand is more accustomed to the sword than to the pen.

PETKOFF: It's very good of you, Bluntschli. It is indeed, to let yourself be put upon in this way. Now are you quite sure I can do nothing?

CATHERINE: *[in a low warning tone]* You can stop interrupting, Paul.

PETKOFF: *[starting and looking round at her]* Eh? Oh! Quite right, my love, quite right. *[He takes his newspaper up again, but presently lets it drop]* Ah, Catherine, you don't know how pleasant it is for us to sit here, after a good lunch, with nothing to do but enjoy ourselves. There's only one thing I want to make me thoroughly comfortable.

CATHERINE: What is that?

PETKOFF: My old coat. I'm not at home in this one. I feel as if I were on parade.

CATHERINE: My dear Paul, how absurd you are about that old coat! It must be hanging in the blue closet where you left it.

PETKOFF: My dear Catherine, I tell you I've looked there. Am I to believe my own eyes or not? *[*CATHERINE *rises and crosses the room to press the button of the electric bell. Nicola presents himself]*

CATHERINE: Nicola, go to the blue closet and bring your master's old coat here.

NICOLA: Yes, madam. *[He goes out]*

PETKOFF: Catherine.

CATHERINE: Yes, Paul?

PETKOFF: I bet you any piece of jewelry you like against a week's housekeeping money that the coat isn't there.

CATHERINE: Done, Paul!

PETKOFF: [excited by the prospect of a gamble] Come. Here's an opportunity for some sport. Who'll bet on it? Bluntschli, I'll give you six to one.

BLUNTSCHLI: [imperturbably] It would be robbing you, major. Madame is sure to be right. [Without looking up, he passes another batch of papers to SERGIUS]

> [NICOLA comes back with the coat, and brings it to PETKOFF who can hardly believe his eyes.]

CATHERINE: Where was it, Nicola?

NICOLA: Hanging in the blue closet, madame.

PETKOFF: Well, I am d—

CATHERINE: [stopping him] Paul!

PETKOFF: I could have sworn it wasn't there. Age is beginning to tell on me. I'm getting hallucinations. [He begins changing coats, NICOLA acting as valet] Ah, now I feel at home at last. [He sits down and takes his newspaper with a grunt of relief]

BLUNTSCHLI: [to SERGIUS, handing a paper] That's the last order.

PETKOFF: [jumping up! What! Finished?

BLUNTSCHLI: Finished.

PETKOFF: [inflating his chest and thumping it] Ah well, I think we've done a thundering good day's work. Can I do anything more?

BLUNTSCHLI: You had better both see the fellows that are to take these. [SERGIUS rises] Pack them off at once; and show them that I've marked on the orders the time they should hand them in by. Tell them that if they stop to drink or tell stories—if they're five minutes late, they'll have the skin taken off their backs.

SERGIUS: [stiffening indignantly] I'll say so. [He strides to the door.] And if one of them is man enough to spit in my face for insulting him, I'll buy his discharge and give him a pension. [He goes out]

BLUNTSCHLI: [confidentially] Just see that he talks to them properly, major, will you?

PETKOFF: [officiously] Quite right, Bluntschli, quite right. I'll see to it. [He goes to the door importantly, but hesitates on the threshold] Catherine, you may as well come too. They'll be far more frightened of you than of me.

CATHERINE: [putting down her embroidery] I daresay I had better. [She goes out, PETKOFF holding the door for her and following her]

> [RAINA, who has risen from the divan, marches slowly down the room with her hands clasped behind her, and looks mischievously at him]

RAINA: *You* look ever so much nicer than when we last met. [He looks up, surprised] What have you done to yourself.

BLUNTSCHLI: Washed, brushed, good night's sleep and breakfast. That's all.

RAINA: Did you get back safely that morning?

BLUNTSCHLI: Quite, thanks.

RAINA: Were they angry with you for running away from Sergius's charge?

BLUNTSCHLI: [grinning] No, they were glad, because they'd all just run away themselves.

RAINA: [going to the table, and leaning over it towards him] It must have made a lovely story for them. All that about me and my room.

BLUNTSCHLI: Capital story. But I only told it to one of them. A particular friend.

RAINA: On whose discretion you could absolutely rely?

BLUNTSCHLI: Absolutely.

RAINA: Hm! He told it all to my father and Sergius the day you exchanged prisoners. [She turns away and strolls carelessly across to the other side of the room]

BLUNTSCHLI: [deeply concerned, and half incredulous] No! You don't mean that, do you?

RAINA: [turning, with sudden earnestness] I do indeed. But they don't know that it was in this house you took refuge. If Sergius knew, he would challenge you and kill you in a duel.

BLUNTSCHLI: Bless me! Then don't tell him.

RAINA: Please be serious, Captain Bluntschli. Can you not realize what it is to me to deceive him? I want to be quite perfect with Sergius. No meanness, no smallness, no deceit. My relation to him is the one really beautiful and noble part of my life. I hope you can understand that I did it to save your life. He would have killed you. That was the second time I ever uttered a falsehood. [BLUNTSCHLI rises quickly and looks doubtfully and somewhat severely at her] Do you remember the first time?

BLUNTSCHLI: I! No. Was I present?

RAINA: Yes. And I told the officer who was searching for you that you were not present.

BLUNTSCHLI: True. I should have remembered it.

RAINA: [greatly encouraged] Ah, it is natural that you should forget it first. It cost you nothing; it cost me a lie! A lie! [She sits down on the ottoman, looking straight before her with her hands clasped round her knee. BLUNTSCHLI, quite touched, goes to the ottoman with a particular reassuring and considerate air, and sits down beside her.

BLUNTSCHLI: My dear young lady, don't let this worry you. Remember, I'm a soldier. Now what are the two things that happen to a soldier so often that he comes to think nothing of them? One is hearing people tell lies. [RAINA recoils] The other is getting his life saved in all sorts of ways by all sorts of people.

RAINA: [rising in indignant protest] And so he becomes a creature incapable of faith and of gratitude.

BLUNTSCHLI: [making a wry face] Do you like gratitude? I don't.

RAINA: Gratitude! [Turning on him] If you are incapable of gratitude you are incapable of any noble sentiment. Even animals are grateful. You were not surprised to hear me lie. To you it was something I probably did every day! Every hour! That is how men think of women. [She paces the room tragically]

BLUNTSCHLI: [dubiously] You said you'd only told two lies in your whole life. Dear young lady, isn't that rather a short allowance? I'm quite a straightforward man myself, but it wouldn't last me a whole morning.

RAINA: [staring haughtily at him] Do you know, sir, that you are insulting me?

BLUNTSCHLI: I can't help it. When you strike that noble attitude and speak in that thrilling voice, I admire you; but I find it impossible to believe a single word you say.

RAINA: [*superbly*] Captain Bluntschli!

BLUNTSCHLI: [*unmoved*] Yes?

RAINA: [*standing over him, as if she could not believe her senses*] Do you mean what you said just now? Do you know what you said just now?

BLUNTSCHLI: I do.

RAINA: [*gasping. She points to herself incredulously, meaning "I"*] "Raina Petkoff, tell lies!" [*He meets her gaze unflinchingly. She suddenly sits down beside him and adds, with a complete change of manner from her heroic to a babyish familiarity*] How did you find me out?

BLUNTSCHLI: [*promptly*] Instinct, dear lady. Instinct, and experience of the world.

RAINA: [*wonderingly*] Do you know, you are the first man I ever met who did not take me seriously?

BLUNTSCHLI: You mean, don't you, that I am the first man that has ever taken you quite seriously?

RAINA: Yes. I suppose I do mean that. [*Cosily, quite at her ease with him*] How strange it is to be talked to in such a way! You know, I've always gone on like that.

BLUNTSCHLI: You mean the—?

RAINA: I mean the noble attitude and the thrilling voice. [*They laugh together*] I did it when I was a tiny child to my nurse. She believed it. I do it before my parents. They believe it. I do it before Sergius. He believes it.

BLUNTSCHLI: Yes, he's a little in that line himself, isn't he?

RAINA: I suppose, now you've found me out you despise me.

BLUNTSCHLI: [*warmly, rising*] No, no, no, no a thousand times. It's part of your charm. I'm like all the rest of them: the nurse, your parents, Sergius. I'm your infatuated admirer.

RAINA: [*pleased*] Really?

BLUNTSCHLI: Really and truly.

RAINA: [*very happy*] But what did you think of me for giving you my portrait?

BLUNTSCHLI: [*astonished*] Your portrait! You never gave me your portrait.

RAINA: [*quickly*] Do you mean to say you never got it?

BLUNTSCHLI: No. [*He sits down beside her, with renewed interest, and says, with some complacency*] When did you send it to me?

RAINA: [*indignantly*] I did not send it to you. [*She turns her head away and adds, reluctantly*] It was in the pocket of that coat.

BLUNTSCHLI: [*pursing his lips and rounding his eyes*] Oh-o-oh! I never found it. It must be there still.

RAINA: [*springing up*] There still! For my father to find the first time he puts his hand in his pocket!

BLUNTSCHLI: [*rising also*] It doesn't matter. I suppose it's only a photograph. How can he tell who it was intended for? Tell him he put it there himself.

RAINA: [*distractedly*] Oh, what shall I do?

BLUNTSCHLI: Ah, I see. You wrote something on it. That was rash.

RAINA: [*vexed almost to tears*] Oh, to have done such a thing for you, who care no more—except to laugh at me—oh! Are you sure nobody has touched it?

BLUNTSCHLI: Well, I can't be quite sure. You see, I couldn't carry it about with me all the time. One can't take such luggage on active service.

RAINA: What did you do with it?

BLUNTSCHLI: When I got through to Pirot I had to put it in safe keeping somehow. So I pawned it.

RAINA: Pawned it!!!

BLUNTSCHLI: It was much the safest plan. I redeemed it the day before yesterday. Heaven only knows whether the pawnbroker cleared out the pockets or not.

RAINA: Oh, I wish I had never met you. [*She flounces away, and sits at the window fuming*]

[*LOUKA comes in with a heap of letters and telegrams on her salver, and crosses, with her bold free gait, to the table. Her left sleeve is looped up to the shoulder with a brooch, showing her naked arm, with a broad gilt bracelet covering the bruise.*]

LOUKA: [*to BLUNTSCHLI*] For you. [*She empties the salver with a fling onto the table*] The messenger is waiting. [*She is determined not to be civil to an enemy, even if she must bring him his letters.*]

BLUNTSCHLI: [*to RAINA*] Will you excuse me? The last postal delivery that reached me was three weeks ago. These are the subsequent accumulations. Four telegrams a week old. [*He opens one*] Oho! Bad news!

RAINA: [*rising and advancing a little remorsefully*] Bad news?

BLUNTSCHLI: My father's dead. [*He looks at the telegram with his lips pursed, musing on the unexpected change in his arrangements. LOUKA crosses herself hastily*]

RAINA: Oh, how very sad!

BLUNTSCHLI: Yes. I shall have to start for home in an hour. He has left a lot of big hotels behind him to be looked after. [*He takes up a letter in a long blue envelope*] Here's a letter from the family solicitor. [*He pulls out the enclosures and glances over them*] Great Heavens! Nine thousand six hundred!!! What on earth am I to do with them all?

RAINA: [*timidly*] Nine thousand hotels?

BLUNTSCHLI: Hotels! Nonsense! If you only knew! Excuse me. I must give my fellow orders about starting. [*He leaves the room hastily, with the documents in his hand*]

LOUKA: [*knowing instinctively that she can annoy RAINA by disparaging BLUNTSCHLI*] He has not much heart, that Swiss. He has not a word of grief for his poor father.

RAINA: [*bitterly*] Grief? A man who has been doing nothing but killing people for years! What does he care? What does any soldier care? [*She goes to the door, restraining her tears with difficulty*]

LOUKA: Major Saranoff has been fighting too, and he has plenty of heart left. [*RAINA, at the door, draws herself up haughtily and goes out*] Aha! I thought you wouldn't get much feeling out of your soldier. [*She is following RAINA when NICOLA enters with an armful of logs for the stove*]

NICOLA: [*grinning amorously at her*] I've been trying all the afternoon to get a minute alone with you, my girl. [*His countenance changes as he notices her arm*] What is that you're wearing on your sleeve, child?

LOUKA: [*proudly*] My own business.

NICOLA: Come! Don't be so contrary with me. I've some good news for you. *[She sits down beside him. He takes out some paper money.* LOUKA, *with an eager gleam in her eyes, tries to snatch it, but he shifts it quickly to his left hand, out of her reach]* See! A twenty leva bill! Sergius gave me that, out of pure swagger. A fool and his money are soon parted. There's ten levas more. The Swiss gave me that for backing up the mistress's and Raina's lies about him. He's no fool, he isn't. You should have heard old Catherine downstairs as polite as you please to me, telling me not to mind the Major being a little impatient, for they knew what a good servant I was—after making a fool and a liar of me before them all! The twenty will go to our savings, and you shall have the ten to spend if you'll talk to me so as to remind me I'm a human being. I get tired of being a servant occasionally.

LOUKA: Yes. Sell your manhood for 30 levas, and buy me for 10! *[rising scornfully]* Keep your money. You were born to be a servant. I was not. When you set up your shop you will only be everybody's servant instead of somebody's servant. *[She goes moodily to the table and seats herself regally in* SERGIUS's *chair]*

NICOLA: *[picking up his logs, and going to the stove]* Ah, wait til you see. I shall be master in my own house, I promise you. *[He throws the logs down and kneels at the stove]*

LOUKA: You shall never be master in mine.

NICOLA: Remember, it was me who taught you to dress right, to modify your make-up, to trim your nails, and keep your hands clean, and be dainty about yourself, like a fine Russian lady? Me. Do you hear that? Me! *[She tosses her head defiantly, and he turns away, adding, more coolly]* I've often thought that if Raina were out of the way, and you just a little less of a fool and Sergius just a little more of one, you might come to be one of my grandest customers, instead of only being my wife and costing me money.

LOUKA: I believe you would rather be my servant than my husband. You would make more out of me.

NICOLA: *[going closer to her for greater emphasis]* If you want to be a lady, your present behavior is too sharp and impudent. Don't be so ready to defy everybody. Act as if you expected to have your own way, not as if you expected to be ordered about.

[SERGIUS *comes in as* NICOLA *exits. He checks himself a moment on seeing* LOUKA, *then goes to the stove.* LOUKA, *without looking at* SERGIUS, *pretends to arrange the papers on the table. He crosses slowly to her, and studies the arrangement of her sleeve reflectively.]*

SERGIUS: Let me see. Is there a mark there? *[He turns up the bracelet and sees the bruise made by his grasp. She stands motionless, not looking at him; fascinated, but on her guard]* Ffff! Does it hurt?

LOUKA: Yes.

SERGIUS: Shall I cure it?

LOUKA: *[instantly withdrawing herself proudly, but still not looking at him]* No. You cannot cure it now.

SERGIUS: *[masterfully]* Quite sure? *[He makes a movement as if to take her in his arms.]*

LOUKA: An officer should not trifle with a servant.

SERGIUS: *[indicating the bruise with a merciless stroke of his forefinger]* That was no trifle, Louka.

LOUKA: *[flinching; then looking at him for the first time]* Are you sorry?

SERGIUS: *[with measured emphasis, folding his arms]* I am never sorry.

LOUKA: *[wistfully]* I wish I could believe a man could be as unlike a woman as that. I wonder are you really a brave man?

SERGIUS: *[unaffected, relaxing his attitude]* Yes, I am a brave man. My heart jumped like a woman's at the first shot, but in the charge I found that I was brave. Yes. That at least is real about me.

LOUKA: You don't know what true courage is.

SERGIUS: *[ironically]* Indeed! I am willing to be instructed. *[He sits on the ottoman, sprawling magnificently]*

LOUKA: Look at me! How much am I allowed to have my own will? I have to get your room ready for you; to sweep and dust, to fetch and carry. But *[with subdued passion]* if I were Empress of Russia, above everyone in the world, then!! Ah then, you should see, you should see.

SERGIUS: What would you do, most noble Empress?

LOUKA: I would marry the man I loved, which no other queen in Europe has the courage to do. If I loved you, though you would be as far beneath me as I am beneath you, I would dare to be the equal of my inferior. Would you dare as much if you loved me? No. You would marry a rich man's daughter because you would be afraid of what other people would say to you.

SERGIUS: *[bounding up]* You lie, by all the stars! If I loved you, and I were Czar, I would set you on the throne by my side. You know that I love another woman, a woman as high above you as heaven is above earth. And you are jealous of her.

LOUKA: I have no reason to be. She will never marry you now. The man I told you of has come back. She will marry the Swiss.

SERGIUS: *[recoiling]* The Swiss!

LOUKA: A man worth ten of you. Then you can come to me; and I will refuse you. You are not good enough for me. *[She turns to the door]*

SERGIUS: *[springing after her and catching her fiercely in his arms]* I will kill the Swiss; and afterwards I will do as I please with you.

LOUKA: *[in his arms, passive and steadfast]* The Swiss will kill you, perhaps. He has beaten you in love. He may beat you in war.

SERGIUS: *[tormentedly]* Do you think I believe that she—she! Whose worst thoughts are higher than your best ones, is capable of trifling with another man behind my back?

LOUKA: Do you think she would believe the Swiss if he told her now that I am in your arms?

SERGIUS: *[releasing her in despair]* Damnation! Oh, damnation! Mockery! Mockery everywhere! Everything I think is mocked by everything I do. *[He strikes himself frantically on the breast]* Coward! Liar! Fool! Shall I kill myself like a man or live and pretend to laugh at myself? *[She again turns to go]* Louka! *[She stops near the door]* Remember: you belong to me.

LOUKA: *[turning]* What does that mean?

SERGIUS: *[commandingly]* It means if I choose to love you, I dare marry you, in spite of all Bulgaria. I will either never touch you again or I will marry you. If these hands ever do touch you again, they shall touch my affianced bride.

LOUKA: We shall see whether you dare keep your word. And take care. I will not wait long.

[BLUNTSCHLI, *much preoccupied, with his papers still in his hand, enters, leaving the door open for* LOUKA *to go out. He goes across to the table, glancing at her as he passes.* SERGIUS, *without altering his resolute attitude, watches him steadily.* LOUKA *goes out, leaving the door open.*]

BLUNTSCHLI: [*absently, sitting at the table as before, and putting down the papers*] That's a remarkable looking young woman.

SERGIUS: [*gravely, without moving*] Captain Bluntschli.

BLUNTSCHLI: Eh?

SERGIUS: You have deceived me. You are my rival. I brook no rivals. At six o'clock I shall be in the drilling ground on the Klissoura road, alone, on horseback, with my sabre. Do you understand?

BLUNTSCHLI: [*staring, but sitting quite at his ease*] Oh, thank you. That's a cavalry man's proposal. I'm in the artillery, and I have the choice of weapons. If I go, I shall take a machine gun. And there shall be no mistake about the cartridges this time.

[RAINA *comes in and hurries forward anxiously*]

RAINA: I have heard what Captain Bluntschli said, Sergius. You are going to fight. Why? [SERGIUS *turns away in silence, and goes to the stove, where he stands watching her as she continues, to* BLUNTSCHLI] What about?

BLUNTSCHLI: I don't know. He hasn't told me. Better not interfere. He won't be able to touch me, and I'll not actually hurt him. In the morning I shall be off home; and you'll never see me or hear from me again. You and he will then make it up and live happily ever after.

RAINA: [*turning away deeply hurt, almost with a sob in her voice*] I never said I wanted to see you again.

SERGIUS: [*striding forward*] Ha! That is a confession.

RAINA: [*haughtily*] What do you mean?

SERGIUS: You love that man!

RAINA: [*scandalized*] Sergius!

SERGIUS: Captain Bluntschli. Denial is useless. You have enjoyed the privilege of being received in her own room, late at night.

BLUNTSCHLI: [*interrupting him pepperily*] Yes, you blockhead! She received me with a pistol at her head. Your cavalry were at my heels. I'd have blown out her brains if she'd uttered a cry. Apologize, man. Apologize. [*He resumes his seat at the table*]

SERGIUS: [*with the old measured emphasis, folding his arms*] I never apologize. Would you have come back here if nothing had passed between you except at the muzzle of your pistol?

RAINA: Who told you? [*Suddenly guessing the truth*] Ah, Louka! My maid! My servant! You were with her this morning all that time after—after—Oh, what sort of god is this I have been worshipping! [*He meets her gaze with sardonic enjoyment of her disenchantment. Angered all the more, she goes closer to him and says, in a lower, intense tone*] Do you know that I looked out of the window as I went upstairs, to have another sight of my hero; and I saw something I did not understand then. I know now that you were making love to her.

SERGIUS: [*with grim humor*] You saw that?

RAINA: Only too well. [*She turns away, and throws herself on the divan under the center window, quite overcome*]

SERGIUS: [*cynically*] Raina, our romance is shattered. Life's a farce.

BLUNTSCHLI: [*to* RAINA, *whimsically*] You see? He's found himself out now.

SERGIUS: [*going to him*] Bluntschli, I have allowed you to call me a blockhead. You may now call me a coward as well. I refuse to fight you. Do you know why?

BLUNTSCHLI: No, but it doesn't matter. I'm a professional soldier. I fight when I have to, and am very glad to get out of it when I haven't to. You're only an amateur. You think fighting's an amusement.

RAINA: [*Rising*] It is not you that he must fight now, but his rival, Nicola.

SERGIUS: Rival! [*bounding half across the room*]

RAINA: Don't you know that they're engaged?

SERGIUS: Nicola!

RAINA: [*getting angrier*] Do you realize what he has done, Captain Bluntschli? He has set this girl as a spy on us; and her reward is that he makes love to her.

SERGIUS: False! Monstrous!

RAINA: Monstrous! [*Confronting him*] Do you deny that she told you about Captain Bluntschli being in my room?

SERGIUS: No, but....

RAINA: [*interrupting*] Do you deny that you were making love to her when she told you?

SERGIUS: No. But I tell you....

RAINA: [*cutting him short contemptuously*] It is unnecessary to tell us anything more. [*quaintly to* BLUNTSCHLI, *with an intuitive guess at his state of mind*] I daresay you think us a couple of grown-up babies, don't you?

BLUNTSCHLI: [*blushing*] Not at all, I assure you. Where is this other young lady?

RAINA: Listening at the door, probably.

SERGIUS: [*shivering as if a bullet had struck him, and speaking with quiet but deep indignation*] I will prove that that, at least, is a lie. [*He goes with dignity to the door and opens it. A yell of fury bursts from him as he looks out. He darts into the passage, and returns dragging in* LOUKA, *whom he flings violently against the table, but she stands there proud and silent.*]

[MAJOR PETKOFF *enters, in his shirtsleeves.*]

PETKOFF: Excuse my shirtsleeves, gentlemen. Raina, somebody has been wearing that coat of mine. I'll swear it. Somebody with a differently shaped back. It's all burst open at the sleeve. Your mother is mending it. I wish she'd make haste. I shall catch cold. [*He looks more attentively at them.*] Is anything the matter?

RAINA: No. [*She sits down at the stove, with a tranquil air*]

BLUNTSCHLI: [*who is already seated*] Nothing, nothing.

PETKOFF: [*sitting down on the ottoman in his old place*] That's all right. [*He notices* LOUKA] Anything the matter, Louka?

LOUKA: No, sir.

PETKOFF: [*genially*] That's all right. [*He sneezes*] Go and ask your mistress for my coat, like a good girl, will you? [NICOLA *enters with the coat.* LOUKA *makes a pretense of having business in the room by taking the little table with the hookah away to the wall near the windows.*]

RAINA: [*rising quickly as she sees the coat on* NICOLA's *arm*] Here it is, papa. Give it to me, Nicola; and do put some more wood on the fire. [*She takes the coat, and brings it to the* MAJOR, *who stands up to put it on.* NICOLA *attends to the fire*]

PETKOFF: Come, give me a kiss. [She kisses him] Now give me the coat.

RAINA: No, I am going to put it on for you. Turn your back. [He turns his back and feels behind him with his arms for the sleeves. She dexterously takes the photograph from the pocket and throws it on the table before BLUNTSCHLI, who covers it with a sheet of paper under the very nose of SERGIUS, who looks on amazed, with his suspicions roused in the highest degree. She then helps PETKOFF on with his coat] There, dear! Now are you comfortable?

PETKOFF: Quite, little love. Thanks. [He sits down, and RAINA returns to her seat near the stove] Oh, by the bye, I've found something funny. What's the meaning of this? [He puts his hand into the picked pocket] Eh? Hallo! [He tries the other pocket] Well, I could have sworn...! [Much puzzled, he tries the breast pocket] I wonder—[trying the original pocket] Where can it—? [he rises, exclaiming] Your mother's taken it!

RAINA: [very red] Taken what?

PETKOFF: Your photograph, with the inscription: "Raina, to her Chocolate Cream soldier; a Souvenir." Now you know there's something more to this than meets the eye; and I'm going to find it out. Come, do you think I don't see it all? [He goes to SERGIUS, and slaps him on the shoulder] Sergius, you're the chocolate cream soldier, aren't you?

SERGIUS: [starting up] A chocolate cream soldier? Certainly not!

PETKOFF: Not! [He looks at them. They are all very serious and very conscious] Do you mean to tell me that Raina sends things like that to other men?

SERGIUS: [enigmatically] The world is not such an innocent place as we used to think, Petkoff.

BLUNTSCHLI: [rising] It's all right, Major. I'm the chocolate cream soldier. [PETKOFF and SERGIUS are equally astonished] The gracious young lady saved my life by giving me chocolate creams when I was starving. Shall I ever forget their flavour! You heard the story at Pirot. I was the fugitive.

PETKOFF: [exasperated] Raina, will you kindly inform me, if I am not asking too much, which of these gentlemen you are engaged to?

RAINA: To neither of them. This young lady [introducing Louka, who faces them all proudly] is the object of Major Saranoff's affections at the present.

PETKOFF: Louka! Are you mad, Sergius? Why, this girl's engaged to Nicola.

NICOLA: I beg your pardon, sir. There is a mistake. Louka is not engaged to me.

PETKOFF: Not engaged to you, you scoundrel! Why, you had twenty-five levas from me on the day of your betrothal; and she had that gilt bracelet from Miss Raina.

NICOLA: [with cool unction] We gave it out so, sir. But was only to give Louka protection. She had a soul above her station; and I have been no more than her confidential servant. I intend, as you know, sir, to set up a shop later on in Sofia; and I look forward to her custom and recommendation should she marry into the nobility. [He goes out with impressive discretion, leaving them all staring after him]

PETKOFF: [breaking the silence] Well, I am—hm!

SERGIUS: This is either the finest heroism or the most crawling baseness. Which is it, Bluntschli?

BLUNTSCHLI: Never mind whether it's heroism or baseness. Nicola's the ablest man I've met in Bulgaria. I'll make him manager of a hotel if he can speak French and German.

LOUKA: [suddenly breaking out at SERGIUS] I have been insulted by everyone here. You set them the example. You owe me an apology.

[SERGIUS, like a repeating clock of which the spring has been touched, immediately begins to fold his arms.]

BLUNTSCHLI: [before he can speak] It's no use. He never apologizes.

LOUKA: Not to you, his equal and his enemy. To me, he will not refuse to apologize.

SERGIUS: [approvingly] You are right. [He bends his knee in his grandest manner] Forgive me.

LOUKA: I forgive you. [She timidly gives him her hand, which he kisses] That touch makes me your affianced wife.

SERGIUS: [springing up] Ah! I forgot that.

LOUKA: [coldly] You can withdraw if you like.

SERGIUS: Withdraw! Never! I never withdraw. You belong to me. [He puts his arm about her]

[CATHERINE comes in and finds LOUKA in SERGIUS's arms, with all the rest gazing at them in bewildered astonishment.]

CATHERINE: What does this mean?

[SERGIUS releases LOUKA]

PETKOFF: Well, my dear, it appears that Sergius is going to marry Louka instead of Raina. [She is about to break out indignantly at him; he stops her by exclaiming testily] Don't blame me. I've nothing to do with it. [He retreats to the stove]

LOUKA: I told Major Saranoff she would never marry him if the Swiss gentleman came back.

BLUNTSCHLI: [rising, much surprised] Hallo?

LOUKA: [turning to RAINA] I thought you were fonder of him than of Sergius. You know best whether I was right.

BLUNTSCHLI: What nonsense! I assure you, my dear Major, my dear Madame, the gracious lady simply saved my life, nothing else. She never cared two straws for me. Why, bless my heart and soul, look at the young lady and look at me. She, rich, young, beautiful, with her imagination full of fairy princes and noble natures and cavalry charges and goodness knows what! And I, a commonplace Swiss Soldier who hardly knows what a decent life is after fifteen years of barracks and battles, a vagabond, a man who has spoiled all his chances in life through an incurably romantic disposition, a man—

SERGIUS: [starting as if a needle had pricked him and interrupting BLUNTSCHLI in incredulous amazement] Excuse me, Bluntschli; what did you say had spoiled your chances in life?

BLUNTSCHLI: [promptly] An incurably romantic disposition. I ran away from home twice when I was a boy. I went into the army instead of into my father's business. I climbed the balcony of this house when a man of sense would have dived into the nearest cellar. I came sneaking back here to have another look at the young lady when any other man of my age would have sent the coat back—

PETKOFF: My coat!

BLUNTSCHLI: —would have sent it back and gone quietly home. Do you suppose I am the sort of fellow a young lady falls in love with? All that adventure which was life or death to me, was only a schoolgirl's game to her—chocolate creams and hide and seek. Here's the proof? *[He takes the photograph from the table]* Now, I ask you, would a woman who took the affair seriously have sent me this and written on it, "Raina, to her Chocolate Cream Soldier; a Souvenir"? *[He exhibits the photograph triumphantly, as if it settled the matter beyond all possibility of refutation]*

PETKOFF: That's what I was looking for. How the deuce did it get there? *[He comes from the stove to look at it, and sits down on the ottoman]*

RAINA: *[going to the table to face him]* I quite agree with your account of yourself. You are a romantic idiot. *[BLUNTSCHLI is unspeakably taken aback]*

SERGIUS: *[with grim enjoyment of his rival's discomfiture]* Incurably romantic? But that's also precisely true of Raina!

BLUNTSCHLI: *[swiftly making up his mind and coming to his host]* In that case, Major Petkoff, I beg to propose formally to become a suitor for your daughter's hand, in place of Major Saranoff retired.

RAINA: You dare!

PETKOFF: We should be most happy, Bluntschli, if it were only a question of your position; but hang it, you know Raina is accustomed to a very comfortable establishment. Sergius keeps twenty horses.

CATHERINE: *[severly]* My daughter, sir, is accustomed to a first-rate stable.

RAINA: Hush, mother; you're making me ridiculous.

BLUNTSCHLI: Oh well, if it comes to a question of an establishment, here goes! *[He darts impetuously to the table; seizes the papers in the blue envelope; and turns to SERGIUS]* How many horses did you say?

SERGIUS: Twenty, noble Switzer.

BLUNTSCHLI: I have two hundred horses. *[they are amazed]* How many carriages?

SERGIUS: Three.

BLUNTSCHLI: I have seventy. Twenty-four of them will hold twelve inside, besides two on the box, without counting the driver and conductor. How many tablecloths have you?

SERGIUS: How the deuce do I know?

BLUNTSCHLI: Have you four thousand?

SERGIUS: No—

BLUNTSCHLI: I have. I have nine thousand six hundred pairs of sheets and blankets, with two thousand four hundred eider-down quilts. I have ten thousand knives and forks, and the same quantity of dessert spoons. I have three hundred servants. I have six palatial establishments, besides two livery stables, a tea garden, and a private house. I have four medals for distinguished services; I have the rank of an officer and the standing of a gentleman; and I have three native languages.

PETKOFF: *[with childish awe]* Are you Emperor of Switzerland?

BLUNTSCHLI: My rank is the highest now in Switzerland. I am a free citizen.

CATHERINE: Then, Captain Blumschli, since you are my daughter's choice—

RAINA: *[mutinously]* He's not.

CATHERINE: *[ignoring her]* I shall not stand in the way of her happiness. *[PETKOFF is about to speak]* That is Major Petkoff's feeling also.

PETKOFF: Oh, I shall be only too glad. Two hundred horses! Whew!

SERGIUS: What says the lady?

RAINA: *[pretending to sulk]* The lady says that he can keep his tablecloths and his omnibuses. I am not here to be sold to the highest bidder. *[She turns her back on him]*

BLUNTSCHLI: I won't take that answer. You accepted me as a fugitive, a beggar, and a starving man. You accepted me. You gave me your hand to kiss, your bed to sleep in, and your roof to shelter me.

RAINA: I did not give them to the Emperor of Switzerland.

BLUNTSCHLI: That's just what I said. *[He catches her by the shoulder and turns her face-to-face with him.]* Now tell us whom you did give them to.

RAINA: *[succumbing with a shy smile]* To my chocolate cream soldier!

[They embrace and kiss]

END OF PLAY

Necessary Targets

by Eve Ensler

Characters

J.S.: A wealthy American psychiatrist

Melissa: her assistant, and a trauma counsler

Jelena: refugee - late 40s

Zlata: refugee - same age as J.S., used to be doctor

Nuna: refugee - very Americanized teen

Seada: refugee - baby doesn't exist, 20s

Doona: Seada's baby

Azra - had a cow

Setting

A Bosnian refugee camp, 1995

SCENE I

Lights up on a posh living room. A coffee table with plates of food. J.S., a stunning, reserved woman near fifty, sits with Melissa, *a young, strong woman who sits awkwardly on the sofa, drinking water.* Melissa *wipes up the excess water that her drink has left on the coffee table. J.S. moves a round wooden object toward her.*

Melissa: Oh, it's a coaster. I thought it was an art object. I'm so sorry

J.S.: Not to worry. It's an old table.

Melissa: It's gorgeous. In such amazing shape. There's not one smudge on it. I could never keep a table like that. It takes so much time.

J.S.: Well, I don't spend my days polishing the table.

Melissa: No, no. I'm sure you have someone who does that. *[They both laugh nervously.]*

J.S.: You're younger than I expected.

Melissa: Well, I've been through a lot.

J.S.: *[unconsciously therapeutic]* Yes?

Melissa: *[sensing she's being analyzed, suddenly]* Oh, I didn't mean it like that.

J.S.: Like what?

Melissa: Like that. Like childhood. Like poor me. I don't feel sorry for myself.

J.S.: Why would I think that?

Melissa: Because you're a shrink. Because I'm sure you'll attribute all I do now to all that happened to me when I was little.

J.S.: I don't know what happened to you when you were little, Melissa.

Melissa: Do you need to know? Is it important for you to know? I'd rather not be identified or determined by that part of my life. It was their life. This is my life.

J.S.: And what makes this your life?

Melissa: That feels very much like a shrink question.

J.S.: Oh, I'm sorry

[They sit awkwardly.]

J.S.: I like your shoes.

Melissa: You do?

J.S.: Yes, very much.

Melissa: Kenneth Cole. I love the zippers.

J.S.: They're very...definitive.

Melissa: Well...yes. They're grounding. I need shoes that are grounding.

J.S.: Yes. I imagine.

Melissa: Not 'cause I'm crazy or off-the-wall or anything. But these situations, these wars. One needs...grounding.

J.S.: Yes. Your resume's impressive. You come highly recommended.

Melissa: Oh, I just made it up for you. I mean, typed it...up for you. All the facts are true. I usually work alone. I don't have to prove myself. So this is new.

J.S.: It's really interesting. You're trained as a therapist and a writer. That's very unusual.

Melissa: Trauma counselor.

J.S.: What?

Melissa: I'm trained as a trauma counselor. It's very specific training. I am not a therapist. I only work with seriously traumatized populations. Oh God, listen to me, "seriously traumatized populations..."

J.S.: Doesn't it frighten you?

Melissa: Yes, definitely. But it scares me more not to see it, not to know what's going on. Why are you going to Bosnia?

J.S.: I am going for the President's commission. I was asked, and it's a huge honor. To be honest, I was a bit surprised. I mean, Bosnia is not a place I know very much about. I read the news, but until about a week ago, the Balkans were not exactly next on my vacation map.

Melissa: Why does this commission want you to be there?

J.S.: Well, they chose a range of professions for the team. I'm the "shrink" piece, as you say. At one time it was my field, trauma.

Melissa: Yes, eating disorders. I am familiar with your books.

J.S.: Yes?

Melissa: You have never been to a war-torn country

J.S.: God, no. That's why I wanted you to be with me,

Melissa. Your experience.

Melissa: War is not exactly the same as anorexia.

J.S.: I am a psychiatrist. Twenty-six years. In private practice. I've been involved in a war of sorts, mental skirmishes and attacks. Trauma is trauma.

Melissa: In Haiti, the psychiatrists were fleeing like flies.

J.S.: Haiti?

Melissa: Yes.

J.S.: How long were you there?

Melissa: Eight months.

J.S.: Weren't you afraid?

Melissa: No. Not in Haiti—in Rwanda, yes...

J.S.: Rwanda.

Melissa: Yes.

J.S.: I can't imagine.

Melissa: No. No one could imagine.

J.S.: Are you sure you're ready to go to Bosnia, to do this again?

Melissa: *[clipped]* It's my work. It's what I do.

J.S.: You are very strong. So young and so strong.

Melissa: Is this commission the real deal? Or is it one of those U.N. situations—observe/witness, but do not go near?

J.S.: They said we would be working directly with the women war refugees. It's very "hands-on." That's why I need you to be my assistant.

Melissa: Is that what you were told?

J.S.: What?

Melissa: That I was an assistant—that I'd be your assistant.

J.S.: Yes, you were to assist me. You are a war specialist and you were to assist me.

Melissa: I am currently writing a book—investigating the effect of war in the creation and development of trauma, focusing primarily on communities of women, on those specific atrocities that traumatize women. It's my first contract with a major publisher. It's actually your publisher. It is essential that I complete the book this *year*. I will need to interview these women.

J.S.: That shouldn't be a problem.

[J.S. offers her a plate of food.]

J.S.: Don't you want something, Melissa? There are some lovely chicken-pesto wraps.

MELISSA: It's hard to eat on an interview. The crumbs. The chewing. Besides, I don't eat meat.

J.S.: Oh, you're a vegetarian.

MELISSA: Yes.

J.S.: That must be difficult when you travel. Isn't it hard to find something to eat?

MELISSA: I eat okay. I eat!

J.S.: Is there something else I can get you—fruit, nuts?

MELISSA: No, I'm fine.

[*They sit awkwardly.*]

J.S.: What does one wear?

MELISSA: Where?

J.S.: In a war-torn country.

MELISSA: You'll need a bulletproof vest, flak jacket, mud-stomping boots.

J.S.: [*unnerved*] Really?

MELISSA: Yes, and a helmet.

J.S.: Really?

MELISSA: No, we're not going as soldiers.

J.S.: What are we going as?

MELISSA: Well, you're going as an appointee of the President, and I, well, I guess I'm going as your assistant. [MELISSA *suddenly spills her drink. She frantically tries to wipe it up.*]

J.S.: Don't worry, MELISSA. It's only water.

MELISSA: But it's on this table...

J.S.: I make you nervous.

MELISSA: Like I said, it's what I can't see that frightens me. [*They stare awkwardly at one another, oddly frozen.*]

J.S.: I think it's insulting. To pretend to be living in these conditions. They know we can leave.

MELISSA: You can go.

J.S.: You'll excuse me, but I need the little comforts. You're younger than I. I welcome a bath, clean sheets, and a place to sit to...

MELISSA: Poop. These women need those same comforts. They had them all before the war.

J.S.: I don't think squatting in filthy footprints will make me a more effective therapist. Frankly, I think it will irritate me. I will be less patient and cranky.

MELISSA: Well, we don't want you cranky.

[*They both laugh.*]

MELISSA: Listen, I can help find you a hotel.

[*J.S. turns to leave, then turns back. She reluctantly throws her suitcase on the bed. She begins to unpack.* MELISSA *stares into her suitcase.*]

MELISSA: God, who packed your bags? Bendel's?

J.S.: I can't help it. I'm organized.

MELISSA: Organized? Even your socks are wrapped in tissue paper! [MELISSA *moves closer to examine. She picks up the socks.*]

MELISSA: What kind of socks are they? [*J.S. grabs her socks back and moves* MELISSA *away from her bag*]

J.S.: Do you have an issue with comfort?

MELISSA: Is that a shrink question?

J.S.: No, it was actually an innocent question.

MELISSA: Is that possible?

J.S.: MELISSA, believe it or not, sometimes I'm just curious about you, as a person. We are traveling together. It's a human thing.

MELISSA: [*pause*] Actually, I'm not big on comfort. It tends to terrorize me.

J.S.: I won't even go there.

SCENE 2

Bosnia. A refugee camp. A barracks-like room. Desolate. Two cots. Emptiness—a feeling of poverty. MELISSA *is making her bed, unpacking. J.S. enters, dressed in her proper New York City clothes.*

J.S.: There are big, dirty footprints in the bathroom.

MELISSA: Yes, you squat in them.

J.S.: You mean to...

MELISSA: [*laughs at her*] Poop. Yes, you squat to poop.

J.S.: In the footprints.

MELISSA: Yes. It's actually better...

J.S.: For...?

MELISSA: Your colon.

J.S.: And the showers.

MELISSA: They're pretty foul, but you'll get used to them.

J.S.: They were used for cattle.

MELISSA: Clean cattle.

J.S.: The hotel would give us some distance.

MELISSA: That's the problem with it. The women will resent us living in such luxury

J.S.: But I am not a refugee.

MELISSA: It will bring us closer to them.

SCENE 3

Barracks room—empty, broken-down. Torn cotton cloths on the window. Very hot. Six chairs in a semicircle, a tray of coffee on the table, little Turkish coffee cups. JELENA, *an earthy woman in her late forties;* ZLATA, *a distinguished and sophisticated woman the same age as J.S.;* NUNA, *a very Americanized teenager;* SEADA, *a beautiful girl in her twenties;* AZRA, *an oldie from the village. J.S. and* MELISSA *sit in the chairs. Most of the women are smoking, staring at J.S., taking in her clothes, etc. After a long time, J.S. finally speaks.*

J.S.: Hello.

WOMEN: Hello.

J.S.: I'm Dr....J.S. And this is my assistant, Melissa. [*uncomfortable, but full of therapist façade*] As most of you already know, we have been brought here by the presidential commission. Although Melissa has a great deal of experience in conflict zones, I must admit that war is new to me.

JELENA: Join the club.

[*The women laugh.*]

J.S.: So I will be learning with you as we go along.

AZRA: So you're a loony doctor.

JELENA: No, she is a doctor for crazy people.

AZRA: Are we crazy?

NUNA: Yes, she heard how you kicked your dog.

AZRA: I did not kick Tessa. I love Tessa more than I love most of you.

J.S.: We thought we'd start off with group sessions in the morning and afternoon. Two hours per session. We'd like to begin and end on time. So we'd appreciate your cooperation.

AZRA: I did not kick Tessa. I love my animals. I had a cow, oh what a cow! She could make enough milk...

EVERYONE: *[all the Bosnian women]* ...to feed a village.

MELISSA: We will also be available to you when we are not in session. As you know, we are staying here in the camp for that purpose. *[looks at J.S.]* So don't hesitate to call on us. Anytime. *[*J.S. *has to put her glasses on in order to read* NUNA's *name tag.]*

J.S.: No-ni. *[mispronounces it, and the women correct her; embarrassed, she begins again]* Nuni. *[the women correct her again; she very nervously tries again]* Nuna, why don't you begin?

NUNA: Begin what?

J.S.: Wherever you are. Start right there.

NUNA: You mean talk.

J.S.: If that's what you'd like to do.

NUNA: Why did you pick me? Do I look sicker than the others?

[The women laugh.]

J.S.: Is that how you feel?

NUNA: I didn't before.

J.S.: Before what?

NUNA: Before you picked me. Before you made me talk. Is it because I'm young? Do I look particularly disturbed? I don't do drugs.

J.S.: Do you normally go through this much when you are asked to speak?

NUNA: There is nothing normal here. Not for a long time.

J.S.: What was normal like for you?

NUNA: What is normal like for anyone? What is normal like for you? You know normal.

J.S.: I'd love for you to tell me about it, Nuna.

NUNA: I don't know. You are asking me so many things. Is this therapy? In America everyone's in therapy, right?

MELISSA: *[laughing]* Well, not everyone.

NUNA: I have heard that the patient—that's what we're called—lies down and goes into a trance and has visions and then they get to be rich.

J.S.: *[stepping in to help]* Are you from Bosnia, Nuna?

MELISSA: Of course she's from Bosnia.

ZLATA: We're all from Bosnia. What do you think we're doing here?

J.S.: *[to* ZLATA*]* What is your name?

JELENA: My name is Jelena. We are very honored that you Americans came all the way here. This is Azra. Azra's from Banja Luka.

AZRA: I need a doctor.

ZLATA: She is not that kind of doctor.

AZRA: I'm sure she knows something about arthritis. All doctors know about arthritis.

ZLATA: She's not that kind of doctor. I've already looked at you. It's simply old age.

JELENA: This is Seada, the gorgeous one. She is from the country. She never went outside her village before the war. And this is our Zlata, a doctor. You will have a hard time winning Zlata. You've already met Nuna. Nuna has seen too many American movies. Oh yes...and, of course, Doona...

*[*SEADA *holds out a wrapped little baby.]*

SEADA: *[to* J.S.*]* You are so pretty and so modern.

ZLATA: *[slightly sarcastic]* There was a war going on in Bosnia. We are refugees.

AZRA: Why don't you get those leaders on the couches? They're the loony ones.

SEADA: Doona is laughing. She is happy you are here.

MELISSA: How old is Doona?

*[*SEADA *holds out her wrapped baby and giggles.]*

ZLATA: What do you want with us?

J.S.: I have come here...well *[looking at* MELISSA*]*, we have come here...to help you.

[Everyone stares at her.]

ZLATA: And how do you plan to do that?

J.S.: I...well...we...I am a clinical therapist and you have...

AZRA: Will you get me my goats and cow? Will you get me my salami? They took my salami.

JELENA: They are not here for that, Azra.

MELISSA: We are here to help you, well...talk.

ZLATA: There is no shortage of talking here.

NUNA: All we do is talk and talk...

ZLATA: We are sick of talking.

J.S.: We are here to help you talk about the war, about the... *[The women laugh.]*

ZLATA: You flew all the way here for that? Two American doctors to "help" a group of poor Bosnian refugees talk about the war? What did you think we were talking about before you came? Our lingerie, our dinner parties...

NUNA: No, our face-lifts...

[The women laugh again.]

MELISSA: We are very moved by what you've been through. We were hoping you would talk to us. You would tell us your stories.

ZLATA: You and everybody else. They came from everywhere at the beginning of the war to hear the gory details.

NUNA: We read about ourselves in the paper. They made us sound deranged.

JELENA: And the scarf, always the scarf. Pictures of Azra with the scarf.

NUNA: They never took pictures of me.

ZLATA: They left and they never came back.

MELISSA: Exactly. That's why I'm writing a book, not an article. It is important that people know your stories the way you want to tell them.

ZLATA: So you are doctors or journalists?

J.S.: We are therapists. Well...Melissa is...

MELISSA: *[overlapping]* I am working on a book composed of the stories of refugees all around the world.

ZLATA: Oh, so we're a chapter.

MELISSA: No, no...

ZLATA: And who do you think will read your book?

MELISSA: I am hoping it will be read everywhere. Would anyone object to my recording our sessions?

ZLATA: I would not like you to record anything I say. I would not like that.

MELISSA: We will...

J.S.: ...not record you, Zlata. Are there others who feel this way?

MELISSA: I know it's difficult, but you will be helping so many people—to know your stories, to get them out.

J.S.: And you do not have to be so generous. You have already been through so much.

ZLATA: We had bad experiences with journalists.

J.S.: We are not journalists.

MELISSA: My writing is not to exploit you. Traumatized war victims...

NUNA: Is that what we're called? Traumatized war victims? Sounds so spooky.

MELISSA: It's not a judgment.

JELENA: No, worse, it's a life sentence. We are not wanted anywhere because we stink.

SEADA: Doona smells so pretty. She smells like doves.

ZLATA: I do not want you recording me.

J.S.: Nothing is being taped today.

NUNA: So this is American therapy?

AZRA: It just feels like another terrible day to me.

SCENE 4

Barracks room with two cots. J.S. is furiously packing when MELISSA *enters.*

MELISSA: What are you doing?

J.S.: Packing. I'm going home. This is ridiculous. Coming to Bosnia to help refugees talk about the war.

MELISSA: I thought you were a trained psychiatrist. Trained to see through denial and well-constructed defenses.

J.S.: That has nothing to do with this.

MELISSA: This is normal, what you're going through.

J.S.: I am totally embarrassed. I feel ludicrous.

MELISSA: And when a patient who's been badly abused comes to you, do you panic, do you give up if you don't have life experiences to compare?

J.S.: Listen. I can't help these women. They need homes, a country, and care.

MELISSA: It's only the first day. We're stirring things up. It means the transference is working.

J.S.: I do not sense transference. I sense their rightful contempt at being patronized.

MELISSA: I thought you were stronger than this.

J.S.: My practice is very limited. I like it that way.

MELISSA: These women need an outlet for their rage and despair. We are necessary targets.

[J.S. looks at MELISSA.*]*

MELISSA: I've been in other wars. It always begins like this.

J.S.: How does it end?

MELISSA: They tell their stories.

J.S.: Yes, but they don't get to go home?

*[*NUNA *comes running in.]*

NUNA: We need you to come. Baby Doona won't stop crying. Seada's worried that Doona's choking, and I'm worried the women are going to choke Seada if Doona doesn't shut up. [MELISSA *runs out.* NUNA *stops and looks at* J.S., *who doesn't move.]*

NUNA: Aren't you coming? We're really very friendly once you get to know us. And you should know, we've already talked and agreed. We think you're a little nervous, but we love the way you dress. You remind us of Meryl Streep.

*[*MELISSA *enters, carrying* DOONA]

J.S.: How's the baby?

MELISSA: She's gonna talk, she's gonna tell us what happened.

[J.S. looks out.]

SCENE 5

AZRA *and* JELENA *sit at a table drinking little shots of alcohol. J.S. listens in the shadows, unseen by them.*

JELENA: Dado. My Dado.

AZRA: What?

JELENA: Dado. Dado. He was so young then and handsome and eager. He was so eager to climb between the sheets, any time of day or night, and he was good there. So tender and...

AZRA: [*cutting her off*] Please, Jelena. Please. Give me my cows. Cows are friendly. Cows are simple. My cow...

JELENA: Dado loved me, Azra. His late-day face returning from the fields. Always he thought to bring me a vegetable, a ripe tomato, a luscious cucumber, or a flower. Always for me. Always for me.

AZRA: My goats ate all the flowers. I didn't mind. Well, I did, but I don't now. Oh what I would give to see my goats eat the flowers.

JELENA: Dado's so tired now.

AZRA: We're all tired now.

JELENA: It's different with Dado. He's changed. He's so angry all the time. He won't touch me except to...he won't talk to me.

AZRA: Cows. Goats. They always talk. They always listen.

JELENA: But sex, Azra, you need a man for sex.

AZRA: Yuck...

JELENA: Have you never had sex, Azra?

AZRA: Yuck...

JELENA: Oh, come on. There must have been someone, once. A kiss? A quick feel in the barn?

AZRA: Cows. Only cows.

JELENA: You would like sex. When we get home, I will get you a man. Believe me, it's better than salami.

[Lights fade on AZRA *and* JELENA, *and J.S. watching and listening in the shadows.]*

SCENE 6

Dark. Nighttime in the barracks. J.S. and MELISSA are asleep. Suddenly a dark shadow appears and grabs J.S. She sits up and screams. The shadow figure screams back and we then see that it's SEADA with her baby, DOONA, in her arms. J.S. tries to gain her composure. MELISSA watches their interaction from her bed, saying nothing.

J.S.: I'm sorry, Seada. I didn't mean to frighten you.

SEADA: *[climbing into* J.S.'s *bed]* Oh, Mama, let me in quickly, please. It's cold in my room. It's so much warmer in your bed. [J.S. *becomes extremely uncomfortable.* J.S. *sits up, preventing* SEADA *from getting into the bed.]*

J.S.: You miss your mother, Seada.

SEADA: *[continuing her need to get into the bed]* Hold me, Mama.

J.S.: You're a little lost, Seada. I think if you could talk about your feelings, we may be able to help you find out where you are.

SEADA: I'm tired, Mama. I don't want to talk. I want to sleep... with you.

J.S.: *[becoming very uptight]* It's not appropriate, Seada.

SEADA: I don't know what that means.

J.S.: It would not help you. It's important you have boundaries. They are essential to help you heal.

SEADA: *[begins to cry]* Doona is freezing, Mama. If we could just lie close like we always do. If we could just lie close, Mama.

[SEADA *defiantly and gently gets into bed.* J.S. *is stiff, trying to remain professional.* SEADA *wraps herself around her.* J.S. *pats her in an awkward, embarrassed kind of way.]*

SEADA: Would you sing to me, Mama?

J.S.: Its late now, Seada. I think it's best you just sleep.

SEADA: Are you afraid, Mama? Are you afraid too?

[SEADA *pats* J.S. *on her head to comfort her and then puts her head on* J.S.'s *very tense breast.* J.S. *looks over at* MELISSA, *who closes her eyes, faking that she's asleep.]*

SCENE 7

A rainstorm. Heat lightning. The same barracks' common room. The entire group of women, including J.S. and MELISSA, sit around a kitchen table in very cramped quarters. There is a lot of smoking. JELENA is making a pot of Turkish coffee, which she eventually brings to the table as the scene progresses. She carries a tray of cups, which sit for some time on the tray before the women drink them. As the scene begins, AZRA is crying. ZLATA holds her hand. The other Bosnian women offer Kleenex and comfort.

AZRA: *[crying[* Those bastards, they took our farms and land and cows...

ZLATA: Oh, Azra, please don't get started.

J.S.: Does Azra upset you, Zlata?

ZLATA: No, Azra upsets Azra. It's what she does.

AZRA: I lived in my Banja Luka for seventy-two years. If I could return to my village I would be happy to die there. I cannot die here. I cannot lie down...You have to lie down in order to die.

MELISSA: Where is your family now?

AZRA: *[begins to cry]* I do not know.

NUNA: We can all tell you what happened to Azra. Each of us knows, each one of us can tell you.

JELENA: Azra is horny. She's never had a man all these years. [MELISSA *turns on her tape recorder.]*

ZLATA: Recording tears, recording refugee tears—sexy business.

NUNA: We can all tell you what happened to each of us. We all know everything.

JELENA: Except Zlata—none of us knows what happened to Zlata.

J.S.: Well, I do not know anything. Perhaps you'd like to tell me.

ZLATA: Why? Why should we want to tell you?

NUNA: They took her brother into a camp.

J.S.: I think we need to address Zlata's question. Do other women have these same concerns?

MELISSA: Azra had begun to share her story. I think she should go on.

J.S.: No, actually, Nuna was sharing Azra's story

NUNA: Do you have movie-star patients in New York? I read that ninety percent of people in the movie business have serious emotional problems. Can you tell us who you see?

J.S.: That's confidential, Nuna.

NUNA: Do you dye your hair?

J.S.: Yes.

NUNA: Do you have a teenage daughter who pierces herself? Does it hurt?

MELISSA: We're getting off track.

NUNA: Are you a Capricorn?

J.S.: I do not think Zlata feels safe. *[AZRA is crying.]*

MELISSA: That's okay. Zlata doesn't have to talk. Azra...

AZRA: I did not leave our village. It was a perfect village. No one hardly raised their voice there except to call their dog or cow. They threatened me for months, but I would not go. I am thick, tough. I decided if they were going to kill me, they'd only kill me once. Then they broke into my house—they stole my cow...

MELISSA: Were you alone?

AZRA: There were just the oldies left, a village of oldies. We did not care if they killed us.

MELISSA: Did they hurt you?

[AZRA *cries more.]*

MELISSA: It's okay to cry.

ZLATA: Azra cries all the time. She does not get better. She just cries more and more. How does that help Azra? How does that help us to hear her cry?

NUNA: Why don't you drink the coffee? Is something wrong with the coffee?

J.S.: The coffee smells delicious. I quit caffeine six months ago.

NUNA: Americans are always quitting things. Why is that? They spend their days quitting things.

MELISSA: Please, Azra was doing so well, we must let Azra tell her story. Azra, tell us about your cow. *[All the women groan.]*

SEADA: Oh look, the sun. It feels so good on my face.

[SEADA *gets up and, holding her baby tight, dances in the*

sun.]

SEADA: *[says into the recorder]* Please, I want you to record that Seada feels safety on her face.

[SEADA goes and touches J.S.'s face and stares into her eyes.]

SEADA: It is because you came. Finally you came. *[SEADA kisses her and giggles.]*

JELENA: Seada thinks she remembers you.

MELISSA: I think it is essential that we focus here. We need to let Azra finish her story.

NUNA: Yes, the patient must tell her story

ZLATA: You keep using that word, Nuna—patient. Are we patients now? I, for one, am a doctor. I am a doctor and a refugee. I have not agreed to be a patient.

NUNA: *[very upset, blurts it out]* *Why* don't you like us, Dr. J.S.? Why have you come all the way here not to be with us?

J.S.: *[a bit taken aback, but gaining her composure]* What do you mean, Nuna?

[JELENA lifts up a coffee. All the women laugh.]

J.S.: I do not understand.

JELENA: Nuna does not understand why you don't drink coffee with us...

[All the women pause and watch J.S., waiting for her next move. J.S. looks to MELISSA for help and MELISSA just watches her too. Finally, J.S. takes a sip of coffee. She smiles and drinks more. The other women smile. J.S. drinks the rest as the lights fade.]

SCENE **8**

Outside the barracks. It is early dawn. ZLATA is sitting on a chair. She has been weeping. She is visibly disturbed, and J.S. feels awkward about interrupting her privacy. J.S. enters. It is very quiet.

J.S.: Hot.

ZLATA: Yes, and hot so late. Usually a breeze comes late.

J.S.: I need a breeze to sleep, the air, the sense of going somewhere.

ZLATA: Yes, the smells. The smells hang. Onion. Old cheese. Garbage. All hanging like a bad mistake.

J.S.: These are difficult circumstances. I am not accustomed to this.

ZLATA: You look different without your makeup.

J.S.: Yes?

ZLATA: Sad. Not so sure. Are you rich?

J.S.: What?

ZLATA: Are you wealthy?

J.S.: Why do you ask?

ZLATA: Because you are wearing a Christian Dior nightgown in a refugee camp. Because you were able to take time off from work.

J.S.: This is my work.

ZLATA: Oh, I see. We are work.

J.S.: Does it bother you that I am a therapist?

ZLATA: You never seem to answer questions.

J.S.: No, that is my work.

ZLATA: Do you make more money not answering questions?

J.S.: I am trained not to get in the way.

ZLATA: Of what?

J.S.: Of you.

ZLATA: How would you be in my way?

J.S.: By offering answers. By suggesting too much.

ZLATA: Wouldn't that just be a conversation? Don't people in America have conversations? Or do they only work?

J.S.: People pay me to listen to them.

ZLATA: People must be very lonely in America. *[pause]* I do not like the night—not anymore, not since the war. It is hard to sleep. I was rich like you before. My parents were very important people. I sleep now in the place of cows.

J.S.: How do you explain what's happened here? How could your neighbors, friends, suddenly behave like this?

ZLATA: I used to think it was the leaders, that men really made this war because of their hunger for power. But now I really believe it's in all of us—this thing, this monster, waiting to be let out. It waits there looking for a reason, a master, an invitation. If we are not aware of it, it can conquer us.

J.S.: Is it true you have such a monster in you, Zlata...?

ZLATA: Oh, I have my ugliness. For example, I can't stand complainers. You know those people who are never happy, never satisfied. *[complaining voice]* It's too hot, it's too slow, but I wanted vanilla ice cream...What about you? What could drive you to violence?

J.S.: Oh, I don't know...

ZLATA: I think you do.

[They sit awkwardly for a bit.]

J.S.: Well, I can't stand people who apologize all the time. They make me crazy. I'm sorry, could you pass the salt? I'm sorry, but I seem to have forgotten my wallet.

ZLATA: What about people who borrow things and conveniently forget to return them? They act like you're selfish or crazy if you ask for your book back.

J.S.: What about the people who don't listen? I despise that. People who don't wait for you to finish a sentence, make up what you're thinking for you. They forget what you've told them because they never listened in the first place. They make me nuts.

ZLATA: Shoot them at once.

J.S.: Well, retraining camps maybe.

ZLATA: Pointless. Just shoot them.

[Both of them laugh at themselves. Suddenly, J.S. realizes that ZLATA is shaking all over.]

J.S.: What is it, Zlata?

ZLATA: Don't, don't do that psychiatrist thing with me. Has this all been a technique, a trick to get me to talk?

J.S.: What is it?

ZLATA: You only care about the story, the gory details of the story. That's all any of you want.

J.S.: I want to be your friend.

ZLATA: You don't understand that this happened to us—to real people. We were just like you, we weren't ready for this—nothing in our experience prepared us—there were no signs—we weren't fighting for centuries—it didn't come out of our perverted lifestyle—you all want it to be logical—you want us to be different than you are so you can convince yourselves it wouldn't happen there, where you are. That's why you turn us into stories, into beasts, Communists, people who live in a strange country and speak a strange language—then you can feel safe, superior. Then, afterward, we become freaks, the stories of freaks—fax, please—get us one raped Bosnian woman, preferably gang-raped, preferably English-speaking.

J.S.: Teach me, Zlata. Teach me how to help you.

ZLATA: Help. Why do you assume I want your help? You Americans don't know how to stop helping. You move so fast, cleaning things up. Fixing.

J.S.: I am a doctor, Zlata.

ZLATA: I was a doctor, too, before the war. I was the head of the pediatrics unit in Prijedor's main hospital. Now I am a refugee. Now I stare off at the stars without explanation. I look out at the beet fields and weep for no reason.

SCENE 9

J.S. and MELISSA*'S room.* MELISSA *is listening to her recorder and taking notes.* SEADA *lies asleep in J.S.'s bed. J.S. enters from outside.*

J.S.: I'm having a hard time with the recorder, MELISSA.

[J.S. goes out. MELISSA *puts on her headphones. J.S. returns, drying her face. She taps* MELISSA *on the shoulder]*

J.S.: *[speaking loudly]* I don't mean just now. The recorder is changing the nature of things. They're either performing for it or resisting. They need to feel safe.

MELISSA: *[referring to* SEADA*]* Right. Safe.

J.S.: It feels invasive.

MELISSA: This recorder has helped women everywhere I've been. It is a device which legitimizes their experience, documents it, heals it...

J.S.: It's a recorder, Melissa.

MELISSA: We're here to trigger, provoke, release. Move in, move out.

J.S.: I appreciate your intensity, but...the way you approach things.

MELISSA: My intensity; you appreciate my intensity...

J.S.: I'm sorry, it is a loaded word.

MELISSA: Intense, that's what they always call women who do their job, who don't apologize, or hand-hold...intense, extreme, hard, difficult, bitch...

J.S.: Melissa, I said I appreciated your intensity. In fact, I do. You're very brave. You don't waste time. You take charge. I admire that. I admire you. It's just I think sometimes you need to hang back a little. You need to watch, wait...

SEADA: *[waking up]* Mommy... it's morning. It's morning, Mommy.

MELISSA: I'm watching, Mommy I'm waiting.

SCENE 10

Laughter. Whole group of the women by the river, dangling toes in water. AZRA, JELENA *have bright green cleansing masks on their faces.* NUNA *is smoothing on the masks like a professional skin-care person. J.S. watches, and* MELISSA *takes photographs, being careful to avoid photographing* ZLATA, *who reads a book.*

NUNA: The most thoughtful refugee item yet. Sent by a French cosmetics company.

ZLATA: Of course it's French. Who else would think of skin cleansing in the middle of ethnic cleansing?

JELENA: So much better than those canned sardines. They send them every day.

NUNA: Took me days to convince most of these women that beauty still matters. I think Azra's stopped bathing altogether.

JELENA: Have you ever noticed a sardine? It's not a fish, really. It's a thing that grows in a can. It no longer has any connection to being alive. It hardly remembers sun or sky or water. Covered in oil, in scum. It survives on the memory of all these things. It survives on the closeness to the other sardines. Sardines/refugines. Or is it surviving? Are we surviving?

ZLATA: Yes.

NUNA: No, we're waiting. Refugees wait.

MELISSA: What are you waiting for?

JELENA: Tomatoes. I haven't had a fresh vegetable for three months.

NUNA: To talk to my friends on the telephone.

ZLATA: Quiet. I am waiting for it to be quiet.

MELISSA: Maybe we could go around. I'd love to know what each of you is waiting for. We could make a kind of group poem out of it. It will allow everyone a chance to share what they're waiting for. Come on.

ZLATA: Maybe everyone doesn't need to *share* or want to *share*, Melissa.

AZRA: Well, I'm waiting to die. If someone would just bring me back to Banja Luka, I'd lie down and die with pleasure. I'd lie down with my cow.

*(*NUNA *begins to put the green mask on J.S.'s face and* SEADA, *in a panic, runs and stops her]*

SEADA: Don't do it. It will hurt her face. She doesn't need it. She has perfect skin.

J.S.: Why don't I do you, Nuna? Not that you need it.

NUNA: People in America have facials all the time, don't they? No one has bad skin. Everyone's beautiful and perfect.

J.S.: You're beautiful, Nuna.

JELENA: She looks like her mother.

NUNA: No, I look like my daddy. I am lean like him, and wiry. I have his mouth and hands. That's how I remember him. *[looks at her hands]* His artistic daddy hands.

MELISSA: Is your father alive, Nuna?

ZLATA: There she goes, story vulture.

NUNA: My father isn't dead. He's in Sarajevo. He is one of them, and so they would not let him leave.

MELISSA: But if he's your father, aren't you one of them, too?

NUNA: Those of us who are both are neither one. We are enemies everywhere.

J.S.: Not here, Nuna.

NUNA: No, not here where we have nothing—no land, no country; no things. There is nothing to kill for. But inside me it's really violent. One part of me hates the other part.

AZRA: Nuna, Nuna, hush...hush...

MELISSA: I think it's good for her to get it out.

NUNA: I used to think before the war how beautiful that all this had come together inside of me. All this history, knowledge, culture. Before the war, we who were mixed were considered the most beautiful, because so much had gone into making us. Now we are dirt—we are smudges. There was a soldier who was half-and-half like me. He slit his own mother's throat to prove to the army that he was one of them. I dream of them sucking the other half out of me with leeches. But I can never decide which part the other would be, Mommy or Daddy. You ask me what I'm waiting for—I'm waiting for someone to respect me, to see me as their own.

JELENA: I am waiting for booze.

AZRA: There is booze. Did you say there was booze?

MELISSA: You want to escape, Jelena, but you still haven't really answered what you're waiting for.

JELENA: I want to get drunk, Melissa, happy, smashed, shit-faced, sloshed. *[The women cheer]*

MELISSA: Yes, drunk, escape...

J.S.: You keep pushing, Melissa. You keep pushing and pushing.

NUNA: That's because she's a Capricorn. They never give up.

J.S.: Sometimes it's important to give up—to just surrender and let things take their course.

JELENA: Sometimes it's important to just get drunk. *[reaches into a bag next to her and pulls out a bottle of booze]* Booze, booze is here.

> *[The women let out a huge cheer. MELISSA is caught off guard. Music from Bosnia-Herzegovina plays. The women sing and dance. J.S. watches. She is totally moved by the singing, suspended as if caught in another time. MELISSA tries to participate, dances a little, but is disturbed by the drinking. J.S. suddenly realizes ZLATA is not there. She goes to find her. MELISSA tries to leave. The women drag her back, urging her to drink and join the fun. Music out.]*

SCENE 11

> *Stars and moonlight and crickets. We hear the women singing, and music continues in the distance. ZLATA sits alone. J.S. enters, excited and moved. She dances and moves to the music.*

J.S.: The honesty, the rawness. The singing in one room, the women...oh my heart. Why didn't I just sing...I wanted to sing. That's all I wanted to do, was sing. Did you know I was named after Bach—yes. J. Johann S. Sebastian. Bach. J.S. Bach. I don't think he could sing.

> *[They laugh.]*

J.S.: My father. Oh boy. I was in awe of him. He was very handsome. Great musician. Perfect. It was his skill that held people. It devastated them. The obsessive, driven nature of his training. I am so goddamn well trained. I'm no different than a soldier. Marching. *[marches]* Marching. Marching through people's brains. I don't murder people, well, I do, really. I kill them with all my boundaries and rules and perfect training. You were all singing. You were just singing. Singing like friends, singing....You must always know where you're going, he said, my father said, particularly in music. You must always take the song. Never let the song take you. That is why we train, practice. So we are not sloppy and sentimental.

ZLATA: Heaven forbid.

J.S.: I would never be a great singer. So I simply stopped singing.

ZLATA: Maybe you didn't want to be a great singer. Maybe you just wanted to sing. Why don't you sing for me?

J.S.: *[vehement]* No, I am no longer a person who can sing. I'm trained. I'm a psychiatrist. I'm not sloppy...no, not *me...[spinning in circles until she collapses]*

> *[The women's singing becomes loud, distinct, emotional, as a fantastically drunk JELENA leads all the women outside, a circus of singing, dancing refugees.]*

ZLATA: Sing. Come on, everybody. Sing.

> *[The women surround J.S. and ZLATA and sing and dance with all their hearts. SEADA is truly wild, stripping away her clothes as she dances. Music out.]*

SCENE 12

> *Lights come up on J.S. peering into a large hole in the ground. Moans come from the hole.*

J.S.: *[worried]* Have you hurt yourself?

AZRA: *[clearly drunk]* No, I am dying. This is my grave.

J.S.: It is cold in there, Azra, and dirty.

AZRA: Death is like that.

J.S.: Are you sick?

AZRA: No, I told you—I am dying.

J.S.: I think it is the vodka, Azra.

AZRA: It is the war. I will close my eyes now. They will come for me soon.

J.S.: But then you never will get home, not to Bosnia.

AZRA: Bosnia is over. Bosnia is a dream.

J.S.: Isn't all of this a dream, really?

AZRA: Don't confuse me. I'm trying to die.

J.S.: I would miss you, Azra. I would feel terrible if you were to die here in this hole.

AZRA: You would get over it. Everyone gets over everything eventually. Everyone forgets.

J.S.: I could not forget you, Azra. Not your face, your kind, deep, welcoming face.

AZRA: I am ugly and old. Let me die.

J.S.: What would it take for you to live?

Azra: I cannot remember.

J.S.: Sure you can, Azra. One thing. Tell me one thing that would get you to live.

Azra: Blossom.

J.S.: What?

Azra: My cow, Blossom. She was full the last time I saw her. She was waiting for me to milk her. I had my pail, and they forced me to leave with my empty pail, to leave Blossom.

J.S.: Can you talk to Blossom?

Azra: From here? I don't know if she can hear me from the grave.

J.S.: I know she can hear you, Azra.

Azra: It's too crazy.

J.S.: Why don't you try it?

> [long silence]

Azra: [as if calling to a cow in a field] Blossom! Blossom! It's me, your old friend Azra. I wanted to say good-bye, Blossom. I wanted to milk you one last time.

J.S.: What is Blossom doing?

Azra: She's staring at me with her big brown eyes. She's just standing there, not moving.

J.S.: Is she afraid?

Azra: Confused. She doesn't know what I'm doing in a hole. She thinks I'm playing a game with her.

J.S.: What do you want to do with her?

Azra: I want to rub her cow skin and walk her into the fields and watch her feed on the grass.

J.S.: But how will you do that if you are in the hole, Azra?

> [Suddenly Azra crawls out from the hole.]

Azra: Blossom, are you here? Where are you, Blossom?

J.S.: She is waiting for you, Azra. And she remembers you.

> J.S. helps Azra get out of the hole. J.S. gradually helps her dust herself off and stand up.]

Azra: Blossom...Blossom...Blossom...

> [J.S. carries a drunk and weary Azra across the lawn as night light fades.]

SCENE 13

Barracks. Morning. Lights comes up at first on Jelena, *who has a terrible black eye.* Zlata *makes an herbal salve for it. Everyone is hungover except* Melissa.

Jelena: I don't mind my eye, really. It's a reminder, a badge of sorts.

Nuna: He hit you, that bastard. He hit you.

Azra: Salami. I stick with salami.

Jelena: I was so happy last night, alive like I used to be before. I woke Dado to dance, to dance with me. This frightened him, as he'd been drinking, and he'd passed out. But this didn't put me off. I felt light-headed and full of a kind of perfect faith, full of God. "Dado," I said last night. "Dado, you must get up and dance with me under the stars, rise up, remember." And I must have pulled at him roughly and I frightened him and he

just went mad, started screaming about not taking him outside, the knives, how he'd do anything; not to hurt him, not to hurt the others—his father, that was his father and brother, to stop with the knives, stop carving his father, his fingers, his chest, his father. To stop. And he started begging, crying like a little boy, and when he found himself all little on the ground, all pathetic and groveling, he went even madder for me to see his weakness, hating that I loved him, worthless coward—and then, of course, proved that he wasn't. But I felt nothing. Nothing. Dado's fists and words, they could not touch me. I was with the old Dado. This new one, this new mutation of war, could not invade my happiness, could not invade my great dance under the stars.

Melissa: The booze was clearly not a good idea.

Jelena: The booze made us happy for the first time in months.

Melissa: You got beaten up. I would not be surprised if she has broken bones.

J.S.: It is my fault. I have not been thinking clearly.

Melissa: We are not doing well here. I don't think vodka is going to be the ticket, ladies, to get you out of this refugee camp. There is no shortage of alcoholic refugees.

Azra: Now we're alcoholics.

Zlata: Traumatized alcoholic war victims.

Nuna: Even more spooky.

Melissa: We need to get serious.

Jelena: Last night was the best thing that has happened to me. I danced. I felt happy.

Melissa: But how long can you go on like that, Jelena? You'll have to be drunk all the time.

Jelena: What's wrong with that?

Melissa: [losing it] This is serious. Your lives are at stake. We are not looking at anything here.

J.S.: Melissa is right. Maybe the booze wasn't a great idea. It wasn't responsible.

Jelena: What is responsible?

Melissa: Please, we need to address what's really going on here. We have big problems. Where is Seada?

Nuna: Seada was too hungover. She couldn't get up. She's really a mess.

Melissa: Seada is borderline and should not be getting drunk.

Zlata: Seada's doing fine.

Nuna: Zlata, come on. Seada is pretty screwed up.

Zlata: Seada's doing fine.

Melissa: Yes, because she has all of us—we support her fantasy world, we agree with her delusions. But she can't rely on us her whole life.

Zlata: Why not?

Melissa: Because she's living a lie. She's in complete denial. It's killing her.

Zlata: No, Melissa. What happened to her during the war is killing her. Her what you call "denial" is keeping her alive.

Melissa: Barely. She has nightmares almost every night. She's hysterical or wildly depressed most of the time.

Azra: Who isn't?

Melissa: Listen, there are ways to get better, to relieve the pain. It's scary to look at things. I know. But I promise it will not kill you—it's actually resisting the truth that is causing the greatest pain.

ZLATA: Again the assumptions—that we are sick and you know better than us what we need.

MELISSA: Zlata, you're very scared. I can feel it. You're holding the whole group back based on your own fear and anger.

AZRA: What is Zlata afraid of?

NUNA: Her story. That's why she hasn't told it to any of us.

JELENA: We are fighting with each other. I don't like that we are fighting.

J.S.: Maybe we should just slow down a little. I understand you want to get to issues, Melissa, but there is a natural human process going on here.

MELISSA: And what does that involve, J.S.? Drinking? Denial? Depression? Battery?

J.S.: Maybe. Maybe we need to be with all that for a while.

MELISSA: No, J.S., no. We can't wait anymore. It's too dangerous. Can you guarantee me that the next time Jelena's happy, Dado will not kill her? Can you assure me that Seada will not kill herself? We need to address some basic issues here.

J.S.: Like what?

MELISSA: Like what the hell happened to Seada. What made her like this?

ZLATA: Why do you, Melissa, need to know? That's up to Seada to tell us.

AZRA: I do not think we should talk about it behind her back. It's bad luck.

MELISSA: Azra, if we know what happened to Seada, we can help her begin to talk about it. We can prepare her for her feelings. Otherwise she will be consumed by what she refuses to remember.

J.S.: Zlata's right. It's Seada's story It's up to her to tell it.

MELISSA: No, it's everyone's story You have never been at war, J.S. It's a completely different dynamic. I thought that's why you wanted me here.

J.S.: I did. I do.

NUNA: Seada lived with her mother and husband.

[MELISSA turns her recorder on. ZLATA gets up to leave.]

J.S.: Where are you going?

[ZLATA stares at everyone and storms out. The group pauses, waits. NUNA continues.]

NUNA: Seada was wildly in love with her husband, who was very handsome. They had a beautiful life in this small village, Donji Vackuf, and a beautiful little three-month-old baby, Doona. You could say it was paradise there. Beautiful mountains, everyone took care of everyone—even the Gypsies came there. When the soldiers came...

AZRA: The soldiers came like that to all the villages. No one could believe they were coming, no one could believe they would hurt their neighbors, people thought they were just crazy kids, crazy boys, no one prepared .... One of the boys who beat me with a stick—I breast-fed him when he was an infant, when his mother was too sick.

NUNA: They got the people to come from their houses. They made them come into the square. It was all casual. *[SEADA suddenly appears in the shadows, holding her baby, overhearing the conversation.]*

JELENA: Seada was the most beautiful girl in the village. Her husband had heard of the rapes, heard how the soldiers had been raping the young girls, so they hid Seada in the house. They did not come out into the square.

NUNA: The soldiers found them, though, at night. They tried to take Seada. Her mother and her husband put up a fight and they shot them just like that, both of them right there, right in the head. Seada saw this happen. She was holding her baby, her baby, Doona, and she went mad. She started running and running. She ran into the night. The soldiers couldn't stop her. They chased her, but she was running like the wind. She ran for hours without stopping.

AZRA: Oh, I think we should stop here. It is wrong.

JELENA: When you are running crazy like that, anything can happen. You can lose your way.

AZRA: You can lose your mind.

NUNA: Or...your baby. You can lose your baby. You can drop your baby.

J.S.: Seada dropped her baby? She dropped her little Doona?

NUNA: She dropped her as she was running. She dropped her in the night, along her way.

J.S.: Oh my God. Oh my God.

[SEADA looks down at her bundle of rags and unfolds it and screams at the top of her lungs.]

SEADA: Doo... Doo... Doona.

[The women scream, stand, shocked.]

SEADA: Doona. Doona. I have to find Doona.

[SEADA runs out. All the women move to follow her. J.S. joins them.]

JELENA: No, J.S....you stay here.

J.S.: I want to come, Nuna. I want to find Seada.

JELENA: We will find her!

[The women quickly exit in search of SEADA.]

J.S.: *[very upset, confronting MELISSA]* Seada heard her story. She was not prepared. This was wrong, Melissa.

MELISSA: You need to get a hold of yourself, J.S. Your emotions are all over the place.

[J.S. loses it. She paces, sees the tape recorder and picks it up. She smashes it to the ground.]

J.S.: These women have suffered terribly and still they are trying to trust us.

MELISSA: Don't lecture me.

J.S.: We are not tape recorders. You do not get to hit and run. Seada didn't have her terrible experience in order to serve your book.

MELISSA: If people don't read Seada's story, they will never know it happened.

J.S.: This isn't about Seada. This is about you and your hunger for fame.

MELISSA: I may want recognition, but only so my work will be seen and these women, their pain, will be heard.

J.S.: And what if no one reads your book, or reads your book and doesn't care, doesn't do anything? What will all of this have meant to you—to you, Melissa?

MELISSA: This isn't about me, J.S. Everything for you is about the I...the big American, self-centered I.... You make thousands of dollars sitting in a room with it, cultivating it, expanding it.

J.S.: What happened to you that you are so numb?

MELISSA: Oh, spare me the pretending-to-be-caring analytical question.

J.S.: Okay. You're a lost little girl trying to find yourself in the middle of big, scary wars...

MELISSA: Maybe I am. Maybe I am. Maybe I'm familiar—too familiar with cruelty and violence—and maybe it came too early. So what? I think you're jealous. I think you would love to be me. I think you're suddenly aware that you waited too long for your life to happen and now you're lonely and old, and you don't know where to begin.

J.S.: [rage exploding] I don't like you, Melissa. I...

[NUNA breaks in, out of breath.]

NUNA: Come fast. Seada is hurting herself. It's very bad.

[NUNA grabs a very embarrassed and emotional J.S. The three of them run out. A wailing sound grows in intensity.]

SCENE 14

Outside, under the stars. SEADA is on the ground, digging madly at the dirt, eating it, pulling her hair, rocking back and forth. MELISSA approaches SEADA right away, and SEADA screams, clearly believing MELISSA is a soldier. MELISSA backs off.

SEADA: Mommy! Mommy!

[SEADA *frantically pulls her hair while eating dirt. J.S., scared, not sure what to do, watches, then suddenly grabs SEADA and stops her from hurting herself. SEADA, terribly lost, stares at her.*]

SEADA: Mommy? Mommy?

[SEADA *throws her arms around her neck and clings.*]

SEADA: Mommy! Mommy!

[J.S. *lets her stay there for a minute. Then she gently takes her arms down and looks SEADA in the face.*]

J.S.: No, Seada, no Mommy. J.S....I'm J.S....I'm right here.

[J.S. *holds on to SEADA.*]

SEADA: No Mommy. No Mommy.

[She starts to hurt herself again, but J.S. stops her. She starts to move away, but J.S. grabs her and holds her back. They struggle a bit.]

SEADA: [wildly anxious] No Mommy. No Mommy.

J.S.: It's okay, Seada. I'm right here.

[SEADA *begins to punch J.S.'s chest.*]

SEADA: Please, I say, please, can't you help me—help me find my baby. Believe me, I was a good mother. Happy until the war came to our village. Please, can't you help me. [*suddenly mad*

and panicked] Those lights, those bright mean lights, and those voices, those loud deep voices laughing, making fun of me. [J.S. *holds her tighter, and Seada connects with her again*] My aching breasts hungry to feed, over-flowing with milk for Doona, as they tear off my blouse, these loud, laughing voices wearing black masks, stinking of shit and meat, tear off my milk-stained blouse and rip at my aching, full breasts, biting them, sucking, "Okay, Mommy, I'll be your little, dirty baby"—as the other one spreads my legs and the other holds my arms—Doona "We'll show you how to make real babies, real clean babies. We'll fill you with the right kind of babies." Then he shoves himself into me, and there is a tearing, a ripping, the center of my dress, my underpants, splitting me apart, and as I'm splitting I can hear her suddenly, hear her crying out for her mother [*wails like her baby*], Doona, crying and crying, I cannot stop it, I cannot get it out of my brain. [*tears at her hair, begins to seriously hurt herself as she continues to wail;* J.S., *terrified, grabs her and rocks her*] Mama. Mama. [*gets quiet, confessional*] Mama, I've lost my baby I've lost our little Doona. [*puts her arms around* J.S.'s *neck and weeps like a baby; as she calms a little, the wailing still continues in her head*]

[J.S. *holds* SEADA. J.S. *weeps. She pauses.* J.S. *and* ZLATA *exchange looks. She rocks* SEADA *slowly and then, tentatively at first,* J.S. *begins to sing a nursery song. She is awkward initially, slightly out of tune, then she gathers herself, gaining her momentum and confidence in her singing.*

As she sings to SEADA *and the women, she finds her spirit, she breaks open, singing with heart and soul in full intensity. As she sings,* SEADA *stops crying. The wailing in her head begins to subside, then stops. The women gather round, appreciating this beautiful song, appreciating* J.S. *singing her song.*

There is silence.]

MELISSA I did not mean to hurt Seada. I did not mean to hurt anyone...this is my job, this is my...I am here to help...I am here to find a way to...I am here to...

SEADA: Hurt. Hurt.

MELISSA: What?

[*The other women start to laugh.*]

NINA: I think she needs you to hurt.

MELISSA: Hurt. Hurt. Do you think I do not hurt? It's not my job to take up space here with my hurt.

[MELISSA *takes a beat, then exits. The women pause.*]

AZRA: At least we don't have to pretend there's a baby anymore.

SCENE 15

J.S. *enters* MELISSA *and* J.S.'s *room in the barracks.* MELISSA *has been packing.* MELISSA *can be heard vomiting offstage.* J.S. *pauses uncomfortably.* MELISSA *comes out of the bathroom, sees J.S., and is embarrassed. She immediately resumes packing.*

J.S.: *You're* leaving?

MELISSA: I got the visa.

J.S.: Visa, to where?

MELISSA: Chechnya. I'm very excited. I'm thinking it will be the final chapter of the book.

J.S.: Chechnya? You're going to Chechnya from here?

MELISSA: Yes.

J.S.: Are you eating?

MELISSA: What?

J.S.: Are you eating?

MELISSA: Don't get involved..

J.S.: We're not in America, where we get paid not to get involved, Melissa. We're here.

MELISSA: I used to have nightmares, violent nightmares all the time. I was paralyzed, then I started traveling and documenting the stories of women. And guess what? The nightmares went away.

J.S.: What do you dream about now?

MELISSA: I don't dream at all. Not my verb. I write, I do, I go.

[MELISSA *quickly finishes packing, grabs her bag, and exits. J.S. is left alone.*]

SCENE 16

J.S. sits outside under the stars, clearly disturbed. It is late. ZLATA comes upon her, embarrassed.

ZLATA: Hot.

J.S.: Yes, and hot so late.

ZLATA: Usually a breeze comes late.

J.S.: I need the breeze to sleep, the air, the sense of going somewhere.

ZLATA: Yes, the smells. The smells hang. Onion. Old cheese. Garbage. All hanging like a bad mistake.

J.S.: Mistakes. Oh, I have learned a lot about mistakes this trip. I am the queen of mistakes.

ZLATA: And what would that make Melissa?

J.S.: Ah, Melissa...

ZLATA: Off to the Russian chapter. *[pause]* I am impressed. Really. Doctor to doctor. You did good.

J.S.: Really?

ZLATA: Really.

J.S.: To be honest, too many of my patients stay the same way year after year. Oh, they learn the language of therapy, they move their neurosis around, rearrange it with new psychoterminology, but their souls, their hearts, do not open. They do not change.

ZLATA: For refugees, things do not change. You were our change.

J.S.: I'm having a hard time packing. I can't seem to organize my things.

ZLATA: What do you think it means, Dr. Freud?

J.S.: I don't want to go there.

ZLATA: Maybe you don't want to leave us.

J.S.: Maybe I'm not sure why I am going back.

[*J.S. scratches herself*]

ZLATA: Why are you scratching? What is it?

J.S.: Nothing. It's nothing.

ZLATA: Let me see.

J.S.: No, no. I'm fine.

ZLATA: Come on, open your shirt. Let me see.

[*J.S. reluctantly opens her shirt, rolls up her sleeves.*]

J.S.: I think I have measles.

[ZLATA *laughs.*]

ZLATA: It is a rare breed of Bosnian heat rash. I have a cure.

J.S.: No, no. I'm fine.

ZLATA: I'll be right back.

[ZLATA *exits and then returns with ointment. She begins to apply it to J.S.'s neck and arms.*]

J.S.: Oh, it's so cool.

ZLATA: *[as she's applying cream]* It's for babies.

[*J.S. begins to cry.*]

ZLATA: What is it?

J.S.: Nothing. This is not your problem.

[*J.S. gets up to go.*]

J.S.: It's the...

ZLATA: ...beauty. Bosnia. Bosnia was beautiful. The song of Bosnia, the world of Bosnia that flows cold clean in the stream and tastes like a full meal. Bosnia, the snowy mountains, the green green hurt heart of Bosnia, the kindness we shared, how we lived in each other's warm kitchens, in sunny cafes, in the room of Bosnia. In the place, my place, my room. Gone. The ancient bridges, the mosques, the churches broken now, blown to bits and pieces. It isn't the cruelty that broke my heart. Cruelty is easy. Cruelty, like stupidity, is quick, immediate. They break in, they wear masks, they smell bad, they have machetes, they chop off the heads of my old parents sitting on their couch. There is blood, lots of it. There is screaming. There are dead, headless bodies. Cruelty is generic. Cruelty is boring, boring into the center of the part of you that goes away. We are dead—all of us—to the suffering. There is too much of it—but remind us of the beauty, the beet fields in full bloom, the redness of the fields. Remind us how we once sang, how the voices echoed as one through the landscape of night and stars. Remind us how often we laughed, how safe we felt, how easy it was to be friends. All of us. I miss everything—Bosnia was paradise.

[*J.S. and ZLATA look at each other and lights fade.*]

SCENE 17

J.S., in her New York apartment, talking into a recorder.

J.S.: Okay, MELISSA. I'm here. I'm talking into a tape recorder. Can you believe it? Hello, hello. Helloooo, Melissa. I'd sing, but I'm not drunk. I still need to be a little drunk to sing. God knows where you are now...Chechnya, Kosovo...

What if I told you that Zlata stopped my life, made my luxurious, advantaged, safe, protected, wellkept, organized, professional life impossible? What if she entered me, and I could not move? Back. Could not return to anything, anyone I'd ever been.

I have amnesia. I am no longer hungry. I am empty. I have lost my desire. America makes no sense to me. I am after nothing. What if this woman, Zlata, her heart, were to bleed into mine and I were to hemorrhage, and we were to bleed together? Would you say I'd lost all boundaries, that I was no longer professional, or would you say BLEED, BLEED?

[The women at the refugee camp gather around the kitchen table in Bosnia to make coffee.]

And then, what if I were to tell you that I was not unhappy? No, my ambition, my need to achieve, have it, have more, was the thing that made me unhappy. Always unhappy, always longing for more. Longing to be someone, to count, to matter, to make it. That was my unhappiness. I am without a country I am without a profession or pursuit. I am without a reason or even a direction. I am there in that refugee camp in the middle of nowhere. I am with Zlata and Jelena and Seada and Nuna and Azra, sometime very early in the morning. We are sitting and we are trying, we are really trying to trust one another, and in between the tears we take little sips of bad, thick coffee.

[J.S. looks to the women. Lights fade.]

THE END

Life Theme 3:

Generations

Life Theme 3: Generations

Parents want their children to follow their lead. Children
want an exciting new world.

Old age and youth cannot live together.

—For Love Alone, *Christina Stead*

Featured plays:

King Lear
   by William Shakespeare
Roosters
   by Milcha Sanchez-Scott

Conflicts between parents and children are an endless source of fascination and frustration. Plays
frequently attempt to make sense and provide wisdom into this perpetual battle between people
who love each other deeply and can nevertheless drive each other crazy, who are torn between
tradition and the need to break boundaries. One very popular theme in drama is what we call the
"rite of passage" play. These explore those vital moments of transition experienced in every life: from
childhood to adulthood, from adulthood to old age, etc.

   We will explore generations through two plays that focus on generational conflict and rites
of passage. First, a tragic, but ultimately wise treatment of generational conflict is found in what
many consider Williams Shakespeare's masterpiece, *King Lear* which is set in the mists of British
pre-history. The second play, the story of a young man's rite of passage into adulthood through
stormy, and sometimes violent, conflict with his parents is told by contemporary Mexican American
playwright, Milcha Sanchez-Scott.

King Lear

Year: 1605
Genre: Elizabethan Tragetdy, predominantly verse
Structure: English neo-classicism
Setting: Ancient Britain

Context:

Fifteen of Shakespeare's 37 plays are set in England, none farther back in time than this one. In fact, Lear is not based on actual history, but myth. It takes place in Celtic Britain, before the invasion of Rome. As in many of Shakespeare's plays, the story had been told numerous times by others before he adapted it. Within the play we even find hints of the popular legend of King Arthur and the Knights of the Round Table. For example King Arthur's famous father took the name Uther Pendragon or Uther "head of the dragon" because a dragon shaped comet was said to have coursed across the sky at his crowning. Celtic warriors who followed favored the symbol of the dragon and Shakespeare uses this image for Lear's description of himself as he threatens one of his lords: *Peace Kent! Come not between the dragon and his wrath!*

Throughout the play we can trace these mythological elements, but Shakespeare was nothing if not a commercial success as a playwright, and this play is not a simple retelling of an old fairy tale. He chose to add an important parallel plot in which a second old father is duped by a conniving child. He also changed the traditional happy ending to one that is powerfully tragic.

A Japanese translation of *King Lear* is reputed to have been published with the subtitle "An Unfortunate Case of Early Retirement." This is funny, reductive and somehow also strangely accurate. Lear, in a position of complete power in the family business, gives it up before he is really ready to let go and gives it to the wrong family members. He then goes through hell, before experiencing enlightenment too late to fix it. The family business happens to be running a country. The results are catastrophic. He gains tremendous personal insight after it is too late to use it to heal and help others.

The play is believed to have been written two years after the death of Elizabeth I. In earlier versions of the story, the Duke of Albany was as actively opposed to the old king as his wife Goneril, sister in law Regan, and her husband Cornwall. But in Shakespeare's lifetime, the title Duke of Albany belonged to his king, James I (formerly James VI of Scotland) who had passed it along to his own son. So the playwright wisely chose to make the character someone deeply sympathetic whom his own king would not mind as ancestor.

While many regard this as Shakespeare's greatest play, surpassing even *Hamlet*, the perception is more about what it is like to read it than to produce it on stage. *Hamlet* has no insurmountable production challenges. *King Lear*, just for starters, has the difficulty of the age of its two central characters. Both old men, while aged, must be "old lions" with strong vestiges of the power and majesty that once made them great. They cannot be pathetic or fragile until life and their children humble them. Someone with the *gravitas* of a Sean Connery or an Anthony Hopkins is important.

Also much of the story takes place during a wild and violent storm—a major technical challenge—the storm needs to rage and howl, but we still must comprehend what each character says and does. One actor (playing the character of Kent) has to appear to be insane and remain nearly naked for much of the play. Another (Gloucester) must have both his eyes gauged out onstage. So while one can read it and imagine, to mount it is an enormous challenge. This is why critics often tend to deem *Hamlet* the greatest piece of theatre and *Lear* the most powerful piece of literature.

The Playwright:

Other biographical details can be found in the Introduction to *Much Ado About Nothing* so here we will concentrate on Shakespeare's major tragedies. Dating the writing and first production of many of Shakespeare's plays can be a daunting task as historical evidence is scant. Plays by definition come and go so quickly and the printing of plays was still in its infancy. We are fortunate indeed to have as many texts of Shakespeare's plays as we do and debates about dates, authorship, and text inconsistencies will no doubt continue as they have done for centuries. However, we can be quite sure that *King Lear* was written and produced when Shakespeare was at the height of his tragic powers. We can be fairly certain that his early plays were primarily histories and comedies. His early attempts at tragedy were *Titus Andronicus* and *Romeo and Juliet*. Then between the years 1600 and 1607 he produced some of the finest tragic plays ever written in the English language: *Hamlet, Troilus and Cressida, Othello, King Lear, Macbeth,* and *Anthony and Cleopatra*. During this same period, his comedies became more complex, more challenging for the reader and the producer as in *Measure for Measure* and *All's Well That End Well*, two plays that almost defy attempts to assign mode and genre. Within a few years of these plays, he retired. As tempting as it is to assign Shakespeare's "happy comedies" to a period of romance and youthful hopefulness in his personal life, so too is it tempting to elicit personal meaning out of this group of dark and troubling plays. We have no clear evidence of anything happening in his personal life to account for the change in tone. One can only be confident in saying that *King Lear* was written during a time when Shakespeare was the master of his craft, a mature artist of the theatre who had established his reputation and fortune and who could now express an adult appreciation of the world and life in all of its light and shadow, simplicity and complexity.

Roosters

> *Year: 1987*
> *Genre: Realismo ("Magic Realism")*
> *Structure: Well-made*
> *Setting: New Mexico*

Context:

Milcha Sanchez-Scott's play, *Roosters*, revolves around the images of machismo, Hispanic Catholicism, and the sport of cock fighting. These bodies of images become the gateways to her larger, more universal study of the conflicts within families, the battles between generations. She calls her play a "tearing away from home play," and uses the cultural images of her own early life to relate the story of a family in its moment of crisis. The more we understand her perceptions of these images, the more accessible the play becomes.

Machismo: This is a cultural institution which is much more complex than the simple idea of posturing men and submissive women. As Ramon A. Flores, artistic director of La Compania Teatro in Albuquerque, New Mexico, explained in 1992, machismo is a system of social organization which was necessary and successful for thousands of years as people lived at a subsistence level in close contact with nature. Though the term machismo is a Spanish derivative, the ideas of machismo have been universal until the very recent past.

The basic idea of machismo culture is that two adults, a man and a woman, are essential to the survival of the family, i.e. the children. The work of survival in a non-technological culture requires a division of labor into male and female strengths. Only if both parents work at full capacity can the children survive. The division of labor is based on two physical facts: 1) men are generally physically stronger than women (and thus more able to do the physically demanding labor of hunting, farming, and defending the home); and 2) women must bear the children and, in pre-"formula" cultures, provide nourishment for at least the first year or two of each child's life. Based on these physical facts, the logical division of labor is that men leave the home to farm, hunt, and protect the family, while women assume the majority of child-rearing and home-based work.

Obviously, the system worked or humans as a species would not have survived. Only a successful system survives for thousands, if not tens of thousands, of years. Theoretically, the division of labor is equal and so is the division of authority. Think of the image of marriage promoted by the Unitarian faith: the man and the woman are each one wing of the same bird. The bird cannot fly, cannot survive, unless both wings work together and equally. According to Flores, the system became corrupt when the subsistence family moved to a technological, urban environment and away from the day to day struggle for survival.

Suddenly, the family's balance of power and labor was disrupted. The man went to work in a factory or office or store, doing work which did not require superior physical endurance. The woman was no longer required to labor all day to provide sustenance for her family. The woman became restless, bored, and demanded a job outside the home. The man found himself without definition, without identity, and began asserting authority at home to compensate.

According to Flores, we should not be surprised if the system has become dysfunctional, carrying now the more negative overtones associated with "machismo." Given time, Flores said, the family will re-define itself in a new and equal relationship. But for now, like the characters in Sanchez-Scott's play, *Roosters,* everyone suffers.

New World Catholicism: According to Sanchez-Scott, her experience of Catholicism in Mexico, South America, and the American Southwest taught her that fundamental differences exist between the Catholicism of the New World and the Catholicism of Europe. She says that the faithful in New World Catholicism are more willing to believe in miracles and the everyday experience of a visceral relationship with God, Jesus, Mary, and the saints. Sanchez-Scott, whose ideas are supported by a number of internationally known scholars, believes that the Catholic community of her childhood perceives their religion in a less intellectual, more experiential way. The rites of the church are taken more literally. Prayers are expected to produce concrete, visible results. The saints, most especially the Virgin Mary, are assumed to be literally present in the church, the community, and the home. Because of this literal faith, Sanchez-Scott says that the community experiences miracles and magic on a regular basis. Scholars have studied the differences in faith between the European community (which includes most "main-stream" American Catholics) and the Hispanic community and have determined several possible explanations for this state of affairs.

First, the New World has been involved in Catholicism for a much shorter period of time than has the European community. Catholicism was the single form of Christian faith in Europe for almost 1500 years. The splintering of European Christians into Protestant and Catholic sects during the sixteenth century did not, at least initially, change the basic tenets of faith. In some ways, European Catholicism has not changed in 2000 years.

In the Western Hemisphere, Catholicism was only introduced about 500 years ago. It was layered on top of existing cultures which were vigorous and thriving and which had well-established religious faiths of their own. Many scholars believe that the introduction of Catholicism into ancient indigenous religions resulted in a blending of the ancient faiths with the new faith. Those ancient faiths were animistic, meaning that inanimate objects were believed to contain spiritual essences and that spirits exist separate from the physical body. Blending of the two faiths resulted in Hispanic Catholicism in which the body of Christ is literally present, the statue of the Virgin Mary can contain her spirit, and miracles can occur regularly without violating church doctrine. The second factor which may have influenced this slightly different approach to Catholicism is the sheer distance from Mexico or South America to Rome. Priests and missionaries sent to the New World might never see their homes in Europe again. The trip to Europe involved a long and hazardous sea voyage, a situation which did not change until the nineteenth century. In such relative isolation and out of the reach of direct papal authority, the church in the New World may have evolved in ways that encouraged conversion of the natives by not dismissing all of their cultural beliefs.

What all of this means in terms of the play, *Roosters*, is that the final image of the play, the miracle of ascension experienced by the character Angela, can be taken to be both literal and symbolic. For the Morales family, an actual miracle occurs. The non-Catholic audience member may not be able to believe in such a literal answer to prayer. But one can still understand the symbolic reference to forgiveness and divine blessing.

Cock fighting: A recent search of the Internet revealed almost 200,000 references to cock fighting that could be accessed on the Web. Almost every region of the world engages in this blood sport, including the United States (despite the fact that it is illegal here). What we need to understand as we approach this play is that cock fighting involves magnificent birds bred to fight. This is not a case of throwing two chickens in a ring. The fighting rooster is only vaguely related to the domestic chicken, actually representing a close genetic link to the original wild fowl which is the ancestor of both species. The dancing bird represented in the first scene of the play should be imagined as a beautifully plumed, very large, strong, aggressive fighter. When Gallo Morales teaches it to fight, we must imagine a contest of two powerful wills.

The place of cock fighting in Hispanic culture must also be understood. It is a male sport dating back for thousands of years. Contemporary concerns about cruelty to animals never were and still are not an issue for men who have engaged in this sport for many generations. If you have never experienced a blood sport (any sport where fighting and potentially killing the opponent is the point, whether its dog fights, bull fighting, bear baiting, or kick boxing), you may find the references to cock fighting distasteful. We must avoid making judgments as we study this play. Whether we agree with the concept of cock fighting or not, the Morales family engages in the sport. The men even define themselves by their success in the ring. We cannot fully appreciate this play if we close our minds to the needs and desires of the characters. For them it is an integral part of their community experience.

The Playwright.

Milcha Sanchez Scott was born in Bali, the daughter of a Colombian agronomist and a Chinese-Indonesian-Dutch mother. This truly international woman was educated at boarding school in London, where she learned English and vacationed on her family's Colombian ranch becoming multilingual as well as multicultural. She moved with her family to the United States where she attended high school in southern California and attended the University of San Diego majoring in philosophy. Upon graduation she worked at a number of jobs, including work at an employment agency that required her to interview recent immigrants. She became so interested in their stories that she started taking notes which eventually formed the spine of her first play, *Latina*. Other plays by Sanchez-Scott include *Dog Lady*, *The Cuban Swimmer*, *Evening Star*, and *City of Angels*. She currently lives and works in southern California.

King Lear

by William Shakespeare
Edited and Adapted by Robert Barton

Characters

LEAR: King of Britain

GONERIL & REGAN: his elder, married daughters

CORDELLA: his youngest, favorite unmarried daughter

THE EARL OF GLOUCESTER: Lear's longtime patient advisor

EDGAR: his legitimate son

EDMUND: his "bastard" son

THE DUKE OF ALBANY: wed to Goneril

THE DUKE OF CORNWALL: wed to Regan

THE DUKE OF BURGUNDY

THE KING OF FRANCE: suitor to Cordelia

THE EARL OF KENT: Lear's most loyal subject

THE FOOL: Lear's all-licensed jester

OSWALD: steward to Goneril

CURAN: a courtier

AN OLD MAN

A DOCTOR

KNIGHTS, CAPTAINS, HERALDS, SOLDIERS, ATTENDANTS

ACT 1, SCENE 1

[Britain. King Lear's palace.]
[Enter **KENT**, **GLOUCESTER**, *and* **EDMUND**.*]*

KENT: I thought the king had more favored the Duke of Albany than Cornwell.

GLOUCESTER: It did always seem so to us; but now, in the division of the kingdom, it appears not which of the dukes he values most.

KENT: Is not this your son, my lord?

GLOUCESTER: His breeding, sir, hath been at my charge. I have so often blush'd to acknowledge him that now I am brazen to it.

KENT: I cannot conceive you.

GLOUCESTER: Sir, this young fellow's mother could. She had a son for her cradle ere she had a husband for her bed. You smell a fault?

KENT: I cannot wish the fault undone, the issue of it being so proper.

GLOUCESTER: I have another son, sir, by order of law, a year elder than this, who yet is no dearer to me. Though this knave came saucily into the world before he was sent for, yet was his mother fair, and there was good sport at his making. Do you know this noble gentleman, Edmund?

EDMUND: No, my lord.

GLOUCESTER: My Lord of Kent; remember him hereafter as my honourable friend.

EDMUND: My services to your lordship.

GLOUCESTER: The king is coming.

[Fanfare. Enter **KING LEAR**, **CORNWALL**, **ALBANY**, **GONERIL**, **REGAN**, **CORDELIA**, *and* **ATTENDANTS**.*]*

LEAR: Attend the Lords of France and Burgundy, Gloucester.

GLOUCESTER: I shall, my liege.

[Exeunt with **EDMUND**]*

LEAR: Meantime we shall express our darker purpose.
Give me the map there. Know we have divided
In three our kingdom; and 'tis our fast intent
To shake all cares and business from our age;
Conferring them on younger strengths, while we
Unburden'd crawl toward death. Our son of Cornwall,
And our son of Albany, we will to publish
This hour our three daughters' separate dowers,
That future strife may be prevented now.
The princes, France and Burgundy, great rivals
In our youngest daughter's love, have made sojourn,
And here are to be answer'd. Tell me, my daughters,
Which of you shall we say doth love us most?
That we there our largest bounty may extend?
Goneril, our eldest-born, speak first.

GONERIL: Sir, I love you more than eyesight, space, and liberty; Beyond what can be valued, rich or rare;
No less than life, grace, health, beauty, and honour;
As much as child e'er loved, or father found.

CORDELIA: *[aside]* what shall Cordelia do? Love, and be silent.

LEAR: Of all these bounds, even from this line to this,

We make thee lady: to thine and Albany's issue
Be this perpetual. What says our second daughter,
Our dearest Regan, wife to Cornwall? Speak.

REGAN: I am made of that same metal as my sister.
And prize me at her worth. In my true heart
I find she names my very deed of love;
Only she comes too short. I do profess
Myself an enemy to all other
Joys, and find I am only made happy
In your dear highness' love.

CORDELIA: *[aside]* Then poor Cordelia!
And yet not so, since, I am sure, my love
Doth weight more than my tongue.

LEAR: To thee and thine we give this ample third,
No less than that conferr'd on Goneril.
Now, our joy, our last, not least; whose love
The vines of France and milk of Burgundy
Strive to claim; what can you say to draw
A third more opulent than your sisters? Speak.

CORDELIA: Nothing, my lord.

LEAR: Nothing!

CORDELIA: Nothing.

LEAR: Nothing will come of nothing; speak again.

CORDELIA: Unhappy that I am, I cannot heave
My heart into my mouth; I love your Majesty
According to my bond; no more nor less.

LEAR: How, how, Cordelia! Mend your speech a little,
Lest you should mar your fortunes.

CORDELIA: Good my Lord,
You have begot me, bred me, lov'd me: I
Return those duties back as are right fit,
Obey you, love you, and most honour you.
Why have my sisters husbands, if they say
They love you all? Happily, when I shall wed,
That lord whose hand must take my plight shall carry
Half my love with him, half my care and duty:
Sure I shall never marry like my sisters,
To love my father all.

LEAR: But goes thy heart with this?

CORDELIA: Ay, my good Lord.

LEAR: So young and so untender?

CORDELIA: So young, my Lord, and true.

LEAR: Let it be so; thy truth then be thy dower:
For, by the sacred radiance of the sun,
Here I disclaim my paternal care.

KENT: Good my Liege—

LEAR: Peace, Kent!
Come not between the dragon and his wrath.
I lov'd her most, and thought to set my rest
On her kind nursery. Call France.[1] Who stirs?
Call Burgundy[2]. Cornwall and Albany,
With my two daughters' dowers digest this third:
Let pride, which she calls plainness, marry her.
I do invest you jointly in my power.
Ourself, by monthly course with an hundred knights,
By you to be sustain'd, shall our abode
Make with you by due turns. We still retain

Only the name of king; yea, all the rest,
Beloved sons, be yours; which to confirm,
This coronet part betwixt you. *[Giving the crown.]*
KENT: Royal Lear,
  Whom I have ever honour'd as my king,
  Loved as my father, as my master follow'd,
  As my great patron thought on in my prayers,
LEAR: The bow is bent and drawn, avoid the shaft.
KENT: Be Kent unmannerly, when Lear is mad.
  What wouldst thou do, old man? Think'st thou that duty
  Shall dread to speak, when power to flattery bows?
  To plainness honour's bound, when majesty falls
  To folly. Check this rashness: by my life,
  Thy youngest daughter does not love thee least.
LEAR: Kent, on thy life, no more.
KENT: My life I never held but as a pawn
  To wage against thine enemies
LEAR: Out of my sight!
  [Laying his hand on his sword.]
ALBANY: Dear sir, forbear.
KENT: I tell thee thou dost evil.
LEAR: Hear me, recreant!
  On thine allegiance, hear me!
  Five days we do allot thee, for provision.
  And, on the sixth, to turn thy hated back
  Upon our kingdom: if, on the tenth day following,
  Thy banish'd trunk be found in our dominions,
  The moment is thy death. Away!
KENT: Fare thee well, king; since thus thou wilt appear,
  Freedom lives hence, and banishment is here.
  [to **CORDELIA***]*
  The gods to their dear shelter take thee, maid,
  That justly think'st, and hast most rightly said!
  [to **REGAN** *and* **GONERIL***]* And your large speeches may
  your deeds approve,
  That good effects may spring from words of love.
  Thus Kent, O princes, bids you all adieu;
  He'll shape his old course in a country new. *[Exit]*
  [Flourish. Enter **GLOUCESTER***, with* **FRANCE***,* **BURGUNDY***,*
  and **ATTENDANTS***]*
GLOUCESTER: Here's France and Burgundy, my noble lord.
LEAR: My Lord of Burgundy, what, in the least,
  Will you require in present dower with her
  Or cease your quest of love?
BURGUNDY: Most royal majesty,
  I crave no more than that your highness offer'd,
  Nor will you tender less.
LEAR: Right noble Burgundy,
  When she was dear to us, we did hold her so;
  But now her price is fall'n. Sir, there she stands,
  And nothing more.
BURGUNDY: I know no answer.
LEAR: Then leave her, sir. *[to* **FRANCE***]* For you, great king,
  I would not from your love make such a stray,
  To match you where I hate.
FRANCE
  This is most strange,

That she, that even but now was your most dear,
Should in so short a time dismantle favour.
Sure, her offence must be unnatural.
CORDELIA: I beseech your majesty to make it known
  It is no vicious blot, murder, or foulness,
  No unchaste action or dishonour'd step,
  That hath deprived me of your grace and favour;
  But yea even for want of such a tongue
  As I am glad I have not, though not to have it
  Hath lost me in your liking.
LEAR: Better thou
  Hadst not been born than not t'have pleased me better.
FRANCE
  Is it but this? A tardiness in nature
  Which often leaves the history unspoken
  That it intends to do?[3] My Lord of Burgundy,
  What say you to the lady? Will you have her?
  She is herself a dowry.
BURGUNDY: Royal Lear,
  Give but that portion which yourself proposed,
  And here I take Cordelia by the hand,
  Duchess of Burgundy.
LEAR: Nothing; I have sworn, I am firm.
BURGUNDY: I am sorry, then, you have so lost a father
  That you must lose a husband.
CORDELIA: Peace be with Burgundy!
  Since that respect and fortune are his love,
  I shall not be his wife.
FRANCE: Fairest Cordelia, that art most rich, being poor;
  Most choice, forsaken; and most loved, despised!
  Thee and thy virtues here I seize upon.
  Thy dowerless daughter, King, thrown to my chance,
  Is queen of us, of ours, and our fair France.
  Not all the dukes of waterish[4] Burgundy
  Can buy this unprized precious maid of me.
  Bid them farewell, Cordelia, though unkind
  Thou losest here, a better where to find.
LEAR: Thou hast her, France; let her be thine; for we
  Have no such daughter, nor shall ever see
  That face of hers again: Come, noble Burgundy.
  [Flourish. Exeunt **LEAR***,* **BURGUNDY***,* **CORNWALL***,* **ALBANY***,*
  GLOUCESTER *and* **ATTENDANTS***.]*
FRANCE: Bid farewell to your sisters.
CORDELIA: The jewels of our father, with wat'ry eyes
  Cordelia leaves you: I know you what you are;
  And, like a sister, am most loathe to call
  Your faults by their true names. Love well our father,
  To your professed bosoms I commit him.
  But yet, alas, stood I within his grace,
  I would prefer him to a better place.
  So, farewell to you both.
REGAN: Prescribe not us our duties.
GONERIL: Let your study
  Be to content your Lord, who hath received you
  At fortune's loss. You have obedience scanted,
  And well deserve the want that you have wanted.
CORDELIA: Time shall unfold what pleated[5] cunning hides.

Covered faults, shame will one day deride.
Well may you prosper!

FRANCE: Come, my fair Cordelia.

[Exeunt **FRANCE** *and* **CORDELIA***]*

GONERIL: Sister, I think our father will hence to-night.

REGAN: That's most certain, and with you; next month with us.

GONERIL: You see how full of changes his age is.
He always loved our sister most, and with such poor judgment he hath now cast her off so grossly.

REGAN: 'Tis the infirmity of his age; yet he hath ever but slenderly known himself.

GONERIL: Even at his best and in his prime, he hath been but rash; we must be alert to receive not alone the unruly waywardness that years bring with him.

REGAN: Such unconstant starts are we like to have from him as this of Kent's banishment.

GONERIL: Pray you, let's agree together if our father continue such dispositions, this last surrender of his power will but mock us.

REGAN: We shall further think on't.

GONERIL: We must do something, and i' the heat.

[Exeunt]

ACT 1, SCENE 2

*[***GLOUCESTER***'s castle]*
[Enter **EDMUND**, *with a letter.]*

EDMUND: Thou, nature, art my goddess; to thy law
My services are bound. Wherefore should I
Stand in the plague of custom, and permit
The curiosity of nations to deprive me,
For that I am some twelve or fourteen moonshines
Lag of a brother? Why bastard? Wherefore base?
When my dimensions are as well compact,
My mind as generous, and my shape as true,
As honest madam's issue? Why brand they us
With base? With baseness? Bastardy? Base, base?
Who, in the lusty stealth of nature, take
More composition and fierce quality
Than doth, within a dull, stale, tired bed,
Go to th' creating a whole tribe of fops,
Got t'ween asleep and wake?—Well, then,
Legitimate Edgar, I must have your land:
Our father's love is to the bastard Edmund
As to th'legitimate: fine word,—legitimate!
Well, my legitimate, if this letter speed,
And my invention thrive, Edmund the base
Shall top th'legitimate—I grow; I prosper—
Now, gods, stand up for bastards!

[enter **GLOUCESTER***]*

GLOUCESTER: Kent banish'd thus! And France in choler parted!

And the king gone tonight! All this done
In a moment!—Edmund, how now! What news?

EDMUND: So please your lordship, none. *[Putting up the letter.]*

GLOUCESTER: Why so earnestly seek you to put up that letter?

EDMUND: I know no news, my lord.

GLOUCESTER: What paper were you reading?

EDMUND: Nothing my Lord

GLOUCESTER: No? What needed then, that terrible dispatch of it into your pocket? The quality of nothing hath not such need to hide itself. Let's see.

EDMUND: I beseech you, sir, pardon me; it is a letter from my brother, that I have not all o'er-read, and for so much as I have perused, I find it not fit for your o'er looking.

GLOUCESTER: Give me the letter, sir.

EDMUND: I shall offend, either to detain or give it.

GLOUCESTER: Let's see, let's see. *[reads]* "Reverence of age keeps our fortunes from us till our oldness cannot relish them. Come to me, that of this I may speak more. If our father would sleep till I waked him, you should enjoy half his revenue forever, and live the beloved of your brother, Edgar "
O- conspiracy!—"Sleep till I waked him, you should enjoy half his revenue!"—My son Edgar! Had he a hand to write this? A heart and brain to breed it in? When came this to you? Who brought it?

EDMUND: It was not brought me, my lord,—there's the cunning of it; I found it thrown in at the casement of my closet.

GLOUCESTER: You know the character to be your brother's?

EDMUND: It is his hand, my lord, but I hope his heart is not in the contents.

GLOUCESTER: O villain, villain! Abhorred villain! Unnatural, worse than brutish—Go, sir, seek him; I'll apprehend him. Where is he?

EDMUND: Suspend your indignation against my brother until you can derive from him better testimony of his intent. By my life, he hath merely writ this to test my honour.

GLOUCESTER: Think you so?

EDMUND: I will place you where you shall hear us confer of this and have satisfaction this very evening.

GLOUCESTER: He cannot be such a monster—

EDMUND: Nor is not, sure.

GLOUCESTER: To his father, that so tenderly and entirely loves him.—Heaven and earth!—Edmund, seek him out; frame the business after your own wisdom. These late eclipses in the sun and moon portend no good. Love cools, friendship falls off, brothers divide; in cities, mutinies, in countries, discord; in palaces, treason; and the bond crack'd twixt child and father. We have seen the best of our time. Machinations, hollowness, treachery, and all ruinous disorders, follow us disquietly to our graves.[6] And true-hearted Kent banish'd! His offence, honesty! *[Exit]*

EDMUND: This is the excellent foppery of the world, that, when we are sick in fortune, often the surfeit of our own behaviour, we make guilty of our disasters the sun, the moon, and the stars; as if we were villains by necessity;

fools by heavenly compulsion; knaves, thieves, and treachers[7], by spherical predominance; drunkards, liars, and adulterers, by an enforced obedience of planetary influence; and all that we are evil in, by a divine thrusting on; an admirable evasion of whoremaster man, to lay his goatish disposition to the charge of a star! My father compounded with my mother under the dragon's tail, and my nativity was under 'ursa major' so that it follows, I am rough and lecherous. Fut, I should have been that I am, had the maidenliest star in the firmament twinkled on my bastardizing. Edgar! Ha! He comes like the catastrophe of the old comedy; my cue is villainous melancholy, with a sigh like Tom o' Bedlam[8]. *[Enter* EDGAR.*] Fa, so la mi.*

EDGAR: How now, brother Edmund! What serious contemplation are you in?

EDMUND: When saw you my father last?

EDGAR: The night gone by.

EDMUND: Spake you with him?

EDGAR: Ay, two hours together.

EDMUND: Parted you in good terms? Found you no displeasure in him by word nor countenance?

EDGAR: None at all.

EDMUND: Bethink yourself wherein you may have offended him. Forbear[9] his presence till some little time hath qualified the heat of his displeasure.

EDGAR: Some villain hath done me wrong.

EDMUND: That's my fear. Retire with me to my lodging, from whence I will fitly bring you to hear my lord speak: pray you, go; there's my key: if you do stir abroad, go arm'd.

EDGAR: Arm'd, brother!

EDMUND: Brother, I advise you to the best. Pray you, away.

EDGAR: Shall I hear from you anon[10]?

EDMUND: I do serve you in this business. *[Exit* EDGAR*]*
   A credulous father! And a brother noble.
   Whose nature is so far from doing harms,
   That he suspects none; on whose foolish honesty
   My practices ride easy!—I see the business-
   Let me, if not by birth, have lands by wit.
   All with me's meet that I can fashion fit.
   [Exit]

ACT 1, SCENE 3

[The DUKE OF ALBANY*'s palace]*
[Enter GONERIL *and* OSWALD, *her steward.]*

GONERIL: Did my father strike my gentleman for chiding of his fool?

OSWALD: Ay, madam.

GONERIL: By day and night, he wrongs me; every hour
   He flashes into one gross crime or other,
   That sets us all at odds. I'll not endure it.
   His knights grow riotous, and himself upbraids us
   On every trifle.—When he returns from hunting,
   I will not speak with him; say I am sick—
   If you fall short of former services,
   You shall do well; the fault of it I'll answer. *[Horns within]*

OSWALD: He's coming madam; I hear him.

GONERIL: Idle old man,
   That still would manage those authorities
   That he hath given away!—Now, by my life,
   Old fools are babes again; and must be so used.
   And let his knights have colder looks among you;
   What grows of it, no matter; I'll write straight to my sister,
   To hold my very course—Prepare for dinner. *[Exeunt.]*

ACT 1, SCENE 4

[A hall in ALBANY*'s palace.]*
[enter KENT, *disguised]*

KENT: Now, banish'd Kent, if thou canst serve where thou
   Dost stand condemn'd, thy master, whom thou lovest,
   May find thee full of labours and good intent.
   [Horns within. Enter LEAR, KNIGHTS, *and* ATTENDANTS.*]*

LEAR: Let me not stay a jot[11] for dinner, go get it ready. *[Exit an* ATTENDANT.*]* How now! What are thou?

KENT: A very honest-hearted fellow, and as poor as the king.

LEAR: If thou be as poor for a subject as he is for a king, thou art poor enough. What wouldst thou?

KENT: Service.

LEAR: Who wouldst thou serve?

KENT: You.

LEAR: Dost thou know me, fellow?

KENT: No, sir, but you have that in your countenance which I would fain call master.

LEAR: What's that?

KENT: Authority

LEAR: What services canst thou do?

KENT: I can keep honest counsel, ride, run, and deliver a plain message bluntly; that which ordinary men are fit for, I am qualified in; and the best of me is diligence.

LEAR: Follow me; thou shalt serve me: if I like thee no worse after dinner, I will not part from thee yet.—Dinner, ho dinner!—Where's my knave, my fool?—Go you, and call my fool hither. *[Exit an* ATTENDANT. *Enter* OSWALD.*]* You, you, sirrah, where's my daughter?

OSWALD: So please you.—*[Exit]*

LEAR: What says the fellow there? Call the clotpoll[12] back. *[Exit a* KNIGHT.*]*—Where's my fool, ho?—I think the world's asleep. *[Enter* KNIGHT.*]* How now! Where's that mongrel?

KNIGHT: He says, my lord, your daughter is not well.

LEAR: Why came not the slave back to me when I call'd him?

KNIGHT: Sir, he answer'd me in the roundest manner, he would not.

LEAR: He would not!

KNIGHT: My lord, I know not what the matter is; but, to my judgment, your Highness is not entertain'd with that ceremonious affection as you were wont. I beseech you, pardon me, my lord, if I cannot be silent when I think your Highness wrong'd.

LEAR: I have perceived a most faint neglect of late.—But where's my fool? I have not seen him this two days.

KNIGHT: Since my young lady's going into France, sir, the fool hath much pined away.

LEAR: No more of that, I have noted it well.—Go you, and tell my daughter I would speak with her. *[Exit an* **ATTENDANT***]*—Go you, call hither my fool. *[Exit an* **ATTENDANT**. *Enter* **OSWALD**.*]* O, you sir, you, come you hither, sir: who am I, sir?

OSWALD: My lady's father.

LEAR: "My lady's father!" my lord's knave: you whoreson dog! You slave! You cur!

OSWALD: I am none of these, my Lord. I beseech your pardon.

LEAR: Do you bandy looks with me, you rascal? *[Striking him.]*

OSWALD: I'll not be struck, my Lord.

KENT: Nor tripp'd neither, you base football[13] player. *[Tripping up his heels.]*

LEAR: I thank thee, fellow; thou servest me, and I'll love thee.

KENT: Come, sir, arise, away! I'll teach you differences: away, away! *[Pushes* **OSWALD** *out.]*

LEAR: Now, my friendly knave, I thank thee; there's earnest of thy service. *[Giving* **KENT** *money. Enter* **FOOL**.*]*

FOOL: Let me hire him too—here's my coxcomb. *[Offering* **KENT** *his cap.]*

LEAR: How now, my pretty knave! How dost thou?

FOOL: Sirrah, you were best take my coxcomb.

KENT: Why, fool?

FOOL: Why, for taking one's part that's out of favour, nay, there, take my coxcomb: why, this fellow hath banish'd two of his daughters and did the third a blessing against his will; if thou follow him, thou must needs wear my coxcomb—How now, nuncle!

LEAR: Why, my boy?

FOOL: There's mine; beg another of thy daughters.

LEAR: Take heed, sirrah,—the whip.

FOOL: Truth's a dog must to kennel; he must be whipp'd out, when falsehood may stand by the fire and stink. I'll teach thee a speech.

LEAR: Do.

FOOL: Mark it, nuncle;
    Have more than thou showest,
    Speak less than thou knowest,
    Lend less than thou owest,
    Ride more than thou goest,
    Leave thy drink and thy whore,
    And keep in-a-door,
    And thou shalt have more
    Than two tens to a score.

KENT: This is nothing, fool.

FOOL: Can you make no use of nothing, nuncle?

LEAR: A bitter fool!

FOOL: Dost thou know the difference between a bitter fool and a sweet fool?

LEAR: No, lad, teach me.

FOOL: That lord that counsell'd thee
    To give away thy land,
    Come place him here by me,—
    Do thou but for him stand:
    The sweet and bitter fool
    Will presently appear;
    The one in motley here,
    The other found out there.

LEAR: Dost thou call me fool, boy?

FOOL: All thy other titles thou hast given away; that thou wast born with.

KENT: This is not altogether fool, my lord.

FOOL: When thou clovest[14] thy crown i' th'middle, and gavest away both parts, thou borest thine ass on thy back o'er the dirt: e'er since thou mad'st thy daughters thy mothers. Prithee, nuncle, keep a schoolmaster that can teach thy fool to lie. I would fain learn to lie.

LEAR: And you lie, sirrah, we'll have you whipp'd.

FOOL: I marvel what kin thou and thy daughters are: they'll have me whipp'd for speaking true, thou'lt have me whipped for lying; and sometimes I am whipp'd for holding my peace. I had rather be any kind o' thing than a fool: and yet I would not be thee, nuncle. *[Enter* **GONERIL**.*]*

LEAR: How now, daughter! What makes that frown?

GONERIL: Not only, sir, this your all-licensed fool,
    But other of your insolent retinue
    Do hourly carp and quarrel; breaking forth
    In rank and not-to-be-endured riots.

LEAR: Are you our daughter?

GONERIL: Come, sir, I would you would put away these dispositions, which transform you from what you rightly are.

LEAR: Doth any here know me? Why, this is not Lear. Who is it that can tell me who I am?

FOOL: Lear's shadow.

GONERIL: I do beseech you
    To understand my purposes aright:
    Here do you keep a hundred knights and squires;
    Men so disorder'd, so debauch'd, and bold,
    That this our court shows like a riotous tavern or a brothel.
    For instant remedy, reduce your train.

LEAR: Darkness and devils!
    Saddle my horses, call my train together!
    Degenerate bastard! I'll not trouble thee.
    Yet have I left a daughter.
    [Enter **ALBANY**.*]*

GONERIL: You strike my people;
    And your disorder'd rabble make servants of their betters.

ALBANY: Pray, sir, be patient.

LEAR *[to* **GONERIL***]*:
    Detested kite! Thou liest.
    My train are men of choice and rarest parts,
    That all particulars of duty know,

And do support—O most small fault,
How ugly didst thou in Cordelia show!
Which, drew from my heart all love, O Lear, Lear!
This gate did let thy folly in, *[Striking his head.]*
And thy dear judgment out!—Go, go, my people.
[Exeunt **KENT** *and* **KNIGHTS**]

ALBANY: My lord, I am guiltless, as I am ignorant
Of what hath moved you.

LEAR: It may be so , my lord—
Hear, Nature, if thou didst intend
To make this creature fruitful!
Into her womb convey sterility!
If she must teem[15]
Create her child of spleen, that it may live,
And be a thwart, disnatured torment to her that she may feel
How sharper than a serpent's tooth it is
To have a thankless child! *[to* **GONERIL**] Life and death! I am ashamed
That thou hast power to shake my manhood thus;
That these hot tears, which break from me perforce,
Should make thee worth them. Blasts and fogs upon thee!
Th'untented woundings[16] of a father's curse
Pierce every sense about thee!
[Exeunt **LEAR**, *and* **ATTENDANTS**]

GONERIL: Do you mark that, my lord?

ALBANY: I cannot be so partial, Goneril,
To the great love I bear you,—

GONERIL: Pray you, content. What, Oswald, ho! *[to the* **FOOL**]
You, sir, more knave than fool, after your master.

FOOL: Nuncle Lear, Nuncle Lear, tarry, and take the fool with thee.
A fox, when one has caught her,
And such a daughter
Should sure to the slaughter,
If my cap would buy a halter;
So the fool follows after. *[Exit]*

GONERIL: This man hath had good counsel.—a hundred knights!
Fifty are too many. I have writ my sister;
She'll ne'er sustain him and his hundred knights.
[Enter **OSWALD**]
How now, Oswald! What, have you writ that letter to my sister?

OSWALD: Ay, madam.

GONERIL: Take you some company, and away to horse:
Inform her full of my particular fear;
And thereto add such reasons of your own
As may compact it more. Get you gone. *[Exit* **OSWALD**]

ALBANY: How far your eyes may pierce I cannot tell:
Striving to better, oft we mar what's well.
[Exeunt.]

ACT 1, SCENE 5

[Before Albany's palace]
[Enter **LEAR**, **KENT** *(as Caius), and* **FOOL**]

LEAR: Go you before to Gloucester with these letters. If your diligence be not speedy, I shall be there afore you.

KENT: I will not sleep, my lord, till I have deliver'd your letter. *[Exit]*

FOOL: O prithee, be merry, thy wit shall ne'er go slip-shod. Shalt see thy other daughter will use thee kindly. I can tell what I can tell.

LEAR: What canst tell, boy?

FOOL: Why doth one's nose stand i' th'middle on's face?

LEAR: I know not.

FOOL: Why, to keep one's eyes of either side's nose; that what a man cannot smell out, he may spy into.

LEAR: I did Cordelia wrong.

FOOL: The reason why the seven stars are no more than seven is a pretty reason.

LEAR: Because they are not eight?

FOOL: Yes, indeed: thou wouldn't make a good fool. If thou wert my fool, nuncle, I'd have thee beaten for being old before thy time.

LEAR: How's that?

FOOL: Thou shouldst not have been old till thou hadst been wise.

LEAR: O, let me not be mad, not mad, sweet heaven! Keep me in temper: I would not be mad! *[Enter* **GENTLEMAN**] How now! Are the horses ready?

GENTLEMAN: Ready, my lord.

LEAR: Come, boy.
[Exeunt]

ACT 2

ACT 2, SCENE 1

[Within the castle of **GLOUCESTER**.]
[Enter **EDMUND**]

EDMUND: The Duke[17] be here tonight? The better! Best!
This weaves itself perforce into my business.
My father hath set guard to take my brother;
And I must act—briefness and fortune, work!
Brother, a word, come out: — brother, I say!
[Enter **EDGAR**]
My father watches—O sir, fly this place;
Intelligence is given where you are hid,
You have now the good advantage of the night.
Have you not spoken 'gainst the Duke of Cornwall
Upon his party 'gainst the Duke of Albany?[18]
Advise yourself.

EDGAR: I am sure on't, not a word.

EDMUND: I hear my father coming: pardon me;
In cunning I must draw my sword upon you:
Draw: seem to defend yourself: now quit you well.
Yield. Come before my father!
Light, ho, here! Fly, brother. Torches! So, farewell.
[Exit EDGAR]
Some blood drawn on me would beget opinion
[Wounds his arm]
Of my more fierce endeavour: I have seen drunkards
Do more than this in sport. Father, father!
Stop, stop! No help?
[Enter GLOUCESTER, and SERVANTS with torches.]

GLOUCESTER: Now, Edmund, where's the villain?

EDMUND: Look, sir, I bleed.

GLOUCESTER: Where is the villain, Edmund?

EDMUND: Fled this way, sir. When by no means he could—

GLOUCESTER: Pursue him, ho! Go after. *[Exeunt some SERVANTS]* By no means what?

EDMUND: Persuade me to the murder of your lordship.

GLOUCESTER: Not in this land shall he remain uncaught.

EDMUND: When I threaten'd to discover him, he replied,
"Thou unpossessing bastard! Dost thou think,
If I would stand against thee, would any.
Trust thy words?"

GLOUCESTER: O strong and fasten'd villain!
[Trumpets within]
Hark! Cornwall's trumpets! I know not why he comes.
All ports I'll bar; the villain shall not scape.
Loyal and natural boy, I'll make thee capable.[19]
[Enter CORNWALL, REGAN, and ATTENDANTS]

CORNWALL: How now, my noble friend!

REGAN: How dost, my lord?

GLOUCESTER: O madam, my old heart is crack'd, it's crack'd!

REGAN: What, did my father's godson seek your life?
He whom my father named? Your Edgar?

GLOUCESTER: O lady, lady, shame would have it hid!

REGAN: Was he not companion with the riotous knights
That tend upon my father?

EDMUND: Yes, madam, he was of that consort.

REGAN: No marvel, then, that he were ill affected:
'Tis they have urged him to seek his father's death.
I have this present evening from my sister
Been well inform'd of them; and if they come to my house,
I'll not be there.

CORNWALL: Nor I, assure thee, Regan.
Edmund, I hear that you have shown your father
A child's true office.

EDMUND: 'Twas my duty, sir.

GLOUCESTER: He received this hurt striving to apprehend him.

CORNWALL: Is he pursued?

GLOUCESTER: Ay, my good lord.

CORNWALL: If he be taken, he shall never more
Be fear'd of doing harm: For you, Edmund,
Whose virtue and obedience doth this instant
So much commend itself, you shall be ours.

EDMUND: I shall serve you, sir.

GLOUCESTER: For him I thank your Grace.

CORNWALL: You know not why we came to visit you.

REGAN: Our father he hath writ, so hath our sister,
Of differences between them which I thought
Fit to answer from our home. Good old friend,
Bestow your needful counsel to our business,
Which craves the instant use.

GLOUCESTER: I serve you, madam:
Your Graces are right welcome *[Exeunt.]*

ACT 2, SCENE 2

[Before GLOUCESTER's castle]
[Enter KENT and OSWALD, severally]

OSWALD: Good dawning to thee, friend: art of this house?

KENT: Ay.

OSWALD: Where may we set our horses?

KENT: I' the mire.

OSWALD: Prithee, if thou lovest me, tell me.

KENT: I love thee not.

OSWALD: Why, then, I care not for thee. Why dost thou use me thus? I know thee not.

KENT: Fellow, I know thee.

OSWALD: What dost thou know me for?

KENT: A knave; a rascal; a base, proud, shallow, beggarly, weakly, filthy, knave, a lily-liver'd whoreson, mirror-gazing, finical rogue slave; one that wouldst be a bawd and art nothing but the composition of a beggar, coward, pander, and the son and heir of a mongrel bitch.

OSWALD: Why, what a monstrous fellow art thou, thus to rail on one that is neither known of thee nor knows thee!

KENT: What a brazen-faced varlet art thou, to deny thou knowest me! Is it two days since I tripp'd up thy heels, and beat thee, before the king? Draw, you rogue: for, though it be night, yet the moon shines; I'll make a sop o' the moonshine of you. Draw, you whoreson, draw. *[Drawing his sword.]*

OSWALD: Away! I have nothing to do with thee.

KENT: Draw, you rascal: you come with letters against the King. Come along!

OSWALD: Help, ho! Murder! Help!

KENT: Stand, slave, strike. *[Beating him]*

OSWALD: Help, ho! Murder! Murder!
[enter CORNWALL, REGAN, GLOUCESTER and SERVANTS]

CORNWALL: Keep peace, upon your lives!
He dies that strikes again. What is the matter?

REGAN: The messengers from our sister and the King.

CORNWALL: What is your difference? Speak.

OSWALD: I am scarce in breath, my lord.

KENT: His countenance likes me not[20].

CORNWALL: No more, perchance, does mine, nor his, nor hers.

KENT: Sir, 'tis my occupation to be plain:

I have seen better faces in my time
Than stands on any shoulder that I see
Before me at this instant.
CORNWALL: This blunt fellow
Effects a saucy roughness. What offence
Gave you him?
OSWALD: I never gave him any;
It pleased the King his master to strike at me,
Then he tripp'd me behind, insulted, rail'd upon me.
And for such acts got praises of the King.
And, in remembrance of this dread exploit,
Drew on me here again.
CORNWALL: Fetch forth the stocks!
We'll teach you.
KENT: Sir, I am too old to learn:
Call not your stocks for me: I serve the King;
On whose employment I was sent to you.
CORNWALL: Fetch forth the stocks! As I have life and honour,
There shall he sit till noon.
REGAN: Till noon! Till night, my lord; and all night too.
KENT: Why madam, if I were your father's dog,
You should not use me so.
REGAN: Sir, being his knave, I will. *[Stocks brought out.]*
GLOUCESTER: Let me beseech your grace not to do so.
His fault is much and the good King his master
Will chick him for't: your purposed low correction
Is such as basest and condemned'st wretches
For pilf'rings and most common trespasses
Are punish'd with: the King must take it ill.
REGAN: My sister may receive it much more worse
To have her gentleman abus'd, assaulted,
For following her affairs. Put in his legs.
[KENT put in the stocks. Exeunt all but GLOUCESTER and KENT.]
GLOUCESTER: I am sorry for thee, friend; I'll entreat for thee.
KENT: Pray, do not, sir: I have watch'd, and travell'd hard;
Some time I shall sleep out, the rest I'll whistle.
[Exit GLOUCESTER]
Approach, thou beacon to this under globe,
That by thy comfortable[21] beams I may
Peruse this letter. Nothing almost see miracles,
But misery: I know 'tis from Cordelia,
Who hath most fortunately been informe'd
Of my obscur'd course; and shall find time
From this enormous state, seeking to give
Losses their remedies.
Fortune, good night: smile once more; turn thy wheel!
[Sleeps]

ACT 2, SCENE 3

[Open country]
[Enter Edgar]

EDGAR: I heard myself proclaim'd;
And by the happy hollow of a tree
Escaped the hunt. No port is free; no place
That guard, and most unusual vigilance,
Does not attend my taking. Whiles I may scape,
I will preserve myself: and am bethought
To take the basest and most poorest shape
That ever penury, in contempt of man,
Brought near to beast: my face I'll grime with filth;
Blanket my loins, elf all my hair in knots;
And with presented nakedness out-face
The winds and persecutions of the sky.
The country gives me proof and precedent
Of Bedlam beggars, who, with roaring voices,
Strike at their numb'd and mortified bare arms
Sometime with lunatic bans, sometime with prayers,
"Poor Turlygod! Poor Tom!" That's something yet:
Edgar I nothing am. *[Exit]*

ACT 2, SCENE 4

[Before GLOUCESTER's castle; KENT in the stocks]
[Enter LEAR, FOOL, and GENTLEMAN]

LEAR: 'Tis strange that they should so depart from home,
And not send back my messenger.
KENT: Hail to thee, noble master!
LEAR: Ha!
Makest thou this shame thy pastime?
KENT: No, my lord.
FOOL: Ha, ha! He wears cruel garters.
LEAR: What's he that hath so much thy place mistook
To set thee here?
KENT: It is both he and she—Your son and daughter.
LEAR: No. They durst not do't,
They could not, would not do't; 'tis worse than murder
To do upon respect such violent outrage.
FOOL: Winter's not gone yet, if the wild geese fly that way.
Fathers that wear rags
Do make their children blind;
But fathers that bear bags
Shall see their children kind.
LEAR: Down, down thou climbing sorrow. Where is this
daughter?
KENT: With the earl, sir, here within.
LEAR: Follow me not *[Exit]*
KENT: How chance the king comes with so small a train?
FOOL: And thou hadst been set i' the stocks for that question,
thou hadst well deserved it.
KENT: Why, fool?
FOOL: When a wise man gives thee better counsel, give me
mine again: I would have none but knaves follow it, since
a fool gives it.
That sir which serves and seeks for gain,

And follows but for form,
Will pack when it begins to rain,
And leave thee in the storm.
But I will tarry; the Fool will stay
And let the wise man fly away.

KENT: Where learn'd you this, fool?

FOOL: Not i' the stocks, fool.

[Enter **LEAR** *with* **GLOUCESTER***]*

LEAR: Deny to speak with me? They are sick?
Fetch me a better answer.
I'd speak with the Duke of Cornwall and his wife.

GLOUCESTER: Well, my good lord, I have inform'd them so.

LEAR: Inform'd them! Dost thou understand me, man?

GLOUCESTER: Ay, my good lord

LEAR: The king would speak with Cornwall; the dear father
Would with his daughter speak, commands her service.
Now, presently: bid them come forth and hear me,
Or at their chamber-door I'll beat the drum
Till it cry sleep to death.

GLOUCESTER: I would have all well betwixt you. *[Exit]*

LEAR: O me, my heart, my rising heart!—But, down!

[Enter **CORNWALL**, **REGAN**, **GLOUCESTER**, *and* **SERVANTS**.
KENT *here set at liberty]*
Good morrow to you both.

CORNWALL: Hail to your Grace!

REGAN: I am glad to see your highness.

LEAR: Regan, I think you are.
Yet thy sister's naught: O Regan, she hath tied
Sharp-tooth'd unkindness, like a vulture, here.*[Points to his heart]*
I can scarce speak to thee; thou'lt not believe
With how depraved a quality—O Regan!

REGAN: I pray you, sir, take patience: I have hope
You less know how to value her desert
Than she to scant her duty.

LEAR: Say, how is that?

REGAN: I cannot think my sister in the least
Would fail her obligation: if, sir, perchance
She have restrain'd the riots of your followers,
Tis on such ground, and to such wholesome end,
As clears her from all blame.

LEAR: My curses on her!

REGAN: O, sir, you are old;
Nature in you stands on the very verge
Of her confine: you should be ruled, and led
By some discretion. Therefore, I pray you,
That to our sister you do make return;
Say you have wrong'd her, sir.

LEAR: *[rising]* Never, Regan.
You nimble lightnings, dart your blinding flames
Into her scornful eyes!

REGAN: O the bless'd gods! So
Will you wish on me, when the rash mood is on.

LEAR: No, Regan, thou shalt never have my curse:
Thou'rt tender; she harsh. Her eyes are fierce; but thine
Do comfort, and not burn.

REGAN: Good Sir, to the purpose.

LEAR: Who put my man i' the stocks?

[Trumpets sound within]

CORNWALL: What trumpet's that?

REGAN: I know't, my sister's: this approves her letter,
That she would soon be here.

LEAR: Who comes here? O heavens. *[Enter* **GONERIL***]*
Art not ashamed to look upon this beard?
O Regan, wilt thou take her by the hand?

GONERIL: Why not by the hand, sir? How have I offended?

LEAR: How came my man i' th'stocks?

CORNWALL: I set him there, sir: but his own disorders
Deserved much less advancement.

LEAR: You! Did you?

REGAN: I pray you, father, being weak, seem so.
If, till the expiration of your month
You will return and sojourn with my sister,
Dismissing half your train, come then to me:
I am now from home, and out of that provision
Which shall be needful for your entertainment.

LEAR: Return to her, and fifty men dismiss'd?
No, rather I abjure all roofs, and choose
To wage against the enmity o' the air;
Comrade to the wolf and owl,—

GONERIL: At your choice, sir.

LEAR: I prithee, daughter, do not make me mad:
I will not trouble thee, my child; farewell:
We'll no more meet, no more see one another;
Mend when thou canst; be better at thy leisure:
I can be patient; I can stay with Regan,
I and my hundred knights.

REGAN: Not altogether so:
I look'd not for you yet, nor am provided
For your fit welcome. Give ear, sir, to my sister;
She knows what she does.

LEAR: Is this well spoken?

REGAN: I dare avouch it, sir: What! Fifty followers?
Is it not well? What should you need of more?
Yea, or so many? How, in one house,
Should many people, under two commands,
Hold amity? 'Tis hard; almost impossible.

GONERIL: Why might not you, my lord, receive attendance
From those that she calls servants or from mine?

REGAN: Why not, my lord? If then they chanced to slack you,
We could control them. If you will come to me,
For now I spy a danger, I entreat you
To bring but five-and-twenty: to no more
Will I give place or notice.

LEAR: I gave you all—

REGAN: And in good time you gave it.

GONERIL: Hear me, my lord:
What need you five-and-twenty, ten, or five,
To follow in a house where twice so many
Have a command to tend you?

REGAN: What need one?

LEAR: O, reason not the need our basest beggars
Are in the poorest thing superfluous:
Allow not nature more than nature needs.

Man's life is cheap as beast's; thou are a lady;
If only to go warm were gorgeous,
Why, nature needs not what thou gorgeous wear'st,
Which scarcely keeps thee warm. But, for true need,
You heavens, give me that patience, patience I need!
You see me here, you gods, a poor old man,
As full of grief as age, wretched in both!
If it be you that stir these daughters' hearts
Against their father, fool me not so much
To bear it tamely; touch me with noble anger,
And let not women's weapons, water-drops,
Stain my man's cheeks! No, you unnatural hags,
I will have such revenges on you both,
That all the world shall—I will do such things,
What they are, yet I know not; but they shall be
The terrors of the earth. You think I'll weep;
No, I'll not weep:
I have full cause of weeping; but this heart
Shall break into a hundred thousand flaws,
Or e'er I'll weep. O fool, I shall go mad!
[*Exeunt* **LEAR**, **GLOUCESTER**, **KENT** *and* **FOOL**. *Storm and tempest*]

CORNWALL: Let us withdraw; 'twill be a storm.

REGAN: This house is little: the old man and his people
   Cannot be well bestow'd.

GONERIL: 'Tis his own blame;
   'Hath put himself from rest, and must taste his folly.

REGAN: For his own person, I'll receive him gladly,
   But not one follower.

GONERIL: So am I purposed.
   Where is my Lord of Gloucester?

CORNWALL: Follow'd the old man forth—he is return'd.
   [*Enter* **GLOUCESTER**]

GLOUCESTER: The king is in high rage.

CORNWALL: Whither is he going?

GLOUCESTER: He calls to horse; but will I know not whither.

CORNWALL: 'Tis best to give him way; he leads himself.

GLOUCESTER: Alack, the night comes on, and the bleak winds
   Do sorely ruffle.

REGAN: O, sir, to willful men
   The injuries that they themselves procure
   Must be their schoolmasters. Shut up your doors.

CORNWALL: Shut up your doors, my lord; 'tis a wild night:
   My Regan counsels well: come out o' the storm.
   [*Exeunt.*]

ACT 3

ACT 3, SCENE 1

[*The heath, a storm with thunder and lightning. Enter* **KENT** *and a* **GENTLEMAN**, *meeting.*]

KENT: Who's there, besides foul weather?

GENTLEMAN: One minded like the storm, most unquietly.

KENT: I know you. Where's the King?

GENTLEMAN: Contending with the fearful elements.

KENT: But who is with him?

GENTLEMAN: None but the Fool, who labours to out-jest
   His heart-stricken injuries.

KENT: Sir, I do know you;
   And dare commend a dear thing to you.
   There is division 'twixt Albany and Cornwall;
   What hath been seen—
   Either in snuffs and packings of the Dukes,
   Or the hard rein which both of them have borne
   Against the old kind King, or something deeper—
   But, true it is, from France there comes a power
   Into this scatter'd kingdom.
   If on my credit you dare to build so far
   To make your speed to Dover, you shall find
   Some that will thank you. Make just report
   Of how unnatural and bemadding sorrow
   The King hath cause to complain.

GENTLEMAN: I will talk further with you.

KENT: No, do not.
   For confirmation that I am much more
   Than I seem, open this purse, and take
   What it contains. If you shall see Cordelia—
   And fear not but you shall—show her this ring,
   And she will tell you who that fellow is
   That yet you do not know. Fie on this storm!
   I will go to seek the King. [*Exeunt severally*]

ACT 3, SCENE 2

[*The heath. Storm still*]
[*Enter* **LEAR** *and* **FOOL**]

LEAR: Blow, winds, and crack your cheeks! Rage! Blow!
   You cataracts and hurricanoes, spout
   Till you have drench'd our steeples, drown'd the cocks!
   You sulphurous and thought-executing fires,
   Vaunt-couriers to oak-cleaving thunderbolts,
   Singe my white head! And thou, all-shaking thunder,
   Strike flat the thick rotundity o' the world!
   Crack nature's moulds, all seeds spill out at once,
   That make ingrateful man!

FOOL: O nuncle, holy-water in a dry house is better than this
   rain-water out o' door. Good nuncle, in, and ask thy
   daughters' blessing! Here's a night pities neither wise man
   nor fool.

LEAR: Rumble thy bellyful! Spit, fire! Spout, rain!
   Nor rain, wind, thunder, fire, are my daughters:
   I tax not you, you elements, with unkindness;
   I never gave you kingdom, call'd you children,
   You owe me no subscription: then let fall

Your horrible pleasure; here I stand, your slave. A poor,
infirm, weak, and despised old man:
But yet I call you servile ministers,
That have with two pernicious daughters join'd
Your high-engender'd battles 'gainst a head
So old and white as this! O! O! 'Tis foul!
[Enter KENT]

KENT: Who's there?
Alas, sir, are you here? Things that love night
Love not such nights as these. Since I was man,
Such sheets of fire, such bursts of horrid thunder,
Such groans of roaring wind and rain, I never
Remember to have heard.

LEAR: Let the great gods,
Find out their enemies now. I am a man
More sinn'd against than sinning.

KENT: Alack, bare-headed!
Gracious my lord, hard by here is a hovel;
Some friendship will it lend you 'gainst the tempest:
Repose you there; while I to this hard house
Return, and force their scanted courtesy.

LEAR: My wits begin to turn.
Come on, my boy: how dost, my boy? Art cold?
I am cold myself. Where is this straw, my fellow?
Necessities can make vile things precious.
Poor fool and knave, I have one part in my heart
That's sorry yet for thee.

FOOL *[singing]*: He that has and a little tiny wit,
With hey, ho, the wind and the rain,
Must make content with his fortunes fit,
Though the rain it raineth every day.

LEAR: True, my good boy. Come, bring us to this hovel.
[Exeunt LEAR, FOOL and KENT]
[Exit]

ACT 3, SCENE 3

[GLOUCESTER's castle]
[Enter GLOUCESTER and EDMUND]

GLOUCESTER: Alack, alack, Edmund, I like not this
unnatural dealing. When I desired their leave that I might
pity him, they took from me the use of mine own house;
charged me, on pain of their perpetual displeasure,
neither to speak of him, entreat for him, nor any way
sustain him.

EDMUND: Most savage and unnatural!

GLOUCESTER: Go to; say you nothing. I have received a
letter this night, 'tis dangerous to be spoken; I have lock'd
the letter in my closet: these injuries the King now bears
will be revenged home; there is a power from France
already footed. I will seek the King, and relieve him. Go
you, and maintain talk with the Duke, that my charity be
not perceived. If he ask for me, I am ill, and gone to bed.

Though I die for it, as no less is threaten'd me, the King
my old master must be relieved. There is some strange
thing toward, Edmund, pray you, be careful.
[Exit]

EDMUND: This courtesy, forbid thee, shall the Duke
Instantly know; and of that letter too:
This seems a fair deserving, and must draw me
That which my father loses,—no less than all.
The younger rises when the old doth fall.
[Exit]

ACT 3, SCENE 4

[The heath, before a hovel]
[Enter LEAR, KENT, and FOOL]

KENT: Here is the place, my lord; good my lord, enter:
The tyranny of the open night's too rough
For nature to endure. *[Storm still]*

LEAR: Let me alone.

KENT: Good my lord, enter here.

LEAR: Wilt break my heart?

KENT: I had rather break mine own. Good my lord, enter.

LEAR: When the mind's free,
The body's delicate: the tempest in my mind
Doth from my senses take all feeling else
Save what beats there. Filial ingratitude!
No, I will weep no more. O Regan, Goneril!
Your old poor father, whose frank heart gave all,
O, that way madness lies, let me shun that;
No more of that.

KENT: Good my lord, enter here.

LEAR *[to the FOOL]*:
In, boy; go first. You houseless poverty,
Nay, get thee in. I'll pray, and then I'll sleep—
[FOOL goes in]
Poor naked wretches, wheresoe'er you are,
That bide the pelting of this pitiless storm,
How shall your houseless heads and unfed sides,
Your loop'd and window'd raggedness, defend you
From seasons such as these? O, I have ta'en
Too little care of this! Take physic, pomp;
Expose thyself to feel what wretches feel,
That thou mayst shake the superflux[22] to them,
And show the heavens more just.

EDGAR *[within]*: Fathom and half, fathom and half! Poor
Tom!
[The FOOL runs out from the hovel.]

FOOL: Come not in here, nuncle, here's a spirit. Help me,
help me!

KENT: Give me thy hand. Who's there?

FOOL: A spirit, a spirit: he says his name's poor Tom.

KENT: What art thou that dost grumble there i' the straw?
Come forth.

[*Enter* EDGAR *disguised as a madman*]

EDGAR: Away! The foul fiend follows me!—Through the sharp hawthorn blows the cold winds.

LEAR: Didst thou give all to thy two daughters? And art thou come to this?

EDGAR: Who gives any thing to poor Tom whom the foul fiend hath led through fire and through flame, through ford and whirlpool, o'er bog and quagmire? Bless thy five wits!—Tom's a-cold,—O, do de, do de, do de.—Bless thee from whirlwinds, star—blasting, and taking! Do poor Tom some charity, whom the foul fiend vexes:—there could I have him now,—and there,— and there again, and there. [*Storm still.*]

LEAR: What, have his daughters brought him to this pass? Couldst thou save nothing? Didst thou give 'em all?

FOOL: Nay, he reserved a blanket, else we had been all shamed.

LEAR: Now, all plagues light on thy daughters!

KENT: He hath no daughters, sir.

LEAR: Death, traitor! Nothing could have subdu'd nature To such a lowness but his unkind daughters. Is it the fashion that discarded fathers Should have thus little mercy on their flesh?

EDGAR: Pillicock sat on Pilicock hill. Halloo, halloo, loo, loo! Take heed o' the foul fiend! Tom's a-cold.

FOOL: This cold night will turn us all to fools and madmen.

LEAR: Thou wert better in a grave than to answer thy uncover'd body this extremity of the skies. Is man no more than this? Thou art the thing itself: unaccommodated man is no more but such a poor, bare, fork'd animal as thou art. Off, off, you lendings! [*Tearing off his clothes*]

FOOL: Prithee, nuncle, be contented; 'tis a naughty night to swim in. [*Enter* GLOUCESTER, *with a torch.*]

EDGAR: This is the foul fiend!

KENT: How fares your Grace?

LEAR: What's he?

KENT: Who's there? What is't you seek?

GLOUCESTER: What are you there? Your names?

EDGAR: Poor Tom; that drinks the green mantle of the standing pool.

GLOUCESTER: What, hath your Grace no better company?

EDGAR: Poor Tom's a-cold.

GLOUCESTER: Go in with me: my duty cannot suffer T'obey in all your daughters' hard commands. Though their injunction be to bar my doors And let this tyrannous night take hold upon you, Yet I have ventured to come seek you out, And bring you where both fire and food is ready.

LEAR: First let me talk with this philosopher. What is the cause of thunder?

KENT: Importune him once more to go, my lord; His wits begin t'unsettle.

GLOUCESTER: Canst thou blame him? His daughters seek his death. Ah! That good Kent; He said it would be thus, poor banish'd man! Thou sayest the king grows mad; I'll tell thee, friend,

I am almost mad myself: I had a son, Now outlaw'd from my blood; he sought my life, But lately, very late: I loved him, friend, No father his son dearer: true to tell thee, The grief hath crazed my wits. What a night's this! I do beseech your Grace.

LEAR: O, cry you mercy, sir. Noble philosopher, your company.

EDGAR: Tom's a-cold.

GLOUCESTER: In fellow, there, into the hovel: keep thee warm.

LEAR: Come, let's in all

KENT: This way, my lord.

LEAR: With him. I will keep still with my philosopher.

KENT: Good my Lord, soothe him; let him take the fellow.

GLOUCESTER: Take him with you.

KENT: Sirrah, come along.

LEAR: Come, good Athenian.

GLOUCESTER: No words, no words, hush. [*Exeunt*]

ACT 3, SCENE 5

[GLOUCESTER'*s castle*]
[*Enter* CORNWALL *and* EDMUND]

CORNWALL: I will have my revenge ere I depart his house.

EDMUND: This is the letter he spoke of, which proves him an intelligent party to the course of France.

CORNWALL: Go with me to the Duchess.

EDMUND: If the matter of this paper be true, you have mighty business in hand.

CORNWALL: True or false, it hath made thee Earl of Gloucester. Seek out where thy traitor father is for apprehension and thou shall find a dearer father in my love. [*Exeunt*]

ACT 3, SCENE 6

[*A farmhouse adjoining the castle*]
[*Enter* LEAR, KENT, GLOUCESTER, FOOL, *and* EDGAR]

GLOUCESTER: Here is better than the open air. I will piece out the comfort with what addition I can: I will not be long from you.

KENT: All the pow'r of his wits have given way to his impatience. The gods reward your kindness! [*Exit* GLOUCESTER]

FOOL: Prithee, nuncle, tell me whether a madman be a
gentleman or a yeoman?

LEAR: A king, a king!

EDGAR: The foul fiend bites my back.

FOOL: He's mad that trusts in the tameness of a wolf, a
horse's health, a boy's love, or a whore's oath.

EDGAR: Bless thy five wits!

KENT: O pity! Sir, where is the patience now
That you so oft have boasted to retain?

EDGAR: *[aside]* My tears begin to take his part so much
They mar my counterfeiting.

LEAR: The little dogs and all,
Tray, Blanch, and Sweetheart, see, they bark at me.

EDGAR: Tom will throw his head at them. Avaunt, you curs!

KENT: Now, my good lord, lie here and rest awhile.

LEAR: Make no noise, make no noise; draw the curtains: so,
so, so: we'll go to supper i' the morning: so, so, so.

FOOL: And I'll go to bed at noon.
[Enter **GLOUCESTER***]*

GLOUCESTER: Come hither, friend, where is the King my
master?

KENT: Here, sir; but trouble him not—his wits are gone.

GLOUCESTER: Good friend, I prithee, take him in thy arms;
I have o'erheard a plot of death upon him:
There is a litter ready; lay him in't,
And drive towards Dover, friend, where thou shalt meet
Both welcome and protection.

KENT *[to the* **FOOL***]:*
Come, help to bear thy master;
Thou must not stay behind.

GLOUCESTER: Come, come, away.
[Exeunt **KENT***,* **GLOUCESTER***, and the* **FOOL***, bearing off*
LEAR*]*

EDGAR: When we our betters see bearing our woes,
We scarcely think our miseries our foes.
How light and portable my pain seems now,
When that which makes me bend makes the king bow,
He childed as I father'd!—Tom, away!
[Exit]

ACT 3, SCENE 7

*[*GLOUCESTER*'s castle]*
[Enter CORNWALL*,* REGAN*,* GONERIL*,* EDMUND*, and*
SERVANTS*.]*

CORNWALL: Post speedily to my lord your husband; show him
this letter: The army of France is landed. Seek out the
traitor Gloucester.
[Exeunt some of the **SERVANTS***]*

REGAN: Hang him instantly.

GONERIL: Pluck out his eyes.

CORNWALL: Leave him to my displeasure. Edmund, keep you
our sister company; the revenges we are bound to take

upon your traitorous father are not fit for you beholding.
Farewell, dear sister—farewell, my Lord of Gloucester.
[Enter **OSWALD***]* How now! Where's the king?

OSWALD: My Lord of Gloucester hath convey'd him hence.
Some of his knights and other of his dependants are gone
with him towards Dover, where they boast to have well-
armed friends.

CORNWALL: Get horses for your mistress.

GONERIL: Farewell, sweet lord, and sister.

CORNWALL: Edmund, farewell.
[Exeunt **GONERIL***,* **EDMUND***, and* **OSWALD***]*
Bring the traitor Gloucester before us. Pinion him like a
thief.
[Enter **GLOUCESTER***, brought in by two or three]*
Is it the traitor?

REGAN: Ingrateful fox! 'tis he.

CORNWALL: Bind fast his arms.

GLOUCESTER: What mean your Graces?—Good my friends,
consider
You are my guests: do me no foul play, friends.

CORNWALL: Bind him, I say. *[*SERVANTS *bind him]*

REGAN: Hard, hard—O filthy traitor!

GLOUCESTER: Unmerciful lady as you are, I'm none.

CORNWALL: To this chair bind him. Villain, thou shalt find—
*[*REGAN *plucks his beard.]*

GLOUCESTER: By the kind gods, 'tis most ignobly done
To pluck me by the beard.

REGAN: So white, and such a traitor!

CORNWALL: Where hast thou sent the king?

GLOUCESTER: To Dover.

REGAN: Wherefore to Dover? Wast thou not charged at
peril—

CORNWALL: Wherefore to Dover? Let him answer that.

GLOUCESTER: I am tied to the stake, and I must stand the
course.

REGAN: Wherefore to Dover?

GLOUCESTER: Because I would not see thy cruel nails
Pluck out his poor old eyes, nor thy fierce sister
In his annointed flesh stick boarish fangs.
The sea, with such a storm as his bare head
In hell-black night endured, would have buoy'd up
And quench'd the fixed stars.
Yet, poor old heart, he helped the heavens to rain.
If wolves had at thy gate howl'd at that time,
Thou shouldst have said, "Good porter, turn the key."
I shall see winged vengeance o'ertake such children.

CORNWALL: See't shalt thou never.—Fellows, hold the
chair.—
Upon these eyes of thine, I'll set my foot.

GLOUCESTER: Give me some help!—O cruel!!—O you gods!

REGAN: One side will mock another; the other too.

CORNWALL: If you see vengeance,—

SERVANT: Hold your hand, my lord:
I have served you ever since I was a child;
But better service have I never done you
Than now to bid you hold.

REGAN: How now, you dog!

SERVANT: If you did wear a beard upon your chin,
   I'd shake it on this quarrel.
REGAN: What do you mean?
CORNWALL: My villain! *[Draws]*
SERVANT: Nay, then, come on, and take the chance of anger.
   [Draws. They fight. CORNWALL *is wounded.]*
REGAN: Give me thy sword.—A peasant stand up thus!
   [Takes a sword from another, and runs at SERVANT *behind]*
SERVANT: O, I am slain!—My lord, you have one eye left
   To see some mischief on him—O! *[Dies.]*
CORNWALL: Lest it see more, prevent it.—Out, vile jelly!
   Where is thy lustre now?
GLOUCESTER: All dark and comfortless. Where's my son
   Edmund?
REGAN: Out, treacherous villain!
   Thou call'st on him that hates thee: it was he
   That gave the knowledge of thy treasons to us;
   He is too good to pity thee.
GLOUCESTER: O my follies! Then Edgar was abused.
   Kind gods, forgive me that, and prosper him!
REGAN: Go thrust him out at gates, and let him smell
   His way to Dover. *[Exit one with* GLOUCESTER.*]*
   How is't, my lord? How look you?
CORNWALL: I have received a hurt.—Follow me, lady.—
   Turn out that eyeless villain;—throw this slave
   Upon the dunghill. Regan, I bleed apace:
   Untimely comes this hurt: give me your arm.
   [Exit CORNWALL, *led by* REGAN*]*

ACT 4

ACT 4, SCENE 1

[The heath.]
[Enter EDGAR*]*

EDGAR: Yet better thus, and known to be contemn'd,
   Than still contemn'd and flatter'd. To be worst,
   The lowest and most dejected thing of fortune,
   Stands still in hope and does not live in fear:
   The lamentable change is from the best;
   The worst returns to laughter. Welcome, then,
   Thou unsubstantial air that I embrac'd!
   The wretch that thou hast blown unto the worst
   Owes nothing to thy blasts. But who comes here?
   [Enter GLOUCESTER, *led by an* OLD MAN*]*
   My father, blinded? World, world, O world!
   But that thy strange mutations make us hate thee,
   Life would not yield to age.[23]
OLD MAN: O my good Lord!
   I have been your tenant, these many years.
GLOUCESTER: Away, get thee away; good friend, be gone:
   Thy comforts can do me no good at all;
   Thee they may hurt.

OLD MAN: You cannot see your way.
GLOUCESTER: I have no way, and therefore want no eyes;
   I stumbled when I saw:—O dear son Edgar,
   Might I but live to see thee in my touch,
   I'd say I had eyes again!
OLD MAN: How now! Who's there?
EDGAR *[aside]*: O gods! Who is't can say, "I am at the worst?"
   I am worse than e'er I was.
OLD MAN: 'Tis poor mad Tom. Fellow, where goest?
GLOUCESTER: Is it a beggar-man?
OLD MAN: Madman and beggar too.
GLOUCESTER: He has some reason, else he could not beg.
   I'th'last night's storm I such a fellow saw,
   Which made me think a man a worm. My son
   Came then into my mind; and yet my mind
   Was scarce friends with him. I have heard more since:
   As flies to wanton boys, are we to the gods,—
   They kill us for their sport.
EDGAR: Bless thee, master!
GLOUCESTER: Is that the naked fellow?
OLD MAN: Ay, my lord.
GLOUCESTER: Bring some covering for this naked soul,
   Which I'll entreat to lead me.
OLD MAN: Alack, sir, he is mad.
GLOUCESTER: 'Tis the times' plague, when madmen lead the
   blind.
   Do as I bid thee, or rather do thy pleasure.
OLD MAN: I'll bring him the best apparel that I have,
   Come on't what will. *[Exit]*
GLOUCESTER: Sirrah, naked fellow,—.
EDGAR: Poor Tom's a-cold—*[aside]* I cannot daub it further[24].
GLOUCESTER: Come hither, fellow.
EDGAR *[aside]*: And yet I must. Bless thy sweet eyes, they
   bleed.
GLOUCESTER: Dost thou know Dover?
EDGAR: Ay, master.
GLOUCESTER: There is a cliff, whose high and bending head
   Looks fearfully at the confined deep;
   Bring me but to the very brim of it,
   I'll repair the misery thou dost bear
   With something rich about me; from that place
   I shall no leading need.
EDGAR: Give me thy arm:
   Poor Tom shall lead thee.
   [Exeunt.]

ACT 4, SCENE 2

[Before Albany's palace]
[Enter GONERIL *and* EDMUND*]*

GONERIL: Welcome, my Lord; I marvel our mild husband
   Not met us on the way.
   [Enter OSWALD*]*

Now, where's your master?

OSWALD: Madam, within; but never man so changed.
I told him of the army that was landed;
He smiled at it, then he call'd me sot,
And told me I had turn'd the wrong side out.—
What most he should dislike seems pleasant to him;
What like, offensive.

GONERIL [to **EDMUND**]:
Back, Edmund, to my brother;²⁵
I must change arms at home, and give the distaff
Into my husband's hands.²⁶
This trusty servant shall pass between us.
You'll hear, if you dare venture in your own behalf,
A mistress's command. Wear this; spare speech;
Decline your head: this kiss, if it durst speak,
Would stretch thy spirits up into the air.
Conceive, and fare thee well.

EDMUND: Yours in the ranks of death.

GONERIL: My most dear Gloucester! [Exit **EDMUND**]
O, the difference of man and man!
To thee a woman's services are due:
A fool usurps my body.

OSWALD: Madam, here comes my lord. [Exit]
[Enter **ALBANY**]

GONERIL: I have been worth the whistling.²⁷

ALBANY: O Goneril!
You are not worth the dust which the rude wind
Blows in your face. What have you done?
Tigers, not daughters, what have you perform'd?
A gracious aged father—most barbarous,
Most degenerate—have you madded.

GONERIL: Milk-liver'd man!
That bear'st a cheek for blows, where's thy drum?
France spreads his banners in our noiseless land;
With plumed helm thy slayer begins to threat;
Whiles thou, a moral fool, sits still, and cries
"Alack, why does he so?"

ALBANY: See thyself, devil!
Deformity shows not in the fiend so horrid
As in woman.

GONERIL: Marry, your manhood! Mew!
[Enter a **MESSENGER**]

ALBANY: What news?

MESSENGER: O, my good lord, the Duke of Cornwall's dead;
Slain by his servant, going to put out
The other eye of Gloucester.

ALBANY: Gloucester's eyes!

MESSENGER: A servant that he bred, thrill'd with remorse,
Oppos'd against the act, bending his sword
To his great master; who, therefore enraged,
Flew on him, and amongst them fell'd him dead;
But not without that harmful stroke, which since
Hath pluck'd him after.

ALBANY: But, O poor Gloucester!
Lost he the other eye?

MESSENGER: Both, both, my Lord.
This letter, madam, craves a speedy answer;

'Tis from your sister.

GONERIL [aside]: One way I like this well;
But being widow, and my Edmund with her,
May all the building in my fancy pluck
Upon my hateful life: another way
The news is not so tart.—[aloud] I'll read, and answer.
[Exit]

ALBANY: Where was Edmund when they did take his eyes?

MESSENGER: My good lord; it was he inform'd against him;
And quit the house on purpose, that their punishment
Might have the freer course.

ALBANY: Old Gloucester, I live
To thank thee for the love thou show'dst the king,
And to revenge thine eyes. [Exeunt.]

ACT 4, SCENE 3

[The French camp near Dover]
[Enter **KENT** and a **GENTLEMAN**]

KENT: Know you the reason why the King of France is so
suddenly gone back?

GENTLEMAN: Something he left imperfect in the state, so
important that his personal return was most requir'd and
necessary.

KENT: Did your letters pierce the Queen to any demonstration
of grief?

GENTLEMAN: Ay, sir; she took them, read them in my
presence;
And now and then an ample tear trill'd down
Her delicate cheek. But she was queen over her passion
Which sought to overwhelm her.

KENT: O, then it moved her!

GENTLEMAN: Not to a rage; patience and sorrow strove
Who should express her goodness.

KENT: Well, sir, the poor distressed Lear's i'th'town
But by no means will yield to see his daughter;
For sovereign shame so elbows him, so stings him
That burning shame detains him from Cordelia.
Of Albany's and Cornwall's powers heard you not?

GENTLEMAN: 'Tis so, they are afoot.

KENT: Well, sir, I'll bring you to Lear,
And leave you to attend him. I pray you,
Go along with me. [Exeunt]

ACT 4, SCENE 4

[The French camp near Dover. A tent.]
[Enter, with drum and colours, **CORDELIA**, **DOCTOR**,
and **SOLDIERS**.]

CORDELIA: Alack, poor father. He was seen e'en now
As mad as the vex'd sea; singing aloud;
And crown'd with idle weeds and flowers. Send forth;
Search every acre in the high-grown field,
And bring him to our eye. *[Exit an* OFFICER*]* What can
man's wisdom do to restore his bereaved sense?
He that helps him take all my outward wealth.
DOCTOR: There is means, madam:
Our foster-nurse of nature is repose,
The which he lacks.
CORDELIA: All bless'd secrets of the earth,
Spring with my tears! Aid and remediate
In this good man's distress!—Seek, seek for him;
Lest his ungovern'd rage dissolve the life
That wants the means to lead it.
[Enter a MESSENGER*]*
MESSENGER: News, madam;
The British powers are marching hitherward.
CORDELIA: 'Tis known before; our preparations stands
In expectation of them.—O dear father,
It is thy business that I go about.
No blown ambition doth our arms incite,
But love, dear love, and our aged father's right.
Soon may I hear and see him! *[Exeunt.]*

ACT 4, SCENE 5

*[*GLOUCESTER*'s castle]*
[Enter REGAN *and* OSWALD*]*

REGAN: But are my brother's powers set forth?
OSWALD: Ay, madam.
REGAN: Himself in person there?
OSWALD: Madam, with much ado:
Your sister is the better soldier.
REGAN: Lord Edmund spoke not with your lord at home?
OSWALD: No, Madam.
REGAN: What might import my sister's letter to him?
OSWALD: I know not, lady.
REGAN: It was great ignorance, Gloucester's eyes being out,
To let him live: where he arrives he moves
All hearts against us. Edmund, I think, is gone,
To dispatch his nighted life and destroy th'enemy.
OSWALD: I must needs after him, madam, with my letter.
REGAN: Our troops set forth tomorrow; stay with us;
The ways are dangerous.
OSWALD: I may not, madam:
My lady charged my duty in this business.
REGAN: Why should she write to Edmund? Might not you
Transport her purposes by word? Belike,
Something- I know not what—I'll love thee much,
Let me unseal the letter.
OSWALD: Madam, I had rather—
REGAN: I know your lady does not love her husband;

I am sure of that: and at her late being here
She gave strange glances and most longing looks
To noble Edmund. I know you are of her bosom.
OSWALD: I, madam?
REGAN: I speak in understanding; you are, I know't.
Therefore I do advise you, take this note:
My lord is dead; Edmund and I have talk'd;
And more convenient is he for my hand
Than for your lady's.—You may gather more.
If you do find him, pray you, give him this;
And when your mistress hears thus much from you,
I pray, desire her call her wisdom to her.
So, fare you well. If you chance upon the blind traitor,
Preferment falls on him that cuts him off.
OSWALD: Would I could meet him, madam! I would show
What party I do follow.

ACT 4, SCENE 6

[Near Dover]
[Enter GLOUCESTER, *and* EDGAR *dressed like a peasant]*

GLOUCESTER: When shall I come to the top of that same hill?
EDGAR: You do climb it up now: look, how we labour.
GLOUCESTER: Methinks the ground is even.
EDGAR: Horrible steep. Hark, do you hear the sea?
GLOUCESTER: No, truly.
EDGAR: Why, then, your other senses grow imperfect
By your eyes' anguish.
GLOUCESTER: So may it be, indeed.
EDGAR: Come on, sir; here's the place: stand still.—How
fearful
And dizzy 'tis to cast one's eyes so low!
The fishermen that walk upon the beach,
Appear like mice; and yon tall anchoring bark,
Almost too small for sight: I'll look no more;
Lest my brain turn, and the deficient sight
Topple down headlong.
GLOUCESTER: Set me where you stand.
EDGAR: Give me your hand. You are now within a foot
Of th' extreme verge: for all beneath the moon
Would I not leap upright.
GLOUCESTER: Let go my hand.
Here, friend, 's another purse; it is a jewel
Well worth a poor man's taking. Go further off;
Bid me farewell, and let me hear thee going.
EDGAR: Now fare you well, good sir.
GLOUCESTER: With all my heart *[kneeling]*
You mighty gods! This world I do renounce.
If Edgar live, O, bless him!
Now, fellow, fare thee well. *[falls forward]*
EDGAR: *[aside]* I trifle with his despair in hopes to cure it.
[aloud] Ho you, sir! Friend!—Hear you, sir! Speak!
What are you, sir?

GLOUCESTER: Away, and let me die.

EDGAR: Thou hast fallen many, many fathoms down.
Thy life's a miracle. Speak yet again.

GLOUCESTER: But have I fall'n, or no?

EDGAR: From the dread summit of this chalky bourn.
Look up a-height pray sir: do but look up.

GLOUCESTER: Alack, I have no eyes.

EDGAR: Give me your arm:
Up, so. How is it? Feel you your legs? You stand.

GLOUCESTER: Too well, too well.

EDGAR: This is above all strangeness.
Upon the crown o'th'cliff what thing was that
Which parted from you?

GLOUCESTER: A poor unfortunate beggar.

EDGAR: As I stood here below methought it was some fiend.
Therefore, thou happy father,
Think that the clearest gods, preserved thee.

GLOUCESTER: I believe it so. Henceforth I'll bear
Affliction till it do cry out itself
"Enough, enough," and die.

EDGAR: Bear free and patient thoughts. But who comes here?
[Enter LEAR, fantastically dressed with wild flowers.]

LEAR: No, they cannot touch me for coining, I am the king
himself. Nature's above art in that respect. Look, look, a
mouse! Peace, peace; this piece of toasted cheese will do't.
O, well flown, bird! Give the word.

GLOUCESTER: I know that voice.

LEAR: Ha! Goneril, with a white beard! When the rain came
to wet me once and the wind to make me chatter and the
thunder would not peace at my bidding, there I found 'em,
there I smelt 'em out; I found they are not men o' their
words: they told me I was everything; 'tis a lie.

GLOUCESTER: I do well remember. Is't not the king?

LEAR: Ay, every inch a king. When I do stare,
See how the subject quakes! I pardon that
Man's life. What was thy cause? Adultery?
Thou shall not die: die for adultery! No.
The wren goes to't, and the small gilded fly
Does lecher in my sight. Let copulation thrive:
Gloucester's bastard son was kinder to his father
Than my daughters got between the lawful sheets.

GLOUCESTER: O, let me kiss that hand!

LEAR: Let me wipe it first; it smells of mortality.

GLOUCESTER: Dost thou know me?

LEAR: I remember thine eyes well enough. No, do thy worst,
Blind Cupid; I'll not love. No eyes in your head, nor no
money in your purse? Your eyes are in a heavy case, your
purse in a light: yet you see how this world goes.

GLOUCESTER: I see it feelingly.

LEAR: A man may see
How this world goes with no eyes. Look with thine ears.
If thou wilt weep my fortunes, take my eyes.
I know thee well enough; thy name is Gloucester.
[Enter a GENTLEMAN, with ATTENDANTS.]

GENTLEMAN: O, here he is: lay hand upon him. Sir,
Your most dear daughter—

LEAR: Let me have a surgeon;

I am cut to the brains.

GENTLEMAN: You shall have anything.

LEAR: No seconds? All myself?

GENTLEMAN: Good sir—

LEAR: I will die bravely; I am a king;
My masters, know you that.

GENTLEMAN: You are a royal one, and we obey you.

KING LEAR: Then there's life in't. Nay, an you get it, you shall
get it by running. Sa, sa sa, sa.
[Exit running. ATTENDANTS follow.]

GLOUCESTER: You ever-gentle gods, take my breath from me.

EDGAR: Well pray you, father.

GLOUCESTER: Now, good sir, what are you?

EDGAR: A most poor man, made tame to fortune's blows;
Give me your hand, I'll lead you to some lodging.

GLOUCESTER: Hearty thanks.
[Enter OSWALD]

OSWALD: A proclaim'd prize! Most happy!
Thou old unhappy traitor, the sword is out
That must destroy thee.

GLOUCESTER: Now let thy friendly hand
Put strength to't. *[EDGAR interposes]*

OSWALD: Wherefore, bold peasant
Durst thou support a publish'd traitor? Let go his arm.

EDGAR: I'll not let go, sir.

OSWALD: Let go, slave, or thou diest!
[They fight]

OSWALD: Slave, thou has slain me: Villain, take my purse:
If ever thou wilt thrive, bury my body;
And give the letters which thou find'st about me
To Edmund Earl of Gloucester; seek him out
Upon the English party:—O, untimely death!
[Dies]

EDGAR: I know thee well: a serviceable villain;
As duteous to the vices of thy mistress
As badness would desire.

GLOUCESTER: What, is he dead?

EDGAR: Sit you down, father; rest you.
Let's see his pockets.
[reads] "Edmund—Let our vows be remember'd. There is
nothing done, if he return the conqueror: then am I the
prisoner, and his bed my prison; from the loathed warmth
whereof deliver me, and supply the place for your labour.
Your wife, so I would say—
Affectionate Servant,
Goneril"
A plot upon her virtuous husband's life;
And the exchange my brother!

GLOUCESTER: The king is mad: better I were distract:
So should my thoughts be sever'd from my griefs.

EDGAR: Give me your hand. *[Drum afar off.]*
Far off, me thinks, I hear the beaten drum:
Come father, I'll bestow you with a friend. *[Exeunt]*

ACT 4, SCENE 7

[A tent in the French camp.]
[Enter **CORDELIA**, **KENT**, **DOCTOR**, *and* **GENTLEMAN**]

CORDELIA: O thou good Kent, how shall I live and work,
To match thy goodness? My life will be too short.
KENT: To be acknowledged, madam, is o'erpaid.
CORDELIA: Then be't so, my good lord. *[to the* **DOCTOR**] How
does the king?
DOCTOR: Madam, sleeps still. So please your majesty
That we may wake the king; he hath slept long.
CORDELIA: Be govern'd by your knowledge, and proceed
I' the sway of your own will. Is he array'd?
[Enter **LEAR** *in a chair carried by* **SERVANTS**]
DOCTOR: Ay, madam; in the heaviness of sleep
We put fresh garments on him.
Be by, good madam, when we do awake him;
I doubt not of his temperance.²⁸
CORDELIA: Very well.
DOCTOR: Please you, draw near. Louder the music there!
CORDELIA: O my dear father! Restoration hang
Thy medicine on my lips; and let this kiss
Repair those violent harms that my two sisters
Have in thy reverence made! Was this a face
To be opposed against the warring winds?
To stand against the deep dread-bolted thunder
And quick, cross lightning? Mine enemy's dog,
Though he had bit me, should have stood that night
Against my fire. Alack, alack!
'Tis wonder that thy life and wits at once
Had not concluded all. He wakes; speak to him.
DOCTOR: Madam, do you: 'tis fittest.
CORDELIA: How does my royal lord? How fares your majesty?
KING LEAR: You do me wrong to take me out o' the grave:—
Thou art a soul in bliss; but I am bound
Upon a wheel of fire, that mine own tears
Do scald like molten lead.
CORDELIA: Sir, do you know me?
LEAR: You are a spirit, I know. Where am I?—Daylight?
CORDELIA: O, look upon me, sir,
And hold your hands in benediction o'er me.
No, sir, you must not kneel.
LEAR: Pray, do not mock me:
I am a very foolish fond old man,
And, to deal plainly, I fear I am not
In my perfect mind. Do not laugh at me;
For, as I am a man, I think this lady
To be my child Cordelia
CORDELIA: And so I am, I am.
KING LEAR: Be your tears wet? Yes, faith. I pray, weep not:
If you have poison for me, I will drink it.
I know you do not love me; for your sisters
Have, as I do remember, done me wrong:
You have some cause, they have not.
CORDELIA: No cause, no cause.

KING LEAR: Am I in France?
KENT: In your own kingdom, sir.
CORDELIA: Will't please your highness walk?
KING LEAR: You must bear with me:
Pray you now, forget and forgive: I am old and foolish.
[Exeunt]

ACT 5

ACT 5, SCENE 1

[The British camp, near Dover.]
[Enter, with drum and colours, **EDMUND**, **REGAN**,
OFFICERS, **SOLDIERS**, *and others.]*

EDMUND: Know of the duke if his last purpose hold,
He's full of alteration. *[To an* **OFFICER**, *who goes out.]*
REGAN: Now, sweet lord,
You know the goodness I intend upon you:
Tell me,—but truly,—but then speak the truth,
Do you not love my sister?
EDMUND: In honour'd love.
REGAN: But have you never found my brother's way
To the forfended²⁹ place?
EDMUND: That thought abuses you.
No, by mine honour, madam.
REGAN: I never shall endure her: dear my Lord,
Be not familiar with her.
EDMUND: Fear me not:
She and the Duke her husband!
[Enter, with drum and colours, **ALBANY**, **GONERIL** *and*
SOLDIERS]
ALBANY: Our very loving sister, well be-met.
Sir, this I hear, the king is come to his daughter;
It toucheth us, as France invades our land.
GONERIL *[aside]*: I had rather lose the battle than that sister
Should loosen him and me.
EDMUND: Sir, you speak nobly.
I shall attend you presently at your tent.
REGAN: Sister, you'll go with us?
GONERIL: No.
REGAN: 'Tis most convenient, pray you, go with us.
GONERIL *[aside]*: O, ho, I know the riddle. I will go.
[As they are going out, enter **EDGAR** *disguised]*
EDGAR: If e'er your Grace had speech with men so poor,
Hear me one word.
ALBANY: I'll overtake you.—Speak.
[Exeunt all but **ALBANY** *and* **EDGAR**.]
EDGAR: Before you fight the battle, ope this letter.
If you have victory, let the trumpet sound
For him that brought it: wretched though I seem,
I can produce a champion that will prove
What is avouched there. Fortune love you!
ALBANY: Why, fare thee well. I will o'erlook thy paper.

[Exit EDGAR. *Enter* EDMUND*]*

EDMUND: The enemy's in view, draw up your powers.
  Here is the guess of their true strength and forces
  By diligent discovery; But your haste
  Is now urged on you.

ALBANY: We will greet the time. *[Exit]*

EDMUND: To both these sisters have I sworn my love;
  Each jealous of the other, as the stung
  Are of the adder. Which of them shall I take?
  Both? One? Or neither? Neither can be enjoy'd,
  If both remain alive: to take the widow
  Makes mad her sister Goneril, whom I shall
  Hardly marry her husband being alive.
  Let her who would be rid of him devise
  His speedy taking off. As for the mercy
  Which he intends to Lear and to Cordelia,
  The battle done, and they within our power,
  They will never see his pardon; for my state
  Stands on me to defend, not to debate.
  [Exit]

ACT 5, SCENE 2

[A field between the two camps. Alarm within. Enter, with drum and colours, French and British forces, skirmish over the stage and exuent. Enter EDGAR *and* GLOUCESTER.*]*

EDGAR: Away, old man,—give me thy hand,—away!
  King Lear hath lost, he and his daughter ta'en
  Give me thy hand; come on.

GLOUCESTER: No further, sir; a man may rot even here.

EDGAR: What, in ill thoughts again? Men must endure
  Their going hence, even as their coming hither;
  Ripeness is all—come on.

GLOUCESTER: And that's true too. *[Exeunt]*

ACT 5, SCENE 3

[The British camp, near Dover. Enter, in conquest, with drum and colours, EDMUND, LEAR *and* CORDELIA *as prisoners;* OFFICERS, SOLDIERS, *etc.]*

EDMUND: Some officers take them away.

CORDELIA: We are not the first
  Who, with best meaning, have incurr'd the worst.
  For thee, oppressed king, am I cast down;
  Myself could else out-frown false fortune's frown.
  Shall we not see these daughters and these sisters?

KING LEAR: No, no, no, no! Come, let's away to prison:
  We two alone will sing like birds i' the cage:

When thou dost ask me blessing, I'll kneel down,
  And ask of thee forgiveness: so we'll live,
  And pray, and sing, and tell old tales, and laugh
  At gilded butterflies, and hear poor rogues
  Talk of court news; and we'll talk with them too,
  Who loses and who wins; who's in, who's out;
  And take upon's the mystery of things,
  As if we were God's spies: and we'll wear out,
  In a wall'd prison, packs and sects of great ones,
  That ebb and flow by th' moon.

EDMUND: Take them away.

KING LEAR: Upon such sacrifices, my Cordelia,
  The gods themselves throw incense! Have I caught thee?
  He that parts us shall bring a brand from heaven,
  Come.
  [Exeunt LEAR *and* CORDELIA, *guarded.]*

EDMUND: Come hither, captain; hark.
  Take thou this note *[giving a paper]*; Go follow them to
  prison.
  One step I have advanced thee; if thou dost
  As this instructs thee, thou dost make thy way
  To noble fortunes: know thou this, that men
  Are as the time is: to be tender-minded
  Does not become a sword: thy great employment
  Will not bear question; either say thou'll do't,
  Or thrive by other means.

OFFICER: I'll do't, my lord.
  [Exit. Flourish. Enter ALBANY, GONERIL, REGAN, OFFICERS, *and* ATTENDANTS.]*

ALBANY: We do require the royal prisoners of you.

EDMUND: Sir, I thought it fit
  To send the old and miserable king
  To some retention. With him I sent the queen.

ALBANY: I hold you but a subject of this war,
  Not as a brother.

REGAN: That's as we list to grace him.
  Methinks our pleasure might have been demanded,
  Ere you had spoke so far. He led our powers;
  Bore the commission of my place and person;
  The which immediacy may well stand up
  And call itself your brother.

GONERIL: Not so hot:
  In his own grace he doth exalt himself,
  More than in your addition.

REGAN: In my rights
  By me invested, he compares the best.

GONERIL: That were the most, if he should husband you.

REGAN: Jesters do oft prove prophets.

GONERIL: Holla, holla!
  That eye that told you so look'd but a-squint.

REGAN: Lady, I am not well; else I should answer
  From a full-flowing stomach. Edmund,
  Take thou my soldiers, prisoners, patrimony;
  Dispose of them, of me; the walls are thine:
  Witness the world that I create thee here
  My lord and master.

GONERIL: Mean you to enjoy him?

ALBANY: Stay yet; hear reason.—Edmund, I arrest thee
  On capital treason; and, I arrest,
  This gilded serpent *[pointing to* **GONERIL***]* as for your
  claim, fair sister.
  I bar it in the interest of my wife;
  'Tis she is sub-contracted to this lord,
  and I, her husband, contradict your banns.
  If you will marry, make your loves to me.
  My lady is bespoke.

GONERIL: An interlude!

ALBANY: Thou art arm'd, Edmund—let the trumpet sound:
  If none appear to prove upon thy person
  Thy heinous, manifest, and many treasons,
  There is my pledge *[throwing down a glove]*; I'll prove it
  on thy heart,
  Ere I taste bread, thou art in nothing less
  Than I have here proclaim'd thee.

REGAN: Sick, O, sick!

GONERIL *[aside]*: If not, I'll ne'er trust medicine.

EDMUND: There's my exchange *[throwing down a glove]*; What
  in the world he is
  That names me traitor, villain-like he lies:
  Call by thy trumpet: I will maintain
  My truth and honour firmly.

DUKE OF ALBANY: A herald, ho!

REGAN: My sickness grows upon me.

ALBANY: She is not well; convey her to my tent.
  [Exit **REGAN***, led. Enter a* **HERALD***]*
  Come hither, herald,—Let the trumpet sound,—
  And read out this.

HERALD *[reads]*: "If any man of quality or degree within the
  lists of the army will maintain upon Edmund, supposed
  Earl of Gloucester, that he is a manifold traitor, let him
  appear by the third sound of the trumpet: he is bold in his
  defense."

EDMUND: Sound! *[First trumpet.]*
  Again! *[Second trumpet.]*
  Again! *[Third trumpet. Trumpet answers within. Enter*
  EDGAR*, at the third sound, arm'd.]*

EDGAR: What's he that speaks for Edmund Earl of
  Gloucester?

EDMUND: Himself: what say'st thou to him?

EDGAR: Draw thy sword,
  That, if my speech offend a noble heart,
  Thy arm may do thee justice: here is mine.
  Despite thy victor sword and fire–new fortune,
  Thy valour and thy heart, thou art a traitor;
  False to thy gods, thy brother, and thy father;
  Conspirant 'gainst this high illustrious prince;
  And, from th' extremest upward of thy head
  To the descent and dust below thy foot,
  A most toad-spotted traitor. Say thou "no,"
  This sword, this arm, and my best spirits are bent.
  To prove upon thy heart, whereto I speak,
  Thou liest.

EDMUND: Back do I toss these treasons to thy head;
  This sword of mine shall speak!

[Alarms. They fight. **EDMUND** *falls.]*

GONERIL: Thou art not vanquish'd,
  But cozen'd and beguiled[30].

ALBANY: Shut your mouth, dame,
  Or with this paper shall I stop it. Most monstrous!
  Know'st thou this paper?

GONERIL: Ask me not what I know. *[Exit]*

ALBANY: Go after her: she's desperate; govern her.
  [to an **OFFICER***, who goes out.]*

EDMUND: What you have charged me with, that have I done.
  And much, much more; the time will bring it out:
  Tis past, and so am I. But what art thou
  That hast this fortune on me? If thou art noble, I forgive
  thee.

EDGAR: Let us exchange charity.
  I am no less in blood than thou art, Edmund;
  My name is Edgar; and thy father's son.
  Thy bloody proclamation taught me to shift
  Into a madman's rags and in this habit
  Met I my father, saved him from despair;
  I reveal'd myself unto him some half-hour past
  And ask'd his blessing, but his heart, alack,
  Torn twixt two extremes of passion, joy and grief,
  Burst smilingly.
  [Enter a **GENTLEMAN** *with a bloody knife.]*
  What means that bloody knife?

GENTLEMAN: It came even from the heart of—O, she's dead!

ALBANY: Who dead? Speak, man.

GENTLEMAN: Your lady, Goneril. And her sister Regan
  By her is poisoned; she hath confess'd it.

EDMUND: I was contracted to them both: all three
  Now marry in an instant. Yet Edmund was beloved.

EDGAR: Here comes Kent.

KENT: I am come to bid my King
  And master good night: Is he not here?

ALBANY: Speak, Edmund, where's the king? And where's
  Cordelia?

EDMUND: I pant for life: some good must I now do,
  Quickly send to the castle; for my writ[31]
  Is on the life of Lear and on Cordelia:—
  Nay, send in time. *[*EDMUND* born off]*

ALBANY: Haste thee, for thy life. *[Exit* EDGAR*]*
  [Enter LEAR*, with* CORDELIA *dead in his arms;* OFFICER*,
  and others]*

LEAR: Howl, howl, howl, howl!—O, you are men of stone:
  Had I your tongues and eyes, I'd use them so
  That heaven's vault should crack.—She's gone forever!—
  I know when one is dead, and when one lives;
  She's dead as earth.

KENT: Is this the promised end?

LEAR: A plague upon you, murderers, traitors all!
  I might have saved her; now she's gone forever!—
  Cordelia, Cordelia! Stay a little. Ha!
  I kill'd the slave that was a-hanging thee.

OFFICER: 'Tis true, my lords, he did.

KING LEAR: Did I not, fellow?
  I have seen the day, with my good biting falchion[32]

I would have made them skip: I am old now,
And these same crosses spoil me.[33] Who are you?
Mine eyes are not o' the best. Are you not Kent?

KENT: The same, your servant Kent and Caius too,
That, from your first of difference and decay,
Have follow'd your sad steps.

LEAR: You are welcome hither.

ALBANY: We will resign, during the life of this old majesty,
To him our absolute power.

LEAR: And my poor fool[34] is hang'd! No, no, no life!
Why should a dog, a horse, a rat, have life,
And thou no breath at all? Thou'll come no more,
Never, never, never, never, never!—
Pray you, undo this button:—thank you, sir.—
Do you see this? Look on her,—look, her lips,—
Look there, look there!—*[Dies]*

EDGAR: He faints!—My lord, my lord!—

KENT: Break, heart; I prithee, break!

EDGAR: Look up, my lord.

KENT: Vex not his ghost: O, let him pass! He doth not

Wish upon the rack of this tough world to
Stretch out longer.

EDGAR: He is gone indeed.

KENT: The wonder is, he hath endured so long:
He but usurp'd his life.

DUKE OF ALBANY: Bear them from hence.—Our present business
Is general woe.—*[To* **KENT** *and* **EDGAR***]* Friends of my soul, you t'wain
Rule in this realm, and the gor'd[35] state sustain.

KENT: I have a journey, sir[36]; shortly to go;
My master calls me, I must not say no.

EDGAR: The weight of this sad time we must obey;
Speak what we feel, not what we ought to say.
The oldest hath borne most: we that are young
Shall never see so much, nor live so long.
[Exeunt, with a dead march.]

END

Notes

[1] France: the king of France, one of Cordelia's suitors.

[2] Burgundy: the Duke of Burgundy and second suitor for Cordelia's hand in marriage.

[3] A tardiness in nature…intends to do? A natural reticence which leads to less talk and more action.

[4] Waterish: quibbling, uncommitted

[5] pleated: folded and therefore dishonest

[6] These late eclipses…to our graves: With this speech Gloucester is describing the Elizabethan sense of cosmic order. Astrology was a serious business, believed to provide reliable guidance and warnings. (Edmund's disrespect for heavenly signs is an indicator of his villainy.) The cosmic order also involved man's place in the hierarchy of being and that hierarchy's essential stability. Chaos was feared if the "chain of being"
was altered or damaged. By giving away and dividing his kingdom, Lear has disrupted the natural God-ordained order of things and Gloucester already sees signs of the chaos to come.

[7] Treachers: traitors

[8] Tom o' Bedlam: generic term referring to poor, often insane, wanderers.

[9] Forbear: avoid

[10] anon: soon

[11] stay a jot: wait a moment

[12] clotpoll: blockhead

[13] football player: football refers to a simple form of street soccer; street urchins who played were considered low and vulgar.

[14] clovest: split

[15] teem: have children

[16] Th'untented woundings: wounds too deep to be bandaged with rolls of lint called "tents".

[17] The Duke: Cornwall and Regan

[18] Have you not…Duke of Albany? Edmund is spreading a whispered rumor that war may be pending between Cornwall and Albany for control of all of England.

[19] capable: able to inherit

[20] His countenance likes me not: His face/appearance pleases me not.

[21] comfortable: comforting

[22] shake the superflux: share the surplus…Lear is beginning to realize that he has not been a good shepherd to his own poor people.

[23] But that thy strange…yield to age.: Only the changes and chances of this hard life, which make us hate it, reconcile us to getting old and approaching death.

[24] daub it further: continue his disguise

[25] my brother: Cornwall

[26] arms/distaff: symbols of gender. She intends to assume a masculine role and reduce her husband to a woman's traditional role of spinning wool.

[27] worth the whistling: worth meeting on the road. Refers to a common proverb: "It is a poor dog that is not worth the whistling."

[28] doubt not his temperance: am not certain of his sanity

[29] forfended: forbidden (in this case, the forbidden place would be Goneril's bed)

[30] cozened and beguil'd: deceived

[31] writ: a legal order (in this case, ordering the murder of Lear and Cordelia)

[32] falchion: a light sword

[33] crosses spoil me: troubles ruin me (as a swordsman)

[34] fool: most experts believe he means Cordelia, not the Fool.

[35] gor'd: bloody, wounded

[36] I have a journey…: to another world or the afterlife.

Roosters

by Milcha Sanchez-Scott

Characters

GALLO: patriarch of the Morales family, just released from prison

JUANA: his wife

HECTOR: his son

ANGELA: his daughter

CHATA: his sister

ADAN: Hector's friend

SHADOW #1

SHADOW #2

ZAPATA: a rooster

SAN JUAN: a rooster

Setting

Time: The present

Place: The Southwest.

ACT 1, SCENE 1

Stage and house are dark. Slowly a narrow pinspot of light comes up. We hear footsteps. Enter **GALLO,** *a very, very handsome man in his forties. He is wearing a cheap dark suit, with a white open-neck shirt. He carries a suitcase. He puts the suitcase down. He faces the audience.*

GALLO: Lord Eagle, Lord Hawk, sainted ones, spirits and winds, Santa Maria Aurora of the Dawn…I want no resentment, I want no rancor….I had an old red Cuban hen. She was squirrel-tailed and sort of slab-sided and you wouldn't have given her a second look. But she was a queen. She could be thrown with any cock and you would get a hard-kicking stag every time. I had a vision, of a hard-kicking flyer, the ultimate bird. The Filipinos were the ones with the pedigree Bolinas, the high flyers, but they had no real kick. To see those birds fighting in the air like dark avenging angels…well like my father use to say, "Son nobles…finos…." I figured to mate that old red Cuban. This particular Filipino had the best. A dark burgandy flyer named MacArther. He wouldn't sell. I began borrowing MacArther at night, bringing him back before dawn, no one the wiser, but one morning the Filipino's son caught me. He pulled out his blade. I pulled out mine. I was faster. I went up on manslaughter….They never caught on…thought I was in the henhouse trying to steal their stags….It took time—refining, inbreeding, cross-breeding, brother to sister, mother to son, adding power, rapid attack…but I think we got him. *[***GALLO** *stands still for a beat, checks his watch, takes off his jacket and faces C. A slow, howling drumbeat begins. As it gradually goes higher in pitch and excitement mounts, we see narrow beams of light, the first light of dawn filtering through chicken wire. The light reveals a heap of chicken feathers which turns out to be an actor/dancer who represents the rooster Zapata. Zapata stretches his wings, then his neck, to greet the light. He stands and struts proudly, puffs his chest and crows his salutation to the sun.* **GALLO** *stalks Zapata, as drums follow their movements.]* Ya, ya, mi lindo…yeah, baby…you're a beauty, a real beauty. Now let's see whatcha got. *[He pulls out a switchblade stiletto. It gleams in the light as he tosses it from hand to hand.]* Come on baby boy. Show Daddy whatcha got *[***GALLO** *lunges at Zapata. Zapata parries with his beak and wings. This becomes a slow, rhythmic fight-dance.* **GALLO** *grabs Zapata by his comb, bending his head backwards until he is forced to sit.* **GALLO** *stands behind Zapata, straddling him. With one hand* **GALLO** *holds Zapata's comb, with the other he holds the knife next to Zapata's neck.]* Oh yeah, you like to fight? Huh? You gonna kill for me baby boy? Huh? *[***GALLO** *sticks the tip of the knife into Zapata. The rooster squawks in pain.]* Sssh! Baby boy, you gotta learn. Daddy's gotta teach you. *[***GALLO** *sticks it to Zapata again. This time the rooster snaps back in anger.]* That's right beauty…Now you got it…Come on, come. *[***GALLO** *waves his knife and hand close to Zapata's face. The*

rooster's head and eyes follow.] Oh yeah…that's it baby, take it! Take it! *[Suddenly Zapata attacks, drawing blood. Gallo's body contracts in orgasmic pleasure/pain. Loudly.]* Ay precioso!…Mi lindo….You like that, eh? Taste good, huh? *[***GALLO** *waves the gleaming knife in a slow hypnotic movement which calms the rooster.]* Take my blood, honey…I'm in you now…Morales blood, the blood of kings…and you're my rooster…a Morales rooster. *[He slowly backs away from the rooster. He picks up his suitcase, still pointing the knife at* **ZAPATA.***]* Kill. You're my son. Make me proud. *[***GALLO** *exits.* **ZAPATA** *puffs his chest and struts U. Lights go up a little on U. L. area as the rooster goes into the chicken-wire henhouse. He preens and scratches. Enter* **HECTOR,** *a young man of about twenty. He is very handsome. He wears gray sweatpants and no shirt. On his forehead is a sweatband. His hair and body are dripping wet. He has been running. Now he is panting as he leans on the henhouse looking at* **ZAPATA.***]*

HECTOR: I saw what you did to those chicks. Don't look at me like you have a mind, or a soul, or feelings. You kill your young…and we are so proud of your horrible animal vigor….But you are my inheritance…Abuelo's gift to me…to get me out. Oh, Abuelo, Grandfather…you should have left me your courage, your sweet pacific strength. *[A ray of light hits D. R. In a semi-shadow, we see a miniature cemetery, with small white headstones and white crosses. We see the profile of a young angel/girl with wings and a pale dress.* **ANGELA** *is kneeling next to a bare desert tree with low scratchy branches. She has a Buster Brown haircut and a low tough voice. She is fifteen, but looks twelve.]*

ANGELA: *[Loudly.]* Angel of God
My Guardian Dear
To whom God's love
Commits me here
Ever this day be
At my side
To light and guard
To rule and guide
Amen.
[Her paper wings get caught in a tree branch.] Aw, shit!
[She exits.]

SCENE 2

As the light changes we hear the clapping of women making tortillas. Lights come up full. Center is a faded wood-frame house, with a porch that is bare except for a table and a few chairs The house sits in the middle of a desert agricultural valley somewhere in the Southwest. Everything is sparse. There is a feeling of blue skies and space. One might see off on the horizon tall Nopales or Century cactus. **JUANA** *a thin, wornout-looking woman of thirty five comes out of the house She is wearing a faded housedress. She goes to mid-yard, faces front and stares out.*

JUANA: It's dry. Bone dry. There's a fire in the mountains…up near Jacinto Pass. [*The clapping stops for a beat, then continues* JUANA *starts to go back into the house, then stops. She sniffs the air, sniffs again, and again.*] Tres Rosas….I smell Tres Rosas. [*She hugs her body and rocks*] Tres Rosas…Ay, St Anthony let him come home…Let him be back. [*The clapping stops.* CHATA *enters from the house. She is a fleshy woman of forty, who gives new meaning to the word blowsy. She has the lumpy face of a hard boozer. She walks with a slight limp. She wears a black kimono, on the back of which is embroidered in red a dragon and the words "Korea, U.S.S. Perkins, 7th Fleet." A cigarette hangs from her lips. She carries a bowl containing balls of tortilla dough.*] I smell Tres Rosas…The brilliantine for his hair…He musta been here. Why did he go?

CHATA: Men are shit.

JUANA: Where could he be?

CHATA: First day out of jail! My brother never comes home first day. You should know that. Gotta sniff around…gotta get use to things. See his friends.

JUANA: Sí, that's right…He just gotta get used to things. I'll feel better when I see him…I gotta keep busy.

CHATA: You been busy all morning.

JUANA: I want him to feel good, be proud of us….You hear anything when you come in yesterday?

CHATA: Who's gonna know anything at the Trailways bus station?

JUANA: You ain't heard anything?

CHATA: Juanita, he knows what he's doing. If there was gonna be any trouble he'd know. Ay, mujer, he's just an old warrior coming home.

JUANA: Ain't that old.

CHATA: For a fighting man, he's getting up there. [JUANA *slaps tortillas* CHATA *watches her.*] Who taught you to make tortillas?

JUANA: I don't remember. I never make 'em. Kids don't ask.

CHATA: Look at this. You call this a tortilla? Have some pride. Show him you're a woman.

JUANA: Chata, you've been here one day, and you already—

CHATA: Ah, you people don't know what it is to eat fresh handmade tortillas. My grandmother Hortensia, the one they used to call "La India Condenada"…she would start making them at five o'clock in the morning. So the men would have something to eat when they went into the fields. Hijo! She was tough…Use to break her own horses…and her own men. Every day at five o'clock she would wake me up. "Buenos pinchi dias," she would say. I was twelve or thirteen years old, still in braids…"Press your hands into the dough," "Con fuerza," "Put your stamp on it" One day I woke up, tú sabes, con la sangre. "Ah! So you're a woman now. Got your cycle like the moon. Soon you'll want a man, well this is what you do. When you see the one you want, you roll the tortilla on the inside of your thigh and then you give it to him nice and warm. Be sure you give it to him and nobody else." Well, I been rolling tortillas on my thighs, on my nalgas, and God only knows where else, but I've been giving my tortillas to the wrong men…and that's been the problem with my life. First there was Emilio. I gave him my first tortilla. Ay Mamacita, he use to say, these are delicious. Aye, he was handsome, a real lady-killer! After he did me the favor he didn't have the cojones to stick around…took my TV set too. They're all shit…the Samoan bartender, what was his name…

JUANA: Nicky, Big Nicky.

CHATA: The guy from Pep Boys—

JUANA: Chata, you really think he'll be back?

CHATA: His son's first time in the pit? With "the" rooster? A real Morales rooster? Honey, he'll be back. Stop worrying.

JUANA: Let's put these on the griddle. Angela, Hector…breakfast.

SCENE 3

ANGELA *slides out from under the house, wearing her wings. She carries a white box which contains her cardboard tombstones, paper and crayons, a writing tablet and a pen. She too sniffs the air. She runs to the little cemetery and looks up, as* HECTOR *appears at the window behind her.*

ANGELA: Tres Rosas…Did you hear? Sweet Jesus, Abuelo, Queen of Heaven, all the Saints, all the Angels. It is true. It is certain. He is coming, coming to stay forever and ever. Amen.

HECTOR: Don't count on it!

ANGELA: [*To Heaven.*] Protect me from those of little faith and substance.

HECTOR: I'm warning you. You're just going to be disappointed.

ANGELA: [*To Heaven*] Guard me against the enemies of my soul.

HECTOR: Your butt's getting bigger and bigger!

ANGELA: And keep me from falling in with low companions.

HECTOR: Listen, little hummingbird woman, you gotta be tough, and grown-up today. [ANGELA *digs up her collection can and two dolls. Both dolls are dressed in nuns' habits One, the St. Lucy doll, has round sunglasses She turns a box over to make a little tea table on which she places a doll's teapot and cups.*]

ANGELA: As an act of faith and to celebrate her father's homecoming, Miss Angela Ester Morales will have a tea party.

HECTOR: No more tea parties.

ANGELA: Dancing in attendance will be that charming martyr St. Lucy.

HECTOR: He will not be impressed.

ANGELA: Due to the loss of her eyes and the sensitivity of her alabaster skin, St. Lucy will sit in the shade. [*She sits St. Lucy in the shade and picks up the other doll.*]

HECTOR: Who's that?

ANGELA: St. Teresa of Avigon, you will sit over here. *[She seats St. Teresa doll.]*

HECTOR: Just don't let him con you Angela.

ANGELA: *[Pouring pretend tea.]* One lump or two, St. Lucy? St. Teresa has hyperglycemia, and only takes cream in her tea. Isn't that right St. Teresa?

HECTOR: He's not like Abuelo. *[Angela animates the dolls like puppets and uses two different voices as St. Lucy and St. Teresa.]*

ANGELA: *[As St. Teresa.]* Shouldn't we wait for St. Luke?

HECTOR: Stop hiding. You can't be a little girl forever.

ANGELA: *[As St. Lucy.]* St. Luke! St. Luke! Indeed! How that man got into Heaven I'll never know. That story about putting peas in his boots and offering the discomfort up to God is pure bunk. I happen to know he boiled the peas first.

HECTOR: I don't want you hurt. It's time to grow up.

ANGELA: *[As St. Teresa.]* St. Lucy! I can only think that it is the loss of your eyes that makes you so disagreeable. Kindly remember that we have all suffered to be saints.

HECTOR: Are you listening to me, Angie?

ANGELA: *[As St. Lucy.]* Easy for you to say! They took my eyes because I wouldn't put out! They put them on a plate. A dirty, chipped one, thank you very much indeed! To this day no true effort has been made to find them.

HECTOR: Excuse me!…Excuse me, St. Teresa, St. Lucy, I just thought I should tell you…a little secret…your hostess, Miss Angela Ester Morales, lies in her little, white, chaste, narrow bed, underneath the crucifix, and masturbates.

ANGELA: Heretic! Liar!

HECTOR: Poor Jesus, up there on the cross, right over her bed, his head tilted down. He sees everything.

ANGELA: Lies! Horrible lies!

HECTOR: Poor saint of the month, watching from the night table.

ANGELA: I hate you! I hate you! Horrible, horrible, Hector.

JUANA: *[From offstage.]* Breakfast! *[Hector leaves the window. Angela sits on the ground writing on a tombstone.]*

ANGELA: *[Lettering tombstone.]* Here lies Horrible Hector Morales. Died at age twenty, in great agony, for tormenting his little sister.

JUANA: *[Offstage.]* You kids…breakfast!

HECTOR: *[Pops up at window.]* Just be yourself. A normal sex-crazed fifteen-year-old girl with a big gigantic enormous butt. *[He exits.]*

ANGELA: *[To Heaven.]* Send me to Alaska

Let me be frozen

Send me a contraction

A shrinking antidote

Make me little again

Please make my legs

Like tiny pink Vienna sausages

Give me back my little butt.

[JUANA and CHATA bring breakfast out on the porch and set it on the table.]

JUANA: Angie! Hector! We ain't got all day. *[ANGELA goes to the breakfast table with the St. Lucy doll and the collection can.]*

And take your wings off before you sit at the table. Ain't you kids got any manners? *[ANGELA removes her wings, sits down, bows her head in prayer. CHATA stares at St. Lucy. St. Lucy stares at CHATA. JUANA shoos flies and stares at the distant fire.]* I hope he's on this side of the fire.

CHATA: That doll's staring at me.

ANGELA: She loves you. *[Lights fade on the women, come up on the henhouse. ADAN, a young man of twenty, is talking to ZAPATA—now a real rooster, not the actor/dancer—and preparing his feed.]*

ADAN: Hola Zapata…ya mi lindo…mi bonito. En Inglés. Tengo que hablar en English…pinchi English…verdad Zapata? En Español más romántico pero Hector say I must learned di English. *[ZAPATA starts squawking.]* Qué te pasa? Orita vas a comer.

[HECTOR enters.]

HECTOR: English, Adan…English.

ADAN: No English…pinchi English.

HECTOR: Good morning, Adan.

ADAN: A que la fregada!…Okay this morning in the fields, I talk English pero this afternoon for fight I talk puro Español.

HECTOR: Good morning, Adan.

ADAN: Si, si, good morning, muy fine…Hector el Filipino he say…*[He moves away from ZAPATA, so bird will not hear him.]* He say to tell you que Zapata no win. Porque Filipino bird fight more y your bird first fight y your first fight y you not no ex…ex…

HECTOR: Experience.

ADAN: Sí eso, he say you sell bird to him y no fight.…He say is not true Morales bird porque Gallo not here. El Filipino say if you fight bird…bird dead. If bird still alive after Filipino bird beat him…Bird still dead porque nobody pay money for bird that lose.

HECTOR: But if he wins, everybody wants him.

Adan: I say, ay di poor Hector. His abuelo leave him bird. He can no sell. El Filipino say, "Good!" Inside, in my heart I am laughing so hard porque he not know Gallo gonna be here. We win, we make much money.

HECTOR: It's my bird, I have to do it myself.

ADAN: You tonto! You stupido! You mulo! Like donkey…He help you, he the king…he you papa. For him all birds fight.

HECTOR: No!

ADAN: Why? Why for you do this? You no even like bird. Zapata he knows this, he feel this thing in his heart. You just want money to go from the fields, to go to the other side of the mountains…to go looking to go looking for what? On the other side is only more stupid people like us.

HECTOR: How could you think I just wanted money? I want him to see me.

ADAN: Sorry…I am sorry my friend…I know…I stay with you y we win vas a ver! Okay Zapata! We win y est a noche estamos tomando Coors, Ripple, Lucky Lager, unas Buds, Johnny Walkers, oh sí, y las beautiful señoritas. *[He gives ZAPATA his food.]* Eat Zapata! Be strong.

HECTOR: I almost forgot, look what I have for you…fresh, warm homemade tortillas.

ADAN: Oh, how nice.

HECTOR: Yes, how nice. Aunt Chata made them.

ADAN: Oh, much nice.

HECTOR: Today she woke up at five o'clock, spit a green booger the size of a small frog into a wad of Kleenex. She wrapped her soiled black "7th Fleet" kimono around her loose, flaccid, tortured, stretch-marked body and put her fat-toed, corned yellow hooves into a pair of pink satin slippers. She slap-padded over to the sink where she opened her two hippo lips and looked into the mirror. She looked sad. I looked at those lips…those lips that had wrapped themselves warmly and lovingly around the cocks of a million campesinos, around thousands upon thousands of Mexicanos, Salvadoreños, Guatemaltecos. For the tide of brown men that flooded the fields of this country, she was there with her open hippo whore's lips, saying "Bienvenidos," "Welcome," "Hola," "Howdy." Those are legendary lips, Adan.

ADAN: Yes…muy yes.

HECTOR: What a woman, what a comfort. Up and down the state in her beat-up station wagon. A '56 Chevy with wood panels on the sides, in the back a sad, abused mattress. She followed the brown army of pickers through tomatoes, green beans, zucchinis, summer squash, winter squash, oranges, and finally Castroville, the artichoke capital of the world, where her career was stopped by the fists of a sun-crazed companero. The ingratitude broke her heart

ADAN: Oh my gooseness!

HECTOR: She was a river to her people, she should be rewarded, honored. No justice in the world.

ADAN: Pinchi world. *[He and* HECTOR *look to mountains]* You look mountains. In my country I look mountains to come here. I am here and everybody still look mountains.

HECTOR: I want to fly right over them.

ADAN: No, my friend, we are here, we belong…la tierra.

JUANA: *[From offstage.]* Hector, I ain't calling you again. *[Light up on the porch.* JUANA *and* CHATA *are sitting at the table. Angela is sitting on the steps. She has her wings back on. St. Lucy and the collection can are by her side. She is writing on her tablet.]* Oh Gallo, what's keeping you?

CHATA: Men are shit! That's all. And it's Saturday. When do they get drunk? When do they lose their money? When do they shoot each other? Saturdays, that's when the shit hits the fan. *[Enter* HECTOR *and* ADAN *with* ZAPATA *in a traveling carrier.]*

JUANA: It's because I'm so plain.

HECTOR: We're better off without him.

CHATA: Buenos días Adan. Un cafecito?

ADAN: Ah. Good morning, Mrs. Chata, no gracias, ah good morning, Mrs. Morales y Miss Angelita *[*ANGELA *sticks out her donation can.* ADAN *automatically drops coins in.]*

JUANA: Angela!

ADAN: No, is good, is for the poor. Miss Angela, she good lady…eh, girl. *[He pats* ANGELA *on the head.]*

JUANA: Why don't you leave the bird, so your father can see him when he gets home.

HECTOR: He's my bird. He can see it later.

JUANA: I can't believe you would do this to your own father. Birds are his life…and he's so proud of you.

HECTOR: This is news. How would he know, he hasn't seen me in years.

JUANA: It isn't his fault

HECTOR: It never is.

JUANA: Your father is with us all the time, he got his eye on us, he knows everything we're doing.

ANGELA: Everything!

JUANA: I brag about you kids in my letters.…His friends they tell him what a smart boy you are…that you're good-looking like him…He's proud… "A real Morales," that's what he says.

HECTOR: And did he call me a winner? A champ? A prince? And did you tell him I was in the fields?

ANGELA: What did he say about me, Mama?

HECTOR: Nothing, you're a girl and a retard. What possible use could he have for you? Grow up!

CHATA: No, you grow up. *[*ANGELA *buries herself in* CHATA's *lap.]*

JUANA: Hector, please, Hector, for me.

HECTOR: No, Mother. Not even for you.

JUANA: You give him a chance.

HECTOR: What chance did he give us? Fighting his birds, in and out of trouble. He was never here for us, never a card, a little present for Angela. He forgot us.

JUANA: You don't understand him. He's different.

HECTOR: Just make it clear to him. Abuelo left the bird to me, not to him, to me.

JUANA: Me, me, me. You gonna choke on this me, me. Okay, okay, I'm not going to put my nose in the bird business. I just ask you for me, for Angie, be nice to him.

HECTOR: As long as we all understand the "bird business," I'll be nice to him even if it kills me, Mother.

JUANA: Now you're feeling sorry for yourself. Just eat. You can feel sorry for yourself later.

HECTOR: Why didn't I think of that. I'll eat now and feel sorry for myself later.

JUANA: Now, you kids gotta be nice and clean, your papa don't like dirty people.

CHATA: Me too, I hate dirty people.

JUANA: Angie, you take a bath.

HECTOR: Oh, Angela, how…how long has it been since you and water came together? *[*ANGELA *hits him.]* Oww!

JUANA: You put on a nice clean dress, and I don't wanna see you wearing no dirty wings.

HECTOR: Right, Angie, put on the clean ones.

JUANA: You say please and excuse me…and you watch your table manners…I don't want to see any pigs at my table.

HECTOR: *[Making pig noises]* What a delicious breakfast! Cold eggs, sunny-side up. How cheery! How uplifting! Hmm, hmmm! *[He turns so* ANGELA *can see him. He picks up the eggs with his hands and stuffs them in his mouth.]* Look, Angela, refried beans in a delicate pool of congealed fat.

[Still making pig noises, he picks up gobs of beans, stuffs them into his mouth.]

CHATA: A que la fregada! Hector, stop playing with your food. You're making us sick

JUANA: *[Looking at watch.]* 7:20, you got ten minutes before work *[**HECTOR** drums his fingers on the table.]*

HECTOR: Nine minutes…I will now put on the same old smelly, shit-encrusted boots, I will walk to the fields. The scent of cow dung and rotting vegetation will fill the air. I will wait with the same group of beaten-down, pathetic men…taking their last piss against a tree, dropping hard warm turds in the bushes. All adding to this fertile whore of a valley. At 7:30 that yellow mechanical grasshopper, the Deerfield tractor, will belch and move. At this exact moment, our foreman, John Knipe, will open his pig-sucking mouth, exposing his yellow, pointy, plaque-infested teeth. He yells, "Start picking, boys." The daily war begins…the intimidation of violent growth…the expanding melons and squashes, the hardiness of potatoes, the waxy purple succulence of eggplant, the potency of ripening tomatoes. All so smug, so rich, so ready to burst with sheer generosity and exuberance. They mock me…I hear them…."Hey Hector," they say, "show us whatcha got," and "Yo Hector we got bacteria out here more productive than you."…I look to the ground. Slugs, snails, worms slithering in the earth with such ferocious hunger they devour their own tails, flies oozing out larvae, aphids, bees, gnats, caterpillars their prolification only slightly dampened by our sprays. We still find eggsacks hiding, ready to burst forth. Their teeming life, their lust, is shameful…Well it's time…Bye Ma. *[He exits]*

JUANA: *[Yelling.]* Hector! You gotta do something about your attitude. *[To herself.]* Try to see the bright side. *[**JUANA** and **CHATA** exit into the house, leaving **ANGELA** on the porch steps. **ADAN** runs up to her.]*

ADAN: Psst! Miss Angelita!…di…di cartas?

ANGELA: Oh, the letters…that will be one dollar.

ADAN: One dollar! Adan very poor man…*[**ANGELA** sticks the donation can out and shakes it. **ADAN** reaches into his pockets and drops coins into the can.]* Oh, si, you are very good. *[**ANGELA** puts on glasses and pulls out a letter.]*

ANGELA: *[Reading letter.]* Adored Senora Acosta: The impulses of my heart are such that they encourage even the most cautious man to commit indiscretion. My soul is carried to the extreme with the love that only you could inspire. Please know that I feel a true passion for your incomparable beauty and goodness. I tremulously send this declaration and anxiously await the result. Your devoted slave, Adan.

ADAN: *[Sighing.]* Ay, que beautiful.

ANGELA: P.S. With due respect Señora, if your husband should be home, do not turn on the porch light.

ADAN: Ah, thank you…thank you very much.

*[**ADAN** hurriedly exits. **ANGELA** gathers her St. Lucy doll and her donation can, and exits quickly. **CHATA** enters from the house wearing "colorful" street clothes. She looks around, then swiftly exits. **HECTOR** enters, picks up **ZAPATA**, hurries off.]*

*The stage darkens, as if smoke from the distant fire has covered the sun. Drum howls are heard. In the distance we hear a rooster crow and sounds of excited chickens as the henhouse comes to life. **GALLO** appears.]*

GALLO: Easy hens, shshsh! My beauties. *[He puts his suitcase down, cups his hands to his mouth, and yells to the house.]* Juana! Juana! Juana! *[**JUANA** opens the door.]* How many times, in the fever of homesickness, have I written out that name on prison walls, on bits of paper, on the skin of my arms….Let me look at you…my enduring rock, my anchor made from the hard parts of the earth—minerals, rocks, bits of glass, ground shells, the brittle bones of dead animals.

JUANA: I never seen you so pale, so thin…

GALLO: I'm home to rest, to fatten up, to breathe, to mend, to you.

JUANA: How long? How long will you stay?

GALLO: Here. Here is where I'll put my chair…I will sit here basking in the sun, like a fat old iguana catching flies, and watching my grandchildren replant the little cemetery with the bones of tiny sparrows. Here. Here I will build the walks for my champions. Morales roosters. The brave and gallant red Cubans, the hard and high-kicking Irish Warhorses, the spirited high-flying Bolinas.

JUANA: Don't say nothing you don't mean…you really gonna stay?

GALLO: *[Gently.]* Here. Here is where I'll plant a garden of herbs. Blessed laurel to cure fright, wild marjoram for the agony of lovesickness, cempauchie flowers for the grief of loneliness. *[Gallo gently kisses **JUANA**, picks her up and carries her into the house. The door slams shut. **ANGELA** enters, her wings drooping behind her. She trips over **GALLO**'s suitcase. She examines it. She smells it.]*

ANGELA: Tres Rosas! *[**ANGELA** looks at the house. She sits on the suitcase, crosses her arms over her chest as if she were ready to wait an eternity. The shadows of two strangers fall on her.]* What do you want? Nobody's home to you, rancor.

SHADOW #1: Just go in, tell him we got something for him.

ANGELA: Nobody's home to you, resentment.

SHADOW #2: Who are you supposed to be?

ANGELA: *[Holding St. Lucy doll.]* I am the angel of this yard
I am the angel of this door
I am the angel of light
I am the angel who shouts
I am the angel who thunders

SHADOW #1: She is pure crazy.

SHADOW #2: Don't play with it, it's serious.

ANGELA: You are the shadow of resentment
You are the shadow of rancor
I am the angel of acid saliva
I will spit on you.

SHADOW #1: There's time.

SHADOW #2: Yeah, later. *[**ANGELA** spits. The shadows leave. Angela crosses her hands over her chest and looks to Heaven.]*

ANGELA: Holy Father…Listen, you don't want him, you want me. Please take me, claim me, launch me and I will be your shooting star woman. I will be your comet woman. I will be your morning-star woman.

SCENE 4

Lights become brighter. **ANGELA** *exits under the house. The door opens.* **GALLO** *comes out in T-shirt and pants and goes to his suitcase.* **JUANA** *comes to the door in slip and tight robe.*

GALLO: I never sent him to the fields.

JUANA: I know.

GALLO: I never said for you to put him there.

JUANA: No, you never said...

GALLO: Then why is my son in the fields? *[They look at each other.* **GALLO** *looks away.]* Don't look at me. I see it in your eyes. You blame me. Just like the old man.

JUANA: Abuelo never said a word against you.

GALLO: I never let him down with the birds, nobody could match me. They were the best

JUANA: He knew that...

GALLO: So, he left the bird to Hector.

JUANA: He wanted him out of the fields. We didn't know when you would be out or maybe something would happen to you.

GALLO: He let the boy into the fields, that was his sin. He allowed a Morales into the fields.

JUANA: He was old, tired, heartbroken.

GALLO: Heartbroken, he wasn't a woman to be heartbroken.

JUANA: His only son was in jail.

GALLO: Yes, we know that, the whole valley knows that. You...what did you do? Didn't you lay out your hard, succulent, bitch's teat at the breakfast table? So he would have the strength to stand behind a hoe, with his back bent and his eyes on the mud for ten hours a day.

JUANA: Hard work never killed anybody.

GALLO: Ay, mujer! Can't you think what you've done, you bowed his head down.

JUANA: What was I suppose to do? There ain't no other work here. I can't see anything wrong with it for a little while.

GALLO: The difference between them and us, is we never put a foot into the fields. We stayed independent—we worked for nobody. They have to respect us, to respect our roosters. *[*HECTOR *and* ADAN *enter. They are both very dirty.* HECTOR *has* ZAPATA, *in his carrier.* ADAN *has a carrier containing a second rooster.* GALLO *and* HECTOR *stare at each other.]* Well...you are taller. This offshoot...this little bud has grown.

HECTOR: Yeah, well...that must be why you seem...smaller.

GALLO: Un abrazo!

HECTOR: I'm dirty. I'm sweaty.

GALLO: I see that.

HECTOR: I'm afraid I smell of the fields.

GALLO: Yes.

HECTOR: Of cheap abundant peon labor...the scent would gag you.

GALLO: It's going to kill you.

HECTOR: Mama says hard work never killed anyone...isn't that right, Mother?

JUANA: It's only for a little while. Your papa thinks that—

GALLO: I'll tell him what I think. Now what about those tamales you promised me?

JUANA: Ah sí, con permiso...I got some work in the kitchen.

ADAN: Oh sí, Mrs. Juana, los tamales...que rico.

JUANA: *[Smiling at* ADAN.*]* I hope they're the kind you like. *[She exits into house.]*

GALLO: Hijo, you always take the bird with you into the fields?

HECTOR: No, not always.

GALLO: This bird has to look like he's got secrets...no one but us should be familiar with him.

HECTOR: This is Adan.

ADAN: Es un honor, Mr. El Gallo *[*ANGELA *sticks her head out from under the house.* ADAN *and* GALLO *shake hands and greet each other.]*

GALLO: *[Referring to* ZAPATA.*]* Let him out...he needs a bigger carrier...he's a flyer.

ADAN: Como Filipino birds?

GALLO: Yes but this baby boy he's got a surprise. He's got a kick.

ADAN: Like Cuban bird?

GALLO: He'll fight in the air, he'll fight on the ground. You can put spurs or razors on that kick and he'll cut any bird to ribbons. You can put money on that.

ADAN: Hijo! Señor...how you know? He never fight. Maybe he only kick in cage.

GALLO: I know because I'm his papa....*[Pointing to the other carrier.]* That your bird?

ADAN: Sí pero no good...no fight. San Juan, he run away.

GALLO: I'll make him fight. Just let him out.

ADAN: Mr. El Gallo, you give this pendejo bird too much honor. Gracias Señor, pero this poor bird, he no can fight.

GALLO: Is it the bird, or you who will not fight?

HECTOR: The bird is too young. He doesn't want him to fight.

GALLO: I've never seen a bird that won't fight, but there are men who are cowards.

HECTOR: He is not a coward.

ADAN: This is true, pero I am not El Gallo. In my country all men who love di rooster know Mr. El Gallo. They tell of di famoso día de los muertos fight in Jacinto Park.

GALLO: Ah, you heard about that fight. You remember that fight, Hector?

HECTOR: No.

GALLO: First time you saw a real cockfight....Abuelo took you...How could you forget your first cockfight? *[To* ADAN.*]* Go on, take your bird out. I'll make him fight. *[*GALLO *takes a drink from a bottle, then blows on San Juan. As he does this, lights go down almost to black. Pinspot comes up C. as other lights come up to a dark red. During this process we hear* GALLO's *voice—"Ready," then a few beats later "Pit!"*

On this cue two dancer/roosters jump into the pinspot. This rooster dance is savage. The dancers wear razors on their feet. The Zapata dancer jumps very high. The poor San Juan dancer stays close to the ground. Throughout the dance, we hear drums and foot-stomping. It every hit, there is a big drum pound. During the fight, **HECTOR** *appears on the porch.]*

HECTOR: *[To himself.]* It was in Jacinto Park…the crowd was a monster, made up of individual human beings stuck together by sweat and spittle. Their gaping mouths let out screams, curses, and foul gases, masticating, smacking, eager for the kill. You stood up. The monster roared. Quasimoto, your bird, in one hand. You lifted him high, "Pit!" went the call. "Pit!" roared the monster. And you threw him into the ring…soaring with the blades on his heels flashing. I heard the mighty rage of his wings and my heart soared with him. He was a whirlwind flashing and slashing like a dark avenging angel then like some distant rainbow star exploding he was hit. The monster crowd inhaled, sucking back their hopes…in that vacuum he was pulled down. My heart went down the same dark shaft, my brains slammed against the earth's hard crust…my eyes clouded…my arteries gushed…my lungs collapsed. "Get up," said Abuelo, "up here with me, and you will see a miracle." You, Father, picked up Quasimoto, a lifeless pile of bloody feathers, holding his head oh so gently, you closed your eyes, and like a great wave receding, you drew a breath that came from deep within your ocean floor. I heard the stones rumble, the mountains shift, the topsoil move, and as your breath slammed on the beaches, Quasimoto sputtered back to life. Oh Papi, breathe on me. *[*ANGELA *appears and stands behind her brother. Her wings are spread very far out. Drums and stomping crescendo as* ZAPATA *brutally kills* SAN JUAN. *Blackout.]*

ACT 2, SCENE 1

Early afternoon. The table is setup in the middle of the yard in a festive away, with tablecloth, flowers, a bowl of peaches, and bottles of whiskey and wine. **GALLO** *is in the henhouse with* **ADAN**, **HECTOR** *is in the bathroom,* **JUANA** *and* **CHATA** *are in the kitchen.* **ANGELA** *is by the little cemetery writing on a tombstone.*

ANGELA: Here lies Angela Ester Morales died of acute neglect. Although she is mourned by many, she goes to a far, far, better place, where they have better food. *[*ANGELA *slides under the house as* JUANA *comes out wearing a fresh housedress and carrying a steaming pot.]*

JUANA: *[Yelling.]* Hector! Angela! You kids wash up, it's time to eat. *[*JUANA *hurries back into the house, almost knocking* CHATA *down as she comes out with a tray of tortillas she is heavily made up, wearing tight clothes, dangling earrings, high heeled shoes. A cigarette dangles from her mouth.]*

CHATA: Why are you eating out here?

JUANA: He wants it. Says he don't wanta hide in the house.

CHATA: Begging for trouble.

JUANA: What can I do, he's the man. *[She goes into the house.]*

CHATA: Ah, they're all shit! Just want trouble. Soup's on! *[*CHATA *pours herself a quick shot of whiskey, shoots it down and makes a face.* JUANA *comes out with another pot.]*

JUANA: You better tell 'em that the food's ready. *[*CHATA *goes to henhouse.]* Hector!

HECTOR: *[Coming out on porch.]* What?

JUANA: It's time to eat…you look real nice honey. Makes me proud to have your papa see you all dressed up.

HECTOR: Okay. Okay. Don't make a big deal about it. I just don't want him to think—

JUANA: I just feel so happy—

HECTOR: I just don't want him to think—

JUANA: Hijito! You love your papa…don't you?

HECTOR: Mother!

JUANA: I know you a little mad at him…pero when he comes home it's like the sun when it—

HECTOR: Shshshsh! *[*CHATA, GALLO *and* ADAN *come out of the henhouse.]*

GALLO: We have to sharpen and polish those spurs. I want them to flash.

JUANA: *[To* GALLO.*]* The food's ready…we fixed what you like…mole, rice, frijolitos…tamales.

GALLO: Tamales estilo Jalisco!

CHATA: *[Looking* HECTOR *over:]* Ay Papi que rico estás! *[*HECTOR *quickly sits down.]* Honey! You gonna have to beat all them women off with a stick, when they see you and that rooster tonight!

ADAN: No worry Hector, I be there…down you mujeres, women leave de Mr. Hector and me alone…Ay Mama! *[He has a giggling fit.]*

GALLO: *[Kissing* JUANA.*]* It's wonderful to be in love…to be touched by the noble fever.

CHATA: Ah, you're better off with a touch of typhoid.

JUANA: I…gracias al Señor que…my whole family is here. *[She looks around. She yells.]*

JUANA: Angela! Angie!

HECTOR: Mom!

JUANA: Where is she? Where is your sister?

HECTOR: Talking to the saints! I don't know. *[*JUANA *gets up, goes to the spot where* ANGELA *slides under the house, gets down on her hands and knees and yells.]*

JUANA: Angela! Angela! You leave them saints alone. You hear me! *[As everybody looks at* JUANA, ANGELA *comes from behind the house and tiptoes toward the henhouse.* HECTOR *is the only one to see her. Using hand signals, she pleads to him to be quiet.* JUANA *peers under the house.]* Angie! Honey…your mama worked for days to fix this food and now it's getting cold. [To* GALLO.*]* You should see how sweet she looks when she's all dressed up. *[To under the house.]* You ain't got no manners…ain't even said hello to your father. *[To* GALLO.*]* She prays a lot…and she's got real pretty eyes.

CHATA: *[To* GALLO.*]* She's sorta…the bashful type…you know.

JUANA: *[To* GALLO.*]* And she ain't spoiled.

CHATA: *[Taking a drink.]* Nah, all them kids smell like that.

JUANA: *[To under the house.]* Angie!

GALLO: Juana leave her alone.

JUANA: Okay. Angie, I'm gonna ignore you, 'cause you spoiled my day, this day that I been looking forward to for years and years and now you making me look like a bad mama, what's your papa gonna think of us.

GALLO: Juana, she'll come out when she's ready. *[*JUANA *goes back to the table.]*

CHATA: Maybe was them roosters fighting got her scared.

ADAN: Poor San Juan.

GALLO: Adan, drink up and I'll see you get one of our famous Champion Morales birds.

HECTOR: What famous Champion Morales birds?

GALLO: The ones I paid for dearly, the ones I came home to raise...isn't that right mi amor?

JUANA: Yes...you see honey your papa's gonna stay home...raise birds...I think Abuelo would want that.

GALLO: And after they see our bird tonight...see first I want them to think it's just you and the bird up there. And the bets are down, I'll take over and they're gonna know we got roosters. A toast...*[As* GALLO *stands up, everybody raises a glass, except* HECTOR. ANGELA *tiptoes from the henhouse carrying* ZAPATA. *She goes behind and under the house. Only* HECTOR *sees her.]* To the finest fighting cocks ever to be seen. *[He slides bottle to* HECTOR.*]*

HECTOR: *[Sliding the bottle back.]* No. *[Pause.]*

GALLO: Too good to drink with your old man.

HECTOR: I only drink with people I trust.

CHATA: Me...I drink with anybody. Maybe that's my problem.

GALLO: I am your father.

CHATA: I like it better when I drink alone. Ya meet a better class of people that way.

HECTOR: But it's my bird. Abuelo left it to me.

GALLO: Abuelo was my father, and you are my son. I see no problem. Now let's eat.

HECTOR: Mother!

JUANA: Let's eat, honey, and we can talk about it later.

ADAN: Ay the mole muy delicious...the mole muy rico...the cole muy beautiful y Mrs. Juana. Today, you look beautiful, like the mole.

GALLO: Hm, sabroso, exquisto.

JUANA: I bet you been in plenty of fancy places got better food than this.

GALLO: This is home cooking, I know that your hands made it....These...these are the hands of a beautiful woman...

HECTOR: Ha! Bullshit.

GALLO: We say your mother is beautiful and you call it bullshit? I find that very disrespectful.

JUANA: Hijo, you're right...it's just the way people talk, I know I ain't beautiful.

ADAN: Sí muy beautiful.

GALLO: Ya ves!...If your son doesn't have the eyes, the soul, the imagination to see it...it's his loss.

HECTOR: That's right. I just can't seem to stretch my imagination that far.

GALLO: This is an insult to your mother.

HECTOR: It's the truth. That is a plain, tired, worn-out woman.

GALLO: Shut up.

HECTOR: The hands of a beautiful woman! Those aren't hands, they're claws because she has to scratch for her living.

JUANA: Please, Hector, let him say what he wants...I know I ain't beautiful. It don't go to my head.

HECTOR: But it goes to your heart which is worse. Did he ever really take care of you? Did he ever go out and work to put food on the table, to buy you a dress? All he has is words, and he throws a few cheap words to you and you come to life. Don't you have any pride?

GALLO: Your mother has great courage to trust and believe in me.

HECTOR: Stupidity!

GALLO: You know nothing!

HECTOR: You don't seem to realize that it is my rooster. And that after the fight, depending on the outcome, I will sell him or eat him. I have made a deal with the Filipinos.

JUANA: Ay Hector! You've spoiled everything. All this food...I worked so hard...for this day.

GALLO: You're not selling anything to anybody. This is nothing to joke about.

HECTOR: I don't want to spend my life training chickens to be better killers. And I don't want to spend my whole life in this valley. Mother, Aunt Chata, excuse me.

CHATA: Ah?...O sí hijo pase...sometimes Hector can be a real gentleman. *[Hector starts to leave.]*

GALLO: Son!...You have no courage, no juice...you are a disgrace to me.

JUANA: Ay, Gallo don't say that to him.

HECTOR: Do you think I care what you think...Father.

JUANA: Hijo no...for me just once for me. I don't wanna be alone no more.

HECTOR: What about me? You have me, you'll always have me, I'll work, I've always worked, I can take care of you. I won't leave you.

JUANA: It ain't the same, honey.

HECTOR: Yeah...He comes first for you, he will always come first.

GALLO: If you sell that bird, it will be over your dead body.

HECTOR: You can't stop me. *[Exit* HECTOR. CHATA *takes a plate of food and bowl of peaches to the under-the-house area and tries to tempt* ANGELA *out.]*

GALLO: He doesn't seem to realize...coward...too bad. *[*GALLO *goes to the henhouse.* JUANA *starts to follow him.]*

JUANA: Talk to him...he's a good boy...if you just talk...*[Seeing* ADAN *still eating.]* Is it good? You really like it?

ADAN: Hm! Sabroso!

CHATA: Come on Angie...it's real good. *[*GALLO *returns running.]*

GALLO: He's gone...the bird is gone...

ADAN: Yo no see nada, nada.

JUANA: He'll bring it back, he's a good boy. He's just a little upset...you know.

GALLO: Nobody fools with my roosters. Not even this over-petted, over-pampered viper you spawned. Go and pray to your Dark Virgin. You know what I'm capable of. *[Exit GALLO. ADAN stops eating and tries to comfort JUANA as she puts her head down on the table and cries.]*

ADAN: No cry, no cry Mrs. Juana. Di women cry y Adan, he not know what to do. *[JUANA cries louder.]* Ay Mrs. Juana, for sure di flowers will die...di trees will be torn from di ground, freshness will leave di morning, softness will leave di night...*[JUANAS cries increase.]* Ay Dios! *[From his pocket, he brings out the letter ANGELA wrote for him. He crosses himself]* Mrs. di Juana...*[Reading with great difficulty.]* Di...impulses...of my...heart...are such...*[Throwing letter aside.]* A que la fregada! Mrs. Juana, Adan have mucho amor for you. My heart break to see you cry. I will not a breathe. When you no cry then I will breathe. *[ADAN takes a big breath and holds it. Slowly JUANA stops crying and lifts her head. ADAN suffering some discomfort, continues to hold his breath.]*

JUANA: I been dreaming. Nothing's gonna change. I gotta face facts. *[ADAN let his breath out in a great whoosh. ANGELA pops out from under the house and takes a peach from CHATA's hand. She stares at the peach with great intensity.]*

CHATA: Angie, ain't it nice to have the family all together again?

ANGELA: There is no pit in this peach. It is hollow. Instead of the pit, there is a whole little world, a little blue-green crystal-clear ocean, with little schools of tiny darting silver fish. On a tiny rock sits a mermaid with little teenie-weenie kinky yellow hair. A tiny sun is being pulled across a little china-blue sky by teenie-weenie white horses with itty-bitty wings. There is an island with tiny palm trees and tiny thatched hut. Next to the hut stand a tiny man and woman. She is wearing flowers and leaves. He is wearing one single leaf. On their heads are little bitty halos. In their arms is a little bitsy baby. He isn't wearing anything.

CHATA: Let me see...*[Looking at peach.]* I can't see dick! *[Blackout.]*

SCENE 2

Later in the afternoon. CHATA sits on the porch steps, her legs spread out, fanning herself. JUANA sits on a straight-back chair, her hands folded on her lap. She rocks herself softly. She watches ANGELA, who is sitting on the ground drawing circles in the dirt, humming softly in time to her circles. The circles get deeper and deeper.

CHATA: It's hot...I am waiting for a cool breeze...

ANGELA: Uh ha uh ha uh ha uh haa.

CHATA: Aire fresco...come on cool breeze, come right over here.

ANGELA: Uh ha uh ha uh haa.

CHATA: Women! We're always waiting. *[ANGELA hums for a beat, then there is silence for a beat.]*

JUANA: It's because I'm so plain.

CHATA: Ah, you just work too much.

JUANA: Plainness runs in my family. My mother was plain, my grandmother was plain, my great-grandmother—

CHATA: It was the hard times...the hard work that did it.

JUANA: My Aunt Chona was the plainest.

CHATA: I don't remember her.

JUANA: The one with the crossed eyes and the little mustache.

CHATA: Ay, Juanita, that woman had a beautiful soul, sewing those little tiny outfits for the statues of the saints. That woman was a saint.

JUANA: She's the one told on you that time you was drinking beer with them sailors at the cockfight.

CHATA: Disgusting old bitch! *[ANGELA hums for a beat as she continues drawing circles.]*

JUANA: I get up at six, I brush my teeth, no creams, no lotions, what they gonna do for me? I work that's all. I take care of people and I work. People look at me, they know that's all I do. I ain't got no secrets. No hidden gardens. I keep busy that's what I do. Don't stop, that's what I say to myself. Don't stop, 'cause you're not pretty enough, exciting enough, smart enough to just stand there.

ANGELA: Mama, I don't wanna be plain.

CHATA: Honey, you're too colorful to be plain.

ANGELA: Yeah, that's what I thought.

CHATA: Your mama forgets...those years when her heart was filled with wild dreams when she use to weave little white star jasmine vines in her hair and drive all the men crazy.

JUANA: It ain't true...she was the one always getting me in trouble.

CHATA: I wasn't the one they called Juanita la Morenita Sabrosita.

JUANA: Oh, Chata. We was young girls together...in the summer, at Jacinto Park...cockfights, fistfights, the music. At night we would jump out of our bedroom windows in our party dresses. With our good shoes in one hand, our hearts in the other, we ran barefoot through the wet grass, above us all the stars twinkling go, go, go.

CHATA: Nothing could stop us...we had such a short time being girls.

JUANA: Now, all I am is an old hag.

CHATA: It ain't true.

JUANA: Sí, it's true enough. I carry burdens, I hang sheets, I scrub, I gather, I pick up, "Here sit down," "I'll wash it," "Here's fifty cents," "Have my chair," "Take my coat," "Here's a piece of my own live flesh"!

CHATA: Es la menopause, that's what it is. You getting it early. I knew this woman once, use to pull out her hair.

JUANA: I don't care, I don't want any stories, I don't care what happens to Fulano Mangano...I just wanna stand still, I wanna be interesting, exciting enough to stand still.

CHATA: Ay, mujer!

JUANA: And I want to look like I got secrets.

CHATA: Juana!

JUANA: Don't call me Juana. Juana is a mule's name.

CHATA: Ah, you're crazy! That new gray hen, the kids named her Juana. See, they think of you.

JUANA: A gray hen! An old gray hen, that's all I am. An old gray hen in a family of roosters. No more! I want feathers, I wanna strut, too. I wanna crow.

ANGELA: Mama!

JUANA: Don't! Don't call me Mama. I am not Mama...I am...I am that movie star, that famous dancer and heartbreaker "Morenita Sabrosita"...and now if my fans will excuse me I'm gonna take a bath in champagne, eat cherry bonbons and paint my toenails. *[She goes into house.]*

CHATA: *[To* JUANA.*]* We got champagne? *[*CHATA *goes into the house as* ANGELA *goes to the little cemetery and puts up a new tombstone.]*

ANGELA: *[Printing on tombstone.]* Here lies Juana Morales. Beloved Wife of El Gallo, Blessed Mother to Angela and Horrible Hector. Died of acute identity crisis sustained during la menopause.

SCENE 3

Lights go down as ANGELA *sits on her box/table at the little cemetery. The long shadows of men fall on* ANGELA *and the cemetery.*

SHADOW #1: There's that spooky kid. You go brother.

SHADOW #2: Ah, it's just a weird kid. Hey! You! Kid! *[*ANGELA *does not acknowledge them.]*

SHADOW #1: Call her "Angel."

SHADOW #2: Hey, Angel. *[*ANGELA *looks up.]*

SHADOW #1: See what I mean.

SHADOW #2: Listen kid, tell your old man, we got business to discuss.

SHADOW #1: Yeah, and you make sure he gets the message.

ANGELA: My old man, my Holy Father, my all powerful Father, sees no problems. If there are problems, I am the angel of this yard. I am the comet. I am the whirlwind. I am the shooting stars. Feel my vibrance.

SHADOW #1: I feel it, right behind my ears, like...like...

ANGELA: Locust wings.

SHADOW #1: Let's get outta here.

SHADOW #2: Tell Gallo some pals dropped by to settle an old score.

SHADOW #1: Come on!

SHADOW #2: *[Voice trailing off.]* Hey! That kid don't scare me, see.

SHADOW #1: *[Voice trailing off.]* I'm telling ya, my ears hurt. *[Exit* SHADOWS. *Lights go back up.* ANGELA *folds her hands in prayer.]*

ANGELA: Holy Father, please help me, I feel the illumination, the fever of grace slipping away. I need to know that you are with me, that you take an interest in my concerns. Send me a little demonstration, a sign. Any sign...I don't care.

Stigmata, visions, voices, send an angel, burn a bush...I am attracted to levitation...but you choose...I'll just lay here and wait. *[*ANGELA *lies down on the ground waiting. After a few beats* HECTOR *enters. He slowly walks up to* ANGELA *and looks down on her for a beat.]*

HECTOR: What are you doing?

ANGELA: *[Sitting up.]* Ohhh...you're no sign.

HECTOR: What is going on?

ANGELA: Weird, shady men came here looking for Gallo. Two of them. They were not polite.

HECTOR: I see...So your reaction is to lay stretched out on the dirt instead of going into the house.

ANGELA: Hector, please, I am scared...I wanted a sign. *[*HECTOR *sits down next to* ANGELA.*]*

HECTOR: Hey, you're the shooting-star woman, you can't be scared.

ANGELA: I am scared. Really scared. If I grow up will I still be scared? Are grown-ups scared?

HECTOR: Always scared, trembling...cowering...this...this second, now...this planet that we are sitting on is wobbling precariously on its lightning path around the sun and every second the sun is exploding...stars are shooting at us from deep distant space, comets zoom around us, meteor rocks are being hurled through distances we measure in light...this very earth which we call our home, our mother, has catastrophic moods, she keeps moving mountains, receding like an overburdened beast trying to shake off...Life is violent.

ANGELA: You're scared about the fight...huh?

HECTOR: No. Whatever happens, Papi will still only care about the rooster. That's his son, that's who gets it all.

ANGELA: Maybe if we gave him the rooster he'd stay here and be happy.

HECTOR: He has to stay for us not the rooster...Angela...you...you were great taking the rooster.

ANGELA: He kept killing the little chicks. How could he do that Hector? He's their papa.

HECTOR: Training. Look Angela, you're the angel of this yard. You keep a close guard on that rooster. Don't let anyone near him...promise me.

ANGELA: Yes.

HECTOR: That's a real promise now. No crossed fingers behind your back

ANGELA: I promise already. *[She spreads her hands out in front of her, then kisses the tip of her thumb.]* May God strike me dumb, make me a plain whiny person and take away my gift of faith. Forever and ever, throughout my mortal years on earth, and throughout the everlasting fires of hell. Amen. Satisfied?

HECTOR: Yes.

ANGELA: Gee, maybe I should have given myself a little leeway, a little room for error. *[*CHATA *enters from the house with a bottle and glass.]*

HECTOR: Too late now. Can't take it back.

CHATA: Oh, oh, look who's here. Angie, your mama needs some cheering up, a nice hug, an angel's kiss, maybe a little song.

ANGELA: Litany to the Virgin. That's her favorite. *[She exits.]*

CHATA: Men are shit. Pure shit.

HECTOR: And you're still drinking.

CHATA: Stay outta my drinking. You hurt your mama, Hector.

HECTOR: Too bad.

CHATA: Ay Dios, what a man he is now.

HECTOR: Yeah, well what about you? Didn't you break Abuelo's heart when you became a whore?

CHATA: They called me the encyclopedia of love. You want to turn a few pages? Your Aunt Chata could show you a few things.

HECTOR: You're disgusting.

CHATA: Is that what fascinates, you, honey? Is that why I always find you peeping at me, mirrors at the keyhole, your eyeballs in the cracks, spying when I'm sleeping, smelling my kimono.

HECTOR: You're drunk

CHATA: I ain't drunk, honey.

HECTOR: You drink too much. It's not…good for you…it makes you ugly.

CHATA: Ain't none of your business. Don't tell me what to do Hector.

HECTOR: I have to, it's for your own good.

CHATA: You got nothing to say about it, you ain't my man, and you ain't your mama's man. The sooner you learn that the better…take your bird, leave it, eat or sell it, but get out of here. *[HECTOR stands alone in the yard, as CHATA goes to the door. She turns They look at each other.]* What are you hanging around here for? Go on! Get out! It ain't your home anymore. *[CHATA takes a broom and shoos HECTOR from the yard.]* Shoo! Shoo! You don't belong here, it ain't your place anymore.

HECTOR: Stop it, stop it, stop it. *[HECTOR goes to the outside boundary of the yard, where he falls to his knees and buries his face in his hands, as CHATA comes slowly up behind him.]*

CHATA: I feel like I'm tearing my own flesh from my bones…He's back. Honey, we got too many roosters in this yard.

HECTOR: Did you sleep with my father? Did he yearn for you as you slept in your little white, chaste, narrow bed? Did he steal you when you were dreaming?

CHATA: *[Embracing him.]* Shshsh…

HECTOR: I'm not like him.

CHATA: You're just like him, so handsome you make my teeth ache.

HECTOR: Whore, mother, sister, saint-woman, moon-woman, give me the shelter of your darkness. Fold me like a fan and take me into your stillness, submerge me beneath the mysteries, baptize me, bear me up, give me life, breathe on me. *[CHATA enfolds him as the lights fade. We hear ANGELA reciting the litany.]*

ANGELA: *[Offstage.]* She is the Gate of Heaven, the Mystical Rose, the Flower of Consolation, the Fire of Transcendence, and the Queen of Love.

SCENE 4

Lights come up to indicate that time has passed. ANGELA *is alone in the yard. She sniffs the air.*

ANGELA: Tres Rosas!

[ANGELA slides under the house as GALLO enters. He sees a brief flash of ANGELA from the corner of his eye. He walks slowly into the yard. He stops by the little cemetery and reads the tombstones. He feels the urge for a drink. He goes to the table and has a shot. He sits.]

GALLO: Acute neglect?…uh-huh…I thought I felt a little spirit, slight, delicate…yes I feel it. A little tenderness…a little greenness…*[Examining the ground]* What's this? Tracks…little tiny paws…there…*[Following tracks.]* and there…*[GALLO pretends to be following tracks to the porch. Then with one great leap he jumps in the opposite direction surprising the hell out of ANGELA, and pulls her from under the house by her heels]* Ah, ha!

ANGELA: Shit! Hey! You're ripping my wings! You shithead! Put me down! Don't touch me! *[GALLO puts ANGELA down, throws his hands up to indicate he won't touch her. They stand and stare at each other. ANGELA goes to the little cemetery, never taking her eyes off GALLO. They continue to stare for a beat, then ANGELA looks up to Heaven slapping her hands together in prayer.]* There is a person here trying to con me, but I don't con that easy.

GALLO: *[Slapping his hands in prayer.]* There is a person here who swallows saints but defecates devils.

ANGELA: *[To Heaven.]* He comes here smelling of rosas using sweet oily words…it's phony, its obnoxious, it's obscene…I wanna throw up.

GALLO: I came here to see my baby, my little angel, my little woman of the shooting stars, my light delicate splendorous daughter. But she is as light, as delicate, as splendid as an angel's fart

ANGELA: Angels do not fart. They do not have a digestive system. That's why they can all scrunch together on the head of a pin.

GALLO: Oh,…I only come with my love—

ANGELA: *[Interrupting.]* You only came with words…well, where were these words on my birthday, Christmas, my saint's day? Where's my Easter outfit, my trip to Disneyland, the orthodontist…You owe me.

GALLO: Sweet Jesus…What a monster! I owe you…but Angela! Angela! Angela! How many times have I written that name on prison walls. On bits of paper, on the skin of my arms.

ANGELA: *[To Heaven.]* He's hopeless! You write everybody's name on your arms.

GALLO: Women like to know that they're on your flesh.

ANGELA: I am not a woman. I'm your baby daughter. You said so yourself.

GALLO: I'm afraid…fathers to daughters…that's so delicate. I don't know…what to do…help me Angela. How do I know what to do?

ANGELA: Instinct! Ain't ya got no instinct? Don't you feel anything?

GALLO: *[Moving closer to* ANGELA.*]* When you were a little baby, you were a miracle of tiny fingers and toes and dimples and you had a soft spot on the top of your head.

ANGELA: I still have it, see.

GALLO: I wanted to take you into my arms and crush you against my chest so that I could keep you forever and nobody, and nothing, could ever, ever hurt you because you would be safe...my little offshoot, my little bud, my little flower growing inside my chest

ANGELA: Papi...

GALLO: Sí, sí, hijita. Your papi's here.

ANGELA: And Papi these men come all the—

GALLO: *[Holding* ANGELA.*]* Shshsh...it's nothing, nothing and you thought I forgot about you...well it just hurt too much, do you understand?

ANGELA: You had to pull down some hard time and the only way to survive was to cut off all feelings and become an animal just like the rest of them.

GALLO: Well, something like that. Honey you know what I wish—

ANGELA: Papa, did the lights really go down when they put the people in the electric chair?

GALLO: Angela, what a...Honey you know what I wish—

ANGELA: Did they force you to make license plates? Hector and I would look real close at the one that started with a G. We thought you made them. "What craftsmanship!" Hector used to say.

GALLO: Don't you have any normal interests?

ANGELA: Like what?

GALLO: Like swimming...you know what I wish? That we could take a trip and see the ocean together.

ANGELA: I've never seen the ocean. When?

GALLO: Just you and me. Laying on our bellies, feeding the seagulls, riding the waves.

ANGELA: I can't swim.

GALLO: I will teach you, that's what fathers are for—

ANGELA: *[To Heaven.]* Angels and saints did you hear? My father's going to teach me to swim!

GALLO: Now Angela, I didn't promise.

ANGELA: But you said—

GALLO: I want to but I have to hurry and fix things. I have to find Hector, talk to him and find that rooster fast before Hector sells him. Honey you pray to St. Anthony, your prayers are powerful...unless...St. Anthony he listen to you?

ANGELA: *[Crossing her fingers.]* Hey, we're like that.

GALLO: Ask St. Anthony, Angela...then we can go to the ocean.

ANGELA: Truly Papi? Just you and me? And will you stay with us forever and ever?

GALLO: Wild horses couldn't drag me away.

ANGELA: Close your eyes. Tony! Tony! Look around, Zapata's lost and can't be found. *[She goes under the house, gets* ZAPATA *and gives him to* GALLO.*]* I found him Papi, he was—

GALLO: Ya lindo, ya. *[To bird.]* Papa's got you now. Angela you keep quiet now honey, this is our secret.

ANGELA: What about Hector?

GALLO: I'm going to talk to Hector now. You go inside and get all dressed up. So I can be proud of my girl. I'll pick you up after the fight. *[He exits.]*

ANGELA: Your girl! *[Singing.]* We are going to the ocean, we are going to the sea, we are going to the ocean to see what we can see...*[*ANGELA *goes into the house. We hear cha-cha music.]*

CHATA: *[Offstage.]* One, two...not like that...I'm getting tired...what time's Zorro on?

JUANA: No, no...Just one more. *[Singing.]* Cha, cha, cha, que rico,...cha, cha, cha...Ay, I could do it all night. *[Enter* GALLO *running breathing hard. He has* ZAPATA'*s carrier. He goes to the door and yells.]*

GALLO: Juana! Juana! *[*JUANA *and* CHATA *come to the door.]* I need money...and my stuff. I gotta leave...something's come up...Do you hear me? I need money now.

JUANA: I hear ya...you ain't even been here a day and already you're gone...nothing's going to change with you...nothing. I was having fun, dancing, remembering old times, do you know how long—

GALLO: I don't have time for this, just give me the money.

JUANA: I ain't got any!

CHATA: I got some. *[She goes in the house.]*

GALLO: The Filipino, somebody told him about the bird. Oh, ya, ya my little hen, don't you ruffle those pretty feathers, I'll be back.

JUANA: No, you always gonna be running.

GALLO: If it was just me, I'd stay. You know that, Juana? You know I'd stay, but I got the bird to think of, gotta hide him, breed him good, soon as I get some good stags I'll come home...this is just a little setback. *[*CHATA *returns with suitcase and money.]*

JUANA: You know how long it's been since I went dancing?

CHATA: Here, you're gonna need this. *[Gives him the suitcase.]* And this is all the cash I got *[*ANGELA *enters as Gallo counts the money. She is dressed in a red strapless dress made tight by large visible safety pin.; high heels, and a great deal of heavy makeup and jewelry. The effect is one of a young girl dressed like a tart for a costume party. She carries a suitcase, purse and her donation can.]*

GALLO: Is this all you got?

ANGELA: *[Shaking the can.]* Don't worry Papa, I got my donation-can money. *[They all stare at her for a beat.]*

JUANA & CHATA: Angela?!!

JUANA: Angie, you got on your mama's old party dress.

CHATA: Yeah, and all my jewelry...where you going?

ANGELA: Papa, didn't you hear me? I have money. *[She shakes the can.]*

GALLO: Oh honey, don't you look pretty...now you got a little bit too much lipstick on, let your mama wipe some off.

ANGELA: Are we leaving now?

JUANA: Gallo!

GALLO: Shshsh Juana…Angela, I gotta talk to your mama for a few minutes. You go in the house and I'll come and get you.

ANGELA: Are you sure?

GALLO: Don't you trust me, Angie?

CHATA: Come on Angie, I'll show you how to draw eyebrows. First you draw a straight line across your forehead and then spit on your finger and rub out the middle. Let's go in and try it.

ANGELA: Really, Aunt Chata, I'm not a child, you don't have to patronize me.

CHATA: Okay, I'll give you the lowdown on blow-jobs. *[ANGELA and CHATA exit into the house.]* Now, don't tell your mama…

GALLO: Juana, keep her in the house until I leave.

JUANA: You promised to take her with you?

GALLO: I had to get the bird. I said I would take her to the ocean.

JUANA: Ay bruto! How could you do it?

GALLO: How was I to know this would happen…and Juanita, it hurts me to say this but that kid is crazy…

JUANA: No, no señor, she is not crazy and I ain't gonna let you call her crazy. She got the spirit they broke in me. I ain't gonna let it happen to her.

GALLO: Shshsh! Don't get so excited. It isn't important.

JUANA: It's important…it's her spirit, her soul and you ain't gonna stomp on it…you hear me. *[ADAN enters running.]*

ADAN: Mr. El Gallo…bad men! Mucho bad, y mucho ugly. Looking for you y Zapata. All ober they look for you…You leave Mr. El Gallo. You go far away. I take you. I go for my truck.

GALLO: You are a good friend Adan, and my new partner.

ADAN: Oh, thank you Mr. El Gallo. I am proud. But is better I come back here to Mrs. Juana y Hector.

JUANA: Thank you, Adan.

GALLO: We better hurry.

ADAN: Sí, sí, I come back with truck. *[He exits. JUANA goes into the house. HECTOR enters as GALLO starts to pack his suitcase.]*

HECTOR: *[Seeing ZAPATA.]* You must have really sold her a bill of goods to get Zapata.

GALLO: Look, there's trouble…the Filipino send you?

HECTOR: No, how could you think I would work for him, but I came to get Zapata.

GALLO: You're the one told him about the bird.

HECTOR: Yes. I made a deal with the Filipino. He'll leave you alone if I give him the rooster.

GALLO: That's a lie and you fell for it.

HECTOR: No, he is an honorable man, we were here unprotected for seven years and he never bothered us. It's his bird, Papi.

GALLO: No, I paid seven years of my life for this baby.

HECTOR: And he lost his son. It's the right thing to do. *[A truck horn is heard. ANGELA comes out of the house with her suitcase, JUANA and CHATA follow after her.]*

ANGELA: Papa? Are we leaving now, Papa?

JUANA: Angie! No!

HECTOR: So that's it…Angela, get back in the house.

ANGELA: I'm going with him, Hector.

HECTOR: Get back in the house, nobody's going anywhere.

ANGELA: No! I don't have to listen to you anymore. You're not my father.

JUANA: Angie…he's not going to the ocean…he can't take you. *[We hear the sound of ADAN's truck. The horn is heard as GALLO starts backing away, picking up ZAPATA's carrier.]*

ANGELA: Papi, wait for me! Papa, you promised.

GALLO: You're all grown up now, you don't need your old man.

CHATA: Hector! *[GALLO turns, tries to run out. Angela grabs him, knocking ZAPATA's carrier out of his hand. HECTOR picks up the carrier.]*

ANGELA: No Papa, we need you and Mama needs you, we've been waiting, and waiting, you can't leave, you promised.

JUANA: They'll kill you Gallo.

GALLO: *[Throwing ANGELA off.]* Stop sucking off me. I got nothing for you.

ANGELA: *[Beating her fists on the ground]* No, no, Papa! You promised me!…Oh, Hector…No, no, I promised Hector *[Drums begin as punctuation of the pounding of ANGELA's fists on the ground. Lights change. A special on ANGELA and another on GALLO and HECTOR come up, as shadows appear. ANGELA sees shadows]* Ah…Holy Father, Abuelo.

GALLO: *[To HECTOR.]* Give me that bird.

ANGELA: Saints, Angels, Mama.

JUANA: *[Trying to pick up ANGELA]* Come on Angie, get up.

GALLO: *[To HECTOR.]* What do you want?

HECTOR: You, alive, Papi.

CHATA: Careful, Hector

ANGELA: I've lost my faith. I am splintered.

GALLO: *[Imitating HECTOR.]* You Papi….Give me life….Make me a man. *[He whips out his stiletto.]* This is how you become a man. *[The drums get louder: We hear howling.]* Come on baby boy, show Daddy whatcha got.

JUANA: Are you crazy! That's your son!

ANGELA: I am cast down! Exiled! *[GALLO stalks HECTOR as drums follow their movements.]*

JUANA: Oh Gallo, you're killing your own children.

CHATA: Move Hector, don't think, move!

GALLO: Oh yeah, mi lindo, you like to fight…eh?

JUANA: No, stop them! Please, please stop this.

ANGELA: Fallen from the light, condemned to the mud, to the shadows.

GALLO: You gotta learn baby boy.

CHATA: Look at him Hector. He's getting old, his hand is shaking…take the knife! Stay down old warrior. Stay down.

ANGELA: Alone and diminished. This loneliness is unendurable.

JUANA: Hector!

HECTOR: Do I have it? Is this what you want me to be…

ANGELA: *[Looking to Heaven.]*
My brains are slammed against the earth's hard crust
My eyes are clouded
My arteries gush

My lungs collapsed.

HECTOR: *[Letting go of* **GALLO**.*]* No! I am your son. *[Drums and cries stop.]*

ANGELA: Holy Father, Abuelo, Hector, breathe on me. *[Celestial sound as a white narrow shaft of light falls on* **ANGELA**. *She levitates, her wings spreading. Only* **CHATA** *and* **JUANA** *see this.]*

HECTOR: *[Taking a deep breath.]* Oh sweet air! *[He gets the rooster and sees* **ANGELA**.*]* Angela!

ADAN: *[Rushing in.]* I am here, I have truck…*[Seeing* **ANGELA**, *he crosses himself]* Ay Dios. *[He kneels]*

JUANA: *[At* **GALLO***'s side.]* Gallo look!

GALLO: Did you see the hands on that kid, just like steel, never seen finer hands….*[Seeing* **ANGELA**.*]* Sweet Jesus, my beautiful monster. *[He crosses himself.]*

CHATA: No, it ain't true.

HECTOR: *[Standing before* **ANGELA** *holding the rooster.]* Oh sweet hummingbird woman, shooting star, my comet, you are launched.

ANGELA: Abuelo, Queen of Heaven, All the Saints, All the Angels. It is true, I am back I am restored. I am…Hector, take me with you.

HECTOR: Everywhere…Over the mountains, up to the stars.

ANGELA: To the very edge.

ADAN: Hector! Angelita! You take Adan. *[He goes to* **ANGELA**.*]*

CHATA: *[Looking at* **ANGELA**.*]* Shit happens…been happening all my life, that's all I know.

JUANA: *[Holding* **GALLO** *like the Pieta.]* We seen it Gallo, with our own eyes.

ANGELA: *[To* **HECTOR** *and* **ADAN**.*]* And I want my doorstep heaped with floral offering…and *[***HECTOR**, **ADAN** *and* **ANGELA** *freeze.* **CHATA** *removes the flower from her hair and holds it in her hand, trying to decide what to do. She freezes.]*

GALLO: Ay Juanaita, I had a vision of a hard-kicking flyer…*[He yawns]* the ultimate bird, noble, fino. *[He falls asleep.* **JUANA** *looks at* **GALLO**, *smiles, then looks out half-smiling.]*

END OF PLAY

Life Theme 4:

Rebellion

Life Theme 4: Rebellion

The status quo isn't working. Social, cultural, or political
upheaval may make things better. Or not.

"…Revolution has its reasons. Its wrath will be pardoned by
the future; its result is a better world. From its most terrible
blow comes a caress for the human race."
    —*Les Miserables,* Victor Hugo

Featured plays:

Antigone
    by Sophocles
"Master Harold" . . . *and the boys*
    by Athol Fugard

The need to rebel, to assert oneself against the status quo, is not confined to the inherent conflict
between generations. The right to rebel against political authority is a cornerstone of the American
experience. This country was born in a violent revolution against British authority and the
right of the people to change or replace political, social, and cultural structures is built into our
Constitution. And yet, even here and even now, rebellion can be met with violent or restrictive
opposition by those currently enjoying positions of power. In other times and other places, the right
to rebel could not be assumed and yet individuals and groups have consistently given their freedom
and their lives to the cause of change.

This impulse to rebel is not new. Our first play, *Antigone* by Sophocles, was written some 2500
years ago in a culture that is only vaguely familiar to most of us. Yet the story of one woman's

struggle to pursue her faith when it is at odds with state law resonates as clearly today as it did all those centuries ago. We still experience clashes of values between individuals/communities and the state. We still struggle to balance the needs of the individual with the needs of the whole.

Our second play, *Master Harold and the boys. . .* by Athol Fugard explores the issue of rebellion in a more contemporary context. Set in South Africa in 1950, this play uses a personal encounter between a black South African man and a white South African boy as a metaphor for the larger struggle of the black South African majority to wrest social, economic and political equality from an entrenched white minority power structure. In an even broader context the play demystifies the mechanism of oppression based on racial and ethnic differences in any time or place by placing the struggle on its most intimate level.

Antigone

> *Year: circa 441* BCE
> *Genre: Greek classical tragedy*
> *Structure: Episodes and Odes*
> *Setting: The city-state of Thebes*

Context:

For the original audience of this particular play, a distinctively Athenian perspective was performed for the benefit of the privileged class and those foreign guests (also privileged) who traveled to Athens for the Great City Dionysia. The play's intent is to affirm the ideals of the status quo while exploring with great sensitivity the burdens of leadership and the catastrophic results that arise from the misuse of power. Universal themes combined with Sophocles' brilliant and persuasive use of language have kept this play current and in production up to our own time. Central to our understanding of this play are the Athenian sense of structure and values.

Social hierarchy is one of the core ideas explored in *Antigone*. This play tells a story from what the Greeks considered their own Golden Age: the Heroic Age, a time when structures of power and leadership were based in both patriarchal lineage and personal prowess. By Theban tradition, the king could choose his successor and most often chose one of his sons: the one best suited, not necessarily the first born. Ideally, the king should be physically powerful, able to defend (or conquer) the city, and also an intellectual man of a philosophical nature. His authority was absolute during the era portrayed in the play, as was also true for much of Greek culture during most of their long history. A king who did not rule with strength of will and purpose, who betrayed a moment's self-doubt, would not sit long on the throne.

A rigid class structure survived even the brief flowering of Athenian democracy that coincided with the life and works of our playwright. The play *Antigone* articulates a struggle amongst the privileged few (the royal family), while the chorus represents the common folk (the chorus of Theban elders). Clearly, the grumbling of the "mob" is influential, but not authoritative in the play. Ultimately, the king answers to no voice but his own in secular matters. The will of the gods will be a topic of discussion below.

The consistent use of the male pronoun in the above paragraphs is neither accident nor oversight. Greek women in the 5th century BCE are essentially absent from social, political, philosophical and artistic life. As the noted historian Will Durant wrote in his benchmark study of Greek history:

> As surprising as anything else in this civilization is the fact that it is brilliant without the aid or stimulus of women. With their help the Heroic Age achieved splendor, the age of dictators a lyric radiance; then, almost overnight married women vanish from the history of the Greeks. . .Greek literature is offensively repetitive about the faults of women and . . . even the kindly Plutarch repeats. . . 'The name of a decent woman, like her person, should be shut up in the house.'"[1]

The central conflict in this play is the battle of wills between two characters at the opposite ends of the power structure, though both are members of the royal family. Antigone is a daughter of the royal house, but as a woman her actual status is little higher than a slave's. Creon, as the newly enthroned king is forced into a virtual and philosophical combat he is not yet ready to undertake. The throne under his posterior is not even warm when he is forced into a public confrontation with a mere woman and, worse yet, a woman of his own household. If he can't control his own niece, how will he ever rule and protect Thebes?

A second relevant contextual issue is found in the area of religious faiths during the Heroic Age and the age of Sophocles. Though philosophers of the 5th century were tending toward the ideals of either secular humanism or a divine Creator, most Athenians still thought of their ancestors as having experienced a visceral, immediate relationship with the Olympian gods (i.e. Zeus, Apollo, Athena, etc.). During the Heroic Age, the Olympians ruled along with lesser gods and spirits, such as those of the underworld, those of nature, and the personal, familial gods sometimes called hearth gods who functioned as protectors of the family. However, by the 5th century, belief systems were moving away from the traditional Olympians and lesser gods. Plato, for example, postulated a single divine creator. For most Athenians watching the play, a prevailing tolerance toward individual belief systems allowed most individuals to worship unmolested. Each city might have its "state religion" with attendant civic duties, but personal faith was usually allowed to be just that: personal.

Antigone is determined that both her brothers will meet her in Hades knowing that she loved them, saying, "Death is eternal, life is fleeting." But while she is focused on the eternal and the will of the gods of the underworld, Creon is forced by his position to defend the people of the city by rewarding loyalty and punishing traitors. His duty is to the finite living and to the Olympians who guide him. What raises the stakes so high in this play is both characters are right. But both cannot win. Neither is able (or willing) to imagine or propose a compromise. Both cannot bend, so both must break.

---

[1] Durant, Will. *The Life of Greece.* Simon and Schuster: NY, p. 305.

The Playwright:

Sophocles was born circa 496 BCE near the city of Athens. The son of a wealthy armor-maker, he received the best traditional aristocratic education available. In 468 BCE, at the age of 28, he defeated Aeschylus in the City Dionysia playwriting contest. As he matured, Sophocles became the preeminent tragic poet of his age usually besting his famous but erratic competitor Euripides. Sophocles won the prize 18 times during his career (including for the trilogy of which *Antigone* was one play), and composed at least 100 tragedies. Seven complete tragedies and fragments of about 80 more are extant. Considered by many to be the greatest of the Greek tragedians, Sophocles lived during the height of Athenian power and prosperity. He also survived and suffered through its decline: Athens fell to the Spartans following a ruinous two decade civil war just months after he died in 406 BCE, at the age of 90.

"Master Harold" . . . and the boys

Year: *1982*
Genre: *Realism*
Structure: *Well-made*
Setting: *Port Elizabeth, South Africa, 1950*

Context:

To understand the context in which this intimate drama takes place, we must look at the political system in South Africa known as *apartheid*. This system evolved over centuries of colonial domination by European powers until in 1948 it was formalized in the South African Constitution. *"Master Harold"* takes place only two years after the formal ratification of the apartheid constitution, yet the play reveals the long standing repression of black South Africans. The beginnings of apartheid can be traced back to the first European incursions into this resource rich land.

In 1652, the Dutch established a colony on the Cape of Good Hope (the southern tip of Africa) to be used as a permanent staging post for Dutch East India Company ships on their passage from Europe to the Far East. At first, the colonists bought fresh meat and vegetables from the indigenous people. The colony was small and the Dutch did not encroach upon land belonging to local peoples. However, the Dutch soon realized that profits could increase enormously if they didn't have to pay for the fresh goods. They quickly conquered the area militarily and imported slaves from other parts of Africa to ensure cheap labor. This state of affairs continued in relative peace and prosperity (for the white colonists at any rate) until events in far away Europe suddenly affected the colony.

During nearly 150 years of residence, the Dutch had established a culture identical in every aspect, governmental, social, religious and economic, to their homeland in Holland. As they spread into the interior of South Africa (continually displacing more native African cultures) they carved out huge plantation farms, manned by slave labor. Because of the relative isolation of these enormous estates and their isolation from Europe, they became an extremely clannish, conservative, and fiercely self-sufficient group. A sense of being a people shaped by South African experience grew and they began to refer to themselves as Afrikaners or Boers (two terms which are used interchangeably) rather than Dutch. This sense of disconnect from Europe may be best illustrated by the fact that South Africa sided with Nazi Germany during WWII, despite the fact that Holland was one of the first nations invaded and occupied by Nazi forces. For the Afrikaners, Germany was at war with England and England was the enemy (see below).

England became immersed in South Africa when the French Revolution of the late 1780s threw Europe into a period of chaos. After the Revolution, France conquered Holland, which disrupted the balance of power in Europe and threatened the lucrative trade routes to the Far East. In 1795, England responded by sending troops to South Africa under the guise of "protecting Dutch interests." By 1814, England took formal control of the Cape Colony and in 1815 paid six million pounds to Holland for ownership of South Africa. English became the official language of the colony in 1822 and slavery was abolished in 1833. British law, religion, and customs conflicted with the Boer/Afrikaner traditions, and a bitter rivalry developed.

One important point to keep in mind is that until the mid-20th century, for a white South African the "troubles" were between the two invading white cultures, the British and the Afrikaners. Neither side considered the condition of the native people a problem as long as these conquered people remained suppressed and powerless. To this day, the descendants of Afrikaner settlers and British settlers have little in common in terms of national goals, political aspirations, or economic security.

Beginning in 1835 and continuing into the 1840s, Afrikaners reacted to British imperialism by moving further inland in a famous journey known as the Great Trek. The Great Trek has become a revered symbol of Afrikaner resistance, which is celebrated and re-enacted each year and to this day retains an aura of mythic proportions. In 1840, after several military successes against the powerful Zulu nation, the Afrikaners established a new republic in the interior of South Africa called Natal. By 1843, the British had gained control over the "republic" of Natal and the Afrikaners simply moved further inland to avoid British influence. Over the next fifty years British and Dutch forces fought for control of the region, with the local Zulu, Basuto, and Grigua nations caught in the middle and crushed in the struggle.

Perhaps this colonial struggle would have faded from the world stage in time. However, in 1866, one of the largest reserves of gold in the world were discovered in the region. As one witness observed, "Never in the history of the world had so much gold been found in one place." By a twist of geological fate, vast diamond reserves were also found, deposits so large that South Africa continues to be the major exporter of diamonds to the world.

Immediate British investment in mining operations led to severe economic disparity between the British who controlled mining and industry, and the Dutch settlers, who for the most part remained farmers. Backed by a British military presence, English settlers controlled the majority of gold and diamond mines and the banking, processing, and shipping industries that supported the export of these commodities. Fortunes were made and the farming Afrikaners fell into an economic, political, and social underclass. Ultimately the increasing power and wealth of the English and the growing anger of the Afrikaners led to all out war in which the British defeated the Boer army and formal control of the region was retained by the British. In 1910, the British parliament passed the South Africa Act, establishing the Union of South Africa as an independent nation with strong economic, military, and political ties with England.

Since that time, the majority of South Africans who could vote were of Afrikaner descent. Though still excluded from the economic prosperity of the gold and diamond industry, and still dominated by British institutions, Afrikaners controlled the Parliament and elected every Prime Minister through their National Party until Nelson Mandela was elected as the first black Prime Minister in the first free elections in South Africa in 1993. Plagued by their losing battle with the British for a bigger piece of the economic pie, Afrikaner rage at some point became misdirected toward native people and in 1948 *apartheid* became the constitutional law of South Africa. The long tradition of black exploitation by both English and Dutch descendants became a rigidly enforced bureaucracy of segregation in all aspects of life.

By 1950, the year in which *"Master Harold"* is set, the formal segregation of the population of South Africa was well established. This process required the enhancement of pre-existing laws by thousands of specific laws and regulations segregating everything from territory to toilets. The following are 6 of the basic and most far-reaching laws of apartheid. Each affects the daily lives of the characters in the play.

1913 – Land Reserve Act

> 7.3% of the land of South Africa, the poorest, least productive sections of the region, was set aside as "National Homelands" intended to be racially pure and theoretically independent enclaves for non-white South Africans.

1948 – Population Registration Act

> Each child born in South Africa was registered at birth in one of four racial categories:
> a. Bantu/Native: descendant from indigenous peoples.
> b. Asian: usually East Indian or Pakistani, can also include people from the Far East.
> c. Colored: mixed race.
> d. White: European descent.
> This registration was fixed at birth and could not be altered under any circumstances. Occasional errors, and stories of insane mislabeling, did not alter the basic premise that skin color is destiny and that the government did not make mistakes.

The Group Areas Act

This Act empowered the government to move anyone, anytime to a racially pure area or "homeland." Forced migration to the homelands displaced millions of families. No member of any other group was allowed to enter a Homelands area.

Pass Cards

This was the most hated of the many restrictive regulations. In the 1980 census, the population of South Africa was identified in the following percentages:

Bantu/Native = 71.9%

Asian = 2.8%

Colored = 9.2%

White = 16.1%

(The white population was 66% Afrikaner and 33% British.)

With about 84% of the population confined on 7.3% of the land, obvious economic difficulties arose. Who was going to work the English mines, labor on Afrikaner plantations, do the domestic and manual labor the elite white population was unwilling to do? Clearly, total segregation was not going to work. Thus the Pass Law was created to allow non-white workers into white enclaves. Every non-white South African was required to carry a Pass Card at all times. This pass must carry the signature of a white employer if the holder was found outside a homeland area. Abuse of this law led to widespread discontent, protest, and rebellion among native South Africans.

The Suppression of Communism Act

Under the guise of defending democracy from communist infiltration, the Suppression of Communism Act became the instrument by which all forms of dissent could be violently crushed. This act allowed for the suspension of all civil liberties at the whim of the government and was often used for indiscriminate arrest and torture of any non-white suspected by the government of trying to undermine apartheid.

The Bureaucracy:

The goal of apartheid was simple. Total segregation of every aspect of life, with power, wealth and privilege reserved for white South Africans. The Afrikaners may have led the National Party that institutionalized apartheid, but the English were not opposed to the system and indeed reaped enormous benefits from it. The Bureaucracy needed to enforce this system grew and grew over the years. Few white South Africans were fully aware of the situation, since news was censored by the government under the Suppression of Communism Act. Every time an aspect of daily life was found to not be specifically, legally segregated, new laws were introduced to make it so.

The life of the average black South African by 1950 was one of misery, isolation, and poverty. As you read the play, be aware that Sam and Willy must have an assigned homeland, that they are likely to live in one of the invisible slum areas that grew up around cities like Port Elizabeth to allow white employers access to black workers, that anyone (including a boy like Hally) could revoke their Pass Cards and send them to prison. For Sam and Willy, the moments of pleasure experienced in the Tea Room or with Hally or at a ballroom dance contest are bright spots in painfully restricted and dangerous lives. When Willy gives up his bus money at the end of play, be aware of what he is risking. Caught walking after dark on the streets of a white city, he is subject to possible imprisonment and even torture. When Sam is driven to want to strike Hally, Willy reminds him of the dangers of hitting a white child. One of the central themes of this play explores the results of a system that rewards one group and punishes another solely on the basis of skin color or ethnic culture.

The Playwright.

Athol Harold Lanigan Fugard (known in his youth as "Hally") was born in Port Elizabeth, South Africa, the son of an Afrikaner mother and a father of British descent. At the age of three, he moved with his family to Port Elizabeth, an industrial city on the Indian Ocean where he was to live off and on for most of his life and where many of his plays are set. His work in the theatre has been controversial over the years as he managed to keep together a racially mixed acting company despite South African apartheid laws. Many of his plays, including *Master Harold* were banned in South Africa and were performed elsewhere (frequently in New York). All of his plays deal with the politics of apartheid, yet he is not considered a political writer except in South Africa. His plays always focus on the tiny miracles, disasters, and triumphs of the ordinary individual and he has continued this work into the present as he now writes plays about post-apartheid South Africa.

Antigone

by Sophocles
Adapted by Annie McGregor

Characters

ANTIGONE: daughter of Oedipus and Jocasta

ISMENE: her sister

THE CHORUS OF THEBAN ELDERS

CREON: newly crowned King of Thebes, brother of Jocasta

HAIMON: his son, fiancé to Antigone

EURYDICE: his wife

TEIRESIAS: the blind prophetl

A GUARD

MESSENGER

Setting: The steps before the palace of Thebes

Time: The day after the battle between the Arigive army and Thebes

PROLOGUE

Scene: A private space near the palace of Creon, King of Thebes

ANTIGONE: Ismene, my sister, in our lifetime haven't we suffered enough for the curse on Oedipus, our father? There is nothing—no pain, nor dishonor—that we have not suffered. And now what is this new edict that they say Creon has just declared? Have you heard of it?

ISMENE: Antigone, our friends have brought no news since we lost both our brothers in a single day. Since the Argive army fled during the night, I have heard nothing.

ANTIGONE: That's as I thought, and so I asked you to come here with me, that we might speak alone.

ISMENE: About what? Clearly, you are troubled by some dark news.

ANTIGONE: Sister, Creon has buried our brother Eteocles with full ceremony and honors, ensuring his place among the dead below. As for our poor Polyneices, however, he has ordered that no one shall bury him or mourn him, but instead leave him lying in a field, a feast for scavenging birds. Such is the law that Creon has laid down for us. They say he is coming here to announce his decision publicly, and that the penalty for defiance is death by public stoning. So, now you can reveal your true nature—whether you are a true daughter of nobility or the corrupt offspring of a fallen house.

ISMENE: Antigone, if this is the law, what can I do?

ANTIGONE: Decide if you will help me or not.

ISMENE: Help you what? What are you going to do?

ANTIGONE: Will you help me lay his corpse to rest?

ISMENE: But Creon has forbid it—how can you bury him?

ANTIGONE: He is still our brother, though you would deny him. I will not betray him now.

ISMENE: How can you when Creon has forbidden it?

ANTIGONE: He cannot stop me. He has no right.

ISMENE: God, no! Think how our father died, scorned and hated. He discovered himself to be guilty of crimes and so stabbed both his eyes with his own hands; then Jocasta, both his mother and his wife, destroyed herself with a twisted noose. Finally, our two brothers in a single day, each shedding the cherished blood of his kinsman, became each other's destroyer. Now, we have been left all alone—if we defy the lawful king's commands, how horribly we will perish! No, we are only women and cannot win in battle against men. Besides which we have no right to defy the strong who have taken control of the city in this time of trouble. I would rather beg forgiveness of the dead, since they will know I had no choice. I will follow Creon's commands, because anything else would be senseless.

ANTIGONE: I did not come here to coerce you—and now, even if you wanted to help me, I would not let you. No, you must live with yourself. I will bury him—I won't mind dying for it because I'll be welcomed by him among the dead, knowing I have loved him. I will be a much longer time among the dead than among the living, for death is eternal and life is fleeting. You prefer to honor the living and ignore the commandments of the gods.

ISMENE: I have no wish to dishonor them but I'm not strong enough to defy the law.

ANTIGONE: Let that be your story to the gods. I will now go and bury the brother that I loved.

ISMENE: My beloved sister, you make me so afraid for you.

ANTIGONE: Be afraid for yourself, not me.

ISMENE: Then please promise you will not tell anyone, and I swear I won't either.

ANTIGONE: Your danger is as great as mine if you conceal it. Go on! Tell the world!

ISMENE: Your heart appears to know no fear…you seem thrilled by the risk!

ANTIGONE: I know that I please those I most want to please.

ISMENE: Yes, if you can. But what you wish is impossible.

ANTIGONE: As long as I have strength to try, I must.

ISMENE: But why attempt the impossible?

ANTIGONE: Do you want to be hated by me, your sister, and by the dead? Well, let me be. I will do this foolish thing and suffer the consequences. If I die, I will at least die with honor.

ISMENE: Go, then, if you must. I only know one thing, ever have you served your loved ones faithfully.

[Exit ANTIGONE on the spectators' left. ISMENE exits into the palace.]

[Enter the Chorus of Theban Elders]

PARADOS

CHORUS: The long shaft of the sun shines forth at last,
Reveals the force from Argos driven back
Upon the road to home, with horses loosed
In headlong flight unchecked by masters' hands.

Led by Polyneices, rival for the throne of Thebes,
The Argive army wheeled and screamed
Like an eagle with bloody claws and wide-spread wings,
Before our fortress gates and cried for vengeance.

But we Thebans did not surrender, though the enemy
Stood fierce before us. And before the towers of our city fell
He turned away and ran. Too fierce the clash of battle rang,
The bird of prey turned back.

For Zeus detests the presumptuous heart, the pride-full heart.
And when He saw the swollen army, arrogant and haughty,
With arms of gleaming gold, He chose the first who shouted victory
And smashed him to the earth with a mighty lightning bolt.

Cloaked in fired he fell to the earth,
And he who was first to rage against us fell silent in the dust.

Among the Argives fell the hard doom of Ares,
As War unleashed its frenzy in their midst.

Seven enemy captains stood before seven gates of Thebes,
Then dropped their arms and turned away
In tribute to Zeus, champion of our cause.

All except one pair, born of one mother and one father,
Sharing one cruel fate,
Who crossed swords against each other,
And now share victory and death.

Now that glorious Victory has smiled on us
We can forget the war and dance
All night in every temple,
Let earth-shaking Dionysius' rule in Thebes.

EPISODE 1

CHORUS: Ah, now Creon, our new crowned king,
Chosen by Fortune, approaches in haste.
What new policy will he declare,
Calling this council of elders to hear?

[Enter CREON, with two attendants.]

CREON: My friends! I have the honor to tell you that our Ship of State, after passing through a fearful storm, has once more found safe harbor by the gods. I have summoned you here because I knew how constant was your loyalty to Laius²; how, again, you were reverent, when Oedipus was guiding our city; and lastly, how, when he was dead, you still maintained loyal thoughts towards his children. Well, now they are dead and I claim the power and the throne by right of succession. It is impossible to know any man's character until he has exercised his authority. I have always believed that the man in power who does not speak out for the good of the state is a coward and a traitor. Equally, I could not put my friend before my country. Zeus, be my witness, I would not be silent if I saw ruin, instead of safety, marching upon the citizens. Nor would I ever make a man who is hostile to my country a friend, because I know this: our country is the ship that bears us safe, and that only when we sail her on a straight course can we thrive. Such are the rules by which I will guide this city and they are the reason I have made the following decision concerning the sons of Oedipus: Eteocles, who died as a man should, defending his city, shall be buried with every honor due to the noblest of the dead. But his brother, Polyneices, who returned from exile with fire and sword against the city of his fathers and his race's gods, and to kill his kindred and sell the rest into slavery—I proclaim to the city that no one shall bury him, but he will remain a sight of shame, carrion for birds and scavenging dogs to find. This is my will, and as long as I am king, no traitor will be honored with the

loyal man. But whoever has good will to Thebes, he shall be honored by me in death as in life.

CHORUS: That is your will, Creon, towards this city's enemy and its friend. And the power is yours, I believe, to make use of every law whatsoever, both concerning the dead and all us who live.

CREON: That is my will. Be sure you do your part.

CHORUS: We are old men; give this heavy task to the young.

CREON: That is not what I meant—sentries have been appointed.

CHORUS: Then what do you mean?

CREON: That you will not support any who defy my commands.

CHORUS: Only a fool is in love with death.

CREON: Yes, death is the price for disobedience, but money has been known to corrupt even the wisest.

[Enter GUARD.]

GUARD: My king, I will not say that I am breathless from running, because every time I stopped and thought about what I was doing, I wanted to turn back. A voice inside me kept saying, "Fool, why do you run straight into trouble and punishment." But then another voice said, "Idiot, are you dallying again? If Creon learns it from another, you'll be punished for that, too." So debating, I made my way here—to you. Even if my report brings no good, still will I tell you, since I come with a good grip on one hope, that I can suffer nothing except what is my fate.

CREON: What is it that so frightens you?

GUARD: I did not do the deed, nor did I see it done. You must not punish me for another's wrong-doing.

CREON: An interesting defense, but perhaps more effective if I knew its purpose. It is clear that you have some serious news to tell.

GUARD: That I do, but I don't know how to tell you.

CREON: Tell me!

GUARD: Yes, well—the corpse—some one has just given it burial and disappeared after sprinkling thirsty dust on the stinking flesh.

CREON: *[with deadly control]* What? What man dared do this?

GUARD: I swear, I don't know! For there was no scar to be seen in the dry earth, the ground was hard and unbroken, no wheel tracks in the dust, no trace of anyone. When the sentry showed it to us, a discomforting amazement fell on us all. The dead man was veiled from us—not shut within a tomb, but a light cover of dust was on him, just enough for the ghost's peace. No beast of prey or any dog had approached or torn him. And then what a scene there was! Guard accusing guard! We were ready to take red-hot iron in our hands, to walk through fire and to swear oaths by the gods. "It was not I! I don't know who it was but it was not I!" At last, someone said a thing that silenced us and made us all stare at the ground. He reminded us that the deed must be reported to you and not hidden. And one of us had to do it! So we threw the dice and it was my miserable luck to win this prize. So here I am, as unwelcome to you as I am unwilling, for no one likes the bearer of bad news.

CHORUS: My king, is it possible this deed is somehow the work of the gods?

CREON: Stop! Your words fill me with rage. Can you doddering old fools claim that the gods have concern for that corpse? Why? How had he served them? Or do you see the gods honoring the wicked? It cannot be. No! From the very beginning certain men of the city were whispering against me, scheming and planning anarchy. Those men, I am certain, have bribed my guard to do this deed. But all they have accomplished is certain punishment. I swear by God, if you do not find the man that made this burial, mere death shall not suffice for you! You'll be hung up alive, and tortured until you reveal your employer.

GUARD: Will you allow me to speak?

CREON: Even your voice sickens me.

GUARD: Is that because of my voice or your conscience?

CREON: And would you define the seat of my pain?

GUARD: It is not my words that hurt you, but what has been done.

CREON: God! You talk too much.

GUARD: Perhaps, but I've done nothing wrong.

CREON: Talk all you like. But, if you fail to bring me the perpetrator of these crimes, you will learn that money basely earned wreaks sorrows.

[Exit CREON.]

GUARD: I'd like nothing better than to bring you the guilty man. But, whether he be caught or not—for fortune must decide that—you've seen the last of me! Saved just now beyond hope and belief, I owe the gods great thanks.

ODE 1

CHORUS: Of all the wonders of the world, none is more wonderful than man.
  Even when sea surges white before the gales of the
      south-wind,
  It must yield before his ships. Earth, too, the eldest of the
      gods,
  Gives way to the furrows of plows woven to and fro year
      after year.

  Speech and thought fast as the wind he fashions to his use.
  His skills deflect the arrows of snow and the spears of the
      storming rain.
  He has made himself secure—from all but one.
  From Death alone he can fashion no escape.

  Possessing resourceful skill, a subtlety beyond expectation
  He moves now to evil, now to good. When he honors the
      law
  His city prospers. But what of his city when the law is
      broken?

Never may he share my home, never think my thoughts,
      any man who breaks the law!

EPISODE 2

[Enter the Guard, leading in Antigone.]

CHORUS: What mystery sent by the gods is this?—I know her! How can I deny that this girl is Antigone? O unhappy child! What can this mean? Why should she be captured?

GUARD: Here she is the one who did the deed. We caught her in the very act of burying him. Where is Creon?

[Enter CREON from the palace.]

CREON: What is it? What has happened?

GUARD: My king, a man should never be too sure of anything. I would have sworn that I would never come here again, because you frightened me with your threats. But since the mystery has been so quickly solved, I am back, bringing this girl who was caught giving burial honors to the dead. This time there was no casting of lots. No, this piece of luck has fallen to me, and me alone. And now, my king, take her, question her, and convict her. I am through with the whole business now.

CREON: But this is Antigone! Why have you brought her to me?

GUARD: She was burying the man.

CREON: Are you sure about what you are saying?

GUARD: I am. I saw her burying the corpse with my own eyes. Is that plain and sufficient?

CREON: But how? The details, quickly!

GUARD: It happened like this. When we had come to the place with those fierce threats of yours still in our ears, we swept away all the dust that covered the corpse and bared the damp body well. We then sat down on a hill to windward, to escape the smell of him. No napping this time! We kept each other awake. So time passed, until the disk of the sun stood bright in mid-sky and the heat began to burn. And then suddenly a whirlwind lifted from the earth a storm of dust, and it filled the plain. We closed our eyes, and endured it. When this storm had passed, the girl was seen, and she wailed aloud with the sharp cry of a grieving bird when she saw the corpse bare. Immediately she took dust in her hands, and from a pitcher of beaten bronze she poured wine three times. We rushed forward and seized her, and she was not afraid. We then charged her with her past and present doings, but she made no denial of anything—at once to my joy and to my pain. For to have escaped from trouble one's self gives the greatest joy, but it hurts to lead a friend to certain death. Yet, as I always say, there is nothing more comfortable than your own safe skin!

CREON: You, Antigone, with your face bent to the ground, do you confess this thing?

ANTIGONE: I do.

CREON: *[To the* GUARD.*]* You can go wherever you please.
[Exit GUARD.*]*
[To ANTIGONE.*]* You, however, tell me—briefly—did you know that an edict had forbidden this?

ANTIGONE: I knew it. How could I not? It was public.

CREON: And yet you dared defy that law?

ANTIGONE: Yes, since it was not God's edict. The final Justice, dwelling below, makes no such law. Nor did I think that your will was strong enough to override the unwritten statutes given us by the gods. For they are eternal. I must die, that I knew well. How could I not? That is true even without your edicts. But if I am to die before my time, that is no hardship. When anyone lives as I do, surrounded by evils, Death seems like a friend. So for me to meet this doom is a grief of no account. But if I had let my brother lie unburied and dishonored, that would have grieved me. You smile at me. Ah, Creon, think me a fool if you like. It may be that it is a fool who accuses me of folly.

CHORUS: She shows herself the wild offspring of a wild father, and does not know how to yield.

CREON: It is the toughest iron that breaks first. And the inflexible heart breaks first. A slave has no use for pride. This girl is twice guilty: first, when she defied the law. And second, that she glories in it. Who is the man, then, if crime brings no penalty. Her or me? My sister's child, or nearer to me in blood than that, she and her sister will not escape. Go! Call Ismene! I charge her with an equal guilt. I saw her weeping inside just now.

ANTIGONE: Creon, what more do you want than my death?

CREON: Nothing. That is all I want.

ANTIGONE: Why then do you wait? I beg you: kill me. Your talk is a great weariness to me. As mine must be to you. And yet, how could I have won a nobler glory than by giving burial to my own brother? These men would praise me, if fear did not grip their tongues. But tyranny has the power to do and say whatever it pleases.

CREON: You alone see it that way.

ANTIGONE: They do, too, but for you they hold their tongues.

CREON: You are ashamed that your beliefs differ from theirs.

ANTIGONE: No, there is nothing shameful in respecting the dead.

CREON: Wasn't Eteocles your brother too, who died in the opposite cause?

ANTIGONE: Yes, my brother.

CREON: Why, then, do you dishonor him?

ANTIGONE: The dead man would not perceive an insult.

CREON: Yes, he will, if you honor him equally with the other one.

ANTIGONE: It was his brother, traitor or not, who died.

CREON: But Polyneices died ravaging this land, while Eteocles fell in its defense.

ANTIGONE: We must honor the dead, nevertheless.

CREON: But the good man deserves more than the wicked.

ANTIGONE: Who knows what the gods hold wicked?

CREON: You do not love someone you have hated, not even after death.

ANTIGONE: It is not my nature to join in hate, but in love.

CREON: Then, love them if you must—in hell! While I live, no woman will rule me.
[Enter ISMENE *from the house, led in by two attendants.]*

CHORUS: Look, here comes Ismene, shedding the tears of a loving sister.

CREON: You, Ismene, a viper in my own house—tell me now, will you also confess your share in this burial?

ISMENE: Yes, I share the burden of guilt, if she will let me.

ANTIGONE: No, since you were not willing to help me, I give you no part in it.

ISMENE: I wish to sail this sea of suffering at your side.

ANTIGONE: Hades[3] and the dead know who did this. A friend in words is not a friend I love.

ISMENE: No, sister, let me die with you and show honor to the dead.

ANTIGONE: Do not share my death. Mine will suffice.

ISMENE: And how can I live without you?

ANTIGONE: Ask Creon.

ISMENE: Tell me, how can I help you?

ANTIGONE: Save yourself. I do not envy you. Your choice was to live, it was mine to die.

ISMENE: But I am equally guilty!

ANTIGONE: Take heart! You live. My life has long been in Death's hands.

CREON: Gentlemen, observe! One of these maidens has just revealed her foolishness; the other has displayed it from the moment of her birth.

ISMENE: Yes, Creon. Grief teaches the strongest mind to waver.

CREON: Yours did, I know, when you sided with the guilty.

ISMENE: What life would there be for me alone?

CREON: She is already dead.

ISMENE: You will kill your own son's bride?

CREON: Why not? There are other fields for him to plow.

ANTIGONE: Haemon, dearest! How your father wrongs you!

CREON: Enough! Enough of you and of your marriage!

CHORUS: Will you really cheat your son of his bride?

CREON: Death will end these nuptials for me.

CHORUS: Then she will die?

CREON: Yes! No more delay! Take them inside! Guard them well, for they are only women and even a brave man will flee when Death closes in.
[Exeunt ATTENDANTS, *guarding* ANTIGONE *and* ISMENE. CREON *remains.]*

ODE 2

CHORUS: Blest are those whose days have not tasted of evil.
For when a house has once been shaken by the gods,
Its ruin is forever: damnation rising behind each child,
Like a wave cresting out of the deep darkness of the sea.

I have seen the ancient sorrows of the house of Labdicus[4].
Suffering heaped upon the sorrows of the dead, generation
to generation.
And now darkness spreads in the last roots of the house of
Oedipus
Turning hope into the blood-stained dust of the gods
infernal.
What human arrogance transcends the wrath of Zeus?
Yours is power that neither Sleep, nor untiring Time can
defeat.
Unaged through time, you rule through the future, both
near and distant,
As through the past. Your law prevails: no pride comes to
mortals without ruin.

The wandering dreams of men bring ghosts of joy and
glory,
But as they drowse the waking embers burn them.
For ancient wisdom tells us:
Fate works most for woe
When evil's face is lovely.

EPISODE 3

[Enter **HAEMON**.*]*

CHORUS: But here is Haemon, the last of your offspring. Does he come grieving for Antigone, his promised bride?

CREON: We will soon know better than seers could tell us.— My son, do you come in rage against your father, having heard my judgement on that girl? Or do I have your love and loyalty, act how I may?

HAEMON: Father, I am yours, and you are my guide. No marriage is more important than your continuing wisdom.

CREON: Good, my son, this is the spirit you should maintain in your heart—to stand behind your father's will in all things. This is what men pray for: children who are obedient. Oh, the misery of a man who raises ungrateful sons. Then, my son, do not lose your head over this evil woman. The pleasures of her bed would soon grown cold. No, spit her out as if she were an enemy, let her go find a husband in Hades. She has shown contempt for the law and for me, and so she will die. If I permit my own kin to defy the law, I will show myself weak before the people. For whoever controls his own household will manage his city as well. Whomever the city chooses to govern, that man must be obeyed in matters small and great and in matters just and unjust. For there is no evil worse than disobedience. This destroys cities; this overturns homes; this scatters armies. Good lives are made by discipline. Therefore we must defend those who respect the law, and we cannot let a woman defeat us. It is better to fall from power by a man's hand, rather than be called weaker than women.

CHORUS: Unless time has stolen our wits, what you say seems wise.

HAEMON: Father, reason is God's gift to man, the highest of all things that we call our own. To say that you are wrong is beyond my power and my desire, yet other men, too, might reason wisely. It is my duty to watch on your behalf all that men say, or do. Fear of you forbids the ordinary citizen to speak such words as would offend your ear. But I can hear these murmurs in the dark, how the city moans for this girl, saying: No woman ever merited death less— none ever died so shamefully for deeds so glorious as hers. They say: Does she not deserve honor? Such is the rumor shrouded in darkness that silently spreads. Father, nothing means more to me than your happiness. What more could any child want? Do not, then, think that your word and no other, must be right. Any man who thinks that he alone is wise—such a man may be empty. No, even when a man is wise, he can learn from others. Father, give way and do not cling to your rage. For even from me, a younger man, you may learn good advice.

CHORUS: My king, he is right, that father and son can learn from each other. On both sides there have been wise words.

CREON: Am I then to be taught by the wisdom of a boy?

HAEMON: Not in anything that is not right. But you should look to my thoughts, not to my years.

CREON: Honoring treason is worthy thought?

HAEMON: I would not advise anyone to show respect for treason.

CREON: And did she not commit treason?

HAEMON: The people of this city say no.

CREON: Shall Thebes teach me how to rule?

HAEMON: Now you speak like a child.

CREON: I am the ruler of this city.

HAEMON: No city belongs to one man.

CREON: Does not the city belong to the man in power?

HAEMON: Only if the city is a desert.

CREON: You are fighting on the side of a woman!

HAEMON: Only if you are a woman, my concern is for you.

CREON: You traitor, attacking your father in public!

HAEMON: Because I see you making a mistake and committing injustice.

CREON: Am I making a mistake when I respect my own authority?

HAEMON: Yes. You do not have the authority to trample on the rights of God.

CREON: Fool! Taken in by a shameless woman!

HAEMON: You will never see me plead for anything wrong.

CREON: You do. Your every word pleads her case.

HAEMON: And yours, and mine, and God's.

CREON: You can never marry her, not while she is still alive.

HAEMON: Then she will die, and in death destroy another.

CREON: What! Is that a threat?

HAEMON: If you were not my father, I'd say you are insane.

CREON: You woman's slave!

HAEMON: I am sorry. You prefer mute obedience.

CREON: Is that so? I swear by all the gods, you will watch her die. Bring out that hated thing, so that she may die right now!

HAEMON: No, she will not die here—do not even imagine it. Nor shall you ever set eyes on my face again. Indulge in your madness now with your friends who can endure it.

[*Exit* HAEMON.]

CHORUS: Your son is gone, King Creon, in anger and haste. A man in a rage is dangerous.

CREON: Let him do or dream to do something more immense than befits a man. He will not save these two girls from death.

CHORUS: Then you really intend to kill them both?

CREON: Not the one who is innocent. You are right.

CHORUS: And the other?

CREON: I will take her into the wilderness and entomb her alive in a rocky vault. She will have food to absolve the city of her death. Perhaps, praying to the gods of Hell, she will obtain immunity from death, or else will learn, at last, that pity shown to the dead is pity wasted.

[*Exit* CREON.]

ODE 3

CHORUS: Love, the unconquerable,
   Love, destroyer of the rich,
   Warm light in the soft face of a girl,
   Sea wanderer, forest visitor,
   Even immortals can not escape you,
   He who has known you is driven to madness.

You seize the minds of just men and drag them to their
      ruin.
   You have made this bright anger between father and son.
   And victory belongs to You shining in the eyes of the
      sweet-bedded bride.
   For in all this divine Aphrodite[5] plays her irresistible game.

EPISODE 4

[*Enter* ANTIGONE *under guard from the palace.*]

CHORUS: But now, I am carried beyond the bounds of loyalty. I can hold back my tears no longer. Here Antigone passes to that chamber where all sleep at last.

ANTIGONE: Look upon me, friends, and pity me seeing my last moment of sunlight. Now, Death who lays all to rest leads me living to Acheron's[6] shore. No bridesong there, nor any music.

CHORUS: In glory and honor you depart to that deep place of the dead, neither struck by wasting sickness, nor having

won the wages of the sword. No woman has ever found your way to death.

ANTIGONE: What of Niobe[7], daughter of Tantalus, encased in stone for all eternity?

CHORUS: But she was the daughter of a god and you are the child of mortals. If her death is like yours, won't that mean glory for you in this world and the world beyond?

ANTIGONE: Ah, you mock me! Can't you wait to abuse me until after I have gone? Oh, gods, witness my fate, doomed without pity, without justice. Send a thought of love to her whose path turns to the underworld, where there are no more human tears.

CHORUS: You have rushed headlong to the far limits of daring, and against the high throne of Justice you have fallen. But in this ordeal you are paying for the crimes of your fathers.

ANTIGONE: You have touched on my most bitter thought. My father's mother as his cursed bride. The doom ordained for us, the famed house of Labdacus. What parents gave me my miserable life! It is to them that I go like this, accursed and unwed, to share their home.

CHORUS: Your reverence for the dead is a virtue, but the city is strong by the rule of law. Your willful disposition is what has destroyed you.

ANTIGONE: Without love, with no one to lament my passing, let me begin this journey of no return. Lead me now to my vigil, locked away from the light of the sun and the warmth of friends.

[*Enter* CREON.]

CREON: Enough! Dirges and wailing would never be given up, if they could put off death. Take her away—now! Put her in the vault and leave her there. She can decide whether to live or die. We wash our hands of this girl.

ANTIGONE: Tomb and bridal chamber in eternal stone. I will meet my family among the dead. Last of them all and in by far the most shameful circumstances, I will descend, even before the fated term of my life is spent. But I cherish strong hopes that I will arrive welcome to my father, mother, and dear brothers. For, when each of you died, with my own hands I washed and dressed you and poured drink-offerings at your graves. But now, Polyneices, it is for tending your corpse that I die. And yet I did no wrong. I have not sinned before God. What law of the gods have I transgressed? Well, then, if Creon's judgment pleases the gods, once I have suffered my doom I will come to know my guilt. But if the guilt lies with my judge, may his punishment equal my own.

CHORUS: Oh, passionate heart. Still gripped by the same tempest of the soul.

CREON: Her guards will have reason to regret their slowness.

ANTIGONE: Ah, no! That voice sounds like the voice of death.

CREON: It's true. I will not console you with any hope of reprieve.

ANTIGONE: O city of Thebes, and you my father's gods. The time is come. Look at me, the last unhappy daughter of a line of kings. See what I suffer, and at whose hands,

because I obeyed the laws of heaven. *[to the guards]* Come, take me away. Let's delay no longer.
*[*ANTIGONE *is led away by the guards.]*

ODE 4

CHORUS: So too endured Danae[8] in her beauty,
In that chamber, both burial and bridal,
she was held in strict confinement.
Yet was she of a line of kings, my daughter,
Zeus poured his love upon her in a rain of gold.
Oh, dreadful is the mysterious power of fate,
No power in wealth or war prevails against it.

So, too, Dryas' son[9], the Edonian king,
Tamed by the will of Dionysus, shut in a rocky prison.
He came to know the danger of mocking the gods.
He tried to prevent the piety of women, profaning their
    sacred revels.
His madness died among the echoes of his stone tomb.

EPISODE 5

[Enter TEIRESIAS, *led by a boy. In his opening speeches,* TEIRESIAS *speaks in a rhythmic chant.]*

TEIRESIAS: Princes of Thebes, we have come on a shared journey
Two scouting the way by the eyes of one.
For this is the way the blind man comes.

CREON: What is it, old Teiresias? What is your news?

TEIRESIAS: I will tell you. Obey the prophet, Creon.

CREON: It has not been my habit to stand apart from your will.

TEIRESIAS: Then you captain this city wisely and well.

CREON: I have benefited from your wisdom. What do you want to tell me?

TEIRESIAS: Creon, you stand poised on fortune's razor-edge.

CREON: What do you mean? I shudder to hear you!

TEIRESIAS: Then listen, Creon. You are the source of the sickness now afflicting the city. For the altars of our city and our hearths have one and all been tainted by birds and dogs with the carrion taken from the corpse of Oedipus' son. The gods are deaf to prayer and sacrifice. Think, therefore, on these things, my son. All men make mistakes. But the wise man sees the errors of his ways and corrects those mistakes: Pride is the only crime. Concede the claim of the dead man. Do not fight with a corpse! What honor is there in killing the dead all over again? Think carefully, I beg you. The sweetest thing is to learn from a good advisor when his advice is to your profit.

CREON: All my life I have been the special target of prophets. They have shot their dull arrows at me again and again. No, Teiresias! Even if the eagles of Zeus carry him piece by piece to heaven, you shall not cover that man with a grave. It is a shameful thing, Teiresias, for the wise man to sell his soul for profit's sake.

TEIRESIAS: Ah Creon! Does any man know, does any consider—

CREON: What? Some universal truth?

TEIRESIAS: Does no man remember that wisdom outweighs any wealth?

CREON: Just as bribed prophecy outweighs any baseness!

TEIRESIAS: Creon, you are sick almost to death!

CREON: I have no desire to trade insults with the prophet.

TEIRESIAS: Yet you say that I am a false prophet.

CREON: Yes, for the generations of prophets were ever fond of gold.

TEIRESIAS: And generations of tyrants love shameful gain.

CREON: Be careful, old man! You are speaking to your king!

TEIRESIAS: I am aware of that. You are king because of me.

CREON: You are a wise seer, but false in this prophecy.

TEIRESIAS: You will drive me to utter the dire secret in my soul.

CREON: Say it! But remember, I will not pay you for it!

TEIRESIAS: If I speak, the cost will be too high for you.

CREON: No doubt. Speak! But know this: I will not change my mind.

TEIRESIAS: Then know this, yes, and know it well! You will not live through many more days before you will give in return one of your own flesh, corpse for corpse. For you have thrust a child of this world into living hell, kept from the gods below a child of their hearts. One in a grave before her death, the other a corpse unburied, unmourned, unholy. For these crimes the avenging destroyers, the Furies of Hades and of the gods, are waiting for you to seize you in terrible sufferings. Do you think my words worth buying now, Creon? A few short days and in your house will be heard the wailing of men and of women. And curses from far cities are flung at you, for their unburied whose mangled corpses, unburied before the walls of Thebes carry their stench to heaven. There, now, are arrows for your heart, since you provoke me. Boy, lead me home, so that he may waste his rage against younger men, and learn to keep a quieter tongue in a wiser head.

[Exit TEIRESIAS.*]*

CHORUS: He is gone, my king, leaving dire prophecies behind. I am old now, and in all my long life I have never known him to be wrong.

CREON: I know this and my mind is troubled. To yield is terrible, but, to resist—this, too, inspires terror.

CHORUS: Creon, you must choose wisely.

CREON: What should I do?

CHORUS: Quickly, let the girl go free. Then raise a tomb for the unburied dead.

CREON: You think that I should yield?

CHORUS: Yes, Creon, and with all possible speed. The gods strike swiftly at the follies of men.

CREON: Ah, it is difficult, but I will obey. We must not wage war with destiny.

CHORUS: Go, do this yourself and do not leave it to others.

CREON: I will go. Go, go, my servants, brings axes, and hurry to the tomb. I will be there to set her free, as I myself confined her. Quickly! I am suddenly full of fear that it is best to honor the gods to life's very end.

PÆAN (HYMN OF PRAISE)

CHORUS: God of many names, Guardian of the West,
God of many names, the Flame of torches,
God of many names, the shadow of plague is upon us.

Come down to us with mercy,
Down the slopes from mighty Olympus,
Across the lamenting waters.
Oh, God of many names, purest voice of the night,
Singer among the throbbing stars,
Come to us in rapture and pity!
Blaze for us, our God of many names.

EXODOS

[Enter MESSENGER*]*

MESSENGER: Men of the house of Cadmus[10], citizens of Thebes, there is no condition of human life that I would ever say is fixed, as "This is good" or "This is bad." Fate raises up and fate casts down from day to day, and no man can predict his Fate. Creon was once blessed: he saved this land from its enemies and won total dominion in the land. He flourished in his noble crop of children. And now all this has been lost. When a man has lost everything, I do not call his continued existence life, but see him as a walking dead man. Get rich if you wish! Live like a tyrant king! But without joy it's worth no more than the shadow of smoke.

CHORUS: What news of sorrow have you come to report?

MESSENGER: They are dead, and the living are guilty of their deaths.

CHORUS: Who is dead? Who is guilty? Tell us!

MESSENGER: Haemon is dead—killed by his own hand.

CHORUS: Ah, Teiresias, you have proven your word!

MESSENGER: That is my news. You must judge its meaning for yourselves.

CHORUS: Wait, I see our unhappy Queen, Eurydice. Did she hear our words?

[Enter EURYDICE.*]*

EURYDICE: My people, I heard your words as I was on my way to prayers. As I was opening the gates of the temple, the sound of a blow to our house struck my ear. In terror I fainted into the arms of my handmaidens. But repeat your news. Whatever it was I can bear it, for I am no stranger to sorrow.

MESSENGER: Dearest Lady, I will tell what I saw and not try to comfort you with soft words. For what good would it do? The truth is always best. I went with Creon to the outer plain where the body of Polyneices still lay. After we had prayed to the gods to restrain their anger in mercy, we washed him with holy water, and with fresh boughs we burned what remains there were. Finally we built a tomb of his native earth. Then we hurried to Antigone's stone vault. From a distance, a servant who had run ahead heard a voice raised in grief and came to tell our master Creon. And as the King moved closer and closer, the air full of wailing, he groaned in bitter lament, "Am I the prophet of evil? Must I walk this path of grief? My son's voice greets me." "Go," he said to us, "hurry closer, and look through the opening where the stones of the mound have been torn away. See if it is Haemon's voice that I recognize, or if I am deceived by the gods."

We ran to do our master's bidding and in the furthest part of the tomb we saw her hanging by the neck, the rope made of her linen veil. And Haemon embraced her around her waist, crying out at the loss of his bride, and for his father's deeds. When Creon saw him, he cried aloud to his son, "Ah, unhappy boy, what have you done! What plan have you seized on that makes your eyes so terrible?" But the boy glared at him with savage eyes, spat in his face, and without a word drew his sword and lunged at his father. He missed his aim and enraged with himself he drove the sword into his own side. As he died, he clasped the maiden in his faint embrace, bright red blood spilled on her pale cheek. Corpse embracing corpse, they lie together married at last in the houses of the Dead.

*[*EURYDICE *departs into the house.]*

CHORUS: What can this mean? The lady has gone without a word.

MESSENGER: I, too, am troubled by this. But perhaps she only thinks it unworthy to grieve in public, and returns home to weep in private for the loss of her son.

CHORUS: Perhaps. But still I fear her deep silence.

MESSENGER: I will find out what she's doing. I will go in, since you are right—this silence may mean more trouble.

[Exit MESSENGER.*]*

[Enter CREON, *attended and carrying the shrouded body of* HAEMON.*]*

CHORUS: Look, here is the King himself approaching, his own damnation in his hands.

CREON: Nothing you say can touch me any more. My own blind heart has brought me from darkness to final darkness. I the murdering father, here the murdered son! All of this caused by my unyielding pride. Haemon, my son, youngest and last of my sons! O God! You have died for my foolishness, not your own!

CHORUS: You are late in seeing the truth.

CREON: Dear God, I have learned a bitter lesson. Too late! And God struck me a crushing blow, and drove me into savage suffering, my last joy trampled. Oh, the pain I worked so hard to earn!

[Enter the MESSENGER *from the house.]*

MESSENGER: My King, you carry a dark and heavy burden. But more is waiting inside your house.

CREON: What more can happen to me?

MESSENGER: Your wife, Creon, is dead.

CREON: O hand of Death, have you no pity for me? What did you say? You have killed a man already dead! What are you saying, boy? Can it be true? God no!—my wife's doom? Death heaped upon death?

[The doors of the palace are opened, and the corpse of EURYDICE *is disclosed.]*

CHORUS: There you can see for yourself.

CREON: Ah, misery! It's true, all true! What destiny can still await me? I have my dead son in my arms, and now my wife? His tormented mother—oh, it's more than I can bear!

MESSENGER: Standing by the altar, she struck herself with a fatal blow. She cried out at the deaths of Megareus[11] and Haimon, her sons both dead. Then, with her last breath, she cursed their father, the slayer of her sons.

CREON: No! I am sick with fear. Will no one end my miserable life with one fatal blow?

MESSENGER: She has cursed you for both this son's death, and the other's.

CREON: Ah, God, she was right to do it. It was I, yes, I, who killed them both. I admit the truth. Lead me inside, my friends. I am already among the dead.

CHORUS: Your words are right, if lessons can be learned by suffering. The quickest way is best in a world of sorrow.

CREON: Let it come, let death appear that brings my final day! Oh, that I would not see tomorrow's light!

CHORUS: That will come in its own time. We must see to the present. The future lies in the hands of the gods.

CREON: All that I desire was in that prayer.

CHORUS: Then pray no more; the gods are deaf.

CREON: Take me away, I beg you! I have murdered my son and my wife—I have been a fool! I know not where to turn. I look for comfort and all my comfort is here, dead before me! Everything I have touched has turned to dust. The gods have crushed me for my arrogance.

[As CREON *is being conducted into the house, the* CHORUS LEADER *speaks the closing verses.]*

CHORUS: There can be no happiness without wisdom,
No wisdom without submission to the gods.
The pride of man is harshly punished
Until, in their suffering, men learn to be wise.

END OF PLAY

Notes:

[1] Dionysius, son of Zeus and god of wine, ecstasy, fertility, and divine madness.

[2] Laius. Former king of Thebes, father of Oedipus.

[3] Hades. The ruler of the underworld (the afterlife), also a name for the underworld itself.

[4] Labdicus. A king of Thebes, father to Laius, grandfather to Oedipus.

[5] Aphrodite. Goddess of love and beauty.

[6] Acheron. The river of woe, one of several rivers in the underworld.

[7] Niobe. A former Queen of Thebes who declared herself the equal of the gods and was punished through the death of her husband and all fourteen of her children. In her grief, she turned to stone, lifeless except for her weeping. "On a mountaintop she weeps but never moves, and even now her tears roll down from the marble statue that was Niobe." (Ovid, Metamorphoses VI)

[8] Danae. Danae's father, King Acrisius of Argos, had been warned that he would be killed eventually by a son born to Danae so he locked Danae in a tower.

[9] Lycurgus. A king of Edon, he attempted to expel Dionysius from his land but was defeated, imprisoned and driven mad by the god until he sliced up his own son thinking he was an ivy plant sacred to Dionysius.

[10] Cadmus. The legendary founder of the city of Thebes.

[11] Megareus. One of Creon's two sons, he fought in the battle against the Argive army and committed suicide in response to a claim by the prophet Tiresias that Thebes would win if one person would voluntarily die to save it.

"Master Harold" . . . and the boys

by Athol Fugard

Characters

HALLY

SAM

WILLIE

Setting

The St. George's Park Tea Room on a wet and windy Port Elizabeth afternoon.

*Tables and chairs have been cleared and are stacked on one side except for one which stands apart with a single chair. On this table a knife, fork, spoon, and side plate in anticipation of a simple meal, together with a pile of comic books. Other elements: a serving counter with a few stale cakes under glass and not a very impressive display of sweets, cigarettes and cool drinks, etc.; a few cardboard advertising hand-outs—Cadbury's Chocolate, Coca-Cola—and a blackboard on which an untrained hand has chalked up the prices of Tea, Coffee, Scones, Milkshakes—all flavors—and Cool Drinks; a few sad ferns in pots; a telephone; an old-style jukebox. There is an entrance on one side and an exit into a kitchen on the other. Leaning on the solitary table, his head cupped in one hand as he pages through one of the comic books, is **SAM**. A black man in his mid-forties. He wears the white coat of a waiter. Behind him on his knees, mopping down the floor with a bucket of water and a rag, is **WILLIE**. Also black and about the same age as **SAM**. He has his sleeves and trousers rolled up. The year: 1950.*

WILLIE *[Singing as he works]*:
> "She was scandalizin' my name,
> She took my money
> She called me honey
> But she was scandalizin' my name.
> Called it love but was playin' a game…"

[He gets up and moves the bucket. Stands thinking for a moment, then, raising his arms to hold an imaginary partner, he launches into an intricate ballroom dance step. Although a mildly comic figure, he reveals a reasonable degree of accomplishment]

Hey, Sam.

[SAM, absorbed in the comic book, does not respond]

Hey, Boet Sam!

[SAM looks up]

I'm getting it. The quickstep. Look now and tell me. *[He repeats the step]* Well?

SAM *[Encouragingly]*: Show me again.

WILLIE: Okay, count for me.

SAM: Ready?

WILLIE: Ready.

SAM: Five, six, seven, eight…*[WILLIE starts to dance]* A-n-d one two three four…and one two three four…. *[Ad libbing as WILLIE dances]* Your shoulders, Willie…your shoulders! Don't look down! Look happy, Willie! Relax, Willie!

WILLIE *[Desperate but still dancing]*: I am relax.

SAM: No, you're not.

WILLIE *[He falters]*: Ag no man, Sam! Mustn't talk. You make me make mistakes.

SAM: But you're too stiff.

WILLIE: Yesterday I'm not straight…today I'm too stiff!

SAM: Well, you are. You asked me and I'm telling you.

WILLIE: Where?

SAM: Everywhere. Try to glide through it.

WILLIE: Glide?

SAM: Ja, make it smooth. And give it more style. It must look like you're enjoying yourself.

WILLIE *[Emphatically]*: I wasn't.

SAM: Exactly.

WILLIE: How can I enjoy myself? Not straight, too stiff and now it's also glide, give it more style, make it smooth…Haai ! Is hard to remember all those things, Boet Sam.

SAM: That's your trouble. You're trying too hard.

WILLIE: I try hard because it is hard.

SAM: But don't let me see it. The secret is to make it look easy. Ballroom must look happy, Willie, not like hard work. It must…Ja!…it must, look like romance.

WILLIE: Now another one! What's romance?

SAM: Love story with happy ending. A handsome man in tails, and in his arms, smiling at him, a beautiful lady in evening dress

WILLIE: Fred Astaire, Ginger Rogers.

SAM: You got it. Tapdance or ballroom, it's the same. Romance. In two weeks' time when the judges look at you and Hilda, they must see a man and a woman who are dancing their way to a happy ending. What I saw was you holding her like you were frightened she was going to run away.

WILLIE: Ja! Because that is what she wants to do! I got no romance left for Hilda anymore, Boet Sam.

SAM: Then pretend. When you put your arms around Hilda, imagine she is Ginger Rogers.

WILLIE: With no teeth? You try.

SAM: Well, just remember, there's only two weeks left.

WILLIE: I know, I know! *[To the jukebox]* I do it better with music. You got sixpence for Sarah Vaughan?

SAM: That's a slow foxtrot. You're practicing the quickstep.

WILLIE: I'll practice slow foxtrot.

SAM *[Shaking his head]*: It's your turn to put money in the jukebox.

WILLIE: I only got bus fare to go home. *[He returns disconsolately to his work]* Love story and happy ending! She's doing it all right, Boet Sam, but is not me she's giving happy endings. Fuckin' whore! Three nights now she doesn't come practice. I wind up gramophone, I get record ready and I sit and wait—What happens? Nothing. Ten o'clock I start dancing with my pillow. You try and practice romance by yourself, Boet Sam. Struesgod, she doesn't come tonight I take back my dress and ballroom shoes and I find me new partner. Size twenty-six. Shoes size seven. And now she's also making trouble for me with the baby again. Reports me to Child Wellfed, that I'm not giving her money. She lies! Every week I am giving her money for milk. And how do I know is my baby? Only his hair looks like me. She's fucking around all the time I turn my back. Hilda Samuels is a bitch! *[Pause]* Hey, Sam!

SAM: Ja.

WILLIE: You listening?

SAM: Ja.

WILLIE: So what you say?

SAM: About Hilda?

WILLIE: Ja.

SAM: When did you last give her a hiding?

WILLIE *[Reluctantly]*: Sunday night.

SAM: And today is Thursday.

WILLIE *[He knows what's coming]*: Okay.

SAM: Hiding on Sunday night, then Monday, Tuesday and Wednesday she doesn't come to practice…and you are asking me why?

WILLIE: I said okay, Boet Sam!

SAM: You hit her too much. One day she's going to leave you for good.

WILLIE: So? She makes me the hell-in too much.

SAM [*Emphasizing his point*]: *Too* much and *too* hard. You had the same trouble with Eunice.

WILLIE: Because she also make the hell-in, Boet Sam. She never got the steps right. Even the waltz.

SAM: Beating her up every time she makes a mistake in the waltz? [*Shaking his head*] No, Willie! That takes the pleasure out of ballroom dancing.

WILLIE: Hilda is not too bad with the waltz, Boet Sam. Is the quickstep where the trouble starts.

SAM [*Teasing him gently*]: How's your pillow with the quickstep?

WILLIE [*Ignoring the tease*]: Good! And why? Because it got no legs. That's her trouble. She can't move them quick enough, Boet Sam. I start the record and before halfway Count Basie is already winning. Only time we catch up with him is when gramophone runs down. [SAM *laughs*] Haaikona, Boet Sam, is not funny.

SAM [*Snapping his fingers*]: I got it! Give her a handicap.

WILLIE: What's that?

SAM: Give her a ten-second start and then let Count Basie go. Then I put my money on her. Hot favorite in the Ballroom Stakes: Hilda Samuels ridden by Willie Malopo.

WILLIE [*Turning away*]: I'm not talking to you no more.

SAM [*Relenting*]: Sorry, Willie...

WILLIE: It's finish between us.

SAM: Okay, okay...I'll stop.

WILLIE: You can also fuck off.

SAM: Willie, listen! I want to help you!

WILLIE: No more jokes?

SAM: I promise.

WILLIE: Okay. Help me.

SAM [*His turn to hold an imaginary partner*]: Look and learn. Feet together. Back straight. Body relaxed. Right hand placed gently in the small of her back and wait for the music. Don't start worrying about making mistakes or the judges or the other competitors. It's just you, Hilda and the music, and you're going to have a good time. What Count Basie do you play?

WILLIE: "You the cream in my coffee, you the salt in my stew."

SAM: Right. Give it to me in strict tempo.

WILLIE: Ready?

SAM: Ready.

WILLIE: A-n-d...[*Singing*] "You the cream in my coffee.
    You the salt in my stew.
    You will always be my necessity.
    I'd be lost without
    you. . . " [*etc.*]

[SAM *launches into the quickstep. He is obviously a much more accomplished dancer than* WILLIE. HALLY *enters. A seventeen-year-old white boy. Wet raincoat and school case. He stops and watches* SAM. *The demonstration comes to an end with a flourish. Applause from* HALLY *and* WILLIE]

HALLY: Bravo! No question about it. First place goes to Mr. Sam Semela.

WILLIE [*In total agreement*]: You was gliding with style, Boet Sam.

HALLY [*Cheerfully*]: How's it, chaps?

SAM: Okay, Hally.

WILLIE [*Springing to attention like a soldier and saluting*]: At your service, Master Harold!

HALLY: Not long to the big event, hey!

SAM: Two weeks.

HALLY: You nervous?

SAM: No.

HALLY: Think you stand a chance?

SAM: Let's just say I'm ready to go out there and dance.

HALLY: It looked like it. What about you, Willie? [WILLIE *groans*] What's the matter?

SAM: He's got leg trouble.

HALLY [*Innocently*]: Oh, sorry to hear that, Willie.

WILLIE: Boet Sam! You promised. [WILLIE *returns to his work*] [HALLY *deposits his school case and takes off his raincoat. His clothes are a little neglected and untidy: black blazer with school badge, gray flannel trousers in need of an ironing, khaki shirt and tie, black shoes.* SAM *has fetched a towel for* HALLY *to dry his hair*]

HALLY: God, what a lousy bloody day. It's coming down cats and dogs out there. Bad for business, chaps... [*Conspiratorial whisper*]...but it also means we're in for a nice quiet afternoon.

SAM: You can speak loud. Your Mom's not here.

HALLY: Out shopping?

SAM: No. The hospital.

HALLY: But it's Thursday. There's no visiting on Thursday afternoons. Is my Dad okay?

SAM: Sounds like it. In fact, I think he's going home.

HALLY [*Stopped short by* SAM's *remark*]: What do you mean?

SAM: The hospital phoned.

HALLY: To say what?

SAM: I don't know. I just heard your Mom talking.

HALLY: So, what makes you say he's going home?

SAM: It sounded as if they were telling her to come and fetch him.

[HALLY *thinks about what* SAM *has said for a few seconds*]

HALLY: When did she leave?

SAM: About an hour ago. She said she would phone you. Want to eat? [HALLY *doesn't respond*] Hally, want your lunch?

HALLY: I suppose so. [*His mood has changed*] What's on the menu?...as if I don't know.

SAM: Soup, followed by meat pie and gravy.

HALLY: Today's

SAM: No.

HALLY: And the soup?

SAM: Nourishing pea soup.

HALLY: Just the soup. [*The pile of comic books on the table*] And these?

SAM: For your Dad. Mr. Kempston brought them.

HALLY: You haven't been reading them, have you?

SAM: Just looking.

HALLY [*Examining the comics*]: Jungle Jim...Batman and Robin...Tarzan...God, what rubbish! Mental pollution. Take them away. [SAM *exits waltzing into the kitchen.* HALLY *turns to* WILLIE]

HALLY: Did you hear my Mom talking on the telephone, Willie?

WILLIE: No, Master Hally. I was at the back.

HALLY: And she didn't say anything to you before she left?

WILLIE: She said I must clean the floors.

HALLY: I mean about my Dad.

WILLIE: She didn't say nothing to me about him, Master Hally.

HALLY [*With conviction*]: No! It can't be. They said he needed at least another three weeks of treatment. Sam's definitely made a mistake. [*Rummages through his school case, finds a book and settles down at the table to read*] So, Willie!

WILLIE: Yes, Master Hally! Schooling okay today?

HALLY: Yes, okay...[*He thinks about it*]
No, not really. Ag, what's the difference? I don't care. And Sam says you've got problems.

WILLIE: Big problems.

HALLY: Which leg is sore? [WILLIE *groans*] Both legs.

WILLIE: There is nothing wrong with my legs. Sam is just making jokes.

HALLY: So then you *will* be in the competition.

WILLIE: Only if I can find me a partner.

HALLY: But what about Hilda?

SAM [*Returning with a bowl of soup*]: She's the one who's got trouble with her legs.

HALLY: What sort of trouble, Willie?

SAM: From the way he describes it, I think the lady has gone a bit lame.

HALLY: Good God! Have you taken her to see a doctor?

SAM: I think a vet would be better.

HALLY: What do you mean?

SAM: What do you call it again when a racehorse goes very fast?

HALLY: Gallop?

SAM: That's it!

WILLIE: Boet Sam!

HALLY: "A gallop down the homestretch to the winning post." But what's that got to do with Hilda?

SAM: Count Basie always gets there first.
[WILLIE *lets fly with has slop rag. It misses* SAM *and hits* HALLY]

HALLY [*Furious*]: For Christ's sake, Willie! What the hell do you think you're doing!

WILLIE: Sorry, Master Hally, but it's him....

HALLY: Act your bloody age! [*Hurls the rags back at* WILLIE] Cut out the nonsense now and get on with your work. And you too, Sam. Stop fooling around.
[SAM *moves away*]
No. Hang on. I haven't finished! Tell me exactly what my Mom said.

SAM: I have. "When Hally comes, tell him I've gone to the hospital and I'll phone him."

HALLY: She didn't say anything about taking my Dad home?

SAM: No. It's just that when she was talking on the phone...

HALLY [*Interrupting him*]: No, Sam. They can't be discharging him. She would have said so if they were. In any case, we saw him last night and he wasn't in good shape at all. Staff, nurse even said there was talk about taking more X-rays. And now suddenly today he's better? If anything, it sounds more like a bad turn to me...which I sincerely hope it isn't. Hang on...how long ago did you say she left?

SAM: Just before two...[*His wrist watch.*]...hour and a half.

HALLY: I know how to settle it. [*Behind the counter to the telephone. Talking as he dials*] Let's give her ten minutes to get to the hospital, ten minutes to load him up, another ten, at the most, to get home and another ten to get him inside. Forty minutes. They should have been home for at least half an hour already. [*Pause—he waits with the receiver to his ear*] No reply, chaps. And you know why? Because she's at his bedside in hospital helping him pull through a bad turn. You definitely heard wrong.

SAM: Okay.
[*As far as* HALLY *is concerned, the matter is settled. He returns to his table, sits down and divides his attention between the book and his soup.* SAM *is at his school case and picks up a textbook* Modern Graded Mathematics for Standards Nine and Ten. *Opens it at random and laughs at something he sees*] Who is this supposed to be?

HALLY: Old fart-face Prentice.

SAM: Teacher?

HALLY: Thinks he is. And believe me, that is not a bad likeness.

SAM: Has he seen it?

HALLY: Yes.

SAM: What did he say?

HALLY: Tried to be clever, as usual. Said I was no Leonardo da Vinci and that bad art had to be punished. So, six of the best, and his are bloody good.

SAM: On your bum?

HALLY: Where else? The days when I got them on my hands are gone forever, Sam.

SAM: With your trousers down!

HALLY: No. He's not quite that barbaric.

SAM: That's the way they do it in jail.

HALLY [*Flicker of morbid interest*]: Really?

SAM: Ja. When the magistrate sentences you to "strokes with a light cane."

HALLY: Go on.

SAM: They make you lie down on a bench. One policeman pulls down your trousers and holds your ankles, another one pulls your shirt over your head and holds your arms...

HALLY: Thank you! That's enough.

SAM: ...and the one that gives you the strokes talks to you gently and for a long time between each one. [*He laughs*]

HALLY: I've heard enough, Sam! Jesus! It's a bloody awful world when you come to think of it. People can be real bastards.

SAM: That's the way it is, Hally.

HALLY: It doesn't *have* to be that way. There is something called progress, you know. We don't exactly burn people at the stake anymore.

SAM: Like Joan of Arc…

HALLY: Correct. If she was captured today, she'd be given a fair trial.

SAM: And then the death sentence.

HALLY *[A world-weary sigh]*: I know, I know! I oscillate between hope and despair for this world as well, Sam. But things will change, you wait and see. One day somebody is going to get up and give history a kick up the backside and get it going again.

SAM: Like who?

HALLY *[After thought]*: They're called social reformers. Every age, Sam, has got its social reformer. My history book is full of them.

SAM: So where's ours?

HALLY: Good question. And I hate to say it, but the answer is: I don't know. Maybe he hasn't even been born yet. Or is still only a babe in arms at his mother's breast. God, what a thought.

SAM: So we just go on waiting.

HALLY: Ja, looks like it. *[Back to his soup and the book]*

SAM *[Reading from the textbook]*: "Introduction: In some mathematical problems only the magnitude…" *[He mispronounces the word "magnitude"]*

HALLY *[Correcting him without looking up]*: Magnitude.

SAM: What's it mean?

HALLY: How big it is. The size of the thing.

SAM *[Reading]*: "…magnitude of the quantities is of importance. In other problems we need to know whether these quantities are negative or positive. For example, whether there is a debit or credit bank balance…"

HALLY: Whether you're broke or not.

SAM: "…whether the temperature is above or below Zero…"

HALLY: Naught degrees. Cheerful state of affairs! No cash and you're freezing to death. Mathematics won't get you out of that one.

SAM: "All these quantities are called…" *[Spelling the word]*…s-c-a-1…

HALLY: Scalars.

SAM: Scalars! *[Shaking his head with a laugh]* You understand all that?

HALLY *[Turning a page]*: No. And I don't intend to try.

SAM: So what happens when the exams come?

HALLY: Failing a math exam isn't the end of the world, Sam. How many times have I told you that examination results don't measure intelligence?

SAM: I would say about as many times as you've failed one of them.

HALLY *[Mirthlessly]*: Ha, ha, ha.

SAM *[Simultaneously]*: Ha, ha, ha.

HALLY: Just remember Winston Churchill didn't do particularly well at school.

SAM: You've also told me that one many times:

HALLY: Well, it just so happens to be the truth.

SAM *[Enjoying the word]*: Magnitude! Magnitude! Show me how to use it.

HALLY *[After thought]*: An intrepid social reformer will not be daunted by the magnitude of the task he has undertaken.

SAM *[Impressed]*: Couple of jaw-breakers in there!

HALLY: I gave you three for the price of one. Intrepid, daunted and magnitude. I did that once in an exam. Put five of the words I had to explain in one sentence. It was half a page long.

SAM: Well, I'll put my money on you in the English exam.

HALLY: Piece of cake. Eighty percent without even trying.

SAM *[Another textbook from* **HALLY***'s case]*: And history ?

HALLY: So-so. I'll scrape through. In the fifties if I'm lucky.

SAM: You didn't do too badly last year.

HALLY: Because we had World War One. That at least had some action. You try to find that in the South African Parliamentary system.

SAM *[Reading from the history textbook]*: "Napoleon and the principle of equality." Hey! This sounds interesting. "After concluding peace with Britain in 1802, Napoleon used a brief period of calm to 'in-sti-tute…'"

HALLY: Introduce.

SAM: "…many reforms. Napoleon regarded all people as equal before the law and wanted them to have equal opportunities for advancement. All ves-ti-ges of the feu-dal system with its oppression of the poor were abolished." Vestiges, feudal system and abolished. I'm all right on oppression.

HALLY: I'm thinking. He swept away…abolished…the last remains…vestiges…of the bad old days…feudal system.

SAM: Ha! There's the social reformer we're waiting for. He sounds like a man of some magnitude.

HALLY: I'm not so sure about that. It's a damn good title for a book, though. A man of magnitude!

SAM: He sounds pretty big to me, Hally.

HALLY: Don't confuse historical significance with greatness. But maybe I'm being a bit prejudiced. Have a look in there and you'll see he's two chapters long. And hell!…has he only got dates, Sam, all of which you've got to remember! This campaign and that campaign, and then, because of all the fighting, the next thing is we get Peace Treaties all over the place. And what's the end of the story? Battle of Waterloo, which he loses. Wasn't worth it. No, I don't know about him as a man of magnitude.

SAM: Then who would you say was?

HALLY: To answer that, we need a definition of greatness, and I suppose that would be somebody who…somebody who benefited all mankind:

SAM: Right. But like who?

HALLY *[He speaks with total conviction]*: Charles Darwin. Remember him? That big book from the library. *The Origin of the Species.*

SAM: Him?

HALLY: Yes. For his Theory of Evolution.

SAM: You didn't finish it.

HALLY: I ran out of time. I didn't finish it because my two weeks was up. But I'm going to take it out again after I've digested what I read. It's safe. I've hidden it away in the Theology section. Nobody ever goes in there. And anyway who are you to talk? You hardly even looked at it.

SAM: I tried. I looked at the chapters in the beginning and I saw one called "The Struggle for an Existence." Ah ha, I thought. At last! But what did I get? Something called the mistiltoe which needs the apple tree and there's too many seeds and all are going to die except one…! No, Hally.

HALLY [Intellectually outraged]: What do you mean, No! The poor man had to start somewhere. For God's sake, Sam, he revolutionized science. Now we know.

SAM: What?

HALLY: Where we come from and what it all means.

SAM: And that's a benefit to mankind? Anyway, I still don't believe it.

HALLY: God, you're impossible. I showed it to you in black and white.

SAM: Doesn't mean I got to believe it.

HALLY: It's the likes of you that kept the Inquisition in business. It's called bigotry. Anyway, that's my man of magnitude. Charles Darwin! Who's yours?

SAM [Without hesitation]: Abraham Lincoln.

HALLY: I might have guessed as much. Don't get sentimental, Sam. You've never been a slave, you know. And anyway we freed your ancestors here in South Africa long before the Americans. But if you want to thank somebody on their behalf, do it to Mr. William Wilberforce. Come on. Try again. I want a real genius. [Now enjoying himself, and so is SAM. HALLY goes behind the counter and helps himself to a chocolate]

SAM: William Shakespeare.

HALLY [No enthusiasm]: Oh. So you're also one of them, are you? You're basing that opinion on only one play, you know. You've only read my Julius Caesar and even I don't understand half of what they're talking about. They should do what they did with the old Bible: bring the language up to date.

SAM: That's all you've got. It's also the only one you've read.

HALLY: I know. I admit it. That's why I suggest we reserve our judgment until we've checked up on a few others. I've got a feeling, though, that by the end of this year one is going to be enough for me, and I can give you the names of twenty-nine other chaps in the Standard Nine class of the Port Elizabeth Technical College who feel the same. But if you want him, you can have him. My turn now. [Pacing] This is a damned good exercise, you know! It started off looking like a simple question and here it's got us really probing into the intellectual heritage of our civilization.

SAM: So who is it going to be?

HALLY: My next man…and he gets the title on two scores: social reform and literary genius…is Leo Nikolaevich Tolstoy.

SAM: That Russian.

HALLY: Correct. Remember the picture of him I showed you.

SAM: With the long beard.

HALLY [Trying to look like Tolstoy]: And those burning, visionary eyes. My God, the face of a social prophet if ever I saw one! And remember my words when I showed it to you? Here's a man, Sam!

SAM: Those were words, Hally.

HALLY: Not many intellectuals are prepared to shovel manure with the peasants and then go home and write a "little book" called War and Peace. Incidentally, Sam, he was somebody else who, to quote, "…did not distinguish himself scholastically."

SAM: Meaning?

HALLY: He was also no good at school.

SAM: Like you and Winston Churchill.

HALLY [Mirthlessly]: Ha, ha, ha.

SAM [Simultaneously]: Ha, ha, ha.

HALLY: Don't get clever, Sam. That man freed his serfs of his own free will.

SAM: No argument. He was a somebody, all right. I accept him.

HALLY: I'm sure Count Tolstoy will be very pleased to hear that. Your turn. Shoot. [Another chocolate from behind the counter] I'm waiting, Sam.

SAM: I've got him.

HALLY: Good. Submit your candidate for examination.

SAM: Jesus.

HALLY [Stopped dead in his tracks]: Who?

SAM: Jesus Christ.

HALLY: Oh, come on, Sam!

SAM: The Messiah.

HALLY: Ja, but still…No, Sam. Don't let's get started on religion. We'll just spend the whole afternoon arguing again. Suppose I turn around and say Mohammed?

SAM: All right.

HALLY: You can't have them both on the same list!

SAM: Why not?, You like Mohammed, I like Jesus.

HALLY: I don't like Mohammed. I never have. I was merely being hypothetical. As far as I'm concerned, the Koran is as bad as the Bible. No. Religion is out! I'm not going to waste my time again arguing with you about the existence of God. You know perfectly well I'm an atheist…and I've got homework to do.

SAM: Okay, I take him back.

HALLY: You've got time for one more name.

SAM [After thought]: I've got one I know we'll agree on. A simple straightforward great Man of Magnitude…and no arguments. And he really did benefit all mankind.

HALLY: I wonder. After your last contribution I'm beginning to doubt whether anything in the way of an intellectual agreement is possible between the two of us. Who is he?

SAM: Guess.

HALLY: Socrates? Alexandre Dumas? Karl Marx? Dostoevsky? Nietzsche?

[SAM shakes his head after each name] Give me a clue.

SAM: The letter P is important…

HALLY: Plato!

SAM: …and his name begins with an F.

HALLY: I've got it. Freud and Psychology.

SAM: No. I didn't understand him.

HALLY: That makes two of us.

SAM: Think of mouldy apricot jam.

HALLY [*After a delighted laugh*]: Penicillin and Sir Alexander Fleming! And the title of the book: *The Microbe Hunters*. [*Delighted*] Splendid, Sam! Splendid. For once we are in total agreement. The major breakthrough in medical science in the Twentieth Century. If it wasn't for him, we might have lost the Second World War. It's deeply gratifying, Sam, to know that I haven't been wasting my time in talking to you. [*Strutting around proudly*] Tolstoy may have educated his peasants, but I've educated you.

SAM: Standard Four to Standard Nine.

HALLY: Have we been at it as long as that?

SAM: Yep. And my first lesson was geography.

HALLY [*Intrigued*]: Really? I don't remember.

SAM: My room there at the back of the old Jubilee Boarding House. I had just started working for your Mom. Little boy in short trousers walks in one afternoon and asks me seriously: "Sam, do you want to see South Africa?" Hey man! Sure I wanted to see South Africa!

HALLY: Was that me?

SAM: ...So the next thing I'm looking at a map you had just done for homework. It was your first one and you were very proud of yourself.

HALLY: Go on.

SAM: Then came my first lesson. "Repeat after me, Sam: Gold, in the Transvaal, mealies in the Free State, sugar in Natal and grapes in the Cape." I still know it!

HALLY: Well, I'll be buggered. So that's how it all started.

SAM: And your next map was one with all the rivers and the mountains they came from. The Orange, the Vaal, the Limpopo, the Zambezi...

HALLY: You've got a phenomenal memory!

SAM: You should be grateful. That is why you started passing your exams. You tried to be better than me.
[*They laugh together.* WILLIE *is attracted by the laughter and joins them*]

HALLY: The old Jubilee Boarding House. Sixteen rooms with board and lodging, rent in advance and one week's notice. I haven't thought about it for donkey's years...and I don't think that's an accident. God, was I glad when we sold it and moved out. Those years are not remembered as the happiest ones of an unhappy childhood.

WILLIE [*Knocking on the table and trying to imitate a woman's voice*]: "Hally, are you there?"

HALLY: Who's that supposed to be?

WILLIE: "What you doing in there, Hally? Come out at once!"

HALLY [*To* SAM]: What's he talking about?

SAM: Don't you remember?

WILLIE: "Sam, Willie...is he in there with you boys?"

SAM: Hiding away in our room when your mother was looking for you.

HALLY [*Another good laugh*]: Of course! I used to crawl and hide under your bed! But finish the story, Willie. Then what used to happen? You chaps would give the game away by telling her I was in there with you. So much for friendship.

SAM: We couldn't lie to her. She knew.

HALLY: Which meant I got another rowing for hanging around the "servants' quarters." I think I spent more time in there with you chaps than anywhere else in that dump. And do you blame me? Nothing but bloody misery wherever you went. Somebody was always complaining about the food, or my mother was having a fight with Micky Nash because she'd caught her with a petty officer in her room. Maud Meiring was another one. Remember those two? They were prostitutes, you know. Soldiers and sailors from the troopships. Bottom fell out of the business when the war ended. God, the flotsam and jetsam that life washed up on our shores! No joking, if it wasn't for your room, I would have been the first certified ten-year-old in medical history. Ja, the memories are coming back now. Walking home from school and thinking: "What can I do this afternoon?" Try out a few ideas, but sooner or later I'd end up in there with you fellows. I bet you I could still find my way to your room with my eyes closed. [*He does exactly that*] Down the corridor...telephone on the right, which my Mom keeps locked because somebody is using it on the sly and not paying...past the kitchen and unappetizing cooking smells...around the corner into the backyard, hold my breath again because there are more smells coming when I pass your lavatory, then into that little passageway, first door on the right and into your room. How's that?

SAM: Good. But, as usual, you forgot to knock.

HALLY: Like that time I barged in and caught you and Cynthia...at it. Remember? God, was I embarrassed! I didn't know what was going on at first.

SAM: Ja, that taught you a lesson.

HALLY: And about a lot more than knocking on doors, I'll have you know, and I don't mean geography either. Hell, Sam, couldn't you have waited until it was dark?

SAM: No.

HALLY: Was it that urgent?

SAM: Yes, and if you don't believe me, wait until your time comes.

HALLY: No, thank you. I am not interested in girls. [*Back to his memories...Using a few chairs he recreates the room as he lists the items*] A gray little room with a cold cement floor. Your bed against that wall...and I now know why the mattress sags so much!...Willie's bed...it's propped up on bricks because one leg is broken...that wobbly little table with the washbasin and jug of water...Yes!...stuck to the wall above it are some pin-up pictures from magazines. Joe Louis...

WILLIE: Brown Bomber. World Title. [*Boxing pose*] Three rounds and knockout.

HALLY: Against who?

SAM: Max Schmeling.

HALLY: Correct. I can also remember Fred Astaire and Ginger Rogers, and Rita Hayworth in a bathing costume which always made me hot and bothered when I looked at it.

Under Willie's bed is an old suitcase with all his clothes in a mess, which is why I never hide there. Your things are neat and tidy in a trunk next to your bed, and on it there is a picture of you and Cynthia in your ballroom clothes, your first silver cup for third place in a competition and an old radio which doesn't work anymore. Have I left out anything?

SAM: No.

HALLY: Right, so much for the stage directions. Now the characters. *[SAM and WILLIE move to their appropriate positions in the bedroom]* Willie is in bed, under his blankets with his clothes on, complaining nonstop about something, but we can't make out a word of what he's saying because he's got his head under the blankets as well. You're on your bed trimming your toenails with a knife—not a very edifying sight—and as for me…What am I doing?

SAM: You're sitting on the floor giving Willie a lecture about being a good loser while you get the checker board and pieces ready for a game. Then you go to Willie's bed, pull off the blankets and make him play with you first because you know you're going to win, and that gives you the second game with me.

HALLY: And you certainly were a bad loser, Willie!

WILLIE: Haai!

HALLY: Wasn't he, Sam? And so slow! A game with you almost took the whole afternoon. Thank God I gave up trying to teach you how to play chess.

WILLIE: You and Sam cheated.

HALLY: I never saw Sam cheat, and mine were mostly the mistakes of youth.

WILLIE: Then how is it you two was always winning?

HALLY: Have you ever considered the possibility, Willie, that it was because we were better than you?

WILLIE: Every time better?

HALLY: Not every time. There were occasions when we deliberately let you win a game so that you would stop sulking and go on playing with us. Sam used to wink at me when you weren't looking to show me it was time to let you win.

WILLIE: So then you two didn't play fair.

HALLY: It was for your benefit, Mr. Malopo, which is more than being fair. It was an act of self-sacrifice. *[To SAM]* But you know what my best memory is, don't you?

SAM: No.

HALLY: Come on, guess. If your memory is so good, you must remember it as well.

SAM: We got up to a lot of tricks in there, Hally.

HALLY: This one was special, Sam.

SAM: I'm listening.

HALLY: It started off looking like another of those useless nothing-to-do afternoons. I'd already been down to Main Street looking for adventure, but nothing had happened. I didn't feel like climbing trees in the Donkin Park or pretending I was a private eye and following a stranger…so as usual: See what's cooking in Sam's room. This time it was you on the floor. You had two thin pieces of wood and

you were smoothing them down with a knife. It didn't look particularly interesting, but when I asked you what you were doing, you just said, "Wait and see, Hally. Wait…and see"…in that secret sort of way of yours, so I knew there was a surprise coming. You teased me, you bugger, by being deliberately slow and not answering my questions!

[SAM laughs]

And whistling while you worked away! God, it was infuriating! I could have brained you! It was only when you tied them together in a cross and put that down on the brown paper that I realized what you were doing. "Sam is making a kite?" And when I asked you and you said "Yes"…! *[Shaking his head with disbelief]* The sheer audacity of it took my breath away. I mean, seriously, what the hell does a black man know about flying a kite? I'll be honest with you, Sam, I had no hopes for it. If you think I was excited and happy, you got another guess coming. In fact, I was shit-scared that we were going to make fools of ourselves. When we left the boarding house to go up onto the hill, I was praying quietly that there wouldn't be any other kids around to laugh at us.

SAM *[Enjoying the memory as much as HALLY]*: Ja, I could see that.

HALLY: I made it obvious, did I?

SAM: Ja. You refused to carry it.

HALLY: Do you blame me? Can you remember what the poor thing looked like? Tomato-box wood and brown paper! Flour and water for glue! Two of my mother's old stockings for a tail, and then all those bits and pieces of string you made me tie together so that we could fly it! Hell, no, that was now only asking for a miracle to happen.

SAM: Then the big argument when I told you to hold the string and run with it when I let go.

HALLY: I was prepared to run, all right, but straight back to the boarding house.

SAM *[Knowing whats coming]*: So what happened?

HALLY: Come on, Sam, you remember as well as I do.

SAM: I want to hear it from you.

[HALLY pauses. He wants to be as accurate as possible]

HALLY: You went a little distance from me down the hill, you held it up ready to let it go… "This is it," I thought. "Like everything else in my life, here comes another fiasco." Then you shouted, "Go, Hally!" and I started to run. *[Another pause]* I don't know how to describe it, Sam. Ja! The miracle happened! I was running, waiting for it to crash to the ground, but instead suddenly there was something alive behind me at the end of the string, tugging at it as if it wanted to be free. I looked back…*[Shakes his head]*…I still can't believe my eyes. It was flying! Looping around and trying to climb even higher into the sky. You shouted to me to let it have more string. I did, until there was none left and I was just holding that piece of wood we had tied it to. You came up and joined me. You were laughing.

SAM: So were you. And shouting, "It works, Sam! We've done it!"

HALLY: And we had! I was so proud of us! It was the most splendid thing I had ever seen. I wished there were hundreds of kids around to watch us. The part that scared me, though, was when you showed me how to make it dive down to the ground and then just when it was on the point of crashing, swoop up again!

SAM: You didn't want to try yourself.

HALLY: Of course not! I would have been suicidal if anything had happened to it. Watching you do it made me nervous enough. I was quite happy just to see it up there with its tail fluttering behind it. You left me after that, didn't you? You explained how to get it down, we tied it to the bench so that I could sit and watch it, and you went away. I wanted you to stay, you know. I was a little scared of having to look after it by myself.

SAM [*Quietly*]: I had work to do, Hally.

HALLY: It was sort of sad bringing it down, Sam. And it looked sad again when it was lying there on the ground. Like something that had lost its soul. Just tomato-box wood, brown, paper and two of my mother's old stockings! But, hell, I'll never forget that first moment when I saw it up there. I had a stiff neck the next day from looking up so much.

[*SAM laughs. HALLY turns to him with a question he never thought of asking before*] Why did you make that kite, Sam?

SAM [*Evenly*]: I can't remember.

HALLY: Truly?

SAM: Too long ago, Hally.

HALLY: Ja, I suppose it was. It's time for another one, you know.

SAM: Why do you say that?

HALLY: Because it feels like that. Wouldn't be a good day to fly it, though.

SAM: No. You can't fly kites on rainy days.

HALLY [*He studies SAM. Their memories have made him conscious of the man's presence in his life*]: How old are you, Sam?

SAM: Two score and five.

HALLY: Strange, isn't it?

SAM: What?

HALLY: Me and you.

SAM: What's strange about it?

HALLY: Little white boy in short trousers and a black man old enough to be his father flying a kite. It's not every day you see that.

SAM: But why strange? Because the one is white and the other black?

HALLY: I don't know. Would have been just as strange, I suppose, if it had been me and my Dad...cripple man and a little boy! Nope! There's no chance of me flying a kite without it being strange. [*Simple statement of fact—no self-pity*] There's a nice little short story there. "The Kite-Flyers." But we'd have to find a twist in the ending.

SAM: Twist?

HALLY: Yes. Something unexpected. The way it ended with us was too straightforward...me on the bench and you going back to work. There's no drama in that.

WILLIE: And me?

HALLY: You?

WILLIE: Yes me.

HALLY: You want to get into the story as well, do you? I got it! Change the title: "Afternoons in Sam's Room"...expand it and tell all the stories. It's on its way to being a novel. Our days in the old Jubilee. Sad in a way that they're over. I almost wish we were still in that little room.

SAM: We're still together.

HALLY: That's true. It's just that life felt the right size in there...not too big and not too small. Wasn't so hard to work up a bit of courage. It's got so bloody complicated since then.

[*The telephone rings. SAM answers it*]

SAM: St. George's Park Tea Room...Hello, Madam...Yes, Madam, he's here...Hally, it's your mother.

HALLY: Where is she phoning from?

SAM: Sounds like the hospital. It's a public telephone.

HALLY [*Relieved*]: You see! I told you. [*The telephone*] Hello, Mom...Yes...Yes no fine. Everything's under control here. How's things with poor old Dad?...Has he had a bad turn?...What?...Oh, God!...Yes, Sam told me, but I was sure he'd made a mistake. But what's this all about, Mom? He didn't look at all good last night. How can he get better so quickly?...Then very obviously you must say no. Be firm with him. You're the boss...You know what it's going to be like if he comes home...Well then, don't blame me when I fail my exams at the end of the year...Yes! How am I expected to be fresh for school when I spend half the night massaging his gammy leg?...So am I!...So tell him a white lie. Say Dr. Colley wants more X-rays of his stump. Or bribe him. We'll sneak in double tots of brandy in future...What?...Order him to get back into bed at once! If he's going to behave like a child, treat him like one...All right, Mom! I was just trying to...I'm sorry....I said I'm sorry...Quick, give me your number. I'll phone you back. [*He hangs up and waits a few seconds*] Here we go again! [*He dials*] I'm sorry, Mom.....Okay...But now listen to me carefully. All it needs is for you to put your foot down. Don't take no for an answer...Did you hear me? And whatever you do, don't discuss it with him...Because I'm frightened you'll give in to him...Yes, Sam gave me lunch...I ate all of it!...No, Mom not a soul. It's still raining here...

Right, I'll tell them. I'll just do some homework and then lock up...But remember now, Mom. Don't listen to anything he says. And phone me back and let me know what happens...Okay. Bye, Mom. [*He hangs up. The men are staring at him*] My Mom says that when you're finished with the floors you must do the windows. [*Pause*] Don't misunderstand me, chaps. All I want is for him to get better. And if he was, I'd be the first person to say: "Bring him home." But he's not, and we can't give him the medical care and attention he needs at home. That's what hospitals are there for. [*Brusquely*] So don't just stand there! Get on with it!

[*SAM clears HALLY's table*]

You heard right. My Dad wants to go home.

SAM: Is he better?

HALLY [Sharply]: No! How the hell can he be better when last night he was groaning with pain? This is not an age of miracles!

SAM: Then he should stay in hospital.

HALLY [Seething with irritation and frustration]: Tell me something I don't know, Sam. What the hell do you think I was saying to my Mom? All I can say is fuck-it-all.

SAM: I'm sure he'll listen to your Mom.

HALLY: You don't know what she's up against. He's already packed his shaving kit and pajamas and is sitting on his bed with his crutches, dressed and ready to go. I know him when he gets in that mood. If she tries to reason with him, we've had it. She's no match for him when it comes to a battle of words: He'll tie her up in knots. [Trying to hide his true feelings]

SAM: I suppose it gets lonely for him in there.

HALLY: With all the patients and nurses around? Regular visits from the Salvation Army? Balls! It's ten times worse for him at home. I'm at school and my mother is here in the business all day.

SAM: He's at least got you at night.

HALLY [Before he can stop himself]: And we've got him! Please! I don't want to talk about it anymore. [Unpacks his school case, slamming down books on the table] Life is just a plain bloody mess, that's all. And people are fools.

SAM: Come on, Hally.

HALLY: Yes, they are! They bloody well deserve what they get.

SAM: Then don't complain.

HALLY: Don't try to be clever, Sam. It doesn't suit you. Anybody who thinks there's nothing wrong with this world needs to have his head examined. Just when things are going along all right, without fail someone or something will come along and spoil everything. Somebody should write that down as a fundamental law of the Universe. The principle of perpetual disappointment. If there is a God who created this world, he should scrap it and try again.

SAM: All right, Hally, all right. What you got for homework?

HALLY: Bullshit, as usual. [Opens an exercise book and reads] "Write five hundred words describing an annual event of cultural or historical significance."

SAM: That should be easy enough for you.

HALLY: And also plain bloody boring. You know what he wants, don't you? One of their useless old ceremonies. The commemoration of the landing of the 1820 Settlers, or if it's going to be culture, Carols by Candlelight every Christmas.

SAM: It's an impressive sight. Make a good description, Hally. All those candles glowing in the dark and the people singing hymns.

HALLY: And it's called religious hysteria. [Intense irritation] Please, Sam! Just leave me alone and let me get on with it. I'm not in the mood for games this afternoon. And remember my Mom's orders...you're to help Willie with the windows. Come on now, I don't want any more nonsense in here.

SAM: Okay, Hally, okay.

[HALLY settles down to his homework; determined preparations...pen, ruler, exercise book, dictionary, another cake...all of which will lead to nothing]

[SAM waltzes over to **WILLIE** and starts to replace tables and chairs. He practices a ballroom step while doing so. **WILLIE** watches. When **SAM** is finished, **WILLIE** tries] Good! But just a little bit quicker on the turn and only move in to her after she's crossed over. What about this one?

[Another step. When **SAM** is finished, **WILLIE** again has a go] Much better. See what happens when you just relax and enjoy yourself? Remember that in two weeks' time and you'll be all right.

WILLIE: But I haven't got partner, Boet Sam.

SAM: Maybe Hilda will turn up tonight.

WILLIE: No, Boet Sam. [Reluctantly] I gave her a good hiding.

SAM: You mean a bad one.

WILLIE: Good bad one.

SAM: Then you mustn't complain either. Now you pay the price for losing your temper.

WILLIE: I also pay two pounds ten shilling entrance fee.

SAM: They'll refund you if you withdraw now.

WILLIE [Appalled]: You mean, don't dance?

SAM: Yes.

WILLIE: No! I wait too long and I practice too hard. If I find me new partner, you think I can be ready in two weeks? I ask Madam for my leave now and we practice every day.

SAM: Quickstep non-stop for two weeks. World record, Willie, but you'll be mad at the end.

WILLIE: No jokes, Boet Sam.

SAM: I'm not joking.

WILLIE: So then what?

SAM: Find Hilda. Say you're sorry and promise you won't beat her again.

WILLIE: No.

SAM: Then withdraw. Try again next year.

WILLIE: No.

SAM: Then I give up.

WILLIE: Haaikona, Boet Sam, you can't.

SAM: What do you mean, I can't? I'm telling you: I give up.

WILLIE [Adamant]: No! [Accusingly] It was you who start me ballroom dancing.

SAM: So?

WILLIE: Before that I use to be happy. And is you and Miriam who bring me to Hilda and say here's partner for you.

SAM: What are you saying, Willie?

WILLIE: You!

SAM: But me what? To blame?

WILLIE: Yes.

SAM: Willie...? [Bursts into laughter]

WILLIE: And now all you do is make jokes at me. You wait. When Miriam leaves you is my turn to laugh. Ha! Ha! Ha!

SAM [He can't take **WILLIE** seriously any longer]: She can leave me tonight! I know what to do. [Bowing before an imaginary partner] May I have the pleasure? [He dances and sings]

"Just a fellow with his pillow...Dancin' like a willow...

In an autumn breeze…"

WILLIE: There you go again! *[SAM goes on dancing and singing]* Boet Sam!

SAM: There's the answer to your problem! Judges' announcement in two weeks' time: "Ladies and gentlemen, the winner in the open section…Mr. Willie Malopo and his pillow!"

[This is too much for a now really angry WILLIE. He goes for SAM, but the latter is too quick for him and puts HALLY's table between the two of them]

HALLY *[Exploding]*: For Christ's sake, you two!

WILLIE *[Still trying to get at SAM]*: I donner you, Sam! Struesgod !

SAM *[Still laughing]*: Sorry, Willie…Sorry…

HALLY: Sam! Willie! *[Grabs his ruler and gives WILLIE a vicious whack on the bum]* How the hell am I supposed to concentrate with the two of you behaving like bloody children!

WILLIE: Hit him too!

HALLY: Shut up, Willie.

WILLIE: He started jokes again.

HALLY: Get back to your work. You too, Sam. *[His ruler]* Do you want another one, Willie?

[SAM and WILLIE return to their work. HALLY uses the opportunity to escape from his unsuccessful attempt at homework. He struts around like a little despot, ruler in hand, giving vent to his anger and frustration]

Suppose a customer had walked in then? Or the Park Superintendent. And seen the two of you behaving like a pair of hooligans. That would have been the end of my mother's license, you know. And your jobs! Well, this is the end of it. From now on there will be no more of your ballroom nonsense in here. This is a business establishment, not a bloody New Brighton dancing school. I've been far too lenient with the two of you.

[Behind the counter for a green cool drink and a dollop of ice cream. He keeps up his tirade as he prepares it] But what really makes me bitter is that I allow you chaps a little freedom in here when business is bad and what do you do with it? The foxtrot! Specially you, Sam. There's more to life than trotting around a dance floor and I thought at least you knew it.

SAM: It's a harmless pleasure, Hally. It doesn't hurt anybody.

HALLY: It's also a rather simple one, you know.

SAM: You reckon so? Have you ever tried?

HALLY: Of course not.

SAM: Why don't you? Now.

HALLY: What do you mean? Me dance?

SAM: Yes. I'll show you a simple step—the waltz—then you try it.

HALLY: What will that prove?

SAM: That it might not be as easy as you think.

HALLY: I didn't say it was easy. I said it was simple—like in simple-minded, meaning mentally retarded. You can't exactly say it challenges the intellect.

SAM: It does other things.

HALLY: Such as?

SAM: Make people happy.

HALLY *[The glass in his hand]*: So do American cream sodas with ice cream. For God's sake, Sam, you're not asking me to take ballroom dancing serious, are you?

SAM: Yes.

HALLY *[Sigh of defeat]*: Oh, well, so much for trying to give you a decent education. I've obviously achieved nothing.

SAM: You still haven't told me what's wrong with admiring something that's beautiful and then trying to do it yourself.

HALLY: Nothing. But we happen to be talking about a foxtrot, not a thing of beauty.

SAM: But that is just what I'm saying. If you were to see two champions doing, two masters of the art…!

HALLY: Oh, God, I give up. So now it's also art!

SAM: Ja.

HALLY: There's a limit, Sam. Don't confuse art and entertainment.

SAM: So then what is art?

HALLY: You want a definition?

SAM: Ja.

HALLY *[He realizes he has got to be careful. He gives the matter a lot of thought before answering]*: Philosophers have been trying to do that for centuries. What is Art? What is Life? But basically I suppose it's…the giving of meaning to matter.

SAM: Nothing to do with beautiful?

HALLY: It goes beyond that. It's the giving of form to the formless.

SAM: Ja, well, maybe it's not art, then. But I still say it's beautiful.

HALLY: I'm sure the word you mean to use is entertaining.

SAM *[Adamant]*: No. Beautiful. And if you want proof, come along to the Centenary Hall in New Brighton in two weeks' time.

[The mention of the Centenary Hall draws WILLIE over to then]

HALLY: What for? I've seen the two of you prancing around in here often enough.

SAM *[He laughs]*: This isn't the real thing, Hally. We're just playing around in here.

HALLY: So? I can use my imagination.

SAM: And what do you get?

HALLY: A lot of people dancing around and having a so-called good time.

SAM: That all?

HALLY: Well, basically it is that, surely.

SAM: No, it isn't. Your imagination hasn't helped you at all. There's a lot more to it than that. We're getting ready for the championships, Hally, not just another dance. There's going to be a lot of people, all right, and they're going to have a good time, but they'll only be spectators, sitting around and watching. It's just the competitors out there on the dance floor. Party decorations and fancy lights all around the walls! The ladies in beautiful evening dresses!

HALLY: My mother's got one of those, Sam, and, quite frankly, it's an embarrassment every time she wears it.

SAM *[Undeterred]*: Your imagination left out the excitement.

[HALLY *scoffs*]

Oh, yes. The finalists are not going to be out there just to have a good time. One of those couples will be the 1950 Eastern Province Champions. And your imagination left out the music.

WILLIE: Mr. Elijah Gladman Guzana and his Orchestral Jazzonions.

SAM: The sound of the big band, Hally. Trombone, trumpet, tenor and alto sax. And then, finally, your imagination also left out the climax of the evening when the dancing is finished, the judges have stopped whispering among themselves and the Master of Ceremonies collects their scorecards and goes up onto the stage to announce the winners.

HALLY: All right. So you make it sound like a bit of a do. It's an occasion. Satisfied?

SAM [*Victory*]: So you admit that!

HALLY: Emotionally yes, intellectually no.

SAM: Well, I don't know what you mean by that, all I'm telling you is that it is going to be the event of the year in New Brighton. It's been sold out for two weeks already. There's only standing room left. We've got competitors coming from Kingwilliamtown, East London, Port Alfred.

[HALLY *starts pacing thoughtfully*]

HALLY: Tell me a bit more.

SAM: I thought you weren't interested…intellectually.

HALLY [*Mysteriously*]: I've got my reasons.

SAM: What do you want to know?

HALLY: It takes place every year?

SAM: Yes. But only every third year in New Brighton. It's East London's turn to have the championships next year.

HALLY: Which, I suppose, makes it an even more significant event.

SAM: Ah ha! We're getting somewhere. Our "occasion" is now a "significant event."

HALLY: I wonder.

SAM: What?

HALLY: I wonder if I would get away with it.

SAM: But what?

HALLY [*To the table and his exercise book*]: "Write five hundred words describing an annual event of cultural or historical significance." Would I be stretching poetic license a little too far if I called your ballroom championships a cultural event?

SAM: You mean…?

HALLY: You think we could get five hundred words out of it, Sam?

SAM: Victor Sylvester has written a whole book on ballroom dancing.

WILLIE: You going to write about it, Master Hally?

HALLY: Yes, gentlemen, that is precisely what I am considering doing. Old Doc Bromely—he's my English teacher—is going to argue with me, of course. He doesn't like natives. But I'll point out to him that in strict anthropological terms the culture of a primitive black society includes its dancing and singing. To put my thesis in a nutshell: The war-dance has been replaced by the waltz. But it still

amounts to the same thing: the release of primitive emotions through movement. Shall we give it a go?

SAM: I'm ready.

WILLIE: Me also.

HALLY: Ha! This will teach the old bugger a lesson. [*Decision taken*] Right. Let's get ourselves organized. [*This means another cake on the table. He sits*] I think you've given me enough general atmosphere, Sam, but to build the tension and suspense I need facts. [*Pencil poised*]

WILLIE: Give him facts, Boet Sam.

HALLY: What you called the climax…how many finalists?

SAM: Six couples.

HALLY [*Making notes*]: Go on. Give me the picture.

SAM: Spectators seated right around the hall. [WILLIE *becomes a spectator*]

HALLY: …and it's a full house.

SAM: At one end, on the stage, Gladman and his Orchestral Jazzonions. At the other end is a long table with the three judges. The six finalists go onto the dance floor and take up their positions. When they are ready and the spectators have settled down, the Master of Ceremonies goes to the microphone. To start with, he makes some jokes to get the people laughing…

HALLY: Good touch! [*As he writes*] "…creating a relaxed atmosphere which will change to one of tension and drama as the climax is approached."

SAM [*Onto a chair to act out the M.C.*]: "Ladies and gentlemen, we come now to the great moment you have all been waiting for this evening…The finals of the 1950 Eastern Province Open Ballroom Dancing Championships. But first—let me introduce the finalists! Mr. and Mrs. Welcome Tchabalala from Kingwilliamstown…"

WILLIE [*He applauds after every name*]: Is when the people clap their hands and whistle and make a lot of noise, Master Hally.

SAM: "Mr. Mulligan Njikelane and Miss Nomhle Nkonyeni of Grahamstown; Mr. and Mrs. Norman Nchinga from Port Alfred; Mr. Fats Bokolane and Miss Dina Plaatjies from East London; Mr. Sipho Dugu and Mrs. Mable Magada from Peddie; and from New Brighton our very own Mr. Willie Malopo and Miss Hilda Samuels."

[WILLIE *can't believe his ears. He abandons his role as spectator and scrambles into position as a finalist*]

WILLIE: Relaxed and ready to romance!

SAM: The applause dies down. When everybody is silent, Gladman, lifts up his sax, nods at the Orchestral Jazzonions …

WILLIE: Play the jukebox please, Boet Sam!

SAM: I also only got bus fare, Willie.

HALLY: Hold it, everybody. [*Heads for the cash register behind the counter*] How much is in the till, Sam?

SAM: Three shillings. Hally…your Mom counted it before she left.

[HALLY *hesitates*]

HALLY: Sorry, Willie. You know how she carried on the last time I did it. We'll just have to pool our combined imaginations and hope for the best. *[Returns to the table]* Back to work. How are the points scored, Sam?

SAM: Maximum of ten points each for individual style, deportment, rhythm and general appearance.

WILLIE: Must I start?

HALLY: Hold it for a second, Willie. And penalties?

SAM: For what?

HALLY: For doing something wrong. Say you stumble or bump into somebody...do they take off any points?

SAM *[Aghast]*: Hally...!

HALLY: When you're dancing. If you and your partner collide into another couple.

[HALLY can get no further. SAM has collapsed with laughter. He explains to WILLIE]

SAM: If me and Miriam bump into you and Hilda...

[WILLIE joins him in another good laugh]

Hally, Hally...!

HALLY *[Perplexed]*: Why? What did I say?

SAM: There's no collisions out there, Hally. Nobody trips or stumbles or bumps into anybody else. That's what that moment is all about. To be one of those finalists on that dance floor is like...like being in a dream about a world in which accidents don't happen.

HALLY *[Genuinely moved by SAM's image]*: Jesus, Sam! That's beautiful!

WILLIE *[Can endure waiting no longer]*: I'm starting! *[WILLIE dances while SAM talks]*

SAM: Of course it is. That's what I've been trying to say to you all afternoon. And it's beautiful because that is what we want life to be like. But instead, like you said, Hally, we're bumping into each other all the time. Look at the three of us this afternoon: I've bumped into Willie, the two of us have bumped into you, you've bumped into your mother; she bumping into your Dad...None of us knows the steps and there's no music playing. And it doesn't stop with us. The whole world is doing it all the time. Open a newspaper and what do you read? America has bumped into Russia, England is bumping into India, rich man bumps into poor man. Those are big collisions, Hally. They make for a lot of bruises. People get hurt in all that bumping, and we're sick and tired of it now. It's been going on for too long. Are we never going to get it right?...Learn to dance life like champions instead of always being just a bunch of beginners at it?

HALLY *[Deep and sincere admiration of the man]*: You've got a vision, Sam!

SAM: Not just me. What I'm saying to you is that everybody's got it. That's why there's only standing room left for the Centenary Hall in two weeks' time. For as long as the music lasts, we are going to see six couples get it right, the way we want life to be.

HALLY: But is that the best we can do, Sam...watch six finalists dreaming about the way it should be?

SAM: I don't know. But it starts with that. Without the dream we won't know what we're going for. And anyway I reckon there are a few people who have got past just dreaming about it and are trying for something real. Remember that thing we read once in the paper about the Mahatma Gandhi? Going without food to stop those riots in India?

HALLY: You're right. He certainly was trying to teach people to get the steps right.

SAM: And the Pope.

HALLY: Yes, he's another one. Our old General Smuts as well, you know. He's also out there dancing. You know, Sam, when you come to think of it, that's what the United Nations boils down to...a dancing school for politicians!

SAM: And let's hope they learn.

HALLY *[A little surge of hope]*: You're right. We mustn't despair. Maybe there's some hope for mankind after all. Keep it up, Willie. *[Back to his table with determination]* This is a lot bigger than I thought. So what have we got? Yes, our title: "A World Without Collisions."

SAM: That sounds good! "A World Without Collisions."

HALLY: Subtitle: "Global Politics on the Dance Floor." No. A bit too heavy, hey? What about "Ballroom Dancing as a Political Vision"?

[The telephone rings. SAM answers it]

SAM: St. George's Park Tea Room...Yes, Madam...Hally, it's your Mom.

HALLY *[Back to reality]*: Oh, God, yes! I'd forgotten all about that. Shit! Remember my words, Sam? Just when you're enjoying yourself, someone or something will come along and wreck everything.

SAM: You haven't heard what she's got to say yet.

HALLY: Public telephone?

SAM: No.

HALLY: Does she sound happy or unhappy?

SAM: I couldn't tell. *[Pause]* She's waiting, Hally.

HALLY *[To the telephone]*: Hello, Mom...No, everything is okay here. Just doing my homework...What's your news?...You've what?...*[Pause. He takes the receiver away from his ear for a few seconds. In the course of HALLY's telephone conversation, SAM and WILLIE discretely position the stacked tables and chairs. HALLY places the receiver back to his ear]* Yes, I'm still here. Oh, well, I give up now. Why did you do it, Mom?...Well, I just hope you know what you've let us in for...*[Loudly]* I said I hope you know what you've let us in for! It's the end of the peace and quiet we've been having. *[Softly]* Where is he? *[Normal voice]* He can't hear us from in there. But for God's sake, Mom, what happened? I told you to be firm with him...Then you and the nurses should have held him down, taken his crutches away...I know only too well he's my father!...I'm not being disrespectful, but I'm sick and tired of emptying stinking chamberpots full of phlegm and piss...Yes, I do! When you're not there, he asks *me* to do it...If you really want to know the truth, that's why I've got no appetite for my food...Yes! There's a lot of things you don't know about. For your information, I still haven't got that science textbook I need. And you know why? He borrowed the money you gave me for it...Because I didn't want to start another fight between you two....He says that every time...All right, Mom! *[Viciously]* Then just remember to start hiding your bag away again, because he'll be at your purse before long for money for booze. And when he's well enough to come down here, you better keep an eye on the till as well, because that is also going to develop a leak…Then don't complain to me when he starts his old tricks…Yes, you do. I get it from you on one side and from him on the other, and it makes life hell for me. I'm not going to be the peacemaker anymore. I'm warning you now: when the two of you start fighting again, I'm leaving home…Mom, if you start crying, I'm going to put down the receiver…Okay…[*Lowering his voice to a vicious whisper*] Okay, Mom. I heard you. [*Desperate*] No…Because I don't want to. I'll see him when I get home! Mom!…[*Pause. When he speaks again, his tone changes completely. It is not simply pretense. We sense a genuine emotional confict*] Welcome home, chum!…What's that?…Don't be silly, Dad. You being home is just about the best news in the world…I bet you are. Bloody depressing there with everybody going on about their ailments, hey!…How you feeling?…Good…Here as well, pal. Coming down cats and dogs…That's right. Just the day for a kip and a toss in your old Uncle Ned…Everything's just hunky-dory on my side, Dad…Well, to start with, there's a nice pile of comics for you on the counter…Yes, old Kemple brought them in. *Batman and Robin, Submariner*…just your cup of tea…I will.…Yes, we'll spin a few yarns tonight…Okay, chum, see you in a little while…No, I promise. I'll come straight home…[*Pause—his mother comes back on the phone*] Mom? Okay. I'll lock up now…What?…Oh, the brandy…Yes, I'll remember!…I'll put it in my suitcase now, for God's sake. I know well enough what will happen if he doesn't get it…[*Places a bottle of brandy on the counter*] I *was* kind to him, Mom. I didn't say anything nasty!…All right. Bye. [*End of telephone conversation. A desolate* HALLY *doesn't move. A strained silence*]

SAM [*Quietly*]: That sounded like a bad bump, Hally.

HALLY [*Having a hard time controlling his emotions. He speaks carefully*]: Mind your own business, Sam.

SAM: Sorry. I wasn't trying to interfere. Shall we carry on? Hally? [*He indicates the exercise book. No response from* HALLY]

WILLIE [*Also trying*]: Tell him about when they give out the cups, Boet Sam.

SAM: Ja! That's another big moment. The presentation of the cups after the winners have been announced. You've got to put that in.
[*Still no response from* HALLY]

WILLIE: A big silver one, Master Hally, called floating trophy for the champions.

SAM: We always invite some big-shot personality to hand them over. Guest of honor this year is going to be His Holiness Bishop Jabulani of the All African Free Zionist Church.
[HALLY *gets up abruptly, goes to his table and tears up the page he was writing on*]

HALLY: So much for a bloody world without collisions.

SAM: Too bad. It was on its way to being a good composition.

HALLY: Let's stop bullshitting ourselves, Sam.

SAM: Have we been doing that?

HALLY: Yes! That's what all our talk about a decent world has been…just so much bullshit.

SAM: We did say it was still only a dream.

HALLY: And a bloody useless one at that. Life's a fuck-up and it's never going to change.

SAM: Ja, maybe that's true.

HALLY: There's no maybe about it. It's a blunt and brutal fact. All we've done this afternoon is waste our time.

SAM: Not if we'd got your homework done.

HALLY: I don't give a shit about my homework, so, for Christ's sake, just shut up about it. [*Slamming books viciously into his school case*] Hurry up now and finish your work. I want to lock up and get out of here. [*Pause*] And then go where? Home-sweet-fucking-home. Jesus, I hate that word.
[HALLY *goes to the counter to put the brandy bottle and comics in his school case. After a moment's hesitation, he smashes the bottle of brandy. He abandons all further attempts to hide his feelings.* SAM *and* WILLIE *work away us unobtrusively as possible*]
Do you want to know what is really wrong with your lovely little dream, Sam? It's not just that we are all bad dancers. That does happen to be perfectly true, but there's more to it than just that. You left out the cripples.

SAM: Hally!

HALLY [*Now totally reckless*]: Ja! Can't leave them out, Sam. That's why we always end up on our backsides on the dance floor. They're also out there dancing…like a bunch of broken spiders trying to do the quickstep! [*An ugly attempt at laughter*] When you come to think of it, it's a bloody comical sight. I mean, it's bad enough on two legs…but one and a pair of crutches! Hell, no, Sam. That's guaranteed to turn that dance floor into a shambles. Why you shaking your head? Picture it, man. For once this afternoon let's use our imaginations sensibly.

SAM: Be careful, Hally.

HALLY: Of what? The truth? I seem to be the only one around here who is prepared to face it. We've had the pretty dream, it's time now to wake up and have a good long look at the way things really are. Nobody knows the steps, there's no music, the cripples are also out there tripping up everybody and trying to get into the act, and it's all called the All-Comers-How-to-Make-a-Fuckup-of-Life Championships. [*Another ugly laugh*] Hang on, Sam! The best bit is still coming. Do you know what the winner's trophy is? A beautiful big chamber-pot with roses on the side, and it's full to the brim with piss. And guess who I think is going to be this year's winner.

SAM [*Almost shouting*]: Stop now!

HALLY [*Suddenly appalled by how far he has gone*]: Why?

SAM: Hally? It's your father you're talking about.

HALLY: So?

SAM: Do you know what you've been saying?
[HALLY *can't answer. He is rigid with shame.* SAM *speaks to him sternly*]

No, Hally, you mustn't do it. Take back those words and ask for forgiveness! It's a terrible sin for a son to mock his father with jokes like that. You'll be punished if you carry on. Your father is your father, even if he is a...cripple man.

WILLIE: Yes, Master Hally. Is true what Sam say.

SAM: I understand how you are feeling, Hally, but even so....

HALLY: No, you don't!

SAM: I think I do.

HALLY: And I'm telling you you don't. Nobody does. *[Speaking carefully as his shame turns to rage at* **SAM***]* It's your turn to be careful, Sam. Very careful! You're treading on dangerous ground. Leave me and my father alone.

SAM: I'm not the one who's been saying things about him.

HALLY: What goes on between me and my Dad is none of your business!

SAM: Then don't tell me about it. If that's all you've got to say about him, I don't want to hear.

[For a moment **HALLY** *is at loss for a response]*

HALLY: Just get on with your bloody work and shut up.

SAM: Swearing at me won't help you.

HALLY: Yes, it does! Mind your own fucking business and shut up!

SAM: Okay. If that's the way you want it, I'll stop trying.

[He turns away. This infuriates **HALLY** *even more]*

HALLY: Good. Because what you've been trying to do is meddle in something you know nothing about. All that concerns you in here, Sam, is to try and do what you get paid for—keep the place clean and serve the customers. In plain words, just get on with your job. My mother is right. She's always warning me about allowing you to get too familiar. Well, this time you've gone too far. It's going to stop right now.

[No response from **SAM***]* You're only a servant in here, and don't forget it.

[Still no response. **HALLY** *is trying hard to get one]* And as far as my father is concerned, all you need to remember is that he is your boss.

SAM *[Needled at last]*: No, he isn't. I get paid by your mother.

HALLY: Don't argue with me, Sam!

SAM: Then don't say he's my boss.

HALLY: He's a white man and that's good enough for you.

SAM: I'll try to forget you said that.

HALLY: Don't! Because you won't be doing me a favor if you do. I'm telling you to remember it.

[A pause. **SAM** *pulls himself together and makes one last effort]*

SAM: Hally, Hally...! Come on now. Let's stop before it's too late. You're right. We are on dangerous ground. If we're not careful, somebody is going to get hurt.

HALLY: It won't be me.

SAM: Don't be so sure.

HALLY: I don't know what you're talking about, Sam.

SAM: Yes, you do.

HALLY *[Furious]*: Jesus, I wish you would stop trying to tell me what I do and what I don't know.

*[***SAM** *gives up. He turns to* **WILLIE***]*.

SAM: Let's finish up.

HALLY: Don't turn your back on me! I haven't finished talking.

[He grabs **SAM** *by the arm and tries to make him turn around.* **SAM** *reacts with a flash of anger]*

SAM: Don't do that, Hally! *[Facing the boy]* All right, I'm listening. Well? What do you want to say to me?

HALLY *[Pause as* **HALLY** *looks for something to say]* To begin with, why don't you also start calling me Master Harold, like Willie.

SAM: Do you, mean that?

HALLY: Why the hell do you think I said it?

SAM: And if I don't?

HALLY: You might just lose your job.

SAM *[Quietly and very carefully]*: If you make me say it once, I'll never call you anything else again.

HALLY: So? *[The boy confronts the man]* Is that meant to be a threat?

SAM: Just telling you what will happen if you make me do that. You must decide what it means to you.

HALLY: Well, I have. It's good news. Because that is exactly what Master Harold wants from now on. Think of it as a little lesson in respect, Sam, that's long overdue, and I hope you remember it as well as you do your geography. I can tell you now that somebody who will be glad to hear I've finally given it to you will be my Dad. Yes! He agrees with my Mom. He's always going on about it as well. "You must teach the boys to show you more respect, my son."

SAM: So now you can stop complaining about going home. Everybody is going to be happy tonight.

HALLY: That's perfectly correct. You see, you mustn't get the wrong idea about me and my Dad, Sam. We also have our good times together. Some bloody good laughs. He's got a marvelous sense of humor. Want to know what our favorite joke is? He gives out a big groan, you see, and says: "It's not fair, is it, Hally?" Then I have to ask: "What, chum?" And then he says: "A nigger's arse"...and we both have good laugh.

[The men stare at him with disbelief]

What's the matter, Willie? Don't you catch the joke? You always were a bit slow on the uptake. It's what is called a pun. You see, fair means both light in color and to be just and decent. *[He turns to* **SAM***]* I thought *you* would catch it, Sam.

SAM: Oh ja, I catch it all right.

HALLY: But it doesn't appeal to your sense of humor.

SAM: Do you really laugh?

HALLY: Of course.

SAM: To please him? Make him feel good?

HALLY: No, for heaven's sake! I laugh because I think it's a bloody good joke.

SAM: You're really trying hard to be ugly, aren't you? And why drag poor old Willie into it? He's done nothing to you except show you the respect you want so badly. That's also not being fair, you know...and I mean just or decent.

WILLIE: It's all right, Sam. Leave it now.

SAM: It's me you're after. You should just have said "Sam's arse"...because that's the one you're trying to kick. Anyway, how do you know it's not fair? You've never seen it. Do you want to? *[He drops his trousers and underpants and presents* *his backside for* **HALLY**'s *inspection]* Have a good look. A real Basuto arse…which is about as nigger as they can come. Satisfied? *[Trousers up]* Now you can make your Dad even happier when you go home tonight. Tell him I showed you my arse and he is quite right. It's not fair. And if it will give him an even better laugh next time, I'll also let *him* have a look. Come, Willie, let's finish up and go.

*[*SAM *and* WILLIE *start to tidy up the tea room.* HALLY *doesn't move. He waits for a moment when* SAM *passes him]*

HALLY *[Quietly]*: Sam

*[*SAM *stops and looks expectantly at the boy.* HALLY *spits in his face. A long and heartfelt groan from* WILLIE*. For a few seconds* SAM *doesn't move]*

SAM *[Taking out a handkerchief and wiping his face]*: It's all right, Willie.

[To HALLY*]*

Ja, well, you've done it…Master Harold. Yes, I'll start calling you that from now on. It won't be difficult anymore. You've hurt yourself, Master Harold. I saw it coming. I warned you, but you wouldn't listen. You've just hurt yourself *bad*. And you're a coward, Master Harold. The face you should be spitting in is your father's…but you used mine, because you think you're safe inside your fair skin…and this time I don't mean just or decent. *[Pause, then moving violently towards* HALLY*]* Should I hit him, Willie?

WILLIE *[Stopping* SAM*]*: No, Boet Sam.

SAM *[Violently]*: Why not?

WILLIE: It won't help, Boet Sam.

SAM: I don't want to help! I want to hurt him.

WILLIE: You also hurt yourself.

SAM: And if he had done it to you, Willie?

WILLIE: Me? Spit at me like I was a dog? *[A thought that had not occurred to him before. He looks at* HALLY*]* Ja. Then I want to hit him. I want to hit him hard!

[A dangerous few seconds as the men stand staring at the boy. WILLIE *turns away, shaking his head]* But maybe all I do is go cry at the back. He's little boy, Boet Sam. Little *white* boy. Long trousers now, but he's still little boy.

SAM *[His violence ebbing away into defeat as quickly as it flooded]*: You're right. So go on, then groan again, Willie. You do it better than me. *[To* HALLY*]* You don't know all of what you've just done…Master Harold. It's not just that you've made me feel dirtier than I've ever been in my life…I mean, how do I wash off yours and your father's filth?…I've also failed. A long time ago I promised myself I was going to try and do something, but you've just shown me…Master Harold…that I've failed. *[Pause]* I've also got a memory of a little white boy when he was still wearing short trousers and a black man, but they're not flying a kite. It was the old Jubilee days, after dinner one night. I was in my room. You came in and just stood against the wall, looking down at the ground, and only after I'd asked you what you wanted, what was wrong, I don't know how many times, did you speak and even then so softly I almost didn't hear you. "Sam, please help me to go and fetch my Dad." Remember? He was dead drunk on the floor of the

Central Hotel Bar. They'd phoned for your Mom, but you were the only one at home. And do you remember how we did it? You went in first by yourself to ask permission for me to go into the bar. Then I loaded him onto my back like a baby and carried him back to the boarding house with you following behind carrying his crutches. *[Shaking his head as he remembers]* A crowded Main Street with all the people watching a little white boy following his drunk father on a nigger's back! I felt for that little boy…Master Harold. I felt for him. After that we still had to clean him up, remember? He'd messed in his trousers, so we had to clean him up and get him into bed.

HALLY *[Great pain]*: I love him, Sam.

SAM: I know you do. That's why I tried to stop you from saying these things about him. It would have been so simple if you could have just despised him for being a weak man. But he's your father. You love him and you're ashamed of him. You're ashamed of so much!…And now that's going to include yourself. That was the promise I made to myself: to try and stop that happening. *[Pause]* After we got him to bed you came back with me to my room and sat in a corner and carried on just looking down at the ground. And for days after that! You hadn't done anything wrong, but you went around as if you owed the world an apology for being alive. I didn't like seeing that! That's not the way a boy grows up to be a man!…But the one person who should have been teaching you what that means was the cause of your shame. If you really want to know, that's why I made you that kite. I wanted you to look up, be proud of something, of yourself…*[Bitter smile at the memory]*…and you certainly were that when I left you with it up there on the hill. Oh, ja…something else!…If you ever do write it as a short story, there was a twist in our ending. I couldn't sit down there and stay with you. It was a "Whites Only" bench. You were too young, too excited to notice then. But not anymore. If you're not careful…Master Harold…you're going to be sitting up there by yourself for a long time to come, and there won't be a kite in the sky. *[*SAM *has got nothing more to say. He exits into the kitchen, taking off his waiter's jacket]*

WILLIE: Is bad. Is all all bad in here now.

HALLY *[Books into his school case, raincoat on]*: Willie…*[It is difficult to speak]* Will you lock up for me and look after the keys?

WILLIE: Okay.

*[*SAM *returns.* HALLY *goes behind the counter and collects the few coins in the cash register. As he starts to leave…]*

SAM: Don't forget the comic books.

*[*HALLY *returns to the counter and puts them in his case. He starts to leave again]*

SAM *[To the retreating back of the boy]*: Stop…Hally…

*[*HALLY *stops, but doesn't turn to face him]*

Hally…I've got no right to tell you what being a man means if I don't behave like one myself, and I'm not doing so well at that this afternoon. Should we try again, Hally?

HALLY: Try what?

SAM: Fly another kite, I suppose. It worked once, and this time I need it as much as you do.

HALLY: It's still raining, Sam. You can't fly kites on rainy days, remember.

SAM: So what do we do? Hope for better weather tomorrow?

HALLY: [Helpless gesture]: I don't know. I don't know anything anymore.

SAM: You sure of that, Hally? Because it would be pretty hopeless if that was true. It would mean nothing has been learnt in here this afternoon, and there was a hell of a lot of teaching going on...one way or the other. But anyway, I don't believe you. I reckon there's one thing you know. You don't have to sit up there by yourself. You know what that bench means now, and you can leave it any time you choose. All you've got to do is stand up and walk away from it.

[HALLY *leaves.* WILLIE *goes up quietly to* SAM]

WILLIE: Is okay, Boet Sam. You see. Is...[He can't find any better words]...is going to be okay tomorrow. . [Changing his tone] Hey, Boet Sam! [He is trying hard] You right. I think about it and you right. Tonight I find Hilda and say sorry. And make promise I won't beat her no more. You hear me, Boet Sam?

SAM: I hear you, Willie.

WILLIE: And when we practice I relax and romance with her from beginning to end. Non-stop! You watch! Two weeks' time: "First prize for promising newcomers: Mr. Willie Malopo and Miss Hilda Samuels" [Sudden impulse] To hell with it! I walk home. [He goes to the jukebox, puts in a coin and selects a record. The machine comes to life in the gray twilight, blushing its way through a spectrum of soft, romantic colors] How did you say it, Boet Sam? Let's dream. [WILLIE sways with the music and gestures for SAM to dance]

[Sarah Vaughan sings] "Little man you're crying,
    I know why you're blue,
    Someone took your kiddy car away;
    Better go to sleep now,
    Little man you've had a busy day." [etc. etc.]
You lead. I follow.

[The men dance together]
    "Johnny won your marbles,
    Tell you what we'll do;
    Dad will get you new ones right away;
    Better go to sleep now,
    Little man you've had a busy day."

END

Life Theme 5:

Dreams

Life Theme 5: Dreams

All of us have ambitions, fantasies and hopes. They may barely resemble the lives for which we settle.

Dreamer of dreams, born out of my due time,
Why should I strive to set the crooked straight?
The Earthly Paradise, William Morris

Featured plays:

The Three Sisters
by Anton Chekhov
Bitter Cane
by Genny Lim

Dreaming of a better life, with less suffering, disappointment, and boredom, is a universal longing. Who hasn't spent hours stuck in one life dreaming of another? Two plays, one by Russia's greatest playwright and a pioneer of realism and the other by a Chinese American playwright, capture very different versions of dashed but indomitable hope.

The Three Sisters

Year: 1900
Genre: Realistic prose drama
Structure: Well-made, three acts
Setting: A remote small town in Russia
Setting: The Prozoroff household in a small provincial Russian town

Context:

At the turn of the 20th century, Russia experienced a growing tidal wave of rebellion and reaction from a long oppressed and angry peasant class. Like most European countries, traditional Russian society was divided into a miniscule elite class of aristocracy, a small but growing "middle class" of professional workers, and a vast underclass of working poor. In Russia, however, the class division was intensified. The aristocracy was fabulously and ostentatiously rich and the poor were virtual slaves. Serfdom, a medieval form of peasant "ownership," was practiced in Russia well into the late 19th century. Even with the passage of laws freeing the serfs from their masters, centuries of poverty, illiteracy, and debt kept the peasant class entrapped. In this play, two life long servants of the family, Anfisa and Ferapont, are too elderly and infirm to work any longer and the brother's new wife Natasha turns them out into the streets.

By 1900, rebellions and violence were breaking out in pockets across Russia as the dreams of the poor were smashed by the army of the elite. The story of the last Czar Nicholas and his family is probably familiar to you. Chekhov's play takes us into the privileged world of the Prozoroff family and the officers of the local regiment, who are their only social equals in their small provincial town. At the time, a man had to purchase his position as an officer and it was very costly. Only the second or third sons of the elite could afford to become officers. While other plays and playwrights of the early 20th century were revealing the appalling conditions of the poor, Chekhov turned his gaze toward members of his own social class – an educated middle class with failing purses and nothing in their pockets but dreams.

Chekhov's plays have had such a profound impact on live theatre and films that it is almost impossible to imagine a time when characters did not speak, act and react like ordinary people whom we might know down the street. Yet the vast majority of plays preceding his were stuck somewhere in the heroic, melodramatic, fantastical mode with little attention to real life. His ideas are now widely accepted, but imagine how revolutionary they must have seemed in that theatrical world. Chekhov wrote:

> *A play should be written in which people arrive, go away, have dinner, talk about the weather, and play cards. Life must be as it is and people as they are – not on stilts! … Let everything on the stage be as complicated and at the same time as simple as it is in life.*

In his works, as in our own lives, characters often fail to understand each other, to connect, and in spite of fleeting connections, remain isolated. Being able to communicate our dreams, to make our dreams more real by talking about them, is an essential human need. But it is frequently most difficult to do so with the people we love the most. This becomes particularly difficult when our dreams and our loved ones' dreams for us are in conflict. In this play, people who love each other drive each other crazy talking about, not talking about, pursuing, or refusing to pursue their conflicting dreams for a better, more fulfilling future.

The Three Sisters captures the poignancy of lifelong frustration, sad meetings and partings, and love that remains unrequited. It is filled with flashes of humor, but is ultimately, infinitely sad. It is this balance of wonderful comic observation and a sense of futility that give Chekhov's works tremendous pathos. He manages to present exquisitely frail and flawed characters without ever passing judgment on them.

Chekhov himself, because of his poor health, was under doctor's orders not to venture to Moscow, but rather to remain in an isolated, provincial town, Yalta in the Crimean, which he described as his "warm Siberia" (the place Russians traditionally regard as the ultimate punishment and dreaded exile). He was even denied the joy of attending the opening of *The Three Sisters* Jan. 31, 1901 at the Moscow Art Theatre and ultimately died of tuberculosis only three years later at the age of 44. While the play was not an immediate hit, it has gone on to become the most widely produced of Chekhov's works. After the Russian Revolution in 1917, *The Three Sisters* was often credited as a major impulse inspiring that event, capturing the lethargy and class conflicts that would ultimately lead to an overthrow of aristocratic governance. Several of the characters predict and long for a future in which everyone has satisfaction through work. The Baron, who has never worked, says:

> *The time is almost here, a mighty clearing storm, an avalanche is coming. It will soon blow away the laziness, the indifference, the distaste for work, the rotten boredom of our society. I swear I am going to work and in another twenty-five or thirty years, everyone will have to work. Every one! That's as it should be.*

Note:

About the varying uses of names among the characters: there are two Russian way of playing with names, Patronymics and Diminutives.

Patronymics- A Russian's middle name is his or her father's first name with feminine and masculine endings: *-yitch* or *-itch* for men, *-ovna*, or *-yevna* for women. Calling a person by his full three names (Alexander Ignatyevitch Vershinin) is usually done under very formal circumstances. Calling someone by his first name and patronymic is usually a form of polite address or it can be done as a kind of ironic, playful endearment.

Diminutives- Turing "Olga" into "Olya" is much like turning John into Johnny. It is proper only among affectionate equals or family members, though never from a child to an adult. Most names are just shortened and then add a "ya' ("Ivan" becomes "Vanya"). The ending *–achka* is a particularly "cutesy" feminine ending. Only someone presumptuous and/or ignorant (like Natasha) would use diminutives without really being entitled to do so.

The Playwright:

Anton Chekhov was born in 1860, the third child of six, the son of a shopkeeper and the grandson of a serf. While still in his teens, he had to financially support his family because his tyrannical, inept father had driven them into bankruptcy and to the brink of social ruin. Chekhov pursued a medical degree while earning extra money by writing amusing character studies, short stories and essays. A true student of people from all classes of the surrounding neighborhood, Chekhov built characters from real experiences. He wrote a number of short plays, generally comic and often farces, and four great masterpieces of modern realism: *The Seagull, Uncle Vanya, The Three Sisters,* and *The Cherry Orchard.* He died in 1904 of tuberculosis in Badenweiler, Germany.

Bitter Cane

Year: 1989
Genre: "Magic" Realism
Structure: Episodic
Setting: Hawaii in the 1880s

Context:

The American cultural landscape has been fundamentally shaped by the hopes and dreams of wave upon wave of emigrants from around the world. Each successive wave of emigrants has dreamed of a better life for their children in what Tony Kushner, an internationally respected playwright, has called "the melting pot where nothing ever melted." Central to the American identity is the struggle of emigrants to reconcile two distinctive dreams: first, to assimilate into American culture and achieve success for their family, community, and especially the next generation; and second, to retain the central tenets of their own cultural identity in a new, strange, and frequently hostile landscape. Many playwrights have dealt with and are still dealing with this paradoxical dream including David Henry Hwang (*M. Butterfly)* and Milcha Sanchez-Scott (*Roosters).* The Irish, Germans, Jews, Italians, Chinese, Japanese, East Indians, etc. have all struggled with the disconnect between their dreams of America and the reality of being the despised "other."

Genny Lim believes that gender and race are two of the most significant issues of our time that create tension in "dominant Western male imperialistic society." She says that the traditional social stigmas attached to women and persons of color are at the heart of the political struggles centered on the environment, AIDS, nuclear arms, technology, homelessness, drugs, guns, and violence. She says:

> *Women are abused, raped, battered, and deserted with their children on a daily basis. Women of color must stand and watch their own sons become involved in wars or imprisoned or killed in their own city streets. If we don't confront these realities squarely and honestly, we, as a culture, will be undermined by them, as we are already witnessing.*
> (Lim, *quoted in The Politics of Life, pg. 154)*

Lim pursues her thematic project in *Bitter Cane* by looking back at a moment in history when Western imperialist powers controlled the islands of Hawaii and brought thousands of poor Chinese workers to the islands to do the back-breaking labor of the sugar cane plantations.

Between 1852 and 1898, 50,000 single Chinese men were lured to the Hawaiian sugar plantations with promises of easy money. Plantation managers also tempted workers from Japan, the Philippines, Portugal and other poor regions of the world, but the Chinese were among the first and largest of the waves of emigration. Agents of the plantation owners went to one of the poorest regions in China, the Kwantung province, which had been ravaged by civil war. (Genny Lim's parents emigrated from Kwantung.) The people of Kwantung province had always lived hard and desperate lives as they struggled to eke an existence out of a harsh and inhospitable environment by cultivating rice (like sugar, a very labor intensive crop). The addition of tribal fighting led to famine and hopelessness, sparking a vulnerability to promises of jobs and wealth to be had elsewhere. Promised easy work, free room and board, passage to Hawaii, and good salaries, tens of thousands of young Chinese men believed the agents who told them they could get rich in the paradise of Hawaii and return home to dignity and honor after a few years' investment.

Sadly, and yet predictably, what they found in Hawaii was more poverty, more hard work, isolation from family and community, and opium. The plantation system in Hawaii was organized in ways that did not differ much from the plantation system in the American Deep South during the years of slavery. Chinese workers were isolated into shanty villages that they were not allowed to leave. They were frequently whipped and punished for insubordination, slow work, and attempting to escape. In contrast to the easy wealth promised by the sugar industry, the average salary of a cane worker was three dollars a month. Committed to a five year contract, many cane workers (or *coolies* as they were called by the white owners) never made it back to China because of illness, injury, death or shame. To return home to China after five years with nothing to show for it was an admission of failure that guaranteed social isolation for the young man.

An extra "Catch-22" was built into the plantation system as workers learned after arriving in Hawaii that they were required to repay their "free" passage to Hawaii and, in some places, their "free" room and board. Like many indentured peoples before them, they discovered that their debt overwhelmed their meager salaries and they might well be caught in the system for the rest of their lives.

Unable to fulfill their dreams or escape from the on-going nightmare of the cane fields, workers became disenchanted and rebellious. In a move specifically designed to control the labor force, plantation owners began including packets of opium in the room and board package. Tragically, many workers became lost in the dreamy twilit world of opium addiction and did not/could not return home even if they survived their five year contract and paid off their debts.

Shortly after the importation of large numbers of men to work the fields, the lack of women and family became an obvious threat to the stability of the work force. The white managers began recruiting young Chinese women by promising them honorable marriages to "wealthy" cane workers. While some women (sometimes called "Picture Brides") were able to fulfill their dreams of marriage, others were placed in virtual enslavement and used for the sexual appeasement of the workers. These women also became desperate to escape when their dreams of marriage and family began to crumble. As with the cane workers, the simple, cost-effective tactic of opium addiction helped control the women.

Despite the hard reality of despair and death in the cane fields, wave upon wave of emigrants continued to flow into Hawaii tempted by dreams of wealth and social standing. As recounted in *Bitter Cane*, the dreams of the men and women of the plantation system were savagely denied. Yet these dreams could not be completely destroyed and the workers struggled to adjust their dreams to the reality of camp life in Hawaii. Further debilitated by opium, some became trapped in a drug-induced dreamscape in which all pain and suffering became a distant ghost image.

The Chinese workers brought to Hawaii the cultural beliefs of their homelands. Ancestor worship dominated the spiritual life of the workers and included the expectation that direct intervention by the dead was a common and expected result of ritual ceremonies. The ghost of Wing's father in *Bitter Cane* is not perceived by the characters as an illusion, delusion, or super-natural event. Ghosts, or the spirits of the ancestors, were an integral part of everyday reality. In addition to ancestor worship, they brought from China a deeply ingrained sense of duty to the community and the family before the self. When Wing sees a chance to escape from the plantation, he is reminded that his duty is to return the bones of his father to China so that his father can at last rest in peace and honor back home. Again, this is a literal reality to Wing, as real as the sugar cane and the foremen who beat him. When Li-Tai, who was in love with Wing's father, finds her final escape in an overdose of opium, her reunion with her lover in the next life is a literal fact. While these cultural realities help foster tension between the plantation owners and the cane workers, they also sustained many of the workers through their ordeal. Genny Lim examines the dreams and nightmares of all emigrant peoples by focusing on a moment in American history when the dreams of riches and respect back home in China are trampled and injured, but never fully defeated.

The Playwright:

Genny Lim was born in 1946, the youngest of seven children in her Chinese American family. She has lived most of her life in San Francisco, where she is a poet, performer, playwright, producer and educator. She says growing up living in San Francisco's Chinatown helped her feel a sense of cultural continuity with her ancestors, and that at the same time her 6 older brothers and sisters introduced her to everything that was "cool" in American culture from Beatnik poetry to country western music. Her works have reflected this multicultural background and Lim continues exploring the cutting edge in theatre and music (esp. jazz) performance, writing, and political activism.

The Three Sisters

by Anton Checkov
Edited and Adapted by Robert Barton
Orginal Production—1901

Characters

The Prozoroff Family, brother and sisters:
  ANDREY
  OLGA
  IRINA
  MASHA

Faithful old family servants:
  ANFISA
  FERAPONT

Andrey's Girlfriend, Later His Wife:
  NATSAHA

Masha's husband:
  KULYGIN

Army officers stationed at the local outpost:
  TUSENBACH
  TCHEBUTYKIN
  SOLYONY
  FEDOTIK
  RODAY
  VERSHININ

Setting

The Prozoroff household in a small provincial Russian town

ACT 1

(The Prozoroff house. A drawing-room with columns and a large dining room beyond. The table in the dining room is being set for lunch. Noon. A bright, sunny day. OLGA, in the blue uniform of a girl's school teacher, correcting school papers, walking to and fro; MASHA, in a black dress with her hat on her knees, sitting reading a book; IRINA, in a white dress, standing lost in thought)

OLGA: It was a year ago today. The day father died. May five—your birthday. But it was cold and snowing then. I thought I'd never live through it. I'll never forget the sight of you lying in a dead faint. But now it's a whole year and well…we can talk about it at least. You're wearing white once again, and you look radiant. *[The clock strikes twelve]* The clock struck twelve then *[a pause]* as they carried Father away. A band was playing, and at the cemetery they fired a three gun salute. Do you think they always do that for a brigadier general? You know what was odd, though, there were very few people walking behind his coffin. I suppose because it was raining… and then snowing.

IRINA: Why bring it up?

[TUSENBACH, TCHEBUTYKIN and SOLYONY appear behind the columns in the dining room near the table.]

OLGA: It's warm today. We can keep the windows wide open, but there are no leaves on the birch trees yet. In Moscow, by this time, everything is in bloom. I remember everything there, even if it has been eleven years. I remember it all as if we'd left only yyesterday. Oh dear God. I woke up this morning, saw brilliant sunlight, saw the spring, and my heart almost burst with joy. And I wanted to go home again.

TCHEBUTYKIN: The devil!

TUSENBACH: It's nonsense. All nonsense.

[MASHA, brooding over a book, softly whistles a song.]

OLGA: Don't whistle, Masha. How can you do? *[a pause]* I'm at the school every day till evening, that's why I always have a headache. I'm starting to think like an old woman. The school has stolen my strength and youth. And only one dream keeps me alive.

IRINA: To go to Moscow! Soon!

OLGA: Yes! To Moscow. Soon!

[TUSENBACH and TCHEBUTYKIN laugh]

IRINA: When AAndreyecomes a professor we can go. The only thing that stops us is poor Masha.

OLGA: But Masha can come to Moscow for the whole summer every year. *[MASHA softly whistles a song.]*

IRINA: Dear God, please let it happen! *[looking out of the window]* What a beautiful day. I don't know why I feel so…light! This morning I remembered it was my birthday and suddenly felt… joy! I remembered being a child. I remembered mama. And felt so alive!

OLGA: You look lovelier than ever today. And Masha is beautiful too. Andrey would be quite attractive if he hadn't gotten so heavy. And me? Older and thinner. But I'm free

of the school today and I have no headache. I feel younger than yesterday. I'm twenty-eight years old and… I don't know… I think I should have been married. I think…*[a pause]* I would have loved my husband.

TUSENBACH: *[to SOLYONY]* You talk such garbage! I'm sick of listening to you. *[entering the drawing room with Kulygin]* Forget to tell you. The new Battery Commander Vershinin is coming to visit today. *[sitting down at the piano]*

OLGA: Well, I'll be glad to meet him.

IRINA: Is he old?

TUSENBACH: No, not very. Fortyish. *[playing softly]* He seems like a good man. Not stupid, that's for sure. Except he talks a lot.

IRINA: Is he interesting?

TUSENBACH: Well, he's got this wife, and a mother-in-law and two daughters. This is his second wife and she's sort of crazy. She wears her hair in long, silky braids, speaks only philosophy, and often tries to commit suicide. To plague the husband, obviously. I'd have left her ages ago, but he puts up with her. And just complains all the time.

SOLYONY: *[entering the drawing room from the dining room with TCHEBUTYKIN]* With one hand I can lift maybe fifty pounds, but with both, 180 or sometimes 200 pounds. So I conclude that two men are more than twice as strong as one. Maybe three times, as strong, maybe more….

TCHEBUTYKIN: *[reading a newspaper as he comes in]* For balding…naphthalene with spirits, two parts to one…dissolve and use daily. Better write that down! *[writing it down in his notebook]*

IRINA: Ivan Romanitch, dear Ivan Romanitch.

TCHEBUTYKIN: What, my child, my sweet girl?

IRINA: Tell me, why am I so happy today? I feel like I'm sailing, with the wide blue sky and great white birds soaring above me. Why is that? Why?

TCHEBUTYKIN: *[kissing both her hands tenderly]* My little white bird.

IRINA: This morning everything seems clear to me and I know how to live. Dear Ivan Romanitch, I know everything! I mightt vork. I might find some way to be of use. It's the only way for anyone to find meaning in life. A shepherd, or a schoolmaster, an engineer or—anyone! My God! Any of them are better than a young woman who wakes up at twelve o'clock, has coffee in bed, and then spends two hours getting dressed! So I'm going to find my meaning. And if I don't get up early and go to work, you give me up as a friend, Ivan Romanitch.

TCHEBUTYKIN: *[tenderly]* I'll give you up, I'll give you up-

OLGA: Irina wakes up early, but then she lies there forever thinking "serious thoughts!" *[laughing]*

IRINA: You still think of me as a little girl. I'm twenty years old *[realizing it fully]* I am! I'm twenty.

TUSENBACH: And longing for work. Now I, on the other hand, have never worked in my life. My family shielded me from work. We had footmen and others to do such things. But you're right. Something is changing. A vast, healing storm is gathering and it's going to clear our class of laziness and indifference. I believe it. I'll work too. And maybe someday, twenty-five years or so, everyone will!

TCHEBUTYKIN: I won't work.

TUSENBACH: You don't count.

SOLYONY: Twenty-five years from now and you won't even be alive, thank God! In a few years you'll die of a stroke, or I'll forget myself and put a bullet through your head. *[taking cologne from his pocket and sprinkling his chest and hands.]*

TCHEBUTYKIN: *[laughing]* I've never really done anything. Since I graduated from the university, I haven't lifted a finger. I haven't read one book, just newspapers…*[taking another newspaper out of his pocket]* Much shorter. *[a servant beckons him]* Ah, somebody here to see me. Be right back… *[he leaves hurriedly, pulling on his beard as he goes.]*

IRINA: He's up to something.

TUSENBACH: Yes. Obviously he'll come right back with a birthday gift for you.

IRINA: Oh, I wish he wouldn't.

OLGA: So do I. He always manages to do something childish.

MASHA: By the curved seashore a green oak, a golden chain upon that oak…a golden chain upon that oak. *[getting up and humming softly.]*

OLGA: You're not exactly cheerful today, Masha.

MASHA: *[hums as she puts on her hat]*

OLGA: Where are you going?

MASHA: Home.

IRINA: Why Masha…

TUSENBACH: Leaving your little sister's birthday party?

MASHA: What does it matter…I'll come back this evening. Goodbye my sweet darling… *[kissing **IRINA**]* I wish you once again good health and happiness. When father was alive, there were as many as forty officers at our birthday parties. It was loud and joyous, but now, here's only a man and a half… It's so quiet….I'm going… I feel blue today. I feel…. So don't listen to me. *[laughing through her tears]* We'll talk. Goodbye now, my dear. *[embraces her]* I'll go somewhere or other.

IRINA: *[vexed]* Oh, you're such a….

OLGA: *[tearfully]* I understand how you feel, Masha.

SOLYONY: Men's ideas are philosophy, but women's are like dentistry.

MASHA: What did you say, you dreadful man?

SOLYONY: Nothing. Quick as a flash, the bear made a dash… *[exit, a pause]*

MASHA: *[to **OLGA** angrily]* Stop blubbering, Olga.
*[Enter **ANFISA**, and after her, **FERAPONT** with a cake.]*

ANFISA: Here, old man. Are your feet clean? Then come in. *[to **IRINA**]* From the County Board, from Mihail Ivanitch Protopopoff…a cake.

IRINA: Thank him for me. *[taking the cake]*

FERAPONT: How's that?

IRINA: *[louder]* Thank him for me.

OLGA: Nursey, give him some pie. Go on, Ferapont. They'll give you some pie.

FERAPONT: How's that?

ANFISA: Come on, little father, Ferapont Spiridonitch. Come on my dear…Come with Anfisa *[goes out with **FERAPONT**.]*

MASHA: I don't like Protopopoff.
*[**TCHEBUTYKIN** enters, behind him servants with a silver samovar; there is a hum of astonishment and displeasure.]*

OLGA: A samovar! On no! How terrible!

IRINA: Ivan Romanitch, what are you doing? What have you done? I'm not your….

TUSENBACH: *[laughing]* I told you so.

TCHEBUTYKIN: My darlings, my sweet girls, you're all I have. You're all that's precious in the world to me. I'm a lonely worthless old man… The only good thing about me is my love for you. *[to **IRINA**]* My dear, little angel, I've known you from the day you were born… I carried you in my arms… I loved your mother... ..

IRINA: But why such excessive presents! This isn't… appropriate.

TCHEBUTYKIN *[through his tears, angrily]* Excessive presents! Why, you're completely…*[to the servants]* Carry the samovar in there… Excessive presents…
[The samovar is carried into the dining room]

ANFISA: *[passing through the drawing room]* My dears, there's a colonel, a stranger. He's coming in here. Irinushka, you be a nice, polite girl. *[as she goes out]* And it was time for lunch long ago…mercy me!

TUSENBACH: This must be Vershinin. *[**VERSHININ** enters]* Lieutenant Colonel Vershinin!

VERSHININ: *[to **MASHA** and **IRINA**]* I'm very glad to visit your house. How you've grown up! My, my….

IRINA: Please sit down. We're delighted to see you, but you know us?

VERSHININ: *[gaily]* You are the three sisters. I remember—three little girls. When I visited your father, the colonel. How time does fly! Oh, oh, my!

TUSENBACH: Alexander Ignatyevitch is from Moscow.

IRINA: From Moscow. You are from Moscow?

VERSHININ: Yes. I was an officer in the same brigade as your father there. *[To **MASHA**]* Now you, I do remember your face.

MASHA: And I you.

IRINA: Olya! Olya! *[calling into dining room]* Olya! Come here.
*[**OLGA** comes in from the dining room]*

IRINA: Lieutenant Colonel Vershinin, it turns out, is from Moscow.

VERSHININ: You must be Olga Sergeyevna, the eldest…and you Maria…and you Irina—the youngest…

OLGA: Are you from Moscow?

VERSHININ: Yes. I used to pay you calls in Moscow. Your father is so fresh in my memory; I can close my eyes now and see him as plain as life. And now here I am in his position as battery commander. And Moscow seems very far away.

OLGA: We're going to move there, you know.

IRINA: We'll be there, oh, probably by Autumn. It's our home town. We were all born there. *[They both laugh delightedly]*

MASHA: What a surprise to see someone from home. *[Vivaciously]* Now I remember! Do you Olya? This is the man they used to call "The lovesick major." You were a lieutenant then and in love and everyone teased you. The lovesick major!

VERSHININ: *[laughing]* Yes, yes! That's right! That's me! The lovesick major.

MASHA: You just had a moustache then. Oh, how much older you look! *[Tearfully]* How much older you look. I'm sorry.

VERSHININ: Yes, well, the lovesick major was young, he was in love. Not so now.

OLGA: But you don't have a single gray hair. You look mature, not old.

VERSHININ: Has it been a long time since you saw Moscow?

IRINA: Eleven years. But why are you crying, Masha, you silly? *[through her tears]* I'm starting to cry too.

MASHA: I'm all right. What street did you live on?

VERSHININ: Old Basmannaya.

OLGA: So did we. Now I remember you too. I remember.

VERSHININ: I knew your mother too, of course.

TCHEBUTYKIN: A lovely woman. God bless her soul.

IRINA: Mother is buried in Moscow.

MASHA: My God, I'm already beginning to forget her face. Well, I suppose others will forget us too, someday.

VERSHININ: Yes. They'll forget us. That's fate. And what seems serious to us, will probably seem silly. *[a pause]* Didn't people first find the discoveries of Copernicus and Columbus nothing more than nonsense? So maybe our present lives will someday be called stupid, even sinful.

TUSENBACH: Who knows? Perhaps we'll be called civilized. There are no more tortures, no executions, no invasions. But not much happiness either.

SOLYONY: *[In a high-pitched voice]* Chick, chick, chick. Don't feed the Baron grain, jut let him philosophize.

TUSENBACH: Vassily Vassilyitch, leave me alone. *[sits at another place]*

SOLYONY: *[In a high-pitched voice]* Chick, chick, chick.

TCHEBUTYKIN: Call our present life civilized? No, we're small. It would only be to console me that anybody would call my life civilized.

[Behind the scenes a violin plays.]

MASHA: It's Andrey playing, our brother.

IRINA: He is the learned one in the family. It looks as if he's going to become a professor, instead of a military man.

MASHA: According to Father's wishes.

OLGA: We've been teasing him. It seems he's a little in love.

IRINA: With a local girl. She'll probably be here today.

MASHA: Oh, how she dresses! Not just unattractive or ugly, but—pathetic. Colors you've never seen together before. And things like—fringe. And her cheeks! Andrey isn't in love—I can't believe it, I just can't. Andrey has taste. Besides, I heard yesterday that she's going to marry Protopopoff, the Chairman of the Board. And that's fine with me *[at the side door]* Andrey, come here! Just for a minute will you darling?

[ANDREY enters]

OLGA: Our brother, Andrey Sergeyitch.

VERSHININ: Alexander IIgnatyevitch Vershinin.

ANDREY: *[he wipes his perspiring face]* You're our new Battery Commander?

OLGA: And from Moscow.

ANDREY: Yes? Well, now my sisters won't give you any peace.

VERSHININ: I think I'm the one who's tired them out.

IRINA: Look at the frame Andrey gave me today! *[showing the frame]* He made it himself.

VERSHININ: *[looking at the frame and not knowing what to say]* Yes, a frame.

IRINA: And the frame over the piano there, he made that, too.

[ANDREY moves his hand in embarrassment and moves away.]

OLGA: IHe is the learned one, he plays the violin and he makes things with wood. He can do anything. Andrey, don't go away! He's always leaving. Come back!

[MASHA and IRINA, laughing take him by the arms and lead him back]

MASHA: Come, sweetheart! Come!

ANDREY: Leave me alone. Please.

MASHA: The colonel here used to be called the lovesick major and he didn't get upset at all.

VERSHININ: Not a bit.

MASHA: We should call you the lovesick fiddler!

IRINA: Or the lovesick professor!

OLGA: Andrusha's in love!

IRINA: *[applauding]* Bravo, bravo! Andrushka is in love!

TCHEBUTYKIN: *[comes up behind ANDREY and puts both arms around his waist]* For love alone did Nature put us in this world.

ANDREY: Well, that's enough, that's enough *[wiping his face]* I haven't slept all night. I'm not myself. I read 'til four o'clock this morning. There's a book I want to translate from English. *[kisses MASHA]*

IRINA: But you already gave me a copy of this book, at Easter.

KULYGIN: *[laughing]* No! Did I? How embarrassing. Well, then give it back, or better still, give it to the Colonel. Take it Colonel. Read it sometimes when you're bored.

VERSHININ: Thank you *[he is about to leave]* I'm very glad to have made your acquaintance, all of you.

OLGA: You're leaving? No,no!

IRINA: Stay for lunch. Please.

OLGA: Oh, please do.

VERSHININ: *[bowing]* I've stumbled in on a birthday party. Forgive me. I didn't know. My congratulations. Of course I'd be honored. *[goes with OLGA to dining room]*

KULYGIN: Today is Sunday, gentlemen, a day of rest, let us rest, each according to his age and position. Now, the Romans they know how to llive. Theyı ad mens sana in corpore sano. Our head master dsays: he important thing in life is form. *[takes MASHA by the waist, laughingly]* Masha loves me. My wife loves me. I am in a good mood today. Masha, at one o'clock today we are due at the headmaster's home. There's an open house for the teachers and their families.

MASHA: I'm not going.

KULYGIN: *[aggrieved]* Dear Masha, why?

MASHA: If you don't *[angrily]* Oh, alright, I'll go, but now just leave me alone, please. *[walks away]*

KULYGIN: In spite of his poor health, our headmaster tries to be sociable. A wonderful man. Yesterday he said to me: "I'm tired, Fyodor Ilyitch: I am tired!" *[looks at the clock on the wall, then at his watch]* Your clock is seven minutes fast. Yes, he says, 'I am tired!'
[Offstage a violin is playing]

OLGA: Ladies and gentlemen, lunch is served! There's a meat pie.

TCHEBUTYKIN: *[puts the newspaper in his pocket, combs his beard]* A meat pie? Splendid!

MASHA: *[to TCHEBUTYKIN, sternly]* Nothing to drink today. Do you hear? Drinking's bad for you.

TCHEBUTYKIN: Oh, go on! I'm past all that. I haven't been drunk for at least two years. *[impatiently]*

MASHA: All the same, don't you dare. *[angrily but so that her husband doesn't hear]* Good Lord, another evening of utter, complete boredom at the head master's house!

TUSENBACH: I wouldn't go if I were you.

TCHEBUTYKIN: Don't go, my dear.

MASHA: Yes, well – this cursed, damnable life *[going to the dining room]*

TCHEBUTYKIN: *[going with her]* Now, now.

SOLYONY: *[taunting the BARON]* Chick, chick, chick.

TUSENBACH: That's enough, Vassily Vassilyitch. Just drop it!

SOLYONY: Chick, chick, chick.

VERSHININ: I'll have some of that vodka *[drinking]* Your health! *[to OLGA]* I feel so at home in your house!
[In the dining room only IRINA and TUSENBACH are left]

IRINA: Masha is in a bad mood today. When she married him, she was eighteen and he seemed the most intelligent man in the world to her. But now it's not the same. He's the kindest but not the most intelligent.

OLGA: *[impatiently]* Andrey, do come, will you?!

ANDREY: Yes, yes, yes. *[enters and goes to the table]*

TUSENBACH: What are you thinking?

IRINA: That Solyony frightens me. I don't like him. Everything he said is warped.

TUSENBACH: Yes, he's strange. I feel sorry for him and annoyed with him. But more sorry, really. When the two of us are alone together, he can be clever, even gentle, but in company, he's a bully and crude. Don't go in yet, please. Stay with me for just a minute. Talk to me. *[a pause]* Here you are, twenty years old. I'm not thirty yet. How many years for us ahead? Every single day full of my love for you.

IRINA: Nikolay Lvovitych, don't talk to me of love.

TUSENBACH: *[not listening]* I feel this great thirst for life, work, change. And it's all tied up in my love for you, Irina. Because you are beautiful, life seems beautiful and possible. Please say something.

IRINA: Life is beautiful? Perhaps. But for us three sisters, life hasn't yet become beautiful. Life has choked us as weeds choke grass. I'm crying. I mustn't. *[quickly wiping her face, smiling]* I honestly think that work is the answer. We're all gloomy and somber, because we don't know how to do anything. How to help and be useful. We come from people who despised work.

[NATASHA IVANOVNA enters; she has on a dress which clashes startlingly with her belt]

NATASHA: Oh dear, they're sitting down to lunch already. I'm late. *[she steals a glance at herself in the mirror and tidies herself]* My hair is all right, I think *[seeing IRINA]* Dear Irina Sergeyevna, happy birthday! *[kissing her vigorously and long]* You have lots of guests. I feel sort of shy. How do you do, Baron!

OLGA: *[entering the living room]* Ah, here is Natasha Ivanovna. Good day, my dear. *[they kiss]*

NATASHA: You have so much company, I feel awfully.

OLGA: Never mind, it's just the family, really. *[In an undertone, alarmed]* Your belt! My dear, it's, well it simply won't….

NATASHA: Do you like it?

OLGA: It looks so, it seems odd, I'm sorry.

NATASHA: *[In a tearful voice]* Yes? It does. But it's not really so bright as it seems, it's more of a neutral color. You need to see it in the light. *[following OLGA into the dining room]* *[In the dining room all are sitting down to lunch; no one is left in the living room]*

KULYGIN: Irina, my birthday wish for you is a good fiance! It's time you got married.

TCHEBUTYKIN: Natasha Ivanovna, I wish you a good fiance too.

KULYGIN: Your conduct gets C minus.

VERSHININ: This liqueur is very good. What's it made of?

SOLYONY: Cockroaches.

IRINA: *[in a tearful voice]* Oh! Ah, How disgusting!

OLGA: For supper there will be roast turkey and apple pie. I'll be at home all day today, thank the Lord. You must all come back this evening.

VERSHININ: May I, too, come this evening?

IRINA: Please do.

NATASHA: They're very informal here.

TUSENBACH: For love alone did nature put us in this world. *[laughing]*

ANDREY: Stop it, everybody! Aren't you sick of it by now?
[FEDOTIK and RODAY enter with a big basket of flowers]

FEDOTIK: But look, they're having lunch.

RODAY: *[loud]* Yes, we're late. I told you.

FEDOTIK: Wait a minute! *[taking a snapshot]* One! Wait, just one more.re. *[taking another snapshot]* Two! Now, ready! *[they pick up the basket and go to the dining room, where they are greeted noisily]*

RODAY: *[loud]* Congratulations. I wish you all good things! You have magnificent weather for your day. All morning, I walked with the high school boys. I teach gymnastics at their….

FEDOTIK: More just a little, Irina Sergeyevna, please. *[taking a snapshot]* You look wonderful today. *[getting a top out of his pocket]* By the way, here's a top for you. It has an amazing sound.

IRINA: Oh, how delightful!

MASHA: By the curved seashore a green oak, a golden chain upon that oak. A golden chain upon that oak. *[tearfully]* why do I keep saying that? That phrase has stuck in my mind ever since early this morning.

KULYGIN: Thirteen at the table! Oh, no!

RODAY: Oh come now. Do you truly believe these superstitious?

KULYGIN: Thirteen at that table is a known sure sign, that there are lovers here. Could it be you Ivan Romanovitch, by any chance? *[laughter]*

TCHEBUTYKIN: Not me. Not the old sinner. But I wonder why Natalia Ivanovna looks embarrassed. I simply have no idea.

[loud laughter, NATASHA runs out from the dining room into the living room. ANDREY follows her]

ANDREY: Natasha! Don't pay any attention to them! Wait! Stop! Please....

NATASHA: I feel so ashamed. They're making fun of me. I know it was bad manners for me to leave the table just now, but I can't, I can't.... *[covers her fce with her hands]*

ANDREY: Oh please, please don't be upset. They're only joking. They mean well. My sweet, beautiful Natasha, these people have good hearts. They love me and you. Come over here. They can't see us here.

[He glances around]

NATASHA: I'm just not used to being in society!

ANDREY: But this isn't society! It's just.... My dear, sweet Natasha, don't be upset! Trust me. I feel so happy with you, as if I can take care of you. Oh they can't see us! Don't worry! You're so innocent and young and I'm in love. Natasha, be my wife! I love you, as I've never loved before! *[a kiss]*

[The two servants enter and seeing the pair kissing, stop surprised]

CURTAIN

ACT 2

(The same setting as Act 1. Eight o'clock in the evening. Offstage, faintly, an accordion, playing in the street. No lights. NATASHA IVANOVNA enters in a dressing gown, with a candle and stops at the door that leads into ANDREY's room.

NATASHA: Andrusha, what are you doing in there? Reading? Alright. *[goes and opens another door and after looking in closes it]* With a light, you never know.

ANDREY: *[enters with a book in his hand]* What, Natasha?

NATASHA: Seeing if there's a candle left lit. It's Carnival week and the servants are beside themselves with neglect. Last night at midnight, I found a candle burning in the dining room. I still haven't found who did it. *[putting down her candle]* What time is it?

ANDREY: *[looking at his watch]* Quarter past eight.

NATASHA: And Olga and Irina not home yet. Still working, poor girls. *[sighing]* 'Take care of yourself,' I always say to Irina. But she won't listen. Off to the telegraph office every morning. Quarter past eight, you say? I'm so worried. Our Bobik is not at all well. Yesterday, he had a fever, and today he is cold all over.

ANDREY: It's nothing, Natasha. The boy's all right.

NATASHA: I'm so anxious! And tonight they say, the gypsies from the carnival will be here to play. It would be better if they didn't come Andrusha.

ANDREY: But they were invited.

NATASHA: This morning our baby boy knew me, I swear. "Bobik," I say, "good morning! Good morning!" And he laughs. So, Andrusha, I'll tell them not to let the gypsies in.

ANDREY: *[indecisively]* But that's for my sisters to say, surely.

NATASHA: Well I'll tell them. They'll understand. *[going]* For supper I ordered some buttermilk. The doctor says, you're to have nothing but buttermilk or you'll never get any thinner. *[stopping]* I'm afraid Bobik is too cold in that room of his. We need to move him. Irina's room is perfect, sunny all day long. I must tell her that. She could be in the same room with Olga for a while. She's not home during the day anyhow, she only spends the night. *[a pause]* Andrushanchik, why don't you say something?

ANDREY: I was just thinking. There's nothing to say, really.

NATASHA: There's something I was supposed to tell you. Oh, yes. Ferapont is here from the County Board. He's asking for you.

ANDREY: *[yawning]* Call him in.

[NATASHA goes out. ANDREY, bending over to the candle, which she has forgotten to take along, reads his book. FERAPONT enters, he is in a shabby old coat, with the collar turned up, a scarf over his ears.]

ANDREY: Good evening, old friend. What is it?

FERAPONT: The Chairman sends you a book and a paper of some kind. Here. *[he gives ANDREY the book and an envelope]*

ANDREY: Good. Thank you. But why so late? It's after eight.

FERAPONT: How's that?

ANDREY: *[louder]* It's after eight.

FERAPONT: Right. It was still light when I got here, but they wouldn't let me in. The master, they said is busy. Well you're busy. I have nowhere to hurry off to. *[Thinking that ANDREY is asking him something]* How's that?

ANDREY: Nothing. *[examining the book]* I'll come tomorrow. It's boring to me anyway. *[a pause]* Dear old man, how life deceives us! Today I picked up this book here—old university lectures, and I felt like laughing. My God! I'm the secretary of the County board, the Board where Protopopoff presides. The very most I can hope for—is to be a *member* of the Board someday! I who dream every night that I'm a professor at Moscow University, a famous scholar, the pride of all Russia!

FERAPONT: I wouldn't know. Don't hear well.

ANDREY: If you could hear well, I might not talk to you. I've got to talk to somebody. My wife doesn't know me. I'm afraid of my sisters, somehow, afraid of their laughter. In

Moscow, you sit in a huge restaurant, you don't know anybody, and nobody knows you, but you don't feel like a stranger. And here you know everybody and everybody knows you, but you're just a lonely stranger.

FERAPONT: How's that? *[a pause]* You know what I heard— maybe it was a lie—that a rope is stretched all the way across Moscow.

ANDREY: What for?

FERAPONT: I wouldn't know. I just heard it.

ANDREY: Ridiculous. *[reading]* Were you ever in Moscow?

FERAPONT: *[after a pause]* No. Never. God didn't give me Moscow. *[pause]* Shall I go?

ANDREY: Um, yes. Goodbye. *[FERAPONT goes out]* Goodbye. *[reading]* Come tomorrow morning to get these papers. And *[a pause]* He's gone. *[a bell rings]* Oh, well, *[stretching and going slowly to his room.]*

[A nurse is heard singing, rocking a child. MASHA and VERSHININ enter talking. In the dining room one of the maids lighting a lamp and candles.]

MASHA: I don't know. *[a pause]* I don't know. The military are in this town, at any rate, the people who are most decent, educated and, honorable.

VERSHININ: I'm thirsty. Is there tea?

MASHA: *[glancing at the clock]* It will be here soon. You know, I was married off when I was eighteen. I was afraid of my husband because he was a teacher, and I had barely finished school. He seersod to learned then, so clever, and important. But now, unfortunately, he doesn't.

VERSHININ: Yes.. 'ell,

MASHA: I don't mean my husband really. I'm used to him. But most of the people in this town are crude and unfriendly. They have no manners. Rudeness upsets me. I see so many men not fine enough, gentle enough, polite enough. My husband's colleagues make me utterly miserable.

VERSHININ: Well, it seems to me they're all equally boring. The local intelligentsia—civilian or military—only talk about how sick they are of their wives, homes, estates, or horses. Russian life never seems to measure up to Russian thought. Why?

MASHA: You're not in a very good mood today.

VERSHININ: Well, my daughter's not well, and when my girls are ill, I get tormented over their having such a mother. Today, we began to quarrel at seven o'clock this morning, and at nine I slammed the door and went out. *[a pause]* I never talk about it. Oddly enough I complain just to you. *[kissing her hand]* Don't be angry with me. If I didn't have you, I'd have—nobody.

[a pause]

MASHA: What a noise howling in the chimney. Just like when Father died.

VERSHININ: Are you superstitious?

MASHA: Yes.

VERSHININ: That's strange. *[kissing her hand]* You're a magnificent, wonderful woman. Even in the dark here, I see the sparkle of your eyes.

MASHA: *[moving to another chair]* There's more light over here.

VERSHININ: I even have dreams about how you—move. You are truly magnificent.

MASHA: *[laughing quietly]* When you talk like that, I laugh, even though I'm frightened. Don't do it anymore, I beg you. *[in a low voice]* But do talk to me. *[covering her face with her hands]* Talk to me. They're coming—talk about something else.

[IRINA and TUSENBACH enter from the dining room]

TUSENBACH: I have a triple name. I am c:Tusenbach-back-Krone-Altschauer—but there's very little German in me, maybe only this patience and stubbornness that makes me see you home every evening.

IRINA: I'm so tired.

TUSENBACH: Every day I'll show up at the telegraph office and see you home. I'll do it for ten, twenty years, for as long as you don't drive me away. *[seeing MASHA and VERSHININ, delightedly]* It's you? Good evening.

IRINA: Home at last. *[to MASHA]* Just now a lady came in to telegraph her brother in Saratoff that her son died today. She couldn't remember the address. So she sent it without the address, simply to Saratoff. She was crying. And I was rude to her for no reason whatsoever. Are the gypsies coming tonight?

MASHA: Yes.

IRINA: *[she sits down in an armchair]* I must rest a bit. I'm exhausted.

TUSENBACH: *[smiling]* When you return from work, you always seem so young and...unhappy.
[a pause]

IRINA: I don't like my work. I don't like it.

MASHA: You're thinner. You look younger and your face looks like a boy.

TUSENBACH: That's because of her hair.

IRINA: I must try to find another job. This is not what I expected. Work without poetry, without thoughts. The doctor and our Andrey were at the club yesterday and lost again. They say Andrey lost two hundred rubles. Something must be done.

MASHA: *[indifferently]* So what's there to do now?

IRINA: He loses all the time. If he loses everything, maybe then we'll go away from this town. O my Lord God, I dream of Moscow every night. I am completely possessed. *[laughing]* We're moving there in June and from now to June is still...February, March, April, May. Almost half a year!

MASHA: The only thing is Natasha mustn't find out about his losses.

IRINA: I doubt if she cares.

[TCHEBUTYKIN just got out of bed—resting after dinner— enters the dining room combing his beard, then sits down at the table and takes a newspaper from his pocket.]

MASHA: Has he paid his rent yet?

IRINA: *[laughing]* No. Not a kopek for eight months. He's forgotten it evidently.
[everybody laughs; a pause] Why are you so quiet, Alexander Ignatyitch?

VERSHININ: I don't know. What I'd like is tea. Half my life for a glass of tea! I've eaten nothing since morning.

TCHEBUTYKIN: Irina Sergeyevna!

IRINA: What is it?

TCHEBUTYKIN: Please come here. Venezci! [IRINA goes and sits down at the table.] I can't do it without you.

[IRINA lays out the cards for Patience.]

VERSHININ: Well? If they are not giving us any tea, let's have philosophy.

TUSENBACH: Yes, let's philosophize. What about?

VERSHININ: What about? Let's dream. Let's dream of the life that will come after us, after we're all dead.

TUSENBACH: After us? After us, they'll learn to fly in balloons. They'll wear new styles of coats, and maybe they'll discover how to develop the sixth sense! But life will be the same, difficult. And mysterious. And sometimes happy. After a thousand years, man will be sighing the same. 'Ah, how hard it is to live!' and, same as now, he will fear death.

VERSHININ: [after a moment's thought] Oh, I think a better life just has to come. We won't share in that life of course, but we are living for it now, starting to create it. I think it's going to grow out of our suffering. I have to believe that.

[MASHA laughs softly]

TUSENBACH: What are you laughing at?

MASHA: I don't know. All day today I've been laughing.

VERSHININ: The longer I live the more I want to know. My hair is turning gray, I'm almost an old man, but I know so little! But I do feel that I know there's no happiness for us. That happiness is something we are trying to create and will our descendants. [a pause] No happiness for me, but surely for my descendants.

[FEDOTIK and RODAY appear in the dining room; they sit down and sing softly, strumming a guitar.]

TUSENBACH: But what if I really am happy?

VERSHININ: No. Impossible.

[laughter]

TUSENBACH: How can I convince you? Life doesn't change, it stays constant no matter what you or I may think. Birds fly and fly no matter what thoughts pass through their heads, and they will always fly and not know where or why. [a pause]

MASHA: It seems to me that we must believe or seek some belief, otherwise life is empty, empty. To live and not know why the bird flies, why children are born, why there are stars in the sky. Either we know what we're living for, or it's all nonsense and waste.

TCHEBUTYKIN: [reading a newspaper] Balzac was married in Berditcheff. [IRINA sings softly.] I'll put that in my book [writing] Balzac was married in Berditcheff. [reading his newspaper.]

[laughter]

IRINA: [as she lays out cards for Patience, musing.] Balzac was married in Berditcheff.

TUSENBACH: The die is cast. You know Maria Sergeyevna, I have tendered my resignation.

MASHA: So I heard. And I don't see anything good in it. I don't like civilians.

TUSENBACH: Just the same [getting up] I'm not handsome, what sort of military man am I if I can't look dashing in a uniform? No, I'm going to find real work and know for once in my life, what it's like to fall in bed exhausted knowing I have done a day's work. [going into the dining room] Workmen must sleep soundly.

FEDOTIK: [to IRINA] I bought you some crayons on Moscoffsky Street, at Phjokoff's, and this penknife.

IRINA: You are still treating me as if I were little, but I'm grown up now. [she takes the crayons and the penknife, gaily.] How delightful!

FEDOTIK: And I bought a knife for myself. Look here, a blade, and another blade, a third, this to pick the ears, these small scissors, this to clean the nails.

RODAY: Doctor, how old are you?

TCHEBUTYKIN: Me? Thirty-two.

[laughter]

FEDOTIK: I'll now show you another game of Patience. [laying out the cards for Patience.]

[The samovar is brought. ANFISA is at the samovar, a little later NATASHA comes in and hovers. SOLYONY enters and after greetings, sits down at the table.]

VERSHININ: What a wind out there!

MASHA: Yes, I'm sick of winter. I've already forgotten what summer is like.

IRINA: The card game is coming out alright. We shall get to Moscow.

FEDOTIK: No, it's not coming out right. Look, the eight falls on the two of spades. [laughing] Colonel, excuse me, sir, your name, I've forgotten.

MASHA: Bring it here, Nurse.

ANFISA: I'm coming!

NATASHA: [to SOLYONY] Bobik understands everything. "Good morning," I say. "Bobik. Good morning, dear!" He gave me a special look. You think I'm only a mother talking, but no, no! He's an unusual child.

SOLYONY: If this child were mine, I would have fried him in a skillet and eaten him.

[general stifled laughter. Goes with his glass into the living room and sits down in the corner.]

NATASHA: Rude, ill-bred man!

MASHA: Happy is he who does not notice whether it's summer now or winter. If I were in Moscow, I think I could scorn the weather.

VERSHININ: The other day I read the journal of a former French diplomat. He mentions with rapture the birds he saw through the prison window and had never noticed before when he was out. Now that he's released, of course, it's the same as it was before, he doesn't notice the birds. And you won't notice Moscow when you live there. Happiness? We don't get it. We only long for it.

TUSENBACH: [taking box from the table] But where's the candy?

IRINA: Solyony ate it all.

TUSENBACH: All of it?

ANFISA: A letter for you dear.

VERSHININ: For me? *[taking the letter]* From my daughter *[reading]* Yes, of course. Forgive me, Maria Sergeyevna, I'll just slip out. Not any tea for me—*[getting up very much disturbed]* Will it ever stop.

MASHA: What is it?

VERSHININ: *[in a low voice]* My wife has taken poison again. Got to go. I'll slip out, won't be seen. *[kissing MASHA's hand]* Dear, kind lovely woman. I'll slip out. *[he goes out.]*

ANFISA: Where is he going now? I have poured his tea. Well, of all the....

MASHA: *[Losing her temper]* Let it be! Stop plaguing us, there's no rest from you. *[going to the table with her cup.]* I am tired of you, old woman.

ANFISA: Why are you offended? Darling!

ANDREY'S VOICE: Anfisa!

ANFISA: *[mocking him]* Anfisa! He sits in there all the time. *[she goes out.]*

MASHA: *[in the dining room at the table, angrily]* Let me sit down! *[musses up the cards on the table]* Cards all over the table. Drink your tea!

IRINA: You're spiteful, Masha.

MASHA: If I'm spiteful, don't talk to me. Don't touch me!

TCHEBUTYKIN: *[laughing]* Don't touch her, don't touch.

MASHA: You are sixty years old, and you're just like a little boy, always full of the Devil.

NATASHA: *[sighing]* Masha, my dear, must you use such expressions? Really. With your wonderful looks, you could do so well in society, if it weren't for some of the ill-bred words you use. Je vous prie, pardonnez-moi, Marie, mais vous avez des manieres un peu grossieres.

TUSENBACH: *[suppressing a laugh]* Give me, I need.. Where's the cognac?

NATASHA: Il prait que mon Bobik deja ne dort pas. He's awakened. He's a little sickish today. I'd better go see.

IRINA: Where's Ignatyevitch tyich?

MASHA: Home. Something very wrong with his wife. Again.

TUSENBACH: *[going to SOLYONY with a decanter of cognac]* You always sit by yourself. God knows what you're thinking. What do you say? Peace? Truce? Let's drink together. *[drinking]* To whatever comes!

SOLYONY: Why make peace? We haven't quarreled.

TUSENBACH: You always make me feel we might. You're a strange man, I must say.

SOLYONY: Me strange? Who isn't! Don't be mad, Aleko.

TUSENBACH: Now you call me Aleko.
[pause]

SOLYONY: I'm really only alright when I'm alone with someone. In groups, I turn gloomy and shy and...say things. Still, I'm a better and more honest man than many.

TUSENBACH: You make me so angry when you plague me in front of others. I can't help like you just the same. Ah well, today I'm going to get drunk! Come, let's drink!

SOLYONY: Let's! *[drinking]* Baron, I have nothing against you really. But I'm a Lermontoff type...everyone says so. *[takes out scent from his pocket and pours it over his hands]*

TUSENBACH: I am submitting my resignation. At last! I've been thinking about it for five years and now I'm going to do it. I'm going to find real work.

SOLYONY: Don't Aleko...forget your dreams...forget them. *[ANDREY comes in quietly with a book and sits down near a candle.]*

TUSENBACH: I'm going to be a working man.

TCHEBUTYKIN: *[entering living room with IRINA]* And they served us food from Caucasus, onion soup and tchehartma meat. rtma meat.

SOLYONY: Tcheremsha is onion, not meat.

TCHEBUTYKIN: No, not onion, mutton roast.

SOLYONY: I tell you tchermermsha—onion!

TCHEBUTYKIN: I tell you tchehartma—mutton!

SOLYONY: Tcheremsha—onion.

TCHEBUTYKIN: Why am I arguing with you? You were never in the Caucasus, you know nothing about things Caucasian, and never ate tchehartma.

SOLYONY: I haven't eaten it because I can't stand it. It smells like garlic!

ANDREY: *[imploringly]* Enough, gentlemen! Please! I beg you!

TUSENBACH: When were the carnival gypsies coming?

IRINA: They promised about nine, which means, right now.

TUSENBACH: *[Embracing ANDREY singing, leading him into a folk dance]* Oh, you porch, my porch, new porch of mine...

ANDREY: *[dancing and singing]* New porch of maple

TCHEBUTYKIN: *[dancing]* With lattice so fine!
[laughter, repetition of chorus and dance]

TUSENBACH: *[kissing ANDREY]* Let's have drink! Andrusha, drink with us, please. And when you go the university in Moscow, Andrusha, I'll go with you!

SOLYONY: To which one? In Moscow, there are two universities.

ANDREY: In Moscow? No there's only one.

SOLYONY: And I tell you—two.

ANDREY: One.

SOLYONY: Two!

ANDREY: Oh hell, let there be three. The more the merrier.

SOLYONY: *[furious]* In Moscow, there are two universities! *[disapproval and hisses from the others]* There are two. And if you will not listen to me, I will stop talking. I will go out of this room. *[he exits]*

TUSENBACH: Bravo! Bravo! *[laughing]* It's just like watching a play. Bravo...
[sits down at the piano and plays a waltz]

MASHA: *[waltzing by herself, singing]* The Baron is drunk, the Baron is drunk, the Baron is drunk as a skunk.
[NATASHA enters]

NATASHA: *[to TCHEBUTYKIN]* Ivan Romanitch! Doctor!
[She says something to TCHEBUTYKIN, then goes out. TCHEBUTYKIN touches TUSENBACH on the shoulder and whispers something to him]

IRINA: What is it?

TCHEBUTYKIN: It's time for us to go.

TUSENBACH: Yes, it's time to go. Goodnight.

IRINA: But you'll miss the gypsies.

ANDREY: *[embarrassed]* There won't be any gypsies. Natasha says Bobik isn't feeling well. So you see, my dear, I don't know, I just don't know.

IRINA: Bobik's not well? But….

MASHA: Oh, who cares! We're being run out. So be it. *[to IRINA]* It's not Bobik, that's ill, it's his mother. Here! *[tapping her forehead]* What a common creature she is! *[ANDREY goes into his room. TCHEBUTYKIN follows him. Good-byes are said in the dining room.]*

FEDOTIK: What a shame. I was really looking forward to it. But if the little boy is sick…of course…I bring him some toys tomorrow.

RODAY: I even took a nap today. I thought I would dance all night.

MASHA: Let's go outside and talk. We'll think of something. *[Sounds of goodbyes, including TEUSENBACH's laughter. Everyone gone. ANFISA and a maid clear the table and put out the lights. A nurse can be heard singing. ANDREY in his coat and hat with TCHEBUTYKIN enter.]*

TCHEBUTYKIN: I never married because life went by too fast. Also because I was in love with your mother, who happened to be already married.

ANDREY: One really shouldn't marry. It's too…boring.

TCHEBUTYKIN: Maybe, but then there's loneliness. A frightful thing. Ah, what does it matter either way.

ANDREY: Quick. Let's go.

TCHEBUTYKIN: What's the hurry. We have plenty of time.

ANDREY: I don't want my wife to stop us.

TCHEBUTYKIN: Ah!

ANDREY: Perhaps I'll just watch tonight and not play. Let's go out through the kitchen. *[They exit. A ring, another. Voices. Laughter. IRINA enters]*

IRINA: What is it?

ANFISA: *[in a whisper]* The Gypsies! *[ring]*

IRINA: Nursey, tell them no one is home. Tell them to please excuse us. *[ANFISA goes out. IRINA paces, thinking, perturbed. SOLYONY enters]*

SOLYONY: *[confused]* Where is everyone?

IRINA: Gone home.

SOLYONY: How odd. Are you alone here?

IRINA: Alone *[pause]* Goodbye.

SOLYONY: I behaved badly earlier. But they're all so…and you are not like them. You are superior and wise. I love you. I love you with all my…

IRINA: Goodnight! Go away, please.

SOLYONY: I can't live without you. I can't! *[following her]* You have such eyes, such extraordinary eyes. I have never seen in any other women.

IRINA: Stop it.

SOLYONY: I've never spoken my love and I…well, you can't force love, I suppose. But I cannot bear rivals…I will not. I swear to you by all that's holy, I'll kill anyone who…I will. *[NATASHA passes by with a candle, looks in at one door, then another, and passes by her husband's room.]*

NATASHA: Andrey must be reading. Well, let him. Excuse me, Vassily Vasilyitch, I didn't know you were here. I'm in my dressing gown.

SOLYONY: Who cares? Goodbye! *[he leaves]*

NATASHA: You look tired, poor dear girl. *[kisses IRINA]* You should go to bed earlier.

IRINA: Is Bobik asleep?

NATASHA: Well, asleep. But not sound asleep. Oh, that reminds me, my dear. His nursery is always cold and damp. And I was thinking that your room would be so good for a child. You could move in with Olga for a while, couldn't you?

IRINA: *[not understanding]* Move where? *[A troika with bells is heard driving up outside]*

NATASHA: You and Olga will share a room for a bit and Bobik will have your room. Oh, he is such an angel. Today I said to him, "Bobik, Bobik, my own!" and he looked up at me with his sweet little eyes. *[a ring]* That must be Olga. She's very late today. *[A maid comes in and whispers in NATASHA's ear]*

NATASHA: Protopopoff? Such a fellow. Protopopoff is out there with a troika and wants me to go riding *[laughing]* Men are so strange! *[ring]* Somebody is at the door. Well, I guess I could go for a quick ride. *[to maid]* Tell him right away. *[ring]* Olga must be here. *[Maid runs out. IRINA sits thinking. KULYGIN, OLGA, VERSHININ enter.]*

KULYGIN: There you are! Where's the party?

VERSHININ: Where are the carnival gypsies?

IRINA: Gone.

KULYGIN: And Masha's gone? Where? And what is Protopopoff doing outside?

IRINA: Don't ask questions. I'm tired.

OLGA: I'm exhausted. Our headmistress is very ill. I'm to take her place. My head aches so…*[sitting down]* Andrey lost two hundred rubles yesterday at cards. The whole town is talking about it. *[KULYGIN sits]*

VERSHININ: My wife decided to scare me again, just now. She almost poisoned herself. It's over now. It better…. Fyodor Ilyitch, let's go somewhere. I can't go home. I jut can't yet.

KULYGIN: No, I'm too tired. *[rises, kisses IRINA's hand]* Goodbye. A two full days of rest ahead *[going]* I really was counting on having tea and pleasant company but oh well, o fallacem, hominum, spem! Accusative case exclamatory.

VERSHININ: Well, I'm going by myself then. *[Exits with KULYGIN whistling]*

OLGA: My head is just throbbing. Andrey, Andrey, Andrey, the whole town talking. I must lie down *[starting to exit]* Tomorrow no school! I'm free! And the day after tomorrow too! Oh god, my head… *[she leaves]*

IRINA: *[Alone]* Gone. All gone. Nobody here. *[An accordian is heard on the street, the nurse is heard singing]*

NATASHA: *[with fur coat, cap and muff, passes through the dining room, behind her a maid]* I'll be home in half an hour or so. Just a little ride. *[She leaves]*

IRINA: *[Alone, dejected]* To Moscow. To Moscow! Moscow!!!

CURTAIN

ACT 3

[OLGA's and IRINA's room. To the left and to the right beds, with screens around them. Nearly three o'clock in the morning. Off-stage a fire-bell ringing for a fire that began a long time back. No one in the house has gone to bed yet. MASHA lies on the sofa. She wears, as usual, a black dress. OLGA and ANFISA enter.]

ANFISA: They're sitting down there under the staircase. I asked them to come upstairs but they're upset and crying. "Daddy," they say, "where's Daddy? What if," they say, "he's burned!" There are some other people in the courtyard too. They don't even have their clothes, poor things.

OLGA: *[Taking some dresses out of the closet.]* Here, this gray one—take it. And this one here…the blouse too. And take the skirt, Nursey. My God, all Kirsanoffsky Street must be burned. Take this… *[throws the dresses for her to catch]* The Vershinins were so frightened. Their house nearly burned up. They will spend the night here. We can't let them go home. And poor Fedotik! Everything he owns was burned.

ANFISA: You'll have to call Ferapont, Olyushka, or I can't carry.

OLGA: *[She rings]* Nobody answers… *[through the door]* Come here, whoever it is! *[Through the open door is seen a window glowing red with the fire; a fire-brigade is heard passing the house. Ferapont enters.]* Here, take this and carry it downstairs. Under the staircase are the young Kolotilin girls. Give it to them. And this…

FERAPONT: Yes, Miss. In the year '12 Moscow burned. My God! Did that ever surprise the French.

OLGA: Go on, move along.

FERAPONT: Yes, Miss. *[He goes out]*

OLGA: Nursey, give everything away. We don't need anything. Give everything away! Nursey, I'm tired, I can barely stand up. The Vershinin girls can sleep in the drawing room, and Alexander Ignatyevitch downstairs at the Baron's. Fedotik at the Baron's too. The Doctor is drunk and we mustn't send anyone to him. Oh, and Vershinin's wife in the drawing-room as well.

ANFISA: *[wearily]* Olyushka, dear, don't send me away! Don't send me away!

OLGA: Don't talk nonsense, Nurse. Nobody's sending you away.

ANFISA: *[Laying her head on OLGA's breast.]* My own, sweet treasure, I do try, I work. I'll get feeble and everybody will say: Get out! And where will I go? I'm over eighty years old!

OLGA: You sit down a while, Nursey. You're tired, poor thing. *[making her sit down]* Rest now, my good old sweet nurse. You look pale!

[NATASHA enters.]

NATASHA: We've been asked to form a relief society for those who have been burned out. Why not! We must help poor people, that's the duty of the rich. Bobik and Sofotchka have just gone to sleep, as if nothing has happened. The house is full of strange people. I hope the children don't catch anything from them.

OLGA: *[not listening to her]* In this room there is no fire, it's peaceful here.

NATASHA: Yes. I must look tres deshabile. *[in front of the mirror]* They say I've gained weight. It's not true! Not a bit! Ah, Masha's sleeping, poor thing is all tired out. *[To ANFISA, coldly]* How dare you sit in my presence! Get up! Get out of here! *[ANFISA goes out, a pause]* Why you keep that old woman I don't understand!

OLGA: *[taken aback]* Pardon me, I don't understand either.

NATASHA: She is a peasant, she should live in the country. I like in a house to have order. Useless people shouldn't be in a house. *[stroking OLGA's cheek]* Poor dear, you are tired! Our headmistress is tired.

OLGA: I shan't be the headmistress.

NATASHA: Of course you'll be elected.

OLGA: I'll turn it down. I can't do it. I don't have the strength. *[Drinking some water.]* You were so rude just now to Nurse. Forgive me, I'm not in any condition to bear…

NATASHA: *[disturbed]* Forgive me, Olga, forgive me. I didn't mean to upset you.

[MASHA gets up, takes a pillow and goes out, angrily.]

OLGA: Understand, my dear…perhaps we were brought up oddly, but I can't bear it. That kind of behavior appalls me. I get ill. I'm simply sick at heart! Rudeness upsets me.

NATASHA: Forgive me *[kisses her]* I talk too much, but you must agree, my dear, she belongs in the country.

OLGA: She's been with us for over thirty years.

NATASHA: But now she can't do anything. She is not up to doing any work, she just sleeps and sits.

OLGA: Well, let her sit.

NATASHA: *[surprised]* How let her sit? *[tearfully]* I don't understand you, Olga. We have a nurse, maids, a cook. Why do we need that old woman?

[A fire alarm rings]

OLGA: I have aged ten years tonight!

NATASHA: We have to reach an understanding, Olga. You're at the high school. I'm at home, you teach, I keep house. When it comes to the servants, I know what I'm saying. And I won't put up with this, this old thief here, this old hag. *[stamping her foot.]* This stupid old witch. Don't cross me! Don't you dare! *[catching herself]* If you don't move downstairs, we'll always be quarreling.

[KULYGIN enters.]

KULYGIN: Where is Masha? It's time to go home. The fire, they say, is subsiding. *[Stretching]* Only one section of the town got burned. *[Sitting down.]* I'm tired out, Olitchka, my dear. I often think if there hadn't been Masha, I'd have married you, Olitchka. You are so good. I'm exhausted. *[Listening for something]* Listen! The doctor is coming. And have you seen him? He's drunk! As if on purpose! *[getting up]* There he is. I'll hide. *[going to the cupboard and standing in the corner]*

OLGA: For two years he hasn't had a drink and tonight all of a sudden he's gotten drunk. *[following* NATASHA *to the back of the room]*

*[*TCHEBUTYKIN *enters; without staggering, walks across the room, stops, looks around, goes to the washstand and begins to wash his hands.]*

TCHEBUTYKIN: The hell with all of 'em—they think I'm a doctor, and can cure any sickness, but I know nothing. I've forgotten everything. *[*OLGA *and* NATASHA *go out, unnoticed by him.]* Last Wednesday, I treated a woman who died and I'm to blame. I knew a little something twenty-five years ago, but now nothing. Perhaps I'm not even a man anymore. Perhaps I don't even exist, and it only seems to me that I walk and eat and sleep. *[crying]* Oh, that I didn't exist! *[no longer crying, crossly]* The banality of life! The meanness of it! That woman I killed Wednesday came back to me today. Everything came back to me, weighing on my soul, my crooked, foul, disgusting soul. So I went and got drunk.

*[*IRINA, VERSHININ *and* TUSENBACH *enter;* TUSENBACH *wears civilian clothes, new and stylish]*

IRINA: Let's sit here. It's quiet here.

VERSHININ: If it weren't for the soldiers, the whole town would be burned up. Good men!

KULYGIN: What's the time, gentlemen?

TUSENBACH: Almost four. It's getting light.

IRINA: Everybody is sitting in the dining room, nobody is going out. And that Solyony of yours is... *[to* TCHEBUTYKIN*]* Doctor, you should go to bed.

TCHEBUTYKIN: No thank you. *[combing his beard]*

KULYGIN: *[laughing]* You're little tipsy, Ivan Romanitchi! *[slapping him on the shoulder]* Bravo! In vino veritas, said the ancients.

TUSENBACH: They want a concert to benefit of the refugees. We could do it. Maria Sergeyevna is a wonderful pianist. Almost a genius.

KULYGIN: She does play beautifully!

IRINA: She has forgotten how. It's three years since she's played. Maybe even four.

TUSENBACH: Well, no wonder. Nobody in this town knows music, at all. Think of being able to play so magnificently and knowing that nobody, absolutely nobody appreciates it!

KULYGIN: *[sighing]* Is it proper for her to take part in a concert? *[a pause]* I think I would have to see what the head master thinks is suitable.

*[*TCHEBUTYKIN *is taking up a china clock in both hands and examining it]*

VERSHININ: I'm covered with dirt from the fire—*[a pause]* I heard our brigade may be transferred to Poland—or maybe to China.

TUSENBACH: I heard that too. The town will be utterly deserted.

IRINA: We'll be leaving too.

TCHEBUTYKIN: *[He drops the clock, shattering it]* Crash!

[A pause, everyone is distressed and embarrassed]

KULYGIN: *[picks up the pieces]* Oh, doctor! What a valuable thing to break! Minus zero to you for conduct.

IRINA: That was Mama's clock.

TCHEBUTYKIN: Maybe, maybe I didn't break it, but only seemed to. Maybe we only seem to exist. I don't know anything. Nobody does. *[by the door]* What are you looking at? Natasha's having an affair with Protopopoff.... Nobody chooses to see it. Maybe it doesn't exist. *[he goes out, humming]*

VERSHININ: Well, what a night! *[a pause]* When the fire started, I ran home and saw our house was safe but my two little girls stood on the porch in their nightgowns, all around them people rushing, horses and dogs running around—and on my little girls' faces was such terror and longing. My heart just ached for them. I thought, my God, what more will these poor babies have to go through in this life! I grabbed them and came here *[fire alarm; a pause]* only to find that their mother was here, shouting, angry, crazy again. What a life.

*[*MASHA *enters with a pillow and sits down on the sofa.]* And while the street was red with the fire and noise, I thought, they, who live in the future will look on this life of ours now with horror and derision. It's as if everybody were asleep now. What a life it will be! When people wake up. You know what kind of people I think will inhabit the future? People more like you, ladies. Everything will veer to you, everyone will think just like you. *[laughing]* I'm in a strange mood today. I want to live. I want to live!

MASHA: Tram-tum-tum....

VERSHININ: Tum-tum...

MASHA: Tra-ra-ra?

VERSHININ: Tra-ta-ta *[laughing]*

*[*FEDOTIK *enters]*

FEDOTIK: *[dancing]* I've lost everything! Up in smoke! Gone! Gone! Gone! *[laughter]*

IRINA: How can you make jokes? Absolutely everything?

FEDOTIK: *[laughing]* Absolutely everything. Nothing left. My guitar, my camera, my letters, all burned! I bought a little notebook for you. It burned up too!

*[*SOLYONY *enters]*

IRINA: No. Please go away. You may not come in here.

SOLYONY: Why is it the Baron may and I may not?

VERSHININ: We must all go. How's the fire?

SOLYONY: Subsiding. Why is the Baron allowed and not me? *[Taking out the cologne bottle, sprinkling himself.]*

VERSHININ: Tram-tum-tum.

MASHA: Tram-tum.

VERSHININ: *[laughing, to* SOLYONY*]* Let's go downstairs.

SOLYONY: I won't forget this. Don't think I will *[quoting]* "we could spell out the moral of this piece, but not without annoying all the geese" *[looking at* TUSENBACH*]* Chick, chick, chick. *[He goes out with* VERSHININ *and* FEDOTIK*]*

IRINA: That Solyony drives me crazy. *[with surprise]* The Baron's asleep! Baron! Baron!

TUSENBACH: *[waking up]* I'm tired. But soon I start work at the brickworks. Then I suppose I'll really know what tired is. [*To* **IRINA**, *tenderly*] You're so pale, so beautiful, so glowing. Your paleness seems to brighten the dark like light. But you're so sad and dissatisfied... Come away with me, let's build a life together!

MASHA: Nikolay Lvovitch, out you go!

TUSENBACH: [*laughing*] Oh, are you here? I didn't see you. [*kissing* **IRINA**'s *hand*] Goodbye, I'm going.... I remember long ago once on your birthday you were so happy and anxious to work. Where have those feelings gone? [*kissing her hand*] Tears in your eyes. Go to bed. It's getting light...morning's here. If only you would let me devote my life to you!

MASHA: Out!

TUSENBACH: I'm going. [*he goes out*]

MASHA: [*lying down*] Are you asleep, Fyodor?

KULYGIN: Huh?

MASHA: You ought to go home.

KULYGIN: Dear Masha, sweet Masha.

IRINA: She's tired. Let her rest, Fedya.

KULYGIN: I'm going, I'm going. My magnificent wife. I love you, my one and only.

MASHA: [*angrily*] Amo, amas, amat, amamus, amatis, amant.

KULYGIN: [*laughing*] No, really, what an amazing woman. Seven years we've been married, but it seems like only yesterday. An amazing woman. I am content, content, content.

MASHA: I'm bored, bored, bored. [*sits up*] There's something I can't get out of my head. I can't stay silent. I mean about Andrey. He's mortgaged this house to the bank and his wife has grabbed all the money! But the house doesn't belong just to him, but to all four of us! How could he?

KULYGIN: Well, he owes a lot of money.

MASHA: But it's outrageous. [*she lies back down*]

KULYGIN: You and I aren't poor.

MASHA: No, I don't need anything. It's the injustice that makes me furious. [*pause*] Go home, Fyodor!

KULYGIN: [*kissing her*] You're tired, rest a bit. I'll sit and wait for you at home. Sleep.... [*going*] I'm content, I am content, I am content. [*he goes out*]

IRINA: Our Andrey has grown petty and small. He's dried up and aged since he married that woman! He has no spark. He's stopped preparing to become a professor altogether. Yesterday he was actually bragging about being on the county council, which is run by Protopopoff. The whole town's talking and laughing and he's the only one who knows nothing and sees nothing. And now, even during the fire, he just sits in his room and plays the violin. [*nervously*] It's a nightmare. [*crying*] I just can't bear any more! I can't! [*sobbing aloud*] I can't...

[**OLGA** *enters*]

OLGA: [*alarmed*] What is the matter, what is it, my darling?

IRINA: [*sobbing*] Where's it all gone? Where is it? Oh, my God, my God! I've forgotten everything. I've forgotten. It's muddled in my head. I don't remember what the Italian word for window is, or the ceiling there. I'm forgetting it all, life's slipping away and we will never go to Moscow. I realize that now—we'll never go.

OLGA: Oh my sweet love....

IRINA: [*restraining herself*] Now I know misery. I thought the answer was work, but I'm sick of it! First telegraph operator, now council secretary and I despise everything they give me to do. My brain's dried up. I'm getting thin, ugly and old, and there's no satisfaction of any kind. Life no longer has any sense of possibility. Why haven't I killed myself? I can't understand why....

OLGA: Don't cry, my little girl, don't cry.

IRINA: I'm not crying. I'm not. I'm sick of it. All that is over.

OLGA: My angel, I'm talking to you as a sister, and friend, if you want my advice, marry the Baron! [**IRINA** *weeps silently*] You respect and value him. He's not good looking, but he's decent. I myself would marry without love. I'd marry anyone who proposed if he was an honorable man. I'd even marry an old man. I would.

IRINA: I kept believing I'd meet the real one in Moscow. But it's no more than a silly dream....

OLGA: [*embracing her sister*] My dear, beautiful sister. I understand it all, when the Baron left the military and came to see us in civilian clothes, he seemed to me so homely that I actually cried. He asked, "Why are you crying?" How could I tell him! But if God grants that he marry you, I'll be so happy.

[**NATASHA** *crosses the stage from the right door to the left, without speaking, a candle in her hand.*]

MASHA: [*sitting up*] She walks about as if she was the one who started the fire.

OLGA: Masha, you old silly! You are the silliest one in our silly family. [*a pause*]

MASHA: I need to confess, my precious sisters. I'll die if I don't say it. [*quietly*] And you know it before I speak it. [*a pause*] I love...that man...Vershinin.

OLGA: [*going behind her screen*] Stop it. I won't listen.

MASHA: What can I do? First I thought he was strange, then I felt sorry for him. Then I began to love him...to love his voice, his words, his little girls, even his misfortunes.

OLGA: [*behind the screen*] I'm not listening!

MASHA: Oh, Olga, you're the silly one. I'm in love—That's my fate. And he loves me. Is it wrong? [*taking* **IRINA** *by the hand and drawing her nearer*] You read novels and think you understand all about love, but when you fall in love yourself, you begin to see that you know nothing. My loves, my sisters. I've confessed to you, now I'll be silent. I will.

[**ANDREY** *enters, followed by* **FERAPONT**]

ANDREY: [*annoyed*] What do you want? I don't understand.

FERAPONT: [*standing in the door impatiently*] Andrey Sergeyevitch, if I've told you once I've told you a dozen times.

ANDREY: First, I am not Andrey Sergeyevitch to you but Your Excellency!

FERAPONT: The firemen, Your Excellentness, want to go to the river through your garden. Now they have to keep going all the way around it.

ANDREY: Alright. Tell them, they may [**FERAPONT** *goes out.*] Where's Olga? [**OLGA** *comes out from behind the screen*] I need the key to the cupboard. I've lost mine. *[OLGA gives him the key without speaking. IRINA goes behind her screen; a pause]* That damn Ferapont made me lose my temper. I said something stupid to him. Your Excellency. *[a pause]* Alright it's time to stop pouting all of you. You're all here. Let's have it out once and for all. What have you three got against me? What?

OLGA: Let it rest, Andrusha.

ANDREY: *[He is very much confused]* Don't get upset. Just tell me.

VERSHININ'S VOICE: Tram-tum-tum!

MASHA: *[Rising. In a loud voice]* Tra-ta-ta! *[To OLGA]* Goodbye, Olga, God be with you! *[she goes behind the screen, kisses IRINA]* Sleep well. Goodbye Andrey. Go away, they're tired. Tomorrow we'll talk. *[She goes out.]*

OLGA: Yes, Andrusha, tomorrow. *[She goes behind her screen.]* It's time for bed.

ANDREY: I'll just say it and go. First, you have something against Natasha, my splendid wife, and I demand that you respect her. *[A pause]* Second, you seem angry that I am not a professor. But I am a member of the City Council, and this service of mine I consider just as sacred. I'm proud of it. *[A pause]* There, I…I mortgaged the house without asking your permission. I ask you to forgive me. My debts…thirty-five thousand…I've stopped playing cards. But remember, you girls each receive a pension and I don't. *[A pause]*

KULYGIN: *[at the door]* Masha not here? *[Perturbed.]* Where is she? That's strange. *[He goes out]*

ANDREY: They're not listening. Natasha is a wonderful… *[walks up and down the stage in silence, then stops.]* When I married, I thought we'd be happy. Everyone happy. But, my God, I… *[crying]* My dear sisters, my own sweet sisters, don't believe me, Don't trust me. *[He goes out.]*

KULYGIN: *[at the door, anxiously]* Where's Masha? *[he goes out]* *[Fire alarm, the stage is empty.]*

IRINA: *[Behind the screen]* What a night! *[a pause]* Olga! *[Looking out from behind the screen.]* Did you hear? They're taking the brigade away from us.

OLGA: That's only a rumor.

IRINA: We'll be all alone…Olga!

OLGA: Yes?

IRINA: I respect the Baron, I value him, I'll marry him, all right? Only let's go to Moscow! I beg you, let's go! There's nothing in the world like Moscow! Let's go, Olga! Please! Let's go!

CURTAIN

ACT 4

[The garden in front of the PROZOROFF house. A long alley of trees, silver birches and maples, at the end of which is a river. On the other side of the river, a wood. On the veranda of the house, a table with bottles and glasses.

People have just been drinking champagne. Noon. Now and then, people cross the garden. TCHEBUTYKIN, in an amiable mood, sits in an easy chair, in the garden, waiting to be called, wearing a military cap and carrying a stick. IRINA, KULYGIN (with a decoration around his neck, with no moustache) and TUSENBACH, are standing on the veranda, saying good bye to FEDOTIK and RODAY. Both officers are in campaign uniform.]

TUSENBACH: *[Exchanging kisses with FEDOTIK.]* You're a good man. We got along well. *[Exchanging kisses with RODAY.]* Once again, Goodbye, my friend.

IRINA: 'Til we meet again.

FEDOTIK: We won't ever meet again.

KULYGIN: Who knows? *[Wiping his eyes, smiling]* Now I'm crying too.

IRINA: Some day…who knows?

FEDOTIK: But will we even know each other? *[Taking a snapshot]* and still…one last picture…

RODAY: *[Embracing TUSENBACH]* We'll never see each other again. *[kissing IRINA's hand]* Thank you for everything, for everything!

FEDOTIK: *[Vexed]* Stand still!

TUSENBACH: Write to us. Be sure to write.

RODAY: *[Casting a glance around the garden.]* Goodbye, trees! *[shouting]* Yoo hoo hoo hoo! *[A pause]* Goodbye, echo!

KULYGIN: You'll probably get married there in Poland and have a little Polish wife! *[laughter]*

FEDOTIK: *[Looking at his watch.]* We've got less than half an hour. Soon peace and quiet will come to this town.…

TUSENBACH: And boredom!

RODAY: And where is Maria Sergeyevna?

KULYGIN: Masha? In the garden.

FEDOTIK: We must say goodbye to her.

RODAY: Goodbye, we must go or I'll be crying. *[He hurriedly embraces TUSENBACH and KULYGIN, kisses IRINA's hand.]* It was wonderful living here. *[They start off. He turns back, shouts]* Yoo hoo hoo hoo!

IRINA: They're gone. *[Sitting down on the bottom step of the veranda]*

TCHEBUTYKIN: They forgot to say goodbye to me.

IRINA: Did you remember to say good-bye to them?

TCHEBUTYKIN: Well, I'll see them soon. I'm leaving tomorrow. One more day is left. In a year they'll retire me. I'll come back here and live out my time with you. *[He puts one newspaper in his pocket and takes out another.]* When I come back, I'll be completely reformed—quiet, proper, even polite.

IRINA: Well, you certainly ought to reform, no doubt about it!

TCHEBUTYKIN: Yes, I know. *[singing softly]* Ta-ra-ra boom-de-aye… Sit on a tomb I may.

IRINA: Fyodor, since you've shaved off his moustache, I can't bear to look at you.

KULYGIN: *[sitting down]*

[at the rear of the stage ANDREY passes, wheeling a baby-carriage with a child asleep in it.]

IRINA: Dear doctor, I'm worried. Tell me what happened yesterday?

TCHEBUTYKIN: What happened? Nothing. All nonsense. *[Reading the newspaper.]*

KULYGIN: Well, I heard that Solyony and the Baron met on the street....

TUSENBACH: Stop it! *[With a wave of his hand he goes into the house]*

KULYGIN: ...And Solyony picked on the Baron, who wouldn't tolerate it, and said something insulting....

TCHEBUTYKIN: I don't know. It's all nonsense.

KULYGIN: They say Solyony is in love with Irina, and that he hates the Baron.... Irina is lovely girl, no doubt about it. She's like Masha...only more...gentle.

[At the rear of the garden off-stage. "Yoo, hoo, hoo, hoo!"]

IRINA: *[shivering]* Everything frightens me today. *[A pause.]* I'm all packed. The baron and I are getting married tomorrow. Then the day after tomorrow I start teaching at the school—a new life! When I passed my teacher's exam, I actually cried for joy...

KULYGIN: Well, I wish you luck with all my heart.

TCHEBUTYKIN: *[tenderly]* My sweet, dear child. My treasure. You have flown far ahead of me and I can't catch up with you. I'm like a bird too old to fly south. Fly on, my precious, and God be with you. *[a pause]* It really was a mistake, Fyodor, to shave off your moustache.

KULYGIN: That's enough! *[sighing]* Well, today the troops are leaving and everything will go back to the way it was. I love Masha no matter what. Who knows why our lives will work out as they do. I often run into one of my old schoolmates, who got expelled because he just couldn't understand ut consecutivum. Now he lives in poverty and sickness. And here I am successful, happy, and am teaching others ut consecutivum. I'm a brighter man than some, but intelligence doesn't guarantee happiness.

[In the house they are playing "The Maiden's Prayer," on the piano.]

IRINA: And tomorrow I won't have to listen to "Maiden's Prayer," any more, and I won't have to see Protopopoff. *[A pause]* He's sitting there in the drawing-room again. He's all but moved in.

KULYGIN: The headmistress not here yet?

IRINA: No. They've sent for her. It has been agony living here without her, now that she lives at the school... So I've decided if it isn't my fate to be in Moscow, then I must accept it. The Baron is a good man, amazingly good. Once I accepted his proposal, suddenly wings grew on my soul. I felt lighter, relieved, and ready to work again. But then yesterday something strange happened.

TCHEBUTYKIN: Nonsense.

NATASHA: *[At the window]* The headmistress!

KULYGIN: The headmistress! Let's go in. *[He goes with Irina into the house]*

TCHEBUTYKIN: *[reading the newspaper, softly singing to himself.]* Ta-ra-ra-boom-de-aye...Sit on a tomb today....

[MASHA approaches, in the background ANDREY is seen pushing the baby carriage.]

MASHA: And there he sits.

TCHEBUTYKIN: And what?

MASHA: *[Sitting down.]* Nothing. *[A pause.]* Were you in love with my mother?

TCHEBUTYKIN: Very much.

MASHA: And was she in love with you?

TCHEBUTYKIN: *[After a pause]* That I don't remember.

MASHA: Is "my man" here? Our cook used to talk about her policeman like that: my man. Is "my man" here?

TCHEBUTYKIN: Not yet.

MASHA: When you grab happiness in bits and pieces, and then lose it, like me, you grow bitter and coarse. *[Pointing to her breast.]* Right here I'm boiling. *[Looking at her brother ANDREY pushing the baby carriage.]* Look at Andrey, our lovely brother. All our hopes gone. Our hopes were with him, but he is completely shattered.

ANDREY: Will they ever be quiet in the house?

TCHEBUTYKIN: Soon.

[Somewhere far off a harp and a violin are playing.]

ANDREY: The town will be empty. *[A pause.]* What happened between the Baron and Solyony yesterday?

TCHEBUTYKIN: Nothing. Nonsense. Solyony challenged him to a duel. *[Looks at his watch.]* It's nearly time for it. *[Laughing]* Solyony thinks he's Lermontov, which is a joke, but the truth is this is his third duel.

MASHA: Whose third duel?

TCHEBUTYKIN: Solyony.

MASHA: This whole thing should be stopped. He might wound the Baron or even kill him.

TCHEBUTYKIN: The Baron's a good man but one baron more, one less—it doesn't really matter.

MASHA: I'm not going into the house. I can't. When Vershinin comes let me know. *[She goes down the walk.]* The birds are flying south already. *[Looking up]* My dear ones, my happy ones—! *[She goes out.]*

ANDREY: Our house will be empty. I'll be all alone here soon.

TCHEBUTYKIN: What about your wife?

[FERAPONT enters with some papers.]

ANDREY: A wife is a wife. She's a good woman—but sometimes she seems not more than a blind animal. She's just not a human being. You're a friend and the only man I can open my soul to. Sometimes she seems so vulgar. I can't understand why I love her so or, at least, did love her.

TCHEBUTYKIN: *[Getting up.]* My friend, I'm going away tomorrow. Here is my advice to you. Put on your hat, pick up a walking-stick and walk—out of here, the farther away the better.

[SOLYONY enters]

SOLYONY: Doctor, it's time! Half past twelve. *[Greeting ANDREY.]*

TCHEBUTYKIN: I'm coming. I'm sick of all of you. *[Sighing]* Oho-ho-ho—

SOLYONY: *[starting off with TCHEBUTYKIN.]* "Quick as a flash the bear made a dash"—Why are you sighing, old man?

TCHEBUTYKIN: That's my business.

SOLYONY: Oh, don't worry. I'll only wing him a bit. *[Takes out the scent and sprinkles it on his hands.]* I've used a whole bottle today and they still smell. They smell like a corpse. [*A pause.*] You know Lermontov's line, "And, rebellious, he seeks the storm, as if in storms one could find peace."

TCHEBUTYKIN: "Quick as a flash the bear made a dash!" [*He goes out with* SOLYONY.*] Let's get this over with.

[*shouts are heard: "Yoo hoo!" Enter* IRINA *and* TUSENBACH, TUSENBACH *in a straw hat,* KULYGIN *crosses the stage.*]

KULYGIN: Yoo-hoo, Masha, yoo-hoo!

TUSENBACH: That's the only man in town who's glad the army is leaving.

IRINA: I think you're right. [*A pause.*] Our town will be empty.

TUSENBACH: [*glancing at his watch*] I must run, but I'll be right back.

IRINA: Where are you going?

TUSENBACH: I have to go into town, then...to see some comrades off.

IRINA: That's not true. Why are you so distracted? [*A pause*] What happened yesterday?

TUSENBACH: [*With an impatient gesture.*] I'll be back in an hour. [*Kissing her hand.*] My beloved. [*Looking into her face*] Five years now I've loved you and I still can't get used to it. You seem to me to just keep growing more beautiful. I'll take you away tomorrow. We'll work, we'll be rich, all our dreams will come true. You're going to be happy. There's just one thing wrong. You don't love me.

IRINA: I can't help that! I'll be your good and faithful wife, but... [*crying*] I have never been in love—not once in my life. Oh, I've dreamed of love, but my heart seems locked up and the key to it lost. [*A pause*] You look restless.

TUSENBACH: That lost key torments me—and won't let me sleep. Say something to me. [*A pause.*] Say something.

IRINA: What? What can I say?

TUSENBACH: Anything.

IRINA: Stop it!

[*A pause*]

TUSENBACH: What little nothings sometimes seem important. Oh, never mind I feel good. I look at these maples and birches now as if I were seeing them for the first time and they're all looking at me with curiosity. What beautiful trees and what a beautiful life there should be under them! [*A shout: "Yoo Hoo!"*] I must go. It's time. There's a tree that's dead, but it still waves with the others in the wind. Maybe it will be so with me. Goodbye, my love. [*Kissing her hands.*] The papers you gave me are on my table, in my room.

IRINA: I'll go with you.

TUSENBACH: [*alarmed*] No,no! [*Going quickly, stopping in the alley.*] Irina!

IRINA: What?

TUSENBACH: [*Not knowing what to say.*] I didn't have any coffee this morning. Will you tell them to make me some.... [*He goes quickly out.*]

[*IRINA stands thinking, then goes to the rear of the stage and sits down in the swing.* ANDREY *comes in with the baby carriage;* FERAPONT *appears.*]

FERAPONT: But Andrey Sergeyitch, the papers aren't mine, they're official. I didn't think them up. Why don't you just sign them?

ANDREY: In this dreary town there isn't one scholar, not one artist, no one who's even faintly remarkable. Just people who eat, drink, sleep, and die...who try to fight boredom with gossip, vodka, cards, and affairs. Wives deceive husbands while husbands pretend not to see anything. And in their children, the divine spark dies. And the children become pitiful corpses like their parents. [*To* FERAPONT, *angrily*] What do you want?

FERAPONT: Eh? Papers to sign.

ANDREY: I've had enough of you.

FERAPONT: [*Handing him the papers.*] I heard that this winter in Petersburg there was a frost of two hundred degrees.

ANDREY: Well if the present is so hateful, the future must be better. Oh God, to be freed from idleness, and sloth....

FERAPONT: Two thousand people frozen. It was either in Petersburg, or it was Moscow—I can't remember which.

ANDREY: [*Seized with a tender feeling*] My dear sisters, my wonderful sisters! [*Tearfully*] Masha, my sister....

NATASHA: [*In the window.*] Who is talking so loud out here? Is it you, Andrusha? You will wake up Sofie. Il ne fut pas faire de bruit, la Sofie est dormie deja. Vous etes un ours. [*Getting angry.*] If you want to talk, give the carriage and child to somebody else. Ferapont, take the carriage from the master.

FERAPONT: Yes, ma'am. [*He takes the carriage.*]

ANDREY: [*Embarrassed.*] I'm speaking quickly.

NATASHA: [*Behind the window, caressing her child.*] Bobik! You little rascal. Naughty Bobik!

ANDREY: [*Glancing through papers.*] Alright, I'll take them in and sign them... [*He goes into the house, reading the papers;* FERAPONT *pushes the baby carriage toward the rear of the garden.*]

NATASHA: [*Behind the window.*] Bobik, who is this? This is Aunt Olya. Say to Auntie: "How do you do, Olya!"

[*ANFISA comes from the house. As she speaks,* OLGA *and* VERSHININ *emerge also.*]

ANFISA: [*To* IRINA] Good morning, Irisha! [*Kissing her*] M-m-m-m, child, I am having the best time! How I live! At the school in an apartment, with my sweet Olyushka—God has given me this in my last years. A huge apartment, and a whole room for me and a little bed all to myself. I wake up in the night and—O Lord, Mother of God, there's nobody happier in this whole world.

VERSHININ: [*Looking at his watch.*] We are leaving, Olga Sergeyevna. It's time. [*A pause.*] I wish you the very best in everything. Where's Masha?

IRINA: She's in the garden. I'll look for her.

VERSHININ: Thank you. Time is short.

ANFISA: I'll help find her. [*Calling*] Mashenka. Ah, oo-oo! [*Going away with* IRINA *to the rear of the garden.*] Ah, oo-oo! Ah, oo-oo!

VERSHININ: All things end. Now we must part. [*Looking at his watch.*] The town gave us a luncheon with champagne and a speech from the Mayor. I ate and listened, but in my heart I was here with all of you.

OLGA: Are we ever to see each other again?

VERSHININ: Probably not. *[A pause]* My wife and daughters will stay on for two more months. Please, if anything happens, if anything is needed....

OLGA: Yes, yes of course. Don't worry. *[A pause]* By tomorrow there won't be an officer in town. *[A pause]* Nothing turns out as we'd plan it. I didn't want to be a headmistress, but I became one. So now I will not live in Moscow.

VERSHININ: Well.... Thank you for everything. Forgive me, I have done anything...not right... *[smiling]* and for talking so much.

OLGA: *[smiling, but wiping her eyes]* Where can Masha be....

VERSHININ: Life is hard. If only the clouds would part more quickly and we could see things clear. *[A pause]* Well, it's time for me....

OLGA: Here she comes.

[MASHA enters]

VERSHININ: I came to say goodbye.

[OLGA moves a little away so as not to disturb their farewell.]

MASHA: *[Looking into his face.]* Goodbye...my love *[A long kiss.]*

[MASHA sobs violently.]

VERSHININ: Write to me, my love. Don't forget me! Let me go. It's time. Take her, please, its time. I'm late—

[Deeply moved, he kisses OLGA's hand, then embraces MASHA again and goes quickly out.]

OLGA: There, there Masha! Hush, darling.

[KULYGIN enters.]

KULYGIN: *[Embarrassed.]* Never mind, let her cry. My dearest Masha. You're my wife and I'm not going to reproach you at all. We'll begin to live again as before, and I won't say one word.

MASHA: *[Stifling her sobs.]* By the curved seashore a green oak, a golden chain upon that oak, golden chain upon that oak. I'm going out of my mind. By the curved seashore, a green oak....

OLGA: Calm down, Masha. Be calm. Give her some water.

MASHA: I'm not crying anymore.

[A shot is heart, faintly, from a distance.]

MASHA: By the curved seashore a green oak, a golden chain upon that oak. The cat's green...the oak's green...I am mixing it up. *[Taking a drink of water]* My life's a failure. I'll be calm soon. What does "By the curved seashore" mean? My thoughts are all mixed up.

[IRINA enters]

OLGA: Be calm, Masha. Now that's a good girl. Let's go in.

MASHA: *[angrily]* I'm not going in there. *[Sobbing, but checking herself at once.]* I don't go in that house any more.

IRINA: Let's sit down together for a moment. Tomorrow I'm going away.

[A pause]

KULYGIN: Look what I took from a boy in the third-grade yesterday. *[Puts on a mustache and beard.]* I look like the German teacher. *[Laughing]* Don't I?

MASHA: *[laughing in spite of herself]* You do look like the German teacher.

OLGA: *[laughing]* Yes.

[MASHA weeps.]

IRINA: There, there, Masha!

KULYGIN: A lot like....

[NATASHA enters]

NATASHA: *[to the maid.]* What? Protopopoff will sit with Sofotchka, and let Andrey wheel Bobik. Children are such a bother.... *[Seeing KULYGIN she gives a shriek; he laughs and takes off the moustache and beard.]* Oh! You scared me! *[To IRINA]* Now that you're leaving, I'm going to put Andrey in your room, with his violin—let him saw away there to his heart's content! And in his room we'll put Sofotchka. What a child she is! Today she looked at me with big eyes and said, "Mama!" *[sighing.]* The first things I'm going to do out here is have all these fir trees chopped down, then this maple here... in the evening it's so ugly. *[to IRINA]* Dear, that belt doesn't suit you at all. It's in very poor taste. You need something light. And I'll order flowers planted and... *[Severely]* What's a fork doing here on the bench? *[She goes into the house, to the maid.]* What's a fork doing here on the bench, I'd like to know? *[shouting]* Shut up!

KULYGIN: She's off again!

[Behind the scenes a band is playing a march, everybody listens.]

OLGA: They're leaving.

[TCHEBUTYKIN enters]

MASHA: Farewell to our friends! *[To her husband]* We must go home. Where are my hat and wrap?

KULYGIN: In the house. I'll get them.

TCHEBUTYKIN: Olga Sergeyevna!

OLGA: What? *[A pause]* What?

TCHEBUTYKIN: Nothing. Don't know how to tell you.... *[Whispering in her ear.]*

OLGA: *[Alarmed]* Oh dear God, no!

TCHEBUTYKIN: Yes. I know. It's dreadful. *[Irritably.]* But then does any of it matter, really?

MASHA: What's happened?

OLGA: *[Putting her arm around IRINA.]* This is a terrible day. I don't know how to tell you, my darling....

IRINA: What? Say it quick. What? For God's sake! *[crying]*

TCHEBUTYKIN: The Baron was killed just now in a duel.

IRINA: *[weeping quietly.]* I knew, I knew it.

TCHEBUTYKIN: *[Sitting down on a bench to the rear of the stage.]* I'm exhausted. *[Taking a newspaper out of his pocket.]* Yes, yes, cry a little. *[Singing softly.]* Ta-ra-ra-boom-de-aye...Sit on a tomb all day....None of it maters.

[The three sisters stand with their arms around one another.]

MASHA: Listen to the music! They're leaving us. Forever. We'll have to start our life over again. We must live...We must live....

IRINA: *[Putting her head on OLGA's breast.]* Someday surely people will know what all this suffering is for. Meanwhile, well, tomorrow I'll go away alone. I'll teach in the school and give my life to those who may have some use for it.

It's autumn now winter will soon come and cover everything with snow, and I'll be working, working....

OLGA: *[Embracing both her sisters.]* The music sounds so brave. It makes one want to live! Oh, dear God! Time will pass and we'll disappear. Our faces, voices, everything. But surely our sufferings can be turned into some kind of joy for those living after us. I must believe that happiness and peace are possible on this Earth and that our lives are not in vain. Oh, dear sisters, our life isn't over yet. We'll live! The music plays so joyously, and perhaps tomorrow—or the day after—we'll know why we live and why we suffer. If we only knew, if we only knew!

[The music plays always softer and softer; **KULYGIN,** *smiling and gay, brings the hat and cape.* **ANDREY** *is pushing the baby carriage with Bobik in it.]*

TCHEBUTYKIN: *[singing softly]* Ta-ra-ra-boom-de-aye. Sit on a tomb and pray. *[reading the newspaper.]* Anyway it doesn't matter! It doesn't matter at all.

OLGA: If we only knew, if we only knew!

CURTAIN

Bitter Cane

by Genny Lim

Characters

LAU HING KUO: the ghost of a middle-aged cane cutter
LI-TAI: a prostitute in her mid-thirties
KAM SU: a cane cutter in his early thirties
WING CHUNG KUO: the sixteen-year-old son of Lau Hing
FOOK MING: a middle-aged Chinese luna (foreman)

Setting

Hawaii in the 1880s

SCENE 1

[China. A bare stage. WING is packing to leave for America. There are several tightly wrapped cloth bundles on the floor, ready to go.]

VOICEOVER OF HIS OLD MOTHER: Listen well, young man, and understand. You are my blood, my color, the offshoot and stem of my bones. There is no place on this earth where you can walk without shadow. The rain will pelt your shoulders like stones. The burning sun shall torment your flesh. Life is difficult and short. But the gods have given us laughter and song to forget our troubles.

You must remember, my only son, never to dishonor yourself. Do not be idle, do not wander aimlessly, without destination. Do not throw dust upon the gods' faces. Do not spill black ink on the ancestral graves. You have been formed, shaped like a thorn from my womb. You grow like the wound in my soul. Now it is up to you, my son. Do not kill me with shame as did your father. Will you break the cycle of pain or will you pursue another grievous lifetime? Beware of tigers everywhere. Snakes lie among the leaves like snares. The sun and wind carry the seeds of memory. Do not forget my words. They are all I have to leave you.

[Enter a funeral procession in a Chinese village during the mid-1800s. The drone of tantric Buddhist chants mingled with the weeping and wailing of women fill the air. White-robed mourners march across the stage bearing a litter with the shrouded body, paper effigies, and palace, symbolizing wealth and status in the afterlife. The objects are lowered to the ground in a funeral pyre. WING approaches and halts apart from the rest. He presses his hands in prayer and bows three times. The mourners turn together and watch him in silence. WING takes up his bundles and exits. Blackout.]

SCENE 2

[Storm over Oahu. Kahuku sugarcane plantation. A weary, middle-aged Chinese traveler, wearing white and a coolie hat, enters carrying a wrapped bundle. His movements should be stylized and suggestive of another world. He stops, listens, and puts down his bundle.]

LAU HING *[attentively]*: Listen to that. Sounds like it's never goin' to stop. Hear it hammering down the tin roofs? Drilling through cracks, dripping down walls, fillin' empty tins on the floor? Yu-chiang, the master of floods, remembers our sins. *[miming]* Sometimes he cups the ocean in his hands and hurls a tidal wave! *[howling of wind]* Hear him growling? *[pauses]* There's nothing more lonely than the sound of wind and rain. But, once it stops, you're back in the fields, knuckling under the sun. Just when you think you'll collapse, you look up and there she'll be, the

cane witch. Smiling at you from behind high stalks; long, black hair shining, naked brown arms beckoning you. You blink your eyes twice to see if you're dreaming and she laughs. You don't know where she came from or who she is, but you want her. You want her so bad you can feel your heart trembling. You chase her through row after row of cane till you're breathless. When you finally catch up to her, she spins around and looks at you. Her two dark eyes are caverns. You reach to enter, but a stabbing pain pierces your heart and she disappears. There's no trace of her. All you see is a lizard darting through the leaves. And the faint smell of pikake.

[Woman's laughter and sound of rain. LAU crosses downstage left, where he remains for the rest of the play. Light goes up on a wooden shack room with a vanity, a bed and a few feminine, Victorian articles. The set should be evocative, not literal. On the bed, LI-TAI is giggling as KAM SU tickles her.]

KAM: Teach me!

LI-TAI: I'm not Hawaiian.

KAM *[lifting her camisole]*: Then you need exposure. *[kisses her navel]*

LI-TAI *[laughing]*: Piko.

KAM *[tickling]*: Piko, piko, piko!

LI-TAI: Diu-mao-gwai!

KAM: Who you calling a drunk?

LI-TAI *[puts out her palm in a no-nonsense manner]*: My money?

[Realizing the rules have changed, KAM irritably picks up a fifth of whiskey from her dresser and takes several snorts. She grabs it from him and puts it back.]

KAM: Payday is Saturday. I'll pay you then.

LI-TAI *[irate]*: What do you think I am? You pay me now!

KAM: I got one year left on my contract. *[digs into his pocket and hands her several coins]* One more lousy year. *[meaningfully]* Then I'm free.

LI-TAI *[looks at the coins with disgust]*: Fifty cents! Is that all you got?

KAM: Have a heart, Li-Tai. I came all this way in the storm!

LI-TAI: And you can go back in it!

KAM: Please...

LI-TAI *[indignant]*: You wouldn't do this to a haole woman!

KAM *[cajoling]*: Just this once. I'm begging you!

LI-TAI *[contemptuously]*: Jawk-gee! Do you think you're catching a pig?

KAM *[desperately]*: As a countryman!

LI-TAI *[throws the coins on the floor in anger]*: Get out.

KAM *[explodes]*: You think you so high and mighty? You think you too good for me, huh? Well I'll tell you something. You and that Pake luna are nothing but a pair of blood-sucking leeches!

LI-TAI: You are dirt!

[She slaps him. He grabs her violently, forces her onto the bed, grabbing her bound feet. She struggles helplessly underneath him.]

KAM *[aroused]*: Crippled woman, where can you go? You have no feet—only petals for toes.

[*She spits at him. He twists her ankles. She clenches her teeth in pain.*]

KAM: You can only submit! [*He bites the tip of her foot as if it was a delicacy.*] Like fish out of water.

[*She struggles free and in a frenzy, gathers his coins and flings them at him.*]

LI-TAI: Take your crumbs and get out!

KAM: Why spit on your own kind? Do you think you're better than me?

LI-TAI [*contemptuously*]: Shit is better than you. [*hysterically*] Get out! Get out!

KAM [*pointing his finger*]: One day, you'll be sorry.

[*He exits, slamming the door violently. She takes his shirt, opens the door, and hurls it out. We hear him yell from outside.*]

KAM [*offstage*]: Pake snake! Mercenary whore!

LI-TAI [*screaming*]: Fook will kill you if you ever come back here!

[*She slams the door shut, leaning against it with eyes shut. She takes big gulps from the whiskey bottle. She goes slowly to the bed, sits, then lights the opium lamp on the bedside table and prepares the pipe. She takes deep tokes. The drug has an almost immediate calming effect on her. She picks up a cricket cage from her bed table and studies it with intense fascination. The room fills with smoke and the crescendo of rain, then the sound of a cane worker singing:*]

Hawaii, Hawaii
so far, far from home,
Hawaii, Hawaii
My bones ache and my heart breaks
thinking about the ones I left behind.

[*The light fades on LI-TAI: and comes up on KAM in the field, holding a machete and singing:*]

Hawaii, Hawaii
so far, far from home,
For every cane I cut, there are a thousand more
With so many days to pay.
Hawaii, Hawaii
Don't let me die of misery.
Don't bury me under the cane fields.

[*LAU HING watches him silently from a distance. KAM wipes his brow with his sleeve, then hacks the stalks with vengeance.*]

KAM: Goddam sonovabitches! [*throws his whole body into cutting motion*] Take that! [*again striking*] And that, son-a-va-bitch!

[*A CHINESE LUNA enters with a new worker.*]

LUNA [*to Kam*]: Less mouth, more action! [*indicating newcomer*] I want you to teach this boy to cut cane. Make sure he doesn't cut the tops high. I want the stubs nice and low. Show him the right way. Stack 'em straight. No sloppy piles. No cheating. I got eyes. We'll have to lop this field by Saturday—otherwise, overtime.

KAM: No overtime! Our contract says no overtime Sunday!

LUNA: I'm boss here! If I say you work, you work. If I say you work overtime, you work overtime. Understand?

KAM [*stubbornly*]: I understand the contract.

LUNA: Well now, I wouldn't want to violate your contract. If you don't like working Sundays, you can work nights.

KAM: No dinner, no work!

LUNA: No work, no pay! You got that, Chinaboy? [*waiting for response*] Now get back to work. That's what we pay you for. [*LUNA exits. KAM takes the machete and lands it with force.*]

KAM: You haole lap-dog! [*strikes*] Profit from the blood of your countrymen! [*strikes*] Traitor to the white devils! [*strikes*] Bastard! [*to WING*] Back up! Look out for flying splinters. You're liable to lose an eye or nose! You want to learn how to cut cane, boy? This is how we cut. Nice and deep. Down to the bone. They want the juice in that stalk. Don't let it run to the ground. The bottom's where the vein's at. Easy. Nice and sweet for the mill to grind. If you can cut one, you can cut eight! Just think of each cane stalk as Fook Ming's skinny neck… Aiii-ee-eee!!!

[*A final angry blow. Fade out.*]

SCENE 3

[*Dinnertime outside the plantation shack. KAM is too wound up to eat. WING, by comparison, wolfs down his bowl as if starved. There are two small packets beside each of their bowls.*]

WING [*with disappointment*]: Is this all we get for dinner?

KAM [*with a bitter laugh*]: What did you expect? A king's nine course banquet? Cod fillet and shark fin soup? Deep-fried quail and tender, boneless barley duck? Ha ha. You'd better get used to limp salt cabbage and cold rice, cause you're gonna be eating a lot of it. [*pushes his bowl toward WING*] Go ahead, eat, friend.

WING [*eagerly seizes KAM's bowl*]: Thank you.

KAM: Welcome to Kahuku, the land of bitter cane. I am Kam Su. Better known as Kam-a Su-tra. And who are you?

WING: Wing. Wing Chun.

KAM: You look like someone I know. [*slapping mosquitoes*] I must have sweet blood. I'm being crucified! [*laughs*] Like Jesus.

WING: I got stung by a wasp in the field. [*rubbing his ear*] Who is Jesus?

KAM: Christ. Wrap your head. The nests are hidden in the leaves. [*points to his unopened packet; WING hands it to him*] Jesus Christ. Nailed on a cross by his own gentle kind. Friendship is a rare thing. Greater love hath no man than this, that a man lay down his life for his friends. [*preparing his pipe*] And there are those who profit from the misery of their own. Judas saith unto him, not Iscariot.

WING [*perplexed*]: What the hell are you talking about?

KAM: Christian delirium. Don't mind me. When the sun hits, I start babbling that holy drivel. [*takes a puff.*] The only book we could get was the Bible. We recited passages from Matthew, Mark, Luke, and John, like little schoolboys, trying to keep our minds off sex. It only made it worse.

[KAM *points to* WING's *unused packet*] Aren't you going to open yours?

[WING *shakes his head disinterestedly.*]

KAM: Then why don't I trade my rice for your powder?

[WING *shrugs and shoves his packet toward* KAM. KAM *eagerly takes it.*]

KAM: I give you a month before you're as depraved as the rest of us. Disciples of the golden poppy.

WING [*offended*]: Don't be so sure.

KAM [*surly*]: Oh? You don't shit?

WING [*stubbornly*]: Every man's different.

KAM [*cynically*]: I don't agree. I say all men are the same. Deaf and dumb. You come out of a hole, you go into a hole. Eventually you disappear. Like the cane. [*takes out his pipe and opens the packet of powder*] You're no different. [*puts the powder in the bowl of the pipe*] You came to make money and return to the village rich. When your contract's up, you'll go home and pick a wife. That's what we all thought. You'll see. The seasons pass without fail. Each day follows the next. You plant, you cut, you harvest, you haul, and you don't ask questions. Like a dumb plow ox. The only thing you got to break the monotony is gambling, opium, or women. Euphoria or Christianity. Take your pick. Can you think of anything more depressing than praying to some limp haole hanging from a cross? [*laughs*] He probably never understood a word of Chinese anyway! [*taps his pipe, then lights it*]

WING: Why did you stop believing?

KAM: When I realized this White God wanted no graven images before him. Father DeCarlo snatched up Kwan Kung and hurled him on the ground. There was no way on earth, I'd let him burn Kwan Kung! I carried him all the way with me from China. Why that'd be like spittin' on my father's grave! Father DeCarlo couldn't believe the endless string of curses I shouted at him. If their God was going to be so greedy, I said, I'd just as soon stay pagan. It was stupid to think of myself as Christian anyway. You can't spin silk out of cotton, no more than you can teach a pigeon to swim. Soon as I pay my debt, I'm going back. I have no illusions about this place. [*cheerfully*] I'll just spend whatever time I have left, playing, not praying. [*shrugs*] If opium is evil, the white man's the devil. He gave it to us and it's him who's keeping us here. [*puffing*] Most of the fellas take any woman they can get their hands on. You can't drain away your manhood. Why wait five or seven years for a village girl? Some of the fellas marry Hawaiian girls. Some even marry prostitutes!

WING: Not me. I'm going to make my village proud.

[WING *takes out a knife and a hunk of wood from his pocket and starts whittling.* LAU *simultaneously takes out an invisible knife and his cutting movements repeat* WING's.]

KAM: Look at the bastard talking! [*mocking him*] I'm going to make my mother proud! What are you anyhow? Mexican? [*amused*] You still a virgin? [*patronizing*] Listen, you don't have to be ashamed. No one's perfect. I was once one too. But once you've tasted wine [*a quick tug at his crotch*], you never lose your thirst. [*smirks*] Know what I mean? You want a woman?

WING: I'll wait till I marry.

KAM [*disgustedly*]: Did you leave your dick in China? Is that what you're carving? Wake up! I got just the woman for you, Chinaboy. She can wrap her gaze around you till you think you're seeing double. She's a snake beauty. With a deadly bite.

WING: She must be a bad woman.

KAM: There are two kinds of women. The kind that reminds you of your mother and the kind every mother fears for her son. The first kind you marry and the other kind you lust. As long as you don't confuse the two, you'll be fine—know what I mean?

WING [*laughs*]: Oh you're a real expert, aren't you, Kam?

KAM [*a casual wave of the hand*]: Ah, I don't trust any woman. I don't let 'em get the better of me. If you're smart, you won't either. You gotta keep your knuckle on 'em. Don't take any chances. When you see a woman cry that's a sign of surrender. She'll be like that piece of wood in your hand. You can carve her into any shape you desire. [WING *laughs with disdain.*] She'll worship you like Jesus.

WING [*laughing*]: You're full of dung!

KAM: Hey take it from me! I know what I'm talking about. Every woman wants you to suck her dainty earlobes. She wants you to caress her creamy thighs and pinch her nipples till she cries with pain. And when you bite those tiny dewdrop feet with your teeth, she'll ache with such pleasure, she'll think she was just born! She'll arch her back up in a half-moon and that's when you'll know, the gate of heaven is open. She's ready for you to plunge into the heart of the flower. [*with a big self-satisfied sigh*] The secret of seduction, according to the analects of Master Kama Sutra, is mystification. [*both are laughing conspiratorially*] Now how about it, country poke? [*lascivious grin*] Ready to dip your brush?

WING [*shaking his head nervously*]: No.

KAM: You turnip, I give you one month before you come sweating!

WING [*stubbornly*]: Not me, I'm no red lotus-chaser!

KAM [*with knowing certainty*]: We'll see about that, Chinaboy. Anyone who whittles the way you do has got to have an itch! [*laughs*]

[*Fade out.*]

SCENE 4

[*Night time. Cicadas. Outside* LI-TAI's *cabin. There is the sound of a couple's laughter from inside. The two men, outside, are hiding behind bushes, spying.* LAU *joins them unnoticed.*]

WING [*anxiously*]: What if he doesn't leave?

KAM: Then you go and knock.

WING *[nervously]*: What do I say?

KAM *[impatiently]*: Why does a man go to a woman in the middle of the night? You don't have to say nothin', stupid!

WING *[misgivings]*: Maybe we should go.

KAM *[irate]*: You think we walked three miles for nothin'? You crazy!

WING *[nervous]*: Maybe this isn't such a good idea.

KAM: Shoot! I do it all the time. The lunas, they know we sneak away. They turn the other way. It just makes their job easier, that's all. *[craning to see]* I wonder who's in there with her?

WING: It sounds like a man's voice!

KAM: Oh, you don't say?

[Lights off on two men and up on **FOOK** *and* **LI-TAI** *in bed, drinking. He is slightly intoxicated. The room is lit by a single kerosene lamp.]*

FOOK *[stroking her in pleased tones]*: You have the body of a virgin. Tight and firm as a stalk of cane. No one would suspect you were over thirty-five.

LI-TAI: I'm not.

FOOK *[grinning possessively]*: You can't keep secrets from me, Li-Tai.

LI-TAI: Did you bring me a treat today?

FOOK: I'm going to wind up in the poorhouse over you, Li-Tai!

LI-TAI: Come on, give Li-Li some candy!

FOOK *[reaches into the pocket of his garment at bedside and takes out an envelope, which he reluctantly hands her]*: That's all you get.

[She grabs the envelope.]

LI-TAI: My delicious poppy!

FOOK *[shaking his head]*: My poor little slave! *[he slowly gets dressed and out of bed]* What will become of you?

LI-TAI *[annoyed]*: Why do you always talk to yourself?

FOOK *[defensively]*: I take good care of you Li-Tai. If it wasn't for me, you'd be stuck in a brothel. You should be grateful.

LI-TAI: Shall I get on my hands and knees?

FOOK: Is that the position you like? *[matter-of-factly]* Do you have my money?

[She crosses to the drawer and takes out some money, which she hands to a suspicious **FOOK**.*]*

FOOK: Is that all?

LI-TAI *[nervously]*: Business is slow.

FOOK: You're smoking up my profits.

LI-TAI *[turns her back]*: Don't start!

FOOK: Then be straight with me!

LI-TAI: I want a cicada.

FOOK: What? Another damn cicada? What happened to the last one?

LI-TAI: It died.

FOOK: I despise those ugly insects!

LI-TAI *[sadly holds the empty cage up]*: That's all I have.

FOOK *[amused]*: You're such a child, Li-Tai. *[he tries to kiss her, but she turns her cheek]* You enjoy wearing me down, don't you? Don't you?

LI-TAI *[wearily]*: Shouldn't you be going?

FOOK *[aroused]*: I ought to turn you over my knees and spank you. Do you realize that in another year, I'll have enough

to buy some land of my own? The rest of these coolies don't have the smarts to do anything but smoke and gamble. They have no ambition. They'll never make a cent because they're not willing to invest time to make money. Not me. Sugar is a good cash crop and prices are climbing. Soon I'll be a planter, not a luna. I'll have my own plantation and I'll hire my own men. We'll have money enough so you won't have to sleep with anyone but me. *[possessively]* I hate the thought of other men touching you. Especially Kam. You're not seeing that scoundrel anymore, are you? *[she shakes her head; he speaks desiringly]* You're spoiled. French perfume, cigarettes, silk stockings… in the middle of nowhere. You fancy yourself a lady, don't you, Li-Tai?

LI-TAI: I have my ways. *[to herself]* Sometimes I wonder which is more oppressive—the heat of the sun or the lust of a man.

FOOK: You know you couldn't survive here without me, Li-Tai. Don't forget where you were when I rescued you. You didn't have one decent outfit to your name and you were frail as a bean thread. It was easy as picking fruit off the ground. If I hadn't taken you, you would have rotted. *[pauses]* We'll be loading the mules tomorrow…I'll be back Sunday. *[pinches her cheek]* Be nice.

LI-TAI: Bring my cicada!

FOOK *[annoyed]*: I'm jealous. *[with amusement]* Imagine that! Jealous of a cicada! A damned cicada. *[He exits.]*

[The porch door opens slightly.]

KAM: Look, someone's coming!

WING: Can you see who?

KAM: Shh.

[The **CHINESE LUNA** *stumbles out drunk and leaves in the darkness.]*

KAM: It's that sonuvabitch Fook Ming! *[under his breath]* That no-good bitch! She goes for that stuffed cock. *[pushes* **WING** *toward the door]* Go on, now's your chance!

WING *[resisting]*: Don't push me!

KAM: You got cold feet?

WING: I just don't like to be pushed.

KAM: Alright, all right. *[starts to leave]*

WING: Hey, where you going?

KAM: To see somebody.

WING: Yeah? Who?

KAM *[giving him the nod]*: What are you waiting for? Someone to take you by the hand? *[reassuringly]* Okay, I'll wait till you go in.

WING *[pats* **KAM** *on shoulder]*: Thanks Kam.

KAM: Remember, take your time, kid. Take a deep breath. Remember what I told you! *[he watches* **WING** *approach her door]* And don't forget to tell her who sent you!

[Light fades on **KAM**. **WING** *takes a deep breath and knocks.]*

LI-TAI *[calling from inside]*: Who is it?

WING *[clearing his throat]*: My name is Wing Chun… Kuo.

[The light inside the cabin comes up as **LI-TAI** *slowly opens the door. She motions him to enter. He stands there awkwardly.]*

LI-TAI *[stares at him with immediate recognition]*: You?

WING *[captivated]*: I hope it's not too late.

LI-TAI *[glancing around nervously]*: I thought I heard voices. *[returning curiously to* **WING***]* You new?

WING: Yes. Three weeks.

LI-TAI: Hoi-ping?

WING [surprised]: Yes. How did you know?

LI-TAI [matter-of-factly]: By the way you talk.

WING [impressed]: You're clever.

LI-TAI [examining him]: You're good-looking. You look mixed.

WING: I'm Chinese, same as you. I was the best farmer back home.

LI-TAI: I believe it. [looks at his hands] Are you good with your hands?

WING [surprised]: Yes. I can carve things.

LI-TAI [impressed]: Ah, an artist! [sounding his name] Wing Chun. My name is Li-Tai.

WING: Li-Tai. That's pretty. [pauses] Where you from?

LI-TAI [abruptly]: Look. I know you're not here to gossip. You have two dollars? [He fumbles in his pocket and without looking hands her several bills. She smirks at his naivete and quickly tucks it in her kimono pocket.]

LI-TAI: Sit down. [He sits.]

LI-TAI: Want something to drink?

WING: Some tea would be nice, thank you.

LI-TAI [amused laugh]: Tea? How old are you?

WING: Twenty.

LI-TAI [frowning]: You're lying.

WING [embarrassed]: Sixteen.

LI-TAI: This your first time? [He nods with embarrassment. She takes a whiskey bottle, uncorks it, pours a glass, and hands it to him.]

LI-TAI: Drink it. It'll give you confidence. [He takes a big swallow and chokes. She laughs at him.]

LI-TAI: Slow down. What's your hurry? [smiling] Talk to me.

WING [still embarrassed]: About what?

LI-TAI: About you.

WING [blushing]: There's not much to tell.

LI-TAI: Why not?

WING [takes a gulp, then blurts]: My name is Wing and I like to eat duck gizzards. [She bursts out laughing, then he laughs, too.]

WING: On the first day of school, I remember the teacher asked us to introduce ourselves.

LI-TAI: And that was what you said.

WING: I couldn't think of anything else!

LI-TAI [mockingly]: You still can't.

WING [frustrated]: I don't know why I'm so tongue-tied. [finishes his glass]

LI-TAI: Talking is not important. [refills his glass] There are other ways to communicate. [pours herself one, clicks his glass, then slumps on the bed with her glass in a provocative manner] Your parents have a bride picked out for you yet?

WING: No. [pauses] My parents are dead.

LI-TAI: I'm sorry.

WING: My father died here. At Kahuku.

LI-TAI: Oh? [surprised] What was his name?

WING: Lau Hing. Kuo Lau Hing. [She freezes at the recognition of his name.]

WING: He was one of those Sandalwood boys who never made it back.

LI-TAI [trembling]: How old were you when he left?

WING: I was just a baby.

[Struck by the resemblance, she cups his face with her hands.]

LI-TAI: Let me look at you!

WING [embarrassed]: What's the matter? Why are you looking at me like that?

LI-TAI [marveling]: You remind me of someone.

WING: I'm as good as any man on Kahuku.

LI-TAI [disdainfully]: The average man here is a pig. You don't want to be like them, do you?

WING: One flop in the family is enough. It's no secret. Lau Hing was a bum.

LI-TAI: How can a son talk about his own father in that way?

WING: And how can a father treat his family that way? Why should I pretend he was somebody he wasn't? [somberly] He was nobody to me. Nothing.

LI-TAI [stung with guilt]: Your mother? She loved him?

WING [disgustedly]: She died. He lied to her. He lied to her every month for two years! When he got tired of lying, he stopped writing altogether. She didn't hear from him again. Then one day, she gets this letter saying he's dead. [bitterly] You want to know what killed him? [pauses] Opium. The money he should have sent home, he squandered on himself! [pauses] They shipped his trunk back. She thought it was his bones. When she opened it, she fainted. The box was empty except for his hat and a few personal belongings. His body was never recovered they said, because he had drowned in the ocean. [with cruel irony] That's why I'm here. To redeem a dead man.

LI-TAI: You think you'll succeed?

WING: I'm not sending my ghost in an empty box home. Life is too short! [listening to the sound of rain] It's raining again.

LI-TAI: It's always raining. There's no escape. [with a sense of foreboding] You do what you can do to forget. And survive. [picks up a fan and begins moodily fanning herself] I can't decide what's more boring. Living out here in the middle of nowhere or raising chickens in a puny plot back home.

WING: Why did you come here?

LI-TAI: A lady in the village told me that Hawai'i was paradise. She said there was hardly anything to do there but suck on big, fat, juicy sugarcane-sweeter than honey. I was crazy for cane and waited for the day to come here. When my mother died, my father remarried. My new mother didn't like a girl with bound feet who talked back. So I told her to send me to Hawai'i. She sold me to a rich old merchant on the Big Island. I cried and begged to go back home. But I was his number four concubine. His favorite. Four is a bad luck number. So when the old man suffered a stroke in my bedroom, they, of course, blamed it on me. Number one wife, who was always jealous of me, picked up my red slippers and threw them at my face. Then she beat me with a bamboo rod and called me a good-for-nothing slave girl! [laughs bitterly] They lit firecrackers when Fook Ming took me. To rid my evil spirit. Some paradise. *[moved by* **WING***'s look of compassion]* Tell me, what do they say about me?

WING *[blushing]*: Who?

LI-TAI: The men. What do the men say about Li-Tai?

*[***LAU HING*** *crosses from the wing toward* **LI-TAI**.*]*

WING: Nothing. *[admiringly]* Just that you're beautiful.

LAU *[passionately]*: You're beautiful!

*[***LI-TAI*** *turns and sees* **LAU**.*]*

LI-TAI: Who sent you here?

WING: No one, I swear!

LI-TAI *[frightened by* **LAU***'s apparition]*: Why do you come? *[cautiously]* What do you want from me?

WING *[apologetic and earnest]*: I came to you because I need a woman.

LAU *[echoing simultaneously]*: I came to you because I need a woman.

LI-TAI *[scornfully]*: How much is your pleasure worth? Two dollars? All the money you have?

WING *[ardently]*: Everything!

LAU: Everything!

LI-TAI *[with a nervous laugh]*: So you need a woman. But not just any woman? *[crosses to a table and lights a candle in a glass holder]* You want one with experience? One who can guide you into manhood? *[puts out the kerosene lamp, picks up the candle, and turns to him]* Someone who can open your eyes and wipe the clouds from them. *[crosses to him]* Because you're not a little boy anymore. *[continues her cross to the bed]* And Mama can't help you. *[places candle on bedside table, then lies down]* But I can. *[coyly]* Come here. *[He takes a nervous breath and crosses to her. He halts in front of her.* **LAU** *turns and watches them.]*

LI-TAI: Are you afraid of me?

[She reaches for him and pulls him down to his knees. She puts his hand to her face and he slowly strokes her cheek as if discovering a woman's skin for the first time. He continues touching and stroking her face, neck, arms, and shoulders, gently and innocently.]

LI-TAI: You're pure as the lily's hidden leaf. *[gazing intently at him]* I see little torches flickering in your eyes!

WING *[with nervous passion]*: They burn for you.

LI-TAI: You should stay away from fire.

WING: Why? We sacrifice to the gods with fire.

LI-TAI: Forget the gods. There's only you and I here. And the huge ocean, which surrounds us.

[She pulls him to her. She takes his hands and examines them as if remembering something from the past. She gently presses them to her cheeks. Then she pulls him alongside her on the bed. He removes her embroidered slippers, gently, then caresses her feet. **LAU** *approaches the pair, mesmerized.]*

WING: Does that feel good? *[she moans softly]* They're so tiny.

LI-TAI *[sighs]*: Oh your hands… they feel like water!

LAU *[echoing]*: …they feel like water!

LI-TAI *[matter-of-factly]*: I'm made for pleasure. Not marriage. Family, cooking, raising babies. I wouldn't be good for that. *[a sad laugh]* I'm only good for one thing. *[provocatively]* And you, what are you good for?

[He kisses her feet. By now, **LAU** *is standing a short distance from the couple, watching and experiencing every nuance of gesture as if reliving it. She leans over and unfastens his shirt. She takes in his young torso and gently runs her fingers over him. He takes her fingertips and gently bites them. She withdraws her hands, unloosens the kimono around her shoulders till it reveals her nakedness.* **LAU HING** *moves in closer to watch.* **WING** *reaches to touch her, but she coyly pulls away and recovers herself with the kimono. He pulls her to him and pulls open her kimono as if unveiling a miracle. Struck by this first experience of womanly beauty, he stares in awe of her.]*

LAU *[passionately]*: You're beautiful!

*[***WING*** *takes her into his arms. We hear the pounding rain amid her soft moans as they kiss. Fade out.]*

SCENE 5

[Downstage left.]

LAU: "When a dog comes, then riches…When a pig comes, then woes…When a cat comes, run quickly…And buy mourning clothes." *[whittles with a carving knife the final touches to a puppet as he speaks]* Chance. Everything, chance! Every gambler knows it. Every farmer knows it. If nature's not with you, you're just out of luck. One flood can wipe your field clean; one disease can finish you off. You see the cane? They grow straight and tall against the wind. Just give them plenty of sunshine and water. But if blight comes *[indicating, with stylized gestures, the puppet's futile struggle with supernatural forces]*, there's nothing can save it. *[to the puppet]* It's the hand of Yuk Wong Dai Dei. Heaven and earth. No man on earth can stop him. If a man does you wrong you can kill him. But once cane rot sets in, who do you blame?

[Fade out.]

SCENE 6

[The next morning. **LI-TAI** *awakens beside* **WING**. *She contemplates his slumbering face. She raises her hand lovingly to stroke his features but refrains to keep from disturbing him. She throws on a light robe and climbs out of bed.* **WING** *stirs.]*

WING *[looks around, disoriented, then horrified]*: Oh my god, it's morning! How could I fall asleep! *[gets up and starts frantically putting on his clothes]* I gotta get back.

LI-TAI *[calmly]*: Wait. I'll fix breakfast. You can't work on an empty stomach.

WING: Next time.

LI-TAI *[resolutely]*: Maybe there won't be a next time.

WING [*confused*]: I don't understand.

LI-TAI [*a bit forcefully*]: Stay here.

WING: I can't. [*reassuringly*] Look, I'll be back.

LI-TAI [*skeptically*]: When?

WING: Next Saturday?

LI-TAI [*demanding*]: Tomorrow!

WING [*embarrassed*]: I—I...can't afford...

LI-TAI [*offended*]: I won't take your money. I don't want it. Just don't treat me like some whore.

WING [*taking her by the shoulder*]: What's gotten into you?

LI-TAI [*pulling away*]: You tell me. [*sarcastically*] You're a man. Oh what's the use! The sun flattens down on you like an iron and all you can do is lie there and whimper. [*a sigh of disgust*] Some paradise.

WING: You give in to bitterness.

LI-TAI: They said, "You will never want to leave!" [*with bitter irony*] I never asked to come. [*reminiscing*] I was only twenty when I came to Kahuku...[*turning away from him*]...and the easy life. I've been here too long! [*gesturing at the landscape*] Like those mountains that never move. [*thinking aloud*] What do you think happens to us when we die?

WING [*decisively*]: We go on living in the afterlife.

LI-TAI: No we don't. We wither and die.

WING: Don't you believe in immortality?

LI-TAI [*firmly*]: No.

WING: Everything lives in the soul.

LI-TAI: Everything dies in the heart.

WING: That's not Chinese!

LI-TAI: Maybe I'm not Chinese.

WING: Don't you believe in fate?

LI-TAI: No.

WING: Why not?

LI-TAI: Because fate is destiny. I don't believe in destiny. It's our own hand that pulls us down, not some god's. We answer to ourselves.

WING: I don't know about that...[*romantically*] I was lying in the dark, unable to sleep, so I listened to sounds. The soft feet of rain, the rustling of boughs and leaves, ten thousand voices of crickets...I heard the grass talk to the wind. I heard the cicada's song.

LI-TAI [*amused*]: What did it sing?

WING: It sang good evening to the stars.

LI-TAI: And what did the stars answer?

WING: The stars answered that they were lonely.

LI-TAI: Why were they lonely?

WING: Because they shined alone in the sky.

LI-TAI [*laughing*]: Did they sing in Chinese?

WING: In a language beyond words. Did you ever try, when you were a kid, to pick out one star in the sky, then try to find that same star the next night? You can't. But you keep looking anyhow. When I first looked at you, I had this feeling fate brought us together. [*looks at her meaningfully*] Things happen for a reason.

LI-TAI: I don't believe that. Things just happen. We make them happen. We stumble into traps. We live, we die.

WING [*intrigued*]: You're not like the women back home.

LI-TAI: They all think like one person. The young girls talk like old women and the old women are ignorant and superstitious. In China you're born old before you can walk. As a woman you're allowed to do only one thing. Please men. I've spent my whole life doing that! [*matter-of-factly*] You see this body? It's not mine. It belongs to Kahuku Plantation. My skin even smells like burnt cane!

WING: And what about your heart?

LI-TAI: I cut it out. Long ago.

WING: Then what was it I felt last night? [*with certainty*] I've known you before.

LI-TAI: Last night I was drunk! So were you. [*begins primping before the mirror*] What happened to all the years? I look in the mirror and count each new gray hair. [*sadly*] Time has no respect for a woman.

WING [*looking at her reflection from behind*]: You have a beautiful face, a true face. With features that sing. [*tenderly*] Your brows describe the mists of Kweilin.

LI-TAI [*laughs*]: What do my wrinkles reveal?

WING: The soft rays of the moon.

LI-TAI: A waning moon?

WING: No. A full one. [*dramatically*] I was reborn last night.

LI-TAI [*laughing*]: Don't make me laugh.

WING: I mean it. [*puts his arms shyly around her*]

LI-TAI: Don't be foolish. [*scoffing*] I'm old enough to be your mother!

WING: The soul has no age.

LI-TAI [*sighs*]: You remind me of a man I loved fifteen years ago.

WING: Who was that?

LI-TAI [*elusively*]: A man who was a cicada. [*thoughtfully*] Did you know the cicada dies after he mates?

WING [*optimistically*]: Yes, but he is resurrected from the grave he leaves behind.

[WING *kisses her, then exits. A spot on* LAU, *kneeling in the cabin. He is folding a red Chinese robe in a ceremonial manner. She gives a start. Fade out*].

SCENE 7

[*Break time. Several weeks have passed.* KAM *enters mopping the sweat off his face as he puts down his machete.* WING *follows exhausted and lays his machete down.* KAM *ladles some water from a barrel for himself, then for* WING.]

WING: Thanks for covering me.

KAM: Sonuvabitch! Is it her again? How can you afford to go so much?

WING [*worried*]: What did you tell the boss?

KAM [*facetiously*]: I said you were in the outhouse with diarrhea.

WING [*gloomily*]: Very funny.

KAM: I'm not covering for you anymore. I'm warning you!

WING: Okay, okay! *[nervously]* What do you know about Li-Tai?

KAM *[suspiciously]*: Why?

WING *[with a deep breath]*: I want to marry her.

KAM *[shocked]*: You're joking! *[contemptuously]* She's a prostitute.

WING: Different flowers have a way with different eyes. *[defensively]* Besides, you said yourself some of the men marry prostitutes.

KAM *[angrily]*: Listen, kid, you don't know what you're talking about. You don't go marry the first prostitute you jump in bed with. That's crazy! Soak your head in cold water and get back to the fields. *[nastily]* Did she tell you who she is?

WING: I don't care about the past.

KAM: Oh you don't, do you? Did she tell you she's Fook Ming's concubine? Huh? Did she tell you how he keeps her in that cabin all to himself? How he visits her on Sundays and Mondays? How the rest of the week he sets her up with the men?

WING *[stubbornly]*: I don't care about him.

KAM *[shaking his head]*: You're not the first you know. Don't think you're the only one who's tried. *[nastily]* More men have crawled into Li-Tai's bed than lice. They don't call her "The Cocoon" for nothing. She's used up. You stay away. I'm telling you, she's no good. She's poison. *[shaming him]* What would your parents think? You chasing after a slut?

WING *[grabs **KAM** angrily by the collar]*: Don't call her names, you hear me? You're jealous because you want her too!

KAM *[confessing guiltily]*: That's right. I want her too. I'd be lying if I said I didn't.

WING: Are you in love with her?

KAM *[angrily]*: What man around here isn't in love with Li-Tai? What man here doesn't want her? The question is what man is crazy enough to give everything up for her?

WING: I am.

KAM *[sighs]*: I know. That's what worries me. *[pauses]* You don't know the danger you're in. I seen one fella waste himself over her. He was a top cutter too. The best on Kahuku. Worked like the devil to buy her off Fook Ming, but when she refused him, he went mad. He deserted one night, went to her cabin, but she just laughed at him. He couldn't take it. Went completely insane. Poor Lau Hing.

WING *[paling]*: Lau Hing Kuo?

KAM *[surprised]*: Yeah, that was his name. Did you know him?

WING *[softly]*: He was my father.

KAM *[hits himself in the head]*: I talk too much.

WING: Then my father never went back to China because of her?

KAM *[shaking his head]*: Li-Tai bewitched him. He was so heartbroken, he killed himself.

WING *[with shame]*: If it's true, then I should hate her.

KAM *[gravely]*: It's true. Everybody knows about Li-Tai and your father.

*[**LAU** crosses behind **WING**. **WING** stands there frozen in utter disbelief and shock. **KAM** shakes his head disparingly.]*

KAM: You ask me, you've jumped from the net into the frying pan! When you think of what you left to come here, it makes no damn difference. Back home you'd plow the field and pray for rain. Even though you might not eat, at least it's your land. Here, you don't starve, but you work like an ox for some other sonuvabitch's land. Not only that, you don't live like a normal man. *[with indignation]* Look at me, I should be married by now. I should have a wife to screw. I should have a roomful of kids to take care of me in my old age. Instead I waste my time gambling, smoking opium, and falling in love with prostitutes. Like Li Tai. *[Fade out.]*

SCENE 8

*[The magical song of a flute fills the air. On stage right, **LAU** is on his hands and knees stalking a cicada. At his side are **LI TAI**'s cricket cage and his wrapped bundle. He mimes catching the insect and carefully putting it in the cage, eyeing it with fascination. As the light comes up on the men stage left, **LAU** sits back in reverie, listening to the cicada's song. It is three months later on the plantation. The men are bedraggled from a long day of cane loading. **WING** ladles water into tin cups for each of them.]*

KAM *[massaging his aching shouder as he grumbles]*: God sits on his holy ass, while we labor like ants! If we die, who cares? *[with disgust]* Look at this hand! Can't even grip the machete. Can't even hold a pair of chopsticks, it's so swollen. *[trying to make a fist to curse the sky]* I may be an insignificant speck, but I got some feelings! *[mopping his forehead with his sleeve]* There must be all of ten suns out there! Each one burns hotter then the rest. We're ants pushing crumbs. No matter how many rows we level, we're always behind. The cane's as endless as sky. *[observing the sullen, hard-working, **WING**]* Except you, you're inhuman. You blast through that jungle like you got a bee up your ass. You got endurance, Wing, but you also got no consideration. *[a warning tone]* Making it hard on the rest of us, you know? No one can pair up with you! They say you cut ahead and cause their cane to fall. *[with begrudging admiration]* You hit the stalk, it falls. Other fellas hit five, six times, it just shakes. You got one swift machete—like you been born to it. You gonna make me lose face, little brother! *[scolding]* All work and no play's unnatural, Wing. Go to town. Relax. *[raising an eyebrow]* Meet some new friends, yeah? *[pauses]* Come with me tonight! There's some tall, yellowhaired wahine with mango breasts and asses like breadfruit. Lots of huluhulu. Hairy legs are beastly.

WING *[disinterested]*: You go ahead, Kam.

KAM *[exasperated]*: Goddam, Wing, Li-Tai's not the only woman in the world! You'd think she was Kwan Yin on earth! There's lots more where she comes from. She's common as opihi!

WING *[spins around with fists clenched]*: Shut your mouth or I'll kill you!

KAM [*holding his arms up to protect himself*]: Hold it, boy! I'm only trying to help. I was the one who introduced you to her! [*guiltily*] That's why I feel responsible. That's why when the fellas talk, I'm the one who defends you.

WING [*annoyed*]: Why should you defend me?

KAM: They say things about you and her.

WING: What do I care what those bastards say?

KAM: They say, "Like father, like son."

WING [*with angry suspicion*]: How do they know Lau's my father? I never told anyone. [*grabbing him angrily by the collar*] Except you.

KAM [*uneasily*]: Maybe she told them!

WING [*threatening*]: You're lying!

KAM [*a matter-of-fact confession*]: Anyhow they were bound to find out, even if I didn't tell. [*struggling free*] Since you came along, she's stopped seeing anybody else. [*pauses*] They say you cursed her.

WING [*confused*]: What the hell are you talking about?

KAM: Li-Tai is fading. She's an opium eater. You haven't been over there, have you? [*no reply*] She's consumed. She's wasted to nothing. The same way your father did. They say you caused it, to avenge him. I told them they were crazy: Fook's the one who's no good. He's the haoles' bootlicker. He's turned her into a ghost.

[FOOK MING *enters, crossing to* WING.]

FOOK: You fellas did decent work. I'm gonna let you off early this afternoon to make up for last night.

BOTH MEN [*mechanically*]: Thank you. [*Both men turn to go.*]

FOOK: Oh, Wing. [WING *remains*] I been watching you. You're strong worker. In fact, one of the best cutters Kahuku's ever had. I like the way you go about your business. No funny stuff. Not like the others. I have to ride whip on 'em to keep 'em awake. You don't give me problems. You're solid, steady. No tricks. The big boss likes you. I like you too. [*studying* WING] I want you to be my back-up boy. You get a raise from three to four dollars a month. You keep the men in line, you see to it the harvest is in on time. Can you handle it?

WING [*with mechanical politeness*]: Yes sir.

FOOK: Good. I think I can trust you. [*confidentially*] Let me warn you. Once you leave China, it's every Chinaman for himself. The minute you turn your back, there's always someone in the shadow, waiting to stick a knife in you. I would be careful of my friends if I were you. That Kam is a troublemaker. Friendship runs thin with him. Take it from me, the only real thing here…[*drops a silver dollar at* WING'*s foot*]…is this. [*Fade out.*]

SCENE 9

[*Nighttime. The song of a cicada fills the silence.* LI-TAI *is lying on the bed in an opium stupor. There is a loud knocking on the door. It is* WING *returning after an absence.* LI-TAI *appears oblivious to the noise, but the banging continues.*]

LI-TAI [*shouting*]: Go away! Go away! [*The door opens.* WING *stands in the doorway staring, shocked at the spectacle of* LI-TAI *in her degenerated, euphoric state. She does not appear aware of his presence.*]

WING: Li-Tai! [*She recognizes his voice but doesn't stir.*]

WING: It's me, Wing. [*approaching tentatively*] I hear you're sick.

LI-TAI [*to herself*]: Three months.

WING [*confessing*]: I tried to put you out of my mind.

LI-TAI: Who are you?

WING [*bewildered at her unkempt state*]: What's happened to you? Why are you doing this?

LI-TAI: What are you doing here?

WING [*with resolve*]: I want to know something. [*demanding*] I need to know. [*She absently picks up the pipe.*]

WING: You knew he was my father.

LI-TAI [*distractedly*]: What are you talking about?

WING [*impatient*]: Quit pretending. Lau Hing Kuo. I told you he was my father! [*seizes the pipe violently*]

LI-TAI [*grabbing for the pipe*]: Give me that! [*He jerks it away from her.*]

LI-TAI: Damn you, give it to me!

WING [*accusatory*]: You were my father's lover, weren't you?

LI-TAI [*evasively*]: I had many lovers!

WING [*resentfully*]: Then he never meant anything to you, did he? You used him. [*hurt*] The same way you used me. [*rage mounting*] You knew he was my father, but you didn't care. I told you who my father was and yet you made love to me. How could you? What kind of a woman are you?

LI-TAI [*coldly*]: You're not man enough to know.

WING: You bitch! [*slaps her on the cheek and then is stunned by his own violence*] I—I never hit a woman before!

LI-TAI [*evenly*]: Lau Hing never hit me.

WING [*jealously*]: How else was my father better than me?

LI-TAI [*acidly*]: He knew how to treat a woman.

WING [*grabs the pipe and plays a sadistic keep-away with her*]: How badly do you want this? Enough to inch over here on your belly? Show your true self, Li-Tai! Show me your white belly! Show me how you can crawl. [*sadistically*] CRAWL! I want you to crawl to me! [*tormenting*] Tell me, lizard woman, I want to know! [*with increasing cruelty*] Tell me how he treated you! [*grabbing her by the hair*] Was he better than me, huh?

[*She fights her tears.*]

WING: Or have you already forgotten? [*lets go of her in disgust, snaps the pipe in two*] Here, bitch! [*throws it on the floor*] [*She crawls to the broken pipe.*]

WING: Why don't you kill yourself. Get it over with!

LI-TAI [*demanding*]: No, you kill me! Kill me! That's what you want, isn't it? [*picks up the broken pipe and stares absently at it*] I waited. I left the porch light on. I listened for your footsteps, your knock. I didn't sleep or eat. All I heard was the cicada. And the wind. Then it struck me that all my life I have done nothing but wait for a man. I waited for your father. And I waited for you.

WING [*accusatory*]: You killed him!

LI-TAI [*with a sad laugh*]: He wanted to marry me. [*cynically*] What kind of a future would we have had? A plantation runaway and a pei-pa girl?

WING: He was obsessed with you.

LI-TAI: He was obsessed with escaping.

WING: You were his dream. He betrayed everything for you.

LI-TAI: Go ahead and believe what you want. What does it matter now? [*listening*] Did you know if there was no sound, there would be nothing to measure time? Sometimes everything becomes so still, even the heart stops beating. Your mind just crawls inside itself like a hole.

WING [*bitterly*]: For you he destroyed mother.

LI-TAI: He never loved her.

WING: You're spiteful. Hateful.

LI-TAI: I thought you were different. But you're not. If I'm spiteful and hateful, it's because you men made me this way. Lau was kind. I thought you were too. But you're cruel. Lau understood me, because he was different too. He had mixed blood. It runs in you too. They called him Heungsan Jai, "Sandalwood Boy," from Sandalwood Mountains. [*pauses*] I knew you were your father's son before you even told me. His face was etched on yours. You came in from his shadow.

WING: My father would have gone back, if it wasn't for you.

LI-TAI [*sadly*]: You hate me, don't you? Don't you think I've suffered? How can you be so righteous? So sure of me. It wasn't because of me. It was your family. Lau swore he'd never go back. They treated him like dirt!

WING: Stop lying!

LI-TAI: Your grandfather brought a Hawaiian mistress back with him to China and she died shortly after giving birth to your father. When your grandfather died, the property was divided, and your father was cheated out of his share of land. Because he was a half-breed. Lau's marriage was arranged by a relative he barely knew. He never loved your mother. Lau loved me!

WING [*yelling*]: Shut up!

LI-TAI: Look at yourself in the mirror, "Sandalwood Boy"! Find what's missing!

WING [*snatches the broken pipe and violently hurls the pieces against the wall*]: SHUT UP! SHUT UP! [*jealously*] He still haunts you.

LI-TAI: He's dead.

WING: Tell me one thing. I've got to know. Do you love me, Li-Tai? Or is it my father you love?

LI-TAI: When you didn't come, I wanted to die. Is that love?

WING: Answer me!

LI-TAI: I love you.

WING: When I came here, I wanted to kill you. I wanted to hurt you. Then I took one look at you and I knew I couldn't pretend. I can't hate you, Li-Tai. [*pauses*] Give this up!

LI-TAI: I can't.

WING: Give up Fook Ming!

LI-TAI [*with a bitter laugh*]: Fook Ming is impotent. I give him the illusion of virility. For that he pays me.

WING [*indicating her state*]: This is how he pays you!

LI-TAI: It's my choice.

WING: Leave him.

LI-TAI: Don't be foolish.

WING: I'll leave Kahuku and take you with me. We'll go to Honolulu.

LI-TAI: Look at me! I'm not a young woman.

WING: You're scared. Everyone on this plantation is scared!

LI-TAI: Yes I am. I look in the mirror, but the lines and shadows don't go away. I think I'm looking at a stranger, then I realize the stranger is me. The young woman I thought I was is gone. Just a memory.

WING [*fervently*]: If we can't change our past lives, then let us, at least, have our future! [*pauses*] Remember what I said about fate bringing us together? I believe it now more than ever.

LI-TAI [*trembling*]: No.

WING: There's nothing to be afraid of. Trust me.

LI-TAI: It's too late.

WING: Don't you want to be happy?

LI-TAI: Happy? I thought only babies and idiots were happy!

WING: I'm good with my hands. I have skills. I can find a job in Honolulu. Back home, I carved the temple statues. I made Kwan Yin so beautiful, she brought tears to the villagers' eyes. My Kwan Kung was so fierce he frightened away temple thieves. If I can't do wood carving I can always farm. I heard about some rice farmers who are doing real well in marshland near Waikiki. And some taro planters in a valley called Manoa too. [*bitterly*] I can do more than cut cane!

LI-TAI [*worried*]: What about Fook Ming?

WING: He won't be able to find us. We'll change our names and our family histories. We'll start all over.

LI-TAI [*thoughtfully*]: I like that. I like the idea of starting over.

WING: I'll build you a house with twenty rooms and a courtyard with fruit trees and night-blooming jasmine. We'll plant seeds wherever we go and I'll carve the eight immortals over our front door so fate will smile upon us.

LI-TAI [*wistful*]: You dream!

WING: I'll come for you on the ninth day of the ninth moon. [*Lights fade on couple and light comes up on* LAU *with his bundle at his feet.*]

LAU: Everything can be understood in a moment, even if nothing is seen. [*holds up the red robe*] This robe belongs to someone on this side. I will take it to her. [*fondles the garment as if it were alive and makes the sleeves dance sensuously before his eyes*] Every night her empty robe dances in the wind and her sleeves get tangled in the boughs. The moon has just come to light her small house. [*he listens*] Listen to the wind. It's the only voice among the leaves. See how quiet the air has become! Darkness awaits her. [*he turns towards cabin*]

[*Fade out.*]

SCENE 10

[Three weeks later in the heavy rain of the afternoon. Distant thunder. LI-TAI is packing. There is a knock on the door.]

LI-TAI *[with nervous anticipation and indecision about what to do with the suitcase]*: Wing?

[The knocking continues. She quickly hides the suitcase under the bed, then opens the door. She is surprised to see a rain-soaked KAM.]

LI-TAI: What are you doing here?

KAM *[awkwardly]*: May I come in, Li-Tai?

LI-TAI: I thought I told you never to come back.

KAM *[with urgency]*: It's important Li-Tai. It concerns you and Wing Chun.

LI-TAI *[suspiciously]*: Come in.

[KAM enters.]

KAM *[brushing wet hair from his forehead]*: Something has been bothering me. *[pauses]* I know the last time we left on bad terms. I have no hard feelings. I hope you don't either. *[groping]* After all, we're all Chinese, aren't we? We all came here for the same reason—why shouldn't we all get along and help each other?

LI-TAI: Get to the point, Kam.

KAM *[nervously]*: Do you have some water?

LI-TAI *[pours him a glass]*: Sit down.

KAM *[gulping gratefully]*: Thank you. *[sits]* I want to apologize.

LI-TAI *[skeptical]*: That's decent of you.

KAM: For those things I said to you. I've come to talk about you and Wing.

LI-TAI *[icily]*: What concern is that of yours?

KAM: I only want to help, Li-Tai. *[rubbing his knees]* You don't know how hard it is for a man. Thousands of miles from home. Nothing to look at but field after rotten field of cane and empty sky. *[painfully]* You're a beautiful woman. Men fall in love with you. *[pauses]* It's no wonder Wing follows his father's footsteps…

LI-TAI *[upset]*: I won't listen to this.

KAM: First Lau Hing, now Wing. Who next, Li-Tai?

LI-TAI: Get out!

KAM: Do you know that Wing is Lau Hing's son?

LI-TAI *[shaken]*: Is this what you've come to tell me?

KAM: You must stop seeing Wing.

LI-TAI: You can't stop me!

KAM *[scrutinizing her]*: It doesn't make a difference to you then? Why did you do it?

LI-TAI *[angrily]*: You were the one who sent him here! Have you forgotten?

KAM *[defensively]*: Do you think I'd be so vile as to do something like that if I'd known? I sent him as a gesture. A kind of peace offering. I know I'm pretty low-down, but I'm not the devil. I don't play with the gods' rules, no more than I can change what's happened. *[pauses]* It's not for me to judge. That is up to heaven. *[pauses]* But think of what you're doing. Think! Wing wants to make good. Not like his father. In ten years he had gone from top cutter at Kahuku to a skeleton. *[pauses]* They blamed you for his suicide, Li-Tai.

[Light on LAU HING standing in the plantation.]

LI-TAI *[bitterly]*: Of course. If a man is weak, it's the fault of the woman. Do you think I have the power to change men's lives? Am I the one who profits from the cane? Am I the one who put you here? Why don't you blame yourself? I'll tell you why. Because you're all scared! *[pauses]* At least Lau Hing had the guts to escape. *[painfully]* He deserted and came to me. He wanted me to run away with him. I refused. I was scared. Not him. He was ready to give up everything for his freedom. But I couldn't. *[ashamed]* I was a coward. What kind of a life would we have? Taking in laundry, shoveling horse dung, scrubbing white folks' dirt? I told him I wanted more than he could give. I told him I didn't want to see him anymore. *[pauses]* He stared at me as if I was mad. Then he left. I didn't see him again. *[pauses]* Then one day I was walking by the water ditch. I heard a moan. When I got close, I saw Lau Hing lying there on the ground…

[A spot on LAU twisting the puppet's limbs as if trying to tear them apart. Then he drops the puppet in a fit of despair and gives a wrenching, soundless cry of pain.]

LI-TAI *[distraught]*: He was rolling in mud, kicking his feet up in the air and drooling like a baby. It was revolting! I turned and ran. I ran all the way home without stopping. I still can see him, lying there, vivid as ever. He disappeared soon after. They said he'd drowned himself. His body was never found.

[Fade on LAU staring absently at the inert puppet.]

KAM *[sadly]*: One cannot trifle with the world. Lau failed his family. He failed you.

LI-TAI *[solemnly]*: No. That's a lie. Lau didn't fail me. *[pauses]* I was the one who failed him. I promised to go with him, but in the end I didn't have the courage.

KAM: You were right not to go with him. What a fool!

LI-TAI: Even though I loved him, even though I wanted to, I couldn't face what was on the other side.

KAM: You've survived. That's enough.

LI-TAI: No, it isn't enough.

KAM: For godsakes, if I can stumble through the day half-awake, I'm ahead! The moment I'm awake, I'm pulled by the smell of cane and the lash of the whip. What choice do I have? I cut that cane and I don't ask questions. I get my four dollars and I spend it. That's life.

LI-TAI: No. Life is going after what you want, no matter what. *[pauses]* I was only six when my mother died. They led me to a small fire. I had to jump over for purification. But I was terrified. I screamed hysterically. I can still see their angry faces. *[pauses]* That day Lau insisted I run away with him to the mainland, I became terrified. The idea of freedom was as frightening as death.

KAM: The problem with you, Li-Tai, is you think too much. You should have been born a man.

LI-TAI: Men want to believe there's a difference between the way men and women think when there isn't.

KAM [*admonishing*]: For a girl, to be without talent is itself a virtue.

LI-TAI [*curtly*]: Virtue without talent is worthless. One may as well be an insect.

KAM [*amused*]: I admire a headstrong woman. [*swallowing*] You've been through a lot. You don't need no more troubles. Neither do I. In nine months my contract will be up. Then I'll be a free man. [*building up courage*] I'm not a rich man. I'm not a young man, but I can take care of you. I can satisfy you…[*puts a nervous hand on her leg; she pulls away*] You won't even let me touch you! Do I repulse you? [*cruelly*] I bet you open up for the young ones…like Wing!

LI-TAI [*pulling away*]: Get out!

KAM [*guiltily*]: I'm sorry. I didn't mean it.

LI-TAI [*contemptuously*]: You're wasting my time. Get out.

KAM [*rising*]: I can give you a decent life. I can take you away from this. [*angrily*] What can that kid give you, huh? A grave in Kahuku? Is that what you want? Don't be stupid. You're no rosebud. Look at yourself.

[*LAU enters carrying the cricket cage in one hand and the red robe folded over his arm. He watches LI-TAI from across the room.*]

KAM: You're a stubborn woman, Li-Tai. [*pauses*] Good afternoon. [*bows stiffly*] Thanks for the water. This rain never lets up, does it? [*wipes his sweaty palms on his pants, then exits*]

[*LI-TAI crosses to the bed and pulls a suitcase out from underneath. LAU crosses with the bundle and folded kimono on top. She looks up, startled, at LAU.*]

LI-TAI: Lau Hing! Why are you here?

LAU: I've left Kahuku.

LI-TAI: You deserted.

LAU: You're coming with me, Li-Tai.

LI-TAI: I'm not going with you, Lau.

LAU: You promised.

LI-TAI: I've changed my mind.

LAU: Why?

LI-TAI: I'm a woman, Lau. There's nothing out there but desolation.

LAU: This life is good enough for you?

LI-TAI: What can you give me?

LAU [*presenting her with the bundle*]: My soul.

LI-TAI [*terrified*]: No!

LAU: You must return my bones. These bones are weary. They have waited so long for the earth. I have carried them all these years. An empty grave awaits me across the ocean. I cannot rest until these bones return to China. I must journey home. Come with me, Li-Tai. It is time. I have come to free you. I was a prisoner of Kahuku, just as you are. Now together we can walk through water and fire. [*extends his arms*] Come!

LI-TAI: I can't go with you Lau. [*with resolve*] I'm going with Wing!

LAU: Wing is my flesh. [*whispering*] He was sent here. You are the only one who can help him. Don't be afraid, Li-Tai! Trust me. Trust yourself. [*approaches her*] Remember the little girl? Go back to her. She needs you. Can't you hear her calling? You must save her. Jump! The flames won't hurt you. From water to fire. Jump! Over ocean into air. Reach! Into your heart. Into the heart of heaven. Redemption lies there. Li-Tai, come!

[*LAU hands her the bundle, which she accepts. He then removes the red robe on top and holds it up for her to wear. She crosses to him in trancelike submission. He helps her slowly and ceremoniously into the open fire robe. Fade out.*]

SCENE 11

[*Outside LI-TAI's cabin. Dusk. WING approaches with a hastily wrapped bundle thrown over his shoulder. He is suddenly cut off by FOOK MING, approaching from the opposite direction.*]

FOOK [*suspiciously*]: You going someplace?

WING: I'm going to see Li-Tai.

FOOK: What are you doing with that goddam bundle? [*no reply*] Are you planning on going somewhere, Wing?

WING: Fook Ming, I don't want any trouble.

FOOK: Don't tell me you're running away? You've only been here a year!

WING: I can't finish my contract.

FOOK: Why, that's too bad. You have only four years to go. You owe Kahuku thirteen hundred dollars for passage, room, and board.

WING: I will pay it back.

FOOK: You will pay it back. Right here on Kahuku! [*anger increasing*] Why did you stop here? [*yells*] Answer me, you sonuvabitch!

WING: I'm taking Li-Tai with me.

FOOK: Over my dead body. [*seething*] You think you can come here, still wet behind the ears and scheme for my woman behind my back?

WING: She doesn't love you.

FOOK [*exploding*]: Li-Tai is mine! I own her. Every hair on her body, every inch of her flesh and bones is paid for in gold.

WING: You don't own her soul.

FOOK [*laughing uproariously*]: So you, Wing Chun, have come to claim her soul, huh? What a hero. Too stupid to know you should never meddle with another man's property. It's a shame you have to learn the hard way. Because now, Wing boy…[*pulls out a knife*]…I will have to kill you!

[*They struggle with the knife. FOOK is about to stab WING, when KAM SU suddenly appears and grabs FOOK from behind. The knife falls to the ground, WING seizes it.*]

FOOK [*desperately*]: Don't do it, Wing. Don't kill me! Please! You won't get away with it. You'll hang!

[*Just as WING is about to plunge the knife into FOOK, WING comes to his senses and drops the knife on the ground. KAM suddenly retrieves the knife and plunges it into FOOK's belly.*]

FOOK *stares at him for one moment before he crumples and falls dead.]*

KAM *[staring at the lifeless body]*: That's for every man who's died on Kahuku. For every goddam wasted life! *[to a shocked* WING*]* I know where you're going! You're making a mistake.

WING: I got nothing against you. Leave me alone.

KAM *[angrily]*: She was mine until you came along! She was mine!!

WING *[steadily]*: I don't want to fight you, Kam.

KAM *[with an ironical laugh]*: When my contract was up, I was going back to China. I was going to take her with me.

WING: She doesn't love you, Kam.

KAM: She would have come, if you hadn't spoiled everything! *[with growing desperation]* I know Li-Tai. She would have come with me. I know she would have!

WING *[trying to reason]*: You could come with us.

KAM *[deeply offended]*: I ought to kill you!

WING: You got one murder on your hands, Kam. You want another? Is it worth it?

KAM *[laughing bitterly]*: I'm a free man today. Do you know what that means? That means I can walk off this plantation and never look back. That means I can change my name and become a new man. Who knows? I might even get rich! *[reaches inside his pocket]* I got nothing holding me back! *[hysterically, he pulls out a fistful of coins, which spills onto the ground]* You see this money? I got more! I been saving for this day, kid! Look at me, look at me! Do I look like a Gold Mountain Boy? Do I look prosperous to you? *[pauses]* Or do I look like some dried-up sinner? *[throws the money on the ground as if it was dirt]* Take it! Take it! Take this dirty money! Take it!

WING: I can't take your money, Kam.

KAM *[commanding]*: Give it to her!

WING: She doesn't want it, either!

KAM *[suspiciously]*: You're speaking for her now, huh? *[a surly nod]* So that's the way it is. I might have known. *[confessing frankly]* I wanted to kill you and her. That's why I came. To put a stop to everything. But when I saw Fook, everything came to a head.

I had to put a stop to everything. I had to. *[sincerely]* You understand? It had to be done. *[*WING *nods]* I don't want to know where you're going or what you're going to do. *[*KAM *turns to leave]*

WING: Where you going?

KAM *[stops to think]*: Honolulu. I like the sound of that name. Hono-lu-lu. Sounds like a woman's name. Maybe I can start a gambling house there. *[grins]* Who knows?

WING *[shaking his head]*: I don't understand you, Kam.

KAM *[with an ironic laugh]*: I don't understand myself! *[an afterthought]* Oh, a word of advice. Watch out for the haoles if you go to Honolulu. They are a two-faced, cunning lot. I heard tell about a fella who bought a plot of land for a taro patch from some haoles. As it turned out, they didn't even own the land. It was owned by the Church. But by the time he found out, he had already planted and seeded the whole damn plot! So watch out. They'll crucify you.

WING: I will. *[They bow farewell to each other.* KAM *runs off. Fade out.]*

SCENE 12

*[*LI-TAI*'s Cabin. Night. Cicadas.* LI-TAI *is dying. She is lying in bed in the red robe and* LAU*'s bundle is at her feet.]*

WING *[rushing over to her in alarm, taking her hands]*: Li-Tai! Li-Tai!

LI-TAI *[very weakly]*: Wing, I'm sorry. I can't go with you. There's little time.

WING *[determinedly]*: I won't leave without you!

LI-TAI: You must. Or everything will have been a loss. I have a message for you. *[points to the bundle at her feet]* You must take this to Kwantung and bury it. They are the bones of your father. He gave them to me for safe burial. Lau died before he could fulfill his duty as a husband and father. Now you must complete his task. Now you are the keeper of his bones. Return home with them. Your father has waited a long time. *[squeezes his hand]* So have I. *[pauses]* Go home, Wing. Go home before it's too late.

WING *[desperately]*: Don't leave me, Li-Tai, don't leave me!

LI-TAI: You were right from the first. We are old souls, you and I. Our destinies were locked. But now you have a chance to be free. Don't wander as your father and I did. Return these bones where they belong. They are part of you, Wing. Part of me. Home. I am ready to go home. Now. Home…

[She loses consciousness. Her fingers fall limp from his hands and she dies. WING *struggles against breaking down. Calmly, he places one final kiss on her lips and covers her slowly with the blanket. He turns his attention then to the bundle, lifts it ceremoniously with the growing revelation of its intrinsic meaning. He carries the bundle in his arms, as if it was alive, outside. He stares sadly into the horizon. We hear the mournful melody of* KAM*'s voice from afar:]*

> Hawaii, Hawaii
> so far, far from home,
> Hawaii, Hawaii
> My bones ache and my heart breaks,
> thinking about the one I left behind.
> Hawaii, Hawaii
> so far, far from home,
> Hawaii, Hawaii
> Don't let me die of misery.
> Don't bury me under the cane fields
> of Hawaii, Hawaii…

[Fade out.]

END OF PLAY

Life Theme 6:

Values

Life Theme 6: Values

What if your most powerful beliefs about what is true are the exact opposite of those with whom you must co-exist? Or even yourself?

It is a peculiar sensation, this double-consciousness, this sense of always looking at one's self through the eyes of others. . . . One feels this twoness—an American, a Negro; two Souls, two thoughts, two unreconciled strivings; two warring ideals in one dark body, whose dogged strength alone keeps it from being torn asunder.

The Souls of Black Folk, W. E. B. DuBois

Featured plays:

He And She
  by Rachel Crothers
The Piano Lession
  by August Wilson

Many of the central conflicts of life, both personal and social, are formed out of a conflict of values. What should we do when our core beliefs are at odds with the rules of society? How can a family be reconciled when their individual senses of truth clash? In the two plays that follow, the struggle to define and defend deeply held values forms the crux of conflict. In *He and She*, an American classic by Rachel Crothers, the values explored are as contemporary as today's headlines though the play is nearly 100 years old. Can a woman be a successful professional and a mother at the same time? Can a man stand behind his wife and enjoy her success without losing his sense of self?

In *The Piano Lesson* by August Wilson a brother and sister fight for possession of the family's piano. Although the piano is carved with the history of the family through slavery times, the brother Boy Willy wants to sell it and buy farm land. The sister Berniece wants to keep the piano as a family heirloom but refuses to touch it or to learn from its story. Both brother and sister are struggling to define the values that will guide them through life: do we focus on the future and build new worlds our ancestors never dreamed of or do we value the past and refuse to look past the present moment? Or does a third path exist?

He and She

Year: 1911
Genre: Realistic prose drama
Structure: Well made three acts
Setting: A middle class home in New York

Context:

Written in the decade preceding the First World War, *He and She* takes the form of a debate over women's rights while telling an emotionally rich story about a family in crisis. During the first two decades of the twentieth century, American women were actively seeking social and political equality. The struggle, however, began with the formation of the American Constitution and was in fact a continuation of women's rights projects from England and Europe. A brief history of the women's movement can help us place the Herford family in context.

One of the first legal decisions concerning the status of women in American society was formulated by colonial authorities in 1769. At that time, the American colonies based their laws on English common law which was summarized in the Blackstone Commentaries as:

> "By marriage, the husband and wife are one person in the law. The very being and existence of the woman is suspended during the marriage, or at least is incorporated into that of her husband under whose wing and protection she performs everything."

In 1777, one year after ratification of the Declaration of Independence and during the first year of the American Revolutionary War, all states in the union (the former colonies) passed laws specifically denying women the right to vote. Not until 62 years later in 1839 did Mississippi become the first state to allow women to own property, but a married woman still needed permission from her husband to do so.

The struggle for women's rights continued in a growing number of arenas. First and foremost was probably the suffrage movement as women actively sought the right to vote. In 1866, the 14th Amendment to the U. S. Constitution granted the vote to former slaves but denied the right to all women by using all male references in the amendment. American women had to wait until 1920, ten years after *He and She* was written, to win the right to vote.

In addition to the right to vote, women were fighting for control over their lives and their bodies. In 1910, few women had access to education, viable professions or financial independence. Their homes, their bodies, and their children were the property of their husbands. An unmarried woman, unless she was very lucky and very rich, had little or no legal status. Birth control was illegal and in fact, until 1918, doctors were barred by law from giving any information about birth control even if the woman's life was in danger from too many pregnancies occurring too close together.

In addition to women's minimal value by law, their social value was imprisoned in archaic patriarchal values. One example of this is the "rule of thumb." Widely held to be an appropriate social value, the rule of thumb stemmed again from English common law that held that a man could only beat his wife with a stick no thicker than his thumb. Although American law never explicitly granted a husband the right to beat his wife and children, a woman's peculiar legal status as an appendage to her husband made such disciplinary measures necessary to protect the reputation and property of the husband. Even today, if a woman is beaten by a man with whom she is having a sexual relationship, the event is called a "domestic dispute" rather than assault and battery.

As we read the story of an extremely liberal-minded family in 1910, we may want to remember that the value of women in today's society is still under review. Not until 1984 did Mississippi ratify the 19th Amendment allowing women the right to vote. Sexual harassment in the work place, the so-called "glass ceiling" restricting women from advancement in their careers, unequal pay and benefits, and personal control over their own bodies are issues which continue to challenge social and political values in this country. In the year 2000, the U. S. Supreme Court reversed sections of the Violence Against Women Act (enacted in 1994) which allowed victims of rape, domestic violence, etc. to sue their attackers in federal court.

Today, we still struggle with conflicting values in sexual politics. Globally, millions of women are still denied the most basic rights. Violence, poverty, illiteracy, and invisibility afflict many women around the world. As a culture, as a species, our values and beliefs are constantly being challenged by forces of change, but despite several thousand years of debate gender values continue to be a flashpoint of conflict in the modern world.

The play *He and She* is perhaps the perfect example of the clash of gender values in contemporary American society. Avoiding the extremes that cry out for immediate, emergency intervention, this family is loving, well-educated, and professional. They treat each other with dignity and respect. Yet they are unable to arrive at a fair and intelligent solution to the clash of gender values that wage war within couples, within families, and within the hearts of women and men of conscience.

The Playwright:

Rachel Crothers lived a remarkable life. She was born in Bloomington, Illinois in 1878 where she completed her studies at the Illinois State Normal School (now Illinois State University) at the age of 14. She then studied theatre arts in Boston and New York, did some acting and writing for the theatre, and in 1906 by age 28 had her first full length play produced on Broadway and it became the hit of the season. For the next 30 years, Crothers maintained the remarkable average of one Broadway show per year, most of them critical and popular successes. She also cast, produced and directed all of these shows. Like *He and She*, her plays were about modern life, modern family, and the modern woman. Sometimes serious, sometimes comic, her work and career are a chronicle of American life in the first 3 decades of the 20th century. She died in 1958.

The Piano Lesson

> *Year: 1990*
> *Genre: Realism*
> *Structure: Well-made*
> *Setting: Pittsburgh in the 1930's*

Context:

Set in a Pittsburgh slum community known as the Hill District, *The Piano Lesson* is one in a series of plays by August Wilson, arguably American theatre's greatest working playwright. He is nearing completion of a massive project, writing one play for each decade of the twentieth century from an African American perspective. Not written in chronological order, each play in the "decology" traces one aspect of the long road from slavery to the end of the twentieth century. Two contextual worlds are surveyed in this particular play, both worlds co-existing during the Great Depression of the 1930's: sharecropping in the Deep South and wage poverty in the urban North. Boy Willy lives in Mississippi where he supports himself through the southern system of subsistence farming known as share-cropping. His sister Berniece and her uncle and daughter live and work in the northern industrial city of Pittsburgh, Pennsylvania.

Following the Civil War and Reconstruction (approx. 1860-1880), land owners in the southern states needed an economically viable way to replace the free (slave) labor that had made them wealthy. One answer was the system of share-cropping, in which former slaves and then their descendants were made economically dependent on the land owners. The family usually lived on the land or in small poor communities near the plantation site. They might receive seed, tools, and farm animals from the land owner given in the form of a loan. After working the land, the share-cropper received a portion of the harvest, usually just enough to sustain life for one more year. Frequently, the only source of supplies in the neighborhood was a store also owned and operated by the land owner. As the family ran charge accounts during the year for necessary supplies, the bill at the store often equaled or exceeded the value of the crop portion received. At the end of the year, after harvest time, the accounting took place and the family might well have found that they owed more than they had earned. They were allowed to start again in the spring with borrowed seed and supplies, but also with the company store debt growing with each passing season. In this way, generations of African American farm families became economically enslaved to the land owner through on-going debt. Legally unable to leave the debt behind (laws being especially rigorous when applied to a black family), the family slipped into a form of virtual slavery, unable to leave the land, unable to buy the land, and unable to pay off the accumulating debt.

By the 1930s, when the Great Depression was at its height, farmers throughout the country were particularly hard hit. If you've ever seen the film or read the book *The Grapes of Wrath*, you know about the fate of many share-cropping families both black and white. Land owners and corporations began evicting share-cropping families in some parts of the country in order to mechanize former family farms into the great agricultural corporations we know today. Others simply cut back on the share of the harvest allotted to the families and increased their debt load at the company store, forcing the families deeper and deeper into economic deprivation and dependence.

Boy Willy arrives in Pittsburgh with a load of watermelons grown on his share-cropping farm in Mississippi. He has enough surplus this year to sell part of his crop, but he is still working land owned by the same family that owned his ancestors as slaves. Since before the Civil War, Boy Willy's family has labored for the Sutter family and now, in 1937, he finally has a chance to buy the land he's been working. He needs more cash, however, and his one avenue to that money is the family's cherished piano. Coming north to claim and sell the piano, he is confronted by the realities of the industrial north.

Pittsburgh, like many northern cities following the Civil War, became a magnet for newly freed slaves seeking greater freedom in the northern states. One of the great steel centers of the industrial north, Pittsburgh promised new economic and social opportunities as factories sought new, cheap sources of labor during a time of rapid growth and expansion. Sadly, those promises were kept only irregularly. Any industry experiences periods of "boom and bust." The Great Depression was a massive bust. As industry faltered and many factories went bankrupt, unemployment rates rose. Perhaps not surprisingly, those first laid off were almost always workers of color.

In the play, Berniece is the housekeeper for a white family, her uncle Doaker works for the railroad, and her boyfriend Avery has an excellent job as an elevator operator (he even gets a turkey at Christmas, as he brags to Boy Willy). The fact that every adult has a job is a remarkable testimony to the family's work ethic and perseverance. The fact that they are all low paying, service jobs points to the lack of economic advancement available to them.

Aside from the economic promises broken, the northern states were also notoriously unwelcoming to the migration of former slaves from the south. Although many northerners were faithful opponents of slavery, it did not necessarily follow that they believed in equality for all. Racism was as pervasive in the north as in the south. African Americans (or "colored folk" as they were called then) were forced into ghettos segregated from white neighborhoods. High paying jobs and management positions went to white applicants. Interest charges on loans were automatically higher for a black family than a white. School districts in black neighborhoods were under-funded and attendance enforcement was lax. Intensely humiliating "courtesy" was required, particularly from black men, which included not looking white people in the eye, bowing to or saluting white persons on the street, and passively accepting wage cuts, unscrupulous business practices, and lack of access to the judicial system. Berniece and her family debate the relative advantages of the north and the south amongst themselves, but the fact is that life was still extremely difficult for African Americans during the Depression whether they were farmers in the south or migrants to the industrial north. In *The Piano Lesson*, August Wilson invites us into one family's struggle to move forward with dignity and independence as they define the values that have sustained them.

The Playwright:

August Wilson was born in 1945 in the Hill District of Pittsburgh, PA, the son of a white father and black mother. His father abandoned the family when Wilson was very young and his mother worked long hours to support them. Wilson left high school at the age of 15 and educated himself in the public library. After a brief stint in the military, he returned to Pittsburgh determined to become a poet. His career as a playwright has been shaped by his association with Lloyd Richards, an internationally respected director and the head of the Yale Drama School when Wilson submitted his play *Ma Rainey's Black Bottom.* Six months after *Ma Rainey's* debut performance at Yale, it moved to Broadway and the rest is history. The winner of many prestigious awards, including two Pulitzer Prizes, Wilson has followed *Ma Rainey* with *Fences, Joe Turner's Come and Gone, The Piano Lesson, Two Trains Running,* and many more Broadway productions.

He and She

by Rachel Crothers

Characters

Tom Herford: a sculptor
Ann Herford: his wife
Daisy Herford: his sister
Millicent: his daughter
Dr. Remington: his father-in-law
Keith McKenzie: his assistant
Ruth Creel: his wife's friend
Ellen: a maid

Setting

1910. New York

ACT 1

The Herford Studio. The room is in the basement of a large old-fashioned house in lower New York—and shows that it has been made over and adapted to the needs of a sculptor. At right center back are double doors opening into the workroom. At right of these doors is a recess showing it has been cut in. The ceiling of the half of the room which is towards the audience is much higher than the other part—showing that the room which is on the floor above has been used to give height to this part of the studio.

The break made in the ceiling is supported by an interesting old carved column—very evidently brought from Italy—and in the overhanging part of the wall is set a very beautiful old Italian frieze in bas relief—a few faded colors showing. At lower left is a large studio window.

At lower right side a single door leading into hall. At upper left corner, a cupboard is built in, in harmony with the construction of the room, and showing, when opened, drawers and compartments for holding sculptors' tools, etc.

Before the window, at right center, is a scaffold built to hold a section of a frieze. At its base is a revolving table, holding modeling clay, tools, etc. In front of the scaffold is a short pair of steps. At center, is a long table holding rolls of sketches, a desk set—a book or two, pencils, compasses, several pieces of modeling. There are a number of chairs about and a piece of rich brocade in vivid coloring thrown over the back of one.

The room is simple, dignified, beautiful, full of taste and strength. Soft afternoon sunshine streams in from the wide window.

KEITH MCKENZIE *and* **TOM HERFORD** *are lifting one section of a bas relief frieze about 3 by 5-and placing in on the scaffolding.* **MCKENZIE** *is about 35, tall, good-looking, in a pleasing, common place way; also wearing a sculptor's working clothes but of a practical and not artistic sort.* **TOM HERFORD** *is 40, a fine specimen of the vigorous American-artist type. Virile, fresh, alive and generous in nature and viewpoint. He wears the stamp of confidence and success.*

TOM: *[as they lift the frieze]* Come on! There she is! Put her over—no, this way, about half a foot. That's right. There! Let's have a look. *[*TOM *goes down to hanging switch and turns on the light. As he does so, he says—]* Wait! *[The lights are turned up. Turning to* KEITH.*]* What do you think?

KEITH: It's a great thing, Governor! Going to be a walk-away for you. You'll win it as sure as guns. I know it. I bet you land the $100,000.00 as sure as you're standing there, Governor.

TOM: Oh, I don't know. The biggest fellows in the country are going in for this competition.

KEITH: Well—you're one of the biggest. I think you're the biggest—and you've turned out the best thing you've ever done in your life. *[Going to stand above table.]*

TOM: That's damned nice of you, McKenzie. It does look pretty good out here. Doesn't it?

[He goes up on the steps-to touch the frieze.]

KEITH: *[after a pause.]* Governor.

TOM: *[working at his frieze]* Um?

KEITH I want to ask you something. Not from curiosity but because—I'd like to know for my own sake. You needn't answer, of course—if you don't want to.

TOM: Go on. Fire away.

KEITH: Have you ever been sorry that Mrs. Herford is a sculptor—instead of just your wife?

TOM: Not for a minute.

KEITH: I've been thinking a lot about it all lately.

TOM: About you and Ruth, you mean?

KEITH: Yes. She'll marry me in the fall if I let her keep on working.

TOM: And?

KEITH: Well—I—Hang it all! I don't want her to. I can take care of her now. At first it was different—when I was grubbing along—but since I've been with you, you've put me on my feet. I'll never be great—I know that all right—but I can take care of her.

TOM: *[working at frieze]* But she wants to keep on, doesn't she?

KEITH: Yes, but—

TOM: Good Heavens, boy—you're not bitten with that bug, I hope. "I want my girl by my own fireside to live for me alone."

KEITH: Oh—

TOM: Why Ruth Creel's a howling success—the way she's climbed up in that magazine—why in the name of Christopher, do you want her to stop?

KEITH: *[at right end of table, figuring mechanically on some papers on table]* How can she keep on at that and keep house, too?

TOM: Well, they do, you know—somehow.

KEITH: Oh, Mrs. Herford's different. She's working right here with you—and her time is her own. But Ruth's tied down to office hours and it's slavery—that's what it is.

TOM: She doesn't think so. Does she?

KEITH: I want a home. I want children.

TOM: Of course. But that doesn't mean she'll have to give up her profession forever.

KEITH: Oh, I'm strong for women doing anything they want to do—in general—but when it's the girl you love and want to marry, it's different.

TOM: It ought not to be.

KEITH: When you come down to brass tacks—

ANN: *[coming quickly in from the workroom, and stopping as she sees the frieze]* Oh, Tom!

*[*ANN HERFORD *is 38. Intensely feminine and a strong, vibrating personality which radiates warmth and vitality. She wears a long linen working smock a soft rich red in color. Her sleeves are rolled up and her general appearance shows that she is at work and has stopped only to look at* TOM'*s frieze.]*

KEITH: Looks great out here—doesn't it, Mrs. Herford?

ANN: Um.

KEITH: Aren't you—more sure now than ever it will win?

ANN: Um—*[Starting to speak and checking herself]*

TOM: What?

ANN: Nothing. Your horses are marvelous, Tom. I wish we could see it all together—now. Don't you? The rest of the twenty sections—so we could see how much we—how much we—feel the running.

TOM: Don't you feel it in this piece?

ANN: Of course.

KEITH: I do—tremendously. I think it's wonderful. *[He goes into the workroom.]*

TOM: Ann—what were you going to say a minute ago about the frieze?

ANN: Ah—I don't know.

TOM: Don't hedge. Several times lately you've started to say something and haven't got it out. What is it? Any suggestions?

ANN: How do you feel about it yourself, boy? Are you satisfied?

TOM: Does that mean you aren't?

ANN: I asked you.

TOM: Well—It's the best that's in me. Why? What's the matter? You don't like it after all.

ANN: Like it? It's a strong—noble—beautiful thing.

TOM: But—

ANN: Dearest—is it—just exactly what your first conception of it was? Has it turned out just as you first felt it?

TOM: Why yes—not absolutely in detail, of course. It's improved a lot, I think—in the working—but in the main, yes—it's just the same. Why do you say that?

ANN: You know, of course, but—

TOM: Say it—Say it. What have you got in your mind?

ANN: I don't know that I can—but in the beginning it had a feeling of swiftness, of rushing, swirling—as if your soul were let loose in it, Tom—too big, too free to be held in and combined. But, somehow, now that it's finished—

TOM: Go on.

ANN: That wild thing has gone out of it. It's crystalized into something magnificent but a little conventional.

TOM: Good Heavens, Ann, you can't call that conventional?

ANN: Well—orthodox, then. It's noble—but that inexplainable thing which made it great—is gone—for me. Perhaps it's just me—my imagination—because I care so much.

TOM: It is imagination. It's much stronger than when I began.

ANN: Is it?

TOM: Of course. You're trying to put something fantastic into it which never was there at all. That's not me. What I've done I've got through a certain strong, solid boldness. That's why I think this stands a good chance. It's the very best thing I've ever done, Ann, by all—

KEITH: [opening the workroom door] Governor—will you show Guido and me about something, please—Just a minute?

[There is a slight pause. TOM looks at the frieze.]

TOM: I don't see what you mean at all, dear girl. Thanks a lot—but I think you're wrong this time.

[He goes into workroom. ANN looks again at the frieze as RUTH CREEL comes in from hall.]

ANN: [going quickly to RUTH] Oh, Ruth—bless you!

[She kisses her warmly.]

RUTH: I came straight from the office and I'm dirty as a pig. *[ANN points to TOM's frieze.]* Is that it? *[ANN nods.]* Well?

ANN: Oh, Ruth—I'm sick in the bottom of my soul. I hope—I hope—I'm wrong. I must be wrong. Tom knows better than I do; but—I can't help it. I tell myself I'm a fool—and the more I try to persuade myself the more it comes back. Ruth, it isn't the same. It isn't. What ever it was that lifted it above good work and made it a thing of inspiration—is gone. It's gone—gone.

RUTH: Have you—told Tom how you feel?

ANN: Just this minute. He says I'm wrong absolutely—that it's the best thing he's ever done.

RUTH: I hope to God you are wrong—but I bet you're not. You know. Did you—have you told him the other thing?

ANN: Not yet. But I've finished it.

RUTH: Absolutely?

ANN: I worked down here last night till three o'clock this morning.

RUTH: Well—how is it?

ANN: Oh, I don't dare think. It can't be as good as it seems to me.

RUTH: Of course it can. Why shouldn't it be? Aren't you going to offer it to him right away—before it's too late?

ANN: How can I? It frightens me to pieces to even think of it—but, oh,—my dear, my dear,—it's alive and fresh and new. It is. It is. If he only would take it—my idea—and put his wonderful work—his wonderful execution into it.

RUTH: Perhaps he'll be fired with it—jump at it.

ANN: I'm afraid, he won't—and I'm afraid of this for him. It would nearly kill him to lose. He's counting on winning. Keith and everybody are so dead sure of him.

RUTH: Show him yours for goodness—

ANN: Be careful. He'll be back in a minute.

RUTH: I'll skip upstairs and make myself presentable.

ANN: Go in my room, dear.

[RUTH goes out through hall. TOM and KEITH come back from workroom. ANN goes to TOM—they stand a moment—looking at the frieze. ANN slaps TOM on the back, without speaking, and goes on into workroom.]

KEITH: [after a pause] I agree with you in general, Governor. But when it comes down to the girl you love and want to marry, it's different.

TOM: Why is it?

KEITH: The world has got to have homes to live in and who's going to make 'em if the women don't do it?

TOM: [smiling at KEITH tolerantly] Oh, come—come.

KEITH: Do you mean to say you wouldn't rather your sister Daisy was married and keeping her own house instead of working here as your secretary?

TOM: But she isn't married—and she won't live with Ann and me unless it's a business proposition. I respect her tremendously for it—tremendously.

KEITH: Well, Daisy's a big, plucky, independent thing, anyway—but Ruth's a little, delicate, fragile—

TOM: With a mind bigger than most of the men you know.

KEITH: Oh, mind be damned. I want a wife.

DAISY: [coming in from the hall] Oh—Tom—it's out here. How corking!

[DAISY HERFORD is 28—strong, wholesome, handsome, with the charm of health and freshness. She wears a severe serge gown and carries a pencil and stenographer's pad.]

TOM: Well—Sis, how do you like it?

DAISY: I adore it. I hope you haven't any doubts now about winning.

TOM: I've plenty of 'em—but somehow today it looks as if it stood a pretty good chance.

DAISY: Chance! I never was so sure of anything in my life!

KEITH: Daisy—maybe you know just what ought to be where with this stuff.

DAISY: I've been itching to get at it. Let's put all the tools on that side.

KEITH: I have started.

DAISY: And throw the trash in here.

[Pushing the box with her foot.]

KEITH: Can you help me now?

DAISY: Yes. Tom, you want me to write to the Ward people about that marble again?

TOM: Yes, I do. Shake them up. Tell 'em if it isn't here by the first of the month, I won't take it.

DAISY: [making a note in her note-book] Um—um.

[MILLICENT HERFORD *rushes in from hall at left.* MILLICENT *is 16—pretty—eager—full of vitality and will—half child, half woman. She is charmingly dressed in an afternoon frock and picture hat and is at the moment happy and exhilarated.*]

MILLICENT: Father, where's Mother?

TOM: In the workroom. But you can't go in.

[*As* MILLICENT *starts to workroom.*]

MILLICENT: Why not?

TOM: She's finishing something and said not to let any one stop her.

MILLICENT: Oh dear! I think I might. It's awfully important. Couldn't I just poke my head in the door a moment?

TOM: Not for a second.

MILLICENT: Sakes, I wish Mother wouldn't work in my Christmas vacation. It's an awful bore. Don't you think she might stop the little while I'm at home, Aunt Daisy?

DAISY: None of my business. Don't ask me.

KEITH: If you ask me—yes, I think she might.

TOM: That's nonsense. Your mother's doing about everything that can be done to make your vacation a success, isn't she?

MILLICENT: Yes, of course.

TOM: Then, I don't see that there's any reason why she shouldn't be allowed a little time for herself.

MILLICENT: But I want her now. Aren't my new pumps stemmy, Aunt Daisy?

DAISY: Aren't they what?

MILLICENT: Stemmy! Wake up, Aunt Daisy. Oh, the luncheon was gorgeous! All the girls were there and the matinee was heavenly.

KEITH: What play?

MILLICENT: *"The Flame of Love."* You needn't laugh, Father. It's the best play in town. The leading man is a peach. Honestly, he's the best looking thing I ever saw in my life. We were all crazy about him. Belle Stevens took off her violets and threw them right at him! She makes me tired, though. I don't think seventeen is so terribly much older than sixteen, do you, Aunt Daisy?

DAISY: [*still at the cupboard*] It depends on whether you're sixteen or seventeen—how much older it is.

MILLICENT: I don't care—I wouldn't want a ring as big as hers if I had one. Oh, Aunt Daisy, may I borrow your earrings? [*Going to* DAISY.]

DAISY: Help yourself.

MILLICENT: Thanks, you're a duck. I could combostulate you for that. How much longer do you think Mother will be, Daddie?

TOM: Couldn't say.

MILLICENT: Well, tell her I have to see her the minute she comes out. Don't forget.

[*She hurries off through hall.*]

TOM: She's grown up over night, somehow. I can't get used to it.

KEITH: And she went away to school a few months ago just a girl. Amazing, isn't it?

DAISY: Not a bit. What do you expect? She's free now—cut loose. Boarding school does that pretty quickly.

TOM: I suppose so—and I suppose it's good for her.

[*Looking at the frieze, he goes into workroom.*]

KEITH: The governor's darned cheerful about the frieze to-day.

DAISY: I should think he would be. It's great!

[KEITH *and* DAISY *go on clearing out cupboard.*]

KEITH: I'd give a good deal to know what Mrs. Herford actually thinks of it.

DAISY: Why, she loves it!

KEITH: She looks at it with such a sort of a—I don't know. I can't help wondering if she is so dead certain of it as the rest of us are.

DAISY: I hope she doesn't discourage Tom. After all, he likes it, and he knows more about it than anybody else. Ann's criticism is wonderful, of course, but still Tom is the artist.

KEITH: You're just as jealous for your brother as you can be, aren't you, Daisy? All right for the missus to be clever, but you want Tom to be supreme in everything, don't you?

DAISY: He is. [*Leaning over the box.*]

KEITH: You're a brick. Daisy, have you ever been in love in your life?

DAISY: What do you mean?

[*Lifting her head—startled and embarrassed.*]

KEITH: I've been thinking an awful lot lately about this business of married women working. What do you think of it—now honestly?

DAISY: What difference does it make—what I think?

KEITH: Of course, there's no reason on earth why you shouldn't be in it. You don't care a hang for men—and—

DAISY: You mean men don't care a hang for me.

KEITH: No, I don't. I don't mean that at all. But you're so independent, men are sort of afraid of you.

DAISY: Oh, don't apologize. You mean I'm a plain, practical girl, meant to take care of myself.

KEITH: Well—that's what you want to be, isn't it?

DAISY: Never mind about me. Let's change the subject.

KEITH: You needn't be so touchy. I talk awfully frankly about my affairs and you never say a word about yourself.

DAISY: Why should I? I'm not interesting, and you're not interested.

KEITH: I am, too. You're the best pal a fellow ever had. I don't know any other girl I could have worked with all this time—day in and day out—and not either been dead sick of or sort of—you know, sweet on, in a way.

DAISY: You needn't rub it in.

KEITH: Why, Daisy, old girl, what is the matter? What in the dickens are you so huffy about?

DAISY: Just let me and my idiosyncrasies alone, please.

KEITH: Heavens! Can't I say what I think?

DAISY: No, you can't. I don't want to hear it. I know just what I seem like to other people—so there's no use explaining me to myself.

KEITH: All I meant was if you were in love would you give up your job and—

DAISY: But I'm not in love, so stop thinking about it.

KEITH: Gosh! I thought you had common sense, but you're just as queer as the rest of them. What I want to know is—

if a girl loves a man well enough to marry him, why in hell she can't stay at home and—

DAISY: What's the matter.

[*As* KEITH *cuts his finger on the tool he is holding.*]

Did you cut your finger?

KEITH: Not much.

DAISY: [*with a sudden tenderness*] Let me see.

KEITH: It's nothing.

DAISY: It is, too. Hold still. I'll tie it up for you.

[*She ties his finger with her own handkerchief.*]

Anything the—hold still! Anything the matter with one of your fingers would put you out of commission.

KEITH: Might be a good idea. I don't think Ruth believes in me much. Doesn't think I'll get much farther.

DAISY: [*warmly*] I don't know why. I think you've got plenty for her to believe in. Well—speaking of angels. How are you, Ruth? [*As* RUTH *comes in from the hall.*]

KEITH: Oh—hello, dear.

RUTH: Hello. What's the matter?

KEITH: Nothing.

DAISY: Keith was waxing emphatic about you and overemphasized a finger. [*She turns back to cupboard.*]

RUTH: I'm sorry.

[*Touching* KEITH'*s hand as he comes down to her.*]

KEITH: How are you?

RUTH: Dead. This day's been twenty-four hours long.

[*Sitting at left end of table.*]

KEITH: [*coming down to* RUTH] Has anything gone wrong?

RUTH: No—but a young author from the eloquent West has been fighting me since nine o'clock this morning.

KEITH: What about?

RUTH: He's got a perfectly magnificent story—or idea for one, rather—but it's so crudely written that it's impossible to publish it.

DAISY: I suppose you can re-write it for him.

RUTH: No, he won't let me. Wants to do it all himself. Oh, he's so stubborn and so funny and so splendid. So outlandishly conceited and so adorably boyish, I wanted to slap him one minute and kiss him the next.

KEITH: Why didn't you do both and you'd have got what you wanted.

RUTH: I was afraid to risk it.

KEITH: [*nodding towards* TOM'*s frieze*] Doesn't that hit you in the eye?

RUTH: Awfully like Tom, isn't it? Strong and splendid.

KEITH: What are you thinking—

RUTH: Oh, nothing—only I wish Ann had—I wish Ann had gone in for this competition, too.

KEITH: What?

DAISY: Why on earth should she?

RUTH: Why shouldn't she?

DAISY: Ruth, you're daffy about Ann. Always have been.

KEITH: She does beautiful work for a woman—but ye gods—she's not in this class.

RUTH: And she never will be if she's held back and told she's limited. I think she has genius and the sooner she makes a bold dash and tries for something big, the better!

DAISY: Nonsense! Tom's pushed her and believed in her always. You can't say he's held her back.

RUTH: [*to* KEITH] I've heard you say she has genius—lots of times.

KEITH: So she has—in a way. She has more imagination than the Governor, but great Peter!—when it comes to execution and the real thing, she isn't in it with him. How could she be? She's a woman.

RUTH: Don't be any more anti-deluvian or prehistoric than you can help, Keith. Don't you think Ann's more original and really inately gifted than Tom is, Daisy?

DAISY: I do not. She's terribly good. Of course—no doubt about that—but, good Lord, Tom's great—a really great artist. [DAISY *starts to hall door.*]

RUTH: Why do you go, Daisy?

DAISY: Must. I have bushels of letters to get off.

RUTH: You look as fresh and rosy as if you were just beginning the day. How do you do it?

DAISY: Oh, I'm not expressing my soul in my job—merely earning my bread and butter. I suppose that's why I look so husky at twilight. [DAISY *goes out through hall.*]

RUTH: [*looking after* DAISY] Do you know—I don't believe Daisy likes me any more.

KEITH: [*sitting on left end of table near* RUTH] Kiss me. [RUTH *leans her head towards* KEITH. *He kisses her cheek.*]

RUTH: She's so marvelously good-natured—queer she's getting snappy at me lately.

KEITH: I'm awfully glad you came.

RUTH: Does it hurt? [*Touching his finger.*]

KEITH: Not much.

RUTH: I wonder why she doesn't like me.

KEITH: What are you talking about? I'm asked to stay to dinner, too.

RUTH: That's nice.

KEITH: I can't bear to see you so tired, dear.

RUTH: I'll be all right when I have some tea.

KEITH: This time next year you could be in your own home—away from those damnable office hours and the drudgery—if you only would. If you only would.

RUTH: It never seems to occur to you that I might be a little less tired but bored to death without my job.

KEITH: If you really cared for me the way you used to—you wouldn't be bored.

RUTH: Oh, let's not begin that.

KEITH: But do you love me, dear? Do you?

RUTH: I've been telling you so for a pretty long time, haven't I?

KEITH: Are you tired of it?

RUTH: There isn't any reason on earth why you should think I am.

KEITH: Well, I do think it. I worry about it all the time. I know you're brilliant and successful—but you—after all you say you love me—and I don't see—

[*He stops with a sigh.*]

You're awful pretty today. Your face is like a flower.

RUTH: Oh—

KEITH: Yes, it is. I love you so.

RUTH: Dear old boy! I love you.

KEITH: Do you, Ruth? Do you?

RUTH: I've never loved anyone else. You've filled all that side of my life and you've made it beautiful. We must hang together, dear—

[Putting both her hands over one of his.]

And understand and give things up for each other. But it must be fifty-fifty, dearest. I can make you happy, Keith—oh, I can. And I'll be so happy and contented with you if you'll only—[KEITH turns away impatiently.]

I've never had a home for a minute—in my whole life—nor a relative since I was three—of any sort or description—not a soul who belonged to me but you.

KEITH: I want you to have the sweetest little home in the world.

RUTH: Think of having our own little dinners and all the nice people we know at our table—ours.

KEITH: Yes—but—how can you do it if you're away all day?

RUTH: Oh, Keith, dear boy, you—the whole trouble is you think housekeeping is making a home—and the two things aren't the same at all—at all, at all.

KEITH: Well, they can't be separated.

RUTH: Oh, yes, they can. Love—love makes a home—not tables and chairs. We can afford more if I work, too. We can pay some one to do the stuff you think I ought to do. And you'll go on climbing up in your work, and I'll go on in mine, and we'll both grow to something and be somebody and have something to give each other. It will be fair—we'll be pulling together—pals and lovers, like Tom and Ann. That's why they're so ideally happy.

KEITH: Yes, but we're different. We couldn't—

RUTH: You're not fair, Keith.

KEITH: Great guns, Ruth—neither are you!

RUTH: I am! I am perfectly. [Their voices rise together.]

TOM: [coming back from the workroom] What's the row? Hello, Ruthie Creel.

RUTH: [giving her hand to TOM] Hello, you nice Tommie Herford. I always lose my heart to you in your working clothes.

TOM: You have my heart in any kind of clothes.

RUTH: Keith's cross with me, Tom. You're much nicer to me than he is.

KEITH: You never spring any of your revolutionary speeches on Herford. You save all your really soothing remarks for him.

RUTH: Tom, am I revolutionary? Aren't I just a little cooing dove?

TOM: Absolutely.

DAISY: [coming to from hall] Dr. Remington's here. Millicent's bringing him down. But he says he wants to sit upstairs on the parlor sofa, not down in the cellar. Tom, will you sign these letters now?

[DAISY puts the letters on the table—TOM goes towards the table as MILLICENT comes in from the hall, bringing DR. REMINGTON by the hand. DR. REMINGTON is 65. He is inclined to portliness and his keen humor and kindliness are combined with an understanding and wisdom which make him a very strong and very lovable man. His manner and speech are a little deliberate. He has a twinkling readiness to tease, but the weight and dignity of a successful and important position.]

TOM: Hello—hello—hello.

REMINGTON: How are you?

KEITH: [taking DR. REMINGTON's coat] How are you, Dr. Remington?

[RUTH comes to the doctor to take his hat and stick.]

REMINGTON: Hello, McKenzie. And here's that pretty little Ruth thing—knowing so much it makes my head ache.

RUTH: So long as it's your head and not mine, I don't mind.

MILLICENT: Oh, thank you for the chocolates, Grandfather! They're just the kind I adore. I could absolutely combostulate you!— [Giving him a violent hug.] Five pounds, Daddie!

TOM: You're a fine doctor!

REMINGTON: Chocolate's about the best medicine I know of if you want a girl to love you. Where's your mother?

MILLICENT: In the cave. [Pointing to workroom.]

REMINGTON: Can't she be excavated? Go and dig her out.

MILLICENT: They won't let me. You do it.

REMINGTON: Hasn't anybody got the courage to do it?

[KEITH starts towards the door with box.]

DAISY: Not me.

REMINGTON: Well, McKenzie, go and tell her to let the work go to thunder and come and see her dad.

[KEITH goes into workroom.]

Is that the thing that's going to get the hundred thousand for you?

TOM: If—yes.

REMINGTON: Well, go to it—boy. I hope you hit it.

[Sitting in the large chair at left.]

TOM: Thanks. I'm doing my durndest. Daisy, you've got some of these dimensions wrong. Keith will have to give them to you again.

DAISY: Oh, I'm sorry.

REMINGTON: It's a good thing you're working for your own brother, Daisy—nobody else would have you.

DAISY: You're the only person in the whole world who isn't impressed with my business ability.

REMINGTON: Stuff! I wager you say in your prayers every night—Oh, Lord, deliver me from this job and get me a good husband.

DAISY: [laughing with the others and going to REMINGTON] That's a very stemmy tie you're wearing. Do you get me?

REMINGTON: Not exactly. All I know is I'd rather be stemmy than seedy.

KEITH: [opening the workroom door] Don't you want me to carry that in for you, Mrs. Herford?

ANN: [from within] No, no—I'd rather do it myself.

KEITH: It's too heavy for you.

ANN: No, it isn't.

[ANN comes in carrying the figure of a woman in the nude—about a foot high. The figure is in wet clay and stands on a modeling board.]

TOM: Steady there! Steady! Let me take it.

ANN: Don't touch it!

REMINGTON: Hello, there!

ANN: Hello, Daddy! I couldn't come out until I finished my lady. Isn't she nice? She's ready to be cast now. Come and look at her, Tom. She isn't so bad?

TOM: She looks pretty good to me.

REMINGTON: She looks a little chilly to me. Why don't you put a full suit of clothes on one of 'em-just for a change, Ann?

ANN: You nice, horrid, sweet, adorable, cross old thing! Why didn't you come yesterday? I don't see why I love you so when you never do anything I want you to.

REMINGTON: If I did, I wouldn't be half as irresistible. Aren't you going to stop for the day now and pay a little attention to me?

ANN: I am.

MILLICENT: Mother, when can I see you? Alone, I mean.

ANN: After a while. Have you had a nice day, dear?

MILLICENT: Gorgeous! But I have to see you about something.

ANN: You do? *[Holding* MILLICENT.*]* Look at her—Dad. Hasn't she grown?

MILLICENT: Mother, may I stay home from school one more day?

ANN: Gracious! Is that what you want to see me about?

MILLICENT: That's just one thing. Can't I, Mother? All the girls are staying over. Mayn't I? Please—please!

ANN: I have to think a little. Let's wait and talk it over. Daisy, aren't we going to have some tea?

DAISY: It will be ready in a minute.

REMINGTON: Thank God! Then we'll go upstairs.

ANN: No, down here—it's much nicer. You'll have to get used to it, Dad.

MILLICENT: Well—you be thinking—but you be thinking—Yes!—for I've just got to stay over. I've just got to. It would be perfectly ridiculous if I didn't.

[She goes out through hall.]

REMINGTON: *[nodding after* MILLICENT*]* Getting more like you every day, Ann.

ANN: She's your grandchild, you know.

REMINGTON: I like 'em that way. I'd rather she was stubborn as a mule than have a wabbly spine.

ANN: *[taking off her smock]* But a little wabbling once in a while is rather a pleasant thing to live with. For instance, it would make me very happy indeed if you wabbled enough to admit that this is a beautiful studio and that having it in the house where we live is the most sensible thing in the world.

REMINGTON: It would be all right if you'd stay upstairs and mind your own business. Tom, if you don't look out, you'll be so mixed up you'll be upstairs keeping house and Ann will be downstairs keeping shop.

TOM: I don't know how I'd keep house—but Ann could keep shop all right.

REMINGTON: Is that the way you feel about it, McKenzie? When you're married, are you going to stay at home and polish up while Ruth goes on running the magazine?

KEITH: It looks as if that's about the way it'll have to be.

RUTH: *[bringing the cake down to table]* That's a splendid suggestion, Dr. Remington. Keith thinks somebody's got to do it for a successful marriage—and I won't-so why not you, dear? *[Pointing at* KEITH.*]*

*[*KEITH *looks at* RUTH *and turns away in hopeless disgust.]*

REMINGTON: *[winking at* RUTH *and lowering his face to her]* Keep at it. He'll come to it.

*[*ANN *laughs as she cuts the cake.]*

KEITH: I don't see that it's so funny.

REMINGTON: *[going to table to get a piece of cake]* You bet it's not funny. Daisy would you like your husband to wash the dishes if you happened to be too much occupied to do it yourself?

DAISY: I'd kill him if he did.

[Bringing the cream and sugar to large table.]

REMINGTON: Oh—well—with one perfectly normal woman in the room, I'm much more comfortable.

[He settles himself elaborately in his chair at left.]

KEITH: I'm serious. I'd like to know if there's anything queer or preposterous in a fellow wanting a girl to give up hard, slavish work and let him take care of her when she marries him.

RUTH: When she wants to do the work. Don't leave that out!

TOM: I don't see that you, Keith, or any other fellow, has got any kick coming, so long as the girl makes you harpy.

KEITH: I'd like to hear your angle on it, if you don't mind, Doctor.

RUTH: Yes. Keith loves to hear his mid-Victorian ideas well supported.

REMINGTON: Oh, I'm not so moth-eaten as I may look. In fact, I'm a damned sight more advanced than you women are. You're still yelling about your right to do anything on land or sea you want to do. We gave you that long ago.

ANN: So nice of you!

RUTH: *[sitting below the table at right]* Why talk about it all, then? What is there to it?

REMINGTON: Put this in your pipe. The more women make good—the more they come into the vital machinery of running the world, the more they complicate their own lives, and the more tragedies they lay up for themselves.

RUTH: The more they escape—you mean.

ANN: *[as she pours the tea]* There isn't a single hard thing that can happen to a woman that isn't made easier by being able to make her own living. And you know it.

REMINGTON: Oh. It's a hopeless subject for conversation. What everybody says is true. There's the rub.

DAISY: Two?

REMINGTON: Three.

*[*KEITH *gives a cup of tea to* REMINGTON.*]*

TOM: Go on. What were you going to say?

ANN: Yes, go on, Dad.

REMINGTON: *[to* ANN*]* You hang on to yourself, then, till I get through. The development of women hasn't changed the laws of creation.

ANN: Oh, yes it has. *[*REMINGTON *looks at her.]* Sorry. Go on.

REMINGTON: Sex is still the strongest force in the world.

[He looks at ANN *again.]*

ANN: *[smiling]* Go on.

REMINGTON: And no matter how far she goes, she doesn't change the fundamental laws of her own—

TOM: Individuality?

RUTH: Type?

DAISY: Character?

KEITH: Ego.

RUTH: Psychology.

ANN: Species.

TOM: Breed.

DAISY: Spots.

REMINGTON: No!—Mechanism—mechanism! And when the sensitive—involved—complex elements of a woman's nature become entangled in the responsibility of a man's work—and the two things fight for first place in her—she's got a hell of a mess on her hands.

ANN: But her psychological mechanism has changed.

REMINGTON: No.

ANN: Yes.

TOM: Yes, I think it has.

KEITH: It couldn't.

RUTH: But it has! Women who are really doing things nowadays are an absolutely different breed from the one-sided domestic animals they used to be.

ANN: But men don't realize how deeply and fiercely creative women love their work.

REMINGTON: That's just it!—Just what I'm getting at. A woman of genius puts in her work the same fierce love she puts into her child or her man. That's where her fight is—for one or the other of 'em has got to be the stronger in her. It isn't a question of her right to do things—nor her ability—God knows—plenty of 'em are beating men at their own jobs now. Why, I sometimes think she'll go so far that the great battle of the future will be between the sexes for supremacy. But I tell you —she has tragedies ahead of her—the tragedy of choice between the two sides of her own nature.

RUTH: Well, thank you—I'll take any and all of the hard things that go with my job—but none of the ones that come from being a dub and giving it up.

REMINGTON: How about you, Daisy? Could any man on earth make you stop typewriting and live for him alone?

DAISY: Oh, I'm not in this class. Ann and Ruth both have men to depend on if they want them. I'm taking care of myself because I've got to—and I must say this soul tragedy of choice stuff makes me a little tired.
[She starts toward hall.]

REMINGTON: *[stopping* DAISY *by taking her hand]* If I were twenty or thirty years younger, I'd go in for you strong.

DAISY: Yes, I know—I'm just the kind that older men appreciate very deeply. *[She goes out.]*

REMINGTON: Poor Daisy.

ANN: Poor Daisy! She's the happiest, most independent thing in the world. *[Straightening the things on the table,* KEITH *having taken the tea tray away.]*

RUTH: Much to be envied. No strings to her independence.

KEITH: And so cocky and spunky—nobody can even ask her if she's ever been in love.

REMINGTON: Sure sign she has been, then.

TOM: But she never has.

REMINGTON: How do you know?

TOM: I've been pretty close to her all my life. No blighted bud about Daisy.

REMINGTON: She's putting up a darned good bluff, I must say.

RUTH: Bluff? What do you mean?

ANN: Father thinks there isn't a girl alive who wouldn't rather have a beau than a job.

REMINGTON: I do. And Daisy looks so self-reliant she *has* to be cocky to keep up appearances. Under her skin, she's not half the man that little lady-like looking thing Ruth is.

RUTH: Now, Dr. Remington, you may go upstairs.

REMINGTON: I haven't time now. I've wasted it all down here.

RUTH: Oh, come and look at the living room just a minute. It's too beautiful!

REMINGTON: Has it got a carpet on it yet?

ANN: Yes, absolutely finished.

REMINGTON: Because I don't mind saying my feet are like ice from this confounded brick floor.

RUTH: Oh, the beautiful tiles!

REMINGTON: I'll take a little less Italian beauty and a little more American comfort in mine.
*[*RUTH, REMINGTON, *and* KEITH *go out through hall.]*

TOM: *[stopping* ANN *as she starts with the others]* Ann—about this thing. Why in the name of Heaven didn't you say you were disappointed in it long ago?

ANN: I kept hoping each day I was mistaken; that what I missed would come back. But when I saw it out here—I'm afraid of it, Tom.

TOM: Afraid of what? That I'll fail? Lose it?
*[*ANN *nods.]*
Nonsense! You're tired of it. There can't be such a change in it as all that. The idea's absolutely the same, and I've worked as I never—

ANN: I know. I know! And oh, the beauty—the beauty of the work! That's the pity.

TOM: Pity?

ANN: I mean somebody without half your skill as an artist may have an idea—an idea that's new.

TOM: Oh bosh! Nothing can be done, anyhow. It's too late. Besides, I don't agree with you. I honestly do not, Ann. I know you're saying this because you're trying to boost me and get the best out of me; but the thing's done, you know. Don't confuse me. I must go on now. What's the use of talking about it? It's too late.

ANN: No, it isn't.

TOM: It is. Of course, it is. You can't expect me to begin all over again and put into it a subtle intangible something I don't even feel. Damn it! It will have to fail then.

ANN: *[taking hold of* TOM *quickly]* It can't. You've got to win, Tom. You've got to. It's the most important thing you've ever done. Think of where it will put you. Think of the money.

TOM: I have thought. I've done the best that's in me, I tell you. It is the best, the very best I've ever—

ANN: But it isn't. It isn't. It isn't as great as your last two things—

TOM: Oh—

ANN: Tom—listen—you don't know how hard it is to say it. I'd rather you won this than anything that could possibly happen. You know that. Don't you?

TOM: Of course. But this isn't getting anywhere. It will have to go in as it stands.

ANN: Wait—I—I've wanted to talk to you about something for a long time—but I wasn't sure—and now I am.

TOM: Well—

MILLICENT: *[coming back through hall]* Thank goodness, Mother. I can't wait any longer.

ANN: *[to MILLICENT]* Oh, just a minute, dear.

TOM: No, that's all right. There's nothing more to be said.

ANN: I appreciate what you mean—yes, I do. But it doesn't get me. And all I can do is to go after it as I see it.

[He goes into workroom. ANN stands looking at the frieze.]

MILLICENT: *[pulling ANN toward table]* Mother—come here. Mother, please. Why—what I wanted to—sit down. *[Putting ANN into a chair above the long table.]* Every one of the girls are staying over tomorrow. It looks as if you were having such a slow time that you didn't have anything to do but go back to school if you don't stay. And I want—Why Fanny's going to have a party tomorrow night—Just a little one, and I want to have eight of them to dinner first.

[Sitting at right end of table.]

ANN: Oh—

MILLICENT: Only eight. You see, Fanny's brother's home, too, and—you see, it's—Everybody has dinners and things, you know, before they go to the dance, you know, and—will you, Mother? Can't I?

ANN: But dearest, you've done so much since you've been home. You can't get back to school too soon. New York is dreadful. It really is! The sensible mothers can't compete with the idiotic ones who let girls do all these silly things.

MILLICENT: Don't be foolish, Mother.

ANN: And school does begin tomorrow. And they expect—

MILLICENT: They don't expect us to be back. All the really smart girls stay over. It's only the deadly slow ones who are there on time. Please, Mother—Please! There'll only be eight of us; and Fanny's done so much for me I think it's as little as I could do to have her brother to dinner. Don't you?

ANN: Is he nice?

MILLICENT: Yes, he is. He's older, you know, and more fun. He got full dress clothes this Christmas—long tails, you know, and he looks perfectly—Mother, you're not listening.

[ANN's eyes have gone back to the frieze again.]

ANN: Yes, I am, dear—Yes, I am. Full dress clothes.

MILLICENT: Well—May I?

ANN: Dearest—I may be frightfully busy tomorrow. I may have to do the most important thing I've ever done in my life, and if I do, it would be awfully hard to have—

MILLICENT: Oh, now, Mother! Fanny's mother's had a party or something for her every single night. She took her to the Plaza to dance after the matinee today, and I've never been to a hotel or any exciting place in my life! You try to keep me so young, Mother, and, Jimmy Cricket, I'm sixteen!

ANN: Positively ancient.

MILLICENT: Well—sixteen's old enough for anything. Will you, Mother—please—please! *[Kissing her mother's throat.]*

ANN: But what would I do if I had to do this other thing?

MILLICENT: What other thing? Can't it wait?

ANN: No, it can't. That's just it. Your father may—I may be working with him all day tomorrow.

MILLICENT: You needn't have such a terribly elaborate dinner, you know, but I'm crazy to do it. In fact, I just have to. I've already asked most of them, and they're dying to come.

ANN: You didn't, Kitten—how could you?

MILLICENT: But, Mother, it's so important—and I don't see how I can get out of it now. You wouldn't want me to be compromised or anything, would you?

ANN: *[laughing and kissing MILLICENT]* You blessed baby—you ought to be spanked.

MILLICENT: You're an angel, Mummie. You will—won't you? *[Putting her cheek against ANN's.]*

ANN: What have you got in your ears?

MILLICENT: Earrings, of course.

ANN: Heavens! Take them off.

MILLICENT: Oh, Mother! All the girls wear them.

ANN: Take them off!

MILLICENT: But they have so much style.

ANN: Style, your granny! Take them off or I'll bite 'em off. *[MILLICENT squirms and giggles as ANN bites her ears.]*

MILLICENT: Wait—wait! I will. I think you're mean to make me. You have such terribly strict ideas.

ANN: Your ears are much prettier than those things. Can't you understand that nothing is so attractive as just being natural? Why cover up with stuff like that?

MILLICENT: You are funny! You'll stay at home and meet everybody tomorrow night, won't you? I want them to see you. You are sweet, Mummie.

ANN: Do you love me a lot?

MILLICENT: Of course. *[Kissing ANN.]*

ANN: *[rising suddenly and going to look at the frieze]* Oh, I'm so unhappy.

MILLICENT: Why? What's the matter? I should think you'd be tickled to death if Father's going to get all that money.

TOM: *[coming to from the workroom quickly]* You say—*[He stops, seeing MILLICENT.]*

MILLICENT: Aren't you coming up, now, to plan it all?

ANN: In a few—

TOM: Go on, Millicent. *[MILLICENT skips out.]* Why didn't you speak the minute you saw it go wrong—thought you did?

ANN: I was never sure, until today, dear.

TOM: I don't agree with you at all, but still, it isn't exactly inspiring—knowing you think I'm going to fail.

ANN: Tom—I'm sorry

TOM: It's all right—but you know I care more what you think than anybody in the world, and—I—it's sort of a knock-out.

ANN: I had to tell you the truth—when I was sure. I had to. Tom—listen—since you've been working at this, an idea has come to me. At first I thought the idea was too big for me—that I never could carry it out—and then I said I won't let myself be afraid—and it's grown and grown night and day. Last night I finished it—down here—

TOM: The—

ANN: The drawings—I want you to look at them—and if—if you like it—if you think the idea is better than yours, I want you to take it—use it, instead of yours.

TOM: Why, Ann, you're not serious. *[She nods.]* Good Heavens, child, you know—you know how tremendous this thing is as well as I do.

ANN: Yes, I do! But I tell you, my idea is big. Oh, I knew you'd look like that when I told you. You can't believe it, of course, but Tom—it's there—something vital and alive—with a strong charm in it. And I offer it to you, dear—if you want it.

TOM: *[taking her in his arms strongly and kissing her passionately]* You generous darling! It's like you to do this. You dear—I love you for it.

ANN: *[responding warmly to his love]* I want you to have it. It's more than I ever dared dream I could do.

TOM: But, darling—you couldn't possibly do anything for a scheme as big as this.

ANN: Why do you take that for granted? Why do you say that—before you've even seen my sketches?

TOM: *[after a pause]* Well—where are they?

ANN: *[taking a key out of her pocket]* In the lower drawer in my cupboard.

TOM: *[taking the key]* No, don't come with me.

ANN: But I—

TOM: I don't want you to explain anything: I want it to strike me fresh. But I'm going to hit hard—right from the shoulder. If it's good—all right. If it's bad—all right. And I expect you to take it like a man.

[ANN nods. TOM hurries into work-room as RUTH comes in from hall.]

RUTH: Have you told him?

ANN: Yes—he s gone to look at my sketches now.

RUTH: Ann—I've been thinking. You're a fool to give away your ideas. Make your models and send them in yourself.

ANN: What?

RUTH: Certainly. Why not?

ANN: Oh, Ruth—I couldn't. Some day I will. Some day.

RUTH: Some day! You've got the biggest idea you've ever had. Do it—send it in yourself—on your own feet!

ANN: Tom would think I was out of my—

RUTH: You know it's good—don't you?

ANN: Yes, I do.

RUTH: It belongs to you—and if you don't take care of it and give it its chance, you kill something which is more important than you are. Don't forget that. You're not just the talented woman, you've got downright genius, and you ought to make everything give way to that. Everything! If you don't, you're weak.

ANN: Wait and see what Tom says. He'll know. He's so dead right about my stuff—always.

RUTH: Oh, you lucky people! Pulling together. If Keith only had a little of it towards me. Ann, what shall I do?

ANN: *[with quick sympathy]* What, dear?

RUTH: He's never, never, never going to know what a sacrifice it will be for me to stop just as I'm getting what I've slaved and struggled for all these years. And I can't bear to hurt him.

ANN: Dear old Keith. He just can't see. And he loves you so.

KEITH: *[coming in from hall]* Why did you come back down here?

RUTH: Just to run away from—you. No, I didn't. *[Going to him sweetly.]* You know I didn't.

ANN: *[as DAISY comes in from hall]* Daisy, tell me the minute Tom comes out.

KEITH: *[to RUTH]* I'll be up in a minute. I've got to cover some stuff in there. *[Exit ANN and RUTH.]* You're a wonder, Daisy. You don't mind sitting up late to get your letters off, do you?

DAISY: Oh, no—I'm healthy.

KEITH: You're a peach. I'm sorry I made you huffy. All I meant was that no man would ever think he could ask you to marry him unless he had an awfully big bankroll to offer.

[REMINGTON comes in from hall to get his hat and stick—just in time to hear KEITH's last remark. DAISY rises, consciously. KEITH goes into workroom. REMINGTON goes to end of table.]

DAISY: I suppose that speech sounded rather queer. He was talking about Ruth, of course.

REMINGTON: Don't apologize or you'll make me suspicious.

DAISY: Now—

REMINGTON: It sounded very much as if he were making love to you.

DAISY: Oh—

REMINGTON: I wish to God he would. You'd—be a much better wife for him than the other one.

DAISY: You—

REMINGTON: You know you would. Why don't you go in and get him? Cut the other one out.

DAISY: How dare you say such a thing to me?

REMINGTON: Why shouldn't I say it?

DAISY: Because you have no right to. I haven't the slightest interest in Keith McKenzie—not the slightest.

REMINGTON: No. I can see that.

DAISY: What do you mean?

REMINGTON: *[suddenly understanding]* Why, my dear girl, I didn't mean anything. I'm sorry.

DAISY: I don't know why in the world you said such a thing to me.

REMINGTON: Well—well—forget it.

DAISY: You don't think from anything I've ever done or said—

REMINGTON: I don't think anything—I don't know anything…

DAISY: I don't see why you said it.

ANN: *[coming from hall]* What's the matter?

[As DAISY *breaks away from* REMINGTON, *who is holding her by the wrists.]*

DAISY: Let me go, please. I'm in a hurry.

*[*DAISY *rushes out through hall.]*

ANN: What on earth are you doing to Daisy?

REMINGTON: She's doing things to me.

ANN: What?

REMINGTON: Convincing me of some of my old-fashioned ideas.

*[*TOM *rushes in from the workroom with a large roll of drawings.]*

TOM: Ann—they're wonderful!

ANN: Oh—Tom!

TOM: *[spreading the roll of sketches on the table—*ANN *helping him]* Beautiful! Astoundingly beautiful! Well as I know you, I didn't think you had it in you.

ANN: I can't believe it. Are you going to use it?

TOM: Oh, my dear girl. That's different. Now, don't be hurt. Why, Ann—it isn't possible. You—you're mistaken—way off—don't know what's got into you. This is imaginative and charming and graceful—full of abandon and and fantasy, and even vitality—but ye gods, child, it isn't in this class.

ANN: But you could strengthen it. It will grow. You'll see more in it. Really, you will! Don't make up your mind yet.

REMINGTON: What are you talking about? What has she done?

TOM: Drawings for a frieze—like this. And they're amazing, Doctor. Positively amazing!

REMINGTON: You don't say.

TOM: Wait—let's see what McKenzie says. McKenzie—!

ANN: *[pounding on the workroom door]* Keith—Keith—come here, quickly!

REMINGTON: Looks beautiful to me, daughter. When did you do all this? Do you mean to say you didn't know anything about it, Tom?

TOM: Not a thing. She's been—*[*KEITH *comes in.]* Here, McKenzie! Look at this. Here's a scheme Mrs. Herford's worked out. Begins here—see—see? Get it? What do you think?

KEITH: Mrs. Herford?

TOM: Yes. Do you get it?

KEITH: Of course.

TOM: Well? What do you say?

KEITH: I say its as beautiful as anything I ever saw.

TOM: Great! And what do you think of it for a big place like mine?

KEITH: For that?

TOM: Yes.

KEITH: Oh—I—too fanciful, isn't it? Will the crowd understand it? Needs a big, clear striking thing like that. Don't you think?

TOM: Then, you don't think it's as good as mine for this competition.

KEITH: As yours? Heavens, no!

ANN: *[standing at right—facing the three men]* Then, do you know what I'm going to do?

KEITH AND TOM: What?

ANN: Make my models and send them in myself.

KEITH, TOM, and REMINGTON: What?

ANN: Why not?

REMINGTON: You don't mean it, daughter.

ANN: I do. I mean it with my whole soul.

REMINGTON: Why do you want to do anything so foolish?

ANN: Because I made it. Because it's my work. You all say it's good. Why shouldn't I send it? I don't mind failure. I only want it to stand its little chance with the rest. I love it. It means more to me than I can possibly—Why shouldn't I? I want to.

TOM: Then, do it. Why not? It's your own affair. Go ahead.

[Putting out the hand of a good pal-ship to her.]

ANN: Oh, Tom—thank you. You're splendid!

THE CURTAIN FALLS.

ACT 2

Scene: Four months later—about nine in the evening. The living room in the Herford house. The room is long and wide, dignified and restful in proportions. At center back a large fireplace with a severe mantel in cream marble. A wide window covers the entire left wall, and wide doors at right lead into library. A single door at back, left of fireplace, leads into hall. The walls are hung in a soft, dull silk which throws out the strong, simple lines of the woodwork.

A bright wood fire is burning, and soft lights throw a warm glow over the gray carpet. The furniture is distinguished and artistic but distinctly comfortable, giving the room the air of being much lived in and used. The room is empty a moment. DAISY *is singing in the library at right.* ELLEN, *a maid, middle-aged and kindly, comes from hall carrying a silver coffee service.*

DAISY: *[as she comes in from library]* Here's your coffee, girls. Come in here. Put the flowers over there, Ellen.

*[*ELLEN *moves the vase of flowers and makes room for the coffee service on table right center.* RUTH *comes in from the library with a book.* ELLEN *goes to fire and pokes it, then straightens the writing things on the desk.]*

Ann, here's your coffee.

ANN: *[calling from library]* I don't want any, thank you. What time is it, Daisy?

DAISY: About nine. Why ?

ANN: Oh, the postman. I'm waiting for the last mail.

DAISY: Well, don't. A watched pot, you know.

[*To* RUTH.]

She's watched every mail for a week. I almost think Ann will be more disappointed than Tom himself if he doesn't get the commission.

[*They take their coffee to the fire.*]

RUTH: I hope to goodness he does. Everybody's so dead sure of him.

DAISY: Almost too sure. I'm beginning to be frightened, myself. The time's about up.

ANN: [*hurrying in from the library*] That's the postman—isn't it?

ELLEN: No, ma'am. Beggin' your pardon. It ain't—I'm listenin', too.

ANN: Are you, Ellen? Keep on, and bring it up the minute it comes.

ELLEN: Faith, I will. I've got the habit meself lately of watchin' for the mail.

ANN: Have you?

ELLEN: Every time I hear the whistle, I drop whatever I'm doin' like it was hot—and run.

ANN: Do you?

ELLEN: And just before I open the door, I say—The Holy Saints be praised, I hope it's come this time—whatever it is they're lookin' fer. [*She goes out through the hall.*]

ANN: Oh, dear! It gets worse as the time grows shorter.

DAISY: Ann, working yourself up like this won't make Tom get the commission. Stop thinking about it.

ANN: But I can't, Daisy Dimple. He ought to hear tonight if he's ever going to.

DAISY: Well, I'll be glad when it's all over and we know one way or the other—and can settle down to ordinary life again. It's almost given me nervous indigestion.

ANN: Listen! There's the postman.

RUTH: [*jumping up so that her cup and saucer almost fall*] Oh, Ann, you're getting me so excited, I'll listen for the postman all the rest of my life.

ANN: I know I shall. Oh, Tom must get it. He must. If he does, I'll wire Millicent.

[*Taking up a picture of* MILLICENT *which stands in a frame on the table.*]

I think I'll run up to school Sunday just to give her a good hug. I get so hungry for her!

RUTH: Isn't it splendid the school is so really what it ought to be?

ANN: Yes. So much that's sweet and right that one can't get in New York for a girl.

DAISY: [*sewing on a frock which is nearly finished*] She seems pretty keen about it herself.

ANN: Yes—rather. Easter vacation when I was working day and night to get my models off, she was perfectly contented to stay at school.

RUTH: She's an adorable kiddie, but I don't envy you your job.

ANN: Why?

RUTH: I think being a mother is the most gigantic, difficult, important, and thankless thing in the world.

DAISY: That's the most sensible remark I ever heard you give vent to, Ruth.

ANN: There's something much more glorious in it than being thanked. You will miss the most wonderful thing in the world, Ruth, if you don't have children.

RUTH: I know. I know. But work has taken that all out of me. It does, you know. It would bore me stiff to take care of a baby.

DAISY: That's a pleasant prospect for Keith. Do you expect him to do it?

RUTH: [*making herself comfortable on the couch*] I'm not going to have children.

ANN: [*going to sit at the fire*] That's perfectly fair, if he knows it. No reason why you should if you don't want 'em.

DAISY: Well, I think it's a rotten way to live.

RUTH: Wait till you decide to marry somebody yourself, young lady, and see how you like giving up everything that interests you most.

DAISY: Well, by Jove, if I ever do marry, I'll marry and do all the things that belong to my side of the game. No halfway business for me. You might as well be a man's mistress and be done with it.

RUTH: [*half serious—half joking*] That's the ideal relationship for a man and a woman. Each to keep his independence in absolutely every way—and live together merely because they charm each other. But somehow we don't seem to be able to make it respectable.

DAISY: I suppose that's very clever and modern.

RUTH: Oh, no—it's as old as the everlasting hills. The trouble is children are apt to set in and mess things up. It's hard on them.

DAISY: So far as I can see, most everything that's modern is hard on children.

ANN: [*laughing*] How's the gown getting on, Daisy?

DAISY: Most finished.

RUTH: That's awfully pretty.

ANN: Slip it on so we can see.

DAISY: Oh, I can't.

ANN: [*rising and walking to* DAISY] Yes, you can—over that one—just to give us an idea.

DAISY: I'll look a tub and it really makes me quite respectably straight up and down.

ANN: You're a perfectly scrumptious size and shape. Isn't she, Ruth?

RUTH: Magnificent!

DAISY: Yes, Ruth, skinny women always enthuse over their fat friends.

RUTH: [*rising and goes to* DAISY] Oh, you aren't fat, Daisy. That is, not too fat. How does this go? It's terribly complicated, isn't it?

DAISY: No—perfectly simple. Wait—this goes over here.

ANN: No, it doesn't, does it?

DAISY: Yes, it does. Right there. Don't you see? The style of the whole gown depends on that.

RUTH: You must have it on wrong side before.

DAISY: Nonsense! Can't you see, Ann? It's as simple as can be.

ANN: Yes, I know, dear—but does this go on the shoulder—or down on your hip? *[They all talk at once for a moment on the subject of where the end of the girdle fastens.]* Oh, here! I see, of course! There!

DAISY: Now, does it make me look big?

RUTH: You want to look big, don't you?

DAISY: Well, I want to look life size. Don't you see how much better I am through here than I was last year, Ann? *[Touching her hip.]*

ANN: Much. The female form divine is improving all the time, anyway—gradually getting back to what it was in the beginning.

DAISY: I don't expect to look like you in it, Ruth.

RUTH: Oh, don't you, dear? Then why don't you have it stick out this way as much as possible so everybody will know you mean to look broad? There's everything in that, you know.

DAISY: I think it would be awfully good on you—to fill out what you haven't got. Then everybody would know you didn't mean to look so narrow—even if you are.

ANN: You're both delightful. Perfect specimens of your types. When I look at Ruth, I think the most alluring charm a woman can have is beautiful bones without a superfluous ounce of flesh on them. And when I look at you, Daisy, I think after all, there's nothing so stunning as a big strong girl with perfectly natural lines—so natural that we know she'd be even better looking with no clothes on at all.

DAISY: Heaven's, Ann! Your sculptor's eye is a little embarrassing.

RUTH: Evidently you think my clothes help me out a good deal. But at least I'm free and comfortable, too. Can you touch the floor, Daisy?

DAISY: Of course.

[The two women bend—touching the floor with the tips of their fingers. TOM, REMINGTON, and KEITH come in from the hall.]

TOM: What's going on?

REMINGTON: What are you trying to do, Ruth—swim or fly?

ANN: We're just saying that the waist measure expands as we broaden in our ideas.

KEITH: Is that the fashion now?

RUTH: Yes—broad and free!

REMINGTON: That's one thing you women have to acknowledge men have more sense about than you have.

ANN, RUTH, AND DAISY: What?

REMINGTON: Our figures. We've had the same shape since the Garden of Eden, and you've had hundreds of absolutely different kinds.

ANN: Turn around, Daisy, I want to try something. *[She accidentally sticks a pin into DAISY's shoulder.]*

DAISY: Ouch!

ANN: Oh, I'm sorry! You seem to be so close to your clothes.

REMINGTON: What are you doing to her?

DAISY: She's sticking pins into me.

ANN: For her own good. Isn't that pretty?

TOM: What?

ANN: The frock.

TOM: Is that new?

KEITH: Which?

DAISY: Do you mean to say you don't realize I have on something different from what I wore at dinner?

RUTH: No use dressing for Keith. He never sees anything.

DAISY: I'm going to undress now. Perhaps that will interest you more. *[ANN begins to unfasten the gown.]*

REMINGTON: Much more.

ANN: Was that the postman?

DAISY: No it was not.

REMINGTON: The postman habit is getting on my nerves. You're all jumping and listening till you'll have St. Vitus Dance if you don't stop.

ANN: How can we help it?

REMINGTON: After all, a few other competitions have been lost and won and people have lived through it. It's not the only thing in life.

TOM: You'd think it was if you had $100,000 at stake. *[ELLEN comes in from hall and takes out the coffee tray.]*

ANN: Aren't we going to have some bridge? Who wants to play? I know you do, Daddie.

REMINGTON: I have to get even with you for that last rubber, Tom.

TOM: You can't do it.

DAISY: I want to play with you, Doctor.

REMINGTON: Come on.

RUTH: I'm afraid to play against you.

REMINGTON: *[turning at the library door]* What's that?

OTHERS: What?

REMINGTON: The postman.

OTHERS: Oh!

[RUTH and DAISY go into library with REMINGTON.]

ANN: *[to TOM and KEITH]* Coming?

TOM: You go, Keith. I want to look at the paper a minute.

KEITH: Oh, my game's no good. You go.

ANN: Now don't stay out here and listen and wait. If there is any mail, Ellen will bring it straight up.

TOM: I won't. I'll be with you—in two minutes.

ANN: Anyway—tonight doesn't necessarily decide it. There may be still two or three more days. Isn't that so, Keith?

KEITH: Yes, I think so.

REMINGTON, RUTH, AND DAISY: *[calling from the library]* Come on! Come on!

ANN: Coming! *[She goes in.]*

KEITH: That's straight. I do think so—*[A pause. TOM reads.]* Don't you?

TOM: I'm trying to—but these last few days of waiting have been—

KEITH: Don't lose your nerve, Herford. I'm just as sure as I was the first day. If by any wild chance you don't get it—it'll be a fluke.

TOM: Oh, no. Oh, no, not by any means. The men judging this know. I'd trust them with anything. The fellows who lose will have no kick coming on that score.

KEITH: Well—I don't see how you can lose.

TOM: A man's a fool to let himself count on an uncertainty. I don't mean that I've lost sight of the fact that I might lose—not for a second—but I confess—as the time has grown shorter I've realized I want it even more than I thought I did.

KEITH: Of course you want it. Aside from the glory—it's an awful lot of money—Governor, an awful lot of money.

TOM: It is. It would put us straight—clear up the house entirely and make it possible to do only the things a fellow wants to do. That's what I'm after. Then—No more competitions for me, thank you. Is that the 'phone? I'm as bad as Ann—jumping and listening. Damn it! I want to know—one way or the other.

KEITH: Of course you do. The cursed waiting is enough to make you cut your throat.

ELLEN: *[opening the hall door]* The telephone for Mr. Herford.

TOM: Who is it?

ELLEN: I couldn't just get the name, sir.

KEITH: Want me to go.

TOM: If you don't mind, old man.

*[*ELLEN *goes out.]*

KEITH: *[starting to the door and turning]* It couldn't be—you wouldn't get word that way—would you?

TOM: Uh?—Oh—nonsense! No—no—nonsense! I'll go—No, I—you go—old man. That's not it—of course.

*[*KEITH *goes out.* TOM *listens a moment—showing a tense anxiety.]*

RUTH: *[coming in from the library]* They're waiting for you, Tom. The cards are dealt. Where's Keith?

TOM: He'll be back in a minute.

RUTH: Aren't you going in?

TOM: Why don't you take my place? I don't feel a bit—

RUTH: I did offer to, but Dr. Remington said he would like to play bridge this evening, not teach it. Wouldn't it be Seventh Heaven to speak the truth on all occasions as unconcernedly as Dr. Remington does? Imagine the sheer bliss of letting go and spitting it all out. Have you ever counted the lies you told in just one day, Tom?

TOM: No—I never had time.

*[*TOM *starts to go into the library and turns to see if* RUTH *is coming.]*

RUTH: No—I'm going to wait for Keith.

*[*TOM *goes in—*RUTH *reads for a moment.]*

KEITH: *[coming back from the hall]* That was—

RUTH: What?

KEITH: Millicent or her school or something. Such a bad connection; they're going to call again in a few minutes. Is that dress new, dear?

RUTH: I've had it three years.

KEITH: It's awfully pretty. I wish you'd wear it all the time.

RUTH: I do.

KEITH: Aren't we going in to play?

RUTH: No, I don't feel like it. Come and sit down, dear. Oh, are you going to sit way over there?

KEITH: Not 'specially. *[Drawing chair near the couch—*KEITH *sits facing* RUTH.*]*

RUTH: Comfortable?

KEITH: Not very.

RUTH: Have you read this?

KEITH: No. Any good?

RUTH: Yes—Good enough. *[She rises, going to the fireplace.]*

KEITH: What's the matter? I thought you wanted to talk. Where are you going?

RUTH: No place.

KEITH: You got the fidgets, too?

RUTH: Sort of.

KEITH: Well, stop it. Herford's going to be all right. There'll be news in a day or so now.

RUTH: I wasn't thinking of that. I have something to tell you.

KEITH: Then why don't you come and tell it?

RUTH: And if you aren't fine about it—it will be the greatest disappointment in my whole life.

[Going to KEITH *and putting a hand on his shoulder.]*

KEITH: You mean if I don't think just what you want me to about it. Go on. I s'pose I know, anyway.

RUTH: Then if you do—but you don't. It's so wonderful you couldn't guess. And you'll just have to see it the right way, because if you don't, it would mean you're what I know you're not. Down in your real soul, Keith, you're generous and fair and right.

KEITH: Suppose you communicate it to me first and discuss my soul afterwards.

RUTH: *[sitting on couch facing* KEITH] Well—Oh, you will be sweet, won't you Keithie?

KEITH: I can see it's going to be something very pleasant for me.

RUTH: It is, if you…

KEITH: It's wonderful if I'm not a fool and a pig. Yes, I know: Go on. Go on.

RUTH: Now don't begin that way,—please, dear. Don't shut up your mind before I even tell you.

KEITH: Suppose you do tell me.

RUTH: Well last week there was a row in the office over a matter concerning the policy of the magazine, and I differed with all the men in my department. At last I was sent for by the Editor-in-Chief. He was terribly severe at first, and I was frightened to pieces—but I stuck to my guns, and—bless your soul!—he sent for me again today and said they had had a meeting of the directors and that they decided—oh, it's too—

KEITH: What? What?

RUTH: They had decided to make me Editor of the Woman's Magazine. *[Fighting back her tears.]* Isn't it funny?

KEITH: And I suppose all this introduction means you accepted—without even asking me?

RUTH: Why, of course! Oh, Keith, don't you understand what this means to me?

KEITH: I understand that unless it means more to you than I do—you wouldn't hesitate a minute to chuck it.

RUTH: It's hopeless—we'll never—never see it the same way.

KEITH: You've never made the slightest effort to see it my way.

RUTH: What you ask of me is to cut off one half of my life and throw it away. What I ask of you is only an experiment—to let me try and see if I can't make things comfortable and smooth and happy for us—and still take this big thing that has come as a result of all my years of hard work and fighting for it.

KEITH: You'll never stop if you don't now. Once you get deeper in it, you'll be swamped—eaten up by it.

RUTH: Don't, Keith. I can't bear it! It's too unutterably selfish.

KEITH: [*rising and pushing his chair away*] All right—I'm selfish—but I'm human—and I'll bet my hat I'm just like every nine men out of ten. What in the name of Heaven does loving a girl amount to if you don't want to take care of her from start to finish? A man's no good if he doesn't feel that way, I tell you. He's a pup—and ought to be shot.

RUTH: [*rising*] But what about me–and what I want and have to have—in order to be happy?

KEITH: That's it. That is the point. You won't be happy without it. You want the excitement of it—that hustle and bustle outside.

RUTH: I want it just as you want your work—and you haven't any more right to ask me to give up mine than I have to ask you to stop yours.

KEITH: You simply don't love me.

RUTH: What rot. What nonsense!

KEITH: You don't love me.

RUTH: It's hopeless. You've decided, then. You won't compromise—so we'll end it.

KEITH: What do you mean?

RUTH: [*going to the hall door*] You've made your own choice. We'll end it now.

KEITH: [*following her*] No—Ruth—I won't give you up!

RUTH: You have. You have given me up.

KEITH: Ruth—wait.

RUTH: It's best, Keith. Don't hate me. You'll see it's best in a little while. We'll learn to be friends. I want you to be happy, dear boy—I do. And I couldn't make you so. We'll end it now. It's the best for us both.

KEITH: Ruth— [*She goes out quickly, closing the door.* KEITH *turns to the fire.*]

DAISY: [*knocking and opening the library door*] Excuse me. May I come in to get my sewing? Where's Ruth?

KEITH: [*with his back to* DAISY] Don't know.

DAISY: Well, don't bite my head off. I can always tell when you and Ruth have been discussing the emancipation of women. [*Sitting below table and taking her dress to sew.*]

KEITH: You all think you're superior beings.

DAISY: Of course.

KEITH: [*beginning to walk about*] Yes, you do. You're just as bad as the rest of them—worse. The minute a woman makes enough to buy the clothes on her back, she thinks she and God Almighty are running the earth and men are just little insects crawling around.

[DAISY *laughs.*]

Oh, you can laugh! It's so—and you know it. Every one of you that have got the bee in your bonnet of doing something—doing something, are through with men. Look at you! You've cut men out entirely, and you think

you're too smart to marry one. Now, don't you? Isn't that the reason?

DAISY: [*threading her needle*] Don't bully-rag me. Say it all to Ruth.

KEITH: I tell you it's all rot—business for women. It spoils every one of you. Why aren't you in a home of your own instead of hustling for your bread and butter? It's because you're too damned conceited. You think you know more than any man you ever saw and you think you don't need one. You wait—You'll see—someday.

[*Going back to the fire.*]

DAISY: You amuse me.

KEITH: There you are—that's about what I'm for.

DAISY: There's a button off your coat. Looks horrid.

KEITH: I know. I've got it.

[*Putting a finger in waistcoat pocket.*]

DAISY: Have you got it there? [KEITH *shows her the button.*] Come here, I'll do it.

KEITH: Never mind. I'll nail it on.

DAISY: Come here. [KEITH *goes slowly to her.*] You'll have to take your coat off. It's bad luck to sew anything on you.

KEITH: Oh—

DAISY: Go on—take it off. [KEITH *takes off his coat reluctantly and watches* DAISY *as she examines the coat.*] Good Gracious, the lining's ripped, too.

KEITH: Yes.

DAISY: Poor old fellow! Are these some of your stitches?

KEITH: [*drawing the chair from center and sitting left before* DAISY] What's the matter with 'em?

DAISY: Looks like carpet thread. [*Snipping some threads.*] See, I'll just draw this together and that'll be all right.

[*She begins to sing an old diddy—*KEITH *gradually hums with her, keeping time with his hands and feet and relaxing into good humor.*]

KEITH: [*soothed for a moment*] How does it happen you're so handy with a needle? I thought you were all for business.

DAISY: Well, I can sew a button on if you can.

KEITH: I tell you it changes all women—business. They make a little money themselves and want luxury and won't live without it.

DAISY: Sometimes—yes. But there are lots and lots and lots of women taking care of themselves—putting up the bluff of being independent and happy—who would be so glad to live in a little flat and do their own work—just to be the nicest thing in the world to some man.

KEITH: Wouldn't you think that Ruth would like that better than the office?

DAISY: No—not the lamplight and the needle for Ruth. Keith, don't ask her to give up her work—don't you see, she's more clever, in her way, than you are in yours. She'll go further, and if you make her stop, she'll hate you some day because she'll think you've kept her back. That's a hard thing to say—but it's the truth.

KEITH: You mean I'm a failure.

DAISY: [*genuinely*] No—no—I don't mean that, Keith.

KEITH: I work—Gosh, how I work, but I'll never do anything. Why haven't I got what Mrs. Herford's got? She sent models off for this frieze that any man would be proud to send. Why couldn't I?

DAISY: Seems kind of mixed up and unfair—doesn't it?

KEITH: You bet it's unfair! I work like a dog and never get anywhere. If Ruth throws me over, I'll never have the home I'm working for. That's what I want—a home. I'll never have it now.

DAISY: Oh, yes you will.

KEITH: I'm done for.

DAISY: No, you're not. There are too many women in the world—who—could—love you.

KEITH: I'm no good.

DAISY: Some woman might think that you—your—the way you work—and your honesty and loyalty are the greatest things a man can have.

KEITH: Um!

DAISY: Some woman might use all her cleverness and ingenuity to make the little flat beautiful—to show you what your own home—could be—to give you a better dinner than you thought you could afford.

KEITH: [sitting with his head in his hands] That kind of a woman is a thing of the past.

DAISY: Oh no, they're not. They're lying around thick. The trouble is—a woman can't ask. Even if a man is—just at her hand—and she knows she could make him happy—she can't tell him—she can't open his eyes—she has to hide what might make things right for both of them. Because she's a woman.

KEITH: Oh—love doesn't cut much ice with a woman. Women are all brain nowadays.

DAISY: [with sudden warmth] That's enough to use all the brains a woman's got—to make a home—to bring up children—and to keep a man's love.

KEITH: [raising his head slowly and looking at DAISY] I never expected to hear you say a thing like that. There's some excuse for you being in business.

DAISY: Yes, of course. [Rising and holding the coat.] I'm not the marrying kind.

KEITH: [getting into the coat] Much obliged. Would you be willing to give up work and marry a man on a small salary—if you loved him?

DAISY: You make me laugh.

KEITH: What's the matter, Daisy?

DAISY: Nothing.

KEITH: I never saw tears in your eyes before. Women are funny things.

DAISY: Yes, we're funny. There's only one thing on earth funnier.

KEITH: What?

DAISY: Men.

REMINGTON: [coming in from the library] Did I leave my other glasses in here?

DAISY: [beginning to look for them] I haven't seen them.

REMINGTON: I've lost one game because I didn't have 'em, and I don't propose to give 'em another.

DAISY: What a shame! Help look for them, Keith.

REMINGTON: I'm pretty blind—but thank God not quite as bad as you, Keith.

KEITH: What? There's nothing the matter with my eyes.

REMINGTON: [looking insinuatingly at DAISY] Don't you think there is, Daisy?

DAISY: [trying to look unconscious] Are you sure you left those glasses in here?

REMINGTON: It's as bad a case of shortsightedness as I ever saw.

DAISY: Oh—[The Doctor holds her and turns her, pushing her toward KEITH.]

REMINGTON: Daisy, don't you see that queer blind look in his eyes?

DAISY: No—I don't.

KEITH: What do you mean? [Remington laughs.] Do you see the joke, Daisy?

REMINGTON: It's no joke—is it, Daisy?

DAISY: I don't know wht on earth you're talking about. I'm going to get those glasses. [Going to hall door.] You probably left them in your hoat in the call. I mean in your hall in the coat—I mean—

REMINGTON: That's all right Daisy—we know what you mean. At least I do.

DAISY: Oh, you—[Ellen comes in from hall.] What is it, Ellen?

ELLEN: The telephone, Miss Herford.

DAISY: For me?

ELLEN: They said any one of the family.

DAISY: I'll go. [She goes out, followed by ELLEN.]

REMINGTON: There's a woman who knows how to take care of a man.

KEITH: I'm afraid that's not her object in life. They all have something else to do.

REMINGTON: What's the matter with you?

KEITH: I'm done for.

REMINGTON: Ruth, you mean?

KEITH: She won't marry me unless she goes on working.

REMINGTON: She's right, too.

KEITH: What?

REMINGTON: Of course. You haven't any more right to ask that clever little woman to throw away half her life and to be the tail of your kite than you have to ask her to cut her throat. Open your eyes and look around. There are always other women.

KEITH: Never. Never in the world for me.

REMINGTON: I give you about three months.

KEITH: Do you think I could ever—

REMINGTON: Certainly, I do. Look at Daisy, for instance. A fine, sweet wholesome girl with no kinks and no abnormal ambitions.

KEITH: Daisy?

REMINGTON: Don't blow your brains out for a couple of days. Talk it over with her. She thinks you're about the finest thing going.

KEITH: What?

REMINGTON: Fact! Don't try to hold on to the woman who's getting away from you, but take the one who is coming your way.

KEITH: You're crazy. Mad as a hatter. What are you giving me?

REMINGTON: Just a little professional advice—free! She's head over heels in love with you, I tell you.

DAISY: [*coming in from hall in great excitement; she has a case for glasses in her hand*] Dr. Remington, that was long distance. They telephoned from school that Millicent has gone.

KEITH: Gone!

REMINGTON: Gone where?

DAISY: Left school suddenly tonight without saying a word to anyone.

REMINGTON AND KEITH: What!

DAISY: As soon as they knew—they 'phoned the station, and found she had taken the train for New York.

REMINGTON: What train?

DAISY: The one that gets here at nine o'clock.

KEITH: [*looking at his watch*] It's 9:15 now.

DAISY: Shall I tell Ann?

REMINGTON: No—no—wait. We'll give her fifteen minutes more to get to the house. No use frightening Ann.

KEITH: Do you think she is coming home?

DAISY: Why do you say that, Keith? What put such an idea into your head?

KEITH: Why wouldn't she say so—wire or write or something?

DAISY: Oh, it's too horrible! Doctor, oughtn't we to tell them now?

REMINGTON: No—no—

DAISY: But we're wasting time. What if she shouldn't come?

KEITH: I think I'll dash down to the station anyway. The train might be late.

REMINGTON: No—no. They'd ask where you'd gone. Wait fifteen minutes—I think she'll be here. I don't want to frighten—

[ANN *comes in from the library.*]

ANN: Well, I never saw people so wildly keen about playing as you are. What's the matter with you?

REMINGTON: I've been waiting all this time—for my glasses. Come on, Daisy. [*Taking the glasses from* DAISY, *he goes into the library.*]

ANN: You look worried, Daisy.

DAISY: No—I'm only-

ELLEN: [*coming in from hall with eight letters on a small tray*] The mail, Mrs. Herford.

ANN: Oh! [*She snatches the letters, taking off the three top ones*] It's come! Tom's letter.

KEITH AND DAISY: What?

[ELLEN *goes out through hall.*]

ANN: It is! It is—as true as I live.

KEITH: Great Scott!

DAISY: Then he's got it. He's got it!

ANN: Sh! Ask him to come here.

DAISY: It's too good to be true. It's too good!

[DAISY *goes into the library.*]

KEITH: I can't tell you how glad I am, Mrs. Herford. I can't tell you.

ANN: [*scarcely able to speak*] Ask him to come here.

KEITH: [*going into library*] Mrs. Herford wants you, Governor.

TOM: [*within*] Come and play, Ann.

ANN: [*throwing the other letters on the table*] Come here just a minute, Tom, please.

TOM: [*coming to door*] What is it?

ANN: Shut the door. It's come! [*Showing the letter.* TOM *opens it and reads it. A look of sickening disappointment comes into his face.*] No? Oh, Tom!

TOM: I was their second choice!

ANN: Oh, Tom, don't take it like that. What difference does it make, after all? You know you did a big thing. It's all luck—anyway.

TOM: I'll pull up in a minute. Well, it means taking hold of something else pretty quick. Going at it again.

ANN: Yes, keeping at it—that's it. What a terrible lot chance has to do with it.

TOM: Oh no, that isn't it.

ANN: Yes, it is, too.

TOM: No—I failed. I didn't get it, that's all.

ANN: You'll do something greater—next time—because of this.

TOM: [*taking her hand*] You're a brick! Now, see here, don't you be cut up about this. It's not the end of everything, you know. Stop that! You're not crying, I hope?

ANN: No, I'm not. Of course, I'm not! [*With passionate tenderness.*]
Oh, my boy. I never loved you so much—never believed in you as I do now. This is only a little hard place that will make you all the stronger.

TOM: Dear old girl! What would I do without you? I'll tell the others and get it over.
[*Rising, he stops, staring at one of the letters on the table.*]
Ann!

ANN: Um?

TOM: [*taking up a letter*] Ann—here's one for you, too.

ANN: What? [*She tears open the letter.*] Tom! They've given the commission to me! Look! Read it! Is that what it says? Is it? Now aren't you glad you let me do it? You haven't lost! We've got it! Say you're glad. Say you're proud of me, dear. That's the best part of it all.

TOM: Of course I am, dear; of course I am.

ANN: Oh, Tom, I wanted you to get it more than I ever wanted anything in my life, but this is something to be thankful for. Doesn't this almost make it right?

TOM: Yes, dear, yes. Don't think of me. That's over—that part of it. Tell the others now.

ANN: Wait!

TOM: Aren't you going to?

ANN: I only want to be sure that you're just as happy that I won, as I would have been if you had.

TOM: Of course I am. You know that. [*Kissing her.*]

ANN: Tell the others, then, Tom—I can't.

TOM: [opening the library doors] What do you think has happened?

DAISY: [rushing in] Tom got it. Didn't you, Tom? You did. You did! Oh, I'm so glad. [She kisses him.]

KEITH: [following DAISY in] Well—Governor—what did I tell you?

REMINGTON: [in doorway] Pretty fine—isn't it?

ANN: You tell them, Tom.

TOM: Ann got it!

DAISY: What?

TOM: Isn't it great?

ANN: You won't believe it. But you can see the letter. Now, Father, don't you think getting that is better than being nursemaid and housekeeper? Now, don't you, honestly—

REMINGTON: I do not.

ANN: What?

REMINGTON: I do not.

ANN: Oh, I can laugh at your theories now. You haven't a leg to stand on. Has he, Tom? Be a dear, Father, and say you're glad.

REMINGTON: I'm not. I'd rather you'd failed a thousand times over—for your own good. What are you going to do with Millicent while you're making this thing?

ANN: How can you be so hard and narrow, Father?

REMINGTON: What if you did win? You've got something far greater than making statues to do.

TOM: Doctor, you're excited.

REMINGTON: Not a bit. I'm only telling the truth. This is your business, you know—and it would have been far better for both of you if you'd won the thing.

TOM: I don't see the argument. Ann got it because she sent in a better model than I did. I don't see that anything else has anything to do with the case.

[TOM goes out through hall.]

ANN: [turning to sit on the couch] At least Tom's glad I got it.

REMINGTON: He's stung to the quick. You've humiliated him in his own eyes. [He goes to the fireplace.]

ANN: I can't understand why you feel this way about it, Father.

DAISY: Oh, it's natural enough.

ANN: [turning to DAISY in amazement] Aren't you glad for me—Daisy?

DAISY: Yes, but—I—I'm awfully sorry for Tom.

[She goes out through hall.]

ANN: What's the matter with them all, Keith?

KEITH: Oh—as Daisy says, it's natural, Mrs. Herford.

[He goes out after DAISY.]

REMINGTON: [coming down to ANN] Daughter, I'm afraid I was a little too stiff just now. I didn't mean to be unkind.

ANN: [rising and starting to hall door] Oh, it doesn't matter.

REMINGTON: [stopping her] Yes, it does matter. I wouldn't hurt you for the world.

ANN: But you've always fought me, Father. You've never thought I had any right to work—never believed in my ability. Now that I've proved I have some—why can't you acknowledge it?

REMINGTON: Ann, this is a dangerous moment in your life. Tom's beaten—humiliated—knocked out. You did it—he can't stand it.

ANN: What have I done? Tom has a big nature. He's not little and petty enough to be hurt because I won.

REMINGTON: You're blind. He's had a blow tonight that no man on earth could stand.

ANN: Not Tom. I won't believe it.

REMINGTON: Yes, I say. I know what I'm talking about. Ann, be careful how you move now. Use your woman's tact, your love. Make Tom know that he is the greatest thing in the world to you—that you'd even give up all this work idea—if—he wanted—you to.

ANN: What? Tom wouldn't let me.

REMINGTON: Ask him. See what he'd say.

ANN: Why, I wouldn't insult him. He'd think I thought he was—

[TOM comes in from hall. ANN checks herself and turns away quickly to fire.]

TOM: [after a pause] What's the matter?

REMINGTON: Nothing!—Nothing. Ann and I were just having a little argument, as usual. I'll be back in a few minutes. [Looking at his watch he goes into hall.]

TOM: [going slowly to ANN] I hope you're not still fighting about the—your frieze?

ANN: They're all so funny, Tom—the way they act about it. It hurts. But so long as you're glad, it doesn't matter what anyone else thinks. Say you're glad, dear. I want you to be as happy as I would be if you had won.

TOM: You know I am dear. You know that.

ANN: [with a sigh of relief ANN sits at left of fire] Think how I'll have to work. I can't even go to the country in the summer.

TOM: [sitting opposite ANN at the fire] And what will you do with Millicent this summer?

ANN: Oh, there are lots of nice things for her to do. The money! Think what it will mean to you!

TOM: Let me tell you one thing, Ann, in the beginning. I'll never touch a penny of the money.

ANN: What?

TOM: Not a cent of it.

ANN: What are you talking about?

TOM: That's your money. Put it away for yourself.

ANN: I never heard you say anything so absolutely unreasonable before in my life.

TOM: If you think I'm unreasonable, all right. But that's understood about the money. We won't discuss it.

ANN: Well, we will discuss it. Why shouldn't you use my money as well as I use ours?

TOM: That's about as different as day and night.

ANN: Why is it?

TOM: Because I'm taking care of you. It's all right if you never do another day's work in your life. You're doing it because you want to; I'm doing it because I've got to. If you were alone, it would be a different thing. But I'm here, and so long as I am, I'll make what keeps us going.

ANN: But I'll help you.

TOM: No, you won't.

ANN: I will. I'm going on just as far as I have ability to go, and if you refuse to take any money I may make—if you refuse to use it for our mutual good, you're unjust and taking an unfair advan—Oh, Tom! What are we saying? We're out of our senses—both of us. You didn't mean what you said. Did you? It would—I simply couldn't bear it, if you did. You didn't—did you?

TOM: I did—of course.

ANN: Tom—after all these years of pulling together, now that I've done something, why do you suddenly balk?

TOM: [rising] Good Heavens! Do you think I'm going to use your money? Don't try to run my end of it. It's the same old story—when you come down to it, a woman can't mix up in a man's business. [He moves away.]

ANN: Mix up in it? Isn't it a good thing for you that I got this commission?

TOM: No. I don't know that it's a good thing from any standpoint to have it known that I failed, but my wife succeeded.

ANN: I thought you said you were glad—proud of me.

TOM: It's too—distracting—too—takes you away from more important things.

ANN: What things?

TOM: Millicent and me.

ANN: Oh, Tom—don't! You know that you and Millicent come before everything on earth to me.

TOM: No.

ANN: You do.

TOM: We don't—now. Your ambition comes first.

ANN: [she rises, going to him] Tom, I worship you. You know that, don't you?

TOM: I'm beginning to hate this work and everything in connection with it.

ANN: But you taught me—helped me—pushed me on. What's changed you?

TOM: I let you do it in the first place because I thought it was right. I wanted you to do the thing you wanted to do.

ANN: Well?

TOM: I was a fool. I didn't see what it would lead to. It's taking you away from everything else—and there'll be no end to it. Your ambition will carry you away till the home and Millicent and I are nothing to you!

ANN: Tom—look at me. Be honest. Are you sorry—sorry I got this commission?

TOM: I'm sorry it's the most important thing in the world to you.

ANN: Oh! Why do you say that to me? How can you?

TOM: Haven't I just seen it? You're getting rid of Millicent now because you don't want her to interfere with your work.

ANN: No!

TOM: You're pushing her out of your life.

ANN: No!

TOM: You said just now you were going to send her away alone in the summer. I don't like that. She's got to be with you—I want you to keep her with you.

ANN: But that's impossible. You know that. If I stop work now, I might as well give up the frieze entirely.

TOM: Then give it up.

ANN: What?

TOM: Give up the whole thing—forever. Why shouldn't you?

ANN: Do you mean that?

TOM: Yes.

ANN: Tom—I love you. Don't ask this sacrifice of me to prove my love.

TOM: Could you make it? Could you?

ANN: Don't ask it! Don't ask it, for your own sake. I want to keep on loving you. I want to believe you're what I thought you were. Don't make me think you're just like every other man.

TOM: I am a man—and you're my wife. And Millicent's our daughter. Unless you come back to the things a woman's always had to do—and always will—we can't go on. We can't go on.

ANN: [Following him around the table] Tom—if you're just a little hurt—just a little jealous because I won—

TOM: Oh—

ANN: That's natural—I can understand that.

TOM: Oh—don't—

ANN: But—Oh, Tom!—the other—to ask me to give it all up. I could never forgive that. Take it back, Tom—take it back.

TOM: Good God, Ann, can't you see? You're a woman and I'm a man. You're not free in the same way. If you won't stop because I ask it—I say you must.

ANN: You can't say that to me. You can't!

TOM: I do say it.

ANN: No!

TOM: I say it because I know it's right.

ANN: It isn't.

TOM: I can't make you see it.

ANN: It isn't.

TOM: I don't know how—but everything in me tells me it's right.

ANN: Tom—listen to me.

TOM: If you won't do it because I ask you—I demand it. I say you've got to.

ANN: Tom—you can kill our love by just what you do now.

TOM: Then this work is the biggest thing in the world to you?

ANN: What is more important to us both—to our happiness than just that?

MILLICENT: [calling outside door] Mother! [A startled pause as ANN and TOM turn toward the hall door.] Mother! I'm home, where are you?

[MILLICENT opens the hall door and rushes into the room.]

ANN: Millicent! What are you doing here?

MILLICENT: I came home, Mother.

ANN: Why?

MILLICENT: Because I had to.

ANN: Are you ill, dear?

MILLICENT: No. No.

TOM: Is anything wrong at school?

MILLICENT: No, but I won't go back.

TOM: But why won't you? What's the trouble?

MILLICENT: I won't go back.

TOM: But you can't do a thing like this. I won't allow it.

MILLICENT: You wouldn't let me come home when I wanted to, and now I can't go back. I won't—everything's different now. I won't go back, and you can't make me. *[She turns and rushes out of the room.]*

[TOM and ANN stare at each other as—]

THE CURTAIN FALLS.

ACT 3

Scene: Same as Act 2, half an hour later.
RUTH *is writing at the desk.* **DAISY** *opens the hall door and stops, listening back into the hall.*

RUTH: *[quickly]* What's the matter?

DAISY: Nothing. I was looking to see who went up the stairs. It's Dr. Remington.

RUTH: How's Millicent now?

DAISY: Ann's with her—getting her to bed.

RUTH: Do you know yet why she came home?

DAISY: I don't know whether Ann's got it out of her yet or not.

RUTH: What do you think? Why on earth didn't she tell them at school?

DAISY: I haven't the dimmest—but she didn't do it without some good reason. I'll bet anything on that. Millicent's a pretty level-headed youngster.

RUTH: She's a pretty self-willed one. Ann will send her right back, of course.

DAISY: I don't know whether she will or not. Millicent's got some rather decided ideas of her own on that.

RUTH: But she'll have to go. Why shouldn't she? Ann will make her.

DAISY: Tom will have something to say about it.

RUTH: It's for Ann to decide, surely.

DAISY: Not at all. I don't see why. She is Tom's child, too, you know, and this is his house and he pays the bills at school and if he doesn't want her to go back, you can bet she jolly well won't go. I only hope Millicent tells the whole business—whatever it is. Ann is so excited over the frieze I don't know whether she'll have the patience to handle Millicent right or not. She's not easy.

RUTH: It's awful for Ann to be upset now—of all times—when she has to begin this gigantic work.

DAISY: Oh—I wish the damned frieze were in Guinea and that Ann had nothing to do but take care of Tom and Millicent—like any other woman. I'd give anything if she hadn't won the competition.

RUTH: Daisy!

DAISY: Oh, I would. I have a ghastly feeling that something horrible is going to come of it—if it hasn't already come.

RUTH: What do you mean?

DAISY: I tell you it is not possible for a man and woman to love each other and live together and be happy—unless the man is—it.

RUTH: Speaking of the dark ages! You ought to live in a harem. How any girl who makes her own bread and butter can be so old fashioned as you are—I can't see.

DAISY: You've got so used to your own ideas you forget that I am the average normal woman the world is full of.

RUTH: Nonsense! You're almost extinct. I'm the average normal woman the world is full of—and it's going to be fuller and fuller.

DAISY: I'll bet on plenty of us—left—*[Indicating herself.]*—on Judgment Day.

RUTH: I want to laugh when I think how mistaken we've been calling you a bachelor girl. Why, you'd make the best wife of anybody I know.

DAISY: I s'pose you mean that as an insult.

RUTH: But you seem so self reliant men are sort of afraid of you—

REMINGTON: *[coming in from hall and feeling a certain restraint in the two girls]* Am I in the wrong camp?

RUTH AND DAISY: No, no. Come in.

REMINGTON: I have to stay someplace. I'm going to hang around till Millicent quiets down—and then I'll clear out.

DAISY: Is she ill?

REMINGTON: Oh, no. Just a little worked up and excited.

RUTH: Why do you think she came home, Dr. Remington?

REMINGTON: I don't know what to think—unless she has "boy" in the head.

DAISY: Goodness no! Not yet!

REMINGTON: She's sixteen. You can't choke it off to save your life.

RUTH: Oh, she's a baby!

REMINGTON: Don't fool yourself. She won't wait as long as you two have to sit by her own fireside with children on her knee.

RUTH: Oh—

REMINGTON: That's the only thing in the game that's worth a cent—anyway. *[As KEITH comes in from hall.]* Isn't that so, Keith?

KEITH: What's that?

REMINGTON: I've just been telling these two that love and children are the greatest things on earth. Ruth doesn't agree with me—but Daisy—

RUTH: I must go.

DAISY: I must go up to Ann.

[RUTH goes out.]

REMINGTON: Let me go. They both seem terribly anxious to get out when you come in, Keith. Or maybe I'm in the way. I'll go.

DAISY: Don't be silly. I really must see if I can do anything for Ann.

REMINGTON: No, you mustn't. She's waiting for me to see Millicent. By the way, Keith—tomorrow's Sunday. I always take a run into the country in the motor on Sunday. Come along and bring either Ruth or Daisy. Take your choice. I know which one I'd take.

DAISY: Isn't he a goose? *[He goes into hall.]*

KEITH: Would it bore you to go, Daisy?

DAISY: Nonsense! Ruth will.

KEITH: It would be awfully good of you. Tomorrow s going to be a hard day for me to get through. Ruth told me tonight that she—I'm afraid it's all over.

DAISY: Why don't you compromise?

KEITH: There's nothing to compromise about. She's all wrong. Don't you think so?

DAISY: Oh, don't ask me. I don't know anything about it.

KEITH: Wait a minute. I—won't you go tomorrow, Daisy?

DAISY: Ask Ruth. It will be a good chance to make up.

KEITH: You're so practical and like such different things—maybe you'd think flying along through the country and lunching at some nice little out-of-the-way place was too frivolous—

DAISY: Oh yes, I don't like anything but being shut up in the house all day, pounding at my typewriter and splitting my head to get the bills straight. To actually go off with a man—for a whole day—and have a little—like any other woman—would be too unheard of. Of course, I couldn't do anything as silly as that.

KEITH: Oh—

DAISY: I wouldn't be amusing, anyway. Dr. Remington—well, he's sixty, and you'd be thinking of Ruth and I'd sit there like a stick—the sensible, practical woman who couldn't possibly be interesting and fascinating because no man would take the trouble to find out how devilish and alluring and altogether exciting I could be if I had the chance.

[She throws open the door and goes out. KEITH *stares after her.]*

TOM: *[coming in from library after a moment]* I thought you'd gone, McKenzie.

KEITH: No, but I'm going.

REMINGTON: *[coming back from hall]* Good night, McKenzie. I'll dig you up in the morning, ten o'clock. Sharp, mind! And I'll call for Daisy first.

KEITH: *[at hall door]* All right. Much obliged, Doctor. *[Turning back.]* How'd you know it was Daisy?

REMINGTON: I didn't—but I do now.

KEITH: Good night. *[He goes out.]*

TOM: Well—how is she? How is Millicent?

REMINGTON: Oh, she's not ill—but the child's nervous as a witch—all strung up. She's worried about something—got something on her mind and naturally her head aches. And she has a little fever—but that won't hurt her.

TOM: Got something on her mind? What?

REMINGTON: She didn't confide in me.

TOM: What could she have on her mind?

REMINGTON: I don't think she's committed murder—but she's got a mind, you know—there's no reason why she shouldn't have something on it.

TOM: Well, I don't know what to do with her.

REMINGTON: If you think she ought not to go back to school, say so. Tell Ann those are your orders.

TOM: I don't give orders to Ann.

REMINGTON: The devil you don't. She'd like it. A woman—a dog and a walnut tree—the more you beat 'em, the better they be.

TOM: The walnut tree business doesn't work with Ann. I made a fool of myself tonight by telling her I wouldn't touch the money she gets out of this thing. She doesn't understand. I've made her think I'm jealous because she won.

REMINGTON: Well, aren't you?

TOM: No! I tell you, it's something else. Something sort of gave way under my feet when she opened her letter.

REMINGTON: I know. I know.

TOM: Doctor, for the Lord's sake, don't think I'm mean. I don't want to drag her back—but she seems gone somehow—she doesn't need me any more. That's what hurts.

REMINGTON: Of course, it hurts.

TOM: Much as I've loved to have her with me—working away at my elbow—wonderful as it all was—sometimes I've wished I hadn't seen her all day—that I had her to go home to—fresh and rested—waiting for me and that I was running the machine alone for her. She'll never understand. I've acted like a skunk.

REMINGTON: Y-e-s-I guess you have—so have I—unjust—pig-headed. No more right to say the things I've said to her than I have to spank her—except that she's—the most precious thing in the world to me—and I'd rather see her happy—as a woman—than the greatest artist in the world.

TOM: That's it. I want her here—mine. But I s'pose that's rotten and wrong.

REMINGTON: Yes—I s'pose it is. But you're despising yourself for something that's been in your bones—boy —since the beginning of time. Men and women will go through hell over this before it shakes down into shape. You're right and she's right, and you're tearing each other like mad dogs over it because you love each other.

TOM: That's it. If another man had got it, I'd take my licking without whining. What's the matter with me? Why can't I be that way to her?

REMINGTON: *[shaking his head with a wistful smile]* Male and female created He them. I don't take back any of the stuff I said to her before she went into this. She's fighting you now for her rights—but she laid her genius at your feet once and she'd do it again if—

ANN: *[coming in from hall and speaking after a pause]* Well, Father—what do you say about Millicent?

REMINGTON: My advice is that you let her stay at home for a while.

ANN: This is only a caprice—and it would be the worst thing in the world to give in to her. Unless you say as a physician—that's she's too ill to.

REMINGTON: I don't say she's too ill—physically. You must decide for yourself. I'll go up an see her again and if she isn't asleep then, I'll give her a mild sleeping powder. Ann, I put her in your arms first—and the look that came into your eyes then was as near divinity as we ever get. Oh, my daughter—don't let the new restlessness and strife of the world about you blind you to the old things—the real things. *[He goes out.]*

ANN: *[after a pause]* You agree with me, don't you, that it's better for her to go back.

TOM: Do whatever you think best.

ANN: But what do you think?

TOM: It doesn't matter what I think, does it?

MILLICENT: *[opening the door]* Mother, aren't you coming back? *[MILLICENT wears a soft robe over her nightgown. Her hair is down her back.]*

ANN: Millicent—why did you get out of bed?

MILLICENT: I couldn't sleep. *[Running and jumping into the middle of the couch.]*

ANN: Run back—quickly.

MILLICENT: In a minute. It's so quiet upstairs, I couldn't sleep. I'm used to the girls.

ANN: You'll catch cold.

MILLICENT: Goodness, Mother, I'm roasting.

ANN: Millicent—what shall I do with you.

MILLICENT: Is that what you and Dad were talking about? What did Grandfather say? I don't care what he says. I'm not going back to school. You're on my side—aren't you, Dad?

TOM: Whatever your mother thinks is right, of course.

MILLICENT: Is it true—what Daisy told me—that you got the contract for a big frieze and not Father? Is it? Is it, Father? *[Looking from one to the other.]*

TOM: Yes. It's quite true.

ANN: Millicent, go to bed.

MILLICENT: I think that's perfectly horrid, Mother. Why should they give it to you? I think Father ought to have it—he's the man. Don't you think people will think it's funny that you didn't get it? I should think it would make them lose confidence in you.

[A pause. TOM stalks out, closing the door.]

Is Father hurt because you got it? I should think he would be.

ANN: Millicent, I've had quite enough of this. Go up to bed at once.

MILLICENT: Will you come up and sleep with me?

ANN: Of course not. *[Walking about restlessly.]*

MILLICENT: Why not?

ANN: Neither one of us would sleep a wink.

MILLICENT: That wouldn't matter. I don't want to be alone.

ANN: Come now—I won't speak to you again.

MILLICENT: What have you decided about school?

ANN: I'll tell you in the morning.

MILLICENT: I won't go up till you tell me.

ANN: Millicent—you will go at once, I say.

MILLICENT: Oh, Mother, don't be cross. Sit down and talk a minute.

ANN: It's late, dear. You must—

MILLICENT: That's nothing. We girls often talk till twelve.

ANN: Till twelve? Do the teachers know it?

MILLICENT: Oh, Mother, you're lovely! Don't you suppose they know that they don't know everything that's going on? Come and sit down, Mummie.

ANN: No! You must go to bed.

MILLICENT: But I won't go back to school.

ANN: *[going to MILLICENT, who is still on the couch]* You make it terribly hard for me, Millicent. You don't know what's good for you, of course. I don't expect you to—but I do expect you to be obedient.

MILLICENT: But, Mother, I tell you I—

ANN: Don't be so rebellious. Now come upstairs, please, dear and—

MILLICENT: But I won't go back to school, Mother dear. I won't.

ANN: You say I treat you like a child. You force me to. If you don't want me to punish you—go upstairs at once and don't say another word.

MILLICENT: I won't go back.

ANN: Stop, I say!

MILLICENT: I know what I want to do. I'm sixteen.

ANN: *[their voices rising together]* You're my child. You will obey me.

MILLICENT: But I won't. You don't understand. I can't, Mother, I can't—I can't!

ANN: Why? Why can't you?

MILLICENT: Because I—I'm going to be married.

ANN: You silly child!

MILLICENT: It's the truth, Mother. I am.

ANN: Don't say a thing like that, even in fun.

MILLICENT: It's the truth, I tell you. I'm going to be married.

ANN: Some time you are, of course—you are.

MILLICENT: No—now—soon. That's why I left. That's why I'm not going back.

ANN: *[after drawing a chair to the couch and sitting before MILLICENT]* What do you mean?

MILLICENT: I—he—we—we're engaged.

ANN: He—who?

MILLICENT: You—you don't know him.

ANN: Who?

MILLICENT: He's—he's perfectly wonderful!

ANN: Who is he?

MILLICENT: Now, Mother, wait. He—he isn't rich—

ANN: Well—

MILLICENT: He's poor—but he's perfectly wonderful—he works and he's so noble about it.

ANN: What does he do?

MILLICENT: He—he—Oh, Mother, it's hard to explain, because he's so different.

ANN: What does he do?

MILLICENT: Well—just now he—he drives the motor at school—because, you see, he's so proud he—

ANN: Drives the motor—a chauffeur, you mean?

MILLICENT: People call him that, of course—but he isn't— *[ANN rises.]*

Mother—*[ANN goes to the door and locks it—going back to MILLICENT, who has risen.]*

Now, Mother, don't look like that.

ANN: Sit down!

MILLICENT: Don't look like that! Let me tell you about it.

ANN: *[sitting again]* Yes, tell me about it.

MILLICENT: Oh, I—hardly know how to begin.

ANN: He drives the motor—the school motor, you say?

MILLICENT: Yes—to the trains, you know—and into town and to church.

ANN: Who is his father?

MILLICENT: Why—I—I don't know who he is. I've never met his father.

ANN: What is his name?

MILLICENT: His father's name? I don't know.

ANN: The boy's.

MILLICENT: Willie Kern.

ANN: How does he happen to drive a motor?

MILLICENT: Well, I don't know just how it happened—he's, so clever, you know, and of course he isn't really a chauffeur at all.

ANN: What is he then?

MILLICENT: Oh, Mother! He just happens to run the school motor.

ANN: And what did he do before that?

MILLICENT: Why he—ran another motor. Oh now, Mother, you don't understand at all!

[She breaks into sobs and throws herself full length on the couch. ANN *sits rigidly.]* Just because he's poor and clever and drives a motor is no reason why you should act this way. *[Sitting up.]*

He's going to do something else. He's going to come to New York to get a different position. And we'll be married as soon as he gets it, and that's why I came home—to tell you. So there—you see I can't go back to school. *[She rises and starts to the door.]*

ANN: Millicent! Come here.

MILLICENT: That's all there is to tell. I'm going to bed now.

ANN: *[rising]* You know this is the most wild and impossible thing in the world.

MILLICENT: I don't. It isn't impossible. I'm going to marry him. I love him better than you or Father or anybody in the world, and I'm going to marry him.

ANN: Stop! Do you want to disgrace us? How any child of mine could speak—even speak to such a—Oh, the disappointment! Where's your pride? How could you? How could you? Millicent, if you'll promise me to give this up, I won't say a word to your father.

MILLICENT: No—no—I'm going.

ANN: Don't unlock that door!

MILLICENT: I want to go now.

ANN: You'll never see this boy again. Never speak to him—never write to him—never hear of him. I shall send you away where he'll never know—

MILLICENT: *[coming back to couch]* You won't! He loves me and I love him. He understands me. All that vacation when you wouldn't let me come home, and all the other girls had gone, he was just as good to me as he could be. He knew how lonely I was, and he—we got engaged that vacation. You wouldn't let me come home.

ANN: Millicent—you don't know what you're saying. You don't know what you're saying.

MILLICENT: Oh yes, I do, Mother. It's you that don't know. You don't understand.

ANN: *[kneeling before* MILLICENT*]* My darling—why—didn't you tell me this when you said you wanted to come home? Why didn't you tell me then?

[Sobbing, ANN *buries her face in* MILLICENT*'s lap.]*

MILLICENT: I would have told you—if you'd let me come home—but you wouldn't—and I was so lonely there without the girls and—we—we got engaged. You don't understand, Mother.

ANN: *[lifting her face to* MILLICENT*]* Oh yes, I do, dear. Yes, I do. Tell me all about it. When did you first know him? How did you—happen to speak to him—I mean, to—to love him?

MILLICENT: Oh, Mother, why I—he—I just did—he's so handsome and so nice. You haven't any idea how nice he is, Mother.

ANN: Haven't I, dear? What is he like? Tell me everything—How did it begin?

MILLICENT: He—the first time I really knew he was so different, you know—

ANN: Yes, dear.

MILLICENT: Was one Sunday morning I was ready for church before anybody else, and I went out to get in the motor, and ran down the steps and fell, and he jumped out and picked me up and put me in the motor, and of course I thanked him, and we had to wait quite a while for the others, and I found out how different and truly wonderful he was. All the girls were crazy about him. Here's his picture. *[Drawing out a locket which is on a chain around her neck.]* It's just a little snapshot which I took myself one morning—and you really can't tell from this just how awfully good looking he is.

*[*ANN *seizes the locket and looks closely at the picture.]*

His eyes are the most wonderful—and his lashes are the longest I ever saw. You can't see his teeth and they are — well, you'd just love his teeth, Mother.

ANN: Would I, dear? Have you seen very much of him? Have you seen him anyplace besides in the motor, I mean? *[*MILLICENT *hesitates.]* Tell me, dear—everything. I shall understand.

MILLICENT: Well, of course, Mother—I had to see him someplace else after school began again and the girls were all back and I wasn't going for the mail anymore.

ANN: Of course; and where did you see him?

MILLICENT: Why, you see, it—it was awfully hard, Mummie, because I couldn't tell anybody. Nobody would have understood—except Fanny. She's such a dear. She's been so sympathetic through the whole thing, and she has helped me a lot. There is a fire escape out of our room, and Mondays and Thursdays at nine o'clock at night—

ANN: Oh—

MILLICENT: What, Mother?

ANN: Nothing—go on, dear.

MILLICENT: At exactly nine I'd put on Fanny's long black coat and go down, and he was always there and we always went down in the arbor just a little while.

ANN: The arbor? Where was the arbor?

MILLICENT: Down the path on the other side of the drive—not far from the house; but of course nobody went near it at that time of night—in cold weather and —and we'd talk a while and then I'd run back. You don't mind, do you, Mother? What else could I do?

ANN: And—he's kissed you—of course?

MILLICENT: Of course.

ANN: And you've kissed him?

MILLICENT: [lowering her eyes] Why yes—Mother—we're engaged.

ANN: And what did he say to you there in the arbor?

MILLICENT: I can't tell you everything he said, Mother.

ANN: Why not, Millicent? I'm your mother. No one on earth is so close to you—or loves you so much—or cares so much for your happiness—and understands so well. I remember when I was engaged to your father—I wasn't much older than you —I know, dear. Tell me what he said.

MILLICENT: He thinks I'm pretty, Mother.

ANN: Yes, dear.

MILLICENT: And he thinks I'm wonderful to understand him and to know what he really is in spite of what he happens to be doing.

ANN: Yes—and how long did you usually stay there in the arbor?

MILLICENT: Oh, not very long, only last time it was longer. He teased so and I couldn't help it. He—he—I—

ANN: How long was it that time?

MILLICENT: Oh—it—it was almost two hours last time.

ANN: And what did you do all that time? Wasn't it cold?

MILLICENT: He made me put on his overcoat—He just made me!

ANN: [holding MILLICENT close in her arms] And he held you close—and kissed you—and told you how much he loved you?

MILLICENT: Yes, I love him so—Mother—but—I—tonight, was the last night to go again—but I——

ANN: [holding MILLICENT off as she searches her face] Yes, dear?

MILLICENT: I—I was—afraid to go.

ANN: [shrieking] Why?

MILLICENT: Oh, Mother—Was it wicked to be afraid? I ran away—I wanted to be with you.

[ANN snatches MILLICENT in her arms. Her head falls against MILLICENT and MILLICENT's arms hold her close as she sobs. Someone tries the door and knocks.]

TOM: [in hall] Ann!—Ann!

ANN: Yes?

TOM: Why is the door locked?

ANN: Millicent and I are talking. Wait just a few minutes. And, Tom—tell her grandfather not to wait to see Millicent again tonight. She's all right.

TOM: Sure?

ANN: I'm sure.

MILLICENT: [in a whisper—after listening a moment] What are you going to tell Father?

ANN: [sitting on the floor] Well—you see, dear—you're too young to be married now—much too young—and—

MILLICENT: Oh now, Mother, if you're going to talk that way, wait till you see him.

ANN: That's just what I want to do. I've got such a lovely plan for us—for the summer.

MILLICENT: But I want to be married as soon as he gets his—

ANN: I know—his position—and while he's looking and getting settled, you and I will go abroad.

MILLICENT: You're awfully good, Mother, but if you really want to do something for me—I'd rather you'd give me that money to be married.

ANN: But, Millicent, my dear child—I have to go. I'm so tired. I've been working awfully hard this winter. You're the only one in the world who could really be with me and take care of me. I need you.

MILLICENT: Poor Mother! I don't want to be selfish and if you need me—I'll go.

ANN: [catching MILLICENT in her arms] Thank you, dear.

MILLICENT: If you'll promise me that I can be married when I get back.

ANN: [getting to her feet] If—you—still—want to—marry him when you come back with me—you may. I promise.

MILLICENT: Mother! I didn't know you loved me so much.

ANN: Didn't you, dear? Now, go to bed.

[They start to the door together. ANN catches MILLICENT again, kissing her tenderly as though she were something new and precious.]

MILLICENT: What's the matter, Mother?

ANN: Nothing, dear—Good night.

MILLICENT: Good night.

TOM: [coming into doorway as MILLICENT unlocks and opens the door] Not in bed yet?

MILLICENT: [throwing her arms about her father's neck] Oh, Dad! I'm so happy! [She goes out.]

ANN: [sitting at the fire] Come in, Tom. I want to talk to you about Millicent.

TOM: [closing the door and going to ANN] What's the matter?

ANN: She thinks she's in love.

TOM: What?

ANN: Our baby. She wants to be married.

TOM: What do you mean?

ANN: That's why she came home.

TOM: Good Heavens, Ann! Married? What has she got mixed up in? How did such a thing happen? How could it?

ANN: Because I didn't let her come home when she wanted to. Don't say anything, Tom. I can't bear it now.

TOM: [putting a hand on her head tenderly] Don't, dear! Don't! It—might have—happened—anyway.

ANN: Oh, the things that can happen!

TOM: Has she told you everything?

ANN: Everything.

TOM: What have you said to her? What are you going to do?

ANN: I'm going to take her away—and win her—till she gives up of her own free will—I shall have to have the wisdom of all the ages. I shall have to be more fascinating than the boy. That's a pretty big undertaking, Tom. I wonder if I'll be equal to it.

TOM: You mean you're going to give up your frieze and go away with her?

[ANN *nods her head.*]

You can't do it, Ann.

ANN: [*rising and moving away*] Oh yes, I can.

TOM: You cannot. Don't lose your head. You've pledged to finish it and deliver it at a certain time. You can't play fast and loose with a big piece of work like that.

ANN: You'll have to make my frieze, Tom.

TOM: I will not! I utterly and absolutely refuse to. You make Millicent behave and break this thing up and you go on with our—

ANN: I can't. I can't. She's been in danger—absolute danger.

TOM: How?

ANN: Oh, I'll tell you. I'll tell you. She ran away to me—to me—and I was pushing her off. My little girl! She's got to be held tight in my arms and carried through.

TOM: Ann, I'm not going to allow this to wipe out what you've done. I'll settle her—

ANN: Tom, you can't speak of it to her—not breathe it—

TOM: Of course I will.

ANN: No, you won't. If we cross her, she'll get at him some way—somehow.

TOM: I'm not going to let you sacrifice yourself for a way-ward—

ANN: It's my job. She is what I've given to life. If I fail her now—my whole life's a failure. Will you make my frieze, dear, will you?

TOM: No. It's yours. You've got to have the glory of it. Ann, I haven't been fair—but you're going to have this and all that's coming to you. I'm not going to let anything take it away from you. It's too important. My God, you've not only beaten me—you've won over the biggest men in the field—with your own brain and your own hands—in a fair, fine, hard fight. You're cut up now—but if you should give this thing up—there'll be times when you'd eat your heart out to be at work on it—when the artist in you will yell to be let out.

ANN: I know. I know. And I'll hate you because you're doing it—and I'll hate myself because I gave it up—and I'll almost—hate—her. I know. I know. You needn't tell me. Why I've seen my men and women up there—their strong limbs stretched—their hair blown back—I've seen the crowd looking up—I've heard people say—"A woman did that"—and my heart has almost burst with pride—not so much that I had done it—but for all women. And then the door opened—and Millicent came in. There isn't any choice, Tom—she's part of my body—part of my soul. Will you make my frieze, dear, will you? [*Falling against him.*]

TOM: [*taking her in his arms*] My darling! I'll do whatever makes it easiest for you. Don't think I don't know all—all—it means to you. My God, it's hard.

ANN: [*releasing herself and going to the hall door*] Put out the light. I hope she's asleep.

[*They go out into the lighted hall.*]

[*After a moment—*]

THE CURTAIN FALLS

The Piano Lesson

by August Wilson

Characters

BOY WILLY

BERNIECE: his sister

DOAKER: their uncle

WINING BOY: another uncle

LYMAN: a friend of Boy Willy's

AVERY: Berniece's boyfriend

BERNIECE'S DAUGHTER

THE TWO WOMEN

Setting

The action of the play takes place in the kitchen and parlor of the house where **DOAKER CHARLES** lives with his niece, **BERNIECE,** and her eleven-year-old daughter, **MARETHA.** The house is sparsely furnished, and although there is evidence of a woman's touch, there is a lack of warmth and vigor. **BERNIECE** and **MARETHA** occupy the upstairs rooms. **DOAKER'S** room is prominent and opens onto the kitchen. Dominating the parlor is an old upright piano. On the legs of the piano, carved in the manner of African sculpture, are mask-like figures resembling totems. The carvings are rendered with a grace and power of invention that lifts them out of the realm of craftsmanship and into the realm of art. At left is a stair-case leading to the upstairs.

ACT 1, SCENE 1

[The lights come up on the Charles household. It is five o'clock in the morning. The dawn is beginning to announce itself, but there is something in the air that belongs to the night. A stillness that is a portent, a gathering, a coming together of something akin to a storm. There is a loud knock at the door.]

BOY WILLIE: *[Off stage, calling.]* Hey, Doaker...Doaker! *[He knocks again and calls.]*

Hey, Doaker! Hey, Berniece! Berniece!

[DOAKER enters from his room. He is a tall, thin man of forty-seven, with severe features, who has for all intents and purposes retired from the world though he works full-time as a railroad cook.]

DOAKER: Who is it?

BOY WILLIE: Open the door, nigger! It's me...Boy Willie!

DOAKER: Who?

BOY WILLIE: Boy Willie! Open the door!

[DOAKER opens the door and BOY WILLIE and LYMON enter. BOY WILLIE is thirty years old. He has an infectious grin and a boyishness that is apt for his name. He is brash and impulsive, talkative and somewhat crude in speech and manner. LYMON is twenty-nine. BOY WILLIE's partner, he talks little, and then with a straightforwardness that is often disarming.]

DOAKER: What you doing up here?

BOY WILLIE: I told you, Lymon. Lymon talking about you might be sleep. This is Lymon. You remember Lymon Jackson from down home? This my Uncle Doaker.

DOAKER: What you doing up here? I couldn't figure out who that was. I thought you was still down in Mississippi.

BOY WILLIE: Me and Lymon selling watermelons. We got a truck out there. Got a whole truckload of watermelons. We brought them up here to sell. Where's Berniece? *[Calls.]* Hey, Berniece!

DOAKER: Berniece up there sleep.

BOY WILLIE: Well, let her get up. *[Calls.]* Hey, Berniece!

DOAKER: She got to go to work in the morning.

BOY WILLIE: Well she can get up and say hi. It's been three years since I seen her.

[Calls.] Hey, Berniece! It's me...Boy Willie.

DOAKER: Berniece don't like all that hollering now. She got to work in the morning.

BOY WILLIE: She can go on back to bed. Me and Lymon been riding two days in that truck...the least she can do is get up and say hi.

DOAKER: *[Looking out the window.]* Where you all get that truck from?

BOY WILLIE: It's Lymon's. I told him let's get a load of watermelons and bring them up here.

LYMON: Boy Willie say he going back, but I'm gonna stay. See what it's like up here.

BOY WILLIE: You gonna carry me down there first.

LYMON: I told you I ain't going back down there and take a chance on that truck breaking down again. You can take the train. Hey, tell him Doaker, he can take the train back. After we sell them watermelons he have enough money he can buy him a whole railroad car.

DOAKER: You got all them watermelons stacked up there no wonder the truck broke down. I'm surprised you made it this far with a load like that. Where you break down at?

BOY WILLIE: We broke down three times! It took us two and a half days to get here. It's a good thing we picked them watermelons fresh.

LYMON: We broke down twice in West Virginia. The first time was just as soon as we got out of Sunflower. About forty miles out she broke down. We got it going and got all the way to West Virginia before she broke down again.

BOY WILLIE: We had to walk about five miles for some water.

LYMON: It got a hole in the radiator but it runs pretty good. You have to pump the brakes sometime before they catch. Boy Willie have his door open and be ready to jump when that happens.

BOY WILLIE: Lymon think that's funny. I told the nigger I give him ten dollars to get the brakes fixed. But he thinks that funny.

LYMON: They don't need fixing. All you got to do is pump them till they catch.

[BERNIECE enters on the stairs. Thirty-five years old, with an eleven-year-old daughter, she is still in mourning for her husband after three years.]

BERNIECE: What you doing all that hollering for?

BOY WILLIE: Hey, Berniece. Doaker said you was sleep. I said at least you could get up and say hi.

BERNIECE: It's five o'clock in the morning and you come in here with all this noise. You can't come like normal folks. You got to bring all that noise with you.

BOY WILLIE: Hell, I ain't done nothing but come in and say hi. I ain't got in the house good.

BERNIECE: That's what I'm talking about. You start all that hollering and carry on as soon as you hit the door.

BOY WILLIE: Aw hell, woman, I was glad to see Doaker. You ain't had to come down if you didn't want to. I come eighteen hundred miles to see my sister I figure she might want to get up and say hi. Other than that you can go back upstairs. What you got, Doaker? Where your bottle? Me and Lymon want a drink.

[To BERNIECE.]

This is Lymon. You remember Lymon Jackson from down home.

LYMON: How you doing, Berniece. You look just like I thought you looked.

BERNIECE: Why you all got to come in hollering and carrying on? Waking the neighbors with all that noise.

BOY WILLIE: They can come over and join the party. We fixing to have a party. Doaker, where your bottle? Me and Lymon celebrating. The Ghosts of the Yellow Dog got Sutter.

BERNIECE: Say what?

Boy Willie: Ask Lymon, they found him the next morning. Say he drowned in his well.

Doaker: When this happen, Boy Willie?

Boy Willie: About three weeks ago. Me and Lymon was over in Stoner County when we heard about it. We laughed. We thought it was funny. A great big old three-hundred-and-forty-pound man gonna fall down his well.

Lymon: It remind me of Humpty Dumpty.

Boy Willie: Everybody say the Ghosts of the Yellow Dog pushed him.

Berniece: I don't want to hear that nonsense. Somebody down there pushing them people in their wells.

Doaker: What was you and Lymon doing over in Stoner County?

Boy Willie: We was down there working. Lymon got some people down there.

Lymon: My cousin got some land down there. We was helping him.

Boy Willie: Got near about a hundred acres. He got it set up real nice. Me and Lymon was down there chopping down trees. We was using Lymon's truck to haul the wood. Me and Lymon used to haul wood all around them parts.
[To **Berniece***.]*
Me and Lymon got a truckload of watermelons out there.
*[***Berniece*** crosses to the window to the parlor.]*
Doaker, where your bottle? I know you got a bottle stuck up in your room. Come on, me and Lymon want a drink.
*[***Doaker*** exits into his room.]*

Berniece: Where you all get that truck from?

Boy Willie: I told you it's Lymon's.

Berniece: Where you get the truck from, Lymon?

Lymon: I bought it.

Berniece: Where he get that truck from, Boy Willie?

Boy Willie: He told you he bought it. Bought it for a hundred and twenty dollars. I can't say where he got that hundred and twenty dollars from...but he bought that old piece of truck from Henry Porter. *[To* **Lymon***.]* Where you get that hundred and twenty dollars from, nigger?

Lymon: I got it like you get yours. I know how to take care of money.
*[***Doaker*** brings a bottle and sets it on the table.]*

Boy Willie: Aw hell, Doaker got some of that good whiskey. Don't give Lymon none of that. He ain't used to good whiskey. He liable to get sick.

Lymon: I done had good whiskey before.

Boy Willie: Lymon bought that truck so he have him a place to sleep. He down there wasn't doing no work or nothing. Sheriff looking for him. He bought that truck to keep away from the sheriff. Got Stovall looking for him too. He down there sleeping in that truck ducking and dodging both of them. I told him come on let's go up and see my sister.

Berniece: What the sheriff looking for you for, Lymon?

Boy Willie: The man don't want you to know all his business. He's my company. He ain't asking you no questions.

Lymon: It wasn't nothing. It was just a misunderstanding.

Berniece: He in my house. You say the sheriff looking for him, I wanna know what he looking for him for. Otherwise you all can go back out there and be where nobody don't have to ask you nothing.

Lymon: It was just a misunderstanding. Sometimes me and the sheriff we don't think alike. So we just got crossed on each other.

Berniece: Might be looking for him about that truck. He might have stole that truck.

Boy Willie: We ain't stole no truck, woman. I told you Lymon bought it.

Doaker: Boy Willie and Lymon got more sense than to ride all the way up here in a stolen truck with a load of watermelons. Now they might have stole them watermelons, but I don't believe they stole that truck.

Boy Willie: You don't even know the man good and you calling him a thief. And we ain't stole them watermelons either. Them old man Pitterford's watermelons. He give me and Lymon all we could load for ten dollars.

Doaker: No wonder you got them stacked up out there. You must have five hundred watermelons stacked up out there.

Berniece: Boy Willie, when you and Lymon planning on going back?

Boy Willie: Lymon say he staying. As soon as we sell them watermelons I'm going on back.

Berniece: *[Starts to exit up the stairs.]* That's what you need to do. And you need to do it quick. Come in here disrupting the house. I don't want all that loud carrying on around here. I'm surprised you ain't woke Maretha up.

Boy Willie: I was fixing to get her now. *[Calls.]* Hey, Maretha!

Doaker: Berniece don't like all that hollering now.

Berniece: Don't you wake that child up!

Boy Willie: You going up there...wake her up and tell her her uncle's here. I ain't seen her in three years. Wake her up and send her down here. She can go back to bed.

Berniece: I ain't waking that child up...and don't you be making all that noise. You and Lymon need to sell them watermelons and go on back.
*[***Berniece*** exits up the stairs.]*

Boy Willie: I see Berniece still try to be stuck up.

Doaker: Berniece alright. She don't want you making all that noise. Maretha up there sleep. Let her sleep until she get up. She can see you then.

Boy Willie: I ain't thinking about Berniece. You hear from Wining Boy? You know Cleotha died?

Doaker: Yeah, I heard that. He come by here about a year ago. Had a whole sack of money. He stayed here about two weeks. Ain't offered nothing. Berniece asked him for three dollars to buy some food and he got mad and left.

Lymon: Who's Wining Boy?

Boy Willie: That's my uncle. That's Doaker's brother. You heard me talk about Wining Boy. He play piano. He done made some records and everything. He still doing that, Doaker?

DOAKER: He made one or two records a long time ago. That's the only ones I ever known him to make. If you let him tell it he a big recording star.

BOY WILLIE: He stopped down home about two years ago. That's what I hear. I don't know. Me and Lymon was up on Parchman Farm doing them three years.

DOAKER: He don't never stay in one place. Now, he been here about eight months ago. Back in the winter. Now, you subject not to see him for another two years. It's liable to be that long before he stop by.

BOY WILLIE: If he had a whole sack of money you liable never to see him. You ain't gonna see him until he get broke. Just as soon as that sack of money is gone you look up and he be on your doorstep.

LYMON: *[Noticing the piano.]* Is that the piano?

BOY WILLIE: Yeah...look here, Lymon. See how it got all those carvings on it. See, that's what I was talking about. See how it's carved up real nice and polished and everything? You never find you another piano like that.

LYMON: Yeah, that look real nice.

BOY WILLIE: I told you. See how it's polished? My mama used to polish it every day. See all them pictures carved on it? That's what I was talking about. You can get a nice price for that piano.

LYMON: That's all Boy Willie talked about the whole trip up here. I got tired of hearing him talk about the piano.

BOY WILLIE: All you want to talk about is women. You ought to hear this nigger, Doaker. Talking about all the women he gonna get when he get up here. He ain't had none down there but he gonna get a hundred when he get up here.

DOAKER: How your people doing down there, Lymon?

LYMON: They alright. They still there. I come up here to see what it's like up here. Boy Willie trying to get me to go back and farm with him.

BOY WILLIE: Sutter's brother selling the land. He say he gonna sell it to me. That's why I come up here. I got one part of it. Sell them watermelons and get me another part. Get Berniece to sell that piano and I'll have the third part.

DOAKER: Berniece ain't gonna sell that piano.

BOY WILLIE: I'm gonna talk to her. When she see I got a chance to get Sutter's land she'll come around.

DOAKER: You can put that thought out your mind. Berniece ain't gonna sell that piano.

BOY WILLIE: I'm gonna talk to her. She been playing on it?

DOAKER: You know she won't touch that piano. I ain't never known her to touch it since Mama Ola died. That's over seven years now. She say it got blood on it. She got Maretha playing on it though. Say Maretha can go on and do everything she can't do. Got her in an extra school down at the Irene Kaufman Settlement House. She want Maretha to grow up and be a schoolteacher. Say she good enough she can teach on the piano.

BOY WILLIE: Maretha don't need to be playing on no piano. She can play on the guitar.

DOAKER: How much land Sutter got left?

BOY WILLIE: Got a hundred acres. Good land. He done sold it piece by piece, he kept the good part for himself. Now he got to give that up. His brother come down from Chicago for the funeral...he up there in Chicago got some kind of business with soda fountain equipment. He anxious to sell the land, Doaker. He don't want to be bothered with it. He called me to him and said cause of how long our families done known each other and how we been good friends and all, say he wanted to sell the land to me. Say he'd rather see me with it than Jim Stovall. Told me he'd let me have it for two thousand dollars cash money. He don't know I found out the most Stovall would give him for it was fifteen hundred dollars. He trying to get that extra five hundred out of me telling me he doing me a favor. I thanked him just as nice. Told him what a good man Sutter was and how he had my sympathy and all. Told him to give me two weeks. He said he'd wait on me. That's why I come up here. Sell them watermelons. Get Berniece to sell that piano. Put them two parts with the part I done saved. Walk in there. Tip my hat. Lay my money down on the table. Get my deed and walk on out. This time I get to keep all the cotton. Hire me some men to work it for me. Gin my cotton. Get my seed. And I'll see you again next year. Might even plant some tobacco or some oats.

DOAKER: You gonna have a hard time trying to get Berniece to sell that piano. You know Avery Brown from down there don't you? He up here now. He followed Berniece up here trying to get her to marry him after Crawley got killed. He been up here about two years. He call himself a preacher now.

BOY WILLIE: I know Avery. I know him from when he used to work on the Willshaw place. Lymon know him too.

DOAKER: He after Berniece to marry him. She keep telling him no but he won't give up. He keep pressing her on it.

BOY WILLIE: Avery think all white men is bigshots. He don't know there some white men ain't got as much as he got.

DOAKER: He supposed to come past here this morning. Berniece going down to the bank with him to see if he can get a loan to start his church. That's why I know Berniece ain't gonna sell that piano. He tried to get her to sell it to help him start his church. Sent the man around and everything.

BOY WILLIE: What man?

DOAKER: Some white fellow was going around to all the colored people's houses looking to buy up musical instruments. He'd buy anything. Drums. Guitars. Harmonicas. Pianos. Avery sent him past here. He looked at the piano and got excited. Offered her a nice price. She turned him down and got on Avery for sending him past. The man kept on her about two weeks. He seen where she wasn't gonna sell it, he gave her his number and told her if she ever wanted to sell it to call him first. Say he'd go one better than what anybody else would give her for it.

BOY WILLIE: How much he offer her for it?

DOAKER: Now you know me. She didn't say and I didn't ask. I just know it was a nice price.

LYMON: All you got to do is find out who he is and tell him somebody else wanna buy it from you. Tell him you can't make up your mind who to sell it to, and if he like Doaker say, he'll give you anything you want for it.

BOY WILLIE: That's what I'm gonna do. I'm gonna find out who he is from Avery.

DOAKER: It ain't gonna do you no good. Berniece ain't gonna sell that piano.

BOY WILLIE: She ain't got to sell it. I'm gonna sell it. I own just as much of it as she does.

BERNIECE: *[Offstage, hollers.]* Doaker! Go on get away. Doaker!

DOAKER: *[Calling.]* Berniece?

[DOAKER and BOY WILLIE rush to the stairs, BOY WILLIE runs up the stairs, passing BERNIECE as she enters, running.]

DOAKER: Berniece, what's the matter? You alright? What's the matter?

[BERNIECE tries to catch her breath. She is unable to speak.]

DOAKER: That's alright. Take your time. You alright. What's the matter?

[He calls.] Hey, Boy Willie?

BOY WILLIE: *[Offstage.]* Ain't nobody up here.

BERNIECE: Sutter...Sutter's standing at the top of the steps.

DOAKER: *[Calls.]* Boy Willie!

[LYMON crosses to the stairs and looks up. BOY WILLIE enters from the stairs.]

BOY WILLIE: Hey Doaker, what's wrong with her? Berniece, what's wrong? Who was you talking to?

DOAKER: She say she seen Sutter's ghost standing at the top of the stairs.

BOY WILLIE: Seen what? Sutter? She ain't seen no Sutter.

BERNIECE: He was standing right up there.

BOY WILLIE: *[Entering on the stairs.]* That's all in Berniece's head. Ain't nobody up there. Go on up there, Doaker.

DOAKER: I'll take your word for it. Berniece talking about what she seen. She say Sutter's ghost standing at the top of the steps. She ain't just make all that up.

BOY WILLIE: She up there dreaming. She ain't seen no ghost.

LYMON: You want a glass of water, Berniece? Get her a glass of water, Boy Willie.

BOY WILLIE: She don't need no water. She ain't seen nothing. Go on up there and look. Ain't nobody up there but Maretha.

DOAKER: Let Berniece tell it.

BOY WILLIE: I ain't stopping her from telling it.

DOAKER: What happened, Berniece?

BERNIECE: I come out my room to come back down here and Sutter was standing there in the hall.

BOY WILLIE: What he look like?

BERNIECE: He look like Sutter. He look like he always look.

BOY WILLIE: Sutter couldn't find his way from Big Sandy to Little Sandy. How he gonna find his way all the way up here to Pittsburgh? Sutter ain't never even heard of Pittsburgh.

DOAKER: Go on, Berniece.

BERNIECE: Just standing there with the blue suit on.

BOY WILLIE: The man ain't never left Marlin County when he was living...and he's gonna come all the way up here now that he's dead?

DOAKER: Let her finish. I want to hear what she got to say.

BOY WILLIE: I'll tell you this. If Berniece had seen him like she think she seen him she'd still be running.

DOAKER: Go on, Berniece. Don't pay Boy Willie no mind.

BERNIECE: He was standing there...had his hand on top of his head. Look like he might have thought if he took his hand down his head might have fallen off.

LYMON: Did he have on a hat?

BERNIECE: Just had on that blue suit...I told him to go away and he just stood there looking at me...calling Boy Willie's name.

BOY WILLIE: What he calling my name for?

BERNIECE: I believe you pushed him in the well.

BOY WILLIE: Now what kind of sense that make? You telling me I'm gonna go out there and hide in the weeds with all them dogs and things he got around there...I'm gonna hide and wait till I catch him looking down his well just right...then I'm gonna run over and push him in. A great big old three-hundred-and-forty-pound man.

BERNIECE: Well, what he calling your name for?

BOY WILLIE: He bending over looking down his well, woman...how he know who pushed him? It could have been anybody. Where was you when Sutter fell in his well? Where was Doaker? Me and Lymon was over in Stoner County. Tell her, Lymon. The Ghosts of the Yellow Dog got Sutter. That's what happened to him.

BERNIECE: You can talk all that Ghosts of the Yellow Dog stuff if you want. I know better.

LYMON: The Ghosts of the Yellow Dog pushed him. That's what the people say. They found him in his well and all the people say it must be the Ghosts of the Yellow Dog. Just like all them other men.

BOY WILLIE: Come talking about he looking for me. What he come all the way up here for? If he looking for me all he got to do is wait. He could have saved himself a trip if he looking for me. That ain't nothing but in Berniece's head. Ain't no telling what she liable to come up with next.

BERNIECE: Boy Willie, I want you and Lymon to go ahead and leave my house. Just go on somewhere. You don't do nothing but bring trouble with you everywhere you go. If it wasn't for you Crawley would still be alive.

BOY WILLIE: Crawley what? I ain't had nothing to do with Crawley getting killed. Crawley three time seven. He had his own mind.

BERNIECE: Just go on and leave. Let Sutter go somewhere else looking for you.

BOY WILLIE: I'm leaving. Soon as we sell them watermelons. Other than that I ain't going nowhere. Hell, I just got here. Talking about Sutter looking for me. Sutter was looking for that piano. That's what he was looking for. He had to die to find out where that piano was at...If I was you I'd get rid of it. That's the way to get rid of Sutter's ghost. Get rid of that piano.

BERNIECE: I want you and Lymon to go on and take all this confusion out of my house!

BOY WILLIE: Hey, tell her, Doaker. What kind of sense that make? I told you, Lymon, as soon as Berniece see me she was gonna start something. Didn't I tell you that? Now she done made up that story about Sutter just so she could tell me to leave her house. Well, hell, I ain't going nowhere till I sell them watermelons.

BERNIECE: Well why don't you go out there and sell them! Sell them and go on back!

BOY WILLIE: We waiting till the people get up.

LYMON: Boy Willie say if you get out there too early and wake the people up they get mad at you and won't buy nothing from you.

DOAKER: You won't be waiting long. You done let the sun catch up with you. This the time everybody be getting up around here.

BERNIECE: Come on, Doaker, walk up here with me. Let me get Maretha up and get her started. I got to get ready myself. Boy Willie, just go on out there and sell them watermelons and you and Lymon leave my house.

[BERNIECE and DOAKER exit up the stairs.]

BOY WILLIE: *[Calling after them.]* If you see Sutter up there...tell him I'm down here waiting on him.

LYMON: What if she see him again?

BOY WILLIE: That's all in her head. There ain't no ghost up there.

[Calls.]

Hey, Doaker...I told you ain't nothing up there.

LYMON: I'm glad he didn't say he was looking for me.

BOY WILLIE: I wish I would see Sutter's ghost. Give me a chance to put a whupping on him.

LYMON: You ought to stay up here with me. You be down there working his land...he might come looking for you all the time.

BOY WILLIE: I ain't thinking about Sutter. And I ain't thinking about staying up here. You stay up here. I'm going back and get Sutter's land. You think you ain't got to work up here. You think this the land of milk and honey. But I ain't scared of work. I'm going back and farm every acre of that land.

[DOAKER enters from the stairs.]

I told you there ain't nothing up there, Doaker. Berniece dreaming all that.

DOAKER: I believe Berniece seen something. Berniece level-headed. She ain't just made all that up. She say Sutter had on a suit. I don't believe she ever seen Sutter in a suit. I believe that's what he was buried in, and that's what Berniece saw.

BOY WILLIE: Well, let her keep on seeing him then. As long as he don't mess with me.

[DOAKER starts to cook his breakfast.]

I heard about you, Doaker. They say you got all the women looking out for you down home. They be looking to see you coming. Say you got a different one every two weeks. Say they be fighting one another for you to stay with them.

[To LYMON.] Look at him, Lymon. He know it's true.

DOAKER: I ain't thinking about no women. They never get me tied up with them. After Coreen I ain't got no use for them. I stay up on Jack Slattery's place when I be down there. All them women want is somebody with a steady payday.

BOY WILLIE: That ain't what I hear. I hear every two weeks the women all put on their dresses and line up at the railroad station.

DOAKER: I don't get down there but once a month. I used to go down there every two weeks but they keep switching me around. They keep switching all the fellows around.

BOY WILLIE: Doaker can't turn that railroad loose. He was working the railroad when I was walking around crying for sugartit. My mama used to brag on him.

DOAKER: I'm cooking now, but I used to line track. I pieced together the Yellow Dog stitch by stitch. Rail by rail. Line track all up around there. I lined track all up around Sunflower and Clarksdale. Wining Boy worked with me. He helped put in some of that track. He'd work it for six months and quit. Go back to playing piano and gambling.

BOY WILLIE: How long you been with the railroad now?

DOAKER: Twenty-seven years. Now, I'll tell you something about the railroad. What I done learned after twenty-seven years. See, you got North. You got West. You look over here you got South. Over there you got East. Now, you can start from anywhere. Don't care where you at. You got to go one of them four ways. And whichever way you decide to go they got a railroad that will take you there. Now, that's something simple. You think anybody would be able to understand that. But you'd be surprised how many people trying to go North get on a train going West. They think the train's supposed to go where they going rather than where it's going.

Now, why people going? Their sister's sick. They leaving before they kill somebody...and they sitting across from somebody who's leaving to keep from getting killed. They leaving cause they can't get satisfied. They going to meet someone. I wish I had a dollar for every time that someone wasn't at the station to meet them. I done seen that a lot. In between the time they sent the telegram and the time the person get there...they done forgot all about them.

They got so many trains out there they have a hard time keeping them from running into each other. Got trains going every whichaway. Got people on all of them. Somebody going where somebody just left. If everybody stay in one place I believe this would be a better world. Now what I done learned after twenty-seven years of railroading is this...if the train stays on the track...it's going to get where it's going. It might not be where you going. If it ain't, then all you got to do is sit and wait cause the train's coming back to get you. The train don't never stop. It'll come back every time. Now I'll tell you another thing...

BOY WILLIE: What you cooking over there, Doaker? Me and Lymon's hungry.

DOAKER: Go on down there to Wylie and Kirkpatrick to Eddie's restaurant. Coffee cost a nickel and you can get two eggs, sausage, and grits for fifteen cents. He even give you a biscuit with it.

BOY WILLIE: That look good what you got. Give me a little piece of that grilled bread.

DOAKER: Here...go on take the whole piece.

BOY WILLIE: Here you go, Lymon…you want a piece?

[He gives **LYMON** *a piece of toast.* **MARETHA** *enters from the stairs.]*

BOY WILLIE: Hey, sugar. Come here and give me a hug. Come on give Uncle Boy Willie a hug. Don't be shy. Look at her, Doaker. She done got bigger. Ain't she got big?

DOAKER: Yeah, she getting up there.

BOY WILLIE: How you doing, sugar?

MARETHA: Fine.

BOY WILLIE: You was just a little old thing last time I seen you. You remember me, don't you? This your Uncle Boy Willie from down South. That there's Lymon. He my friend. We come up here to sell watermelons. You like watermelons?

*[*MARETHA *nods.]*

We got a whole truckload out front. You can have as many as you want. What you been doing?

MARETHA: Nothing.

BOY WILLIE: Don't be shy now. Look at you getting all big. How old is you?

MARETHA: Eleven. I'm gonna be twelve soon.

BOY WILLIE: You like it up here? You like the North?

MARETHA: It's alright.

BOY WILLIE: That there's Lymon. Did you say hi to Lymon?

MARETHA: Hi.

LYMON: How you doing? You look just like your mama. I remember you when you was wearing diapers.

BOY WILLIE: You gonna come down South and see me? Uncle Boy Willie gonna get him a farm. Gonna get a great big old farm. Come down there and I'll teach you how to ride a mule. Teach you how to kill a chicken, too.

MARETHA: I seen my mama do that.

BOY WILLIE: Ain't nothing to it. You just grab him by his neck and twist it. Get you a real good grip and then you just wring his neck and throw him in the pot. Cook him up. Then you got some good eating. What you like to eat? What kind of food you like?

MARETHA: I like everything…except I don't like no black-eyed peas.

BOY WILLIE: Uncle Doaker tell me your mama got you playing that piano. Come on play something for me.

*[*BOY WILLIE *crosses over to the piano followed by* **MARETHA***.]*
Show me what you can do. Come on now. Here…Uncle Boy Willie give you a dime…show me what you can do. Don't be bashful now. That dime say you can't be bashful.

*[*MARETHA *plays. It is something any beginner first learns.]*
Here, let me show you something. *[*BOY WILLIE *sits and plays a simple boogie-woogie.]*
See that? See what I'm doing? That's what you call the boogie-woogie. See now…you can get up and dance to that. That's how good it sound. It sound like you wanna dance. You can dance to that. It'll hold you up. Whatever kind of dance you wanna do you can dance to that right there. See that? See how it go? Ain't nothing to it. Go on you do it.

MARETHA: I got to read it on the paper.

BOY WILLIE: You don't need no paper. Go on. Do just like that there.

BERNIECE: Maretha! You get up here and get ready to go so you be on time. Ain't no need you trying to take advantage of company.

MARETHA: I got to go.

BOY WILLIE: Uncle Boy Willie gonna get you a guitar. Let Uncle Doaker teach you how to play that. You don't need to read no paper to play the guitar. Your mama told you about that piano? You know how them pictures got on there?

MARETHA: She say it just always been like that since she got it.

BOY WILLIE: You hear that, Doaker? And you sitting up here in the house with Berniece.

DOAKER: I ain't got nothing to do with that. I don't get in the way of Berniece's raising her.

BOY WILLIE: You tell your mama to tell you about that piano. You ask her how them pictures got on there. If she don't tell you I'll tell you.

BERNIECE: Maretha!

MARETHA: I got to get ready to go.

BOY WILLIE: She getting big, Doaker. You remember her, Lymon?

LYMON: She used to be real little.

[There is a knock on the door. **DOAKER** *goes to answer it.* **AVERY** *enters. Thirty-eight years old, honest and ambitious, he has taken to the city like a fish to water, finding in it opportunities for growth and advancement that did not exist for him in the rural South. He is dressed in a suit and tie with a gold cross around his neck. He carries a small Bible.]*

DOAKER: Hey, Avery, come on in. Berniece upstairs.

BOY WILLIE: Look at him…look at him…he don't know what to say. He wasn't expecting to see me.

AVERY: Hey, Boy Willie. What you doing up here?

BOY WILLIE: Look at him, Lymon.

AVERY: Is that Lymon? Lymon Jackson?

BOY WILLIE: Yeah, you know Lymon.

DOAKER: Berniece be ready in a minute, Avery.

BOY WILLIE: Doaker say you a preacher now. What…we supposed to call you Reverend? You used to be plain old Avery. When you get to be a preacher, nigger?

LYMON: Avery say he gonna be a preacher so he don't have to work.

BOY WILLIE: I remember when you was down there on the Willshaw place planting cotton. You wasn't thinking about no Reverend then.

AVERY: That must be your truck out there. I saw that truck with them watermelons, I was trying to figure out what it was doing in front of the house.

BOY WILLIE: Yeah, me and Lymon selling watermelons. That's Lymon's truck.

DOAKER: Berniece say you all going down to the bank.

AVERY: Yeah, they give me a half day off work. I got an appointment to talk to the bank about getting a loan to start my church.

BOY WILLIE: Lymon say preachers don't have to work. Where you working at, nigger?

DOAKER: Avery got him one of them good jobs. He working at one of them skyscrapers downtown.

AVERY: I'm working down there at the Gulf Building running an elevator. Got a pension and everything. They even give you a turkey on Thanksgiving.

LYMON: How you know the rope ain't gonna break? Ain't you scared the rope's gonna break?

AVERY: That's steel. They got steel cables hold it up. It take a whole lot of breaking to break that steel. Naw, I ain't worried about nothing like that. It ain't nothing but a little old elevator. Now, I wouldn't get in none of them airplanes. You couldn't pay me to do nothing like that.

LYMON: That be fun. I'd rather do that than ride in one of them elevators.

BOY WILLIE: How many of them watermelons you wanna buy?

AVERY: I thought you was gonna give me one seeing as how you got a whole truck full.

BOY WILLIE: You can get one, get two. I'll give you two for a dollar.

AVERY: I can't eat but one. How much are they?

BOY WILLIE: Aw, nigger, you know I'll give you a watermelon. Go on, take as many as you want. Just leave some for me and Lymon to sell.

AVERY: I don't want but one.

BOY WILLIE: How you get to be a preacher, Avery? I might want to be a preacher one day. Have everybody call me Reverend Boy Willie.

AVERY: It come to me in a dream. God called me and told me he wanted me to be a shepherd for his flock. That's what I'm gonna call my church…The Good Shepherd Church of God in Christ.

DOAKER: Tell him what you told me. Tell him about the three hobos.

AVERY: Boy Willie don't want to hear all that.

LYMON: I do. Lots a people say your dreams can come true.

AVERY: Naw. You don't want to hear all that.

DOAKER: Go on. I told him you was a preacher. He didn't want to believe me. Tell him about the three hobos.

AVERY: Well, it come to me in a dream. See…I was sitting out in this railroad yard watching the trains go by. The train stopped and these three hobos got off. They told me they had come from Nazareth and was on their way to Jerusalem. They had three candles. They gave me one and told me to light it…but to be careful that it didn't go out. Next thing I knew I was standing in front of this house. Something told me to go knock on the door. This old woman opened the door and said they had been waiting on me. Then she led me into this room. It was a big room and it was full of all kinds of different people. They looked like anybody else except they all had sheep heads and was making noise like sheep make. I heard somebody call my name. I looked around and there was these same three hobos. They told me to take off my clothes and they give me a blue robe with gold thread. They washed my feet and combed my hair. Then they showed me these three doors and told me to pick one.

I went through one of them doors and that flame leapt off that candle and it seemed like my whole head caught fire. I looked around and there was four or five other men standing there with these same blue robes on. Then we heard a voice tell us to look out across this valley. We looked out and saw the valley was full of wolves. The voice told us that these sheep people that I had seen in the other room had to go over to the other side of this valley and somebody had to take them. Then I heard another voice say, "Who shall I send?" Next thing I knew I said, "Here I am. Send me." That's when I met Jesus. He say, "If you go, I'll go with you." Something told me to say, "Come on. Let's go." That's when I woke up. My head still felt like it was on fire…but I had a peace about myself that was hard to explain. I knew right then that I had been filled with the Holy Ghost and called to be a servant of the Lord. It took me a while before I could accept that. But then a lot of little ways God showed me that it was true. So I became a preacher.

LYMON: I see why you gonna call it the Good Shepherd Church. You dreaming about them sheep people. I can see that easy.

BOY WILLIE: Doaker say you sent some white man past the house to look at that piano. Say he was going around to all the colored people's houses looking to buy up musical instruments.

AVERY: Yeah, but Berniece didn't want to sell that piano. After she told me about it…I could see why she didn't want to sell it.

BOY WILLIE: What's this man's name?

AVERY: Oh, that's a while back now. I done forgot his name. He give Berniece a card with his name and telephone number on it, but I believe she throwed it away.

[BERNIECE and MARETHA enter from the stairs.]

BERNIECE: Maretha, run back upstairs and get my pocketbook. And wipe that hair grease off your forehead. Go ahead, hurry up.

[MARETHA exits up the stairs.]

How you doing, Avery? You done got all dressed up. You look nice. Boy Willie, I thought you and Lymon was going to sell them watermelons.

BOY WILLIE: Lymon done got sleepy. We liable to get some sleep first.

LYMON: I ain't sleepy.

DOAKER: As many watermelons as you got stacked up on that truck out there, you ought to have been gone.

BOY WILLIE: We gonna go in a minute. We going.

BERNIECE: Doaker. I'm gonna stop down there on Logan Street. You want anything?

DOAKER: You can pick up some ham hocks if you going down there. See if you can get the smoked ones. If they ain't got that get the fresh ones. Don't get the ones that got all that fat under the skin. Look for the long ones. They nice and lean.

[He gives her a dollar.]

Don't get the short ones lessen they smoked. If you got to get the fresh ones make sure that they the long ones. If they ain't got them smoked then go ahead and get the short ones.

[Pause.]

You may as well get some turnip greens while you down there. I got some buttermilk...if you pick up some cornmeal I'll make me some cornbread and cook up them turnip greens.

*[*MARETHA *enters from the stairs.]*

MARETHA: We gonna take the streetcar?

BERNIECE: Me and Avery gonna drop you off at the settlement house. You mind them people down there. Don't be going down there showing your color. Boy Willie, I done told you what to do. I'll see you later, Doaker.

AVERY: I'll be seeing you again, Boy Willie.

BOY WILLIE: Hey, Berniece...what's the name of that man Avery sent past say he want to buy the piano?

BERNIECE: I knew it. I knew it when I first seen you. I knew you was up to something.

BOY WILLIE: Sutter's brother say he selling the land to me. He waiting on me now. Told me he'd give me two weeks. I got one part. Sell them watermelons get me another part. Then we can sell that piano and I'll have the third part.

BERNIECE: I ain't selling that piano, Boy Willie. If that's why you come up here you can just forget about it.

[To DOAKER.*]*

Doaker, I'll see you later. Boy Willie ain't nothing but a whole lot of mouth. I ain't paying him no mind. If he come up here thinking he gonna sell that piano then he done come up here for nothing.

*[*BERNIECE, AVERY, *and* MARETHA *exit the front door.]*

BOY WILLIE: Hey, Lymon! You ready to go sell these watermelons?

*[*BOY WILLIE *and* LYMON *start to exit. At the door* BOY WILLIE *turns to* DOAKER.*]*

Hey, Doaker...if Berniece don't want to sell that piano...I'm gonna cut it in half and go on and sell my half.

*[*BOY WILLIE *and* LYMON *exit.]*

[The lights go down on the scene.]

SCENE 2

[The lights come up on the kitchen. It is three days later. WINING BOY *sits at the kitchen table. There is a half-empty pint bottle on the table.* DOAKER *busies himself washing pots.* WINING BOY *is fifty-six years old.* DOAKER*'s older brother, he tries to present the image of a successful musician and gambler, but his music, his clothes, and even his manner of presentation are old. He is a man who looking back over his life continues to live it with an odd mixture of zest and sorrow.]*

WINING BOY: So the Ghosts of the Yellow Dog got Sutter. That just go to show you I believe I always lived right. They say every dog gonna have his day and time it go

around it sure come back to you. I done seen that a thousand times. I know the truth of that. But I'll tell you outright...if I see Sutter's ghost I'll be on the first thing I find that got wheels on it.

*[*DOAKER *enters from his room.]*

DOAKER: Wining Boy!

WINING BOY: And I'll tell you another thing...Berniece ain't gonna sell that piano.

DOAKER: That's what she told him. He say he gonna cut it in half and go on and sell his half. They been around here three days trying to sell them watermelons. They trying to get out to where the white folks live but the truck keep breaking down. They go a block or two and it break down again. They trying to get out to Squirrel Hill and can't get around the corner. He say soon as he can get that truck empty to where he can set the piano up in there he gonna take it out of here and go sell it.

WINING BOY: What about them boys Sutter got? How come they ain't farming that land?

DOAKER: One of them going to school. He left down there and come North to school. The other one ain't got as much sense as that frying pan over yonder. That is the dumbest white man I ever seen. He'd stand in the river and watch it rise till it drown him.

WINING BOY: Other than seeing Sutter's ghost how's Berniece doing?

DOAKER: She doing alright. She still got Crawley on her mind. He been dead three years but she still holding on to him. She need to go out here and let one of these fellows grab a whole handful of whatever she got. She act like it done got precious.

WINING BOY: They always told me any fish will bite if you got good bait.

DOAKER: She stuck up on it. She think it's better than she is. I believe she messing around with Avery. They got something going. He a preacher now. If you let him tell it the Holy Ghost sat on his head and heaven opened up with thunder and lightning and God was calling his name. Told him to go out and preach and tend to his flock. That's what he gonna call his church. The Good Shepherd Church.

WINING BOY: They had that joker down in Spear walking around talking about he Jesus Christ. He gonna live the life of Christ. Went through the Last Supper and everything. Rented him a mule on Palm Sunday and rode through the town. Did everything...talking about he Christ. He did everything until they got up to that crucifixion part. Got up to that part and told everybody to go home and quit pretending. He got up to the crucifixion part and changed his mind. Had a whole bunch of folks come down there to see him get nailed to the cross. I don't know who's the worse fool. Him or them. Had all them folks come down there...even carried the cross up this little hill. People standing around waiting to see him get nailed to the cross and he stop everything and preach a little sermon and told everybody to go home. Had enough nerve to tell them to come to church on Easter Sunday to celebrate his resurrection.

DOAKER: I'm surprised Avery ain't thought about that. He trying every little thing to get him a congregation together. They meeting over at his house till he get him a church.

WINING BOY: Ain't nothing wrong with being a preacher. You got the preacher on one hand and the gambler on the other. Sometimes there ain't too much difference in them.

DOAKER: How long you been in Kansas City?

WINING BOY: Since I left here. I got tied up with some old gal down there. [Pause.] You know Cleotha died.

DOAKER: Yeah, I heard that last time I was down there. I was sorry to hear that.

WINING BOY: One of her friends wrote and told me. I got the letter right here.

[He takes the letter out of his pocket.]

I was down in Kansas City and she wrote and told me Cleotha had died. Name of Willa Bryant. She say she know cousin Rupert.

[He opens the letter and reads.]

Dear Wining Boy: I am writing this letter to let you know Miss Cleotha Holman passed on Saturday the first of May she departed this world in the loving arms of her sister Miss Alberta Samuels. I know you would want to know this and am writing as a friend of Cleotha. There have been many hardships since last you seen her but she survived them all and to the end was a good woman whom I hope have God's grace and is in His Paradise. Your cousin Rupert Bates is my friend also and he give me your address and I pray this reaches you about Cleotha. Miss Willa Bryant. A friend.

[He folds the letter and returns it to his pocket.]

They was nailing her coffin shut by the time I heard about it. I never knew she was sick. I believe it was that yellow jaundice. That's what killed her mama.

DOAKER: Cleotha wasn't but forty-some.

WINING BOY: She was forty-six. I got ten years on her. I met her when she was sixteen. You remember I used to run around there. Couldn't nothing keep me still. Much as I loved Cleotha I loved to ramble. Couldn't nothing keep me still. We got married and we used to fight about it all the time. Then one day she asked me to leave. Told me she loved me before I left. Told me, Wining Boy, you got a home as long as I got mine.

And I believe in my heart I always felt that and that kept me safe.

DOAKER: Cleotha always did have a nice way about her.

WINING BOY: Man that woman was something. I used to thank the Lord. Many a night I sat up and looked out over my life. Said, well, I had Cleotha. When it didn't look like there was nothing else for me, I said, thank God, at least I had that. If ever I go anywhere in this life I done known a good woman. And that used to hold me till the next morning.

[Pause.]

What you got? Give me a little nip. I know you got something stuck up in your room.

DOAKER: I ain't seen you walk in here and put nothing on the table. You done sat there and drank up your whiskey. Now you talking about what you got.

WINING BOY: I got plenty money. Give me a little nip.

[DOAKER carries a glass into his room and returns with it half-filled. He sets it on the table in front of WINING BOY.]

WINING BOY: You hear from Coreen?

DOAKER: She up in New York. I let her go from my mind.

WINING BOY: She was something back then. She wasn't too pretty but she had a way of looking at you made you know there was a whole lot of woman there. You got married and snatched her out from under us and we all got mad at you.

DOAKER: She up in New York City. That's what I hear.

[The door opens and BOY WILLIE and LYMON enter.]

BOY WILLIE: Aw hell…look here! We was just talking about you. Doaker say you left out of here with a whole sack of money. I told him we wasn't going see you till you got broke.

WINING BOY: What you mean broke? I got a whole pocketful of money.

DOAKER: Did you all get that truck fixed?

BOY WILLIE: We got it running and got halfway out there on Centre and it broke down again. Lymon went out there and messed it up some more. Fellow told us we got to wait till tomorrow to get it fixed. Say he have it running like new. Lymon going back down there and sleep in the truck so the people don't take the watermelons.

LYMON: Lymon nothing. You go down there and sleep in it.

BOY WILLIE: You was sleeping in it down home, nigger! I don't know nothing about sleeping in no truck.

LYMON: I ain't sleeping in no truck.

BOY WILLIE: They can take all the watermelons. I don't care. Wining Boy, where you coming from? Where you been?

WINING BOY: I been down in Kansas City.

BOY WILLIE: You remember Lymon? Lymon Jackson.

WINING BOY: Yeah, I used to know his daddy.

BOY WILLIE: Doaker say you don't never leave no address with nobody. Say he got to depend on your whim. See when it strike you to pay a visit.

WINING BOY: I got four or five addresses.

BOY WILLIE: Doaker say Berniece asked you for three dollars and you got mad and left.

WINING BOY: Berniece try and rule over you too much for me. That's why I left. It wasn't about no three dollars.

BOY WILLIE: Where you getting all these sacks of money from? I need to be with you. Doaker say you had a whole sack of money…turn some of it loose.

WINING BOY: I was just fixing to ask you for five dollars.

BOY WILLIE: I ain't got no money. I'm trying to get some. Doaker tell you about Sutter? The Ghosts of the Yellow Dog got him about three weeks ago. Berniece done seen his ghost and everything. He right upstairs.

[Calls.] Hey Sutter! Wining Boy's here. Come on, get a drink!

WINING BOY: How many that make the Ghosts of the Yellow Dog done got?

BOY WILLIE: Must be about nine or ten, eleven or twelve. I don't know.

DOAKER: You got Ed Saunders. Howard Peterson. Charlie Webb.

WINING BOY: Robert Smith. That fellow that shot Becky's boy...say he was stealing peaches . . .

DOAKER: You talking about Bob Mallory.

BOY WILLIE: Berniece say she don't believe all that about the Ghosts of the Yellow Dog.

WINING BOY: She ain't got to believe. You go ask them white folks in Sunflower County if they believe. You go ask Sutter if he believe. I don't care if Berniece believe or not. I done been to where the Southern cross the Yellow Dog and called out their names. They talk back to you, too.

LYMON: What they sound like? The wind or something?

BOY WILLIE: You done been there for real, Wining Boy?

WINING BOY: Nineteen thirty. July of nineteen thirty I stood right there on that spot. It didn't look like nothing was going right in my life. I said everything can't go wrong all the time...let me go down there and call on the Ghosts of the Yellow Dog, see if they can help me. I went down there and right there where them two railroads cross each other...I stood right there on that spot and called out their names. They talk back to you, too.

LYMON: People say you can ask them questions. They talk to you like that?

WINING BOY: A lot of things you got to find out on your own. I can't say how they talked to nobody else. But to me it just filled me up in a strange sort of way to be standing there on that spot. I didn't want to leave. It felt like the longer I stood there the bigger I got. I seen the train coming and it seem like I was bigger than the train. I started not to move. But something told me to go ahead and get on out the way. The train passed and I started to go back up there and stand some more. But something told me not to do it. I walked away from there feeling like a king. Went on and had a stroke of luck that run on for three years. So I don't care if Berniece believe or not. Berniece ain't got to believe. I know cause I been there. Now Doaker'll tell you about the Ghosts of the Yellow Dog.

DOAKER: I don't try and talk that stuff with Berniece. Avery got her all tied up in that church. She just think it's a whole lot of nonsense.

BOY WILLIE: Berniece don't believe in nothing. She just think she believe. She believe in anything if it's convenient for her to believe. But when that convenience run out then she ain't got nothing to stand on.

WINING BOY: Let's not get on Berniece now. Doaker tell me you talking about selling that piano.

BOY WILLIE: Yeah...hey, Doaker, I got the name of that man Avery was talking about. The man what's fixing the truck gave me his name. Everybody know him. Say he buy up anything you can make music with. I got his name and his telephone number. Hey, Wining Boy, Sutter's brother say he selling the land to me. I got one part. Sell them watermelons get me the second part. Then...soon as I get them watermelons out that truck I'm gonna take and sell that piano and get the third part.

DOAKER: That land ain't worth nothing no more. The smart white man's up here in these cities. He cut the land loose and step back and watch you and the dumb white man argue over it.

WINING BOY: How you know Sutter's brother ain't sold it already? You talking about selling the piano and the man's liable to sold the land two or three times.

BOY WILLIE: He say he waiting on me. He say he give me two weeks. That's two weeks from Friday. Say if I ain't back by then he might gonna sell it to somebody else. He say he wanna see me with it.

WINING BOY: You know as well as I know the man gonna sell the land to the first one walk up and hand him the money.

BOY WILLIE: That's just who I'm gonna be. Look, you ain't gotta know he waiting on me. I know. Okay. I know what the man told me. Stovall already done tried to buy the land from him and he told him no. The man say he waiting on me...he waiting on me. Hey, Doaker...give me a drink. I see Wining Boy got his glass.

[DOAKER exits into his room.]

Wining Boy, what you doing in Kansas City? What they got down there?

LYMON: I hear they got some nice-looking women in Kansas City. I sure like to go down there and find out.

WINING BOY: Man, the women down there is something else.

[DOAKER enters with a bottle of whiskey. He sets it on the table with some glasses.]

DOAKER: You wanna sit up here and drink up my whiskey, leave a dollar on the table when you get up.

BOY WILLIE: You ain't doing nothing but showing your hospitality. I know we ain't got to pay for your hospitality.

WINING BOY: Doaker say they had you and Lymon down on the Parchman Farm. Had you on my old stomping grounds.

BOY WILLIE: Me and Lymon was down there hauling wood for Jim Miller and keeping us a little bit to sell. Some white fellows tried to run us off of it. That's when Crawley got killed. They put me and Lymon in the penitentiary.

LYMON: They ambushed us right there where that road dip down and around that bend in the creek. Crawley tried to fight them. Me and Boy Willie got away but the sheriff got us. Say we was stealing wood. They shot me in my stomach.

BOY WILLIE: They looking for Lymon down there now. They rounded him up and put him in jail for not working.

LYMON: Fined me a hundred dollars. Mr. Stovall come and paid my hundred dollars and the judge say I got to work for him to pay him back his hundred dollars. I told them I'd rather take my thirty days but they wouldn't let me do that.

BOY WILLIE: As soon as Stovall turned his back, Lymon was gone. He down there living in that truck dodging the sheriff and Stovall. He got both of them looking for him. So I brought him up here.

LYMON: I told Boy Willie I'm gonna stay up here. I ain't going back with him.

BOY WILLIE: Ain't nobody twisting your arm to make you go back. You can do what you want to do.

WINING BOY: I'll go back with you. I'm on my way down there. You gonna take the train? I'm gonna take the train.

LYMON: They treat you better up here.

BOY WILLIE: I ain't worried about nobody mistreating me. They treat you like you let them treat you. They mistreat me I mistreat them right back. Ain't no difference in me and the white man.

WINING BOY: Ain't no difference as far as how somebody supposed to treat you. I agree with that. But I'll tell you the difference between the colored man and the white man. Alright. Now you take and eat some berries. They taste real good to you. So you say I'm gonna go out and get me a whole pot of these berries and cook them up to make a pie or whatever. But you ain't looked to see them berries is sitting in the white fellow's yard. Ain't got no fence around them. You figure anybody want something they'd fence it in. Alright. Now the white man come along and say that's my land. Therefore everything that grow on it belong to me. He tell the sheriff, "I want you to put this nigger in jail as a warning to all the other niggers. Otherwise first thing you know these niggers have everything that belong to us."

BOY WILLIE: I'd come back at night and haul off his whole patch while he was sleep.

WINING BOY: Alright. Now Mr. So and So, he sell the land to you. And he come to you and say, "John, you own the land. It's all yours now. But them is my berries. And come time to pick them I'm gonna send my boys over. You got the land…but them berries, I'm gonna keep them. They mine." And he go and fix it with the law that them is his berries. Now that's the difference between the colored man and the white man. The colored man can't fix nothing with the law.

BOY WILLIE: I don't go by what the law say. The law's liable to say anything. I go by if it's right or not. It don't matter to me what the law say. I take and look at it for myself.

LYMON: That's why you gonna end up back down there on the Parchman Farm.

BOY WILLIE: I ain't thinking about no Parchman Farm. You liable to go back before me.

LYMON: They work you too hard down there. All that weeding and hoeing and chopping down trees. I didn't like all that.

WINING BOY: You ain't got to like your job on Parchman. Hey, tell him, Doaker, the only one got to like his job is the waterboy.

DOAKER: If he don't like his job he need to set that bucket down.

BOY WILLIE: That's what they told Lymon. They had Lymon on water and everybody got mad at him cause he was lazy.

LYMON: That water was heavy.

BOY WILLIE: They had Lymon down there singing:

[Sings.]

> O Lord Berta Berta O Lord gal oh-ah

> O Lord Berta Berta O Lord gal well

[LYMON and WINING BOY join in.]

> Go 'head marry don't you wait on me oh-ah
> Go 'head marry don't you wait on me well
> Might not want you when I go free oh-ah
> Might not want you when I go free well

BOY WILLIE: Come on, Doaker. Doaker know this one.

[As DOAKER joins in the men stamp and clap to keep time. They sing in harmony with great fervor and style.]

> O Lord Berta Berta O Lord gal oh-ah
> O Lord Berta Berta O Lord gal well
> Raise them up higher, let them drop on down oh-ah
> Raise them up higher, let them drop on down well
> Don't know the difference when the sun go down oh-ah
> Don't know the difference when the sun go down well
> Berta in Meridan and she living at ease oh-ah
> Berta in Meridan and she living at ease well
> I'm on old Parchman, got to work or leave oh-ah
> I'm on old Parchman, got to work or leave well
> O Alberta, Berta, O Lord gal oh-ah
> O Alberta, Berta, O Lord gal well
> When you marry, don't marry no farming man oh-ah
> When you marry, don't marry no farming man well
> Everyday Monday, hoe handle in your hand oh-ah
> Everyday Monday, hoe handle in your hand well
> When you marry, marry a railroad man, oh-ah
> When you marry, marry a railroad man, well
> Everyday Sunday, dollar in your hand oh-ah
> Everyday Sunday, dollar in your hand well
> O Alberta, Berta, O Lord gal oh-ah
> O Alberta, Berta, O Lord gal well

BOY WILLIE: Doaker like that part. He like that railroad part.

LYMON: Doaker sound like Tangleye. He can't sing a lick.

BOY WILLIE: Hey, Doaker, they still talk about you down on Parchman. They ask me, "You Doaker Boy's nephew?" I say, "Yeah, me and him is family." They treated me alright soon as I told them that. Say, "Yeah, he my uncle."

DOAKER: I don't never want to see none of them niggers no more.

BOY WILLIE: I don't want to see them either. Hey, Wining Boy, come on play some piano. You a piano player, play some piano. Lymon wanna hear you.

WINING BOY: I give that piano up. That was the best thing that ever happened to me, getting rid of that piano. That piano got so big and I'm carrying it around on my back. I don't wish that on nobody. See, you think it's all fun being a recording star. Got to carrying that piano around and man did I get slow. Got just like molasses. The world just slipping by me and I'm walking around with that piano. Alright. Now, there ain't but so many places you can go. Only so many road wide enough for you and that piano. And that piano get heavier and heavier. Go to a place and they find out you play piano, the first thing they want to do is give you a drink, find you a piano, and sit you right down. And that's where you gonna be for the next eight hours. They ain't gonna let you get up! Now, the first three or four years of that is fun. You can't get enough whiskey and you can't get enough women and you don't never get tired of playing that piano. But that only last so long. You look up one day and you hate the whiskey, and you hate the women, and you hate the piano. But that's all you got. You can't do nothing else. All you know how to do is play that piano. Now, who am I? Am I me? Or am I the piano player? Sometime it seem like the only thing to do is shoot the piano player cause he the cause of all the trouble I'm having.

DOAKER: What you gonna do when your troubles get like mine?

LYMON: If I knew how to play it, I'd play it. That's a nice piano.

BOY WILLIE: Whoever playing better play quick. Sutter's brother say he waiting on me. I sell them watermelons. Get Berniece to sell that piano. Put them two parts with the part I done saved…

WINING BOY: Berniece ain't gonna sell that piano. I don't see why you don't know that.

BOY WILLIE: What she gonna do with it? She ain't doing nothing but letting it sit up there and rot. That piano ain't doing nobody no good.

LYMON: That's a nice piano. If I had it I'd sell it. Unless I knew how to play like Wining Boy. You can get a nice price for that piano.

DOAKER: Now I'm gonna tell you something, Lymon don't know this…but I'm gonna tell you why me and Wining Boy say Berniece ain't gonna sell that piano.

BOY WILLIE: She ain't got to sell it! I'm gonna sell it! Berniece ain't got no more rights to that piano than I do.

DOAKER: I'm talking to the man…let me talk to the man. See, now…to understand why we say that…to understand about that piano…you got to go back to slavery time. See, our family was owned by a fellow named Robert Sutter. That was Sutter's grandfather. Alright. The piano was owned by a fellow named Joel Nolander. He was one of the Nolander brothers from down in Georgia. It was coming up on Sutter's wedding anniversary and he was looking to buy his wife…Miss Ophelia was her name…he was looking to buy her an anniversary present. Only thing with him…he ain't had no money. But he had some niggers. So he asked Mr. Nolander to see if maybe he could trade off some of his niggers for that piano. Told him he would give him one and a half niggers for it. That's the way he told him. Say he could have one full grown and one half grown. Mr. Nolander agreed only he say he had to pick them. He didn't want Sutter to give him just any old nigger. He say he wanted to have the pick of the litter. So Sutter lined up his niggers and Mr. Nolander looked them over and out of the whole bunch he picked my grandmother…her name was Berniece…same like Berniece…and he picked my daddy when he wasn't nothing but a little boy nine years old. They made the trade off and Miss Ophelia was so happy with that piano that it got to be just about all she would do was play on that piano.

WINING BOY: Just get up in the morning, get all dressed up and sit down and play on that piano.

DOAKER: Alright. Time go along. Time go along. Miss Ophelia got to missing my grandmother…the way she would cook and clean the house and talk to her and what not. And she missed having my daddy around the house to fetch things for her. So she asked to see if maybe she could trade back that piano and get her niggers back. Mr. Nolander said no. Said a deal was a deal. Him and Sutter had a big falling out about it and Miss Ophelia took sick to the bed. Wouldn't get out of the bed in the morning. She just lay there. The doctor said she was wasting away.

WINING BOY: That's when Sutter called our granddaddy up to the house.

DOAKER: Now, our granddaddy's name was Boy Willie. That's who Boy Willie's named after…only they called him Willie Boy. Now, he was a worker of wood. He could make you anything you wanted out of wood. He'd make you a desk. A table. A lamp. Anything you wanted. Them white fellows around there used to come up to Mr. Sutter and get him to make all kinds of things for them. Then they'd pay Mr. Sutter a nice price. See, everything my granddaddy made Mr. Sutter owned cause he owned him. That's why when Mr. Nolander offered to buy him to keep the family together Mr. Sutter wouldn't sell him. Told Mr. Nolander he didn't have enough money to buy him. Now…am I telling it right, Wining Boy?

WINING BOY: You telling it.

DOAKER: Sutter called him up to the house and told him to carve my grandmother and my daddy's picture on the piano for Miss Ophelia. And he took and carved this…*[*DOAKER *crosses over to the piano.]*
See that right there? That's my grandmother, Berniece. She looked just like that. And he put a picture of my daddy when he wasn't nothing but a little boy the way he remembered him. He made them up out of his memory. Only thing…he didn't stop there. He carved all this. He got a picture of his mama…Mama Esther…and his daddy, Boy Charles.

WINING BOY: That was the first Boy Charles.

DOAKER: Then he put on the side here all kinds of things. See that? That's when him and Mama Berniece got married. They called it jumping the broom. That's how you got married in them days. Then he got here when my daddy was born…and here he got Mama Esther's funeral…and down here he got Mr. Nolander taking Mama Berniece and my daddy away down to his place in Georgia. He got all kinds of things what happened with our family. When Mr. Sutter seen the piano with all them carvings on it he got mad. He didn't ask for all that. But see…there wasn't nothing he could do about it. When Miss Ophelia seen it…she got excited. Now she had her piano and her niggers too. She took back to playing it and played on it right up till the day she died. Alright…now see, our brother Boy Charles…that's Berniece and Boy Willie's daddy…he was the oldest of us three boys. He's dead now. But he would have been fifty-seven if he had lived. He died in 1911 when he was thirty-one years old. Boy Charles used to talk about that piano all the time. He never could get it off his mind.

Two or three months go by and he be talking about it again. He be talking about taking it out of Sutter's house. Say it was the story of our whole family and as long as Sutter had it,...he had us. Say we was still in slavery. Me and Wining Boy tried to talk him out of it but it wouldn't do any good. Soon as he quiet down about it he'd start up again. We seen where he wasn't gonna get it off his mind...so, on the Fourth of July, 1911...when Sutter was at the picnic what the county give every year...me and Wining Boy went on down there with him and took that piano out of Sutter's house. We put it on a wagon and me and Wining Boy carried it over into the next county with Mama Ola's people. Boy Charles decided to stay around there and wait until Sutter got home to make it look like business as usual.

Now, I don't know what happened when Sutter came home and found that piano gone. But somebody went up to Boy Charles's house and set it on fire. But he wasn't in there. He must have seen them coming cause he went down and caught the 3:57 Yellow Dog. He didn't know they was gonna come down and stop the train. Stopped the train and found Boy Charles in the boxcar with four of them hobos. Must have got mad when they couldn't find the piano cause they set the boxcar afire and killed everybody. Now, nobody know who done that. Some people say it was Sutter cause it was his piano. Some people say it was Sheriff Carter. Some people say it was Robert Smith and Ed Saunders. But don't nobody know for sure. It was about two months after that that Ed Saunders fell down his well. Just upped and fell down his well for no reason. People say it was the ghost of them men who burned up in the boxcar that pushed him in his well. They started calling them the Ghosts of the Yellow Dog. Now, that's how all that got started and that why we say Berniece ain't gonna sell that piano. Cause her daddy died over it.

BOY WILLIE: All that's in the past. If my daddy had seen where he could have traded that piano in for some land of his own, it wouldn't be sitting up here now. He spent his whole life farming on somebody else's land. I ain't gonna do that. See, he couldn't do no better. When he come along he ain't had nothing he could build on. His daddy ain't had nothing to give him. The only thing my daddy had to give me was that piano. And he died over giving me that. I ain't gonna let it sit up there and rot without trying to do something with it. If Berniece can't see that, then I'm gonna go ahead and sell my half. And you and Wining Boy know I'm right.

DOAKER: Ain't nobody said nothing about who's right and who's wrong. I was just telling the man about the piano. I was telling him why we say Berniece ain't gonna sell it.

LYMON: Yeah, I can see why you say that now. I told Boy Willie he ought to stay up here with me.

BOY WILLIE: You stay! I'm going back! That's what I'm gonna do with my life! Why I got to come up here and learn to do something I don't know how to do when I already know how to farm? You stay up here and make your own way if that's what you want to do. I'm going back and live my life the way I want to live it.

[WINING BOY gets up and crosses to the piano.]

WINING BOY: Let's see what we got here. I ain't played on this thing for a while.

DOAKER: You can stop telling that. You was playing on it the last time you was through here. We couldn't get you off of it. Go on and play something.

[WINING BOY sits down at the piano and plays and sings. The song is one which has put many dimes and quarters in his pocket, long ago, in dimly remembered towns and way stations. He plays badly, without hesitation, and sings in a forceful voice.]

WINING BOY: [Singing.]

I am a rambling gambling man
I gambled in many towns
I rambled this wide world over
I rambled this world around
I had my ups and downs in life
And bitter times I saw
But I never knew what misery was
Till I lit on old Arkansas.

I started out one morning
to meet that early train
He said, "You better work for me
I have some land to drain.
I'll give you fifty cents a day,
Your washing, board and all
And you shall be a different man
In the state of Arkansas."

I worked six months for the rascal
Joe Herrin was his name
He fed me old corn dodgers
They was hard as any rock
My tooth is all got loosened
And my knees begin to knock
That was the kind of hash I got
In the state of Arkansas.

Traveling man
I've traveled all around this world
Traveling man
I've traveled from land to land
Traveling man
I've traveled all around this world
Well it ain't no use
writing no news
I'm a traveling man.

[The door opens and BERNIECE enters with MARETHA.]

BERNIECE: Is that...Lord, I know that ain't Wining Boy sitting there.

WINING BOY: Hey, Berniece.

BERNIECE: You all had this planned. You and Boy Willie had this planned.

WINING BOY: I didn't know he was gonna be here. I'm on my way down home. I stopped by to see you and Doaker first.

DOAKER: I told the nigger he left out of here with that sack of money, we thought we might never see him again. Boy Willie say he wasn't gonna see him till he got broke. I looked up and seen him sitting on the doorstep asking for two dollars. Look at him laughing. He know it's the truth.

BERNIECE: Boy Willie, I didn't see that truck out there. I thought you was out selling watermelons.

BOY WILLIE: We done sold them all. Sold the truck too.

BERNIECE: I don't want to go through none of your stuff. I done told you to go back where you belong.

BOY WILLIE: I was just teasing you, woman. You can't take no teasing?

BERNIECE: Wining Boy, when you get here?

WINING BOY: A little while ago. I took the train from Kansas City.

BERNIECE: Let me go upstairs and change and then I'll cook you something to eat.

BOY WILLIE: You ain't cooked me nothing when I come.

BERNIECE: Boy Willie, go on and leave me alone. Come on, Maretha, get up here and change your clothes before you get them dirty.

[BERNIECE exits up the stairs, followed by MARETHA.]

WINING BOY: Maretha sure getting big, ain't she, Doaker. And just as pretty as she want to be. I didn't know Crawley had it in him.

[BOY WILLIE crosses to the piano.]

BOY WILLIE: Hey, Lymon…get up on the other side of this piano and let me see something.

WINING BOY: Boy Willie, what is you doing?

BOY WILLIE: I'm seeing how heavy this piano is. Get up over there, Lymon.

WINING BOY: Go on and leave that piano alone. You ain't taking that piano out of here and selling it.

BOY WILLIE: Just as soon as I get them watermelons out that truck.

WINING BOY: Well, I got something to say about that.

BOY WILLIE: This my daddy's piano.

WINING BOY: He ain't took it by himself. Me and Doaker helped him.

BOY WILLIE: He died by himself. Where was you and Doaker at then? Don't come telling me nothing about this piano. This is me and Berniece's piano. Am I right, Doaker?

DOAKER: Yeah, you right.

BOY WILLIE: Let's see if we can lift it up, Lymon. Get a good grip on it and pick it up on your end. Ready? Lift!

[As they start to move the piano, the sound of SUTTER's GHOST is heard. DOAKER is the only one to hear it. With difficulty they move the piano a little bit so it is out of place.]

BOY WILLIE: What you think?

LYMON: It's heavy…but you can move it. Only it ain't gonna be easy.

BOY WILLIE: It wasn't that heavy to me. Okay, let's put it back.

[The sound of SUTTER's GHOST is heard again. They all hear it as BERNIECE enters on the stairs.]

BERNIECE: Boy Willie…you gonna play around with me one too many times. And then God's gonna bless you and West is gonna dress you. Now set that piano back over there. I done told you a hundred times I ain't selling that piano.

BOY WILLIE: I'm trying to get me some land, woman. I need that piano to get me some money so I can buy Sutter's land.

BERNIECE: Money can't buy what that piano cost. You can't sell your soul for money. It won't go with the buyer. It'll shrivel and shrink to know that you ain't taken on to it. But it won't go with the buyer.

BOY WILLIE: I ain't talking about all that, woman. I ain't talking about selling my soul. I'm talking about trading that piece of wood for some land. Get something under your feet. Land the only thing God ain't making no more of. You can always get you another piano. I'm talking about some land. What you get something out the ground from. That's what I'm talking about. You can't do nothing with that piano but sit up there and look at it.

BERNIECE: That's just what I'm gonna do. Wining Boy, you want me to fry you some pork chops?

BOY WILLIE: Now, I'm gonna tell you the way I see it. The only thing that make that piano worth something is them carvings Papa Willie Boy put on there. That's what make it worth something. That was my great-granddaddy. Papa Boy Charles brought that piano into the house. Now, I'm supposed to build on what they left me. You can't do nothing with that piano sitting up here in the house. That's just like if I let them watermelons sit out there and rot. I'd be a fool. Alright now, if you say to me, Boy Willie, I'm using that piano. I give out lessons on it and that help me make my rent or whatever. Then that be something else. I'd have to go on and say, well, Berniece using that piano. She building on it. Let her go on and use it. I got to find another way to get Sutter's land. But Doaker say you ain't touched that piano the whole time it's been up here. So why you wanna stand in my way? See, you just looking at the sentimental value. See, that's good. That's alright. I take my hat off whenever somebody say my daddy's name. But I ain't gonna be no fool about no sentimental value. You can sit up here and look at the piano for the next hundred years and it's just gonna be a piano. You can't make more than that. Now I want to get Sutter's land with that piano. I get Sutter's land and I can go down and cash in the crop and get my seed. As long as I got the land and the seed then I'm alright. I can always get me a little something else. Cause that land give back to you. I can make me another crop and cash that in. I still got the land and the seed. But that piano don't put out nothing else. You ain't got nothing working for you. Now, the kind of man my daddy was he would have understood that. I'm sorry you can't see it that way. But that's why I'm gonna take that piano out of here and sell it.

BERNIECE: You ain't taking that piano out of my house. *[She crosses to the piano.]*

Look at this piano. Look at it. Mama Ola polished this piano with her tears for seventeen years. For seventeen years she rubbed on it till her hands bled. Then she rubbed the blood in…mixed it up with the rest of the blood on it. Every day that God breathed life into her body she rubbed and cleaned and polished and prayed over it. "Play something for me, Berniece. Play something for me, Berniece." Every day. "I cleaned it up for you, play something for me, Berniece." You always talking about your daddy but you ain't never stopped to look at what his foolishness cost your mama. Seventeen years' worth of cold nights and an empty bed. For what? For a piano? For a piece of wood? To get even with somebody? I look at you and you're all the same. You, Papa Boy Charles, Wining Boy, Doaker, Crawley…you're all alike. All this thieving and killing and thieving and killing. And what it ever lead to? More killing and more thieving. I ain't never seen it come to nothing. People getting burned up. People getting shot. People falling down their wells. It don't never stop.

DOAKER: Come on now, Berniece, ain't no need in getting upset.

BOY WILLIE: I done a little bit of stealing here and there, but I ain't never killed nobody. I can't be speaking for nobody else. You all got to speak for yourself, but I ain't never killed nobody.

BERNIECE: You killed Crawley just as sure as if you pulled the trigger.

BOY WILLIE: See, that's ignorant. That's downright foolish for you to say something like that. You ain't doing nothing but showing your ignorance. If the nigger was here I'd whup his ass for getting me and Lymon shot at.

BERNIECE: Crawley ain't knew about the wood.

BOY WILLIE: We told the man about the wood. Ask Lymon. He knew all about the wood. He seen we was sneaking it. Why else we gonna be out there at night? Don't come telling me Crawley ain't knew about the wood. Them fellows come up on us and Crawley tried to bully them. Me and Lymon seen the sheriff with them and give in. Wasn't no sense in getting killed over fifty dollars' worth of wood.

BERNIECE: Crawley ain't knew you stole that wood.

BOY WILLIE: We ain't stole no wood. Me and Lymon was hauling wood for Jim Miller and keeping us a little bit on the side. We dumped our little bit down there by the creek till we had enough to make a load. Some fellows seen us and we figured we better get it before they did. We come up there and got Crawley to help us load it. Figured we'd cut him in. Crawley trying to keep the wolf from his door…we was trying to help him.

LYMON: Me and Boy Willie told him about the wood. We told him some fellows might be trying to beat us to it. He say let me go back and get my thirty-eight. That's what caused all the trouble.

BOY WILLIE: If Crawley ain't had the gun he'd be alive today.

LYMON: We had it about half loaded when they come up on us. We seen the sheriff with them and we tried to get away. We ducked around near the bend in the creek…but they

was down there too. Boy Willie say let's give in. But Crawley pulled out his gun and started shooting. That's when they started shooting back.

BERNIECE: All I know is Crawley would be alive if you hadn't come up there and got him.

BOY WILLIE: I ain't had nothing to do with Crawley getting killed. That was his own fault.

BERNIECE: Crawley's dead and in the ground and you still walking around here eating. That's all I know. He went off to load some wood with you and ain't never come back.

BOY WILLIE: I told you, woman…I ain't had nothing to do with…

BERNIECE: He ain't here, is he? He ain't here! [*BERNIECE hits* **BOY WILLIE**.]

I said he ain't here. Is he?

[*BERNIECE continues to hit* **BOY WILLIE**, *who doesn't move to defend himself, other than back up and turning his head so that most of the blows fall on his chest and arms.*]

DOAKER: [*Grabbing* **BERNIECE**.] Come on, Berniece…let it go, it ain't his fault.

BERNIECE: He ain't here, is he? Is he?

BOY WILLIE: I told you I ain't responsible for Crawley.

BERNIECE: He ain't here.

BOY WILLIE: Come on now, Berniece…don't do this now. Doaker get her. I ain't had nothing to do with Crawley…

BERNIECE: You come up there and got him!

BOY WILLIE: I done told you now. Doaker, get her. I ain't playing.

DOAKER: Come on. Berniece.

[**MARETHA** *is heard screaming upstairs. It is a scream of stark terror.*]

MARETHA: Mama!…Mama!

[*The lights go down to black. End of Act 1.*]

ACT 2, SCENE 1

[*The lights come up on the kitchen. It is the following morning.* **DOAKER** *is ironing the pants to his uniform. He has a pot cooking on the stove at the same time. He is singing a song. The song provides him with the rhythm for his work and he moves about the kitchen with the ease born of many years as a railroad cook*]

DOAKER:
Gonna leave Jackson Mississippi
and go to Memphis
and double back to Jackson
Come on down to Hattiesburg
Change cars on the Y.D.
coming through the territory to
Meridian
and Meridian to Greenville
and Greenville to Memphis
I'm on my way and I know where

groom

Change cars on the Katy
Leaving Jackson
and going through Clarksdale
Hello Winona!
Courtland!
Bateville!
Como!
Senitobia!
Lewisberg!
Sunflower!
Glendora!
Sharkey!
And double back to Jackson
Hello Greenwood
I'm on my way Memphis
Clarksdale
Moorhead
Indianola
Can a highball pass through?
Highball on through sir
Grand Carson!
Thirty First Street Depot
Fourth Street Depot
Memphis!

[WINING BOY enters carrying a suit of clothes.]

DOAKER: I thought you took that suit to the pawnshop?

WINING BOY: I went down there and the man tell me the suit is too old. Look at this suit. This is one hundred percent silk! How a silk suit gonna get too old? I know what it was he just didn't want to give me five dollars for it. Best he wanna give me is three dollars. I figure a silk suit is worth five dollars all over the world. I wasn't gonna part with it for no three dollars so I brought it back.

DOAKER: They got another pawnshop up on Wylie.

WINING BOY: I carried it up there. He say he don't take no clothes. Only thing he take is guns and radios. Maybe a guitar or two. Where's Berniece?

DOAKER: Berniece still at work. Boy Willie went down there to meet Lymon this morning. I guess they got that truck fixed, they been out there all day and ain't come back yet. Maretha scared to sleep up there now. Berniece don't know, but I seen Sutter before she did.

WINING BOY: Say what?

DOAKER: About three weeks ago. I had just come back from down there. Sutter couldn't have been dead more than three days. He was sitting over there at the piano. I come out to go to work...and he was sitting right there. Had his hand on top of his head just like Berniece said. I believe he broke his neck when he fell in the well. I kept quiet about it. I didn't see no reason to upset Berniece.

WINING BOY: Did he say anything? Did he say he was looking for Boy Willie?

DOAKER: He was just sitting there. He ain't said nothing. I went on out the door and left him sitting there. I figure as long as he was on the other side of the room everything be alright. I don't know what I would have done if he had started walking toward me.

WINING BOY: Berniece say he was calling Boy Willie's name.

DOAKER: I ain't heard him say nothing. He was just sitting there when I seen him. But I don't believe Boy Willie pushed him in the well. Sutter here cause of that piano. I heard him playing on it one time. I thought it was Berniece but then she don't play that kind of music. I come out here and ain't seen nobody, but them piano keys was moving a mile a minute. Berniece need to go on and get rid of it. It ain't done nothing but cause trouble.

WINING BOY: I agree with Berniece. Boy Charles ain't took it to give it back. He took it cause he figure he had more right to it than Sutter did. If Sutter can't understand that...then that's just the way that go. Sutter dead and in the ground...don't care where his ghost is. He can hover around and play on the piano all he want. I want to see him carry it out the house. That's what I want to see. What time Berniece get home? I don't see how I let her get away from me this morning.

DOAKER: You up there sleep. Berniece leave out of here early in the morning. She out there in Squirrel Hill cleaning house for some bigshot down there at the steel mill. They don't like you to come late. You come late they won't give you your carfare. What kind of business you got with Berniece?

WINING BOY: My business. I ain't asked you what kind of business you got.

DOAKER: Berniece ain't got no money. If that's why you was trying to catch her. She having a hard enough time trying to get by as it is. If she go ahead and marry Avery...he working every day...she go ahead and marry him they could do alright for themselves. But as it stands she ain't got no money.

WINING BOY: Well, let me have five dollars.

DOAKER: I just give you a dollar before you left out of here. You ain't gonna take my five dollars out there and gamble and drink it up.

WINING BOY: Aw, nigger, give me five dollars. I'll give it back to you.

DOAKER: You wasn't looking to give me five dollars when you had that sack of money. You wasn't looking to throw nothing my way. Now you wanna come in here and borrow five dollars. If you going back with Boy Willie you need to be trying to figure out how you gonna get train fare.

WINING BOY: That's why I need the five dollars. If I had five dollars I could get me some money.

[DOAKER goes into his pocket.] Make it seven.

DOAKER: You take this five dollars...and you bring my money back here too.

[BOY WILLIE and LYMON enter. They are happy and excited. They have money in all of their pockets and are anxious to count it.]

DOAKER: How'd you do out there?

BOY WILLIE: They was lining up for them.

LYMON: Me and Boy Willie couldn't sell them fast enough. Time we got one sold we'd sell another.

BOY WILLIE: I seen what was happening and told Lymon to up the price on them.

LYMON: Boy Willie say charge them a quarter more. They didn't care. A couple of people give me a dollar and told me to keep the change.

BOY WILLIE: One fellow bought five. I say now what he gonna do with five watermelons? He can't eat them all. I sold him the five and asked him did he want to buy five more.

LYMON: I ain't never seen nobody snatch a dollar fast as Boy Willie.

BOY WILLIE: One lady asked me say, "Is they sweet?" I told her say, "Lady, where we grow these watermelons we put sugar in the ground." You know, she believed me. Talking about she had never heard of that before. Lymon was laughing his head off. I told her, "Oh, yeah, we put the sugar right in the ground with the seed." She say, "Well, give me another one." Them white folks is something else...ain't they, Lymon?

LYMON: Soon as you holler watermelons they come right out their door. Then they go and get their neighbors. Look like they having a contest to see who can buy the most.

WINING BOY: I got something for Lymon.

[WINING BOY goes to get his suit. BOY WILLIE and LYMON continue to count their money.]

BOY WILLIE: I know you got more than that. You ain't sold all them watermelons for that little bit of money.

LYMON: I'm still looking. That ain't all you got either. Where's all them quarters?

BOY WILLIE: You let me worry about the quarters. Just put the money on the table.

WINING BOY: *[Entering with his suit.]* Look here, Lymon...see this? Look at his eyes getting big. He ain't never seen a suit like this. This is one hundred percent silk. Go ahead...put it on. See if it fit you.

[LYMON tries the suit coat on.]

Look at that. Feel it. That's one hundred percent genuine silk. I got that in Chicago. You can't get clothes like that nowhere but New York and Chicago. You can't get clothes like that in Pittsburgh. These folks in Pittsburgh ain't never seen clothes like that.

LYMON: This is nice, feel real nice and smooth.

WINING BOY: That's a fifty-five-dollar suit. That's the kind of suit the bigshots wear. You need a pistol and a pocketful of money to wear that suit. I'll let you have it for three dollars. The women will fall out their windows they see you in a suit like that. Give me three dollars and go on and wear it down the street and get you a woman.

BOY WILLIE: That looks nice, Lymon. Put the pants on. Let me see it with the pants.

[LYMON begins to try on the pants.]

WINING BOY: Look at that...see how it fits you? Give me three dollars and go on and take it. Look at that, Doaker...don't he look nice?

DOAKER: Yeah...that's a nice suit.

WINING BOY: Got a shirt to go with it. Cost you an extra dollar. Four dollars you got the whole deal.

LYMON: How this look, Boy Willie?

BOY WILLIE: That look nice...if you like that kind of thing. I don't like them dress-up kind of clothes. If you like it, look real nice.

WINING BOY: That's the kind of suit you need for up here in the North.

LYMON: Four dollars for everything? The suit and the shirt?

WINING BOY: That's cheap. I should be charging you twenty dollars. I give you a break cause you a homeboy. That's the only way I let you have it for four dollars.

LYMON: *[Going into his pocket.]* Okay...here go the four dollars.

WINING BOY: You got some shoes? What size you wear?

LYMON: Size nine.

WINING BOY: That's what size I got! Size nine. I let you have them for three dollars.

LYMON: Where they at? Let me see them.

WINING BOY: They real nice shoes, too. Got a nice tip to them. Got pointy toe just like you want.

[WINING BOY goes to get his shoes.]

LYMON: Come on, Boy Willie, let's go out tonight. I wanna see what it looks like up here. Maybe we go to a picture show. Hey, Doaker, they got picture shows up here?

DOAKER: The Rhumba Theater. Right down there on Fullerton Street. Can't miss it. Got the speakers outside on the sidewalk. You can hear it a block away. Boy Willie know where it's at. *[DOAKER exits into his room.]*

LYMON: Let's go to the picture show, Boy Willie. Let's go find some women.

BOY WILLIE: Hey, Lymon, how many of them watermelons would you say we got left? We got just under a half a load...right?

LYMON: About that much. Maybe a little more.

BOY WILLIE: You think that piano will fit up in there?

LYMON: If we stack them watermelons you can sit it up in the front there.

BOY WILLIE: I'm gonna call that man tomorrow.

WINING BOY: *[Returns with his shoes.]* Here you go...size nine. Put them on. Cost you three dollars. That's a Florsheim shoe. That's the kind Staggerlee wore.

LYMON: *[Trying on the shoes.]* You sure these size nine?

WINING BOY: You can look at my feet and see we wear the same size. Man, you put on that suit and them shoes and you got something there. You ready for whatever's out there. But is they ready for you? With them shoes on you be the King of the Walk. Have everybody stop to look at your shoes. Wishing they had a pair. I'll give you a break. Go on and take them for two dollars. *[LYMON pays WINING BOY two dollars.]*

LYMON: Come on, Boy Willie...let's go find some women. I'm gonna go upstairs and get ready. I'll be ready to go in a minute. Ain't you gonna get dressed?

BOY WILLIE: I'm gonna wear what I got on. I ain't dressing up for these city niggers.

[LYMON exits up the stairs.]

That's all Lymon think about is women.

WINING BOY: His daddy was the same way. I used to run around with him. I know his mama too. Two strokes back and I would have been his daddy! His daddy's dead now...but I got the nigger out of jail one time. They was fixing to name him Daniel and walk him through the Lion's Den. He got in a tussle with one of them white fellows and the sheriff lit on him like white on rice. That's how the whole thing come about between me and Lymon's mama. She knew me and his daddy used to run together and he got in jail and she went down there and took the sheriff a hundred dollars. Don't get me to lying about where she got it from. I don't know. The sheriff looked at that hundred dollars and turned his nose up. Told her, say, "That ain't gonna do him no good. You got to put another hundred on top of that." She come up there and got me where I was playing at this saloon...said she had all but fifty dollars and asked me if I could help. Now the way I figured it...without that fifty dollars the sheriff was gonna turn him over to Parchman. The sheriff turn him over to Parchman it be three years before anybody see him again. Now I'm gonna say it right...I will give anybody fifty dollars to keep them out of jail for three years. I give her the fifty dollars and she told me to come over to the house. I ain't asked her. I figure if she was nice enough to invite me I ought to go. I ain't had to say a word. She invited me over just as nice. Say, "Why don't you come over to the house?" She ain't had to say nothing else. Them words rolled off her tongue just as nice. I went on down there and sat about three hours. Started to leave and changed my mind. She grabbed hold to me and say, "Baby, it's all night long." That was one of the shortest nights I have ever spent on this earth! I could have used another eight hours. Lymon's daddy didn't even say nothing to me when he got out. He just looked at me funny. He had a good notion something had happened between me an' her. L. D. Jackson. That was one bad-luck nigger. Got killed at some dance. Fellow walked in and shot him thinking he was somebody else.

[DOAKER enters from his room.]

Hey, Doaker, you remember L. D. Jackson?

DOAKER: That's Lymon's daddy. That was one bad-luck nigger.

BOY WILLIE: Look like you ready to railroad some.

DOAKER: Yeah, I got to make that run.

[LYMON enters from the stairs. He is dressed in his new suit and shoes, to which he has added a cheap straw hat.]

LYMON: How I look?

WINING BOY: You look like a million dollars. Don't he look good, Doaker? Come on, let's play some cards. You wanna play some cards?

BOY WILLIE: We ain't gonna play no cards with you. Me and Lymon gonna find some women. Hey, Lymon, don't play no cards with Wining Boy. He'll take all your money.

WINING BOY: *[To* LYMON.*]* You got a magic suit there. You can get you a woman easy with that suit...but you got to know the magic words. You know the magic words to get you a woman?

LYMON: I just talk to them to see if I like them and they like me.

WINING BOY: You just walk right up to them and say, "If you got the harbor I got the ship." If that don't work ask them if you can put them in your pocket. The first thing they gonna say is, "It's too small." That's when you look them dead in the eye and say, "Baby, ain't nothing small about me." If that don't work then you move on to another one. Am I telling him right, Doaker?

DOAKER: That man don't need you to tell him nothing about no women. These women these days ain't gonna fall for that kind of stuff. You got to buy them a present. That's what they looking for these days.

BOY WILLIE: Come on, I'm ready. You ready, Lymon? Come on, let's go find some women.

WINING BOY: Here, let me walk out with you. I wanna see the women fall out their window when they see Lymon.

[They all exit and the lights go down on the scene.]

SCENE 2

[The lights come up on the kitchen. It is late evening of the same day. BERNIECE *has set a tub for her bath in the kitchen. She is heating up water on the stove. There is a knock at the door.]*

BERNIECE: Who is it?

AVERY: It's me, Avery. *[*BERNIECE *opens the door and lets him in.]*

BERNIECE: Avery, come on in. I was just fixing to take my bath.

AVERY: Where Boy Willie? I see that truck out there almost empty. They done sold almost all them watermelons.

BERNIECE: They was gone when I come home. I don't know where they went off to. Boy Willie around here about to drive me crazy.

AVERY: They sell them watermelons...he'll be gone soon.

BERNIECE: What Mr. Cohen say about letting you have the place?

AVERY: He say he'll let me have it for thirty dollars a month. I talked him out of thirty-five and he say he'll let me have it for thirty.

BERNIECE: That's a nice spot next to Benny Diamond's store.

AVERY: Berniece...I be at home and I get to thinking you up here an' I'm down there. I get to thinking how that look to have a preacher that ain't married. It makes for a better congregation if the preacher was settled down and married.

BERNIECE: Avery...not now. I was fixing to take my bath.

AVERY: You know how I feel about you, Berniece. Now...I done got the place from Mr. Cohen. I get the money from the bank and I can fix it up real nice. They give me a ten cents a hour raise down there on the job...now Berniece, I ain't got much in the way of comforts. I got a hole in my pockets near about as far as money is concerned. I ain't never found no way through life to a woman I care about like I care about you. I need that. I need somebody on my bond side. I need a woman that fits in my hand.

BERNIECE: Avery, I ain't ready to get married now.

AVERY: You too young a woman to close up, Berniece.

BERNIECE: I ain't said nothing about closing up. I got a lot of woman left in me.

AVERY: Where's it at? When's the last time you looked at it?

BERNIECE: [Stunned by his remark.] That's a nasty thing to say. And you call yourself a preacher.

AVERY: Anytime I get anywhere near you...you push me away.

BERNIECE: I got enough on my hands with Maretha. I got enough people to love and take care of.

AVERY: Who you got to love you? Can't nobody get close enough to you. Doaker can't half say nothing to you. You jump all over Boy Willie. Who you got to love you, Berniece?

BERNIECE: You trying to tell me a woman can't be nothing without a man. But you alright, huh? You can just walk out of here without me—without a woman—and still be a man. That's alright. Ain't nobody gonna ask you, "Avery, who you got to love you?" That's alright for you. But everybody gonna be worried about Berniece. "How Berniece gonna take care of herself? How she gonna raise that child without a man? Wonder what she do with herself. How she gonna live like that?" Everybody got all kinds of questions for Berniece. Everybody telling me I can't be a woman unless I got a man. Well, you tell me, Avery—you know—how much woman am I?

AVERY: It wasn't me, Berniece. You can't blame me for nobody else. I'll own up to my own shortcomings. But you can't blame me for Crawley or nobody else.

BERNIECE: I ain't blaming nobody for nothing. I'm just stating the facts.

AVERY: How long you gonna carry Crawley with you, Berniece? It's been over three years. At some point you got to let go and go on. Life's got all kinds of twists and turns. That don't mean you stop living. That don't mean you cut yourself off from life. You can't go through life carrying Crawley's ghost with you. Crawley's been dead three years. Three years, Berniece.

BERNIECE: I know how long Crawley's been dead. You ain't got to tell me that. I just ain't ready to get married right now.

AVERY: What is you ready for, Berniece? You just gonna drift along from day to day. Life is more than making it from one day to another. You gonna look up one day and it's all gonna be past you. Life's gonna be gone out of your hands—there won't be enough to make nothing with. I'm standing here now, Berniece—but I don't know how much longer I'm gonna be standing here waiting on you.

BERNIECE: Avery, I told you...when you get your church we'll sit down and talk about this. I got too many other things to deal with right now. Boy Willie and the piano...and Sutter's ghost. I thought I might have been seeing things, but Maretha done seen Sutter's ghost, too.

AVERY: When this happen, Berniece?

BERNIECE: Right after I came home yesterday. Me and Boy Willie was arguing about the piano and Sutter's ghost was standing at the top of the stairs. Maretha scared to sleep up there now. Maybe if you bless the house he'll go away.

AVERY: I don't know, Berniece. I don't know if I should fool around with something like that.

BERNIECE: I can't have Maretha scared to go to sleep up there. Seem like if you bless the house he would go away.

AVERY: You might have to be a special kind of preacher to do something like that.

BERNIECE: I keep telling myself when Boy Willie leave he'll go on and leave with him. I believe Boy Willie pushed him in the well.

AVERY: That's been going on down there a long time. The Ghosts of the Yellow Dog been pushing people in their wells long before Boy Willie got grown.

BERNIECE: Somebody down there pushing them people in their wells. They ain't just upped and fell. Ain't no wind pushed nobody in their well.

AVERY: Oh, I don't know. God works in mysterious ways.

BERNIECE: He ain't pushed nobody in their wells.

AVERY: He caused it to happen. God is the Great Causer. He can do anything. He parted the Red Sea. He say I will smite my enemies. Reverend Thompson used to preach on the Ghosts of the Yellow Dog as the hand of God.

BERNIECE: I don't care who preached what. Somebody down there pushing them people in their wells. Somebody like Boy Willie. I can see him doing something like that. You ain't gonna tell me that Sutter just upped and fell in his well. I believe Boy Willie pushed him so he could get his land.

AVERY: What Doaker say about Boy Willie selling the piano?

BERNIECE: Doaker don't want no part of that piano. He ain't never wanted no part of it. He blames himself for not staying behind with Papa Boy Charles. He washed his hands of that piano a long time ago. He didn't want me to bring it up here—but I wasn't gonna leave it down there.

AVERY: Well, it seems to me somebody ought to be able to talk to Boy Willie.

BERNIECE: You can't talk to Boy Willie. He been that way all his life. Mama Ola had her hands full trying to talk to him. He don't listen to nobody. He just like my daddy. He get his mind fixed on something and can't nobody turn him from it.

AVERY: You ought to start a choir at the church. Maybe if he seen you was doing something with it—if you told him—you was gonna put it in my church—maybe he'd see it different. You ought to put it down in the church and start a choir. The Bible say "Make a joyful noise unto the Lord." Maybe if Boy Willie see you was doing something with it he'd see it different.

BERNIECE: I done told you I don't play on that piano. Ain't no need in you to keep talking this choir stuff. When my mama died I shut the top on that piano and I ain't never opened it since. I was only playing it for her. When my daddy died seem like all her life went into that piano. She used to have me playing on it...had Miss Eula come in and teach me…say when I played it she could hear my daddy talking to her. I used to think them pictures came alive and walked through the house. Sometime late at night I could hear my mama talking to them. I said that wasn't gonna happen to me. I don't play that piano cause I don't want to wake them spirits. They never be walking around in this house.

AVERY: You got to put all that behind you, Berniece.

BERNIECE: I got Maretha playing on it. She don't know nothing about it. Let her go on and be a schoolteacher or something. She don't have to carry all of that with her. She got a chance I didn't have. I ain't gonna burden her with that piano.

AVERY: You got to put all of that behind you, Berniece. That's the same thing like Crawley. Everybody got stones in their passway. You got to step over them or walk around them. You picking them up and carrying them with you. All you got to do is set them down by the side of the road. You ain't got to carry them with you. You can walk over there right now and play that piano. You can walk over there right now and God will walk over there with you. Right now you can set that sack of stones down by the side of the road and walk away from it. You don't have to carry it with you. You can do it right now. *[AVERY crosses over to the piano and raises the lid.]*

Come on, Berniece…set it down and walk away from it. Come on, play "Old Ship of Zion." Walk over here and claim it as an instrument of the Lord. You can walk over here right now and make it into a celebration.

[BERNIECE moves toward the piano.]

BERNIECE: Avery…I done told you I don't want to play that piano. Now or no other time.

AVERY: The Bible say, "The Lord is my refuge…and my strength!" With the strength of God you can put the past behind you, Berniece. With the strength of God you can do anything! God got a bright tomorrow. God don't ask what you done…God ask what you gonna do. The strength of God can move mountains! God's got a bright tomorrow for you…all you got to do is walk over here and claim it.

BERNIECE: Avery, just go on and let me finish my bath. I'll see you tomorrow.

AVERY: Okay, Berniece. I'm gonna go home. I'm gonna go home and read up on my Bible. And tomorrow…if the good Lord give me strength tomorrow…I'm gonna come by and bless the house…and show you the power of the Lord.

[AVERY crosses to the door.]

It's gonna be alright, Berniece. God say he will soothe the troubled waters. I'll come by tomorrow and bless the house.

[The lights go down to black.]

SCENE 3

*[Several hours later. The house is dark. **BERNIECE** has retired for the night. **BOY WILLIE** enters the darkened house with **GRACE**.]*

BOY WILLIE: Come on in. This my sister's house. My sister live here. Come on, I ain't gonna bite you.

GRACE: Put some light on. I can't see.

BOY WILLIE: You don't need to see nothing, baby. This here is all you need to see. All you need to do is see me. If you can't see me you can feel me in the dark. How's that, sugar? *[He attempts to kiss her.]*

GRACE: Go on now…wait!

BOY WILLIE: Just give me one little old kiss.

GRACE: *[Pushing him away.]* Come on, now. Where I'm gonna sleep at?

BOY WILLIE: We got to sleep out here on the couch. Come on, my sister don't mind. Lymon come back he just got to sleep on the floor. He run off with Dolly somewhere he better stay there. Come on, sugar.

GRACE: Wait now…you ain't told me nothing about no couch. I thought you had a bed. Both of us can't sleep on that little old couch.

BOY WILLIE: It don't make no difference. We can sleep on the floor. Let Lymon sleep on the couch.

GRACE: You ain't told me nothing about no couch.

BOY WILLIE: What difference it make? You just wanna be with me.

GRACE: I don't want to be with you on no couch. Ain't you got no bed?

BOY WILLIE: You don't need no bed, woman. My granddaddy used to take women on the backs of horses. What you need a bed for? You just want to be with me.

GRACE: You sure is country. I didn't know you was this country.

BOY WILLIE: There's a lot of things you don't know about me. Come on, let me show you what this country boy can do.

GRACE: Let's go to my place. I got a room with a bed if Leroy don't come back there.

BOY WILLIE: Who's Leroy? You ain't said nothing about no Leroy.

GRACE: He used to be my man. He ain't coming back. He gone off with some other gal.

BOY WILLIE: You let him have your key?

GRACE: He ain't coming back.

BOY WILLIE: Did you let him have your key?

GRACE: He got a key but he ain't coming back. He took off with some other gal.

BOY WILLIE: I don't wanna go nowhere he might come. Let's stay here. Come on, sugar. *[He pulls her over to the couch.]* Let me heist your hood and check your oil. See if your battery needs charged.

[He pulls her to him. They kiss and tug at each other's clothing. In their anxiety they knock over a lamp.]

BERNIECE: Who's that…Wining Boy?

BOY WILLIE: It's me...Boy Willie. Go on back to sleep. Everything's alright.

[*To* GRACE.]

That's my sister. Everything's alright, Berniece. Go on back to sleep.

BERNIECE: What you doing down there? What you done knocked over?

BOY WILLIE: It wasn't nothing. Everything's alright. Go on back to sleep.

[*To* GRACE.] That's my sister. We alright. She gone back to sleep.

[*They begin to kiss.* BERNIECE *enters from the stairs dressed in a nightgown. She cuts on the light.*]

BERNIECE: Boy Willie, what you doing down here?

BOY WILLIE: It was just that there lamp. It ain't broke. It's okay. Everything's alright. Go on back to bed.

BERNIECE: Boy Willie, I don't allow that in my house. You gonna have to take your company someplace else.

BOY WILLIE: It's alright. We ain't doing nothing. We just sitting here talking. This here is Grace. That's my sister Berniece.

BERNIECE: You know I don't allow that kind of stuff in my house.

BOY WILLIE: Allow what? We just sitting here talking.

BERNIECE: Well, your company gonna have to leave. Come back and talk in the morning.

BOY WILLIE: Go on back upstairs now.

BERNIECE: I got an eleven-year-old girl upstairs. I can't allow that around here.

BOY WILLIE: Ain't nobody said nothing about that. I told you we just talking.

GRACE: Come on...let's go to my place. Ain't nobody got to tell me to leave but once.

BOY WILLIE: You ain't got to be like that, Berniece.

BERNIECE: I'm sorry, Miss. But he know I don't allow that in here.

GRACE: You ain't got to tell me but once. I don't stay nowhere I ain't wanted.

BOY WILLIE: I don't know why you want to embarrass me in front of my company.

GRACE: Come on, take me home.

BERNIECE: Go on, Boy Willie. Just go on with your company.

[BOY WILLIE *and* GRACE *exit.* BERNIECE *puts the light on in the kitchen and puts on the teakettle. Presently there is a knock at the door.* BERNIECE *goes to answer it.* BERNIECE *opens the door.* LYMON *enters.*]

LYMON: How you doing, Berniece? I thought you'd be asleep. Boy Willie been back here?

BERNIECE: He just left out of here a minute ago.

LYMON: I went out to see a picture show and never got there. We always end up doing something else. I was with this woman she just wanted to drink up all my money. So I left her there and came back looking for Boy Willie.

BERNIECE: You just missed him. He just left out of here.

LYMON: They got some nice-looking women in this city. I'm gonna like it up here real good. I like seeing them with their dresses on. Got them high heels. I like that. Make them look like they real precious. Boy Willie met a real nice one today. I wish I had met her before he did.

BERNIECE: He come by here with some woman a little while ago. I told him to go on and take all that out of my house.

LYMON: What she look like, the woman he was with? Was she a brown-skinned woman about this high? Nice and healthy? Got nice hips on her?

BERNIECE: She had on a red dress.

LYMON: That's her! That's Grace. She real nice. Laugh a lot. Lot of fun to be with. She don't be trying to put on. Some of these woman act like they the Queen of Sheba. I don't like them kind. Grace ain't like that. She real nice with herself.

BERNIECE: I don't know what she was like. He come in here all drunk knocking over the lamp, and making all kind of noise. I told them to take that somewhere else. I can't really say what she was like.

LYMON: She real nice. I seen her before he did. I was trying not to act like I seen her. I wanted to look at her a while before I said something. She seen me when I come into the saloon. I tried to act like I didn't see her. Time I looked around Boy Willie was talking to her. She was talking to him kept looking at me. That's when her friend Dolly came. I asked her if she wanted to go to the picture show. She told me to buy her a drink while she thought about it. Next thing I knew she done had three drinks talking about she too tired to go. I bought her another drink, then I left. Boy Willie was gone and I thought he might have come back here. Doaker gone, huh? He say he had to make a trip.

BERNIECE: Yeah, he gone on his trip. This is when I can usually get me some peace and quiet, Maretha asleep.

LYMON: She look just like you. Got them big eyes. I remember her when she was in diapers.

BERNIECE: Time just keep on. It go on with or without you. She going on twelve.

LYMON: She sure is pretty. I like kids.

BERNIECE: Boy Willie say you staying...what you gonna do up here in this big city? You thought about that?

LYMON: They never get me back down there. The sheriff looking for me. All because they gonna try and make me work for somebody when I don't want to. They gonna try and make me work for Stovall when he don't pay nothing. It ain't like that up here. Up here you more or less do what you want to. I figure I find me a job and try to get set up and then see what the year brings. I tried to do that two or three times down there...but it never would work out. I was always in the wrong place.

BERNIECE: This ain't a bad city once you get to know your way around.

LYMON: Up here is different. I'm gonna get me a job unloading boxcars or something. One fellow told me say he know a place. I'm gonna go over there with him next week. Me and Boy Willie finish selling them watermelons I'll have enough money to hold me for a while. But I'm gonna go over there and see what kind of jobs they have.

BERNIECE: You shouldn't have too much trouble finding a job. It's all in how you present yourself. See now, Boy Willie couldn't get no job up here. Somebody hire him they got a pack of trouble on their hands. Soon as they find that out they fire him. He don't want to do nothing unless he do it his way.

LYMON: I know. I told him let's go to the picture show first and see if there was any women down there. They might get tired of sitting at home and walk down to the picture show. He say he wanna look around first. We never did get down there. We tried a couple of places and then we went to this saloon where he met Grace. I tried to meet her before he did but he beat me to her. We left Wining Boy sitting down there running his mouth. He told me if I wear this suit I'd find me a woman. He was almost right.

BERNIECE: You don't need to be out there in them saloons. Ain't no telling what you liable to run into out there.

This one liable to cut you as quick as that one shoot you. You don't need to be out there. You start out that fast life you can't keep it up. It makes you old quick. I don't know what them women out there be thinking about.

LYMON: Mostly they be lonely and looking for somebody to spend the night with them. Sometimes it matters who it is and sometimes it don't. I used to be the same way. Now it got to matter. That's why I'm here now. Dolly liable not to even recognize me if she sees me again. I don't like women like that. I like my women to be with me in a nice and easy way. That way we can both enjoy ourselves. The way I see it we the only two people like us in the world. We got to see how we fit together. A woman that don't want to take the time to do that I don't bother with. Used to. Used to bother with all of them. Then I woke up one time with this woman and I didn't know who she was. She was the prettiest woman I had ever seen in my life. I spent the whole night with her and didn't even know it. I had never taken the time to look at her. I guess she kinda knew I ain't never really looked at her. She must have known that cause she ain't wanted to see me no more. If she had wanted to see me I believe we might have got married. How come you ain't married? It seem like to me you would be married. I remember Avery from down home. I used to call him plain old Avery. Now he Reverend Avery. That's kinda funny about him becoming a preacher. I like when he told about how that come to him in a dream about them sheep people and them hobos. Nothing ever come to me in a dream like that. I just dream about women. Can't never seem to find the right one.

BERNIECE: She out there somewhere. You just got to get yourself ready to meet her. That's what I'm trying to do. Avery's alright. I ain't really got nobody in mind.

LYMON: I get me a job and a little place and get set up to where I can make a woman comfortable I might get married. Avery's nice. You ought to go ahead and get married. You be a preacher's wife you won't have to work. I hate living by myself. I didn't want to be no strain on my mama so I left home when I was about sixteen. Everything I tried seem like it just didn't work out. Now I'm trying this.

BERNIECE: You keep trying it'll work out for you.

LYMON: You ever go down there to the picture show?

BERNIECE: I don't go in for all that.

LYMON: Ain't nothing wrong with it. It ain't like gambling and sinning. I went to one down in Jackson once. It was fun.

BERNIECE: I just stay home most of the time. Take care of Maretha.

LYMON: It's getting kind of late. I don't know where Boy Willie went off to. He's liable not to come back. I'm gonna take off these shoes. My feet hurt. Was you in bed? I don't mean to be keeping you up.

BERNIECE: You ain't keeping me up. I couldn't sleep after that Boy Willie woke me up.

LYMON: You got on that nightgown. I likes women when they wear them fancy nightclothes and all. It makes their skin look real pretty.

BERNIECE: I got this at the five-and-ten-cents store. It ain't so fancy.

LYMON: I don't too often get to see a woman dressed like that.
[There is a long pause. LYMON *takes off his suit coat.]*
Well, I'm gonna sleep here on the couch. I'm supposed to sleep on the floor but I don't reckon Boy Willie's coming back tonight. Wining Boy sold me this suit. Told me it was a magic suit. I'm gonna put it on again tomorrow. Maybe it bring me a woman like he say.
[He goes into his coat pocket and takes out a small bottle of perfume.]
I almost forgot I had this. Some man sold me this for a dollar. Say it come from Paris. This is the same kind of perfume the Queen of France wear. That's what he told me. I don't know if it's true or not. I smelled it. It smelled good to me. Here…smell it see if you like it. I was gonna give it to Dolly. But I didn't like her too much.

BERNIECE: *[Takes the bottle.]* It smells nice.

LYMON: I was gonna give it to Dolly if she had went to the picture with me. Go on, you take it.

BERNIECE: I can't take it. Here…go on you keep it. You'll find somebody to give it to.

LYMON: I wanna give it to you. Make you smell nice.
[He takes the bottle and puts perfume behind BERNIECE'*s ear.]*
They tell me you supposed to put it right here behind your ear. Say if you put it there you smell nice all day.
*[*BERNIECE *stiffens at his touch.* LYMON *bends down to smell her.]*
There…you smell real good now.
[He kisses her neck.]
You smell real good for Lymon.
[He kisses her again. BERNIECE *returns the kiss, then breaks the embrace and crosses to the stairs. She turns and they look silently at each other.* LYMON *hands her the bottle of perfume.* BERNIECE *exits up the stairs.* LYMON *picks up his suit coat and strokes it lovingly with the full knowledge that it is indeed a magic suit. The lights go down on the scene.]*

SCENE 4

[It is late the next morning. The lights come up on the parlor. LYMON *is asleep on the sofa.* BOY WILLIE *enters the front door.]*

BOY WILLIE: Hey, Lymon! Lymon, come on get up.

LYMON: Leave me alone.

BOY WILLIE: Come on, get up, nigger! Wake up, Lymon.

LYMON: What you want?

BOY WILLIE: Come on, let's go. I done called the man about the piano.

LYMON: What piano?

BOY WILLIE: *[Dumps* LYMON *on the floor.]* Come on, get up!

LYMON: Why you leave, I looked around and you was gone.

BOY WILLIE: I come back here with Grace, then I went looking for you. I figured you'd be with Dolly.

LYMON: She just want to drink and spend up your money. I come on back here looking for you to see if you wanted to go to the picture show.

BOY WILLIE: I been up at Grace's house. Some nigger named Leroy come by but I had a chair up against the door. He got mad when he couldn't get in. He went off somewhere and I got out of there before he could come back. Berniece got mad when we came here.

LYMON: She say you was knocking over the lamp busting up the place.

BOY WILLIE: That was Grace doing all that.

LYMON: Wining Boy seen Sutter's ghost last night.

BOY WILLIE: Wining Boy's liable to see anything. I'm surprised he found the right house. Come on, I done called the man about the piano.

LYMON: What he say?

BOY WILLIE: He say to bring it on out. I told him I was calling for my sister, Miss Berniece Charles. I told him some man wanted to buy it for eleven hundred dollars and asked him if he would go any better. He said yeah, he would give me eleven hundred and fifty dollars for it if it was the same piano. I described it to him again and he told me to bring it out.

LYMON: Why didn't you tell him to come and pick it up?

BOY WILLIE: I didn't want to have no problem with Berniece. This way we just take it on out there and it be out the way. He want to charge twenty-five dollars to pick it up.

LYMON: You should have told him the man was gonna give you twelve hundred for it.

BOY WILLIE: I figure I was taking a chance with that eleven hundred. If I had told him twelve hundred he might have run off. Now I wish I had told him twelve-fifty. It's hard to figure out white folks sometimes.

LYMON: You might have been able to tell him anything. White folks got a lot of money.

BOY WILLIE: Come on, let's get it loaded before Berniece come back. Get that end over there. All you got to do is pick it up on that side. Don't worry about this side. You wanna stretch you' back for a minute?

LYMON: I'm ready.

BOY WILLIE: Get a real good grip on it now.

[The sound of SUTTER'S GHOST *is heard. They do not hear it.]*

LYMON: I got this end. You get that end.

BOY WILLIE: Wait till I say ready now. Alright. You got it good? You got a grip on it?

LYMON: Yeah, I got it. You lift up on that end.

BOY WILLIE: Ready? Lift! *[The piano will not budge.]*

LYMON: Man, this piano is heavy! It's gonna take more than me and you to move this piano.

BOY WILLIE: We can do it. Come on—we did it before.

LYMON: Nigger—you crazy! That piano weighs five hundred pounds!

BOY WILLIE: I got three hundred pounds of it! I know you can carry two hundred pounds! You be lifting them cotton sacks! Come on lift this piano!

[They try to move the piano again without success.]

LYMON: It's stuck. Something holding it.

BOY WILLIE: How the piano gonna be stuck? We just moved it. Slide you' end out.

LYMON: Naw—we gonna need two or three more people. How this big old piano get in the house?

BOY WILLIE: I don't know how it got in the house. I know how it's going out though! You get on this end. I'll carry three hundred and fifty pounds of it. All you got to do is slide your end out. Ready?

[They switch sides and try again without success. DOAKER *enters from his room as they try to push and shove it.]*

LYMON: Hey, Doaker…how this piano get in the house?

DOAKER: Boy Willie, what you doing?

BOY WILLIE: I'm carrying this piano out the house. What it look like I'm doing? Come on, Lymon, let's try again.

DOAKER: Go on let the piano sit there till Berniece come home.

BOY WILLIE: You ain't got nothing to do with this, Doaker. This my business.

DOAKER: This is my house, nigger! I ain't gonna let you or nobody else carry nothing out of it. You ain't gonna carry nothing out of here without my permission!

BOY WILLIE: This is my piano. I don't need your permission to carry my belongings out of your house. This is mine. This ain't got nothing to do with you.

DOAKER: I say leave it over there till Berniece come home. She got part of it too. Leave it set there till you see what she say.

BOY WILLIE: I don't care what Berniece say. Come on, Lymon. I got this side.

DOAKER: Go on and cut it half in two if you want to. Just leave Berniece's half sitting over there. I can't tell you what to do with your piano. But I can't let you take her half out of here.

BOY WILLIE: Go on, Doaker. You ain't got nothing to do with this. I don't want you starting nothing now. Just go on and leave me alone. Come on, Lymon. I got this end. *[*DOAKER *goes into his room.* BOY WILLIE *and* LYMON *prepare to move the piano.]*

LYMON: How we gonna get it in the truck?

BOY WILLIE: Don't worry about how we gonna get it on the truck. You got to get it out the house first.

LYMON: It's gonna take more than me and you to move this piano.

BOY WILLIE: Just lift up on that end, nigger!

[DOAKER comes to the doorway of his room and stands.]

DOAKER: *[Quietly with authority.]* Leave that piano set over there till Berniece come back. I don't care what you do with it then. But you gonna leave it sit over there right now.

BOY WILLIE: Alright…I'm gonna tell you this, Doaker. I'm going out of here…I'm gonna get me some rope…find me a plank and some wheels…and I'm coming back. Then I'm gonna carry that piano out of here…sell it and give Berniece half the money. See…now that's what I'm gonna do. And you…or nobody else is gonna stop me. Come on, Lymon…let's go get some rope and stuff. I'll be back, Doaker.

[BOY WILLIE and LYMON exit. The lights go down on the scene.]

SCENE 5

[The lights come up. BOY WILLIE sits on the sofa, screwing casters on a wooden plank. MARETHA is sitting on the piano stool. DOAKER sits at the table playing solitaire.]

BOY WILLIE: *[To MARETHA.]* Then after that them white folks down around there started falling down their wells. You ever seen a well? A well got a wall around it. It's hard to fall down a well. You got to be leaning way over. Couldn't nobody figure out too much what was making these fellows fall down their well…so everybody says the Ghosts of the Yellow Dog must have pushed them. That's what everybody called them four men what got burned up in the boxcar.

MARETHA: Why they call them that?

BOY WILLIE: Cause the Yazoo Delta railroad got yellow boxcars. Sometime the way the whistle blow sound like an old dog howling so the people call it the Yellow Dog.

MARETHA: Anybody ever see the Ghosts?

BOY WILLIE: I told you they like the wind. Can you see the wind?

MARETHA: No.

BOY WILLIE: They like the wind you can't see them. But sometimes you be in trouble they might be around to help you. They say if you go where the Southern cross the Yellow Dog…you go to where them two railroads cross each other…and call out their names…they say they talk back to you. I don't know, I ain't never done that. But Uncle Wining Boy he say he been down there and talked to them. You have to ask him about that part. *[BERNIECE has entered from the front door.]*

BERNIECE: Maretha, you go on and get ready for me to do your hair.

[MARETHA crosses to the steps.]

Boy Willie, I done told you to leave my house. *[To MARETHA.]*

Go on, Maretha. *[MARETHA is hesitant about going up the stairs.]*

BOY WILLIE: Don't be scared. Here, I'll go up there with you. If we see Sutter's ghost I'll put a whupping on him. Come on, Uncle Boy Willie going with you.

[BOY WILLIE and MARETHA exit up the stairs.]

BERNIECE: Doaker—what is going on here?

DOAKER: I come home and him and Lymon was moving the piano. I told them to leave it over there till you got home. He went out and got that board and them wheels. He say he gonna take that piano out of here and ain't nobody gonna stop him.

BERNIECE: I ain't playing with Boy Willie. I got Crawley's gun upstairs. He don't know but I'm through with it. Where Lymon go?

DOAKER: Boy Willie sent him for some rope just before you come in.

BERNIECE: I ain't studying Boy Willie or Lymon—or the rope. Boy Willie ain't taking that piano out this house. That's all there is to it.

[BOY WILLIE and MARETHA enter on the stairs. MARETHA carries a hot comb and a can of hair grease. BOY WILLIE crosses over and continues to screw the wheels on the board.]

MARETHA: Mama, all the hair grease is gone. There ain't but this little bit left.

BERNIECE: *[Gives her a dollar.]* Here…run across the street and get another can. You come straight back, too. Don't you be playing around out there. And watch the cars. Be careful when you cross the street.

[MARETHA exits out the front door.] Boy Willie, I done told you to leave my house.

BOY WILLIE: I ain't in you' house. I'm in Doaker's house. If he ask me to leave then I'll go on and leave. But consider me done left your part.

BERNIECE: Doaker, tell him to leave. Tell him to go on.

DOAKER: Boy Willie ain't done nothing for me to put him out of the house. I told you if you can't get along just go on and don't have nothing to do with each other.

BOY WILLIE: I ain't thinking about Berniece.

[He gets up and draws a line across the floor with his foot.] There! Now I'm out of your part of the house. Consider me done left your part. Soon as Lymon come back with that rope, I'm gonna take that piano out of here and sell it.

BERNIECE: You ain't gonna touch that piano.

BOY WILLIE: Carry it out of here just as big and bold. Do like my daddy would have done come time to get Sutter's land.

BERNIECE: I got something to make you leave it over there.

BOY WILLIE: It's got to come better than this thirty-two-twenty.

DOAKER: Why don't you stop all that! Boy Willie, go on and leave her alone. You know how Berniece get. Why you wanna sit there and pick with her?

BOY WILLIE: I ain't picking with her. I told her the truth. She the one talking about what she got. I just told her what she better have.

BERNIECE: That's alright, Doaker. Leave him alone.

BOY WILLIE: She trying to scare me. Hell, I ain't scared of dying. I look around and see people dying every day. You got to die to make room for somebody else. I had a dog that died. Wasn't nothing but a puppy. I picked it up and put it in a bag and carried it up there to Reverend C. L. Thompson's church. I carried it up there and prayed and asked Jesus to make it live like he did the man in the Bible. I prayed real hard. Knelt down and everything. Say ask in Jesus' name. Well, I must have called Jesus' name two hundred times. I called his name till my mouth got sore. I got up and looked in the bag and the dog still dead. It ain't moved a muscle! I say, "Well, ain't nothing precious." And then I went out and killed me a cat. That's when I discovered the power of death. See, a nigger that ain't afraid to die is the worse kind of nigger for the white man. He can't hold that power over you. That's what I learned when I killed that cat. I got the power of death too. I can command him. I can call him up. The white man don't like to see that. He don't like for you to stand up and look him square in the eye and say, "I got it too." Then he got to deal with you square up.

BERNIECE: That's why I don't talk to him, Doaker. You try and talk to him and that's the only kind of stuff that comes out his mouth.

DOAKER: You say Avery went home to get his Bible?

BOY WILLIE: What Avery gonna do? Avery can't do nothing with me. I wish Avery would say something to me about this piano.

DOAKER: Berniece ain't said about that. Avery went home to get his Bible. He coming by to bless the house see if he can get rid of Sutter's ghost.

BOY WILLIE: Ain't nothing but a house full of ghosts down there at the church. What Avery look like chasing away somebody's ghost?

[MARETHA enters the front door.]

BERNIECE: Light that stove and set that comb over there to get hot. Get something to put around your shoulders.

BOY WILLIE: The Bible say an eye for an eye, a tooth for a tooth, and a life for a life. Tit for tat. But you and Avery don't want to believe that. You gonna pass up that part and pretend it ain't in there. Everything else you gonna agree with. But if you gonna agree with part of it you got to agree with all of it. You can't do nothing halfway. You gonna go at the Bible halfway. You gonna act like that part ain't in there. But you pull out the Bible and open it and see what it say. Ask Avery. He a preacher. He'll tell you it's in there. He the Good Shepherd. Unless he gonna shepherd you to heaven with half the Bible.

BERNIECE: Maretha, bring me that comb. Make sure it's hot.

[MARETHA brings the comb. BERNIECE begins to do her hair.]

BOY WILLIE: I will say this for Avery. He done figured out a path to go through life. I don't agree with it. But he done fixed it so he can go right through it real smooth. Hell, he

liable to end up with a million dollars that he done got from selling bread and wine.

MARETHA: OWWWWWW!

BERNIECE: Be still, Maretha. If you was a boy I wouldn't be going through this.

BOY WILLIE: Don't you tell that girl that. Why you wanna tell her that?

BERNIECE: You ain't got nothing to do with this child.

BOY WILLIE: Telling her you wished she was a boy. How's that gonna make her feel?

BERNIECE: Boy Willie, go on and leave me alone.

DOAKER: Why don't you leave her alone? What you got to pick with her for? Why don't you go on out and see what's out there in the streets? Have something to tell the fellows down home.

BOY WILLIE: I'm waiting on Lymon to get back with that truck. Why don't you go on out and see what's out there in the streets? You ain't got to work tomorrow. Talking about me…why don't you go out there? It's Friday night.

DOAKER: I got to stay around here and keep you all from killing one another.

BOY WILLIE: You ain't got to worry about me. I'm gonna be here just as long as it takes Lymon to get back here with that truck. You ought to be talking to Berniece. Sitting up there telling Maretha she wished she was a boy. What kind of thing is that to tell a child? If you want to tell her something tell her about that piano. You ain't even told her about that piano. Like that's something to be ashamed of. Like she supposed to go off and hide somewhere about that piano. You ought to mark down on the calendar the day that Papa Boy Charles brought that piano into the house. You ought to mark that day down and draw a circle around it…and every year when it come up throw a party. Have a celebration. If you did that she wouldn't have no problem in life. She could walk around here with her head held high. I'm talking about a big party!

Invite everybody! Mark that day down with a special meaning. That way she know where she at in the world. You got her going out here thinking she wrong in the world. Like there ain't no part of it belong to her.

BERNIECE: Let me take care of my child. When you get one of your own then you can teach it what you want to teach it.

[DOAKER exits into his room.]

BOY WILLIE: What I want to bring a child into this world for? Why I wanna bring somebody else into all this for? I'll tell you this…If I was Rockefeller I'd have forty or fifty. I'd make one every day. Cause they gonna start out in life with all the advantages. I ain't got no advantages to offer nobody. Many is the time I looked at my daddy and seen him staring off at his hands. I got a little older I know what he was thinking. He sitting there saying, "I got these big old hands but what I'm gonna do with them? Best I can do is make a fifty-acre crop for Mr. Stovall. Got these big old hands capable of doing anything. I can take and build something with these hands. But where's the tools? All I got is these hands. Unless I go out here and kill me somebody and take what they got…it's a long row to hoe for me to get something of my own. So what I'm gonna do with these big old hands? What would you do?"

See now…if he had his own land he wouldn't have felt that way. If he had something under his feet that belonged to him he could stand up taller. That's what I'm talking about. Hell, the land is there for everybody. All you got to do is figure out how to get you a piece. Ain't no mystery to life. You just got to go out and meet it square on. If you got a piece of land you'll find everything else fall right into place. You can stand right up next to the white man and talk about the price of cotton…the weather, and anything else you want to talk about. If you teach that girl that she living at the bottom of life, she's gonna grow up and hate you.

BERNIECE: I'm gonna teach her the truth. That's just where she living. Only she ain't got to stay there.

[To **MARETHA.***]* Turn you' head over to the other side.

BOY WILLIE: This might be your bottom but it ain't mine. I'm living at the top of life. I ain't gonna just take my life and throw it away at the bottom. I'm in the world like everybody else. The way I see it everybody else got to come up a little taste to be where I am.

BERNIECE: You right at the bottom with the rest of us.

BOY WILLIE: I'll tell you this…and ain't a living soul can put a come back on it. If you believe that's where you at then you gonna act that way. If you act that way then that's where you gonna be. It's as simple as that. Ain't no mystery to life. I don't know how you come to believe that stuff. Crawley didn't think like that. He wasn't living at the bottom of life. Papa Boy Charles and Mama Ola wasn't living at the bottom of life. You ain't never heard them say nothing like that. They would have taken a strap to you if they heard you say something like that.

[**DOAKER** *enters from his room.]*

Hey, Doaker…Berniece say the colored folks is living at the bottom of life. I tried to tell her if she think that…that's where she gonna be. You think you living at the bottom of life? Is that how you see yourself?

DOAKER: I'm just living the best way I know how. I ain't thinking about no top or no bottom.

BOY WILLIE: That's what I tried to tell Berniece. I don't know where she got that from. That sound like something Avery would say. Avery think cause the white man give him a turkey for Thanksgiving that makes him better than everybody else. That's gonna raise him out of the bottom of life. I don't need nobody to give me a turkey. I can get my own turkey. All you have to do is get out my way. I'll get me two or three turkeys.

BERNIECE: You can't even get a chicken let alone two or three turkeys. Talking about get out your way. Ain't nobody in your way.

[To **MARETHA.***]*

Straighten your head, Maretha! Don't be bending down like that. Hold your head up!

[To **BOY WILLIE.***]*

All you got going for you is talk. You' whole life that's all you ever had going for you.

BOY WILLIE: See now…I'll tell you something about me. I done strung along and strung along. Going this way and that. Whatever way would lead me to a moment of peace. That's all I want. To be as easy with everything. But I wasn't born to that. I was born to a time of fire.

The world ain't wanted no part of me. I could see that since I was about seven. The world say it's better off without me. See, Berniece accept that. She trying to come up to where she can prove something to the world.

Hell, the world a better place cause of me. I don't see it like Berniece. I got a heart that beats here and it beats just as loud as the next fellow's. Don't care if he black or white. Sometime it beats louder. When it beats louder, then everybody can hear it. Some people get scared of that. Like Berniece. Some people get scared to hear a nigger's heart beating. They think you ought to lay low with that heart. Make it beat quiet and go along with everything the way it is. But my mama ain't birthed me for nothing. So what I got to do? I got to mark my passing on the road. Just like you write on a tree, "Boy Willie was here."

That's all I'm trying to do with that piano. Trying to put my mark on the road. Like my daddy done. My heart say for me to sell that piano and get me some land so I can make a life for myself to live in my own way. Other than that I ain't thinking about nothing Berniece got to say.

[There is a knock at the door. **BOY WILLIE** *crosses to it and yanks it open thinking it is* **LYMON.** **AVERY** *enters. He carries a Bible.]*

BOY WILLIE: Where you been, nigger? Aw…I thought you was Lymon. Hey, Berniece, look who's here.

BERNIECE: Come on in, Avery. Don't you pay Boy Willie no mind.

BOY WILLIE: Hey…Hey, Avery…tell me this…can you get to heaven with half the Bible?

BERNIECE: Boy Willie…I done told you to leave me alone.

BOY WILLIE: I just ask the man a question. He can answer. He don't need you to speak for him. Avery…if you only believe on half the Bible and don't want to accept the other half…you think God let you in heaven? Or do you got to have the whole Bible? Tell Berniece…if you only believe in part of it…when you see God he gonna ask you why you ain't believed in the other part…then he gonna send you straight to Hell.

AVERY: You got to be born again. Jesus say unless a man be born again he cannot come unto the Father and who so ever heareth my words and believeth them not shall be cast into a fiery pit.

BOY WILLIE: That's what I was trying to tell Berniece. You got to believe in it all. You can't go at nothing halfway. She think she going to heaven with half the Bible.

[To **BERNIECE.***]* You hear that…Jesus say you got to believe in it all.

BERNIECE: You keep messing with me.

BOY WILLIE: I ain't thinking about you.

DOAKER: Come on in, Avery, and have a seat. Don't pay neither one of them no mind. They been arguing all day.

BERNIECE: Come on in, Avery.

AVERY: How's everybody in here?

BERNIECE: Here, set this comb back over there on that stove.

[To AVERY.]

Don't pay Boy Willie no mind. He been around here bothering me since I come home from work.

BOY WILLIE: Boy Willie ain't bothering you. Boy Willie ain't bothering nobody. I'm just waiting on Lymon to get back. I ain't thinking about you. You heard the man say I was right and you still don't want to believe it. You just wanna go and make up anythin'. Well there's Avery…there's the preacher…go on and ask him.

AVERY: Berniece believe in the Bible. She been baptized.

BOY WILLIE: What about that part that say an eye for an eye a tooth for a tooth and a life for a life? Ain't that in there?

DOAKER: What they say down there at the bank, Avery?

AVERY: Oh, they talked to me real nice. I told Berniece…they say maybe they let me borrow the money. They done talked to my boss down at work and everything.

DOAKER: That's what I told Berniece. You working every day you ought to be able to borrow some money.

AVERY: I'm getting more people in my congregation every day. Berniece says she gonna be the Deaconess. I get me my church I can get married and settled down. That's what I told Berniece.

DOAKER: That be nice. You all ought to go ahead and get married. Berniece don't need to be by herself. I tell her that all the time.

BERNIECE: I ain't said nothing about getting married. I said I was thinking about it.

DOAKER: Avery get him his church you all can make it nice.

[To AVERY.]

Berniece said you was coming by to bless the house.

AVERY: Yeah, I done read up on my Bible. She asked me to come by and see if I can get rid of Sutter's ghost.

BOY WILLIE: Ain't no ghost in this house. That's all in Berniece's head. Go on up there and see if you see him. I'll give you a hundred dollars if you see him. That's all in her imagination.

DOAKER: Well, let her find that out then. If Avery blessing the house is gonna make her feel better…what you got to do with it?

AVERY: Berniece say Maretha seen him too. I don't know, but I found a part in the Bible to bless the house. If he is here then that ought to make him go.

BOY WILLIE: You worse than Berniece believing all that stuff. Talking about…if he here. Go on up there and find out. I been up there I ain't seen him. If you reading from that Bible gonna make him leave out of Berniece imagination, well, you might be right. But if you talking about . . .

DOAKER: Boy Willie, why don't you just be quiet? Getting all up in the man's business. This ain't got nothing to do with you. Let him go ahead and do what he gonna do.

BOY WILLIE: I ain't stopping him. Avery ain't got no power to do nothing.

AVERY: Oh, I ain't got no power. God got the power! God got power over everything in His creation. God can do anything. God say, "As I commandeth so it shall be." God

said, "Let there be light," and there was light. He made the world in six days and rested on the seventh. God's got a wonderful power. He got power over life and death. Jesus raised Lazareth from the dead. They was getting ready to bury him and Jesus told him say, "Rise up and walk." He got up and walked and the people made great rejoicing at the power of God. I ain't worried about him chasing away a little old ghost!

[There is a knock at the door. BOY WILLIE goes to answer it. LYMON enters carrying a coil of rope.]

BOY WILLIE: Where you been? I been waiting on you and you run off somewhere.

LYMON: I ran into Grace. I stopped and bought her drink. She say she gonna go to the picture show with me.

BOY WILLIE: I ain't thinking about no Grace nothing.

LYMON: Hi, Berniece.

BOY WILLIE: Give me that rope and get up on this side of the piano.

DOAKER: Boy Willie, don't start nothing now. Leave the piano alone.

BOY WILLIE: Get that board there, Lymon. Stay out of this, Doaker.

[BERNIECE exits up the stairs.]

DOAKER: You just can't take the piano. How you gonna take the piano? Berniece ain't said nothing about selling that piano.

BOY WILLIE: She ain't got to say nothing. Come on, Lymon. We got to lift one end at a time up on the board. You got to watch so that the board don't slide up under there.

LYMON: What we gonna do with the rope?

BOY WILLIE: Let me worry about the rope. You just get up on this side over here with me.

[BERNIECE enters from the stairs. She has her hand in her pocket where she has Crawley's gun.]

AVERY: Boy Willie…Berniece…why don't you all sit down and talk this out now?

BERNIECE: Ain't nothing to talk out.

BOY WILLIE: I'm through talking to Berniece. You can talk to Berniece till you get blue in the face, and it don't make no difference. Get up on that side, Lymon. Throw that rope around there and tie it to the leg.

LYMON: Wait a minute…wait a minute, Boy Willie. Berniece got to say. Hey, Berniece…did you tell Boy Willie he could take this piano?

BERNIECE: Boy Willie ain't taking nothing out of my house but himself. Now you let him go ahead and try.

BOY WILLIE: Come on, Lymon, get up on this side with me.

[LYMON stands undecided.]

Come on, nigger! What you standing there for?

LYMON: Maybe Berniece is right, Boy Willie. Maybe you shouldn't sell it.

AVERY: You all ought to sit down and talk it out. See if you can come to an agreement.

DOAKER: That's what I been trying to tell them. Seem like one of them ought to respect the other one's wishes.

BERNIECE: I wish Boy Willie would go on and leave my house. That's what I wish. Now, he can respect that. Cause he's leaving here one way or another.

BOY WILLIE: What you mean one way or another? What's that supposed to mean? I ain't scared of no gun.

DOAKER: Come on, Berniece, leave him alone with that.

BOY WILLIE: I don't care what Berniece say. I'm selling my half. I can't help it if her half got to go along with it. It ain't like I'm trying to cheat her out of her half. Come on, Lymon.

LYMON: Berniece…I got to do this…Boy Willie say he gonna give you half of the money…say he want to get Sutter's land.

BERNIECE: Go on, Lymon. Just go on…I done told Boy Willie what to do.

BOY WILLIE: Here, Lymon…put that rope up over there.

LYMON: Boy Willie, you sure you want to do this? The way I figure it…I might be wrong…but I figure she gonna shoot you first.

BOY WILLIE: She just gonna have to shoot me.

BERNIECE: Maretha, get on out the way. Get her out the way, Doaker.

DOAKER: Go on, do what your mama told you.

BERNIECE: Put her in your room.

[MARETHA exits to Doaker's room. BOY WILLIE and LYMON try to lift the piano. The door opens and WINING BOY enters. He has been drinking.]

WINING BOY: Man, these niggers around here! I stopped down there at Seefus…. These folks standing around talking about Patchneck Red's coming. They jumping back and getting off the sidewalk talking about Patchneck Red this and Patchneck Red that. Come to find out…you know who they was talking about? Old John D. from up around Tyler! Used to run around with Otis Smith. He got everybody scared of him. Calling him Patchneck Red. They don't know I whupped the nigger's head in one time.

BOY WILLIE: Just make sure that board don't slide, Lymon.

LYMON: I got this side. You watch that side.

WINING BOY: Hey, Boy Willie, what you got? I know you got a pint stuck up in your coat.

BOY WILLIE: Wining Boy, get out the way!

WINING BOY: Hey, Doaker. What you got? Gimme a drink. I want a drink.

DOAKER: It look like you had enough of whatever it was. Come talking about "What you got?" You ought to be trying to find somewhere to lay down.

WINING BOY: I ain't worried about no place to lay down. I can always find me a place to lay down in Berniece's house. Ain't that right, Berniece?

BERNIECE: Wining Boy, sit down somewhere. You been out there drinking all day. Come in here smelling like an old polecat. Sit on down there, you don't need nothing to drink.

DOAKER: You know Berniece don't like all that drinking.

WINING BOY: I ain't disrespecting Berniece. Berniece, am I disrespecting you? I'm just trying to be nice. I been with strangers all day and they treated me like family. I come in here to family and you treat me like a stranger. I don't need your whiskey. I can buy my own. I wanted your company, not your whiskey.

DOAKER: Nigger, why don't you go upstairs and lay down? You don't need nothing to drink.

WINING BOY: I ain't thinking about no laying down. Me and Boy Willie fixing to party. Ain't that right, Boy Willie? Tell him. I'm fixing to play me some piano. Watch this.

[WINING BOY sits down at the piano.]

BOY WILLIE: Come on, Wining Boy! Me and Lymon fixing to move the piano.

WINING BOY: Wait a minute…wait a minute. This a song I wrote for Cleotha. I wrote this song in memory of Cleotha.

[He begins to play and sing.]

Hey little woman what's the matter with you now
Had a storm last night and blowed the line all down

Tell me how long
Is I got to wait
Can I get it now
Or must I hesitate

It takes a hesitating stocking in her hesitating shoe
It takes a hesitating woman wanna sing the blues

Tell me how long
Is I got to wait
Can I kiss you now
Or must I hesitate.

BOY WILLIE: Come on, Wining Boy, get up! Get up, Wining Boy! Me and Lymon's fixing to move the piano.

WINING BOY: Naw…Naw…you ain't gonna move this piano!

BOY WILLIE: Get out the way, Wining Boy.

[WINING BOY, his back to the piano, spreads his arms out over the piano.]

WINING BOY: You ain't taking this piano out the house. You got to take me with it!

BOY WILLIE: Get on out the way, Wining Boy! Doaker get him!

[There is a knock on the door.]

BERNIECE: I got him, Doaker. Come on, Wining Boy. I done told Boy Willie he ain't taking the piano.

[BERNIECE tries to take WINING BOY away from the piano.]

WINING BOY: He got to take me with it! [DOAKER goes to answer the door. GRACE enters.]

GRACE: Is Lymon here?

DOAKER: Lymon.

WINING BOY: He ain't taking that piano.

BERNIECE: I ain't gonna let him take it.

GRACE: I thought you was coming back. I ain't gonna sit in that truck all day.

LYMON: I told you I was coming back.

GRACE: [Sees BOY WILLIE.] Oh, hi, Boy Willie. Lymon told me you was gone back down South.

LYMON: I said he was going back. I didn't say he had left already.

GRACE: That's what you told me.

BERNIECE: Lymon, you got to take your company someplace else.

LYMON: Berniece, this is Grace. That there is Berniece. That's Boy Willie's sister.

GRACE: Nice to meet you. *[To* LYMON.*]*

I ain't gonna sit out in that truck all day. You told me you was gonna take me to the movie.

LYMON: I told you I had something to do first. You supposed to wait on me.

BERNIECE: Lymon, just go on and leave. Take Grace or whoever with you. Just go on get out my house.

BOY WILLIE: You gonna help me move this piano first, nigger!

LYMON: *[To* GRACE.*]* I got to help Boy Willie move the piano first.

[Everybody but GRACE *suddenly senses* SUTTER's *presence.]*

GRACE: I ain't waiting on you. Told me you was coming right back. Now you got to move a piano. You just like all the other men.

*[*GRACE *now senses something.]*

Something ain't right here. I knew I shouldn't have come back up in this house.

*[*GRACE *exits.]*

LYMON: Hey, Grace! I'll be right back, Boy Willie.

BOY WILLIE: Where you going, nigger?

LYMON: I'll be back. I got to take Grace home.

BOY WILLIE: Come on, let's move the piano first!

LYMON: I got to take Grace home. I told you I'll be back.

*[*LYMON *exits.* BOY WILLIE *exits and calls after him.]*

BOY WILLIE: Come on, Lymon! Hey…Lymon! Lymon…come on!

[Again, the presence of SUTTER *is felt.]*

WINING BOY: Hey, Doaker, did you feel that? Hey, Berniece…did you get cold? Hey, Doaker…

DOAKER: What you calling me for?

WINING BOY: I believe that's Sutter.

DOAKER: Well, let him stay up there. As long as he don't mess with me.

BERNIECE: Avery, go on and bless the house.

DOAKER: You need to bless that piano. That's what you need to bless. It ain't done nothing but cause trouble. If you gonna bless anything go on and bless that.

WINING BOY: Hey, Doaker, if he gonna bless something let him bless everything. The kitchen…the upstairs. Go on and bless it all.

BOY WILLIE: Ain't no ghost in this house. He need to bless Berniece's head. That's what he need to bless.

AVERY: Seem like that piano's causing all the trouble. I can bless that. Berniece, put me some water in that bottle.

*[*AVERY *takes a small bottle from his pocket and hands it to* BERNIECE, *who goes into the kitchen to get water.* AVERY *takes a candle from his pocket and lights it. He gives it to* BERNIECE *as she gives him the water.]*

Hold this candle. Whatever you do make sure it don't go out.

O Holy Father we gather here this evening in the Holy Name to cast out the spirit of one James Sutter. May this vial of water be empowered with thy spirit. May each drop of it be a weapon and a shield against the presence of all evil and may it be a cleansing and blessing of this humble abode.

Just as Our Father taught us how to pray so He say, "I will prepare a table for you in the midst of mine enemies," and in His hands we place ourselves to come unto his presence. Where there is Good so shall it cause Evil to scatter to the Four Winds.

[He throws water at the piano at each commandment.]

AVERY: Get thee behind me, Satan! Get thee behind the face of Righteousness as we Glorify His Holy Name! Get thee behind the Hammer of Truth that breaketh down the Wall of Falsehood! Father. Father. Praise. Praise. We ask in Jesus' name and call forth the power of the Holy Spirit as it is written ….

[He opens the Bible and reads from it.]

I will sprinkle clean water upon thee and ye shall be clean.

BOY WILLIE: All this old preaching stuff. Hell, just tell him to leave.

*[*AVERY *continues reading throughout* BOY WILLIE's *outburst.]*

AVERY: I will sprinkle clean water upon you and you shall be clean: from all your uncleanliness, and from all your idols, will I cleanse you. A new heart also will I give you, and a new spirit will I put within you: and I will take out of your flesh the heart of stone, and I will give you a heart of flesh. And I will put my spirit within you, and cause you to walk in my statutes, and ye shall keep my judgments, and do them.

*[*BOY WILLIE *grabs a pot of water from the stove and begins to fling it around the room.]*

BOY WILLIE: Hey Sutter! Sutter! Get your ass out this house! Sutter! Come on and get some of this water! You done drowned in the well, come on and get some more of this water!

*[*BOY WILLIE *is working himself into a frenzy as he runs around the room throwing water and calling* SUTTER's *name.* AVERY *continues reading.]*

BOY WILLIE: Come on, Sutter! *[He starts up the stairs.]*

Come on, get some water! Come on, Sutter!

[The sound of SUTTER's GHOST *is heard. As* BOY WILLIE *approaches the steps he is suddenly thrown back by the unseen force, which is choking him. As he struggles he frees himself, then dashes up the stairs.]*

BOY WILLIE: Come on, Sutter!

AVERY: *[Continuing.]* A new heart also will I give you and a new spirit will I put within you: and I will take out of your flesh the heart of stone, and I will give you a heart of flesh. And I will put my spirit within you, and cause you to walk in my statutes, and ye shall keep my judgments, and do them.

[There are loud sounds heard from upstairs as BOY WILLIE *begins to wrestle with* SUTTER's GHOST. *It is a life-and-death struggle fraught with perils and faultless terror.* BOY WILLIE *is thrown down the stairs.* AVERY *is stunned into silence.* BOY WILLIE *picks himself up and dashes back upstairs.]*

AVERY: Berniece, I can't do it.

*[There are more sounds heard from upstairs. **DOAKER** and **WINING BOY** stare at one another in stunned disbelief. It is in this moment, from somewhere old, that **BERNIECE** realizes what she must do. She crosses to the piano. She begins to play. The song is found piece by piece. It is an old urge to song that is both a commandment and a plea. With each repetition it gains in strength. It is intended as an exorcism and a dressing for battle. A rustle of wind blowing across two continents.]*

BERNIECE: *[Singing.]*

I want you to help me
I want you to help me
I want you to help me
I want you to help me
I want you to help me
I want you to help me
Mama Berniece
I want you to help me
Mama Esther
I want you to help me
Papa Boy Charles
I want you to help me
Mama Ola
I want you to help me

I want you to help me
I want you to help me
I want you to help me
I want you to help me
I want you to help me
I want you to help me
I want you to help me
I want you to help me

[The sound of a train approaching is heard. The noise upstairs subsides.]

BOY WILLIE: Come on, Sutter! Come back, Sutter!

*[**BERNIECE** begins to chant:]*

BERNIECE:

Thank you.
Thank you.
Thank you.

*[A calm comes over the house. **MARETHA** enters from **DOAKER**'s room. **BOY WILLIE** enters on the stairs. He pauses a moment to watch **BERNIECE** at the piano.]*

BERNIECE:

Thank you.
Thank you.

BOY WILLIE: Wining Boy, you ready to go back down home? Hey, Doaker, what time the train leave?

DOAKER: You still got time to make it.

*[**MARETHA** crosses and embraces **BOY WILLIE**.]*

BOY WILLIE: Hey Berniece…if you and Maretha don't keep playing on that piano…ain't no telling…me and Sutter both liable to be back.

[He exits.]

BERNIECE: Thank you.

[The lights go down to black.]

END OF PLAY